The Novels of
THOMAS DELONEY

line, for I remember an olde saying : Loue and Lordship brookes no fellowship: But when this matter was
made known to the rest of the iorneymen: Tom Drums
entertainment was spoke of in euery place, insomuch
that it is to this day a prouerbe amongst vs, that where
it is supposed a man shall not be welcomed, they will say
he is like to haue Tom Drums entertainment. And to
auoide the flouts that were dayly giuen him, poore Tom
Drum forsooke Fléetestréete, and at last went into Scotland, being prest for a drummer at Muskeloborough field,
where the noble Duke of Sommerset and the Earle of
Warwicke were sent with a noble armie: where the
Englishmen and Scotes méeting, there was fought a
cruell battle, the victorie whereof fel to the Englishmen:
at what time there was slaine of the Scotes to the number of fouretéene thousand, and fiftéene hundred taken
prisoners: where we will leaue Tom Drum till his returne, making mention how Harry Neuell behaued
himselfe in the meane space in London.

Chap. 9.

❧ How Harry Neuell, wooed mistres Farmer and de-
ceaued Doctor Burket: and how they were both beguiled by a prentice that dwelt in the house, who in the
end married her.

Istres Farmer stering the hearts
of many with her faire beautie,
was wondrously wooed by Doctor Burket, who would giue vnto her diuers rich gifts, the which
though they were faire and costly, yet Mistres Farmer would
hardly accept them, but euen
what he in a manner by perforce

L   con-

A page from *The Gentle Craft, Part II,* probably 1598.
(*Courtesy of The Folger Shakespeare Library*)

The Novels of
THOMAS DELONEY

Edited by

MERRITT E. LAWLIS

INDIANA UNIVERSITY PRESS
Bloomington   1961

94604

In Memory of
Hyder Edward Rollins

ACKNOWLEDGMENTS

I wish to express my gratitude to the Graduate School of Indiana University for several research grants.

To Professors Philip B. Daghlian, Horst Frenz, Rudolf B. Gottfried, and William R. Parker of Indiana University, and to Professor William A. Jackson of Harvard University, I am indebted for countless suggestions offered in pleasant daily contact.

All the libraries with Deloney materials have been most helpful, but I especially wish to thank the ones holding the editions that I have used as copy texts: the Henry E. Huntington Library for *Jack of Newbury* and *Thomas of Reading;* the University of Sheffield Library for *The Gentle Craft, Part I;* and the British Museum for *The Gentle Craft, Part II.*

Libraries have a way of attracting people who are at once kind, efficient, and intelligent. I wish to thank particularly E. Lingle Craig, Reference Librarian, and Robert A. Miller, Director, Indiana University Library; David A. Randall, Librarian, Lilly Library; James G. McManaway, Consultant in Literature and Bibliography, Folger Shakespeare Library; Mary Isabel Fry, Reference Librarian, Henry E. Huntington Library; J. E. Tolson, Librarian, University of Sheffield; F. C. Francis, Director and Principal Librarian, British Museum; and L. W. Hanson, Department of Printed Books, Bodleian Library.

It was my good luck to have as guide and master the late Hyder Edward Rollins. As graduate teacher, editor, and friend, he had no equal.

M. E. L.

Bloomington, Indiana
September, 1960

CONTENTS

Acknowledgments   vii

Introduction

   1. Deloney as Novelist: His Use of the Drama and the
       Jestbook   xi

   2. Characterization   xviii

   3. Biographical Sketch   xxiii

   4. The Text   xxx

Jack of Newbury   1

The Gentle Craft, Part I   89

The Gentle Craft, Part II   171

Thomas of Reading   265

Explanatory Notes   345

Collation Notes   387

Index   427

INTRODUCTION

1. Deloney as Novelist: His Use of the Drama and the Jestbook

By the time Thomas Deloney in the last few years of the sixteenth century turned to what we now call the novel form, he knew what his public wanted. All four of his novels immediately became so popular that the early editions of them were read completely out of existence. To the twentieth-century reader such a flattering catastrophe is not at all difficult to understand, for Deloney's writing is still fresh and exciting.

His characters come alive quickly and easily. How, the reader asks, did he learn to write crisp and life-creating dialogue? Unfortunately, our knowledge of Deloney's life, as we shall see below, is very sketchy; and when we turn to the novels written by his contemporaries, we find little evidence that he so much as glanced at them.

True, such idealized characters as Duke Robert and Margaret in *Thomas of Reading* may remind us vaguely of Musidorus and Pamela in Sir Philip Sidney's *Arcadia* (1590 and 1593). But the resemblance is entirely superficial. In his only specific reference to Arcadia, Deloney has Tom Drum remark that the place abounds in asses. Tom may not have Sidney's romance in mind, but his incidental remark nevertheless serves to remind us that Sidney and Deloney are poles apart. The *Arcadia, Old* or *New,* has little to offer a novelist who is concerned primarily with the everyday life of artisans.

Yet the realism of Thomas Nashe and Robert Greene apparently was not to his taste either. Nashe's witty, biting, satirical manner in his pamphlets and in *The Unfortunate Traveler* (1594) is alien to Deloney; and although he frequently calls a spade a spade, Deloney is not interested in the ramifications of the underworld that Greene describes in his pamphlets about conies and cony-catchers (1591-92).

Nor did John Lyly offer a suitable model. That Deloney was well acquainted with euphuism is clear, but by 1597 there was no need to read *Euphues* (1578) to become acquainted with it. By the end of the century Lyly's influence was so pervasive that Deloney, along with many another writer, must have felt its impact. Yet his only direct borrowings are not from Lyly, but from such compendiums as Thomas Fortescue's translation of *The Forest* (1571). In *The Forest* Deloney found various bits of information, usually erroneous and often fantastic, phrased neatly in paramoion and isocolon.

Deloney's novels contrast so strongly with *Euphues,* and with other Elizabethan novels, that the reader immediately recognizes them as something new, as a different order of fiction. *Jack of Newbury* (1597 or 1598) is the first really dramatic novel in English. It is dramatic in every sense. A story more vivid and exciting would be difficult to find. Deloney's vision of life is dramatic: he chooses to write about people of action, people in the act of accomplishing certain material things. Perhaps his basic attitude toward people is what attracted him to the drama and what then led him to make his novels dramatic in the sense of drama-like.

To understand Deloney's use of the play form, all one has to do is contrast Shakespeare's use of the novel form. When Shakespeare borrows from Thomas Lodge's *Rosalynde* and Robert Greene's *Pandosto* for *As You Like It* and *The Winter's Tale,* he takes not only the incident but the actual wording. Yet it is clear that he already knows what genre he is going to write in: it is the play. Different as the play is from the novel, especially in Elizabethan times, there is not the slightest tendency in Shakespeare to write in the manner of Lodge and Greene. Whatever he uses he "makes his own," as we say, because the novel and the play are so different in form and structure that his act of creation is not diminished by the extensive literal borrowing.

Deloney's indebtedness to the drama is of another kind. He never filches a whole scene; nor does he copy the dialogue word for word. He likes the dramatic form so well that he simply takes it over. He puts a scene before us the way a playwright does; and, especially in the first three novels, he seldom analyzes omnisciently in his own words. Although *Jack of Newbury* begins with omniscient analysis, the point of view quickly changes; and we rarely get Jack's thoughts any longer. Instead, we are an audience viewing a stage, and we know only what we see and hear.

But if the view usually is limited, as in a play, Deloney nevertheless finds one way of letting a character express his own thoughts and feelings directly to the reader. He uses the soliloquy, an accepted device in plays. Meg's catechism on grief, in Chapter III of *The Gentle Craft, Part II,* is a good example:

Meg being merily inclined, shooke off sorrow in this sort, and gently taking the willow Garland, said: wherefore is griefe good? can it recall folly past? no: can it helpe a matter remedilesse? no: can it restore losses, or draw us out of danger? no: what then? can griefe make unkind men curteous? no: can it bring long life? no: for it doth rather hasten our death, what then can it do: can it call our friends out of their graves? no: can it restore virginity if we chance to lose our maidenhead? no: Then wherefore should I grieve? except I went to kill my selfe: Nay seeing it is so, hang sorrow, I will never care for them that care not for me, and therefore a Figge for the Cocke of *Westminster.*

The actual wording of her soliloquy is different from the wording of Falstaff's soliloquy on honor in *1 Henry IV* (V, i, 128 ff.). Yet there can be little question, as Alexis F. Lange and others have pointed out, that Deloney has Falstaff's questions and answers in mind. The pattern is exactly the same. Meg is on a "stage" before us, and for the moment she has forgotten Casteler, Robin, and Gillian in her successful effort to engage the reader's sympathy for her plight.

Again and again Deloney seems to have a stage in mind as he groups his characters for an important scene. He learned well what no other Elizabethan novelist learned: some episodes in a novel need to be emphasized more than others; and an episode that is to be emphasized in prose fiction needs to be handled the same way it is handled on the stage—by giving the reader a close view of the characters through a carefully defined and well limited setting. Often Deloney arranges a duologue. First he describes a homely setting that is easy to visualize—a bedroom, a dining room, a shop, or a tavern—and then he has two persons engage each other in conversation. The exchange between Meg and Gillian in Chapter I of *The Gentle Craft, Part II,* is typical.

Wherefore then doe you not marry (quoth *Margaret*)? in my opinion it is the most pleasingst life that may be, when a woman shall have her husband come home and speake in this sort vnto her. How now Wife? how dost thou my sweet-heart? what wilt thou have? or what dost thou lacke? and therewithall kindly embracing her, gives her a gentle kisse, saying: speake my prettie mouse, wilt thou have a cup of Claret-wine

. . . ? O how sweet doe these words sound in a womans eares? But when they are once close betweene a paire of sheetes, O Gillian then, then.

Why what of that (quoth she)?

Nay nothing (saith *Margaret*) but they sleep soundly all night.

This interchange is characteristic of stage humor. There is the careful build-up to Gillian's "straight line," which is followed promptly by Margaret's "punch line."

When Jack first meets his prospective father-in-law, there is a brief description of the old man's arrival in Newbury from Alesbury in Buckinghamshire. After looking over Jack's estate, including the warehouses with various kinds of cloth in them, the old man accosts Jack:

Sir (quoth the olde man) Iwis che zee you bee bominable rich, and cham content you shall haue my daughter, and Gods blessing and mine light on you both.

But Father (quoth *Iack* of *Newbery*) what will you bestow with her?

Mary hear you (quoth the old man) I vaith cham but a poore man, but I thong God, cham of good exclamation among my neighbours, and they will as zoone take my vice for any thing as a richer mans: thicke I will bestowe, you shall haue with a good will: because che heare very good condemnation of you in euery place, therefore chill giue you twenty Nobles and a weaning Calfe, and when I dye and my Wife, you shall haue the reuelation of all my goods.

As Ernest A. Baker has noted, this bit of dialogue is historically important; it contains the first use of dialect and the first use of malapropism in English prose fiction.[1]

Deloney employs dialogue so naturally, and so much the way we are accustomed to it in the twentieth-century novel, that his achievement at first escapes us. More than four-fifths of *Jack of Newbery* is in dialogue form. The story begins with two brief paragraphs of introduction. Then comes a chorus-like interchange, a distant "quoth one" and "quoth another." But before long Jack is sitting on a cushion beside the widow, his employer; and what we "hear" is an intimate conversation as racy and colloquial as a scene from *The Alchemist*. Some chapters, like Chapter X of *Jack* —the wonderful episode in which Tweedle gets sweet revenge on Mistress Frank—are entirely in dialogue except for a brief comment at the beginning and the end.

[1] *The History of the English Novel* (London, 1924-39), II, 175.

Introduction

Often Deloney prefers even to introduce characters through dialogue. Instead of giving the reader brief analyses of Tom Drum and Harry Nevell, he simply has the two characters meet and start talking. They introduce themselves.

Deloney is best at comedy and farce; but he has one excellent tragic scene, and dialogue is the making of it. In Chapter XI of *Thomas of Reading* the innkeeper and his wife are about to murder Thomas Cole. The three of them are alone at the inn. Feeling premonitions of death, Cole looks at his host, starts back, and exclaims:

What aile you to looke so like pale death? good Lord, what haue you done, that your hands are thus bloudy?

What my hands, said his host? Why you may see they are neither bloudy nor foule: either your eies do greatly dazell, or else fancies of a troubled mind do delude you.

Alas my hoast, you may see, saide he, how weake my wits are, I neuer had my head so idle before. Come, let me drinke once more, and then I will to bed, and trouble you no longer.

With that he made himselfe vnready, and his hostesse was very diligent to warme a kerchefe, and put it about his head.

Good Lord said he I am not sicke, I prayse God, but such an alteration I find in my selfe as I neuer did before.

With that the scritch owle cried pitteously, and anone after the night rauen sate croking hard by his window.

Iesu haue mercy vpon me, quoth he, what an ill fauored crie do yonder carrion birds make!

And therewithall he laid him downe in his bed, from whence he neuer rose againe.

There would seem to be a few "echoes" here from such Jacobean tragedies as *Macbeth* and *The Duchess of Malfi*. But of course *Thomas of Reading* was written at least eight years before *Macbeth* and fifteen years before *The Duchess of Malfi;* if any borrowing is involved, Shakespeare and Webster are the borrowers.

Whether the scene to be emphasized is comedy or tragedy, Deloney always manages to be vivid. His focus is on the details of everyday life. The dialogue, in fact, is so concrete that it is a mine of information about the artisans of the Elizabethan period. Love and marriage are the main topics of conversation; but since Deloney is a materialist to the core, his characters talk freely of money, food, and other business and household matters.

XV

Like Dickens, Deloney has such a gift for particularity that he occasionally is able to give us the very heart of a situation without benefit of analysis. Consider the opening chapter of *Thomas of Reading*. Deloney nowhere says, in his own words or through the dialogue of his characters, that the rise of the middle class came with the development of certain industries, such as the clothing industry in the days of Henry I. The action speaks for itself. As King Henry I rides along the narrow road from London to Wales, he sees cartloads of cloth coming from the opposite direction. Instinctively, he gets off the road and into the hedge—and watches the carts go by. The scene is historically inaccurate, of course, as Deloney must have known; but it is dramatically perfect.

Still another aspect of Deloney's vividness derives from his use of the contemporary jestbook, the best model of the period for racy, vigorous, and often scatological concreteness. That he was the "T.D." who translated Des Périers' *Les contes* in 1583 is a real possibility, as we shall see below. But whether he was the translator or not, it is clear that he was well acquainted with "detached jests" as well as "jest-biographies," to use the generally accepted terminology of Ernst Schulz.[2]

The collection of detached jests and the jest-biography are basically much alike. In the latter the tales or anecdotes relate to one person, but otherwise they are as unconnected structurally as they are in a collection of detached jests, in which the subject and characters differ from one tale to the next. *The Merie Tales of Skelton* (1567), for example, is almost as loose in form as *A C. mery Talys* (1525). An exception is the anonymous *Dobsons Drie Bobbes* (1607), a jest-biography in which the hero's character develops convincingly from boyhood to manhood as he moves about in Durham and Cambridge. As F. P. Wilson has contended, *Dobsons Drie Bobbes* leads very naturally to Defoe's long biographical novels.[3]

In structure, Deloney's first three novels are similar to jest-biographies. Occasionally he inserts completely irrelevant episodes; and at these points his narrative breaks down, reminding one of jestbooks like *The Merie Tales of Skelton*. But usually he keeps the action under control, the way it is in *Dobsons Drie Bobbes,* which,

[2] *Die englischen Schwankbücher bis herab zu Dobson's Drie Bobs* (Berlin, 1912), p. 2.

[3] F. P. Wilson, "The English Jestbooks of the Sixteenth and Early Seventeenth Centuries," *Huntington Library Quarterly,* II (1939), 143.

incidentally, is one of the truly significant Renaissance novels. It is inferior to *Jack of Newbury* and *Thomas of Reading* in dialogue and scene management, but is superior to them in its grasp of the total plot situation. One is tempted to say that a combination of the two techniques might have produced a novel like *Tom Jones* long before 1749.

Of Deloney's novels, *Jack of Newbury* is most like a jest-biography; *Thomas of Reading*, with its cleverly woven plot and subplot, smacks more of the play than the jestbook. But both novels show a double relationship. The story of Will Sommers in Chapter IV of *Jack of Newbury*, for example, can be traced both to the jestbooks of the *Skelton* type and to the drama. The incident—Jack's "maiden weauers" play a practical joke on Will Sommers for disturbing their spinning wheels—is irrelevant to the plot as a whole in the manner of the careless jest-biography, where laughter is all; and yet the dialogue is far superior to that of the jestbooks: it rivals the dialogue in the better comedies of the London stage.

There are a few other such irrelevant incidents in Deloney's novels; but the only incident that seems to be patterned after a particular, extant jest completely transcends its original in every way and fits snugly into the biographical structure of *Jack of Newbury*. Chapter I is, in part of its bare outline, taken from a jest in *A C. mery Talys* called "The Burning of John." [4] In both stories (1) there is a middle-aged and unnamed woman whose husband has died recently, leaving her well-to-do; (2) the widow falls in love with her young apprentice, whose name is John; (3) the widow's maid has a minor role in furthering the love affair between the widow and John; (4) eventually the two lovers spend a night together in the widow's bedroom; and (5) the next morning they have a sumptuous breakfast together. These are rather specific details, and it would seem to be no accident that all five of them appear in the jest and also in *Jack of Newbury*. Yet Deloney radically transforms the very tone and meaning of the jest. While expanding and developing the plot, he bases the illicit love scene on the character of the widow. She remains throughout a "flat" character in the purely descriptive sense that implies no derogation. We do not know her well, but we know her as well as we need to; and she makes a strong impact upon us. We look over her shoulder, as it were, as

4 See W. Carew Hazlitt, ed., *Shakespeare Jest-Books* (London, 1846), I, 119-121.

she sees Jack kiss a girl at the fair; and we understand her feeling of jealousy. We know that somehow she will get rid of her three fervent suitors—the tailor, the parson, and the tanner. For like Mistress Eyre, she has commendable initiative and manages to get what she wants. Jack, on the other hand, is a passive young apprentice. He is as virtuous and industrious as Ben Franklin, but he is also self-righteous and not nearly so innocent as he pretends. In short, the reader feels that Jack's eventual marriage to the widow is more lucky than unlucky.

Yet there is just enough doubt. The relationship between the widow and Jack is not obvious, as it is in "The Burning of John." Nor is it merely laughable. Deloney has converted the raw jest into an exciting episode that moves along smoothly while it gives us a convincing insight into the widow's character.

2. *Characterization*

Deloney's handling of historical material is one of the most interesting aspects of his method. Writing more than two hundred years before Sir Walter Scott, he makes his characters function as we have become accustomed to see them function in the historical novel: the truly historical characters (Henry VIII, for example) are figureheads, and the admittedly fictional characters (such as Old Bosom) are depicted with complete freedom.[5]

Deloney's kings actually do so little that, like the Duke of Argyle in *Heart of Midlothian,* they need not stray very far from the history books. But Deloney is not interested primarily in historical accuracy. Henry VIII needs only to be convincing as royalty and have the dignity appropriate to his high station. In most episodes he is the passive observer; over his shoulder we, too, may look at the action, but he himself acts only when Deloney is in need of an arbiter or a *deus ex machina*. In *Thomas of Reading* the main outlines of Henry I's conflict with his brother, Duke Robert, are historical—as any Elizabethan familiar with the chronicles of Richard Grafton and Raphael Holinshed would know. But Henry is larger than real life. Deloney goes beyond history to idealize him and

---

[5] In 1812 the firm of J. Ballantyne, in Edinburgh, published *Thomas of Reading*. Was Scott responsible for selecting the novel? Perhaps he even chose the 1632 edition as copy text and performed the other necessary editorial tasks (learning a thing or two from Deloney in the process).

speak through him with authority. There is one exception: in the conflict between Henry and his brother, Duke Robert, Deloney's sympathies are with Duke Robert. But in his relations with the clothiers Henry is the ideal governor; and his function is to establish standards and to pass judgments that are true and final. When the King recognizes that a clothing industry is important to the well-being of the commonwealth, then the clothing industry gains stature. The King's judgment is a standard of reference. When Henry VIII chooses to visit John Winchcomb in Newbury, everyone recognizes that John henceforth is to be considered a success. Neither his thriving business nor his election to Parliament had carried the same weight.

For the figurehead, vague and general detail is better than realistic detail, which Deloney saves for some of his other characters. In general, he avoids realistic detail whenever he feels that a character would be compromised by it. That is why the tradesmen heroes are almost as idealized as the kings. They reward virtue and punish vice, but they themselves are allowed only a passive role in the action of the story. Young Jack of Newbury is wooed by a designing widow; Simon Eyre achieves great wealth through a rather shady plan engineered by Mistress Eyre. In each case the hero reaches a desired goal without having to turn a hand. Presumably if he had turned a hand, he would have soiled it.

If Deloney's talent for characterization extended only to his handling of kings and tradesmen, his talent would be negligible, even though the kings and tradesmen fulfill very well indeed their creator's purpose. The trouble with them is that they are mainly presiders; and it is necessary that they preside over something vital and interesting, since they themselves are rather colorless.

Color and vitality in great measure come naturally to Deloney's heroines—Mistress Eyre, the first Mistress Winchcomb, Long Meg of Westminster, Gillian of the George, and Mistress Farmer—and to the minor characters, both male and female—Randoll Pert, Tom Drum, Round Robin, Old Bosom, Tom Dove, and Mistress Frank. In creating this gallery of portraits, Deloney leaves the other Elizabethan novelists far behind and rivals the very best Elizabethan comedy.

According to the title pages, Deloney's novels are "pleasant histories" of "famous and worthy" men. But as the plots unfold, women are in the thick of the action while the famous and worthy men look on. Nominally it is a man's world; but the wife often is responsible for her husband's success, as Deloney illustrates when he has the clever Mistress Eyre arrange the purchase of a cargo that makes Simon rich. In the story of Crispine and Crispianus, women initiate all the action. The widowed mother of Crispine and Crispianus disguises her sons to keep them from the wicked Emperor; the Emperor's daughter, Ursula, proposes to Crispine; and the boys' mistress at the shoe shop, where they are apprenticed, is the one who thinks of a plan to get Ursula from the palace to the shoe shop.

All these women come alive the instant Deloney touches them. He appears merely to observe and record, passing but few judgments, though giving the impression generally that he would not have women any different from the way they are. "Women are not Angels," Long Meg contends, "though they haue Angels faces." They are made essentially of fine stuff, or at least they appear to be; yet they have definite weaknesses that are peculiar to their sex. But Deloney accepts their whole nature, considering each trait sympathetically and understandingly.

He thinks that some women *are* angels. Winifred is unswerving in her devotion to Christianity, finally dying a martyr. Another paragon of virtue is Margaret, the daughter of the Earl of Shrewsbury. Her love for the imprisoned Duke Robert is so great that she decides never to marry and enters the abbey at Gloucester. Fortunately, Winifred and Margaret are Deloney's only two ventures into the realm of angelic women. Very likely he was never in a position to know, even remotely, any women of so high a rank. Their portraits show a consequent idealization and stylization. We hear them speak occasionally, but only in the most high-flown euphuistic dialogue and monologue. They are two characters apart from the everyday world, with no particular relevance to human affairs. Deloney found Winifred in a saint's legend and never completely takes her out of it.

For a knowledge of middle-class women, however, he does not turn to literary sources. He knows them firsthand and records all their little foibles. He recognizes the foibles by their deviation from a "norm" of ideal conduct; and the "norm" appears to stem from Proverbs XXXI, verses 10 to 31. That Deloney was well acquainted with these verses is evident from his ballad, "Salomons good houswife in the 31 of his Proverbes," in the 1607 edition of

Introduction

Strange Histories. The ballad is a close paraphrase of Proverbs XXXI, several verses of which are as follows:

10 Who can find a virtuous woman? for her price is far above rubies.

11 The heart of her husband doth safely trust in her, so that he shall have no need of spoil.

12 She will do him good, and not evil, all the days of her life. . . .

16 She considereth a field, and buyeth it; with the fruit of her hands she planteth a vineyard.

17 She girdeth her loins with strength, and strengtheneth her arms. . . .

23 Her husband is known in the gates, when he sitteth among the elders of the land. . . .

31 Give her of the fruit of her hands: and let her own works praise her in the gates.

Proverbs XXXI is perhaps behind Deloney's idealistic, often sentimental, attitude toward women and his conception of woman's part in family life. Doctor Burket, after losing out in his suit for the hand of Mistress Farmer, remarks philosophically that it is much better to have a virtuous woman than one who has "much gold in her coffers." The Green King, though perhaps less deserving, is lucky: "God blest him with the gift of a good wife." And for Deloney a good wife, as in Proverbs XXXI, is never idle. She runs the household, which is her province. Her main function, day in and day out, is the performance or superintendence of chores; but she is also wise, and offers, when the occasion arises, a bit of advice to her husband that he does well to take. At other times she is rather silent, not "brabling" like some women. She rarely strays beyond her own home. "Gadding abroad" and "carelesse spending" are furthest from her mind, because they are the two cardinal sins in an industrious middle-class wife. Jack and his first wife make no headway at all until she finally decides to stay home and manage the household the way a good wife should.

Deloney's ability to individualize a host of minor characters is just as impressive as his delineation of the heroines. His success with both groups suggests that his eye is mainly on action. If the minor characters are less subtle than the heroines, they strike with greater impact. As E. M. Forster has observed, Dickens' flat characters each may be summed up in one sentence, like "I shall never desert Mr. Micawber"; but at the same time they somehow sug-

xxi

gest human depth.[6] The method is to single out a trait and exaggerate it. But the secret is to choose the right trait, the one that will represent the whole man and therefore give the impression that his essence is laid open to the reader. Of course, in reality no man has an essence; the flat character is an oversimplification. But he is nevertheless most satisfying, and the talent for creating him is rare indeed. As Forster observes, Russian novels could use many more flat characters, those "little luminous disks of a prearranged size" that "never run away, have not to be watched for development, and provide their own atmosphere."

John Winchcomb's father-in-law is one of Deloney's most memorable flat characters. His "tag" is his manner of speech, a combination of dialect and malapropism. We recognize him instantly each time he appears. Similarly, we recognize Simon of Southampton by his love of pottage, Tom Dove by his calling for music, Tom Drum by his "sin of cogging," and Round Robin by his ceaseless rhyming.

Randoll Pert—incidentally, Deloney's genius is about equal to Dickens' in naming characters—is a little more complicated than most of the flat characters. Recently out of debtors' prison, Pert, formerly a successful draper, becomes a porter because he can find no other means of supporting his family. When Jack of Newbury arrives in London, he happens to stay at the Spread Eagle and hire Pert to carry his trunk. But when Pert recognizes Jack as a man whom he owes £500, he drops the trunk and runs away. Jack fails to recognize Pert, but he sends a servant in close pursuit to find out why such an unusual looking man is running away. Pert indeed looks odd enough; he is wearing

an old ragged doublet, and a torne payre of breeches, with his hose out at the heeles, and a paire of olde broken slip shooes on his feet, a rope about his middle instead of a girdle, and on his head an old greasie cap, which had so many holes in it, that his haire started through it.

Such an exaggerated description contains possibilities for pathetic as well as comic interpretation. Deloney chooses to develop both. The chase begins pathetically. As soon as Pert sees the servant running after him, he runs faster and faster, "euer looking behinde him, like a man pursued with a deadly weapon, fearing euery twinkling of an eye to bee thrust thorow." But comic things begin

[6] *Aspects of the Novel* (New York, 1927), pp. 104-109.

to happen to him. First he loses his shoes, and then the whole race suddenly ends as his trousers fall down and shackle his churning legs. Sprawling headlong in the street, he is overtaken by the servant and both of them stand "blowing and puffing a great while ere they could speake one to another."

The whole episode, including the sentimental part where Jack agrees not to collect the £500 until Pert is sheriff of London, is excellent comedy; and we laugh all the more because it is sharpened by pathos. All the characters, but especially the porter and the scrivener, come alive. As E. A. Baker has said: "When we turn to character-drawing, neither Lyly nor Sidney, not even Nashe . . . has a leg to stand on in comparison to Deloney." [7] Baker is right. On his own ground Deloney compares favorably with the best English novelists of the eighteenth and nineteenth centuries. Who besides Dickens is his superior in drawing flat characters?

3. Biographical Sketch

Of Thomas Deloney the man we know very little indeed. J. W. Ebsworth, in *The Dictionary of National Biography*, suggests 1543 as the possible date of his birth. No evidence is available; but a considerably later date, say 1560, would seem to be a better guess, making Deloney twenty-six when his earliest extant ballads appeared in 1586.

The place of his birth was once thought to be Norwich, but the only evidence was a misquoting of a passage in Thomas Nashe's *Have with You to Saffron-Walden* (1596). Nashe called Deloney "the Balletting Silke-weauer," but not "the Balletting Silke-weauer of Norwich."

Of one vital statistic, however, we may be fairly certain: Deloney died early in 1600. Will Kemp, the comic actor and morris dancer, noted in *Nine Daies Wonder* (entered in the Stationers' Register on 22 April 1600) that "the late generall Tho. dyed poorely" and was "honestly buried." In the same pamphlet Kemp gives us proof that "T.D." on the title pages of the novels is indeed Thomas Deloney:

I haue made a priuie search, what priuate Iigmonger of your iolly number, hath been the Author of these abhominable ballets written of me: I was told it was the great ballet-monger T. D., alias Tho. Deloney, Chronicler of the memorable liues of the 6. yeomen of the west, Iack of

[7] *History of the English Novel*, II, 191.

Newbery, the Gentle-craft, and such like honest men. . . . (*Nine Daies Wonder*, ed. Dyce, p. 30.)

Kemp is referring to all four of Deloney's novels—*Jack of Newbury; The Gentle Craft, Part I; The Gentle Craft, Part II;* and *Thomas of Reading or The Six Worthy Yeomen of the West.*

Deloney probably had no such background as Harry Nevell, a semi-historical character in *The Gentle Craft, Part II,* who works at a trade after receiving the education of a gentleman; but it is true that Deloney's earliest known literary activity shows a kind of learning unusual for a weaver. In 1583 he translated from Latin into vigorous English three separate items that appeared together in one volume. The first, dated 16 January 1583, bore the title, "A declaration made by [Gebhard,] the Archbishop of Collen, vpon the deede of his mariage"; the second, dated 17 December 1582, is a letter from Pope Gregory XIII to Gebhard; and the third, undated, is Gebhard's answer to Pope Gregory's letter. Archbishop Gebhard Truchsess von Waldburg (1547-1601) was Elector and Archbishop of Cologne from 1577 to 1583. After his conversion to reformed doctrines and his marriage to Agnes, Countess of Mansfeld, Gebhard decided to retain his see and convert his subjects to Protestantism. But in the end he was deposed and excommunicated (April, 1583) by the Pope. To Deloney the controversy is symbolic of the fight between the Pope and Protestantism; and he leaves no doubt, in his dedication to the Bishop of London, that his own sympathies are with Protestantism. Gebhard is one of "many worthy personages, lately liuing in darknes and ignorance [who have] now turned to the trueth, with most earnest repentance of their former life." According to the title page, "A declaration" and the two letters were printed in London by John Wolfe in 1583.

Deloney may be the "T. D." who in the same year, 1583, translated parts of *Les contes ou les nouvelles récréations et joyeux devis* by Bonaventure Des Périers (1500?-1544). The title in the English translation became *The Mirrour of Mirth and pleasant Conceits.* F. P. Wilson was the first to suggest Deloney as the translator,[8] and no other "T. D." of the period has a better claim. Judg-

8 F. P. Wilson, "The English Jestbooks," p. 139. See also J. Woodrow Hassell, Jr., "An Elizabethan Translation of the Tales of Des Périers: *The Mirrour of Mirth,* 1583 and 1592," *Studies in Philology,* LII (1955), 172-185. Mr. Hassell agrees that Deloney probably is the translator and finds the translation "generally faithful and ably executed."

ing from his novels, Deloney was well acquainted with jestbook literature; and Des Périers' short tales form what Ernst Schulz would call a "collection of detached jests." [9] They show, as a whole, more sensitivity and more narrative skill than such English collections as *A C. mery Talys* (1525?). The first edition of *The Mirrour of Mirth* (1583) consisted of thirty-nine tales translated from Des Périers; for the second edition of 1592, nine tales were dropped and one added to make a total of thirty-one. According to the title page of the 1583 edition the translator was "R.D.," but the address to the reader bore the initials "T.D." In the second edition "R.D." on the title page was changed to "T.D."

Nothing is known about Deloney between 1583 and 1586, when a broadside ballad entitled "The Lamentation of Beckles" was printed by Nicholas Colman of Norwich. Since it was printed in Norwich, Francis Oscar Mann thought that Norwich may have been Deloney's residence. But the other extant 1586 ballads were printed in London; furthermore, two frustratingly brief entries in the parish register of St. Giles, Cripplegate, seem to indicate that Deloney was living in London by the end of 1586. The first entry reveals that on 16 October 1586 "Richarde, the sonne of Thomas Delony, weauer" was baptized. The other is for the 21 December following: "Richard, the sonne of John Deloney (weauer)" was buried. John Payne Collier contended in his *Memoirs of the Principal Actors in the Plays of Shakespeare* (1846) that the two Richards are one and the same child and that "John" in the later entry is an error for "Thomas" in the first entry. Collier probably was right, but in any case "Thomas Delony, weauer" definitely was the ballad writer and future novelist. Unfortunately, the St. Giles register yields no further information of any kind about the Deloney family.

"The Lamentation of Beckles" reminds one that the broadside ballad was the sixteenth-century newspaper and that Deloney's apprenticeship, like many a later novelist's, was in journalism. From his journalistic experience he may have learned how to write concisely and how to choose popular subjects. The cause of the "lamentation" was a fire on the previous Saint Andrew's Eve that destroyed a great portion of Beckles, a market town in Suffolk; some eighty houses burned to the ground at a loss of over £20,000, according to Deloney's report. In another broadside published in the

[9] *Die englischen Schwankbücher*, p. 2.

same year, 1586, Deloney "covers" the Babington conspiracy. "A proper new Ballad breefely declaring the Death and Execution of fourteen most wicked Traitors" is a description of the hanging and quartering of Anthony Babington, John Ballard, and twelve others. Deloney makes no attempt to give an objective report in the manner of a twentieth-century journalist. In his opinion Babington, a "cursed catife," deserved having his carcass quartered and his heart thrown into a fire. But Deloney is scrupulous in presenting the external details. Seven of the culprits were executed on 20 September 1586 and the remaining seven on the following day. The place was Lincoln's Inn Fields. Since Deloney could not work the names of the alleged traitors into the ballad proper, he tacked them on at the end.

"The Lamentation of Mr. Pages Wife" (1591) is very much like a "human interest story" on the front page of a modern American newspaper. Again Deloney reports the available facts. A young lady is in love with George Strangewidge; but her father forces her to marry Page, a dull old miser of Plymouth. After the marriage the girl begins to loathe her husband. Finally she and Strangewidge murder him—and must die at Barnstable in Devonshire for the crime. The most interesting aspect of this ballad is Deloney's attitude toward his subject. He has great sympathy for Mrs. Page, from whose point of view he tells the story. Surely here is material for a novel as well as a ballad.

But current events were not Deloney's only ballad subjects. Through the works of Grafton and Holinshed he drew upon English history; and a study of *The Mirrour for Magistrates,* in its seventh edition by 1587, probably helped him not only in the choosing but also in the treatment of his material. Ballads with such titles as "The faire Lady Rosamond" and "Shores Wife" were bound to be popular in the Elizabethan period; these two ballads, incidentally, may have appeared first as broadsides, but we have them now only in a collection of Deloney's ballads called *The Garland of Good Will,* the earliest extant edition of which is 1631.[10] The

10 Assuming that *The Garland* contained the same ballads in the earlier editions that it contained in the 1631 edition, 1596 was the earliest possible date for the first edition. "The Winning of Cales," the third ballad in Part III of the 1631 edition, concerns an incident that occurred on 21 June 1596. Nashe refers playfully to *The Garland,* and perhaps also to a few lost Deloney ballads, in *Have with You to Saffron-Walden* (1596). See Ronald B. McKerrow, ed., *The Works of Thomas Nashe* (London, 1904-[1910]), III, 84.

early editions of another Deloney ballad collection, *Strange Histories,* were not read out of existence so completely; both the Bodleian and the Huntington Libraries have copies of a 1602 edition.

By 1592 Deloney succeeded William Elderton as the principal ballad maker in England. Elderton's death occurred in 1591 or early in 1592. Robert Greene died about the same time; and Gabriel Harvey, in *Four Letters* (1592), lumps them together—"Elderton for Ballating: Greene for pamphletting"—as a pair of ne'er-do-wells whom the world can dispense with. Harvey's disparaging remark about Elderton, incidentally, drew Deloney's name into the Harvey-Nashe quarrel. Nashe, ever the opportunist, in *Strange News* (late 1592 or early 1593) tried to get Deloney to attack Harvey for attacking Elderton.

Hough *Thomas Delone, Phillip Stubs, Robert Armin,* &c. Your father *Elderton* is abus'd. Reuenge, reuenge on course paper and want of matter, that hath most sacriligiously contaminated the diuine spirit & quintessence of a penny a quart.

Helter skilter, feare no colours, course him, trounce him, one cup of perfect bonauenture licour will inspire you with more wit and Schollership than hee hath thrust into his whole packet of Letters.[11]

But there is no record of Deloney's having taken Nashe's bait. He chose his own controversies. The Archbishop of Cologne affair he had entered wholeheartedly, and he took sides again in 1595 when the weavers needed a spokesman.

In the early months of 1595 Deloney and fourteen other freemen-weavers decided that something had to be done about their "great decaye and ympoverishinge."[12] They thought that foreign labor, especially French and Dutch, was the cause; under the pretense of immigrating to England for religious reasons, great numbers of foreigners were coming to England each year to earn their livelihood in the clothing industry. Despite the competition, however, English freemen still could make profits if only the foreigners would observe the rules laid down by the Weavers' Company, especially the rules concerning apprenticeship. In an attempt to effect a rem-

11 *Works of Nashe,* I, 280.

12 For all the information contained in this paragraph see Frances Consitt, *The London Weavers' Company* (Oxford, 1933), I, 146-147 and 312-318. Note especially the texts of three important documents: the complaint of the weavers, a letter (dated 27 June 1595) from the Lord Mayor to the Lord Treasurer, and a petition from the imprisoned weavers to the Lord Chief Justice.

edy, the group of freemen drew up, in June of 1595, a complaint against the immigrant weavers; the leaders of the group in drafting the complaint were "one Willington," William Muggins, and Deloney. After a printer by the name of Gabriell Sympson set the type, the entire group of fifteen read the proof in Muggins' house. They decided to print forty copies, eleven for the pastors and elders of the French church, an equal number for the Dutch church, and one copy each for the mayor and the aldermen of London. Apparently the freemen thought that the pastors would call their errant parishioners on the carpet and demand that the rules be obeyed. But instead the pastors had the mayor clap the freemen into Newgate. Undaunted, the weavers while in jail wrote to Sir John Popham, the Lord Chief Justice. The petition was successful, and the prisoners were released "with good Commendacions." (Chapter VI of *Jack of Newbury* seems to reflect Deloney's experiences of 1595. The problem is entirely different; but there is a letter of complaint, the complainers are imprisoned for a short time, and then after petitioning high authority they are released.)

Slightly more than a year later Deloney was in trouble again. This time the offending publication was not a pamphlet but a ballad that is now lost. The incident can be reconstructed from a letter written by the mayor of London, Stephen Slany, to the Lord Treasurer, William Cecil, on 26 July 1596.[13] According to Slany, Deloney in his ballad complained of the scarcity of grain in England; and such a complaint tended to occasion "some Discontentment" among the poor. One can only guess at the nature of Deloney's complaint. The mayor perhaps gives a clue when he reports that Queen Elizabeth in the ballad speaks "with her people in dialogue wise in very fond and vndecent sort." Could it be that Deloney in the ballad has Elizabeth speak the way Henry VIII and Henry I do in the novels? The ideal governor in the novels is a person who transcends the differences in rank; his great concern is the best interests of the commonwealth. Henry VIII in Chapter VI of *Jack* states the basic principle:

As the Clergie for the Soule, the Souldier for defence of his Countrie, the Lawyer to execute iustice, the husbandman to feede the belly: So is the skilfull Clothier no lesse necessary for the clothing of the backe. . . .

When the King needs advice on the clothing industry, he calls in

[13] The letter is in the British Museum, Landsdowne MSS. 81.30.

the clothiers, who naturally know the most about their own trade.

the clothiers, who naturally know the most about their own trade. Each trade and profession makes an important contribution to the total welfare and therefore should be kept in a healthy condition. Thus the King not only countenances a petition of grievances; he actually encourages it, for according to his vision of government each group of the commonwealth should lobby freely in its own behalf. He himself supplies the power. When Henry I receives recommendations from Thomas Cole and eight other clothiers (in *Thomas,* Chapter IV), he immediately translates the recommendations into action.

Perhaps Deloney implied such an idealistic conception of government in his ballad on the scarcity of grain. From Slany's point of view, it may have been "vndecent" for Queen Elizabeth to converse with her subjects and to learn what they wanted. Slany may have found the dialogue in the novels "vndecent," too; but by the time they came out, between 1597 and 1600, he was no longer mayor. Yet there is some question whether he would have objected to the novels. Their settings are all in the past, as though Deloney had decided to profit from the official reaction to his ballad and stay clear of direct contemporary allusion.

Slany goes on to say, in his letter of 1596 to Cecil, that he has apprehended the publisher and printer of the ballad but that as yet he has not found the author. Apparently Deloney never was found; and in his desire to escape the authorities, he kept burning his bridges so thoroughly that between 1596 and 1600 there seems to be no record of him.

Of his work during this time, however, there is some record. Between 1597 and 1600 appeared four novels of almost exactly the same length. They were *Jack of Newbury; The Gentle Craft, Part I; The Gentle Craft, Part II;* and *Thomas of Reading,* very likely written and published in that order, though in the absence of first editions and contemporary references one cannot be certain. Only two of the novels were entered in the Stationers' Register—*Jack of Newbury* on 7 March 1597 and *The Gentle Craft, Part I,* on 19 October of the same year. Presumably they were printed shortly afterward, perhaps a year before the final two novels. Judging from the dedication "To the Master and Wardens of the worshipfull company of the Cordwaynors," *Part I* became immediately so popular that Deloney was "the more bolde to proffer" *Part II.* If he had wanted to follow the path of least resistance, he could have projected the same characters into different situations. But he had a trilogy in mind, three separate novels dealing with shoemaking in England. *Part I* was designed to give the origins of the trade; *Part II* was to show how it flourished in London; and then *Part III*, if he had lived to write it, was to trace the development of shoemaking in the country.

There is no way of knowing whether *The Gentle Craft, Part II*, appeared before or after *Thomas of Reading;* all we know about the latter is contained in Deloney's dedication to *Jack of Newbury*, where he says that if *Jack* is well received, he will

shortly . . . set to your sight the long hidden Historie of *Thomas* of *Redding, George* of *Glocester, Richard* of *Worcester,* and *William* of *Salsburie,* with diuers others. . . .

Enough time, however, must have elapsed between Deloney's writing of this dedication and his actual writing of *Thomas* for him to change some of the names. "George" became "Gray" of Gloucester, "Richard" became "William" of Worcester, and "William" became "Sutton" of Salisbury, all the changes involving the alliteration characteristic of Deloney's style.

4. The Text

I am using the earliest extant editions of Deloney's four novels as my copy texts, for in each case the earliest edition happens to be the most authoritative. I attempt to show what I mean by authoritative in the explanatory notes. Briefly, it is a matter of establishing relationship, of deciding which editions are "substantive" (those not derived from any other extant edition) and which "derivative" (those derived from some other extant edition or editions). Having chosen a copy text, I follow it exactly in spelling, punctuation, and capitalization, except for the emendations noted below.

The copy text has been collated with other editions of the early and middle seventeenth century. Modern editions have been collated, too, but receive attention only when an emendation is accepted in the present text (or is not accepted for reasons that appear in the explanatory notes).

I agree with Fredson Bowers, in his edition of Dekker's dramatic works, that the textual footnotes should not include all the variant readings of the early and modern editions. The editor should distract the reader's attention as little as possible. Accordingly, in the present edition there are just two kinds of footnote. The first calls attention to an emendation and gives the rejected reading of the copy text. An example is

ill] Q2-5; til Q1

where the compositor of Q1, the copy text, makes a typographical error that is corrected in all four of the succeeding editions. If the emendation is mine, the footnote simply reads

ill] til Q1

If Mann is responsible for the emendation, the footnote reads

ill] Mann; til Q1

The second kind of footnote calls attention to readings of the copy text that are retained in the present edition despite creditable emendations that appear in later editions. An example is

*them] him Q4,5

where "him" is an emendation worthy of consideration, but "them," the reading of Q1-3, has a better claim. The asterisk before the footnote indicates that there is a note, in the section called "Explanatory Notes," giving my reason for accepting the reading that appears to the left of the bracket.

All the variant readings for each novel are listed together, with appropriate page and line numbers, in the section called "Collation Notes." Most of the entries are "substantive" in that they involve differences in wording. But differences in "accidentals"— spelling, punctuation, and capitalization—are recorded if the meaning could be affected in any way. An example is

seruants at that time:] Q2,3; seruants: at that time Q1

where a shift in the position of the colon alters the meaning of the sentence.

Variants in punctuation need to be singled out quickly, and therefore I am following McKerrow in using two handy symbols—the wavy dash (~) and the caret (ᐱ).[14] The above entry should read

seruants ᐱ at that time:] Q2,3; ~: ~ ᐱ Q1

[14] See *Prolegomena for the Oxford Shakespeare* (Oxford, 1939), pp. 86-87.

to show at a glance that the wording is not involved at all, but only the punctuation. The carets indicate immediately that no punctuation appears after "seruants" in Q2 and Q3 or after "time" in Q1. The wavy dash indicates that the wording is exactly the same in all the editions; the first wavy dash stands for "seruants" and the second for "at that time."

Finally, there remains a statement of policy regarding silent emendations. Modern s replaces the Elizabethan ſ, and w replaces vv. Evident misprints, including turned or damaged letters, are corrected silently only when there is no ambiguity. For example, "madien" in Q1 is changed to "maiden" in Q2-5 and, without footnote or collation note, in the present edition. But if the supposed misprint is not completely obvious, it is retained in a footnote and also placed with the collation notes in the back.

Where the copy text uses black letter, I use roman; where the copy text has roman, bold, or italics for emphasis, I use italics only. Verse in the copy text appears in italics, but some of the ballads are so long that I am putting them all in roman. No attempt is made to reproduce the ornamental initials at the beginnings of chapters, and the capital following an ornamental initial is set in lower case throughout the present edition. Running headlines, catchwords, and signatures are omitted. A lower-case letter at the beginning of a sentence or of a line of verse is capitalized silently, except where lower case consistently was intended by the printer of the copy text, and where Elizabethan printers usually did not capitalize (after a question mark or an exclamation mark). Contractions are expanded. Customary abbreviations like L. for Lord have been retained, but all other abbreviations (such as &, which merely helped the printer justify lines) are spelled out. I make no attempt to modernize either the punctuation or the spelling.

In all the early editions, Deloney's crisp dialogue appears in solid blocks of type. Although I have not used quotation marks, I have taken the liberty of starting a new paragraph with each change of speaker, though as a consequence I have had to make slight changes in punctuation in order to have a full stop at the end of each paragraph.

JACK OF NEWBURY

THE
PLEASANT HI-
STORY OF IOHN

Winchcomb, in his younger yeares
called Iack of Newberie, *the famous*
and worthy Clothier of England: declaring
his life and loue, together with his charitable
deeds and great hospitality;

And how hee set continually fiue
hundred poore people at worke, to the
great benefit of the Common-wealth:
worthy to be read and regarded.

Now the eight time Imprinted, corrected, and inlarged,
by *T. D.*

Haud curo inuidiam.

AT LONDON,
Printed by *Humfrey Lownes*, and are to bee sould at the
signe of the Star on Bredstreet hill.
1619.

TO ALL FAMOVS

Cloth workers in England, I wish all happiness of life, prosperity and brotherly affection.

Among all manuall Arts vsed in this Land, none is more famous 5
for desert, or more beneficiall to the Commonwealth, than is the
most necessarie Art of Cloathing. And therefore as the benefit thereof
is great, so are the professors of the same to bee both loued and
maintained. Many wise men therfore, hauing deeply considered the
same, most bountifully haue bestowed their gifts for vpholding of 10
so excellent a commoditie, which hath been, and yet is the nourish-
ing of many thousands of poore People. Wherefore to you most
worthy Clothiers doe I dedicate this my rude worke, which hath
raised out of the dust of forgetfulnesse a most famous and worthie
man, whose name was *John Winchcombe*, alias *Iacke* of *Newberie;* of 15
whose life and loue I haue briefly written, and in a plain and humble
manner, that it may be the better vnderstood of those for whose sake
I take paines to compile it, that is, for the well minded Clothiers,
that herein they may behold the great worship and credit which
men of this trade haue in former time come vnto. If therefore it bee 20
of you kindly accepted, I haue the end of my desire, and thinke my
paines well recompenced: and finding your gentlenes answering my
hope, it shall moue mee shortly to set to your sight the long hidden
Historie of *Thomas* of *Redding, George* of *Glocester, Richard* of
Worcester, and *William* of *Salsburie,* with diuers others, who were 25
all most notable members in the Commonwealth of this Land, and
men of great fame and dignitie. In the meane space I commend you
all to the most high God; who euer increase, in all perfection and
prosperous estate, the long honoured trade of English Clothiers.

Yours in all humble seruice, 30

T. D.

3

The Most Pleasant
and delectable Historie of
Iohn Winchcombe, *otherwise* called
Iacke of *Newberie:* and first of his
loue and pleasant life.

5

CHAPTER I.

In the daies of King *Henery* the eight that most noble and vic-
torious Prince, in the beginning of his reigne, *Iohn Winchcomb,*
a broad cloth Weauer, dwelt in *Newberie,* a towne in *Barkshire:* who
for that he was a man of a merry disposition, and honest conuersa- 10
tion, was wondrous wel-beloued of Rich and Poore, especiallie because in euery place where hee came, hee would spend his money
with the best, and was not at any time found a churle of his purse.
Wherefore beeing so good a companion, he was called of old and
young *Iack* of *Newbery:* a man so generally well knowne in all his 15
countrey for his good fellowship, that hee could goe in no place but
hee found acquaintance; by meanes whereof *Iack* could no sooner
get a Crowne, but straight hee found meanes to spend it: yet had
hee euer this care, that hee would alwaies keepe himselfe in comely
and decent apparell, neither at any time would hee bee ouer- 20
come in drinke, but so discreetly behaue himselfe with honest
mirth, and pleasant conceits, that hee was euery Gentlemans companion.

After that *Iacke* had long led this pleasant life, beeing (though
hee were but poore) in good estimation; it was his Masters chance 25
to die, and his Dame to bee a Widow, who was a very comely auncient Woman, and of reasonable Wealth. Wherefore she hauing a
good opinion of her man *Iohn,* committed vnto his gouerment the
guiding of all hir Workefolkes, for the space of three yeares together: In which time shee found him so carefull and diligent, 30
that all things came forward and prospered wondrous well. No man
could intice him from his businesse all the weeke, by all the in-

5

treaty they could vse: Insomuch that in the end some of the wild
youths of the Towne, began to deride and scoffe at him.

Doubtlesse quoth one, I doubt some female spirit hath inchaunted
Iack to hir treadles, and coniured him within the compasse of his
5 Loome, that hee can stir no further.

You say truth quoth *Iack,* and if you haue the leisure to stay
till the Charme bee done, the space of sixe dayes and fiue nights,
you shall find mee ready to put on my holy daie apparell, and on
Sunday morning for your paines I will giue you a pot of Ale ouer
10 against the Maypole.

Nay quoth another, Ile lay my life, that as the *Salamander* cannot liue without the fire, so *Iack* cannot liue without the smel of
his Dames smocke.

And I maruell quoth *Iacke,* that you beeing of the nature of the
15 Herring (which so soone as hee is taken out of the Sea streight dyes)
can liue so long with your nose out of the pot.

Nay *Iacke* leaue thy testing quoth another, and goe along with
vs, thou shalt not stay a iot.

And because I will not stay, nor make you a lyer (quoth *Iacke*)
20 Ile keepe me here still: and so farewell.

Thus then they departed, and after they had for halfe a score
times tried him to this intent, and saw hee would not be led by their
lure, they left him to his owne will. Neuerthelesse, euery Sunday in
the afternoone, and euery Holy day, *Iacke* would keepe them com-
25 panie, and bee as merrie as a Pie, and hauing still good store of
money in his purse one or other would euer be borrowing of him,
but neuer could hee get pennie of it againe: which when *Iack* perceiued, he would neuer after carry aboue twelue pence at once in
his purse, and that being spent, hee would streight returne home
30 merily, taking his leaue of the company in this sort.

My Masters I thank you, its time to pack home,
For he that wants money is counted a Mome:
And twelue pence a Sunday being spent in good cheare,
To fifty two shillings amounts in the yeare;
35   Enough for a crafts man that liues by his hands,
And he that exceedes it shall purchase no lands.
For that I spend this day, Ile work hard to morrow,
For woe is that party that seeketh to borrow.
My money doth make me full merry to be,

6

And without my money none careth for mee:
Therefore wanting money what should I do heere?
But haste home, and thanke you for all my good cheer.

Thus was *Iacks* good gouernment and discretion noted of the best
and substantiallest men of the Towne, so that it wrought his great 5
commendations, and his dame thought herselfe not a little blest to
haue such a seruant, that was so obedient vnto her, and so carefull
for her profit; for she had neuer a Prentise that yeelded her more
obedience then hee did, or was more dutifull: so that by his
good example, he did as much good as by his diligent labour 10
and trauaile: which his singular vertue beeing noted by the widow,
shee began to cast very good countenance to her man *Iohn,* and to
vse very much talk with him in priuate: and first by way of communication, shee would tell vnto him what suters shee had, and
the great offers they made her, what gifts they sent her, and the 15
great affection they bare her, crauing his opinion in the matter.
    When *Iacke* found the fauour to bee his dames Secretarie, he
thought it an extraordinary kindnesse: and ghessing by the yarne
it would prooue a good Web, began to question with his dame in
this sort. 20
    Although it becommeth not mee your seruant to prie into your
secrets, nor to bee busie about matters of your loue: yet for so much
as it hath pleased you to vse conference with mee in those causes,
I pray you let me intreat you to know their names that bee your
sutors, and of what profession they bee. 25
    Marie *Iohn* saith she that you shall, and I pray thee take a cush-
ion and sit downe by mee.
    Dame quoth hee I thanke you, but there is no reason I should
sit on a cushion till I haue deserued it.
    If thou hast not thou mightest haue done said shee: but faint 30
souldiers neuer find fauour.
    Iohn replied, that makes mee indeed to want fauour: for I durst
not trie Maydens because they seeme coy, nor Wiues for feare of
their Husbands, nor Widowes, doubting their disdainfullnesse.
    Tush *Iohn* (quoth shee) hee that feares and doubts Womankind, 35
cannot bee counted Mankind: and take this for a principle, all
things are not as they seeme: but let vs leaue this and proceed to

---

[8] profit;] Q4,5; ~? Q1 ; ~: Q2,3
[35] Womankind] Q2-5; Womenkind Q1

7

Jack of Newbury

our former matter. My first sutor dwels at *Wallingford,* by Trade
a Tanner, a man of good wealth and his name is *Craftes,* of comly
personage, and very good behauiour, a Widower, well thought of
amongst his neighbours: hee hath proper land, a faire house and
5 well furnished, and neuer a childe in the world, and hee loues me
passing well.

Why then Dame quoth *Iohn,* you were best to haue him.

Is that your opinion quoth shee? now trust me, so it is not mine.
For I finde two speciall reasons to the contrary: the one is, that hee
10 being ouerworne in yeares makes mee ouerloth to loue him: and
the other, that I know one neerer hand.

Beleeue me dame (quoth *Iack*) I perceiue store is no sore, and
profered ware is worse by ten in the hundred than that which is
sought: but I pray ye who is your second sutor?

15 *Iohn* quoth shee, it may seeme immodesty in me to bewray my
loue secrets: yet seeing thy discretion, and being perswaded of thy
secrecy, I will shew thee: the other is a man of middle yeares, but
yet a Batcheler, by occupation a Taylor, dwelling at *Hungerford:*
by report a very good husband, such a one as hath crownes good
20 store, and to mee he professes much good will, for his person he
may please any woman.

I dame quoth *Iohn,* because he pleaseth you.

Not so said she, for my eies are vnpartiall Iudges in that case:
and albeit my opinion may be contrary to others, if his Art deceiue
25 not my eye-sight, hee is worthie of a good wife, both for his person and conditions.

Then trust mee Dame (quoth *Iohn*) for so much as you are without doubt of your selfe that you will proue a good wife, and so
well perswaded of him, I should thinke you could make no better
30 a choice.

Truly *Iohn* (quoth shee) there be also two reasons that mooue
me not to like of him: the one, that being so long a ranger, he
would at home be a stranger; and the other, that I like better of
one nearer hand.

35 Who is that, quoth *Iacke?*

Saith shee, the third Suter is the Parson of *Spinhome-land,* who
hath a proper liuing, hee is of holy conuersation and good estimation, whose affection to me is great.

16 loue] Q5; loues Q1,4; louers Q2,3

8

No doubt Dame (quoth *Iohn*) you may doe wondrous well with him, where you shall haue no care but to serue G O D and to make ready his meats.

O *Iohn* (quoth shee) the flesh and the spirit agrees not; for hee will bee so bent to his books, that he will haue little minde of his bed: for one moneths studying for a Sermon, will make him forget his wife a whole yeer.

Truely Dame (quoth *Iohn*) I must needes speake in his behalfe, and the rather for that he is a man of the Church, and your neere neighbour, to whom (as I guesse) you beare the best affection: I doe not thinke that hee will bee so much bound to his booke, or subiect to the spirit, but that he will remember a woman at home or abroad.

Well *Iohn* (quoth she) I wis my minde is not that way, for I like better of one nearer hand.

No maruell (quoth *Iacke*) you are so peremptorie seeing you haue so much choice: but I pray ye Dame (quoth he) let me know this fortunate man that is so highly placed in your fauour?

Iohn (quoth shee) they are worthy to knowe nothing, that cannot keepe something: that man (I tell thee) must goe namelesse: for he is Lord of my loue, and King of my desires: there is neither Tanner, Taylor, nor Parson may compare with him, his presence is a preseruatiue to my health, his sweete smiles my hearts solace, and his words heauenly musike to my eares.

Why then Dame (quoth *Iohn*) for your bodies health, your hearts ioy, and your eares delight, delay not the time, but entertaine him with a kisse, make his bed next yours, and chop vp the match in the morning.

Well, quoth shee, I perceiue thy consent is quickly got to anie, hauing no care how I am matcht so I bee matcht: I wis, I wis I could not let thee goe so lightly, beeing loath that any one should haue thee, except I could loue her as well as my selfe.

I thanke you for your kindnesse and good will good Dame quoth hee, but it is not wisedome for a young man that can scantly keepe himselfe, to take a wife: therefore I hould it the best way to leade a single life: for I haue heard say, that manie sorrowes followe mariage, especially where want remaines: and beside, it is a hard matter to finde a constant woman: for as young maides are fickle, so are old women iealous: the one a griefe too common, the other a torment intolerable.

9

What *Iohn* (quoth she) consider that maidens ficklenesse proceedes of vaine fancies, but old womens iealousie of superabounding loue, and therefore the more to bee borne withall.

But Dame, quoth hee, many are iealous without cause: for is it
5 sufficient for their mistrusting natures to take exceptions at a shadow, at a word, at a looke, at a smile, nay at the twinkle of an eye, which neither man nor woman is able to expell? I knewe a woman that was readie to hang her selfe, for seeing but her husbands shirt hang on a hedge with her maides smocke.

10 I grant that this furie may haunt some, quoth shee, yet there be many other that complaine not without great cause.

Why, is there any cause that should moue iealousie, quoth *Iohn*?

I by S. *Mary* is there quoth she: for would it not grieue a woman (being one euery way able to delight her husband) to see him
15 forsake her, despise and contemne her, being neuer so merrie as when he is in other company, sporting abroad from morning till noone, from noone till night, and when he comes to bed, if hee turne to his wife, it is in such solemnesse, and wearisome drowsie lamenesse, that it brings rather lothsomnesse than any delight: can
20 you then blame a woman in this case to bee angrie and displeased? Ile tell you what, among brute beasts it is a griefe intolerable: for I heard my Grandame tell that the Bel-weather of her flocke fancying one of the Eawes aboue the rest, and seeing *Gratis* the Shepheard abusing her, in abhominable sort (subuerting the lawe of
25 Nature) could by no meanes beare that abuse; but watching opportunity for reuenge, on a time found the said Shepheard sleeping in the field, and suddenly ranne against him in such violent sort, that by the force of his wreathen hornes, hee beat the braines out of the Shepheards head and slewe him. If then a Sheepe could
30 not endure that iniurie, thinke not that women are so sheepish to suffer it.

Beleeue mee (quoth *Iohn*) if euery horne-maker should be so plagued by a horned beast, there should bee less hornes made in *Newberie* by many in a yeare. But Dame (quoth hee) to make an end
35 of this prattle, because it is an argument too deepe to be discussed betweene you and I, you shal heare me sing an ould song, and so wee will depart to supper.

A maiden faire I dare not wed,
For feare to haue *Acteons* head.
A maiden blacke is often proud:
A maiden little will be loud.
A maiden that is high of groath,   5
They say is subiect vnto sloath.
Thus, faire or foule, little or tall,
Some faults remaine among them all,
But of all the faults that be,
None is so bad as iealousie.   10
For iealousie is fierce and fell,
And burnes as hot as fire in hell:
It breedes suspicion without cause,
And breakes the bondes of reasons lawes.
To none it is a greater foe,   15
Than vnto those where it doth grow.
And God keepe me both day and night,
From that fell, fond, and vgly spright:
For why? of all the plagues that be,
The secret plague is iealousie.   20
Therefore I wish all womenkinde,
Neuer to beare a iealous minde.

Well said *Iohn* (quoth she) thy song is not so sure, but thy voice
is as sweet: but seeing the time agrees with our stomackes, though
loth yet will wee giue ouer for this time, and betake our selues to our   25
suppers.

Then calling the rest of her seruants, they fell to their meate
merrily, and after supper, the Goodwife went abroad for her recreation, to walke awhile with one of her neighbours. And in the
meane space *Iohn* got him vp into his chamber, and there began   30
to meditate on this matter, bethinking with himselfe what hee were
best to doe: for well he perceiued that his Dames affection was
great towarde him: knowing therefore the womans disposition, and
withall that her estate was reasonable good, and considering beside
that he should finde a house ready furnished, seruants readie taught,   35
and all other things for his trade necessarie, he thought it best not

---

[1] faire I dare] Q2-5; fare I daire Q1

11

to let slip that good occasion, least hee should neuer come to the like. But againe, when hee considered her yeares to bee vnfitting to his youth, and that she that sometime had beene his Dame, would (perhaps) disdaine to be gouerned by him that had beene her poore
5 seruant, that it would proue but a badde bargaine, doubting many inconueniences that might growe thereby, hee therefore resolued to be silent rather than to proceed further: wherefore hee got him straight to bed, and the next morning settled him selfe close to his businesse.

10   His Dame comming home and hearing that her man was gone to bed, tooke that night but small rest, and early in the morning hearing him vp at his worke merrily singing, shee by and by arose, and in seemely sort attyring her selfe, she came into the worke-shop, and sat her downe to make quills.

15   Quoth *Iohn*, Good morow Dame, how do you to day?

God a mercie *Iohn* (quoth shee) euen as well as I may: for I was sore troubled in my Dreames. Mee thought two Doues walked to-gether in a corne field, the one (as it were) in communication with the other, without regard of pecking vp any thing to sustaine them-
20 selues: and after they had with many nods spent some time to their content, they both fell hard, with their pretie bils, to pecke vp the scattered corne, left by the wearie Reapers hand. At length (finding themselues satisfied) it chaunced another Pigion to light in that place, with whome one of the first Pigions at length kept companie:
25 and after, returning to the place where she left her first companion, perceiued he was not there, shee kindly searching vp and downe the high stubble to finde him, lighted at length on a hogge fast asleep, wherewith me thought the poore Doue was so dismaid, that presently shee fell downe in a trance. I seeing her legges faile, and
30 her wings quiuer, yeelding her selfe to death, moued with pittie ranne vnto her, and thinking to take vp the Pigion, mee thought I had in my hands my owne heart, wherein me thought an arrow stucke so deepe, that the bloud trickled downe the shaft, and lay vpon the feathers like the siluer pearled deawe on the greene grasse,
35 which made me to weepe most bitterly. But presently mee thought there came one to me crowned like a Queene, who tould mee my heart would die, except in time I got some of that sleeping hogges grease to heale the wounds thereof. Whereupon I ranne in all haste

*19 pecking] Q4,5; picking Q1-3

to the Hog with my heart bleeding in my hand, who (mee thought)
grunted at mee in most churlish sort, and vanisht out of my sight.
Whereupon comming straite home, me thought I found this Hog
rustling among my Loomes, wherewith I presently awaked, sodainely
after midnight, beeing all in a sweate and very ill: and I am sure 5
you could not choose but heare mee groane.

Trust mee Dame I heard you not (quoth *Iohn*) I was so sound
asleepe.

And thus (quoth shee) a woman may die in the night before you
will haue the care to see what shee ailes, or aske what she lackes. 10
But truly *Iohn* (quoth she) all is one, for if thou shouldest haue
come, thou couldest not haue got in, because my chamber door was
lockt: but while I liue this shall teach mee wit, for henceforth I
will haue no other lock but a latch, till I am married.

Then Dame (quoth he) I perceiue though you bee curious in your 15
choise, yet at length you will marrie.

I truly (quoth shee) so thou wilt not hinder me.

Who I quoth *Iohn*? on my faith Dame not for a hundred pounds,
but rather will further you to the vttermost of my power.

Indeede (quoth she) thou hast no reason to shew any discurtesie 20
to me in that matter, although some of our neighbours do not stick
to say, that I am sure to thee alreadie.

If it were so (quoth *Iohn*) there is no cause to denie it, or to bee
ashamed thereof, knowing my selfe farre vnworthie of so high a
fauour. 25

Well let this talke rest quoth shee, and take there thy quils, for
it is time for me to goe to market.

Thus the matter rested for two or three dayes, in which space
she daily deuised which way shee might obtaine her desire, which
was to marrie her man. Many things came in her head, and sundrie 30
sleights in her minde, but none of them did fit her fancie, so that
shee became wondrous sad, and as ciuill as the nine *Sibbels;* and
in this melancholie humour she continued three weekes, or a
moneth, till at last it was her lucke vpon a *Bartholmew* day (hauing
a Fayre in the towne) to spie her man *Iohn* giue a paire of Gloues 35
to a proper maide for a Fayring, which the maiden with a bashfull
modestie kindly accepted, and requited it with a kisse: which kin-

5 ill] Q2-5; til Qı
33 humour she continued] Q4,5; humour continued Qı-3
35 towne)] Q2-5; ~∧ Qı

dled in her an inward iealousie: but notwithstanding very discreetly shee couered it, and closely past along vnspied of her man or the maid.

Shee had not gone farre but shee met with one of her sutors
5 namely the Taylor, who was verie fine and briske in his apparell, and needes hee would bestow the wine vpon the Widow: and after some faint deniall, meeting with a Gossip of hers, to the Tauerne they went, which was more curtesie than the Taylor could euer get of her before, shewing her selfe verie pleasant and merrie: and
10 finding her in such a pleasing humour, the Tailor after a new quart of wine renewed his old sute: the Widow with patience heard him, and gently answered, that in respect of his great good will long time borne vnto her, as also in regard of his gentlenesse, cost and curtesie, at that present bestowed, shee would not flatly denie him.

15 Therefore (quoth shee) seeing this is not a place to conclude of such matters; if I may intreate you to come to my poore house on Thursday next, you shall be heartily welcome, and be further satisfied of my minde: and thus preferred to a touch of her lips, hee payed the shot and departed.

20 The Taylor was scant out of sight, when shee met with the Tanner: who albeit hee was aged, yet lustily he saluted her, and to the wine she must, there was no nay. The Widow seeing his importunacie, calles her gossip, and along they walked together. The olde man called for wine plentie, and the best cheere in the house: and in
25 hartie manner hee biddes the Widow welcome. They had not sitten long, but in comes a noyse of Musitions in tawnie coates, who (putting off their caps) asked if they would haue any Musicke.

The Widow answered no, they were merrie enough.

Tut quoth the oldeman, let vs heare good fellowes what you can
30 doe, and play mee *The beginning of the World*.

Alas, quoth the widow, you had more need to harken to the ending of the world.

Why Widowe, quoth hee, I tell thee the beginning of the world was the begetting of Children: and if you find mee faultie in that
35 occupation, turne mee out of thy bed for a bungler, and then send for the Sexton.

Hee had no sooner spoke the word, but the Parson of *Speen* with his corner cap, popt in at the doore, who seeing the widow sitting at the table craued pardon and came in.

⁷ hers, to] Q2-5; hers ∧ to Q1

14

Quoth shee, for want of the Sexton, heere is the Priest if you need him.

Mary (quoth the Tanner) in good time, for by this meanes wee need not goe farre to bee married.

Sir quoth the Parson, I shall doe my best in conuenient place. 5
Wherein, quoth the Tanner?

To wed her my selfe quoth the Parson.

Nay soft, sayde the Widow, one Swallow makes not a Sommer, nor one meeting a marriage: as I lighted on you vnlookt for, so came I hither vnprouided for the purpose. 10

I trust quoth the Tanner, you came not without your eyes to see, your tongue to speake, your eares to heare, your hands to feele, nor your legs to goe.

I brought my eyes, quoth she, to discerne colours, my tongue to say No to questions I like not, my hands to thrust from me the 15 things that I loue not, my eares to iudge twixt flatterie and friend-ship, and my feet to run from such as would wrong me.

Why then quoth the Parson by your gentle abiding in this place, it is euident that here are none but those you like and loue.

God forbid I should hate my friends (quoth the widow) whom I 20 take all these in this place to bee.

But, there be diuers sorts of loues, quoth the Parson.

You say truth, quoth the Widow: I loue your selfe for your pro-fession, and my friend the Tanner, for his curtesie and kindnesse, and the rest for their good company. 25

Yet (quoth the Parson) for the explaining of your loue, I pray you drinke to them you loue best in the company.

Why (quoth the Tanner) haue you any hope in her loue?

Beleeue me (saith the Parson) as much as another.

Why then Parson sit downe, said the Tanner: for, you that are 30 equall with mee in desire, shall surely be halfe with mee in the shotte: and so Widow, on Gods name fulfill the Parsons request.

Seeing (quoth the widow) you are so pleasantly bent, if my cour-tesie might not breede contention betweene you, and that I may haue your fauour to shewe my fancie, I will fulfill your request. 35

Quoth the Parson, I am pleased howsoeuer it bee.

And I, quoth the Tanner.

Why then (quoth shee) with this cup of Claret wine and Sugar, I heartily drinke to the Ministrels boy.

*27 them] him Q4,5

Why, is it hee you loue best, quoth the Parson?

I haue reason, sayd shee, to like and loue them best, that will bee least offended with my doings.

Nay Widow (quoth they) wee meant you should drinke to him
5 whom you loued best in the way of marriage.

Quoth the Widow, you should haue sayd so at first: but, to tell you my opinion, it is small discretion for a woman to disclose her secret affection in an open assembly: therefore, if to that purpose you spake, let mee intreat you both to come home to my house on
10 Thursday next, where you shall be heartily welcome, and there be fully resolued of my mind: and so, with thankes at this time, Ile take my leaue.

The shot being paid, and the Musitians pleased, they all departed, the Tanner to *Wallingford,* the Parson to *Speen,* and the
15 widow to her own house: where in her wonted solemnes shee settled her selfe to her businesse.

Against Thursday shee drest her house fine and braue, and set her selfe in her best apparell: the Taylor nothing forgetting his promise sent to the Widowe a good fat Pigge, and a Goose. The
20 Parson beeing as mindfull as hee, sent to her house a couple of fat Rabbets and a Capon: and the Tanner came himselfe and brought a good shoulder of Mutton, and halfe a dozen Chickens, beside hee brought a good gallon of Sacke, and halfe a pound of the best sugar. The Widowe receiuing this good meate, set her maide to dresse it
25 incontinent, and when dinner time drew neere, the Table was couered, and euery other thing prouided in conuenient and comely sort.

At length the guests being come, the Widow bad them al heartily welcome. The Priest and the Tanner seeing the Taylor, mused what
30 hee made there: the Taylor on the oher side, maruelled as much at their presence. Thus looking strangely one at another, at length the widow came out of the kitchin, in a faire traine gowne stucke full of siluer pinnes, a fine white cap on her head, with cuts of curious needle worke vnder the same, and an apron before her as white as
35 the driuen snowe: then verie modestly making curtsie to them all, shee requested them to sit downe. But they straining curtsie the one with the other, the Widow with a smiling countenance, tooke the Parson by the hand saying: Sir, as you stand highest in the Church, so is it meet you should sit highest at the Table: and there-
40 fore I pray you sit downe there on the bench side. And sir said shee

to the Tanner, as age is to bee honoured before youth for their experience, so are they to sit aboue Batchelers for their grauitie, and so she set him downe on this side the Table, ouer against the Parson. Then comming to the Taylor shee sayd: Batchler, though your lot bee the last, your welcome is equall with the first, and seeing 5 your place points out it selfe, I pray you take a cushion and sit downe. And now (quoth shee) to make the boord equall, and because it hath beene an ould saying, that three things are to small purpose, if the fourth be awaie: if so it may stand with your fauours, I will call in a Gossip of mine to supplie this voide place. 10

With a good will quoth they.

With that shee brought in an olde woman with scant euer a good tooth in her head, and placed her right against the Bachelor. Then was the meate brought to the boorde in due order by the Widowes seruants, her man *Iohn* beeing chiefe seruitor. The Widow sate 15 downe at the Tables end between the Parson and the Tanner, who in very good sort carued meate for them all, her man *Iohn* waiting on the table.

After they had sitten a while, and wel refreshed themselues, the Widow taking a Crystall glasse fild with claret Wine, drunke vnto 20 the whole companie, and bade them welcome. The Parson pledged her, and so did all the rest in due order; but still in their company the cup past ouer the poor olde Womans nose: insomuch that at length the olde Woman (in a merrie vaine) spake thus vnto the companie: I haue had much good meate among you; but as for the 25 drinke I can nothing commend it.

Alas good Gossip (quoth the Widow) I perceiue no man hath drunke to thee yet.

No truly quoth the old Woman, for Churchmen haue so much minde of young Rabbets, old men such ioie in young Chickens, and 30 Bachelors in Pigs flesh take such delight, that an old Sow, a tough Henne, or a gray Coney are not accepted: and so it is seene by mee, else I should haue beene better remembred.

Well old woman quoth the Parson, take heere the leg of a Capon to stop thy mouth. 35

Now by S. *Anne* I dare not, quoth she.

No? wherefore said the Parson?

Marie for feare least you should goe home with a Crutch, quoth shee.

The Taylor said, then taste here a peece of Goose. 40

17

Now God forbid, sayde the old Woman, let Goose goe to his kinde: you haue a young stomacke, eate it your selfe, and much good may it doo your hart sweet young man.

The old woman lacks most of her teeth, quoth the Tanner, and 5 therefore a peece of tender Chicke is fittest for her.

If I did lacke as many of my teeth, quoth the olde woman, as you lacke points of good husbandrie, I doubt I should starue before it were long.

At this the Widow laught heartily, and the men were stricken 10 into such a dumpe, that they had not a word to say. Dinner being ended, the widow with the rest rose from the Table, and after they had sitten a pretie while merrily talking, the Widow called her man *Iohn* to bring her a bowle of fresh ale, which he did.

Then sayd the Widow: My masters, now for your curtesie and 15 cost I heartily thanke you all, and in requitall of all your fauour, loue and good-will, I drinke to you, giuing you free libertie when you please to depart.

At these wordes her sutors looked so sowrely one vpon another, as if they had beene newly champing of Crabs. Which when the 20 Taylor heard, shaking vp himselfe in his new russet Ierkin, and setting his hat on one side, hee began to speake thus.

I trust sweete widow (quoth hee) you remember to what ende my comming was hither to day, I haue long time beene a sutor vnto you, and this day you promised to giue me a direct an-25 swer.

Tis true, quoth shee, and so I haue: for your loue I giue you thankes, and when you please you may depart.

Shall I not haue you said the Taylor?

Alas (quoth the Widow) you come too late.

30 Good friend (quoth the Tanner) it is manners for young men to let their elders bee serued before them: to what end should I bee here if the widow should haue thee? a flat deniall is meete for a saucie sutor: but what saist thou to mee faire widow (quoth the Tanner)?

35 Sir said shee, because you are so sharp set, I would wish you as soon as you can to wed.

Appoint the time your self quoth the Tanner.

Euen assoone (quoth shee) as you can get a Wife, and hope not after mee, for I am alreadie promised.

[18] sutors] Q2-5; sutor Q1

Now Tanner you may take your place with the Taylor, quoth the Parson, for indeede the widow is for no man but my selfe.

Master Parson (quoth shee) many haue runne neere the goale, and yet lost the game, and I cannot helpe it though your hope bee in vaine: besides, Parsons are but newly suffered to haue 5 wiues, and for my part I will haue none of the first head.

What (quoth the Taylor) is our merriment growne to this reckoning? I neuer spent a Pig and a Goose to so bad purpose before: I promise you when I came in, I verilie thought that you were inuited by the Widowe to make her and me sure together, and that 10 the iolly Tanner was brought to bee a witnesse to the contract, and the old Woman fetcht in for the same purpose; else I would neuer haue put vp so many drie bobs at her hands.

And surely quoth the Tanner, I knowing thee to bee a Taylor, did assuredly think that thou wast appointed to come and take 15 measure for our wedding apparell.

But now we are all deceiued quoth the Parson, and therefore as wee came fooles, so wee may depart hence like asses.

That is as you interpret the matter, said the Widow: for I euer doubting that a concluding answer would breede a iarre in the 20 end among you euery one, I thought it better to bee done at one instant, and in mine owne house, than at sundry times and in common Tauernes: and as for the meate you sent, as it was vnrequested of mee, so had you your part thereof, and if you think good to take home the remainder, prepare your wallets and you 25 shall haue it.

Nay Widow quoth they, although wee haue lost our labours, wee haue not altogether lost our manners: that, which you haue keepe, and God send to vs better lucke, and to you your hearts desire, and with that they departed. 30

The Widow being glad shee was thus rid of her guestes, when her man *Iohn* with all the rest sate at supper, she sitting in a chaire by, spake thus vnto them.

Well my masters, you sawe that this day your poore Dame had her choise of husbands, if shee had listed to marrie, and such as 35 would haue loued and maintained her like a woman.

Tis true quoth *Iohn,* and I pray God you haue not withstoode your best fortune.

8 before:] Q2-5; ~? Qi
35 husbands] Q2-5; husbads Qi
37 you] Q2-5; yun Qi

19

Trust me (quoth shee) I know not, but if I haue I may thank mine owne foolish fancie.

Thus it past on from *Bartholomewtide,* till it was neere Christmas, at what time the weather was so wonderfull cold, that all the
5 running Riuers round about the Towne were frozen very thicke. The Widowe beeing very loath any longer to lie without companie, in a colde winters night made a great fire, and sent for her man *Iohn:* hauing also prepared a chaire and a cushion, shee made him sit downe therein, and sending for a pinte of good Sacke, they both
10 went to supper.

In the ende bed time comming on, shee caused her maide in a merriment to plucke off his hose and shooes, and caused him to bee laide in his masters best bed, standing in the best Chamber, hung round about with very faire curtaines. *Iohn* being thus pre-
15 ferred, thought himselfe a Gentleman, and lying soft, after his hard labour and a good supper, quickly fell asleepe.

About midnight, the Widow being cold on her feet, crept into her mans bed to warme them. *Iohn* feeling one lift vp the cloathes, asked who was there?

20 O good *Iohn* it is I, quoth the widow, the night is so extreame colde, and my Chamber walles so thin, that I am like to be starued in my bed: wherefore rather then I would any way hazard my health, I thought it much better to come hither and trie your curtesie, to haue a little roome beside you.

25 *Iohn* being a kind young man would not say her nay, and so they spent the rest of the night both together in one bed. In the morning betime shee rose vp and made her selfe ready, and willed her man *Iohn* to runne and fetch her a Link with all speede: for quoth shee, I haue earnest businesse to do this morning.

30 Her man did so. Which done shee made him to carrie the Linke before her, vntill she came to Saint *Bartholomewes* Chappell, where Sir *Iohn* the Priest with his Clark and Sexton, stoode wayting for her.

Iohn quoth shee, turne into the Chappell, for before I goe fur-
35 ther, I will make my prayers to S. *Bartholmew,* so shall I speed the better in my businesse.

When they were come in, the Priest according to his order came to her, and asked where the Bridegroome was?

Quoth she, I thought he had beene here before me. Sir (quoth
40 shee) I will sit downe and say ouer my beades, and by that time hee will come.

20

Chapter One

Iohn mused at this matter, to see that his Dame should so sodainly bee married, and hee hearing nothing thereof before. The Widowe rising from her prayers, the Priest toulde her that the Bridegroome was not yet come.

Is it true, quoth the widow? I promise you I will stay no longer 5
for him if he were as good as *George a Green:* and therefore dispatch quoth shee, and marrie me to my man *Iohn.*

Why Dame (quoth he) you doe but iest I trowe.

Iohn (quoth shee) I iest not: for so I meane it shall bee, and stand not strangely, but remember that you did promise mee on 10
your faith not to hinder mee, when I came to the Church to bee married, but rather to set it forward: therfore set your link aside and giue mee your hand, for none but you shall be my husband.

Iohn seeing no remedy consented, because he sawe the matter coulde not otherwise bee amended; and married they were pres- 15
ently. When they were come home, *Iohn* entertained his Dame with a kisse: which the other seruants seeing, thought him something sawcie. The Widow caused the best cheere in the house to bee set on the Table, and to breakfast they went, causing her new husband to bee set in a chaire at the Tables end, with a faire 20
napkin laid on his trencher: then shee called out the rest of her seruants, willing them to sit downe and take part of their good cheere. They wondring to see their fellow *Iohn* sit at the Tables end in their old masters chaire, began heartily to smile, and openly to laugh at the matter, especially because their Dame so kindly 25
sate by his side: which shee perceiuing, asked if that were all the manners they could shew before their master: I tell you quoth shee, he is my husband, for this morning we were maried, and therefore hence forward looke you acknowledge your duty towardes him. 30

The folkes looked one vpon another, maruelling at this strange newes. Which when *Iohn* perceiued, hee said: My masters muse not at all: for although by Gods prouidence and your Dames fauour, I am preferred from being your fellow to bee your Master, I am not thereby so much puft vp in pride, that any way I will 35
forget my former estate: Notwithstanding, seeing I am now to holde the place of a Master, it shall bee wisedome in you to forget what I was, and to take mee as I am; and in dooing your diligence, you shall haue no cause to repent that God made mee your master.

The seruants hearing this, as also knowing his good gouernment before time, past their yeares with him in dutifull manner.

The next daie the report was ouer all the Towne, that *Iacke* of *Newbery* had married his Dame: so that when the Woman walked
5 abroad, euery one bad God giue her ioy: some said that shee was matcht to her sorrow, saying, that so lustie a young man as he, would neuer loue her being so auncient. Whereupon the Woman made answer, that shee would take him downe in his wedding shooes, and woulde trie his patience in the prime of his lustinesse:
10 whereunto many of her Gossips did likewise encourage her. Euery daie therefore for the space of a moneth after shee was married, it was her ordinarie custome, to goe forth in the morning among her gossips and acquaintance to make merrie, and not to returne home till night, without any regarde of her houshold. Of which,
15 at her comming home, her husband did very oftentimes admonish her in very gentle sort, shewing what great inconuenience would grow thereby: the which sometime shee would take in gentle part, and somtime in disdaine, saying:

I am now in very good case, that hee which was my seruant but
20 the other day, will now bee my master: this it is for a Woman to make her foot her head. The day hath beene when I might haue gone forth when I would, and come in againe when it had pleased me without controulement: and now I must bee subiect to euery Iackes checke. I am sure (quoth she) that by my gadding abroad,
25 and carelesse spending I waste no goods of thine. I pittying thy pouertie, made thee a man, and maister of the house, but not to the end I woulde become thy slaue. I scorne, I tel thee true, that such a youngling as thy selfe should correct my conceit, and giue mee instructions, as if I were not able to guide my selfe: but yfaith
30 yfaith, you shall not vse me like a babe, nor bridle me like an asse: and seeing my going abroad greeues thee, where I haue gone forth one day I will goe abroad three, and for one houre I will stay fiue.

Well (quoth her husband) I trust you will be better aduised: and with that hee went from her about his businesse, leauing her
35 swearing in her fustian furies.

Thus the time past on, till on a certaine day shee had beene abroad in her wonted manner, and staying forth very late he shut the dores and went to bed. About midnight shee comes to the

---

¹³ returne] Q2-5; returns Q1

doore and knockes to come in: to whom he looking out of the window, answered in this sort.

What, is it you that keepes such a knocking? I pray you get hence and request the Constable to prouide you a bed, for this night you shall haue no lodging heere.   5

I hope quoth shee, you will not shut me out of doores like a dogge, or let me lie in the streetes like a strumpet.

Whether like a dogge or drab, quoth hee, all is one to mee, knowing no reason but that as you haue stayed out all day for your delight, so you may lie foorth all night for my pleasure. Both birds   10
and beestes at the nights approach prepare to their rest, and obserue a conuenient time to returne to their habitation. Looke but vpon the poore spider, the frogge, the flie, and euery other silly worme, and you shell see all these obserue time to returne to their home: and if you beeing a woman will not doe the like, content   15
your selfe to beare the brunt of your owne folly, and so farewell.

The Woman hearing this, made pitious moane, and in verie humble sort intreated him to let her in, and to pardon this offence, and while shee liued vowed neuer to doe the like. Her husband at length beeing mooued with pittie towardes her, slipt on his   20
shooes and came downe in his shirt: the doore being opened, in shee went quaking, and as hee was about to locke it againe, in very sorrowfull manner she said:

Alacke husband, what hap haue I? My wedding Ring was euen now in my hand, and I haue let it fall about the doore, good sweet   25
Iohn come forth with the Candle and help mee to seeke it.

The man incontinent did so, and while hee sought for that which was not there to bee found, shee whipt into the house, and quickly clapping to the doore, she lockt her husband out. He stood calling with the candle in his hand to come in, but shee made as if shee   30
heard not. Anon shee went vp into her chamber, and carried the key with her: but when hee sawe she would not answere, he presently began to knock as lowd as hee could at the doore.

At last shee thrust her head out at the window, saying: who is there?   35

Tis I quoth *Iohn,* what meane you by this? I pray you come downe and open the doore that I may come in.

⁴ night ͜] Q2-5; ∼, Q1
¹⁹ like.] Q2-5; ∼ ͜ Q1
²² as hee was] Q2-5; as hee as was Q1

What sir, quoth shee, is it you? haue you nothing to doe but daunce about the streetes at this time of night, and like a Spirit of the Butterie hunt after Crickets? are you so hot that the house cannot hold you?

5 Nay I pray thee, sweet heart quoth he doe not gibe any longer, but let me in.

O sir, remember quoth she, how you stood euen now at the window, like a Iudge on the bench, and in taunting sort kept me out of my owne howse. How now *Iacke*, am I euen with you? What 10 *Iohn* my man, were you so lustie to lock your Dame out of doores? Sirra, remember you bad me goe to the Constable to get lodging: now you haue leisure to trie if his wife will preferre you to a bed. You sir Sawce, that made me stand in the colde till my feete did freeze, and my teeth chatter, while you stood preaching of birds 15 and beasts telling mee a tale of spiders, flyes, and frogges: goe trie now if any of them will be so friendly to let thee haue lodging. Why go you not man? feare not to speake with them, for I am sure you shall finde them at home: thinke not they are such ill husbands as you, to bee abroad at this time of night.

20 With this, *Iohns* patience was greatly moued, insomuch that hee deeply swore that if shee woulde not let him in hee would break downe the doore.

Why *Iohn* quoth she, you neede not bee so hot, your clothing is not so warme: and because I thinke this will bee a warning vnto 25 yee against another time how you shut mee out of my house, catch, there is the key, come in at thy pleasure, and look you go to bed to your fellowes, for with mee thou shalt not lie to night.

With that shee clapt to the casement, and got her to bedde, locking the chamber doore fast. Her husband that knew it was in 30 vaine to seeke to come into her Chamber, and beeing no longer able to endure the colde, got him a place among his Prentices, and there slept soundly. In the morning his wife rose betime, and merily made him a Cawdell, and bringing it vp to his bed, asked him how he did.

35 Quoth *Iohn*, troubled with a shrewe, who the longer she liues the worse shee is: and as the people of *Ilyris* kill men with their lookes, so shee kils her husbands hart with vntoward conditions.

---

³ Crickets?] Q4,5; ∼, Q1-3
*²⁶⁻²⁷ you . . . your] thou . . . thy Q2-5

Chapter One

But trust mee wife, quoth hee, seeing I finde you of such crooked qualities, that (like the Spider) ye turne the sweete flowers of good counsell into venemous poyson, from henceforth I will leaue you to your own wilfulnes, and neither vexe my minde nor trouble my selfe to restraine you: the which if I had wisely done last night, I 5 had kept the house in quiet, and my selfe from cold.

Husband (quoth shee) thinke that women are like Starlings, that will burst their gall before they will yeelde to the Fowler: or like the fish *Scolopendra,* that cannot be touched without danger. Notwithstanding, as the hard steele doth yeelde to the hammers 10 stroke, being vsed to his kinde, so will women to their husbands, where they are not too much crost. And seeing yee haue sworne to giue mee my will, I vowe likewise that my wilfulnesse shall not offend you. I tell you husband, the noble nature of a woman is such, that for their louing friends they will sticke (like the Pellican) 15 to pearce their owne hearts to doo them good. And therefore forgiuing each other all iniuries past, hauing also tried one anothers patience, let vs quench these burning coales of contention, with the sweete iuice of a faithfull kisse; and shaking hands, bequeath all our anger to the eating vp of this Cawdle. 20

Her husband curteously consented: and after this time, they liued long together, in most godly, louing and kind sort, till, in the end she died, leauing her husband wondrous wealthie.

[1] mee ∧ wife,] ~, ~ ∧ Q1

25

CHAPTER II.

Of *Iacke* of *Newbery* his great wealth, and number of
seruants: and also how hee brought the Queen *Kath-*
erin one hundred and fifty men prepared for the warre
5   at his owne cost against the King of Scots at *Flodden*
field.

Now *Iacke* of *Newberie* beeing a widower, had the choise of many
Wiues, mens daughters of good credit and widowes of great
wealth. Notwithstanding he bent his onely like to one of his owne
10 seruants, whom hee had tried in the guiding of his house a yeere or
two: and knowing her carefull in her businesse, faithfull in her dealing, and an excellent good huswife, thought it better to haue her
with nothing, than some other with much treasure. And besides, as
her qualities were good, so was she of very comely personage, of a
15 sweete fauour, and faire complexion. In the end hee opened his mind
vnto her, and craued her good will. The maid (though shee tooke
this motion kindly) said shee would do nothing without consent of
her Parents. Whereupon a Letter was writ to her Father, being a
poore man dwelling at *Alesburie* in *Buckinghamshire:* who being
20 ioyfull of his daughters good fortune speedily came to *Newbery,*
where of her master he was frendly entertained: who after hee
had made him good chear, shewed him all his seruants at worke,
and euery office in his house.

        Within one roome being large and long,
25   There stood two hundred Loomes full strong:
        Two hundred men, the truth is so,
        Wrought in theese Loomes all in a rowe,
        By euery one a pretty boy,
        Sate making quils with mickle ioie.
30   And in another place hard by,

*4 one] two Q1-5
19 *Alesburie*] Q2,3; *Alisburie* Q4,5; *Alseburie* Q1

Chapter Two

An hundred women merrily,
Were carding hard with ioyfull cheere,
Who singing sate with voices cleare.
And in a chamber close beside,
Two hundred maidens did abide,   5
In peticoates of stammel red,
And milke-white kerchers on their head:
Their smocke sleeues like to winter snow,
That on the Westerne mountaines flow,
And each sleeue with a silken band,   10
Was feately tyed at the hand.
These prety maides did neuer lin,
But in that place all day did spin:
And spinning so with voices meete,
Like Nightingales they sung full sweet.   15
Then to another roome came they,
Where children were in poore aray:
And euery one sate picking wooll,
The finest from the course to cull:
The number was seauen score and ten,   20
The children of poore silly men:
And these, their labours to requite,
Had euery one a penny at night:
Beside their meate and drink all day,
Which was to them a wondrous stay.   25
Within another place likewise,
Full fiftie proper men he spies,
And these were Shearemen euery one,
Whose skill and cunning there was showne:
And hard by them there did remaine,   30
Full foure score Rowers taking paine.
A Dye-house likewise had he then,
Wherein he kept full forty men:
And likewise in his Fulling mill,
Full twenty persons kept he still.   35
Each weeke ten good fat Oxen he
Spent in his house for certainty:
Beside good butter, cheese, and fish,
And many another holesome dish.
He kept a Butcher all the yeere,   40

27

A Brewer eke for Ale and Beere:
A Baker for to bake his bread,
Which stood his houshold in good stead.
Fiue Cookes within his kitchin great,
5 Were all the yeare to dresse his meate.
Six scullian boyes vnto their hands,
To make cleane dishes, pots and pans:
Beside poore children that did stay,
To turne the broaches euery day.
10 The olde man that did see this sight,
Was much amaz'd, as well he might:
This was a gallant Cloathier sure,
Whose fame for euer shall endure.

When the olde man had seene this great houshold and familie,
15 then hee was brought into the Ware-houses, some being fild with
wooll, some with flockes, some with woad and madder, and some
with broad cloathes and kersies readie dyed and drest, beside a
great number of others, some stretcht on the Tenters, some hanging on poles, and a great many more lying wet in other places.
20 Sir (quoth the olde man) Iwis che zee you bee bominable rich,
and cham content you shall haue my daughter, and Gods blessing
and mine light on you both.

But Father (quoth *Iack* of *Newbery*) what will you bestow with
her?

25 Mary hear you (quoth the old man) I vaith cham but a poore
man, but I thong God, cham of good exclamation among my
neighbours, and they will as zoone take my vice for any thing as a
richer mans: thicke I will bestowe, you shall haue with a good
will: because che heare very good condemnation of you in euery
30 place, therefore chill giue you twenty Nobles and a weaning Calfe,
and when I dye and my Wife, you shall haue the reuelation of all
my goods.

When *Iack* heard his offer hee was straight content, making
more reckning of the womans modestie, than her Fathers money.
35 So the marriage day beeing appointed, all things were prepared
meet for the wedding, and royal cheere ordained; most of the
Lordes, Knights, and Gentlemen therabout, were inuited thereunto: the Bride being attired in a Gowne of sheepes russet, and a
kertle of fine wosted, her head attired with a billiment of gold,

28

Chapter Two

and her haire as yellow as golde hanging downe behind her, which
was curiously combd and pleated; according to the manner in
those dayes, shee was led to Church betweene two sweet boyes, with
Bride laces and Rosemary tied about their silken sleeues, the one
of them was sonne to Sir *Thomas Parrie,* the other to Sir *Francis* 5
Hungerford. Then was there a faire Bride-cup of siluer and gilt
caried before her, wherein was a goodly branch of Rosemary gilded
very faire, hung about with silken Ribonds of all colours: next was
there a noyse of Musicians that played all the way before her: after
her came all the chiefest maydens of the Countrie, some bearing 10
great Bride Cakes, and some Garlands of wheate finely gilded,
and so shee past vnto the Church.

It is needelesse for mee to make any mention heere of the Bridegroome: who being a man so well beloued, wanted no companie,
and those of the best sort, beside diuers Marchant Strangers of the 15
Stilyard, that came from London to the Wedding. The marriage
being solemnized, home they came in order as before, and to dinner
they went, where was no want of good cheere, no lacke of melodie:
Rhennish Wine at this wedding was as plentifull as Beere or Ale,
for the Marchants had sent thither ten Tunnes of the best in the 20
Stilyard.

This wedding endured ten dayes, to the great reliefe of the poore,
that dwelt all about: and in the ende the Brides Father and Mother
came to pay their Daughters portion: which when the Bridegroome
had receiued, hee gaue them great thankes: Notwithstanding hee 25
would not suffer them yet to depart: and against they should goe
home, their sonne in law came vnto them, saying: Father, and
Mother, all the thankes that my poore heart can yeeld, I giue you
for your good will, cost, and curtesie, and while I liue make bolde
to vse me in any thing that I am able; and in requitall of the gift 30
you gaue mee with your daughter, I giue you heere twenty pound
to bestowe as you find occasion; and for your losse of time, and
charges riding vp and downe, I giue you here as much broade cloath
as shall make you a cloake and my mother a holiday gowne, and
when this is worne out, come to mee and fetch more. 35

O my good zonne (quoth the old woman) Christs benizon bee
with thee euermore: for to tell thee true, we had zold al our kine
to make money for my Daughters marriage, and this zeauen yeare

⁶ faire] Q2-5; farie Q1

29

we should not haue been able to buy more: Notwithstanding wee
should haue zold all that euer wee had, before my poore wench
should haue lost her marriage.

I (quoth the olde man) chud haue zold my coate from my back,
5 and my bed from vnder me, before my Girle should haue gone
without you.

I thank you good father and mother, said the Bride, and I pray
God long to keep you in health: then the Bride kneeled down
and did her dutie to her Parents; who weeping for very ioy, de-
10 parted.

Not long after this, it chaunced while our Noble King was making
warre in *France*, that *Iames,* king of *Scotland,* falsly breaking his
oath inuaded *England* with a great army and did much hurt vpon
the Borders: whereupon on the sodaine euerie man was appointed
15 according to his abilitie to be readie with his men and furniture at
an houres warning, on paine of death. *Iacke* of *Newberie* was commanded by the Iustices to set out sixe men, foure armed with Pikes
and two Calieuers, and to meete the Queene in *Buckinghamshire,*
who was there raising a great power to goe against the faithlesse
20 king of Scots.

When *Iacke* had receiued this charge, hee came home in all haste,
and cut out a whole broadcloth for horsemens coats, and so much
more as would make vp coates for the number of a hundred men:
in short time hee had made readie fiftie tall men well mounted in
25 white coates, and red caps with yellowe Feathers, Demilances in
their hands, and fiftie armed men on foot with Pikes, and fiftie shot
in white coats also, euery man so expert in the handling of his
weapon, as fewe better were found in the field. Himselfe likewise
in compleat armour on a goodly Barbed Horse, rode formost of the
30 companie, with a launce in his hand, and a faire plume of yellow
feathers in his crest, and in this sort hee came before the Iustices:
who at the first approach did not a little wonder what hee should
be.

At length when he had discouered what he was, the Iustices and
35 most of the Gentlemen gaue him great commendations for this
his good and forward mind shewed in this action: but some other
enuying heereat gaue out words that hee shewed himselfe more
prodigall then prudent, and more vaine glorious then well aduised,

*34 he had discouered] they had discouered Q3; he discouered Q5

seeing that the best Nobleman in the Countrie would scarce haue done so much: and no maruell (quoth they) for such a one would call to his remembrance, that the King had often occasions to vrge his subiects to such charges, and therefore woulde do at one time as they might bee able to doe at another: but *Iacke* of *Newbery,* 5 like the Stork in the Spring time, thinks the highest Cedar too lowe for him to build his neast in, and eare the yeare bee halfe done, may bee glad to haue his bed in a bush.

These disdainefull speeches being at last brought to *Iacke* of *Newberies* eare, though it grieued him much, yet patiently put 10 them vp till time conuenient. Within a while after, all the Souldiers in *Barkshire, Hampshire,* and *Wilshire,* were commanded to shew themselues before the Queene at *Stonny Stratford,* where her Grace with many Lords, Knights, and Gentlemen were assembled, with tenne thousand men. Against *Iacke* should goe to the Queen, hee 15 caused his face to bee smeared with bloud, and his white coate in like manner.

When they were come before her Highnesse, she demanded (aboue all the rest) what those white coates were?

Wherupon Sir *Henery Englefield* (who had the leading of the 20 *Barkshire* men) made answere: Maie it please your Maiestie to vnderstand, that hee which rideth formost there, is called *Iacke* of *Newbery,* and all those gallant men in white, are his owne seruants, who are maintained all the yeare by him, whom hee at his owne cost hath set out in this time of extremitie, to serue the King against 25 his vaunting Foe: and I assure your Maiesty there is not, for the number, better Souldiers in the field.

Good sir *Henry* (quoth the Queene) bring the man to mee that I may see him: which was done accordingly. Then *Iacke* with all his men alighted, and humbly on their knees fell before the Queene: 30 Her Grace said, Gentleman arise, and putting forth her lillie white hand, gaue it him to kisse.

Most gratious Queene quoth hee, Gentleman I am none, nor the sonne of a Gentleman, but a poore Clothier, whose lands are his Loomes, hauing no other Rents but what I get from the backes 35 of little sheepe, nor can I claime any cognisance but a wodden shuttle. Neuerthelesse, most gratious Queene, these my poore servants and my selfe, with life and goods are readie at your Maiesties commaund, not onely to spend our blouds, but also to lose our liues in defence of our King and Countrey. 40

31

Welcome to mee *Iacke* of *Newberie,* saide the Queene, though
a Clothier by trade, yet a Gentleman by condition, and a faithfull
subiect in heart: and if thou chance to haue any sute in Court,
make account the queene will bee thy friend, and would to God
5 the King had many such Clothiers. But tell mee, how came thy
white coate besmeared with bloud, and thy face so bescratcht?

May it please your Grace (quoth hee) to vnderstand, that it was
my chaunce to meete with a Monster, who like the people *Cynomolgy,* had the proportion of a man, but headed like a dogge, the
10 biting of whose teeth was like the poysoned teeth of a Crocodile,
his breath like the Basilisks, killing afarre off. I vnderstand, his
name was Enuie, who assailed mee inuisibly, like the wicked spirit
of *Mogunce,* who flung stones at men and could not bee seene: and
so I come by my scratcht face, not knowing when it was done.

15 What was the cause this monster should afflict thee aboue the
rest of thy companie, or other men in the field?

Although most Souereigne Queen, quoth hee, this poysoned
curre snarleth at many, and that few can escape the hurt of his
wounding breath, yet at this time hee bent his force against mee,
20 not for any hurt I did him, but because I surpast him in heartie
affection to my Souereigne Lord, and with the poore Widowe
offered all I had to serue my Prince and Countery.

It were happy for *England,* sayd the Queene, if in euery market
Towne there were a Iybbet to hang vp curres of that kind: who
25 like *Æsops* dogge lying in the maunger, will doe no good himselfe,
nor suffer such as would to doe any.

This speech beeing ended, the Queene caused her Army to bee
set in order, and in warlike manner to march toward *Flodden,* where
King *Iames* had pitcht his field. But as they passed along with Drum
30 and Trumpet, there came a Post from the valiant Earle of *Surrey,*
with tydings to her Grace, that now shee might dismisse her Army,
for that it had pleased *God* to grant the noble Earle victorie ouer
the Scots: whome hee had by his wisedome and valiancie vanquisht
in fight, and slayne their King in battel. Upon which newes her
35 Maiestie discharged her Forces, and ioyfully tooke her iourney to
London, with a pleasant countenance, praysing *God* for her famous
victorie, and yeelding thankes to all the Noble Gentlemen and
Souldiers for their readinesse in the action, giuing many giftes to
the Nobilitie, and great rewards to the Souldiers: among whom shee

---

[10] poysoned teeth] Q2-5; poysoned tooth Q1
[16] field?] Q2-5; ~. Q1

nothing forgot *Iacke* of *Newberie,* about whose necke shee put a
rich chaine of gold: at what time he with all the rest gaue a great
shout, saying *God* saue *Katherin* the noble Queene of *England.*

Many Noble men of *Scotland* were taken prisoners at this battell,
and manie more slaine: so that there neuer came a greater foyle to 5
Scotland this this: for you shall vnderstand that the Scottish King
made full account to bee Lord of this land, watching opportunitie
to bring to passe his faithlesse and trayterous practise: which was
when our King was in *France,* at *Turney,* and *Turwin:* in regard
of which warres, the Scots vaunted there was none left in *England,* 10
but shepheards and ploughmen, who were not able to lead an army,
hauing no skill in martiall affaires. In consideration of which
aduantage, hee inuaded the Countrey, boasting of victorie befor
hee had wonne: which was no small griefe to Queene *Margaret* his
wife, who was eldest Sister to our noble King. Wherefore in dis- 15
grace of the Scots, and in remembrance of the famous atchieued
victorie, the Commons of *England* made this Song: which to this
day is not forgotten of many.

The Song.

King *Iamie* had made a vowe,
  Keepe it well if hee may:
That he will be at louely *London,*
  vpon Saint *Iames* his day.   20

Vpon Saint *Iames* his day at noon,
  at faire *London* will I bee;
And all the Lords in merrie *Scotland,*   25
  they shall dine there with me.

Then bespoke good Queene *Margaret,*
  the teares fell from her eye:
Leaue off these warres most noble King,
  keepe your fidelitie.   30

The water runnes swift and wondrous deepe,
  from bottome vnto the brimme:
My brother *Henry* hath men good enough,
  England is hard to winne.   35

24 *Iames* his day] Q2-5; *Iames* day Q1

33

Away quoth he with this silly foole,
    in prison fast let her lie:
For she is come of the English bloud,
    and for these words she shall dye.

5   With that bespake Lord *Thomas Howard,*
    The Queenes Chamberlaine that day:
If that you put Queene *Margaret* to death,
    Scotland shall rue it alway.

Then in a rage King *Iamie* did say,
10   away with this foolish Mome:
He shall be hanged, and the other bee burned,
    so soone as I come home.

At *Floden Field* the Scots came in,
    which made our English men faine:
15   At *Bramstone-greene* this battaile was seene;
    there was King *Iamie* slaine.

Then presently the Scots did flie,
    their Cannons they left behinde:
Their Ensignes gay were woon all away,
20   our Souldiers did beate them blinde.

To tel you plaine, twelue thousand were slaine,
    that to the fight did stand:
And many prisoners tooke that day,
    the best in all *Scotland.*

25   That day made many a fatherlesse child,
    and many a Widow poore:
And many a Scottish gay lady,
    sate weeping in her bowre.

Iacke with a feather was lapt all in leather,
30   His boastings were all in vaine:
He had such a chance with a new morrice dance,
    He neuer went home againe.

FINIS.

CHAPTER III.

How *Iack* of *Newberie* went to receiue the King, as hee
went a progresse into Barkeshire: and how hee made
him a banquet in his owne house.

About the tenth year of the kings reign, his Grace made his 5
progresse into *Barkshire,* against which time *Iacke* of *Newberie*
cloathed 30. tall fellowes, being his houshold seruants, in blewe
coates, faced with Sarcenet, euerie one hauing a good sword and
buckler on his shoulder, himselfe in a plaine russet coate, a paire
of white kersie breeches, without welt or gard, and stockings of the 10
same peece sowed to his slops, which had a great codpeece, wheron
hee stucke his pinnes: who knowing the King would come ouer a
certaine meadow neer adioyning to the Towne, got himselfe thither
with all his men; and repairing to a certaine Ant-hill, which was in
the field, tooke vp his seate there, causing his men to stand round 15
about the same with their swords drawne.

The King comming neere the place with the rest of his Nobilitie,
and seeing them stand with their drawne weapons, sent to know
the cause. *Garter* King at armes was the Messenger, who spake in
this sort. Good fellowes, the Kings maiestie would know to what 20
end you stand heere with your swords and bucklers prepared to
fight.

With that, *Iacke* of *Newberie* started vp and made this answere.
Harrold (quoth he) returne to his Highnesse, it is poore *Iacke* of
Newberie, who beeing scant Marquesse of a mole hill, is chosen 25
Prince of Ants, and heere I stand with my weapons and Guard
about mee, to defend and keep these my poore and painefull sub-
iects from the force of the idle Butterflyes, their sworne enemies,
least they should disturbe this quiet Common wealth, who this
Sommer season are making their winters prouision. 30

The Messenger returning, told his Grace that it was one *Iacke* of

*19 *Garter*] Q5; *Garret* Q1-4

35

Newbery that stoode there with his men about him to guard (as they say) a company of Ants, from the furious wrath of the Prince of Butterflies. With this newes the King heartily laught, saying: Indeede it is no maruel hee stand so well prepared, considering
5 what a terrible tyrant he hath to deale withall. Certainly my Lords (quoth hee) this seemes to bee a pleasant fellow, and therefore we will send to talke with him.

The Messenger being sent, told *Iack* he must come speake with the King.
10 Quoth hee, his Grace hath a horse, and I am on foote, therefore will him to come to mee: beside that, while I am away, our enemies might come and put my people in hazard as the Scots did *England,* while our King was in *France.*

How dares the Lambe bee so bolde with the Lyon, quoth the
15 Herald?

Why quoth hee, if there bee a Lyon in the field, here is neuer a cocke to feare him: and tell his Maiestie, hee might thinke me a very bad Gouernour that would walke aside vpon pleasure, and leaue my people in perill. Herald (quoth hee) it is written, Hee
20 that hath a charge must looke to it, and so tell thy Lord my King.

The Message being done, the King sayd: My Lords, seeing it will bee no other, wee will ride vp to the Emperour of Ants, that is so careful in his gouernment. At the Kings approach, *Iack* of *Newbery* and his seruants put vp all their weapons, and with a ioy-
25 full crie flung vp their caps in token of victorie.

Why how now my masters (quoth the King) is your wars ended? Let mee see where is the Lord Generall of this great Campe?

With that, *Iack* of *Newberie* with all his seruants fell on their knees, saying: God saue the King of *England,* whose sight hath put
30 our foes to flight, and brought great peace to the poore labouring people.

Trust me (quoth our King) here bee pretie fellowes to fight against Butterflies: I must commend your courage, that dares withstand such mightie gyants.
35 Most dread Soueraigne (quoth *Iacke*) not long agoe, in my conceit, I saw the most prouident Nation of the Ants, summoned their cheefe Peeres to a Parliament, which was helde in the famous citie *Dry Dusty,* the one and thirtith day of September: whereas,

*38 thirtith] twentith Q2,3

by their wisdomes, I was chosen their King; at what time also
manie billes of complaint were brought in against diuers ill members in the common-wealth: among whome the Moule was at-
tainted of high treason to their state, and therefore was banished
for euer from their quiet Kingdome: so was the Grashopper and the 5
Caterpiller, because they were not onely idle, but also liued vpon
the labours of other men: amongst the rest, the Butterflie was very
much misliked, but fewe durst say anie thing to him because of
his golden apparell: who through sufferance grewe so ambitious
and malapert, that the poore Ant could no sooner get an egge into 10
her nest, but hee would haue it away, and especially against Easter,
which at length was misliked. This painted Asse tooke snuffe in
the nose, and assembled a great many other of his owne coate, by
windie warres to roote these painefull people out of the land, that
hee himselfe might bee seated aboue them all. 15

(These were proud Butterflies, quoth the King.)

Whereupon I with my men (quoth *Iacke*) prepared our selues to
withstand them till such time as your Maiesties royall presence
put them to flight.

Tush (said the King) thou must think that the force of flies is 20
not great.

Notwithstanding (quoth *Iacke*) their gaie gownes make poore
men afraid.

I perceiue (quoth Cardinall *Wolsey*) that you being King of Ants,
doe carry a great grudge to the Butterflies. 25

I, quoth *Iack*, wee bee as great foes, as the Foxe and the Snake
are friends: for the one of them being subtile, loues the other for
his craft: but now I intend to be no longer a prince, because the
maiestie of a king hath eclipst my glorie: so that looking like the
Peacocke on my blacke feet, makes mee abase my vain glorious 30
feathers, and humbly I yeeld vnto his Maiestie all my souereigne
rule and dignitie, both of life and goods, casting up my weapons at
his feete, to doe any seruice wherein his Grace shall command me.

God a mercy good *Iack* (quoth the king) I haue often heard of
thee, and this morning I mean to visite thy house. 35

Thus the King with great delight rode along vntill hee came
to the townes end, where a great multitude of people attended,

¹¹ haue] Q2,4,5; haus Q1,3
³⁵ visite thy] Q2-5; visity the Q1

to see his Maiestie: where also Queene *Katherine* with all her traine met him. Thus with great reioycing of the Commons, the King and Queene passed along to this iolly Clothiers house, where the good wife of the house with threescore maidens attending on her, pre-
5 sented the king with a Bee hiue, most richly gilt with gold, and all the Bees therein were also of gold curiously made by Art, and out of the top of the same Hiue sprung a flourishing green tree, which bore golden Apples, and at the roote thereof lay diuers Serpents, seeking to destroy it, whom Prudence and Fortitude trode vnder
10 their feet, holding this inscription in their hands;

> Loe here presented to your Royall sight,
> The figure of a flourishing Common-wealth:
> Where vertuous subiects labour with delight,
> And beate the drones to death which liue by stealth.
> 15   Ambition, Enuie, Treason loathsom Serpents bee,
> Which seeke the downefall of a fruitfull tree.

> But Lady Prudence with deep searching eye,
> Their ill intended purpose doth preuent:
> And noble Fortitude standing alwayes nye,
> 20   Disperst their power prepar'd with bad intent
>   Thus are they foyld that mount by meanes vnmeet,
>   And so like slaues are troden vnder feet.

The King fauourably accepted this Embleme, and receiving it at the womans hands, willed Cardinall *Wolsey* to look thereon, com-
25 manding it should bee sent to *Windsor* Castle. This Cardinall was at that time Lord Chauncellor of *England,* and a wonderfull proude Prelate, by whose meanes great variance was set betwixt the King of *England* and the French King, the Emperour of *Almaine,* and diuers other Princes of Christendome, whereby the trafficke
30 of those Merchants was vtterly forbidden, which bred a generall woe through *England,* especially among Clothiers: insomuch that hauing no sale for their cloath, they were faine to put away many of their people which wrought for them, as hereafter more at large shall be declared.
35 Then was his Maiestie brought into a great Hall, where foure long Tables stoode readie couered: and passing through that place, the King and Queene came into a faire and large Parlour hung

38

about with goodly Tapistrie, where was a Table prepared for his Highnesse and the Queenes Grace. All the floore where the king sate, was couered with broadcloathes in stead of greene rushes: these were choice peeces of the finest wool, of an Azure colour, valued at an hundred pound a cloath, which afterward was giuen 5 to his Maiestie.

The king beeing set with the chiefest of his Councell about him, after a delicate dinner, a sumptuous Banquet was brought in, serued all in glasse: the description whereof were too long for mee to write, and you to read. The great Hall was also filled with 10 Lords, Knights, and Gentlemen, who were attended by no other but the seruants of the house. The Ladies of Honour and Gentlewomen of the Court were all seated in an other Parlour by themselues: at whose table the maidens of the house did waite in decent sort. The seruingmen by themselues, and the pages and foot men 15 by themselues, vpon whom the Prentizes did attend most diligently. During the kings abiding in this place, there was no want of delicates: Renish wine, Claret wine, and Sacke, was as plentifull as small Ale. Then from the highest to the lowest, they were serued in such sort, as no discontent was found anie waie, so that great 20 commendations redounded vnto the Good-man of the house.

The L. Cardinall that of late found himselfe gall'd by the Allegorie of the Ants, spoke in this wise to the King. If it would please your Highnesse (quoth he) but to note the vaine glory of these Artificers, you should find no small cause of dislike in many of their 25 actions. For an instance, the fellow of this house, hee hath not stucke this day to vndoo himselfe onely to become famous by receiuing of your Maiestie: like *Herostratus* the Shoomaker, that burned the Temple of *Diana,* onely to get himselfe a name, more than for any affection hee beares to your Grace, as may well bee 30 prooued by this: Let there be but a simple Subsidie leuied vpon them for the assistance of your Highnesse Wars, or anie other weightie affaires of the Common wealth and state of the Realme, though it bee not the twentith part of their substance, they will so grudge and repine, that it is wonderfull; and like people desper- 35 ate crie out, They be quite vndone.

My Lord Cardinall quoth the Queene, (vnder correction of my

*15 pages ∧] Q2,3,5; ∼, Q1,4
*27 stucke] Q2-5; stocke Q1

Lord the King) I durst lay an hundred pound *Iacke* of *Newberie* was neuer of that mind, nor is not at this instant: if ye ask him, I warrant hee will say so. My self also had a proofe thereof at the Scottish inuasion, at what time this man, being seassed but at 5 sixe men, brought (at his owne cost) an hundred and fiftie into the field.

I woulde I had moe such subiects saide the King, and many of so good a minde.

Ho, ho *Harry* (quoth *Will Sommers*) then had not *Empson* and 10 *Dudley* beene chronicled for knaues, or sent to the Tower for treason.

But then they had not knowne the paine of imprisonment quoth our King, who with their subtiltie grieued many others.

But their subtiltie was such that it broke their necks quoth *Will* 15 *Sommers*.

Whereat the King and Queen laughing heartily, rose from the Table. By which time, *Iacke* of *Newberie* had caused all his folkes to goe to their worke, that his Grace and all the Nobilitie might see it, so indeed the Queene had requested. Then came his High- 20 nesse where hee saw an hundred Loomes standing in one roome, and two men working in euery one, who pleasantly sung in this sort.

The Weauers Song.

When *Hercules* did vse to spin,
    and *Pallas* wrought vpon the Loome,
25
Our Trade to flourish did begin,
    While Conscience went not selling Broome.
      Then loue and friendship did agree,
      To keepe the band of amitie.

When Princes sonnes kept sheep in field,
30
    and Queenes made cakes of wheaten flower,
Then men to lucre did not yeeld,
    which brought good cheare in euery bower.
      Then loue and friendship did agree,
35
      To hold the bands of amitie.

But when that Giants huge and hie,
    did fight with speares like Weauers beames,

Then they in Iron beds did lie,
    and brought poore men to hard extreames.
        Yet loue and friendship did agree,
        To hold the bands of amitie.

Then *Dauid* tooke his Sling and stone,   5
    not fearing great *Golias* strength:
He pearc't his braines and broke the bone,
    though he were fifty foote of length.
        For loue and friendship &c.

But while the Greekes besieged *Troy,*   10
    Penelope apace did spin,
And Weauers wrought with mickle ioy,
    though little gaines were comming in.
        For loue and friendship, &c.

Had *Helen* then sate carding wooll   15
    (whose beautious face did breed such strife)
Shee had not been sir *Paris* trull,
    nor caused so many lose their life.
        Yet we by loue did still agree, &c.

Or had King *Priams* wanton sonne,   20
    beene making quils with sweet content,
He had not then his friends vndone,
    when he to *Greece* a gadding went.
        For loue and friendship did agree, &c.

The Cedar trees indure more stormes,   25
    than little shrubs, that sprout on hie:
The Weauers liue more voyd of harmes,
    Than Princes of great dignitie,
        While loue and friendship doth agree, &c.

The Shepheard sitting in the field,   30
    doth tune his pipe with hearts delight:
When Princes watch with speare and shield,

22 not] Q2-5; nor Q1

the poore man soundly sleepes all night.
While loue and friendship doth agree, &c.

Yet this by proofe is daily tride,
for *Gods* good gifts wee are ingrate:
5   And no man through the World so wide,
liues well contented with his state.
No loue and friendship wee can see,
To hold the bands of amitie.

Well sung good fellowes, said our King: Light hearts and merrie
10 mindes liue long without gray haires.

But (quoth *Will Sommers*) seldome without red noses.

Well, said the King, there is a hundred angels to make good
chear withal: and looke that euery yeare once you make a feast
among your selues, and frankly (euery yeare) I giue you leaue to
15 fetch foure Buckes out of *Dunnington* parke, without any mans let
or controulement.

O I beseech your Grace (quoth *Will Sommers*) let it be with a
condition.

What is that, said our King?

20 My Liege, quoth hee, that although the Keeper will haue the
skins, that they may giue their wiues the hornes.

Goe to, said the Queene, thy head is fuller of knauerie, then thy
purse is of crownes.

The poore workemen humbly thanked his Maiestie for his boun-
25 tifull liberalitie: and euer since it hath beene a custome among
the Weauers, euery yeare presently after *Bartholomewtide,* in remembrance of the Kings fauor to meete together, and make a merrie
feast. His Maiestie came next among the spinners, and carders, who
were merrily a working: whereat *Will Sommers* fell into a great
30 laughter.

What ayles the foole to laugh, sayd the King?

Marrie (quoth *Will Sommers*) to see these maidens get their
liuing, as buls doe eate their meate.

How is that, said the Queen?

35 By going still backward quoth *Will Sommers:* and I will laie a
wager, that they that practise so well being maides to goe backward, will quickly learne ere long to fall backward.

But sirra said the Cardinall, thou didst fall forward when thou
brokest thy face in maister *Kingsmiles* cellar.

But you my Lord sate forward (quoth *Will Sommers*) when you
sate in the stockes at Sir *Amias Paulets.*

Whereat there was greater laughing than before. The King and
Queene and all the Nobilitie heedfully beheld these Women, who
for the most part were very faire and comly creatures, and were all
attired alike from top to toe. Then (after due reuerence) the maidens in dulcet manner chaunted out this song, two of them singing
the Dittie, and all the rest bearing the burden.

The Maidens Song.

It was a Knight in *Scotland* borne,   10
  follow my loue, leape ouer the strand:
Was taken prisoner and left for lorne,
  euen by the good Earle of *Northumberland.*

Then was he cast in prison strong,
  follow my loue, leape ouer the strand: 15
Where he could not walke nor lie along,
  euen by the good Earle of *Northumberland.*

And as in sorrow thus he lay,
  follow my loue, come ouer the strand;
The Earles sweete Daughter walkt that way, 20
  and she the faire flower of *Northumberland.*

And passing by like an Angell bright,
  follow my loue, come ouer the strand:
This Prisoner had of her a sight,
  and she the faire flower of *Northumberland.* 25

And loud to her this Knight did crie,
  follow my loue, come ouer the strand:
The salt teares standing in his eye,
  and she the faire flower of *Northumberland.*

Faire Lady he sayd, take pitty on me, 30
  follow my loue, come ouer the strand:
And let me not in prison dye,
  and you the faire flower of *Northumberland,*

Faire Sir how should I take pittie on thee,
    follow my loue, come ouer the strand:
Thou being a foe to our Country,
    and I the faire flower of *Northumberland?*

5   Faire Lady I am no foe he said,
    follow my loue, come ouer the strand:
Through thy sweet loue here was I stayd,
    for thee the faire flower of *Northumberland.*

Why shouldst thou come here for loue of me,
10   follow my loue, come ouer the strand;
Hauing wife and Children in thy Countrie,
    and I the faire flower of *Northumberland?*

I sweare by the blessed Trinitie,
    follow my loue, come ouer the strand:
15   I haue no wife nor children I,
    nor dwelling at home in merry *Scotland.*

If curteously you will set me free,
    follow my loue, come ouer the strand:
I vow that I will marrie thee,
20   so soone as I come in faire *Scotland.*

Thou shalt be a Lady of Castles and Towers:
    follow my loue, come ouer the strand:
And sit like a Queene in princely bowers,
    when I am at home in faire *Scotland.*

25   Then parted hence this Lady gay,
    follow my loue, come ouer the strand:
And got her fathers ring away,
    to helpe this sad Knight into faire *Scotland.*

Likewise much gold she got by sleight,
30   follow my loue, come ouer the strand:
And all to helpe this forlorne Knight
    to wend from her father to faire *Scotland.*

44

Chapter Three

Two gallant steedes both good and able,
  follow my loue, come ouer the strand:
She likewise tooke out of the stable,
  to ride with this Knight into faire *Scotland*.

And to the Iaylor she sent this ring,   5
  follow my loue, come ouer the strand:
The Knight from prison forth to bring,
  to wend with her into faire *Scotland*.

This token set the prisoner free,
  follow my loue, come ouer the strand: 10
Who straight went to this faire Lady,
  to wend with her into faire *Scotland*.

A gallant steed he did bestride,
  follow my loue, come ouer the strand:
And with the Lady away did ride,   15
  and she the faire flower of *Northumberland*.

They roade till they came to a water cleare,
  follow my loue, come ouer the strand:
Good sir how should I follow you here,
  and I the faire flower of *Northumberland*?   20

The water is rough and wonderfull deepe,
  follow my loue, come ouer the strand:
And on my saddle I shall not keep,
  and I the faire flower of *Northumberland*.

Feare not the foord faire Lady quoth he,   25
  follow my loue, come ouer the strand:
For long I cannot stay for thee:
  and thou the faire flower of *Northumberland*.

The Lady prickt her wanton steed,
  follow my loue, come ouer the strand: 30
And ouer the Riuer swom with speede,
  and she the faire flower of *Northumberland*.

From top to toe all wet was shee,
  follow my loue, come ouer the strand:
This haue I done for loue of thee,
  and I the faire flower of *Northumberland.*

5   Thus rode shee all one wintersnight,
  follow my loue, come ouer the strand:
Till *Edenborow* they saw in sight,
  the chiefest towne in all *Scotland.*

Now chuse (quoth he) thou wanton flower,
10   follow my loue, come ouer the strand:
Where thou wilt be my paramour,
  or get thee home to *Northumberland.*

For I haue wife and children fiue,
  follow my loue, come ouer the strand:
15 In *Edenborow* they be aliue,
  then get thee home to faire *England.*

This fauour shalt thou haue to boote,
  follow my loue, come ouer the strand:
Ile haue thy horse, goe thou on foote,
20   goe get thee home to *Northumberland.*

O false and faithlesse Knight quoth shee,
  follow my loue, come ouer the strand:
And canst thou deale so bad with me,
  and I the faire flower of *Northumberland?*

25 Dishonour not a Ladies name,
  follow my loue, come ouer the strand:
But draw thy sword and end my shame,
  and I the faire flower of *Northumberland.*

He tooke her from her stately steed,
30   follow my loue, come ouer the strand:

---

[24] *Northumberland?*] Q2-5; ∼. Q1

46

And left her there in extreame need,
  and she the faire flower of *Northumberland*.

Then sate she downe full heauily,
  follow my loue, come ouer the strand:
At length two Knights came riding by,   5
  two gallant Knights of faire *England*.

Shee fell downe humbly on her knee,
  follow my loue, come ouer the strand:
Saying curteous Knights take pitty on mee,
  and I the faire flower of *Northumberland*.   10

I haue offended my father deere,
  follow my loue, come ouer the strand:
And by a false Knight that brought me heere,
  from the good Earle of *Northumberland*.

They tooke her vp behind them then,   15
  follow my loue, come ouer the strand:
And brought her to her Fathers agen,
  and he the good Earle of *Northumberland*.

All you faire Maidens be warned by me,
  follow my loue, come ouer the strand,   20
Scots were neuer true, nor neuer will be,
  To Lord, to Lady, nor faire *England*.

FINIS.

  After the Kings Maiestie and the Queene had heard this song
sweetely sung by them, hee cast them a great rewarde: and so de- 25
parting thence, went to the Fulling mills, and Dyehouse, where a
great many also were hard at worke: and his Maiesty perceiuing
what a great number of people were by this one man set on worke,
both admired, and commended him, saying further, that no Trade
in all the Land was so much to bee cherished and maintained as 30
this, which quoth he may well be called The life of the poor. And

---

³¹ The life] Q2-5; the life Q1

as the King returned from this place with intent to take horse and depart, there met him a great many of children in garments of white silke fringed with gold, their heads crowned with golden Baies, and about their armes each one had a scarfe of green sarcenet
5 fast tyed, in their hands they bore siluer Boawes, and vnder their girdles golden arrowes.

The formost of them represented *Diana*, goddesse of Chastitie, who was attended vpon by a trayne of beautifull Nymphes, and they presented to the King foure prisoners: The first was a sterne
10 and grisly Woman, carrying a frowning countenance: and her forehead full of wrinkles, her hair as blacke as pitch; and her garments all bloudie, a greate sworde shee had in her hand all stayned with purple gore: they called her name *Bellona*, Goddesse of warres, who had three daughters: the first of them was a tall Woman, so
15 leane and ill fauoured, that her cheek bones were ready to start out of the skinne, of a pale and deadly colour, her eyes sunke into her head: her legges so feeble, that they could scantly carrie the body, all along her armes and hands through the skin you might tel the sinowes, ioyntes, and bones: her teeth were very strong and
20 sharpe withall: shee was so greedy that shee was readie with her teeth to teare the skin from her owne armes: her attyre was black, and all torne and ragged, shee went bare footed and her name was *Famine.* The second was a strong and lustie Woman, with a looke pittilesse, and vnmercifull countenance: her garments were all
25 made of Iron and Steele, and she carried in her hand a naked weapon and shee was called the *Sword.* The third was also a cruell creature, her eyes did sparkle like burning coales: her hayre was like a flame: and her garments like burning brasse: shee was so hot that none could stand neere her, and they called her name *Fyre.*
30 After this they retyred againe, and brought vnto his Highnesse two other Personages, their countenaunce was Princely and amiable, their attyre most rich and sumptuous: The one carried in his hand a golden trumpet, and the other a Palmetree, and these were called *Fame* and *Victory,* whom the goddesse of Chastitie charged to waite
35 vpon this famous Prince for euer. This done, each child after other with due reuerence gaue vnto his Maiestie a sweete smelling Gilliflower, after the manner of the Persians, offering something in token of loyalty and obedience. The King and Queene behould-

---

[24] pittilesse,] Q2,3,5; ~∧ Q1,4

48

ing the sweet fauour and countenance of these children, demaunded of *Iack* of *Newbery* whose children they were? Who answered: It shall please your Highnesse to vnderstand, that these are the children of poore people: that do get their liuing by picking of woll, hauing scant a good meale once in a weeke.   5

With that the King began to tell his Gilliflowers, whereby hee found that there was 96. children. Certainely said the Queene I perceiue God gives as faire children to the poore as to the rich, and fairer manie times: and though their dyet and keeping bee but simple, the blessing of God doth cherish them. Therefore sayd the   10 Queene I will request to haue two of them to waite in my Chamber.

Faire *Katherine* said the King, thou and I haue iumpt in one opinion, thinking these children fitter for the Court than the Countrey: whereupon he made choyse of a dozen more: foure he ordained to be Pages to his royall person, and the rest hee sent to Uniuersi-   15 ties, allotting to euery one a Gentlemans liuing. Diuers of the Noble men did in like sort entertaine some of those children into their seruices, so that (in the end) not one was left to picke wool, but were all so prouided for, that their Parents neuer needed to care for them: and God so blessed them, that each of them came to be   20 men of great account and authority in the land, whose posterities remaine to this day worshipfull and famous.

The King, Queene, and Nobles being ready to depart, after great thankes and gifts giuen to *Iack* of *Newbery,* his Maiestie would haue made him Knight, but hee meekely refused it, saying: I be-   25 seech your Grace let me liue a poore Clothier among my people, in whose maintenance I take more felicity, then in all the vaine titles of Gentilitie: for these are the labouring Ants whom I seeke to defend, and these bee the Bees which I keepe: who labour in this life, not for our selues, but for the glory of God, and to do seruice to   30 our dread Soueraigne.

Thy knighthood need be no hinderance of thy faculty, quoth the King.

O my drad Soueraigne said *Iacke,* honour and worship may be compared to the Lake of *Laethe,* which makes men forget them-   35 selues that taste thereof: and to the end I may still keepe in minde from whence I came, and what I am, I beseech your Grace let mee rest in my russet coat a poore Clothier to my dying day.

[37] whence] Q2-4; when Q1,5

Seeing then (said the King) that a mans minde is a Kingdome to himselfe, I will leaue thee to the riches of thy owne content, and so farewell.

The Queenes Maiesty taking her leaue of the good wife with a
5 Princely kisse, gaue her in token of remembrance a most precious and rich Dyamond set in gold, about the which was also curiously set sixe Rubies, and sixe Emeralds in one peece, valued at nine hundred Marks: and so her Grace departed.

But in this meane space *Will Sommers* kept company among the
10 maids, and betooke himselfe to spinning as they did, which among them was held as a forfeit of a gallon of wine: but *William* by no meanes would pay it except they would take it out in kisses, rating euery kisse at a farthing.

This paiment we refuse for two causes quoth the Maidens: the
15 one, for that we esteem not kisses at so base a rate: and the other, because in so doing we should giue as much as you.

CHAPTER IV.

How the maidens serued *Wil Sommers* for his sawsinesse.

The maidens consented together, seeing *Will Sommers* was so
20 busie both with their worke, and in his wordes, and would not pay his forfeiture, to serue him as he serued: first therefore they bound him hand and foote, and set him vpright against a poste, tying him thereto, which he tooke in ill part, notwithstanding he could not resist them: and because hee let his tongue runne at
25 randome, they set a faire gagge in his mouth, such a one as he could not for his life put away: so that he stood as one gaping for winde. Then one of them got a couple of dogs droppings, and putting them in a bagge, laide them in soke in a bason of water, while the rest turned downe the coller of his Ierkin, and put an hoste
30 cloath about his necke in stead of a fine towell: then came the

---

⁵ kisse,] ∼: Q1
²² hand and foote] Q5; hand and feete Q1,4; hands and feete Q2,3

other maide with a bason and water in the same, and with the perfume in the pudding-bagge, flapt him about the face and lips, till he looked like a tawnie Moore, and with her hand washt him very orderly: the smell being somwhat strong, *Will* could by no meanes abide it, and for want of other language, cryed *Ah ha ha ha.* Faine 5 hee would haue spet, and could not, so that he was faine to swallow down such liquor as hee neuer tasted the like.

When hee had a pretty while been washed in this sort, at the length he croucht downe vpon his knees, yeelding himselfe to their fauor: which the maidens perceiuing, pulled the gag out of his 10 mouth. He had no sooner the liberty of his tongue, but that he curst and swore like a diuel: the maides that could scant stand for laughing, at last askt how hee liked his washing?

Washing, quoth hee? I was neuer thus washt, nor euer met with such Barbers since I was borne: let mee goe quoth hee, and I will 15 giue you whatsoeuer you will demand: wherewith hee cast them an English Crowne.

My quoth one of the maides, you are yet but washt, but wee will shaue you ere yee goe.

Sweete Maides quoth hee pardon my shauing, let it suffice that 20 you haue washt mee: if I haue done a trespasse to your trade, forgiue it mee, and I will neuer hereafter offend you.

Tush said the Maides you haue made our wheeles cast their bands and bruzed the teeth of our cards in such sort, as the offence may not bee remitted without great penance. As for your gold wee re- 25 garde it not: therefore as you are perfumed fit for the dogges, so we enioine you this night to serue all our hogs, which penance if you will sweare with all speede to performe, we will let you loose.

O quoth *Will,* the huge Elephant was neuer more fearefull of the silly sheepe, than I am of your displeasures: therefore let mee 30 loose and I will doo it with all diligence.

Then they vnbound him, and brought him among a great companie of Swyne, which when *Will* had well viewed ouer, hee draue out of the yard all the sowes. Why how now quoth the maides, what meane you by this? 35

Mary quoth *Will,* these be all sowes, and my pennance is but to serue the hogs.

It is true quoth they: haue you ouertaken vs in this sort? Well looke there bee not one hog vnserued wee would aduise you.

Will Sommers stript vp his sleeues very orderly, and clapt an apron 40

about his motley hosen, and taking a paile serued the hogs hand-
somely. When he had giuen them all meate, he sayd thus:

> My taske is duly done,
> My libertie is won:
> 5   The hogs haue eate their crabs.
> Therefore farewell yee drabs.

Nay soft friend quoth they, the veriest hog of all hath yet had
nothing.

Where the diuell is he said *Will* that I see him not?

10 Wrapt in a motley Ierkin quoth they, take thy selfe by the nose,
and thou shalt catch him by the snout.

I was neuer so verie a hog quoth hee, but I would always spare
from my own bellie to giue to a Woman.

If thou do not (say they) eate (like the prodigall Childe) with
15 thy fellow hogs, wee will so shaue thee, as thou shalt dearely repent
thy disobedience.

He seeing no remedie, committed himselfe to their mercie: and
so they let him goe. When hee came to the Court, hee shewed to the
King al his aduenture among the Weauers maidens, wherat the
20 King and Queene laughed heartily.

CHAPTER V.

Of the pictures which *Iacke* of *Newbery* had in his house,
whereby hee encouraged his seruants to seeke for fame
and dignitie.

25 In a faire large Parlour which was wainscotted about, *Iacke* of
Newbery had 15. faire Pictures hanging, which were couered
with curtaines of green silke, fringed with gold, which hee would
often shew to his friends and seruants. In the first was the picture

12 but I] Q2-5; I Q1

of a sheepheard before whom kneeled a great King named *Viriat,* who sometime gouerned the people of *Portugal.*

See heere quoth *Iacke,* the father a Shepheard, the sonne a Soueraigne. This man ruled in *Portugall,* and made great warres against the Romanes, and after that inuaded *Spaine,* yet in the end was 5 traiterously slaine.

The next was the Portraiture of *Agathocles,* which for his surpassing wisedome and manhood, was created King of *Sicilia,* and maintained battaile against the people of *Carthage.* His Father was a poore Potter, before whom he also kneeled. And it was the 10 vse of this King, that whensoeuer he made a banquet, he would haue as well vessels of earth as of golde set vpon the Table, to the intent hee might alwaies beare in mind the place of his beginning, his Fathers house and family.

The third was the picture of *Iphicrates* an Athenian borne, who 15 vanquished the Lacedemonians in plaine and open battaile. This man was Captaine generall to *Artaxerxes,* King of Persia, whose father was notwithstanding a Cobler, and there likewise pictured. *Eumenes* was also a famous Captaine to *Alexander* the great, whose father was no other then a Carter. 20

The fourth was the similitude of *Aelius Pertinax,* sometime Emperor of Rome, yet was his father but a Weauer: and afterward to giue example to others of lowe condition, to beare minds of worthy men, he caused the shop to be beautified with marble curiously cut, wherein his father before him was wont to get his liuing. 25

The fift was the picture of *Dioclesian,* that so much adorned Rome with his magnificall and triumphant victories. This was a most famous Emperour, although no other than the sonne of a Book-binder.

Valentinian stood the next, painted most artificially: who also 30 was crowned Emperor, and was but the sonne of a poore Rope-maker, as in the same picture was expressed, where his father was painted by him vsing his trade.

The seuenth was the Emperor *Probus,* whose father being a Gardener, was pictured by him houlding a spade. 35

---

[15] third] Q2-5; 3. Q1
[17] man] Q2-5; then Q1
[27] This was] *not a new paragraph* Q2,3,5; *begins a new paragraph* Q1,4
[30] *Valentinian*] *begins a new paragraph* Q5; *not a new paragraph* Q1-4

The eighth picture was of *Marcus Aurelius,* whom euery age honoureth, he was so wise and prudent an Emperour: yet was he but a cloth-weauers sonne.

The ninth was the portraiture of the valiant Emperour *Maximi-*
5 *nus,* the son of a Black-smith, who was there painted as he was wont to worke at the Anuill.

In the tenth table was painted the Emperour *Galerus,* who at the first was but a poore shepheard.

Next to this picture was placed the pictures of two Popes of
10 Rome, whose wisedome and learning aduanced them to that digni- tie. The first was the liuely counterfeit of Pope *Iohn* the twenty two, whose father was a Shoomaker: he beeing elected Pope, in- creased their rents and patrimonie greatly.

The other was the picture of Pope *Sextus* the fourth of that
15 name, being a poore Mariners sonne.

The thirteenth picture was of *Lamusius,* King of *Lombardie,* who was no better then the son of a common strumpet, being painted like a naked childe walking in water, and taking hold of the point of a Launce, by the which hee hung fast, and saued himselfe.
20 The reason whereof is this. After his lewde mother was deliuered of him, shee vnnaturally threw him into a deepe stinking ditch, wherein was some water. By hap, King *Agilmond* passed that way, and found this childe almost drowned, who mouing him somewhat with the point of his Launce, the better to perceiue what he was,
25 the child (though newly borne) took hold thereof with one of his pretty hands, not suffering it to slide or slip away againe: which thing the king considering, beeing amazed at the strange force of this young little infant, caused it to bee taken vp, and carefully to be fostered, and because the place where hee found it, was called
30 *Lama,* he named the child *Lamusius:* who after grew to be so braue a man, and so much honoured of Fortune, that in the end hee was crowned King of the Lombards, who liued there in honour, and in his succession after him, euen vnto the time of the vnfortu- nate King *Albouina,* when all came to ruine, subuersion and de-
35 struction.

In the fourteenth picture, *Primislas* King of *Bohemia,* was most artificially drawne, before whom there stood an horse without bridle or saddle, in a field where husbandmen were at plough.

¹ eighth] Q2-5; eight Q1   * ⁷ *Galerus*] *Gabienus* Q1,4,5; *Gabianus* Q2,3
²⁷ king] Q2,3; prince Q1,4,5

The cause why this King was thus painted (quoth *Iack*) was this. At that time the King of the *Bohemians* died without issue, and great strife being among the Nobility for a new King, at length they all consented that a horse should be let into the field, without bridle or saddle, hauing all determined with a most assured pur- 5 pose to make him their King, before whom this horse rested: At what time it came to passe, that the horse first stayed himselfe be- fore this *Primislas*, being a simple creature, who was then busie driuing the plough: they presently made him their Soueraigne, who ordered himselfe and his Kingdome very wisely. Hee ordained 10 many good Lawes, he compassed the Citty of Prague with strong walles, besides many other things, meriting perpetuall laud and commendations.

The fifteenth was the picture of *Theophrastus,* a Philosopher, a counsellor of Kings, and companion of Nobles, who was but sonne 15 of a Taylor.

Seeing then my good seruants, that these men haue been ad- uanced to high estate and Princely dignities by wisedome, learning, and diligence, I would wish you to imitate the like vertues, that you might attaine the like honors: for which of you doth know 20 what good fortune God hath in store for you? there is none of you so poorly born, but that men of baser birth haue come to great honors: the idle hand shall euer goe in a ragged garment, and the slothfull liue in reproach: but such as do leade a vertuous life, and gouerne themselues discreetely, shall of the best bee esteemed, and 25 spend their dayes in credit.

*8 *Primislas*] *Brimislas* Q5
20 of] Q2-5; if Q1
26 their] Q2,3,5; his Q1,4

CHAPTER VI.

How all the Clothiers in England ioyned together, and with
one consent complayned to the King of their great
hinderance sustayned for want of traffique into other
5　Countries, whereupon they could get no sale for their
Cloath.

By meanes of the warres our King had with other countries,
many Merchaunt strangers were prohibited for comming to
England, and also our owne Merchants (in like sort) were forbidden
10　to haue dealing with *France,* or the *Low-countries:* by meanes
whereof, the Clothiers had most of their cloth lying on their hands,
and that which they sold was at so low rate, that the money
scarcely paide for the wooll, and workemanship. Whereupon they
thought to ease themselues by abating the poore workemens wages,
15　and when that did not preuaile they turned away their people;
Weauers, Shearemen, Spinners and Carders: so that where there
was a hundred loomes kept in one towne, there was scant 50. and
hee that kept twenty, put downe ten. Many a poore man (for want
of worke) was hereby vndone with his wife and children, and it
20　made many a poore widow to sit with an hungry belly: This bred
great woe in most places in *England.* In the end *Iack* of *Newbery*
intended (in the behalfe of the poore) to make a supplication to the
King: and to the end he might do it the more effectually, he sent
Letters to all the chiefe clothing townes in *England* to this effect.

25　　　　　　　　*The Letter.*

Welbeloued friends and brethren, hauing a taste of the generall griefe,
and feeling (in some measure) the extreamitie of these times, I fell into
consideration by what means we might best expell these sorrowes, and
recouer our former commodity. When I had well thought thereon, I

12 that the money] Q2-5; that money Q1
28 means] Q2-5; meane Q1

56

found that nothing was more needefull herein then a faithfull vnity among our selues. This sore of necessity can no way be cured but by concord: for like as the flame consumes the candle, so men through discorde waste themselues. The poore hate the rich, because they will not set them on worke: and the rich hate the poore, because they seeme 5 burdenous: so both are offended for want of gaine. When *Belinus* and *Brennus* were at strife, the Queene their mother in their greatest furie perswaded them to peace, by vrging her conception of them in one wombe, and mutuall cherishing of them from their tender yeeres: so let our Art of Clothing, which like a kinde mother hath cherished vs with 10 the excellency of her secrets, perswade vs to an vnity. Though our occupation be decayed, let vs not deale with it as men doe by their old shoes, which after they haue long borne them out of the mire, doe in the end fling them on the dunghill: or as the husbandman doth by his Bees, who for their honey burnes them. Deare friends, consider that our Trade 15 will mainetaine vs, if wee will vphold it, and there is nothing base, but that which is basely vsed. Assemble therefore your selues together, and in euery Town tell the number of those that haue their liuing by meanes of this Trade: note it in a Bill, and send it to me: and because suits in Court are like winter nights long and wearisome, let there be in each place a 20 weekely collection made to defray charges: for I tell you. Noble mens Secretaries and cunning Lawyers haue slow tongues and deafe eares: which must daily bee nointed with the sweete oyle of Angels. Then let two honest discreete men be chosen, and sent out of euery Towne to meet me at *Blackwell* hall in *London,* on *All Saints* Eue, and then wee will 25 present our humble petition to the King: Thus I bid you heartily farewell.

Copies of this Letter being sealed, they were sent to all the clothing Townes of *England,* and Weauers both of Linnen and Wollen gladly receiued them: so that when all the Bills were brought together, there were found of the Clothiers, and those they main- 30 tained, threescore thousand and six hundred persons. Moreouer euery clothing Towne, sending vp two men to *London,* they were found to bee an hundred and twelue persons, who in very humble sort fell downe before his Maiesty, walking in S. *Iames* his Parke, and deliuered vnto him their petition. The King presently perusing 35 it, asked if they were all Clothiers? who answered (as it were one man) in this sort:

Wee are (most gracious King) all poore Clothiers, and your Maiesties faithfull subiects.

My Lords, quoth the King, let these mens complaint bee 40 throughly lookt vnto, and their griefe redressed: for I account them

in the number of the best Common wealths men. As the Clergie for
the Soule, the Souldier for defence of his Countrie, the Lawyer to
execute iustice, the husbandman to feede the belly: So is the skilfull
Clothier no lesse necessary for the clothing of the backe, whom wee
may reckon among the chiefe Yeomen of our Land: and as the
Crystall sight of the eye is tenderly to bee kept from harmes, because
it giues to the whole body light; so is the clothier, whose cunning
hand prouides garments to defend our naked parts from the winters nipping frost. Many more reasons there are which may mooue
vs to redresse their griefes, but let it suffice that I command to
haue it done.

With that his grace deliuered the petition to the Lord Chauncellor, and all the Clothiers cried, God saue the King. But as the King
was ready to depart, hee suddenly turned about, saying I remember there is one *Iack* of *Newbery,* I muse hee had not his hand in
this businesse, who profest himselfe to bee a defender of true la-
bourers.

Then said the Duke of *Sommerset:* It may bee his purse is answerable for his person.

Nay (quoth the Lord Cardinall) all his treasure is little enough
to maintaine wars against the Butterflies.

With that *Iack* shewed himselfe vnto the King, and priuately
told his Grace of their griefe anew. To whom his Maiesty said:
Giue thy attendance at the Councell Chamber, where thou shalt
receiue an answere to thy content. And so his highnes departed.
Finally, it was agreed that the Marchants should freely traffique
one with another: and that proclamation thereof shold bee made
as well on the other side of the sea, as in our Land, but it was long
before this was effected, by reason the Cardinall beeing Lord Chan-
cellor, put off the matter from time to time. And because the
Clothiers thought it best not to depart before it was ended, they
gaue their daily attendance at the Cardinals house: but spent many
dayes to no purpose. Sometimes they were answered, my Lord was
busie: and could not bee spoke withall, or else hee was asleepe,
and they durst not wake him: or at his study, and they would not
disturbe him: or at his prayers, and they durst not displease him:
and still one thing or other stood in the way to hinder them. At
last, *Patch* the Cardinals foole, beeing (by their often repaire

*⁷ clothier] Q4,5; clothiers Q1-3

thither) well acquainted with the Clothiers, came vnto them and saide: what, haue you not spoken with my Lord yet?

No truly (quoth they) we heare say he is busy and wee stay till his Grace bee at leasure.

It is true, saide *Patch:* and with that in all hast hee went out of the hall, and at last came in againe with a great bundle of straw on his back.

Why how now *Patch* (quoth the Gentlemen) what wilt thou doe with that straw?

Mary (quoth hee) I will put it vnder these honest mens feete, least they should freeze ere they finde my Lord at leisure. This made them all to laugh, and caused *Patch* to cary away his straw againe.

Well, well (quoth hee) if it cost you a groats worth of faggots at night, blame not mee.

Trust me (said *Iack* of *Newbery*) if my Lord Cardinals father had beene no hastier in killing of Calues then he is in dispatching of poore mens sutes, I doubt he had neuer worne a Myter. Thus he spake betwixt themselues softly: but yet not so softly but that hee was ouerheard by a flattering fellow that stood by, who made it knowne to some of the Gentlemen, and they straight certified the Cardinall thereof.

The Cardinall (who was of a very high spirit, and a lofty aspiring minde) was maruailously displeased at *Iack* of *Newbery:* wherefore in his rage hee commanded and sent the Clothiers all to prison, because the one of them should not sue for the others releasement. Foure dayes lay these men in the Marshalsey, till at last they made their humble Petition to the King for their release: but some of the Cardinals friends kept it from the kings sight. Notwithstanding the Duke of *Sommerset* knowing thereof, spake with the Lord Cardinall about the matter, wishing he should speedily release them, least it bred him some displeasure: for you may perceiue (quoth the Duke) how highly the King esteemes men of that facultie.

Sir (quoth the Cardinall) I doubt not but to answere their imprisonment well enough, being perswaded that none would haue giuen mee such a quip but an heretique: and I dare warrant you, were this *Iack* of *Newbery* well examined, hee would be found to bee infected with *Luthers* spirit, against whom our king hath of late written a most learned booke: in respect whereof the Popes

holinesse hath entituled his Maiesty, *Defender of the Faith:* therefore I tell you such fellowes are fitter to bee faggots for fire, then
Fathers of families: notwithstanding (at your Graces request) I
will release them.

5 Accordingly the Cardinall sent for the Clothiers before him to
White-hall, his new built house by *Westminster,* and there bestowing his blessing vpon them, said: Though you haue offended mee
I pardon you: for as *Steuen* forgaue his enemies that stoned him,
and our Sauiour those sinfull men that crucified him, so doe I
10 forgiue you that high trespasse committed in disgrace of my birth:
for herein do men come neerest vnto God, in shewing mercy and
compassion. But see hereafter you offend no more. Touching your
suite it is granted, and to morrow shall bee published through
London.

15 This being said, they departed: and according to the Cardinalls
words, their businesse was ended. The Stil-yard Marchants ioyfull
thereof, made the Clothiers a great banquet. After which each man
departed home, carying tidings of their good successe: so that in
short space, Clothing againe was very good, and poore men as well
20 set on worke as before.

CHAPTER VII.

How a yong Italian Marchant comming to *Iack* of *New-beries* house, was greatly enamoured of one of his maidens, and how he was serued.

25 Among other seruants which *Iack* of *Newbery* kept, there were
in his house threescore maydens, which euery Sunday waited
on his Wife to Church and home againe, who had diuers offices.
Among other, two were appointed to keepe the beames and
waights, to waighe out wooll to the Carders and Spinners, and to
30 receiue it in againe by waight: one of them was a comely mayden,

*17 thereof] hereof Q2-5

fayre and louely, borne of wealthy parents, and brought vp in good qualities, her name was *Ione:* so it was that a yong wealthie Italian Marchant, comming oft from *London* thither to bargaine for cloth (for at that time clothiers most commonly had their cloth bespoken, and halfe payd for aforehand.) This Master *Benedicke* 5 fell greatly enamoured of this mayden, and therefore offered much courtesie to her, bestowing many gifts on her, which she receiued thankefully: and albeit his outward countenance shewed his inward affection, yet *Ione* would take no knowledge thereof. Halfe the day sometime, would he sit by her, as she was waighing wooll, 10 often sighing and sobbing to himselfe, yet saying nothing, as if hee had beene tonguelesse, like the men of *Coromandae;* and the loather to speake, for that hee could speake but bad english. *Ione* on the other side that well perceiued his passions, did as it were triumph ouer him, as one that were bondslaue to her beauty: and 15 although shee knew well enough before that shee was faire; yet did she neuer so highly esteeme of her selfe as at this present: so that when she heard him eyther sigh, sob, or groane, shee would turne her face in a carelesse sort, as if shee had beene borne (like the women of *Taprobana*) without eares. 20

When master *Benedick* saw shee made no reckoning of his sorrows, at length he blabbered out this broken English, and spoke to her in this sort: Mettressa *Ione,* be mee tra and fa, mee loue you wod all mine heart, and if you no shall loue mee againe, mee know me shall die, sweete Mettressa loue a mee; and by my fa and 25 tra you shall lack nothing: First me will giue you de silke for make you a Frog. Second de fin Camree for make you ruffes, and de turd shall be for make fin hankercher, for wipe your nose.

She mistaking his speech began to be cholerick, wishing him to keepe that bodkin to pick his teeth. Ho, ho Mettressa *Ione* (quoth 30 he) be Got, you are angry. Oh Mettressa *Ione* be not chafe with your friene for noting.

Good sir (quoth shee) keepe your friendship for them that care for it and fixe your loue on those that can like you: as for mee I tell you plaine, I am not minded to marry. 35

O tis no matter for marrie, if you will come to my chamber, beshit my bed, and let me kisse you.

The maide though she were very much displeased, yet at these words shee could not forbeare laughing for her life.

Ahah, Mettressa *Ione,* mee is very glad to see you merry, hould 40

Mettressa *Ione,* holde your hand I say, and there is foure crowne
because you laugh on mee.

I pray you Sir, keepe your crowns, for I neede them not.

Yes be Got you shall haue them Mettressa *Ione,* to keepe in
5 box for you.

She that could not well vnderstand his broken language, mistook
his meaning in many things, and therfore wild him not to trouble
her any more: Notwithstanding such was his loue toward her, that
he could not forbeare her company, but made many iournies
10 thither for her sake: and as a certain spring in *Arcadia,* makes men
to starue that drinke of it: so did poore *Bennedicke* feeding his
fancie on her beautie: for when he was in *London,* he did nothing
but sorrow, wishing he had wings like the monsters of *Tartaria*
that he might fly to and fro at his pleasure.

15 When any of his friends did tel her of his ardent affection toward
her, she wisht them to rub him with the sweate of a mule, to
asswage his amorous passion, or to fetch him some of the water
in *Boetia,* to coole and extinguish the heate of his affection: for
quoth she, let him neuer hope to be helpt by mee.

20 Well quoth they, before he saw thy alluring face, hee was a man
reasonable and wise, but is now a stark foole, being by thy beautie
bereft of wit, as if he had drunke of the riuer *Cea,* and like bewitching *Circes* thou hast certainly transformed him from a man
to an Asse. There are stones in *Pontus* quoth they, that the deeper
25 they bee layd in the water, the fiercer they burne: vnto the which,
fond Louers may fitly be compared, who the more they are denyed,
the hotter is their desire: but seeing it is so, that he can finde no
fauor at your hands, we will shew him what you haue said, and
either draw him from his dumpes, or leaue him to his owne will.

30 Then spake one of the Weauers that dwelt in the Towne, and
was a kinsman to this maid. I muse (quoth hee) that maister *Bennedicke* will not be perswaded, but like the Moath, will play with
the flame that will scorch his wings. Mee thinkes he should forbeare to loue, or learne to speake, or else woo such as can answer
35 him in his language, for I tell you that *Ione* my kinswoman is no
taste for an Italian.

These speeches were told to *Benedicke* with no small addition.
When our yong marchant heard the matter so plain, he vowd to be

*5 box] pox Q2-5

reuenged of the Weauer, and to see if he could finde any more friendship of his wife: therefore dissembling his sorrow, and couering his griefe, with speed he tooke his iourney to *Newbery,* and pleasantly saluted mistris *Ione,* and hauing his purse full of crownes, hee was very liberall to the workefolkes, especilly to *Iones* kins- 5 man, in so much that hee got his fauour many times to goe forth with him, promising him very largely to doe great matters, and to lend him a hundreth pound, wishing him to be a seruant no longer, beside hee liberally bestowed on his wife many gifts, and if she washt him but a band, hee would giue her an angel: if hee 10 did but send her child for a quart of Wine, hee would giue him a shilling for his paines. The which his curtesie changed the weauers mind: saying hee was a very honest Gentleman, and worthie to haue one far better then his kinswoman.

This pleased Master *Bennedick* well to heare him say so, not- 15 withstanding hee made light of the matter, and many times when the weauer was at his masters at worke, the Marchant would bee at home with his wife, drinking and making merrie. At length time bringing acquaintance, and often conference breeding familiaritie, master *Bennedicke* began somewhat boldly to iest with *Gillian,* 20 saying that her sight, and sweet countenance had quite reclaimed his loue from *Ione,* and that shee only was the mistris of his hart: and if shee would lend him her loue, hee would giue her gold from *Arabia,* orient pearls from *India,* and make her bracelets of precious diamonds. Thy garments shall bee of the finest silke that is made in 25 *Venice,* and thy purse shall still be stuft with angels. Tell mee thy mind my loue, and kill me not with vnkindnes, as did thy scornefull kinswoman; whose disdain had almost cost mee my life.

O master *Bennedicke,* thinke not the wiues of England can bee wonne by rewards, or intised with faire words, as children are with 30 Plums, it may bee that you being merily disposed, do speak this to try my constancie. Know then that I esteeme more the honour of my good name, than the sliding wealth of the world.

Master *Bennedicke* hearing her say so, desired her, that considering it was loue which forced his tongue to bewray his harts affec- 35 tion, that yet shee would bee secret, and so for that time tooke his leaue.

When hee was gone, the woman began to call her wits together,

<hr/>

15 him] Q2,3; them Q1,4,5

and to consider of her poore estate, and withall the better to note the comelines of her person, and the sweet fauour of her face: which when she had well thought vpon, shee began to harbour new thoughts, and to entertaine contrarie affections, saying: shall
5 I content my selfe to be wrapt in sheepes russet that may swim in silks, and sit all day carding for a groat, that may haue crowns at my command? No quoth shee, I will no more beare so base a mind, but take fortunes fauours while they are to bee had. The sweet Rose doth florish but one moneth, nor Womens beauties but in
10 young yeers: as the winters frost consumes the Summer flowers, so doth old age banish pleasant delight. O glorious gold quoth shee, how sweete is thy smell? how pleasing is thy sight? Thou subduest Princes, and ouerthrowest kingdomes, then how should a silly woman withstand thy strength? thus shee rested meditating on
15 preferment, minding to hazard her honestie to maintaine her selfe in brauerie, euen as occupiers corrupt their consciences to gather riches.

Within a day or two, master *Bennedick* came to her again, on whom she cast a smiling countenance: hee perceiuing that, (accord-
20 ing to his old custome) sent for Wine, and very merrie they were. At last in the midst of their cups hee cast out his former question: and after farther conference she yeelded, and appointed a time when he should come to her: for which fauour hee gaue her halfe a dozen portigues: within an houre or two after, entring into her
25 owne conscience, bethinking how sinfully shee had sould her selfe to folly, began thus to expostulate.

Good Lord quoth shee, shall I breake that holy vow which I made in marriage, and pollute my bodie which the Lord hath sanctified? Can I breake the commandement of my God, and not
30 rest accursed? or bee a traytor to my husband, and suffer no shame? I heard once my brother read in a book, that *Bucephalus, Alex-anders* steed, being a beast, would not bee backt by any but the Emperour, and shal I consent to any but my husband? *Artemisia* being a heathen Lady, loued her husband so well, that shee drunke
35 vp his ashes, and buried him in her owne bowels: and should I being a Christian, cast my husband out of my heart? The Women of Rome were wont to Crowne their husbands heads with bayes, in token of victory, and shall I giue my husband hornes in token of

31 *Bucephalus*,] Q2,3; ∼∧ Q1,4,5

infamy? An harlot is hated of all vertuous people, and shall I make my selfe a whore? O my God forgiue me my sin, quoth shee, and cleanse my heart from these wicked imaginations: and as she was thus lamenting, her husband came home. At whose sight her teares were doubled, like a Riuer whose streame is increased by showers of raine. Her husband seeing this, would needs know the cause of her sorrow: but a great while she would not show him, casting many a pitious looke vpon him, and shaking her head, at last she said: O my deare husband, I haue offended against God and thee, and made such a trespasse by my tongue, as hath cut a deepe scarre in my conscience, and wounded my heart with griefe like a sword: like *Penelope* so haue I beene wooed, but like *Penelope* I haue not answered.

Why woman quoth hee, what is the matter? If it be but the bare offence of the tong why shouldst thou so greeue? considering that womens tongues are like Lambes tayles, which sildome stand still: And the wise man saith, where much talke is, must needes bee some offence. Womens beauties are faire markes for wandring eyes to shoot at: but as euery Archer hits not the white, so euery wooer wins not his mistris fauour. All Cities that are besieged, are not sackt, nor all women to be misliked that are loued. Why Wife, I am perswaded thy faith is more firme, and thy constancie greater to withstand Louers alarums, than that any other but my selfe should obtaine the fortresse of thy heart.

O sweet husband (quoth shee) wee see the strongest Tower at length falleth downe by the Canons force, though the bullets be but Iron: then how can the weake Bulwarke of a womans breast make resistance, when the hot Canons of deepe perswading words are shot off with golden bullets, and euery one as big as a Portigue?

If it bee so wife, I may think my selfe in a good case, and you to bee a very honest woman. As *Mars* and *Venus* daunst naked together in a net, so I doubt, you and some knaue haue playd naked together in a bed: but in faith you queane, I will send thee to salute thy friends without a nose, and as thou hast sold thy honestie, so will I sell thy company.

Sweete Husband, though I haue promised, I haue performed nothing: euery bargaine is not effected, and therefore as *Iudas*

---

⁹ said] Q2-5; sad Q1
²¹ Wife,] Q2,3; ∼? Q1,4,5
³⁰ selfe ∧] Q2-5; ∼, Q1

brought againe the thirtie siluer plates, for the which he betrayed his Maister: so repenting my folly, Ile cast him againe his gold, for which I should haue wronged my husband.

Tell me quoth her husband what hee is?

5 It is master *Bennedicke* quoth shee, which for my loue hath left the loue of our kinswoman, and hath vowed himselfe for euer to liue my seruant.

O dissembling Italian, quoth he, I will be reuenged on him for this wrong. I know that any fauour from *Ione* my kinswoman,
10 will make him runne like a man bitten with a mad dog: therefore be ruled by me, and thou shalt see me dresse him in his kinde: the woman was verie well pleased, saying he would be there that night.

All this works well with mee, quoth her husband, and to supper
15 wil I inuite *Ione* my kinswoman, and in the meane space make vp the bed in the Parlour very decently.

So the good man went forth, and got a sleepy drench from the Potecaries, the which hee gaue to a young Sow, which he had in his yard, and in that euening laid her downe in the bed in the
20 Parlour, drawing the curtaines round about. Supper time being come, master *Bennedick* gaue his attendance, looking for no other company but the good wife: Notwithstanding at the last mistresse *Ione* came in with her kinsman, and sate downe to supper with them. Maister *Bennedicke* musing at their sudden approach,
25 yet neuerthelesse glad of mistresse *Iones* company, past the supper time with many pleasant conceits, *Ione* shewing her selfe that night more pleasant in his company than at any time before: therefore he gaue the good man great thankes.

Good master *Bennedicke,* little do you thinke how I haue trau-
30 elled in your behalfe to my kinswoman, and much adoe I had to bring the peeuish Wench into any good liking of your loue: not-withstanding by my great diligence and perswasions, I did at length win her good will to come hither, little thinking to finde you here, or any such good cheare to entertaine her, all which I see is
35 fallen out for your profit. But trust mee all the world cannot alter her minde, nor turne her loue from you: In regard whereof she hath promised mee to lie this night in my house, for the great de-sire shee hath of your good companie: and in requitall of all your great curtesies shewed to mee, I am very well content to bring you

66

to her bed. Marrie this you must consider, and so she bad me tel
you, that you shold come to bed with as little noise as you could,
and tomble nothing that you find, for feare of her best gowne and
her hat, which shee will lay hard by the bed side, next her best
partlet, and in so doing you may haue company with her all night, 5
but say nothing in any case till you bee a bed.

O quoth hee, Mater *Ian*, bee Got Mater *Ian,* mee will not spoyle
her clothes for a towsand pound, ah mee loue Matres *Ione* more
then my wife.

Well, supper being done, they rose from the table. Master *Benne-* 10
dick imbracing mistresse *Ione,* thankt her for her great curtesie and
company, and then the good man and hee walkt into the towne,
and *Ione* hied hir home to her masters, knowing nothing of the
intended iest. Master *Bennedick* thought euerie houre twaine till
the sun was downe, and that hee were a bed with his beloued. 15
At last hee had his wish, and home hee came to his friends house.

Then said *Iohn,* master *Bennedick* you must not in any case
haue a candle when you goe into the chamber, for then my kinswoman will bee angrie, and dark places fit best Louers desires.

O Mater *Ian* quoth hee, tis no such matter for light, mee shall 20
find Metres *Ione* will enough in the darke.

And entring in the parlour, groping about, hee felt a gowne
and hat. O Metres *Ione* (quoth hee) here is your gowne and hat,
me shall no hurt for a tousand pound.

Then kneeling down by the beds side, in stead of mistris *Ione,* 25
hee saluted the sow in this sort.

O my loue and my delight, it is thy faire face that hath wounded
my hart, thy gray sparkling eyes, and thy lilly white hands, with the
comely proportion of thy prity body, that made mee in seeking thee
to forget my selfe, and to find thy fauor lose my owne freedome: 30
but now is the time come wherein I shall reape the fruits of a
plentifull haruest. Now mee deare, from thy sweet mouth let me
sucke the hony balme of thy breath, and with my hand stroke
those Rosie cheekes of thine, wherein I haue tooke such pleasure.
Come with thy prittie lips and entertaine me into thy bed with one 35
gentle kisse (why speakest thou not my sweet hart?) and stretch out

---

¹ to her bed] Q2,3; to bed Q1,4,5
³⁶ (why . . . hart?)] Q4,5; (∼∧) Q1; Why . . hart, Q2,3 *parentheses*
omitted

thy Alabaster armes to infoulde thy faithfull friend. Why should
ill pleasing sleepe close vp the crystall windowes of thy bodie so
fast, and bereaue thee of thy fine Lordly attendants, wherewith
thou was wont to salute thy friends? let it not offend thy gentle
5 eares that I thus talk to thee. If thou hast vowed not to speak, I
will not break it, and if thou wilt command mee to bee silent, I
will be dumbe: but thou needest not feare to speake thy mind,
seeing the cloudy night concealeth euery thing.

By this time master *Bennedick* was vnready, and slipt into bed,
10 where the sow lay swathed in a sheet, and her head bound in a
great linnen cloth. As soon as hee was laid, he began to embrace
his new bedfellow, and laying his lips somwhat neere her snowt
he filt her draw her breath very short.

Why how now loue (quoth hee) bee you sicke? Mistris *Ione*
15 your breath bee very strong: haue you no cacke a bed?

The sow feeling her selfe disturbed, began to grunt and keepe a
great stirre: whereat master *Bennedick* (like a mad man) ran out of
bed crying, de diuel, de deuill. The good man of the house (being purposely prouided) came rushing in with halfe a dosen of his
20 neighbors, asking what was the matter.

Poh mee (quoth *Bennedick*) here be the great diuel, crie hoh,
hoh, hoh, bee Gossen I tink dee play the knaue uid mee, and mee
wil bee reuenged on you.

Sir quoth hee I knowing you loue mutton thought porke nothing
25 vnfit, and therfore prouided you a whole sow, and as you like this
entertainment, spend Portegues. Walk, walk, *Barkshire* maids will
bee no Italians strumpets, nor the wiues of *Newbery* their baudes.

Barkshire dog (quoth *Bennedick*) owleface, shacke, hang dou and
dy wife, haue it not bee for mee loue to sweete Metresse *Ione*, I
30 will no come in your houz: but farewell till I cash you, I shall make
your hog nose bud.

The good man and his neighbours laught aloud, away went
master *Bennedick,* and for very shame departed from *Newbery*
before day.

*3 fine] fiue Q2,3
*15 cacke] cake Q4,5

CHAPTER VIII.

How *Iack* of *Newbery* keeping a very good house, both for his seruants and reliefe of the poore, won great credit therby, and how one of his wiues gossips found fault therwith.   5

Good morrow Gossip, now by my truely I am glad to see you in health. I pray you how dooth Maister *Winchcombe?* What neuer a great belly yet? now fie, by my fa your husband is waxt idle.

Trust mee Gossip, saith mistresse *Winchcombe,* a great belly comes sooner then a new coate, but you must consider wee haue   10
not beene long married: but truly gossip you are welcome, I pray you sit down and we will haue a morsell of something by and by.

Nay truely Gossip I cannot stay quoth she, indeede I must be gone: for I did but euen step in to see how you did.

You shall not chuse but stay a while quoth mistris *Winchcombe,*   15
and with that a fayre Napken was layd vpon the little Table in the Parlour, hard by the fire side, whereon was set a fine cold Capon, with a great deale of other good cheare, with Ale and Wine plentie.

I pray you Gossip eate, and I beshrew you if you spare quoth   20
the one.

I thanke you heartily Gossip saith the other. But hear you Gossip, I pray you tell mee: doth your husband loue you well, and make much of you?

Yes truly I thanke God quoth shee.   25

Now by my truth sayd the other, it were a shame for him if hee should not: for though I say it before your face, though he had little with you, yet you were worthy to bee as good a mans wife as his.

Trust me I would not change my *Iohn* for my Lord Marquesse,   30
quoth she: a woman can be but well, for I liue at hearts ease, and haue all things at will, and truly hee will not see mee lacke any thing.

69

Gods blessing on his heart quoth her Gossip, it is a good hearing: but I pray you tell mee, I heard say your husband is chosen for our Burgesse in the Parliament house, is it true?

Yes verily quoth his wife. I wis it is against his will; for it will
5 be no small charges vnto him.

Tush woman, what talke you of that? thankes be to God, there is neuer a Gentleman in all *Barkshire* that is better able to beare it. But heare you Gossip, shall I bee so bold to aske you one question more?

10 Yes, withall my heart quoth shee.

I heard say that your husband would now put you in your hood, and silke gowne, I pray you is it true?

Yes in truth, quoth mistresse *Winchcomb,* but farre against my mind, Gossip: my french hood is bought already, and my silke
15 gowne is a making, likewise the Goldsmith hath brought home my chayne and bracelets: but I assure you Gossip, if you will be-leeue mee, I had rather go an hundred miles then weare them, for I shall bee so ashamed that I shall not looke vpon any of my neighbors for blushing.

20 And why I pray you? quoth her Gossip. I tell you deare woman, you need not be any thing abashed or blush at the matter, espe-cially seeing your husbands estate is able to maintaine it: now trust me truly, I am of opinion you will become it singular well.

Alas quoth mistresse *Winchcombe,* hauing neuer beene vsed to
25 such attyre, I shall not know where I am, nor how to behaue my selfe in it: and beside, my complexion is so blacke, that I shall carry but an ill fauoured countenance vnder a hood.

Now without doubt (quoth her Gossip) you are to blame to say so: beshrew my heart if I speake it to flatter; you are a very faire
30 and well fauored young woman as any is in *Newbery.* And neuer feare your behauiour in your hood: for I tel you true, as old and withered as I am my selfe, I could become a hood well enough, and behaue my selfe as well in such attyre as any other whatso-euer, and I would not learne of neuer a one of them all: what
35 woman, I haue beene a pretty wench in my dayes, and seene some fashions. Therefore you need not to feare, seeing both your beauty and comely personage deserues no lesse then a french hood, and bee of good comfort. At the first (possible) folkes will gaze some-

6 you of] Q2-5; of you Q1

thing at you: but bee not you abashed for that, it is better they
should wonder at your good fortune, then lament at your miserie:
but when they haue seene you two or three times in that attyre
they will afterward little respect it: for euery new thing at the first
seemes rare, but being once a little vsed, it growes common.   5

Surely gossip you say true, (quoth shee) and I am but a foole to
bee so bashfull: it is no shame to vse Gods gifts for our credites:
and well might my husband thinke me vnworthy to haue them,
if I would not weare them: and though I say it, my hoode is a
fayre one, as any woman weares in this countrey, and my gold   10
chaine and bracelets are none of the worst sort, and I will shew
them you, because you shall giue your opinion vpon them: and
therewithall shee stept into her chamber and fetcht them foorth.

When her Gossip saw them, shee sayd: Now beshrew my fingers
but these are fayre ones indeede. And when doe you meane to   15
weare them Gossip?

At Whitsontide (quoth shee) if God spare mee life.

I wish that well you may weare them, sayd her Gossip, and I
would I were worthie to bee with you when you dresse your selfe,
it should bee neuer the worse for you: I would order the matter   20
so, that you should set euery thing about you in such sort as
neuer a Gentlewoman of them all should staine you.

Mistresse *Winchcombe* gaue her great thankes for her fauour,
saying, that if she needed her helpe, she would be bold to send
for her.   25

Then beganne her gossip to turne her tongue to another tune,
and now to blame her for her great house keeping. And thus she
beganne: Gossip, you are but a young woman, and one that hath
had no great experience of the World, in my opinion you are something too lauish in expences: pardon me good gossip, I speake but   30
for good will; and because I loue you, I am the more bolde to
admonish you: I tell you plain, were I the Mistresse of such a house,
hauing such large allowance as you haue, I would saue 20. pound
a yeare that you spend to no purpose.

Which way might that be (quoth mistres *Winchcombe?*) indeed   35
I confesse I am but a greene housewife, and one that hath but small
tryall in the world, therefore I should bee verie glad to learne any
thing that were for my husbands profite, and my commoditie.

Then listen to mee quoth shee: You feede poor folkes with the
best of the beefe, and the finest of the wheate, which in my opinion   40

is a great ouersight: neither do I heare of any Knight in this countrey that doth it. And to say the truth, how were they able to beare that port which they doe, if they saued it not by some meanes? Come thither, and I warrant you that you shall see but
5 browne bread on the boord: if it be wheate and rie mingled together, it is a great matter, and the bread highly commended: but most commonly they eate either barlybread, or rie mingled with pease, and such like course graine: which is doubtlesse, but of small price, and there is no other bread allowed, except at their
10 owne boord. And in like manner for their meate: it is well knowne that neckes and poynts of beefe is their ordinarie fare: which because it is commonly leane, they seeth therewith now and then a peece of bacon or porke, whereby they make their pottage fat, and therewith driues out the rest with more content. And thus must you
15 learne to doe. And beside that, the midriffes of the Oxen, and the cheekes, the sheepes heads, and the gathers, which you giue away at your gate, might serue them well enough: which would be a great sparing to your other meat, and by this meanes you would saue in the yeare much mony, whereby you might the better main-
20 taine your hood and silke gowne. Againe, you serue your folkes with such superfluities, that they spoyle in manner as much as they eate: beleeue me were I their Dame, they should haue things more sparingly, and then they would thinke it more daintie.

Trust mee gossip (quoth Mistresse *Winchcombe*) I know your
25 wordes in many things to bee true: for my folkes are so corne fed, that wee haue much adoe to please them in their dyet: one doth say this is too salt: and another saith this is too grosse, this is too fresh, and that too fat, and twentie faults they will finde at their meales: I warrant you they make such parings of their cheese, and
30 keepe such chipping of their bread, that their very ortes would serue two or three honest folkes to their dinner.

And from whence I pray you proceedes that (quoth her Gossip) but of too much plentie? but yfaith were they my seruants, I would make them glad of the worst crumme they cast away, and there-
35 upon I drinke to you, and I thanke you for my good cheere with all my heart.

Much good may it doe you good gossip, sayd mistress *Winch-comb:* and I pray you when you come this way let vs see you.

That you shall verily quoth she, and so away she went.
40 After this, mistresse *Winchcomb* tooke occasion to giue her folks

shorter commons, and courser meate then they were wont to haue: which at length being come to the good mans eare, hee was very much offended therewith, saying: I will not haue my people thus pincht of their victuals. Emptie platters make greedy stomackes, and where scarcitie is kept, hunger is nourished: and therefore wife as you loue mee let me haue no more of this doings.

Husband (quoth she) I would they should haue enough: but it is a sinne to suffer, and a shame to see the spoyle they make: I could bee verie well content to giue them their bellyes full, and that which is sufficient, but it grieues me, to tell you true, to see how coy they are, and the small care they haue in wasting of things: and I assure you, the whole towne cryes shame of it, and it hath bred me no small discredit for looking no better to it. Trust me no more, if I was not checkt in my owne house, about this matter, when my eares did burne to heare what was spoken.

Who was it that checkt thee, I pray thee tell mee? was it not your old gossip, dame dayntie, mistresse trip and go? I beleeue it was.

Why man if it were she, you know shee hath beene an old housekeeper, and one that hath known the world; and that shee told mee was for good will.

Wife (quoth hee) I would not haue thee to meddle with such light braind huswiues, and so I haue told thee a good many times, and yet I cannot get you to leaue her company.

Leaue her company? why husband so long as she is an honest woman, why should I leaue her company? Shee neuer gaue mee hurtfull counsell in all her life, but hath alwayes been ready to tell me things for my profit, though you take it not so. Leaue her company? I am no gyrle I would you should well know, to bee taught what company I should keepe: I keepe none but honest company I warrant you. Leaue her company ketha? Alas poore soule, this reward she hath for her good will. I wis I wis, she is more your friend, then you are your owne.

Well let her be what she will sayd her husband: but if shee come any more in my house, shee were as good no. And therefore take this for a warning I would aduise you: and so away he went.

73

CHAPTER IX.

How a Draper in *London,* who owed *Iacke* of *Newberry*
much money became bankrout, whom *Iack* of *Newbery*
found carrying a porters basket on his neck, and how
5   he set him vp again at his owne cost, which draper
afterward became an Alderman of *London.*

There was one *Randoll Pert* a Draper, dwelling in *Watling
streete,* that owed *Iacke* of *Newbery* fiue hundred pounds at
one time, who in the ende fell greatly to decay, in so much that hee
10 was cast in prison, and his wife with her poore children turned out
of doores. Al his creditors except *Winchcomb* had a share of his
goods, neuer releasing him out of prison, so long as he had one
penny to satisfie them. But when this tidings was brought to *Iack*
of *Newberies* eare, his friends counselled him to lay his action
15 against him.

Nay (quoth he) if he be not able to pay me when hee is at
libertie, hee will neuer be able to pay me in prison: and therfore
it were as good for me to forbear my mony with out troubling him,
as to adde more sorrow to his grieued hart, and be neuer the
20 neerer. Misery is troden downe by many, and once brought low
they are seldome or neuer relieued: therfore he shall rest for me
vntoucht, and I would to God he were cleare of all other mens debts,
so that I gaue him mine to begin the world again.

Thus lay the poore Draper a long time in prison, in which space
25 his Wife which before for dayntinesse would not foule her fingers,
nor turne her head aside, for feare of hurting the set of her neckenger, was glad to goe about and wash buckes at the Thames side,
and to bee a chare-Woman in rich mens houses, her soft hand was
now hardened with scowring, and in steade of gold rings vpon her
30 lillie fingers, they were now fild with chaps, prouoked by the sharpe
lee and other drudgeries.

At last, master *Winchcombe* being (as you heard) chosen against
the Parliament a Burgesse for the towne of *Newbery,* and comming

vp to *London* for the same purpose, when hee was alighted at his Inne, hee left one of his men there, to get a Porter to bring his trunke vp to the place of his lodging. Poore *Randoll Pert,* which lately before was come out of prison, hauing no other meanes of maintenance, became a Porter to carry burthens from one place 5 to another, hauing an old ragged doublet, and a torne payre of breeches, with his hose out at the heeles, and a paire of olde broken slip shooes on his feet, a rope about his middle instead of a girdle, and on his head an old greasie cap, which had so many holes in it, that his haire started through it: who assoone as hee heard one call 10 for a Porter, made answere straight: here Master, what is it that you would haue caryed?

Mary (quoth hee) I would haue this Trunke borne to the spread Eagle at Iuiebridge.

You shall master (quoth hee) but what will you giue me for my 15 paines?

I will giue thee two pence.

A penny more and I will carry it, sayd the Porter: and so being agreed, away he went with his burthen till he came to the spread Eagle doore, where on a sudden espying Master *Winchcombe* 20 standing, hee cast downe the Trunke and ran away as hard as euer hee could.

Master *Winchcombe* wondring what hee meant thereby, caused his man to runne after him, and to fetch him againe: but when he saw one pursue him, he ranne then the faster, and in running, 25 here he lost one of his slip shooes, and there another: euer looking behinde him, like a man pursued with a deadly weapon, fearing euery twinkling of an eye to bee thrust thorow. At last his breech, being tyed but with one poynt, what with the haste he made, and the weakenesse of the thong, fell about his heeles: which so shackled 30 him, that downe hee fell in the streete all along, sweating and blowing, being quite worne out of breath: and so by this meanes the Seruing man ouertooke him, and taking him by the sleeue, being as windlesse as the other, stood blowing and puffing a great while ere they could speake one to another. 35

Sirra, quoth the Seruingman, you must come to my maister, you haue broken his Trunke all to peeces, by letting it fall.

O for Gods sake (quoth he) let me go, for Christs sake let me goe, or else Master *Winchcombe* of *Newbery* will arrest me, and then I am vndone for euer. 40

Now by this time *Iack* of *Newbery* had caused his Trunke to be carryed into the house, and then he walked along to know what the matter was: but when he heard the Porter say that he would arrest him, he wondred greatly and hauing quite forgot *Perts*
5 fauour, being so greatly changed by imprisonment and pouertie, he said, Wherefore should I arrest thee? tell me good fellow: for mine owne part I know no reason for it.

O Sir (quoth he) I would to God I knew none neither.

Then asking him what his name was: the poore man falling
10 downe on his knees, sayd: Good Maister *Winchcombe* beare with me and cast me not into prison: my name is *Pert,* and I do not deny but I owe you fiue hundred pound: yet for the loue of God take pittie vpon mee.

When Maister *Winchcombe* heard this, hee wondred greatly at
15 the man, and did as much pittie his miserie, though as yet hee made it not knowne, saying: Passion of my heart man, thou wilt neuer pay mee thus: neuer thinke being a Porter to pay fiue hundred pound debt. But this hath your prodigalitie brought you to, your thriftlesse neglecting of your busines, that set more by your
20 pleasure than your profite. Then looking better vpon him, he said: What neuer a shoo to thy foot, hose to thy legge, band to thy necke, nor cap to thy head? O *Pert* this is strange; but wilt thou be an honest man, and giue me a bill of thy hand for my mony?

Yes sir, with all my heart, quoth *Pert.*

25 Then come to the Scriueners (quoth he) and dispatch it, and I will not trouble thee.

Now when they were come thither, with a great many following them at their heeles, master *Winchcomb* said: Hearest thou Scriuener? this fellow must giue mee a bill of his hand for fiue hundred
30 pounds, I pray thee make it as it should bee.

The Scriuener looking vpon the poore man, and seeing him in that case, said to master *Winchcombe:* Sir, you were better to let it bee a Bond, and haue some sureties bound with him.

Why Scriuener (quoth hee) doest thou thinke this is not a suf-
35 ficient man of himselfe for fiue hundred pound?

Truly Sir (sayd the Scriuener) if you thinke him so, you and I am of two minds.

Ile tell thee what (quoth master *Winchcombe*) were it not that we are all mortall, I would take his word assoone as his Bill or
40 Bond; the honystie of a man is all.

76

And wee in *London* (quoth the Scriuener) doe trust Bonds farre better then honestie. But Sir when must this money bee payd?

Marry Scriuener when this man is Sheriffe of *London.*

At that word the Scriuener and the people standing by laughed heartily, saying: In truth Sir make no more adoe but forgiue it him: as good to doe the one as the other.

Nay beleeue mee (quoth hee) not so: therefore do as I bid you.

Whereupon the Scriuener made the Bill to be payd when *Randoll Pert* was Sheriffe of *London,* and thereunto set his owne hand for a witnesse, and twentie persons more that stoode by set their handes likewise. Then hee asked *Pert* what hee should haue for carrying his trunk.

Sir (quoth hee) I should haue three pence, but seeing I finde you so kinde, I will take but two pence at this time.

Thanks good *Pert* quoth he, but for thy three pence, there is three shillings: and looke thou come to mee to morrow morning betimes.

The poore man did so, at what time Master *Winchcombe* had prouided him out of Birchin lane, a faire sute of apparell, Marchantlike, with a faire blacke cloake, and all other thinges fit to the same: then he tooke him a shop in *Canweeke* streete, and furnisht the same shop with a thousand pounds worth of cloath: by which meanes, and other fauours that master *Winchcombe* did him, hee grew againe into great credite, and in the end became so wealthy, that while maister *Winchcombe* liued hee was chosen Sheriffe, at what time he payed fiue hundred pounds euery pennie, and after dyed an Alderman of the Citie.

CHAPTER X.

How *Iack* of *Newberies* Seruants were reuenged of their Dames tattling Gossip.

5 Vpon a time it came to passe, when Master *Winchcombe* was farre from home, and his Wife gone abroad: That Mistris many-better, dame tittle-tattle, gossip pinte-pot, according to her old custome came to Mistris *Winchcombes* house, perfectly know-ing of the good mans absence, and little thinking the good wife was from home: where knocking at the gate, *Tweedle* stept out and 10 askt who was there? where hastily opening the wicket, he sodainly discouered the full proportion of this foule beast, who demanded if their Mistris were within.

What, mistris *Franke* (quoth he) in faith welcome: how haue you done a great while? I pray you come in.

15 Nay, I cannot stay quoth shee: Notwithstanding, I did call to speake a word or two with your Mistris, I pray you tell her that I am heere.

So I will (quoth he) so soone as shee comes in.

Then said the woman, what is shee abroad? Why then farewell 20 good *Tweedle*.

Why what haste, what haste, mistris *Frank* (quoth he) I pray you stay and drinke ere you goe, I hope a cup of newe Sacke will doe your old belly no hurt.

What (quoth shee) haue you new sacke alreadie? Now by my 25 honestie I drunke none this yeare, and therefore I do not greatly care if I take a taste before I go: and with that shee went into the wine cellar with *Tweedle,* where first hee set before her a piece of poudred biefe as greene as a leeke: And then going into the kitchen, he brought her a piece of rosted beefe hot from the spit.

30 Now certaine of the Maidens of the house and some of the young men, who had long before determined to bee reuenged of this pratling huswife: came into the Cellar one after another, one of them bringing a great piece of a gambon of Bacon in his hand:

78

and euerie one bad mistresse *Franke* welcome: and first one dranke
to her, and then another, and so the third, the fourth, and the
fift: so that Mistresse *Franks* braines waxt as mellow as a pippin
at Michaelmas, and so light, that sitting in the Cellar she thought
the world ran round. They seeing her to fall into merry humors, 5
whetted her on in merriment as much as they could, saying: mistresse *Frank,* spare not I pray you, but thinke your selfe as welcome as any woman in *Newberie,* for we haue cause to loue you,
because you loue our mistris so well.

Now assure you quoth shee (lisping in her speech) her tongue 10
waxing somwhat too big for her mouth, I loue your mistresse well
indeed, as if she were my owne daughter.

Nay but hear you quoth they, she begins not to deal well with
vs now.

No my Lamb quoth shee, why so? 15

Because quoth they, she seekes to bar vs of our allowance, telling
our Master that hee spends too much in housekeeping.

Nay then (quoth she) your mistresse is an Asse, and a foole: and
though she goe in her hood, what care I? she is but a girle to mee:
twittle twattle, I know what I know: Go to, drinke to mee. Wel 20
Tweedle, I drinke to thee with all my hart: why thou whoreson
when wilt thou be maried? O that I were a young wench for thy
sake: but tis no mater though I be but a poore woman, I am a true
woman. Hang dogs, I haue dwelt in this Towne these thirtie
winters. 25

Why then quoth they, you haue dwelt here longer than our
Maister.

Your Master, quoth shee? I knew your Master a boy, when he
was called *Iacke* of *Newbery;* I *Iacke,* I knew him called plaine
Iack: and your Mistresse, now she is rich and I am poor, but tis 30
no matter, I knew her a draggle tayle girle, marke yee?

But now quoth they, she takes vpon her lustily, and hath forgot
what shee was.

Tush, what will you haue of a greene thing quoth shee. Heere
I drink to you, so long as she goes where she list a gossipping: and 35
tis no matter, little said is soone amended: but heare you my maisters, though mistresse *Winchomb* goe in her hood, I am as good
as shee, I care not who tell it her: I spend not my husbands money

---

*10 Now assure you] Now I assure you Q4,5; Now by my troth Q2,3

in cherries and codlings, go to, go to, I know what I say well enough: I am sure I am not drunk: mistresse *Winchcomb,* mistresse? No, *Nan Winchcombe,* I will call her name, plain *Nan:* what, I was a woman, when she was se-reuerence a paltrie girle,
5 though now she goes in her hood and chaine of gold: what care I for her? I am her elder, and I know more of her tricks: nay I warrant you I know what I say, tis no matter, laugh at me and spare not. I am not drunke I warrant: and with that being scant able to hold open her eyes, shee began to nodde and to spill the
10 wine out of the glasse: which they perceiuing let her alone, going out of the cellar till shee was sound asleepe, and in the meane space they deuised how to finish this peece of knauery. At last they consented to laie her forth at the backside of the house, halfe a mile off, euen at the foote of a stile, that whosoeuer came next ouer
15 might finde her: notwithstanding, *Tweedle* stayed hard by to see the end of this action.

At last comes a notable clowne from *Greenham,* taking his way to *Newbery,* who comming hastily ouer the stile stumbled at the Woman, and fell down cleane ouer her: but in the starting vp,
20 seeing it was a woman, cryed out, alas, alas.

How now, what is the matter quoth *Tweedle?*

O quoth hee here lies a dead woman.

A dead woman quoth *Tweedle:* thats not so I trow, and with that hee tumbled her about: bones of mee quoth *Tweedle,* its a
25 drunken Woman, and one of the Towne vndoubtedly: surelie it is great pittie shee should lie heere.

Why? do you know her quoth the Clowne?

No not I, quoth *Tweedle:* neuerthelesse, I will giue thee halfe a groat and take her in thy Basket, and carry her throughout the
30 Towne and see if any body know her.

Then said th'other, let me see the money and I will: For by the Masse che earnd not halfe a groat this great while.

There it is quoth *Tweedle.*

Then the fellow put her in his basket, and so lifted her vpon
35 his back. Now by the masse shee stinkes vilely of drinke or wine, or some thing: but tell mee, what shall I say, when I come into the towne, quoth hee?

First quoth *Tweedle,* I would haue thee so soone as euer thou canst go to the townes end, with a lustie voice, to crie O yes; and
40 then say, who knowes this woman, who? And though possible

some will say, I know her, and I know her, yet do not thou set her downe till thou comest to the market Crosse, and there vse the like words: and if any bee so friendly, to tell thee where shee dwels, then iust before her doore crie so againe: and if thou performe this brauely, I will giue thee halfe a groat more.

Maister *Tweedle* (quoth he) I know you well enough, you dwell with Maister *Winchcomb,* do you not? Well, if I do it not in the nick, giue mee neuer a pennie: And so away hee went till hee came to the Townes end, and there hee cryes out as boldly as anie Baylifes man, O yes, who knowes this woman, who?

Then said the drunken woman in the Basket, her head falling first on one side, and then on the other side, Who co mee, who?

Then said hee againe, Who knowes this woman, who?

Who co mee, who (quoth shee) and looke how oft hee spake the one, she spake the other: saying still Who co mee, who co me, who? Whereat all the people in the streete fell into such a laughing, that the teares ran downe againe.

At last one made answer, saying: goodfellow she dwels in the North brooke street, a little beyond master *Winchcombes.*

The fellow hearing that, goes downe thither in all haste, and there in the hearing of a hundred people, cries: Who knowes this woman, who? whereat her husband comes out, saying: Marrie that doe I too well God helpe mee.

Then sayd the Clowne, if you know her, take her: for I know her not but for a drunken beast.

And as her husband tooke her out of the Basket, shee gaue him a sound boxe on the eare, saying: What you Queanes, do you mocke mee, and so was caried in.

But the next day, when her braines were quiet, and her head cleared of these foggie vapours shee was so ashamed of her selfe, that shee went not forth of her doores a long time after: and if any body did say vnto her, Who co me who? She would bee so mad and furious, that shee would bee ready to draw her knife and to stick them, and scold as if she stroue for the best game at the cucking stools. Moreouer, her prattling to Mistresse *Winchcombes* folks of their mistresse, made her on the other side to fall out with her, in such sort that shee troubled them no more, either with her companie or her counsell.

CHAPTER XI.

How one of *Iack* of *Newberies* maydens became a Ladie.

At the winning of *Morlesse* in *France,* the noble Earle of *Surrey* beeing at that time Lord high Admirall of *England,* made
5 manie Knights: among the rest was Sir *George Rigley,* brother to Sir *Edward Rigley,* and sundrie other, whose valours farre surpassed their wealth: so that when peace bred a scarcity in their purses that their credits grew weak in the Citie, they were inforced to ride into the country, where at their friends houses they might
10 haue fauourable welcome, without coyne or grudging. Among the rest, *Iacke* of *Newbery* that kept a table for all commers, was neuer lightly without many such guests: where they were sure to haue bold welcome and good cheere, and their mirth no lesse pleasing then their meat was plentie. Sir *George* hauing lyen long at boord
15 in this braue yeomans house, at length fell in liking of one of his maidens, who was as faire as she was fond.

This lustie wench hee so allured with hope of marriage, that at length shee yeelded him her loue, and therwithall bent her whole studie to work his content: but in the end she so much contented
20 him, that it wrought altogether her owne discontent: to become high, she laid her selfe so low, that the Knight suddenly fell ouer her, which fall became the rising of her belly: but when this wanton perceiued her selfe to bee with child, shee made her moane vnto the Knight, saying:

25 Ah sir *George,* now is the time to perform your promise, or to make me a spectacle of infamy to the whole world for euer: in the one, you shall discharge the duty of a true Knight; but in the other, shew your selfe a most periured person: small honour will it bee to boast in the spoyle of poore maidens, whose innocencie all good
30 Knights ought to defend.

Why thou leud paltrie thing quoth hee: commest thou to father thy bastard vpon mee? A way ye dunghill carrion, awaie: heare you good huswife, get you among your companions, and lay your litter where you list, but if you trouble me any more, trust mee thou shalt dearely abie it: and so bending his browes like the angry god of warr, he went his waies leauing the child breeding wench to the hazard of her fortune, either good or bad.

The poore maiden seeing her selfe for her kindnesse thus cast 5 off, shed many teares of sorrow for her sinne, inueighing with manie bitter groanes, against the vnconstancie of loue-alluring men. And in the end, when shee saw no other remedie, shee made her case knowne vnto her mistresse: who after she had giuen her many checkes and taunts, threatening to turne her out of doores, shee 10 opened the matter to her husband.

So soone as he heard thereof, he made no more to do, but presently poasted to *London* after Sir *George,* and found him at my Lord Admirals. What master *Winchcombe* (quoth hee) you are heartily welcome to *London,* and I thank you for my good cheere: 15 I pray you how doth your good wife, and all our friends in *Barkshire?*

All well and merrie, I thank you good Sir *George,* quoth hee: I left them in health, and hope they do so continue. And trust me sir (quoth he) hauing earnest occasion to come vp to talke with a 20 bad debter, in my iourney it was my chance to light in company of a gallant widow: a Gentlewoman shee is of wondrous good wealth, whom grisly death hath bereft of a kinde husband, making her a Widow ere shee had been halfe a yeare a wife: her land, sir *George,* is as well worth a hundred pound a yeare as one penny, being as 25 faire and comely a creature as any of her degree in our whole countrey: Now sir, this is the worst, by the reason that she doubtes her selfe to bee with child, she hath vowed not to marrie these xii. moneths: but because I wish you well, and the Gentlewoman no hurt: I came of purpose from my businesse to tell you thereof: 30 Now sir *George,* if you thinke her a fit wife for you, ride to her, woo her, winne her, and wed her.

I thanke you good Maister *Winchcombe* (quoth he) for your fauour euer toward mee: and gladly would I see this young Widow if I wist where. 35

Shee dwels not halfe a mile from my house quoth Maister *Winchcombe,* and I can send for her at any time if you please.

*2 abie] abide Q2-5
27 this is the] Q2-5; this the Q1

Sir *George* hearing this, thought it was not best to come there, fearing *Ioane* would father a child vpon him, and therefore said, hee had no leasure to come from my Lord: But quoth hee, would I might see her in *London,* on the condition it cost me twenty
5 nobles.

Tush, sir *George* (quoth Maister *Winchcombe*) delay in loue is dangerous, and hee that will woo a widow, must take time by the forelocke, and suffer none other to stop before him, least hee leape with out the Widowes loue. Notwithstanding, seeing now I haue
10 toulde you of it, I will take my gelding and get me home, if I heare of her comming to *London* I will send you word, or perhaps come my selfe: till when adieu good sir *George.*

Thus parted Master *Winchcombe* from the knight: and being come home, in short time hee got a faire Taffetie gowne, and a
15 french hood for his maide, saying: Come ye drab, I must be faine to couer a foule fault with a faire garment, yet all will not hide your great belly: but if I finde meanes to make you a Lady, what wilt thou say then?

O Maister (quoth she) I shall be bound while I liue to pray for
20 you.

Come then minion (quoth her mistris) and put you on this gown and french hood: for seeing you haue lien with a Knight, you must needes bee a gentlewoman.

The maid did so, and being thus attired, shee was set on a faire
25 gelding, and a couple of men sent with her vp to *London:* and be- ing well instructed by her maister and dame what shee should do, shee tooke her iourney to the Cittie in the Terme time, and lodged at the Bell in the Strand: and mistresse *Louelesse* must be her name, for so her Master had warned her to call her selfe: neither
30 did the men that waited on her, know the contrary, for Master *Winchcombe* had borrowed them of their Maister, to wait vpon a frend of his to *London,* because he could not spare any of his owne seruants at that time: notwithstanding they were appointed, for the Gentlewomans credit, to say they were her owne men. This being
35 done, Master *Winchcombe* sent sir *George* a Letter, that the Gen- tlewoman which hee toulde him of, was now in *London,* lying at the Bell in the Strand, hauing great busines at the Terme.

---

*32 *London,* because he] Q2,3; *London* ∧ who Q1
    33 seruants ∧ at that time:] Q2,3; ~: ~ ∧ Q1

Chapter Eleven

With which newes Sir *Georges* heart was on fire, till such time
as he might speake with her: three or foure times went hee thither,
and still shee would not bee spoken withall: the which close keeping of her selfe, made him the more earnest in his sute.

At length he watcht her so narrowly, that finding her going forth 5
in an euening, hee followed her, shee hauing one man before, and
another behinde: carrying a verie stately gate in the street, it draue
him into the greater liking of her, beeing the more vrged to vtter
his minde.

And suddenly stepping before her, hee thus saluted her, Gentle- 10
woman God saue you, I haue often beene at your lodging and could
neuer finde you at leisure.

Why sir quoth shee (counterfeting her naturall speech) haue you
any businesse with me?

Yes faire Widow quoth he, as you are a clyent to the law, so am 15
I a sutor for your loue: and may I find you so fauorable to let me
plead my owne case at the bar of your beautie, I doubt not but to
vnfold so true a tale as I trust will cause you to giue sentence on
my side.

You are a merry Gentleman quoth shee: But for my own part I 20
know you not: neuerthelesse, in a case of loue, I will bee no let
to your sute, though perhaps I helpe you little therein. And therefore Sir, if it please you to giue attendance at my lodging, vpon
my returne from the Temple, you shall knowe more of my minde,
and so they parted. 25

Sir *George* receiuing hereby som hope of good happe, stayed
for his dear at her lodging doore: whom at her comming she
frendly greeted, saying: Surely Sir, your diligence is more then the
profit you shall get thereby: but I pray you how shall I call your
name? 30

George Rigley (quoth hee) I am called, and for some small
deserts I was knighted in *France*.

Why then Sir *George* (quoth shee) I haue done you too much
wrong to make you thus dance attendance on my worthlesse person. But let mee bee so bold to request you to tell mee, how you 35
came to know mee: for my owne part I cannot remember that euer
I saw you before.

Mistris *Louelesse* (sayd Sir *George*) I am well acquainted with a

[31] *Rigley*] Q2,3,5; *Regly* Q1,4

good neighbour of yours, called Maister *Winchcombe,* who is my very good friend, and to say the truth you were commended vnto mee by him.

Truly sir *George* sayd shee, you are so much the better welcome:
5 Neuerthelesse, I haue made a vowe not to loue any man for this tweluemoneths space. And therefore Sir, till then I would wish you to trouble your selfe no further in this matter till that time be expired: and then if I finde you bee not intangled to any other, and that by triall I finde out the truth of your loue, for Master
10 *Winchcombes* sake your welcome shall bee as good as any other Gentlemans whatsoeuer.

Sir *George* hauing receiued this answere was wonderous woe, cursing the day that euer he meddled with *Ioane* whose time of deliuerance would come long before a tweluemoneth were expired,
15 to his vtter shame, and ouerthrowe of his good fortune: for by that meanes should hee haue maister *Winchcombe* his enemie, and therewithall the losse of this faire Gentlewoman. Wherefore to pre-uent this mischiefe he sent a Letter in all haste to maister *Winch-combe,* requesting him most earnestly to come vp to *London,* by
20 whose perswasion hee hoped straight to finish the marriage. Maister *Winchcomb* fulfilled his request, and then presently was the mar-riage solemnized at the Tower of *London,* in presence of many gentlemen of Sir *Georges* friends. But when hee found it was *Ione* whome hee had gotten with child, hee fretted and fumed, stampt,
25 and star'd like a diuell.

Why (quoth M. *Winchcomb*) what needs all this? Came you to my table to make my maid your strumpet? had you no mans house to dishonor but mine? Sir, I would you should well know, that I account the poorest wench in my house too good to be your whore,
30 were you ten knights: and seeing you tooke pleasure in making her your wanton, take it no scorne to make her your wife: and vse her well too, or you shall heare of it. And hould thee *Ione* (quoth he) there is a hundred pounds for thee: And let him not say thou comst to him a begger.

35 Sir *George* seeing this, and withall casting in his minde what friend Maister *Winchcombe* might bee to him, taking his wife by the hand gaue her a louing kisse, and Master *Winchcombe* great thankes. Whereupon hee willed him for two yeres space to take his diet and his Ladies at his house: which the Knight accepting rode

straight with his wife to *Newbery*. Then did the Mistris make curtsie to the Maid, saying: you are welcome Madam, giuing her the vpper hand in all places. And thus they liued afterward in great ioy: and our King, hearing how *Iacke* had matcht sir *George,* laughing heartily thereat, gaue him a liuing for euer, the better to maintain my Lady his Wife.

FINIS.

THE GENTLE CRAFT, PART I

THE
GENTLE CRAFT.
A
DISCOVRSE CON-
TAINING MANY MAT-
TERS OF DELIGHT, VERY
pleaſant to be read : ſhewing what
famous men haue beene Shoomakers
in time paſt in this Land, with their worthy *deeds and great Hoſpitality.*

DECLARING THE CAVSE WHY
it is called the GENTLE CRAFT: and
alſo how the Prouerbe firſt grew;
A Shoomakers ſonne is a Prince borne. T.D.

With gentleneſſe iudge you,
At nothing here grudge you;
   The merry Shoomakers delight in good ſport :
What here is preſented,
Be therewith contented;
   And as you doe like it, ſo giue you report.

Hand cure inuidiam.

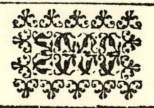

Printed at London for E. Brewſter. 1627.

To all the good Yeomen of the Gentle Craft.

You that the Gentle Craft professe, list to my words both more and
    lesse.
And I shall tell you many things, of worthy and renowned Kings:
And diuers Lords and Knights also, that were shoomakers long 5
    agoe,
Some of them in their distresse, delighted in this businesse:
And some, for whom great wait was laid, did saue their liues by
    this same Trade:
Other some, in sport and game, delighted much to leaue the same. 10
No other Trade in all this Land, they thought so fit vnto their
    hand,
For euermore they still did find, that shoomakers bore a gallant
    mind.
Men they were of high conceit, the which wrought many a merry 15
    feat:
Stout of courage were they still, and in their weapons had great
    skill.
Trauellers by sea and land, each country guise to vnderstand:
Wrong they wrought not any man, with reason all things did they 20
    scan,
Good houses kept they euermore, releeuing both the sicke and
    poore.
In law no mony would they spend, their quarrels friendly wold
    they end.   25
No malice did they beare to any, but shew'd great fauour vnto
    many;
Offences soone they would forgiue, they would not in contention
    liue.
Thus in ioy they spent their daies, with pleasant songs and roun- 30
    delaes,
And God did blesse them with content; sufficient for them he sent:
And neuer yet did any know, a shoomaker a begging goe:
Kinde are they one to another, vsing each stranger as his brother.
Thus liu'd shoomakers of old, as ancient writers haue it told: 35
And thus shoomakers still should be, so Fame from them shall
    neuer flee.

To all courteous Readers, health.

How Saint *Hugh* was sonne vnto the renowned King of *Powis,*
a noble Britaine borne, who in the prime of his yeares loued
the faire Virgin *Winifred,* who was the onely daughter of *Don-*
5 *wallo,* which was the last King that euer reigned in *Tegina,* which
is now called Flint-shire. But she refusing all offers of loue, was
onely pleased with a religious life. Her father was sent to *Rome,*
and dyed; whose Lady left her life long before. This Virgin therefore forsooke her fathers Princely Palace in *Pont Varry,* and made
10 her whole abiding in the most sweet pleasant Valley of *Sichnaunt,*
and liued there solitarily, and carelesse of all companie or comfort.
It chanced that in Summers heate, this faire Virgin being greatly
distressed for lacke of drinke, and not knowing where to get any,
there sprung vp suddenly a christal stream of most sweet and pleas-
15 ant water out of the hard ground, whereof this Virgin did daily
drinke: Vnto the which God himselfe gaue so great a vertue, that
many people hauing beene washed therein, were healed of diuers
and sundry infirmities wherewith they were borne. Moreouer, round
about this well, where this Virgin did vse to walke, did grow a
20 kinde of Mosse, which is of a most sweet sauour, and the colour
thereof is as fresh in Winter as in Summer; so that lying thereon,
you would suppose your selfe to be vpon a bed of Downe, perfumed with most precious odours. And what of all this? Marry
reade the booke and you shall know; but reade nothing except
25 you reade all. And why so? Because the beginning shewes not the
middle, nor the middle shewes not the latter end.

And so farewell.

19 where] Q2-4; wherein Q1

92

CHAPTER I.

The Pleasant Historie of S. *Hvgh;* and first of all, his most constant loue to the faire Virgin *Winifred.*

Conquering and most imperious Loue, hauing seized on the heart of young sir *Hugh,* all his wits were set on worke, how for to compasse the loue of the faire Virgin *Winifred,* whose disdaine was the chiefe cause of his care, hauing receiued many infinite sorrowes for her sake: but as a streame of water being stopt, ouerfloweth the banke; so smothered desire doth burst out into a great flame of fire, which made this malecontented Louer to seeke some meanes to appease the strife of his contentious thoughts; whereupon he began to incourage himselfe.

Tush *Hugh,* let not a few froward words of a woman dismay thee, for they loue to be intreated, and delight to bee wooed, though they would make the world beleeue otherwise; for their denyals proceed more of nicenesse then niggardlinesse, refusing that they would fainest haue: What if sometimes *Winifred* frowne on thee? yet her fauours may exceed her frowardnesse. The Sunne is sometimes ouercast with clouds, so that his brightnesse is not seene. In warres, the sorer the fight is, the greater is the glory of the victorie; and the harder a woman is to be wonne, the sweeter is her loue when it is obtained: wherefore Ile once againe try my fortune, and see what successe my sute shall find. On this resolution sir *Hugh* returned to *Winifred,* greeting her thus: Now faire Lady, hauing slept away the remembrance of your sharpe answers, I come againe into a new conceit, to reuiue an old sute, and to see if the change of the day will yeeld a change of my dolours.

Truly Sir *Hugh* (quoth shee) if with the change of the day you haue changed your opinion, your dolour will bee driuen away well enough: but as touching your sute it shall be needlesse to repeate it because I am not willing to preferre it.

¹ CHAPTER I.] *heading om.* Q1-4

93

Stay there (quoth sir *Hugh*) I will preferre it, so that you will accept.

No quoth she, I will accept it, if you will preferre it, in sending it backe to the place from whence it proceeded, and I would to
5 God I could send you away as soone as your sute.

Why then belike I am not welcome, said sir *Hugh*.

Yes quoth she, as welcome to me, as a storme to a distressed Mariner: I muse greatly that reason will not rule you, nor words win you from your wilfulnesse: if you were as weary to wooe as I
10 am wearied to heare you, I am perswaded that long since you would haue ceased your vaine sute. You thinke by these perswasions to remoue my opinion, but as well you may thinke that you may quench fire with oyle; therefore I pray you good sir *Hugh*, be not so tedious vnto me, nor troublesome to your selfe.

15 Come, come, quoth he, all this will not serue your turne, ponder with thy selfe *Winifred* that thou art faire. O that thou wert as fauorable! thy beauty hath bound me to bee thy seruant, and neuer to cease till I see another obtaine thee, or my selfe be possessed of my hearts content. Thou art a Kings daughter, and I a
20 Princes sonne: staine not the glory of true Nobility with the foule sin of obstinacie, but be thou as kind, as thou art courtly, and gentle as thou art noble, and then shall our strife soone end.

Winifred perceiuing that the farther off she was to grant loue, the more eager he was to desire, shifted him off thus: Sir although
25 your ouerhastinesse driue me into the greater doubtfulnesse, yet let me intreat you, if you loue me, to giue me but one moneths respite to consider on this matter; and it may be that vpon my better deliberation it shall be pleasing vnto you, and nothing at all discontent me.

30 Faire loue, quoth he, farre be it from my heart to denie so kind a request; I am content to stay a moneth from thy sight, were it two or three, vpon condition that thou wouldst then grant mee thy good will: three moneths, although it bee very long, yet it will come at last; and I could be content for that time to bee
35 dead for thy sake, insomuch that my life might be renewed by thy loue.

Nay (quoth *Winifred*) stay three months, and stay for euer; by this a Maid may see how readie men are vpon a light occasion to take

³⁴ I] Q3,4; *om.* Q1,2

94

long daies, whose loues are like a Ferne bush, soone set on fire, and
soone consumed: and seeing it is so, in faith sir *Hugh* I doe meane
to try you better before I trust you.

Pardon me faire *Winifred,* said sir *Hugh,* if my tongue doe out-   5
slip my wit: in truth I speake but to please thee, though to displease my selfe: but I pray thee, let it not be three houres, nor
three quarters of an houre, if thou wilt.

Nay, nay (quoth she) your first word shall stand: after three
months come to me againe, and then you shall know my minde to
the full, and so good sir *Hugh* be gone: but if I doe euer heare   10
from thee, or see thee betwixt this time and the time prefixed, I
will for euer hereafter blot thy name out of my booke of Remem-
brances, and neuer yeeld thee that courtesie which thou at this
time so earnestly intreatest for.

Sir *Hugh* vpon these words departed, betwixt hope and dread,   15
much like to a man committing a trespasse, that stayed for the
sentence of life or death.

O vnhappy man, quoth he, how hath my ouer-slippery tongue
lengthened the time of my sorrow! she of her selfe most curteously
requested of me but one months stay, and I most willingly and   20
vndiscreetly added thereto eight weekes more of misery: much like
the Hinde, that hauing a knife giuen him to paire his nailes, did
therewith murder himselfe.

Now I could wish that the Sunne had Eagles wings, swiftly to
fly through the faire firmament, and finish sixe dayes in one dayes   25
time: With that he began to count the daies and houres that were
in three months, falling (in a manner) to despare with himselfe
when he found them so many in number: and therewithall melan-
cholily and sadly he went to his fathers house, where his brother
Griffith found by his countenance the perfect map of a pensiue   30
louer.

Wherupon he said vnto him: Why how now brother? hath *Winifreds* faire beauty so greatly wounded you, as you cannot speake
a merry word to your friends, but sit in a corner, as if you were
tonguelesse like a Storke? tush brother, women are like shadowes,   35
for the more a man followes them the faster they run away: but
let a man turne his course, and then they will presently follow him.

*35 Storke?] Mann; Stocke; Q1; Stocke: Q2; Stocke? Q3,4
37/. him. What] Q2-4; ~, ~ Q1

What man? plucke vp a good heart: for there are more women now, then liued in the time of our old father *Adam*.

O, said *Hugh*, were there ten thousand times more then there are now, what were that to me, if *Winifred* be vnkinde? yet is she
5 the oile that still maintaines the lampe of my light, and without her there is nothing comfortable to my sight.

Then (replied *Griffith*) you are as much troubled in loue, as a Goat in an ague, and as blind as a Flie in October, that will stand still while a man cuts off his head. Come, goe a hunting with me,
10 that will driue away your ouerfond conceits, and you shall see that these three months will come vpon you as a quarter day vpon a poore man that hath neuer a pennie ready towards the paiment of his rent.

CHAPTER II.

15 How beautifull *Winifred* being ouermuch superstitious, forsooke her fathers wealth and liued poorely by a springing fountaine, from whence no man could get her to goe; which Spring to this day is called *Winifreds* Well.

20 *Winifred*, who had but of late yeeres, with her owne father, receiued the Christian Faith, became so superstitious, that shee thought the wealth of the world for euer would haue beene an heauie burthen for her soule, and haue drawne her minde from the loue of her Maker; wherfore forsaking all manner of earthly pomp,
25 she liued a long time very poorelie, hard by the side of a most pleasant springing well; from which place, neither her friends by intreaty, nor her foes by violence could bring her: which sir *Hugh* hearing, he went thither immediately after vnto her, which was the time limited by them both, and finding her minde altogether
30 altered, hee wondred not a little what shee meant. And when he approached neare vnto the place where she sate, all suted in simple attire, he saluted her with these words:

Chapter Two

All health to faire *Winifred:* I trust (my deare) that now the Destinies haue yeelded a conuenient oportunity for mee to finish my
long begun sute, with the end of my former sorrowes. Long and
tedious hath the winter of my woes bin, which with nipping
care hath blasted the beautie of my youthfull delight which is 5
like neuer againe to florish except the bright Sun-shine of thy
fauour doe renew the same: therefore (faire loue) remember thy
promise made vnto me, and put me no more off with vnpleasing
delaies.

She (which all this while sat solemnlie reading in her booke) 10
lent little eare vnto his words; which he perceiuing, pluckt her by
the arme, saying: Wherefore answereth not my faire Loue, to her
dearest perplexed friend?

What would you haue, quoth she? can I neuer be quiet for you?
is there no corner of content in this world to be found? 15

Yes *Winifred,* said he, content dwells here, or no where: content
me, and I will content thee.

If my content may be thy content, then read this booke, and
there rests content, said *Winifred;* and if thou refuse this, then
thinke not to find content on earth. 20

Sir *Hugh* replied, What, is this all the reward I shall haue for
obeying your heart-cutting commandement? Haue I thus long hoped,
and find no better hap? You wot well that it is now three long
months since these eyes tooke comfort of thy beauty, and since
that time that my bleeding heart hath receiued ioy in thy great 25
gentlenesse.

I haue forgot you quite, said she; what three months is that you
speake of? for my part I assure you, that it is as farre out of my
mind, as you are from the mount of *Caluarie.*

Faire *Winifred* (quoth he) haue you forgotten me, and there- 30
withall my loue, which was so effectually grounded vpon your
good liking? you told me that now I should receiue an answer to
my content.

O Sir (quoth she) you have staied ouerlong, and your words are
in my hearing, as vnprofitable as snow in haruest: my loue is fled 35
to heauen, from whence no earthly man can fetch it, and therefore
build not in vaine hope, nor doe thou deceiue thy selfe by following an vnprofitable suite: if euer I loue earthly man, it shall be

---

[10] reading in] Q2-4; reading on Q1

97

thee, insomuch as thou hast deserued an earthly Ladies loue; but my loue is setled for euer, both in this world and in the world to come: and this I most earnestly intreat thee to take for a finall answer.

5   With that Sir *Hugh* turning his head aside, wept most bitterly; and in going away, he glansed his eye still backe againe after his loue, saying to himselfe: O vnconstant women, wauering and vncertaine, how many sorrowes are fond men drawne into by your wilie inticements? who are also swallowed vp in the gaping gulfe
10 of Care, while they listen after the heartliking sound of your inchanting voices. O *Winifred,* full little did I thinke that so hard a heart could haue been shrouded vnder so sweet and louing a countenance: but seeing that my good will is thus vnkindly requited, I will altogether abhorre the sight of women, and I will
15 seeke the world throughout, but I will find out some blessed plot, where no kind of such corrupt cattell doe breed.

   Hereupon all in hot hastie humour he made preparation for to goe beyond the Seas, suting himselfe after the nature of a melancholy man; and ariuing in *France,* he tooke his iourney towards *Paris,*
20 which citie (at that time) was well replenished with many goodly faire women, as well as *Brittaine,* though to his thinking nothing so louely, but neuerthelesse what they wanted in beauty, they had in brauery: which when sir *Hugh* saw, he suddenly departed from that place, counting it the most pernicious place in the whole
25 Countrie; and from thence hee went into *Italy,* where he found such stately Dames, and louely Ladies, whom Nature had adorned with all perfection of outward beauty, whose right put him againe in remembrance of his faire Loue, which like fresh fuell newly augmented the flame of his burning desire.

30   O (said he) how vnhappie am I to be haunted by these hearttormenting fiends, bewitching the eies of simple men with Angellike faces, and like enchanting *Circes,* bring them to a labyrinth of continuall woes.

   O *Winifred,* thy peeuishnesse hath bred my dangers, and done
35 thy selfe no good at all. Thou sittest weeping by a Christall streame, where is no need of water, while I wander vp and downe, seeking to forget thee, thou neuer remembrest me, hauing drawne the fountaine of mine eies drie through thy discourteous disdaine. Might I neuer see any of thy sexe, my heart would be more at

quiet, but euery place where I come puts me in mind of thy perfections, and therewithall renewes my paine: but I will from hence as soon as possible I can, though not so soon as I wold, for feare lest these sweet serpents should sting me to death with delight.

Hereupon he passed on so far, that at length he came to a City 5 situated in the Sea, and compassed with the wide Ocean.

Here (quoth sir *Hugh*) is a fit place for a melancholy man; where it is supposed no women doe liue, insomuch that their delicate bodies cannot abide the salt sauor of the mounting waues: if it bee so, there will I make my residence, counting it the most 10 blessed place vnder heauen.

But he was no sooner set on land, but he beheld whole troopes of louely Ladies, passing vp and downe in most sumptuous attire, framing their iestures answerable vnto their beauties and comely personages. 15

Nay now I see (quoth sir *Hugh*) that the whole world is infected with these deceiuing *Syrens,* and therfore in vaine it is for me to seek for that I shall neuer find; and therewithall sought for some house wherein hee might hide himselfe from them. But by that time he was set to supper, comes a crue of courtlike dames richly attired, 20 and with wanton eies and pleasant speech they boldly sate downe by him; and perceiuing him to be a stranger, they were not strange to allure him to their delight: wherefore while he sate at meate, they yeelded him such mirth as their best skill could affoord; and stretching their nimble fingers, playing on their sweet sounding instru- 25 ments, they sung this ensuing song, with such cleare and quauering voices, as had been sufficient to allure chaste hearted *Xenocrates* vnto folly: and still as they did sing, sir *Hugh* answered in the last line, insomuch as it seemed to be a dialogue between them; and in this manner following, the women began their song. 30

The Curtizans Song of Venice.

Ladies. Welcome to *Venice,* gentle courteous Knight,
    Cast off fond Care, and entertaine Content:
If any here be gracious in thy sight,
    Doe but request, and she shall soone consent: 35
Loues wings are swift, then be not thou so slow.

Hugh.   Oh that faire *Winifred* would once say so.

Ladies. Within my lap lay downe thy comely head,
          And let me stroke those golden lockes of thine:
          Looke on the teares that for thy sake I shed,
5   And be thou Lord of any thing is mine;
          One gentle looke vpon thy loue bestow.

Hugh.   Oh that faire *Winifred* would once say so.

Ladies. Embrace with ioy thy Ladie in thine armes,
          And with all pleasures passe to thy delight:
10   If thou doest thinke the light will worke our harmes,
          Come, come to bed, and welcome all the night;
          There shalt thou find, what Louers ought to know.

Hugh.   Oh that faire *Winifred* would once say so.

Ladies. Giue me those pearles as pledges of thy loue,
15   And with those pearles the fauour of thy heart:
          Doe not from me thy sugred breath remoue,
          That double comfort giues to euery part.
          Nay stay sir Knight, from hence thou shalt not goe.

Hugh.   Oh that faire *Winifred* would once say so.

20   When sir *Hugh* had heard this Song, and there withall noted
their wanton gestures, he began to grow suspicious of their profers,
and thinking in himselfe, that either they thought his destruction,
as the *Sirens* did to *Vlisses;* or that they intended to make a prey of
his purse, as *Lais* did of her louers: and therefore supposing some
25 adder to lie lurking vnder the faire flowers of their proffered pleasures, he determined the next morning after (with all speed) to
depart from the Citie. So when he had with good discretion auoided
their company, while he lay tormented with restles thoughts on
his stil-tossed bed, began thus to meditate:
30   Now I well see mine own vanity, that is as ill pleased with
womens fauours as their frownes; how often haue I with heart-
sighing sorrow complained of womens vnkindnesse, making large
inuectiues against their discourtesies? and yet here where I find
women as kinde as they are faire, and courteous as they are comely,

[30] well] Q2-4; will Qı

Chapter Two

I ran into a world of doubts, and as suspitious of their faire profers, as I was earnest to win *Winifreds* fauour: it may be (quoth he) that it is the nature of this gentle soile to breed as kind creatures, as the Country of *Brittaine* breeds coy dames.

Undoubtedly, had my loue first taken life in this kinde and 5 curteous climate, shee would haue beene as kinde as they. If I mis-iudge not of their gentlenesse, because I haue alwaies beene inured to scornfulnesse, me thinks they are too faire to bee harlots, and too bold to bee honest: but as they haue no cause to hate me that neuer hurt them, so haue they little cause to loue me, being a far 10 stranger borne, and to them a man altogether vnknowne.

But it may be that this time of the yeare is onely vnfortunate for louers; as it is certainly known to all men, that euery season of the yeare breeds a sundry commodity, for Roses flourish in Iune, and Gilliflowers in August, and neither of them both do so in the 15 cold winter. Such as seeke for fruit on the saplesse trees in the month of Ianuary lose their labors as well as their longing: then why should I couet to gather fruits of loue, when I see that loue is not yet ripe? Now let me obserue the season that yeelds the sweetest comfort to loue-sicke persons, and so I may reape the 20 ioyfull fruits of hearts content: I will therefore returne to my former loue, hoping now to find her as friendly, as at my departure she was froward; I will once againe intreat her, and speake her exceeding faire; for, with many drops the hardest stone is pierced; so also with many importunate intreaties a flinty hart may be 25 moued to some remorse. I take no pleasure at al in any place, but onely in her presence, with the which she continually graceth a run-ning streame; farre be it from her mind to kisse her owne shadow in the christall spring, and to be in loue with her own similitude, for so she might be spoiled as *Narcissus* was: for it is commonly 30 seene, that sudden danger followes fond opinions: so with this and the like thoughts he droue out the night, till the Suns bright eye began to peepe at his chamber window; at what time dressing himself he went to the water side, where he found a ship ready to transport rich merchandise into the Westerne Ilands, in the which 35 sir *Hugh* became a passenger. But when they were put off to sea, there arose so sudden a storme, and of so long continuance, that no

---

8 scornfulnesse,] Lange; ~; Q1-4
14 breeds] Q2-4; breede Q1

man looked for life, but expected euery moment present death;
so that the Mariners quite forsooke the tackle, and the Master the
helme, committing themselues to God, and their ship to the mercy
of the swelling seas, by whose furious waues they were sometime
5 tossed vp towards heauen, and anon throwne downe to the deepe
of hell: in which extremitie sir *Hugh* made this lamentation: O
vnhappy man, how eagerly doth mischance pursue me at my heeles,
for betwixt my loue on the land, and danger of life on the sea, it
hath made me the wretchedst man breathing on earth.

10 Here we may see that miseries haue power ouer men, and not
men ouer miseries. Now must I die farre from my friends, and bee
drenched in the deepe, where my bodie must feed the fishes that
swim in the rich bottome of the Sea. Therefore faire *Winifred,* the
chiefe ground of my griefes, here will I sacrifice my last teares
15 vnto thee, and powre forth my complaints.

Oh how happie should I count my selfe, if those fishes which
shall liue on my bodies food, might bee meate for my Loue! it
grieueth mee much to thinke that my poore bleeding heart, wherein
thy picture is ingrauen, should bee rent in peeces in such greedie
20 sort; but thrice accursed bee that fish, that first setteth his nimble
teeth thereon, except hee swimme therewith vnto my Loue, and so
deliuer it as a present taken from me.

Had my troubled starres allotted me to leaue my life in the
pleasant valley of *Sichnaunt,* then no doubt but my Loue with
25 her faire hands would haue closed vp my dying eyes, and perhaps
would haue rung a peale of sorrowfull sighs for my sake.

By this time was the weather-beaten Barke driuen vpon the
shore of *Cicilie,* where the men had safety of their liues, although
with losse of their ship and spoile of their goods: but they had no
30 sooner shaken off their dropping wet garments on the shore, but
that they were assaulted by a sort of monstrous men that had but
one eie a piece, and that placed in the midst of their foreheads,
with whom the tempest beaten souldiers had a fierce fight, in which
many of them were slaine, and diuers of them fled away to saue
35 themselues; so that in the end sir *Hugh* was left alone to Fortune
in a double fray: and hauing at last quite ouercome all his aduer-
saries, hee went his way, and so passing vp the country in darke

---

[29] ship] Q3,4; ships Q1,2
[32] that placed] Q2-4; were placed Q1
[37] in darke] Q2-4; the darke Q1

night, in the end he lost his way, and was so farre entred into a great darke wildernesse, that hee could not deuise with himselfe which way he should take to get out, where hee was so cruelly affrighted with the dreadfull cry of fierce Lyons, Beares, and wilde Bulls, and many thousand more of other dangerous and cruell rauenous beasts, 5 which with greedie mouths ranged all about for their prey: in which distresse, sir *Hugh* got him vp to the top of a tree, and being there, brake out into this passion.

O Lord (quoth he) hast thou preserued me from the great perill and danger of the Sea, and deliuered me out of the cruell hands 10 of monstrous men, and now suffer me to be deuoured of wilde beasts? Alas, that my foule sins should bring so many sundry sorrowes on my head.

But for all this may I thanke vnkind *Winifred,* whose disdaine hath wrought my destruction. Woe worth the time that euer my 15 eyes beheld her bewitching beauty. But hereby we may see that the path is smooth that leadeth to danger. But why blame I the blamelesse Ladie? Alas, full little did she know of my desperate courses in trauell. But such is the fury that hants franticke Louers, that neuer feare danger vntill it fall and light vpon their owne heads. 20

But by that time that the day began to appeare, he perceiued an huge Elephant with stiffe ioynts stalking towards him, and presently after came a fiery tongued Dragon, which suddenly assaulted the peacefull Elephant, in whose subtile encounter the wrathfull Dragon with his long wrinkling taile did so shackle the hinder feet 25 of the Elephant together, that like a prisoner fast fettered in irons, hee could not stirre a foot for his life; at what time the furious Dragon neuer left till he had thrust his slender head into the Elephants long hooked nose, out of which he neuer once drew it, vntill by sucking the Elephants blood, he had made him so feeble 30 and weake, that he could stand no longer vpon his feet; at which time the fainting Elephant with a grieuous cry, fell downe dead vpon the Dragon: so with the fall of his weighty body, burst the Dragon in pieces, and so killed him; whereby their bloods being mingled together, it stained all the ground where they both lay, 35 changing the greene grasse into a rich scarlet colour.

This strange fight betwixt these two beasts, caused good sir *Hugh* to iudge that nature had planted betwixt them a deadly

[30] blood,] Q2-4; ~: Q1

hatred, the fire whereof could not bee quenched, but by the shedding of both their hearts blood. Now when sir *Hugh* saw that grim Death had ended their quarrell, and perceiuing no danger neere, he came downe from the tree, and sought to find out some inhabited
5 towne, but being intangled in the woods, like the *Centaure* in his labyrinth, hee could by no meanes get out, but wandring in vnknowne passages, leading him to many perills.

At last another Elephant met him, who according to his kinde nature neuer left him till hee had conducted him out of all danger,
10 and brought him out of the Wildernesse into the way againe; whereby sir *Hugh* at the length came in sight of a Port-towne, where in foure dayes after hee imbarked himselfe in a ship bound for *Brittaine,* and at last obtained the sight of his natiue Country, where hee arriued in safetie, though in very poore sort, comming
15 on shoare at a place called *Harwich,* where for want of money he greatly lamented, and made much moane. But meeting with a merry Iourney-man Shoomaker dwelling in that towne, and after some conference had together, they both agreed to trauell in the Country, where we will leaue them, and speake of *Winifred,* and of
20 her great troubles and calamities.

[2] hearts blood] Q2-4; heart bloods Q1
[7] passages] Q2-4; passage Q1
[19] where] Q2-4; were Q1

CHAPTER III.

How faire *Winifred* was imprisoned, and condemned to
  dye for her Religion: and how sir *Hugh* became a
  Shoomaker, and afterward came to suffer death with
  his Loue: shewing also how the Shoomakers tooles 5
  came to be called Saint *Hughs* bones, and the trade
  of Shoomaking, *The Gentle Craft.*

Anon after that the Doctrine of Christ was made knowne in *Brittaine,* and that the worship of heathen Idols was forbidden,
yet many troubles did the Christians endure by the outragious 10
blood-thirstinesse of diuers woluish tyrants, that by the way of inuasion set footing in this Land, as it fell out in the dayes of
Dioclesian, that with bloudie mindes persecuted such as would not
yeeld to the Pagan law: amongst which the Virgin *Winifred* was
one, who for that shee continued constant in faith, was long im- 15
prisoned. During which time Sir *Hugh* wrought in a Shoomakers
shop, hauing learned that trade through the courteous directions
of a kind Iourney-man, where hee remained the space of one whole
yeere; in which time hee had gotten himselfe good apparell, and
euery thing comely and decent. Notwithstanding though hee were 20
now contented to forget his birth, yet could hee not forget the
beautie of his Loue, who although shee had vtterly forsaken him,
yet could hee not alter his affection from her, because indeed affections alter not like a palefaced coward.

The wildest Bull (quoth hee) is tamed being tyed to a Fig-tree; 25
and the coyest Dame (in time) may yeeld like the stone *Carchaedonis,* which sparkles like fire, and yet melts at the touch of soft
waxe. Though Roses haue prickles, yet they are gathered; and
though women seeme froward, yet will they shew themselues kinde

[1] III] Q4; II Q1-3
[10] by the] Q3,4; by diuers the Q1,2
[11] of diuers woluish] Q3,4; of woluish Q1,2

and friendly. Neither is there any waxe so hard, but by often tempering, is made apt to receiue an impression: Admit she hath heretofore beene cruell, yet now may she be courteous. A true hearted Louer forgets all trespasses: and a smile cureth the wounding of a
5 frowne. Thus after the manner of fond Louers he flattered himselfe in his owne folly, and in the praise of his faire Lady, hee sung this pleasant Ditty here following.

> The pride of Britaine is my hearts delight,
>   My Lady liues, my true loue to requite:
10 And in her life I liue that else were dead,
>   Like withered Leaues in time of Winter shead.
>
> She is the ioy and comfort of my minde,
>   She is the Sunne that clearest sight doth blinde;
> The fairest flower that in the world doth grow,
15 Whose whitenesse doth surpasse the driuen snow.
>
> Her gentle words more sweet then hony are,
>   Her eyes for clearenesse dims the brightest starre:
> O were her heart so kind as she is faire,
>   No Lady might with my true loue compare.
>
20 A thousand griefes for her I haue sustained,
>   While her proud thoughts my humble sute disdained:
> And though she would my heart with torments kill,
>   Yet would I honour, serue, and loue her still.
>
> Blest be the place where she doth like to liue:
25 Blest be the light that doth her comfort giue:
> And blessed be all creatures farre and neer,
>   That yeeld reliefe unto my Lady deere.
>
> Neuer may sorrow enter where she is,
>   Neuer may she contented comfort misse:
30 Neuer may she my proffered loue forsake,
>   But my good will in thankfull sort to take.

Thus feeding his fancy with the sweet remembrance of her beauty, being neuer satisfied with thinking and speaking in her praise, at length hee resolued himselfe to goe into *Flint-shire,* where hee might solicite his sute anew againe: but comming neere to the place of her residence; and hearing report of her troubles, he so highly commended her faith and constancy, that at length he was clapt vp in prison by her, and in the end he was condemned to 5 receiue equall torment, for a tryall of his owne truth.

But during the time that they lay both in prison, the Iourneymen Shoomakers neuer left him, but yeelded him great reliefe continually, so that hee wanted nothing that was necessary for him; in requitall of which kindnesse he called them *Gentlemen of the* 10 *Gentle Craft* and a few dayes before his death, he made this Song in their due commendations.

Of Craft and Crafts-men more and lesse,
    The *Gentle Craft* I must commend:
Whose deeds declare their faithfulnesse,   15
    And hearty loue unto their freind:
The *Gentle Craft* in midst of strife,
    Yeelds comfort to a carefull life.

A Prince by Birth I am indeed,
    The which for Love forsooke this Land: 20
And when I was in extreme need,
    I tooke the *Gentle Craft* in hand,
And by the *Gentle Craft* alone,
    Long time I liu'd, being still unknowne,

Spending my dayes in sweet content,   25
    With many a pleasant sugred Song:
Sitting in pleasures complement,
    Whilst we recorded Louers wrong:
And while the *Gentle Craft* we us'd,
    True Love by vs was not abus'd.   30

Our shooes we sowed with merry notes,
    And by our mirth expell'd all mone:
Like Nightingales, from whose sweet throats,

---

[10] Sig. C1 is missing in Q1; beginning with "of which kindnesse" and ending with "miseries, and in-" (page 109, line 20) the copy text is Q2.
  [33] throats,] Q3; ~. Q2 [*This stanza omitted in Q4*]

Most pleasant tunes are nightly blowne;
The *Gentle Craft* is fittest then,
   For poore distressed Gentlemen:

Their minds doe mount in courtesie,
   And they disdaine a niggards feast:
Their bodies are for Chivalrie,
   All cowardnesse they doe detest.
For Sword and Sheild, for Bow and Shaft,
   No man can staine the *Gentle Craft*.

Yea sundry Princes sore distrest,
   Shall seeke for succour by this Trade:
Whereby their greifes shall be redrest,
   Of foes they shall not be afraid.
And many men of fame likewise,
   Shall from the *Gentle Craft* arise.

If we want money ouer night,
   Ere next day noone, God will it send,
Thus may we keepe our selues upright,
   And be no churle vnto our freind:
Thus doe we live where pleasure springs,
   In our conceit like petty Kings.

Our hearts with care we may not kill,
   Mans life surpasseth worldly wealth,
Content surpasseth riches still,
   And fie on knaves that live by stealth:
This Trade therefore both great and small,
   The *Gentle Craft* shall ever call.

When the Iourney-men Shoomakers had heard this Song, and
the faire Title that Sir *Hugh* had giuen their Trade, they ingraued
the same so deeply in their minds, that to this day it could neuer
be razed out: like a remembrance in a Marble stone which continueth time out of mind.

But not long after came that dolefull day, wherein these two

---

²⁵ on] Q3,4; one Q2

Chapter Three

Louers must loose their liues, who like two meeke Lambes were
led to the slaughter: the bloody performance thereof was to bee
done hard by that faire Fountaine, where the Loue-despising Lady
made her most abode: and because she was a kings daughter, the
bloody Tyrant gaue her the priuiledge to chuse her owne death: 5
to the which she passed with as good a countenance, as if she had
been a faire yong Bride prepared for marriage.

(*viz.*) When they were come to the place of execution, and
mounted vpon the Scaffold, they seemed for beauty like two bright
Stars, *Castor* and *Pollux,* there they embraced each other with 10
such chaste desires, as all those that beheld them, admired to see
how stedfast and firme both these Louers were, ready in hearts
and minds to heauen itselfe.

At what time the Lady turned herselfe to Sir *Hugh,* and spake
to this effect: Now doe I find thee a perfect Louer indeed, that 15
hauing setled thy affection aboue the Skies, art ready to yeeld thy
life for thy Loue, who in requitall thereof, will giue thee life for
euer.

The Loue of earthly creatures is mixed with many miseries, and
interlaced with sundrie sorrowes: and here griefe shall abate the 20
pleasures of Loue, but be well assured that ioy shall follow the
same.

Thou didst wooe me for loue, and now haue I wonne thee to
loue: where setling both our loues vpon God his loue, we will loue
one another; and in token of that heauenly loue, receiue of mee I 25
pray thee a chaste and louing kisse from my dying lips.

Faire *Winifred* (quoth he) it is true indeed; I neuer loued truly,
vntill thou taughtest me to loue, for then my loue was full of discontent, but now altogether pleasing, and more sweet is the thought
thereof then any tongue can expresse.   30

The thing that I euer before called Loue, was but a shadow of
loue, a sweetnesse tempered with gall-dying life, and a liuing
death, where the heart was continually tossed vpon the seas of
tempestuous sorrowes, and wherein the minde had no calme quietnesse: and therefore blessed bee the time that I euer learned this 35
loue.

With that hee was interrupted by the Tyrant, who sayd, You are
not come hither to talke but to dye; and I haue sworne you both
shall die at this instant.

Thou Tyrant (sayd Sir *Hugh*) the very like sentence is pro- 40

109

nounced against thy selfe; for Nature hath deemed that thou shalt die likewise, and albeit the execution thereof be something deferred, yet at length it will come, and that shortly, for neuer did Tyrant carry gray haires to the graue.

5 The young Lady desired first to die, saying to Sir *Hugh,* Come deare friend and learne magnanimitie of a Maide: now shalt thou see a silly woman scorne death to his teeth, and make as small account of his crueltie, as the Tyrant doth of our liues, and there withall stript vp her silken sleeues, and committed her Alabaster
10 armes into the Executioners foule hands, hauing made choice to die in bleeding: at what time being pricked in euery veine, the scarlet blood sprung out in plentifull sort, much like a pretious fountaine lately filled with Claret Wine.

And while she thus bled, she said, Here doe I sacrifice my blood
15 to him that bought mee, who by his blood washt away all my sinnes, O my sweet Sauiour, thus were thy sides pierced for my transgressions, and in this sort sprung thy precious blood from thee, and all for the loue thou bearest vnto mankinde: I feele my heart to faint, but my soule receiueth strength, I come sweet Christ, I come.

20 And therwithall her body fainting, and the blood failing, like a Conduit suddenly drawne drie, the young Princesse fell downe dead, at what time a pale colour ouer-spread her faire face, in such comely sort, as if a heape of Roses had beene shadowed with a sheet of pure Lawne.

25 But it is to bee remembred, that all the while the young Princesse bled, her blood was receiued into certaine basons, which being in that sort saued together, the Tyrant caused it to bee tempered with poyson, and prepared it to bee the last drinke that Sir *Hugh* should haue, saying; That by her loue whom hee so
30 dearely loued, hee should receiue his death. And thereupon incontinently, without any further delaying of time, he caused a cup of that most deadly poysoned blood to bee deliuered into his hands, who with a louely and chearefull countenance receiued the same, and then vttered his minde in this manner.

35 O thou cruell tyrant (quoth he) what a poore spite is this to inflict vpon a dying man, that is as carelesse how he dies, as when hee dies? Easie it is for thee to glut me with blood, although with blood thou art not satisfied. Sweet blood (quoth he) precious and pure, how faire a colour dost thou cast before mine eies? Sweet

110

Chapter Three

I say wast thou, before such time as this ill-sauoring poyson did infect thee: and yet as thou art, I nothing despise thee. O my deere *Winifred,* full little did I think, that euer I should come to drinke of thy heart blood.

My greedie eie that glutton-like did feed vpon thy beautie, and 5 yet like the Sea was neuer satisfied, is now with thy gore blood fully gorged. Now may I quench my thirsty desire with loue, that like hot burning coales set my heart in such an extreme heate, that it could not be quenched before this time; for if faire *Winifred* could spare any loue from heauen, assuredly she left it in her blood, her 10 sweet heart blood I meane, that nourished her chast life: see, here is a Caudle to coole my vaine affections. Farre bee it that any true Louer should euer taste the like.

But this punishment haue the iust heauens poured vpon mee: for the preferring the loue of an earthly creature, before the loue 15 of an heauenly Creator; Pardon, O Lord, the foule sinnes of super-stitious Louers, that while they make Idols of their Ladies, they forget the honour of thy Diuine Maiestie. Yet doth it doe my heart much good to thinke that I must bury sweet *Winifreds* blood in my body, whose loue was lodged long agoe in my heart: and 20 therewithall, drinking the first draught, hee said, O Lord, me seemeth this potion hath a comfortable taste, farre doth it surpasse that Nectar wherewith the gods were nourished.

Well (said the Tyrant) seeing it pleaseth thee so well, thou shalt haue more, and therewith another cup of the same blood was giuen 25 him to drinke.

Yes come (quoth he) my thirst is not quenched; for the first draught gaue me but a taste of sweetnesse, and like a longing woman, I desire the rest; and with that he dranke the second draught. 30

The third being deliuered him, he tooke the cup into his hand, and looking about, he said: Loe here, I drinke to all the kind Yeomen of the *Gentle Craft,* the dearest draught of drinke that euer man tasted of.

I drinke to you all (quoth he) but I cannot spare you one drop 35

---

¹ ill-sauoring] Q2-4; insauoring Q1
⁸ coales] Q2-4; cooles Q1
¹² Caudle] Q2-4; Candle Q1
²⁶ him] Q2,4 (*sig. C3 missing in Q3*); me Q1

111

to pledge me. Had I any good thing to giue, you should soone receiue it: but my life the tyrant doth take, and my flesh is bequeathed to the Fowles, so that nothing is left but onely my bones to pleasure you withall; and those, if they will doe you any good, 5 take them: and so I humbly take my leaue, bidding you all farewell.

There with the last draught he finished his life, whose dead carkasse after hanged vp where the Fowles deuoured his flesh, and the yong Princesse was contemptuously buried by the Well where 10 she had so long liued. Then had he the title of Saint *Hugh* giuen him, and she of Saint *Winifred,* by which termes they are both so called to this day.

CHAPTER IV.

How the Shoomakers stole away Saint *Hughes* bones, and
15   made them working tooles thereof, and the vertue
that they found in the same: whereby it came, that
when any man saw a Shoomaker trauelling with a
packe at his backe, they would presently say: There
goes Saint *Hughes* bones.

20 **V**pon a time it chanced, that a company of Iourney-men Shoomakers passed along by the place where Saint *Hughes* dead body was hanging, and finding the flesh pickt cleane off from the bones, they entred thus into communication among themselues.

Neuer was Saint *Hugh* so bare (quoth one) to carry neuer a 25 whit of skin vpon his bones; nor thou neuer so bare (said another) to beare neuer a penny in thy purse.

But now seeing you talke of Saint *Hugh,* it brings mee in remembrance of the Legacie that hee gaue vs at his death.

What was that said the rest?

30 Marry (quoth he) I will tell you. When the gentle Prince saw

----

[18] backe,] Q4; ~: Q1,2

112

that the crueltie of the time would not suffer him to be liberall to
his friends, but that his life was taken away by one, and his flesh
giuen to others, he most kindly bequeathed his bones vnto vs.

Tush (quoth another) that was but to shew his minde towards the
Shoomakers, because he had of them receiued so many fauours: 5
for alas, what can the dead mans bones pleasure the liuing?

No (quoth another) I can tell you there may bee as great vertue
found in his bones, as the braines of a Weasill, or the tongue of
a Frog.

Much like (answered the rest) but I pray thee shew vs what 10
vertue is in those things you speake of.

Quoth he, I will tell you. The braines of a Weasill hath this
power, *experientia docet,* that if the powder thereof bee mingled
with the Runnet, wherewith women make their Cheese, no mouse
dares euer touch it: In like manner, the tongue of a water-frog 15
hath such great force in it, that if it be laid vpon the breast of any
one sleeping, it will cause them tell whatsoeuer you shall demand;
for by that meanes *Dicke Piper* knew hee was a Cuckold. Againe,
I know that those that are trauellers are not ignorant, that whosoeuer puts but six leaues of Mugwort in his shooes, shall neere 20
bee wearie, though hee trauell thirty or forty miles on foot in a
forenoone.

That indeed may be true, quoth one, for by the very same hearbe
my last Dame kept her Ale from sowring: and it is said, that where
houseleeke is planted, the place shall neuer bee hurt with thunder. 25
Pimpernell is good against Witchcraft; and because my sister *Ioane*
carrieth alwaies some about her, Mother *Bumby* could not abide
her: Therefore what vertue a dead mans bones may haue, wee
know not till wee haue tryed it.

Why then said the third man, let vs soone at night steale Saint 30
Hughes bones away, and albeit the Tyrant will bee displeased, yet
it is no theft, for you say they were giuen vs, and therefore wee
may the bolder take them, and because wee will turne them to
profit, and auoyd suspition, wee will make diuers of our Tooles with
them, and then if any vertue doe follow them, the better wee shall 35
finde it.

To this motion euery one gaue his consent, so that the same night
Saint *Hughes* bones were taken downe, and the same being brought
before a sort of shoomakers, there they gaue their opinion, That
it was necessary to fulfill the will of the dead, and to take those 40

bones in as good a part, as if they were worth ten thousand pounds; whereupon one steps out, and thus did say:

My freinds, I pray you list to me,
   And marke what S. *Hughs* bones shall be.
First a Drawer and a Dresser,
   two Wedges, a more and a lesser:
A pretty blocke three inches high,
   in fashion squared like a Die,
Which shall be called by proper name,
   a Heeleblocke, the very same.
A Hand-leather and a Thumb-leather likewise,
   to pull out shoo-threed we must despise;
The Needle and the Thimble,
   shal not be left alone
The Pincers and the pricking Aule
   and the rubbing Stone.
The Aule steele and Tackes,
   the Sow-haires beside,
The Stirrop holding fast,
   while we sowe the Cow-hide,
The whetstone, the stopping sticke,
   and the Paring knife:
All this doth belong,
   to a Journeymans life.
Our Apron is the Shrine,
   to wrap these bones in:
Thus shrowd we Saint *Hugh*
   in gentle Lambes skinne.

5 · 10 · 15 · 20 · 25

Now all you good Yeomen of the *Gentle Craft,* tell me now (quoth he) how like you this?

As well (replyed they) as Saint *George* doth of his Horse, for as long as we can see him fight with the Dragon, we will neuer part from this Posie.

And it shall bee concluded that what Iourney-man soeuer hee

---

³ Sig. C4 is missing in Q1; beginning with "My freinds" and ending with "swift time ouerslip" (page 116, line 15) the copy text is Q2.
⁸ squared] Q3,4; sqared Q2
*¹² despise] devise Q3,4

bee hereafter, that cannot handle the Sword and Buckler, his Long
Sword, or a Quarter staffe, sound the Trumpet, or play vpon the
Flute and beare his part in a three mans Song: and readily reckon
vp his tooles in Rime; except he haue borne Colours in the field,
being a Lieutenant, a Sergeant or Corporall, shall forfeit and pay a   5
pottle of wine, or be counted for a colt: to which they answered
all *viua voce* Content, content, and then after many merry Songs,
they departed. And neuer after did they trauell without these tooles
on their backes: which euer since were called Saint *Hughes* bones.

CHAPTER V.   10

How *Crispianus* and his brother *Crispine,* the two sons of
the King of *Logria,* through the cruelty of the Tyrant
Maximinus, were faine in disguised manner to seeke
for their lives safety, and how they were entertained
by a Shoomaker in *Feversham.*   15

When the Roman *Maximinus* sought in cruel sort, to bereaue
this Land of all her noble youth or youth of noble blood,
The vertuous Queene of *Logria* (which now is called *Kent*) dwelling in the Citie *Durovernum, alias Canterbury,* or the Court of
Kentishmen, hauing at that time two young Sons, sought all the   20
meanes she could possible to keepe them out of the Tyrants clawes;
and in this manner she spake vnto them.

My deare and beloued sonnes, the ioy and comfort of my age,
you see the danger of these times and the stormes of a Tyrants
raigne, who hauing now gathered together the most part of the   25
young Nobility, to make them slaues in a forraigne Land, that are
free borne in their owne Country, seeketh for you also, thereby to
make a cleare riddance of all our borne Princes, to the end he
might plant strangers in their stead. Therefore (my sweet sons)
take the counsell of your mother, and seeke in time to preuent   30

---

⁸ departed.] Q4; ∼ ‸ Q2 [*This section of leaf torn off in Q3*]

ensuing danger, which will come vpon vs suddenly as a storme at
sea, and as cruelly as a Tyger in the wildernesse: therfore suiting
your selues in honest habites, seeke some poore seruice to sheild
you from mischance, seeing necessity hath priuiledged those places
5 from Tyranny. And so (my sons) the gracious Heauens may one
day raise you to deserued dignity and honour.

The young Lads seeing their mother so earnest to haue them
gone, fulfilled her commandement, and casting off their attire, put
homelie garments on, and with many bitter teares, took leaue of
10 the Queene their mother, desiring her before they went, to bestow
her blessing vpon them.

O my sons (quoth she) stand you now vpon your ceremonies?
had I leasure to giue you one kisse, it were somthing; The Lord
blesse you, get you gone, away, away, make hast I say, let not swift
15 time ouerslip you, for the Tyrant is hard by: with that shee pushed
them out of a backe doore, and then set her selfe downe to weepe.

The two yong Princes, which like prettie lambes went straying
they knew not whither, at length, by good fortune, came to *Feuer-
sham*, where before the daies peepe, they heard certaine Shoo-
20 makers singing, being as pleasant as their notes, as they sate at
their businesse, and this was their Song:

Would God that it were holiday,
　hey dery downe downe dery:
That with my Love I might goe play,
25 　with woe my heart is wearie:
My whole delight is in her sight,
　would God I had her company,
　　her company,
Hey dery downe, downe a downe.

30 My Loue is fine, my Loue is faire,
　hey dery downe, downe dery:
No Maid with her may well compare,
　in Kent or Canterbury:
From me my loue shall neuer moue,
35 　would God I had her company,
　　her company,
Hey dery downe, downe a downe.

116

To see her laugh, to see her smile,
  hey dery downe, downe dery:
Doth all my sorrowes cleane beguile,
  and make my heart full merry;
No griefe can grow where she doth goe,   5
  would God I had her company, &c.
Hey dery downe, downe a downe.

When I doe meet her on the greene,
  hey dery downe, downe dery:
Me thinkes she lookes like beauties Queene,   10
  which makes my heart full merry:
Then I her greet with kisses sweet,
  would God I had her company, &c.
Hey dery downe, downe a downe.

My love comes not of churlish kinde,   15
  hey dery downe, downe dery;
But beares a gentle courteous minde,
  which makes my heart full merry,
She is not coy, she is my ioy,
  would God I had her company, &c.   20
Hey dery downe, downe adowne.

Till Sunday come, farewell my deare,
  hey dery downe, downe dery.
When we doe meet weele have good cheare,
  and then I will be merry: 25
If thou loue me, I will loue thee,
  and still delight thy company, thy company,
Hey dery downe, downe adowne.

The yong Princes perceiuing such mirth to remaine in so homely a cottage, iudged by their pleasant Notes, that their hearts 30 were not cloyed with ouer many cares, and therefore wished it might bee their good hap to be harboured in a place of such great content.

But standing a long time in doubt what to doe, like two distressed strangers, combating twixt hope and feare; at length taking 35 courage, *Crispianus* knocked at the doore.

What knaue knockes there (quoth the Iourney-man) and by and by, downe he takes his quarter Staffe and opens the doore, being as readie to strike as speake, saying: What lacke you?

To whom *Crispianus* made this answer: Good sir, pardon our
5 boldnesse, and measure not our truth by our rudenesse; we are two poore boyes that want seruice, stript from our friends by the fury of these warres, and therefore are wee enforced succourlesse to craue seruice in any place.

What, haue you no friends or acquaintaince in these parts to goe
10 to (said the shoemaker) by whose meanes you might get prefer- ment?

Alas sir (sayd *Crispianus*) necessitie is despised of euery one, and misery is troden downe of many; but seldome or neuer re- lieued: yet notwithstanding, if our hope did not yeeld vs some
15 comfort of good happe, wee should grow desperate through dis- tresse.

That were great pittie (said the Shoomaker) bee content, for as our Dame often tells our Master, A patient man is better than a strong man. Stay a while and I will call our Dame to the doore,
20 and then you shal heare what shee will say.

With that he went in, and forth came his Dame, who beholding the said youths, said: Now alas, poore boyes, how comes it to passe that you are out of seruice? What, would you be Shoomakers, and learne the *Gentle Craft*?
25 Yes forsooth (said they) with all our hearts.

Now by my troth (quoth she) you do looke with honest true faces. I will intreat my husband for you, for we would gladly haue good boyes; and if you will be iust and true, and serue God, no doubt you may doe well enough: Come in my lads, come in.
30 *Crispianus* and his brother, with great reuerence, gaue her thankes; and by that time they had stayed a little while, downe came the good man, and his wife hard at his heeles, saying: See husband, these be the youths I told you of, no doubt but (in time) they will bee good men.
35 Her husband looking wishlie vpon them, and conceiuing a good opinion of their fauors, at length agreed that they should dwel with him, so that they would be bound for seuen yeeres. The

---

⁶ seruice] Q2-4; seruices Q1

youths being contented, the bargaine was soone ended, and so set
to their businesse; wherat they were no sooner setled, but that
great search was made for them in all places; and albeit the Officers
came to the house where they dwelt, by the reason of their disguise
they knew them not: hauing also taken vpon them borrowed names 5
of *Crispianus* and *Crispine.*

Within a few daies after, the Queene their mother was by the
tyrant taken; and for that shee would not confesse where her sons
were: shee was laid prisoner in *Rochester* Castle: whereunto she
went with as chearefull a countenance, as *Cateratus* did, when hee 10
was led captiue to *Rome:* and comming by the place where her
sonnes sate at worke, with a quicke eie she had soone spyed them,
and looke how a dying cole reuiues in the wind, euen so at this
sight she became suddenly red: but making signes that they should
hold their tongues, she was led along: whom seuen yeeres after her 15
sons did neuer see. But as men stand amazed at the sight of Appari-
tions in the aire, as ignorant what successe shall follow, euen so
were these two Princes agast to see their owne mother thus led
away, not knowing what danger would insue thereof.

Notwithstanding, they thought good to keepe their seruice as 20
their liues surest refuge: at what time they both bent their whole
minds to please their Master and Dame, refusing nothing that was
put to them to doe, were it to wash Dishes, scoure Kettles, or any
other thing, whereby they thought their Dames fauour might be
gotten, which made her the readier to giue them a good report to 25
their Master, and to doe them many other seruices, which otherwise they should haue missed; following therein the admonition of
an old Iourneyman, who would alwaies say to the Apprentices:

> *Howsoever things doe frame,*
> *Please well thy Master, But chiefly thy Dame.* 30

Now by that time, these two young Princes had truely serued
their Master the space of foure or fiue yeeres, he was growne something wealthy, and they very cunning in the trade; whereby the
house had the name to breed the best workmen in the Countrey:
which report in the end preferd their Master to be the Emperours 35
Shoomaker: and by this meanes, his seruants went to *Maximinus*
Court euery day: but *Crispianus* and *Crispine* fearing they should

haue beene knowne, kept themselues from thence as much as they could. Notwithstanding, at the last perswading themselues, that Time had worne them out of knowledge, they were willing in the end to goe thither, as well to heare tidings of the Queene their
5 Mother, as also for to seeke their owne preferment.

CHAPTER VI.

How the Emperors faire daughter *Vrsula,* fell in loue with
young *Crispine,* comming with Shooes to the Court;
and how in the end they were secretly maried by a
10 blind Frier.

N̲ow among all the Shoomakers-men that came to the Court with shooes, young *Crispine* was had in greatest regard with the faire Princesse, whose mother being lately dead, she was the only ioy of her father, who alwaies sought meanes to match her with
15 some worthy Romane, whose renowne might ring throughout the whole world.

But faire *Vrsula,* whose bright eies had intangled her heart with desire of the Shoomakers fauour, despised all profers of loue, in regard of him. And yet notwithstanding shee would oft checke
20 her owne opinion, in placing her loue vpon a person of such low degree, thus reasoning with herselfe.

Most aptly is the god of Loue by cunning Painters drawne blind, that so equally shoots forth his fiery shafts: for had hee eies to see, it were vnpossible to deale in such sort, as in matching faire *Venus*
25 with foule *Vulcan,* yoaking the Emperiall hearts of Kings to the loue of beggars, as he did by *Cofetua,* and as now in my selfe I finde how mad a thing it would seem to the eies of the world, that an Emperors daughter should delight in the fauor of a simple Shoomaker.

30 O *Vrsula* take heed what thou dost, staine not thy royaltie with such indignitie. O that *Crispines* birth were agreeable to his person! for in mine eie, there is no Prince in the world comparable

to him: if then while he is clothed in these rags of seruitude, hee appeare so excellent, what would he bee, were he in Princely attire. O *Crispine,* either thou are not as thou seemest, or else Nature, in disgrace of Kings, hath made thee a Shoomaker.

In these humors would the Princesse often be, especially at *Crispines* approach, or at his departure: For, as soone as euer he came within her sight with shooes, a sudden blush like vnto a flame of lightning would strike in her face, and at his departure an earthly pale colour, like to the beames of the bright Sunne obscured by cole blacke clouds. But after many weary conflicts with Fancy, shee fully resolued, at his next comming, to enter in communication with him, but imagining his stay from Court ouer long, on the sudden she sent presently for him, finding great fault in the last shooes he brought her. At which time *Crispine* most humbly on his knee gently craued pardon for all such faults as she then found, promising amendment in the next shooes she should haue.

Nay (quoth she) Ile shew thee, they are too low something in the instep; also the heele is bad, and besides that, they are too strait in the toes.

You shall haue a paire made (said he) shall fit you better, for none shall set a stitch in them but mine owne selfe.

Doe, sayd the Princesse, but let me haue them so soone as thou canst; and therewith *Crispine* departed.

The Princesse then all solitarie, got her selfe into her chamber, entred there into consideration, how shee might breake out her mind at *Crispines* next comming, and found within her selfe great trouble and sorrow, while her tongue, the hearts aduocate, was not suffered to speake. At last she heard *Crispines* voice, enquiring of the Ladies in the great Chamber for the Princesse, who answered, That hauing taken little rest the night before, shee was now laid downe to sleepe, and therefore they willed him to come againe some other time.

Asleepe, replied the Princesse! I am not asleepe, bid him stay: what hastie huswife was that which sent him hence? Call him againe quickly I would aduise you. And therewithall changing melancholy into mirth, shee arose vp from out of her bed, and as a bright star shooting in the Element, she swiftly got her forth to meet the shoomaker, whose faire sight was to her as great a comfort as Sun-shine is before a shower of raine.

How now (quoth she) hast thou brought me a paire of shooes?
I haue, gracious Madam (quoth he).

Then (quoth the Princesse) come thy selfe and draw them on:
therwith she sitting downe, lifted vp her well proportioned leg
5 vpon his gentle knee. Where, by that time her shooes were drawne
on, she had prepared a good reward for her shoomaker, and giuing
him a handfull of gold, she said: Thou hast so well pleased me in
making of these shooes, that I cannot but reward thee in some good
sort, therefore shoomaker, take this, and from henceforth let no
10 man make my shooes but thy self. But tell me *Crispine,* art thou
not in loue, that thou dost smug vp thy selfe so finely, thou wast
not wont to go so neatly: I pray thee tel me what pretty wench
is it that is mistresse of thy heart?

Truely, faire Madam (quoth he) If I should not loue, I might be
15 counted barbarous, for by natures course there is a mutuall loue
in all things: the Doue and the Peacocke loue intirely, so doth
the Turtle and the Popiniay; the like affection the fish *Musculus*
beareth vnto the hugh Whale, insomuch that hee leadeth him from
all danger of stonie rocks, and as among birds and fishes, so amongst
20 plants and trees the like concord is to be found, for if the male of
palme trees be planted from the female, neither of both prosper:
and being set one neere another, they doe flourish accordingly, imbracing with ioy the branches one of another. And for mine owne
part, I am in loue too; for first of all, I loue my Maker, and next,
25 my good Master and Dame. But as concerning the loue of pretty
wenches, verily Madam, I am cleere: and the rather doe I abstaine
from fixing my fancy on women, seeing many sorrowes doe follow
the maried sort, that for a dram of delight haue a pound of paine.

That is (answered the Princesse) where Contention setteth the
30 house on fire, but where true loue remaines, there is no discontent: and what can a man more desire for this worlds comfort, but a
vertuous wife, which is reported to be a treasure inestimable.
Therefore *Crispine,* say thy minde, if I preferre thee to a wife,
euery way deseruing thy loue, wouldst thou take it well?

35 Truely Madame, (said *Crispine*) if I should not accept of your
good will, I should shew my selfe more vnmannerly then well nur-
tured: but seeing it pleaseth you to grace me with your Princely
countenance, and to giue me libertie to speake my minde, this is
my opinion: If I were worthy to choose a wife, then would I haue

one faire, rich, and wise; first, to delight mine eie; secondly, to
supply my want; and thirdly, to gouerne my house.

Then (said the Princesse) her beauty I will refer vnto the iudgement of thine owne eies, and her wisedome vnto the triall of Time;
but as concerning her portion, I dare make some report, because
it well deserueth to be praised: For at her marriage thou shalt
haue a bag full of rare vertues with her.

Truely Madam (quoth *Crispine*) such coines goe not currant
among Tanners; and I know, if I should goe therewith to the
Market, it will buy me no soale leather. Notwithstanding, when I
do see her, I will tel you more of my mind.

The Princesse taking him aside, priuately walking with him in a
faire Gallery, said, In looking vpon mee, thou maist iudge of her,
for she is as like me as may be.

When *Crispine* heard her say so, he right prudently answered:
I had rather Madam shee were your owne selfe, then like your
selfe: and although my words sauour of presumption, yet with your
fauour I dare boldly pronounce it, that I hold my selfe worthy of
a Queene, if I could get her good will. And were it not danger to
match with your Excellency, if so it shold please you it should not
dislike me.

Then said the Princesse, Now Shoomaker I see thou hast some
courage in thee: and doubt thou not, that if I were of that mind,
but I would be as readie to guide thee from the dangerous rocks of
my fathers wrath, as the fish called *Musculus* is for the Whale. But,
couldst thou not bee contented to die for a Ladies loue?

No Madam (quoth he) if I could keepe her loue, and liue.

Then liue faire friend (answered she) enioy my loue, for I will
die rather then liue without thee.

Crispine hearing this, was stricken into an extasie of ioy, in such
sort, as he wist not whether he were asleepe, or dreamed: But by
that time hee had summoned his wits together, with the plighting
of his faith, he opened his estate and high birth vnto her, shewing
all the extremities that hee and his brother had been put vnto
since the death of their royall Father, and of the imprisonment
of the Queene their Mother.

The which when faire *Vrsula* with great wonder heard, giuing

---

⁸ goe not] Q2,3; goes not Q1; goe out Q4

him an earnest of her loue, with a sweet kisse; she said, My deare
Loue, and most gentle Prince, euer did I thinke, that more then
a common man was shrowded in these poore habiliments, which
made me the bolder to impart my minde vnto thee, and now
5 dread no more my Fathers wrath, for the fire thereof was long
agoe quenched.

No, no, (quoth *Crispine*) an Eagles thirst is neuer expelld, but
by blood. And albeit your father haue now (perhaps) qualified the
heate of his furie by the length of time, yet if he should vnderstand
10 of this my loue to thee, it would cause him to rake out of ashes,
hote burning coales of displeasure againe: and then might my life
pay a deare price for thy loue.

Therefore (my deare *Vrsula*) I desire thee, euen by the power
of that loue thou bearest to me, to keepe secret what I haue shewed
15 thee, nothing doubting but that in time, I may finde release of
these miseries; in the meane space wee will bee secretly maried, by
which holy knot, wee may as well in bodie, as in heart, be vnsep-
arately tyed together.

To this *Vrsula* consented most gladly, and thereupon told him
20 that shee would meet him in her fathers Parke, at any houre hee
would appoint, which she might doe the more easily, in respect
shee had a key to one of the garden doores, which gaue present
passage into the Parke. The day and houre being concluded vpon,
they parted for this time, both of them indued with such content,
25 as in all their liues they neuer found the like.

And at this time there was in *Canterbury* a blinde Frier that in
many yeeres had neuer seen the Sun, to this man did *Crispine*
goe, thinking him the fittest Chapplaine to chop vp such a mariage,
who meeting with him at Christ-church one euening after the An-
30 theme, broke with him after this manner.

God speed good father: there is a certaine friend of mine that
wold be secretly maried in the morning betimes; for which purpose
hee thinkes you the fittest man to performe it in all the Cloister:
and therefore, if you will be diligent to doe it, and secret to con-
35 ceale it, you shall haue foure angells for your paines.

The Frier being fired with the desire of his gold, rubbing his
elbow and scratching his crowne, swore by the blessed booke that
hung by his knee, that hee would be both willing and constant to
keepe it in secret.
40 Tush young man, you may trust mee, I haue done many of these

124

feats in my daies; I know that youth are youth, but they would not haue all the world wonder at their doings: and where shall it be, said the Frier?

Quoth *Crispine,* at Saint *Gregories* Chappell, and because you shall not make your boy acquainted therewith, I my selfe will call 5 you in the morning. Good father be not forgetfull to obserue the time, at two of the clocke is the houre, and therefore looke you be ready when I shall call you.

I warrant you (replied the Frier:) and because I will not ouer-sleepe my selfe, I will for this night lie in my cloathes, so that as 10 soone as euer you call, I will straight be ready.

Then father I will trust you (quoth *Crispine*) and so departed.

When he came to his Masters, he made not many words, but so soone as he had supt on Sunday at night, he went to his chamber, and laid him downe vpon his bed, making no creature in the house 15 priuy to his intent, not his owne brother, his mind still running on his faire mistris, and the happy houre that should tie them both in one: neuer was there hunger-starued man that did long more for the sweet approch of wholesome food, than did *Crispine* for two a clocke. And so soone as the silent night had drawne all 20 things to rest, *Crispine* got him vp, and to *Canterburie* goes he, to meet his Rose cheeked Lady in her fathers Parke, who also tooke hold of Times forlocke, and like cleere *Cinthia* shaped her course to seeke out *Sol* in the Meridian. But so soone as her searching eie had spied him, she commended his vigilancy, saying: He well ob- 25 serued his houre.

O my deere (quoth he) rich preyes do make true men theeues: but finding thee here so happily, I wil fetch the Frier straight: he had no sooner called at the Friers doore, but hee presently heard him; and groaping the way downe, he opened the doore, and 30 along they went together.

But the Frier, finding his iourney longer then he expected, said; That either Saint *Gregories* Chappell was remoued, or else he was not so good a footman as he was wont to be.

That is likely enough (said *Crispine:*) for how much the older 35 you are since you went this way last, so much the weaker you are to trauell. But be you content, now we are at the last come to the place, and therefore good Frier, make what speed you may.

[23] forlocke] Q2-4; foreclock Q1

I warrant you (quoth he) and therewithall he puts his Spectacles on his nose.

The faire Princesse perceiuing that, laughed heartily, saying, Little need hath a blind man of a paire of Spectacles.

5 True Mistris, said he, as little need hath an old man of a yong wife; but you may see what vse is: Though I bee blind and can see neuer a letter, yet I cannot say Masse without my Booke and my Spectacles, and then he proceeded to solemnize their mariage, which being finished, the Frier had his gold, and home he was led.

10 In the meane time the Princesse stayed still in the Parke for her bridegroome; where when he came, on a banke of sweet primroses, he pluckt the rose of amorous delight: and after, the Princesse came to her Fathers Palace, and *Crispine* to his Masters shop.

CHAPTER VII.

15 How *Crispianus* was prest to the warres, and how he fought with *Iphicratis* the renowned Generall of the *Persians,* who made warre vpon the Frenchmen: shewing also the occasion that a Shoomakers sonne is said to be a Prince borne.

20 In the meane time that *Crispine* was secretly busie about his marriage, his brother *Crispianus* the same night, with many other, was prest to wars into the Countrey of *Gaule,* now called *France,* which made his Master and Dame full woe, who had committed to his gouernment the whole rule of the house. And when *Crispine* 25 came home, they told him what chance had hapned, and demanded where he had bin. They said, they were glad he had so well escaped.

Crispine excusing himselfe so well as he could, said he was sorrie for his brothers sudden departure: notwithstanding, the ioy of his late mariage mittigated much of his sorrow; to whom in his broth-30 ers absence, his Master gaue the ouersight of his houshold, which

25 hapned, and] hapned. And Q1-4
26 bin. They] been, they Q1-4

place he guided with such discretion, as therby he got both the good will of his Master, and the loue of the houshold. And as he sate one day at his worke, he sung this song in commendation of mariage: himselfe sung the Ditty, and his fellowes bore the burthen.

Among the ioyes on earth, though little ioy there bee,   5
    hey downe downe adowne, fine is the silken twist,
Among the maried sort most comfort I doe see:
    hey downe downe adowne, beleeue it they that list.

He that is a maried man, hath beauty to embrace,
    hey downe downe a downe, and therefore mickle woe: 10
He liueth in delight, and is in happy case,
    hey downe downe adowne, in faith we thinke not so.

His wife doth dresse his meate, with euery thing most meet,
    hey downe downe adowne, faire women loue good cheare:
And when he comes to bed, she giues him kisses sweet,   15
    hey downe downe adowne, for thankes he paies full deare.

A hundred hony sweets, he hath when that is done,
    hey downe downe adowne, the truth is seldome knowne:
He hath in a little time a daughter or a sonne,
    hey downe downe adowne, God grant they be his owne.   20

A wife is euermore, both faithfull true and iust,
    hey downe downe adowne, 'tis more then you doe know:
Her husband may be sure, in her to put his trust,
    hey downe downe adowne, most are deceiued so.

While he doth ride abroad, she lookes vnto his house,   25
    hey downe downe a downe, the finest cloth is torne:
And when he comes, she giues him brawne and sowse,
    hey downe downe adowne, and oftentimes the horne.

How now, what is that you say (quoth *Crispine?*)
Nothing (quoth they) but only beare the burden of your Song. 30
And surely we think it great pitty that you are not maried, seeing you can sing so well in the praise of mariage.
Truely (quoth he) were it not for that holy Institution, what

would the world be but a brood of haplesse bastards, like to the cursed seed of *Cain,* men fit for all manner of villany, and such as would leaue behind them a race of runnagates, persons that would liue as badly as they were lewdly begotten.

5 The rest of the Iourney-men hearing him enter into such a deep discourse of the matter, began thereof to demand many questions: but seeing it appertains not to our matter, weele leaue them to their disputation: and in the meane space I will shew you some thing of *Crispianus,* who is now in *France,* with many other Noble

10 *Britaines,* whom *Maximinus* sent thither to aide the *Gaules* against the mightie force of *Iphicratis* the *Persian* Generall, who had at this time inuaded their country with a great power. The day of battell being appointed, the Armies met in the field, at what time both the Generals like two Lions filled with wrath in their proud

15 march viewed one another, breathing forth on both sides words of disdain, and thus the Generall of the *Gaules* began:

Thou insolent Commander of the Easterne troupes, how durst thou set thy ambitious foot within our territories? Cannot the confines of *Persia* content thee, nor those conquered kingdomes al-

20 ready in they hand, but that with vnsatiate desire thou must come to vsurp our right? Know thou, that the vndaunted *Gaules* doe scorne thee: for albeit that *Alexander*-like, thou seekest to subdue the whole world, flattering thy selfe in thy fortunes, yet neuer thinke that the son of a Shoomaker shall bend our neck to a

25 seruile yoke. Therefore in our iust right we are come to giue thee hire for thy pride, and by the force of our swords to beate downe the Scepter of thy proud thoughts.

The renowned *Iphicratis* vpon these words made this replie: Now may I report, that the *Gaules* can do something, finding them

30 such good scolds: But know this that I come not to raile, but to reuenge these contemptuous speeches, and with the points of sturdie Lances to thrust them downe your throats againe. Indeed, my fathers trade is a reproach vnto me, but thou art a reproach to thy father: but thou shalt vnderstand that a Shoemakers son is a Prince

35 borne, his fortunes made him so, and thou shalt find no lesse. And hereupon the trumpets sounding to a charge, and the drums striking alarum, there followed a sore and cruell fight: wherein *Crispianus* like a second *Hector* laid about him, hewing downe his foes

4 lewdly] Q2-4; lewly Q1

128

on euery side. Whose valiancy and Princely courage was noted of all the *Gaules*. And this fierce fight ended with the nights approach, each Army tooke their rest. At what time the Noble Generall of the *Gaules* sent for *Crispianus,* and receiuing him with sundry kind imbracements into his Tent, he demanded of what 5 birth he was.

To whom *Crispianus* shaped this answer: Most worthy Generall, my birth is not meane, and my secrets lesse, but by trade I am a Shoomaker in *England.*

A Shoomaker (said the Generall!) If such fame waite vpon shoo- 10 makers, and such magnanimity follow them, well were it for vs, if all the people in the Kingdome were Shoomakers. And as great thanks I am to give *Maximinus* for sending me such a Souldier, as he may be proud to haue such a subiect: and now right sorrie am I, that euer I reproached famous *Iphicratis,* with his Fathers trade, 15 seeing I find it true that Magnanimitie and Knightly Prowesse, is not alwaies tyed within the compasse of Noble blood. And for my owne part, I will so honourably requite thy deseruings, that thou shalt blesse the time thou euer camest into these wars.

The next morning the Generalls ioyned battell againe, resoluing 20 in this fight either by death or victory, to make an end of these troubles, where the souldiers on each side stroue for the golden wreath of renowne. The two Generals meeting in the battell, fought most couragiously together; in which bloodie conflict the Prince of the *Gaules* was thrice by *Iphicratis* vnhorsed, and as many times of 25 *Crispianus* mounted againe: but in the end the great Commander of the Easterne Army, so mightily preuail'd, that he had seized on the person of the French Prince, and was carying him captiue to his Colours.

But so highly was *Crispianus* fauoured of fortune, that he and 30 his followers met him in the pride of his conquest: who then al besmeared in the *Persian* blood, set upon *Iphicratis,* and so manly behaued himselfe, that hee recouered the Prince againe, and in despite of the *Persians,* brought him to his Royall Tent: in which incounter the Noble *Iphicratis* was sore wounded, by reason 35 whereof the Souldiers had rest for three or foure daies: in which space *Iphicratis* sent to the Prince of *Gaules,* to know what kin he was, that in such valiant sort rescued him out of his hands, saying;

---

29 his Colours] Q4; that Colours Q1-3

that if he would serue him, he would make him ruler ouer a mighty Kingdome.

The *French* Prince sent him word, that it was a right hardy *Britaine,* which had performed that honorable seruice; but no
5 Knight, though wel deseruing greater dignity, but a Shoomaker in *England:* and thus (quoth he) a Shoomakers son was by a Shoomaker foyled.

When *Iphicratis* vnderstood this, hee sent word againe to the *Gaules,* that for the fauour of that worthy man, he would not
10 onely cease the wars, but for euer after bee a friend to the *Gaules:* which ioyfull message when the *French* King vnderstood, most willing he imbraced the vnlooked for tydings of happy peace: and thereupon made *Crispianus* a Knight.

After the which there was a great feast ordained, whereunto the
15 renowned *Iphicratis* was inuited, and the two Generalls, with *Crispianus,* friendly met together. Thus the sowre warre was ended with sweet feasting: and *Iphicratis* soone after departed out of the Country with his Army, and neuer after annoyed them.

Then the *French* King, writing his Letter of thanks vnto the
20 Emperor *Maximinus,* did therein certifie him of the Princely acts of *Crispianus,* whereby he was brought into the Emperours fauour; and with these Letters *Crispianus* returned into *England.*

CHAPTER VIII.

How the Lady *Vrsula* finding her selfe to be with child,
25 made her great mone vnto her husband *Crispine,* and how he prouided for her a secret place, where she was deliuered.

In the meane space the Lady *Vrsula* finding her self to be with childe, and her vnknowne husband coming one day with Shooes
30 vnto her, she made her moan vnto him, saying: O *Crispine* how shall we doe? the time of my sorrow and shame groweth on; I

feele that liuing in my Wombe, which, I feare, will bring death vpon vs all.

Why my dere Lady (answered he) art thou with child? Keep thy chamber close, and wittily excuse thy grief, vntill I haue found means to procure our safety.   5

But dost thou mean faithfully (sayd she) wilt thou not deceiue me, and for feare of my fathers wrath fly the Country: if thou shouldest doe so, then were I the wretchedst Lady aliue. Forsake me not sweet *Crispine,* whatsoeuer thou dost, but take me with thee wheresoeuer thou goest: it is not my fathers frownes that I 10 regard, so I may haue thy fauour, what doe I care for a Princely Pallace: an homely Cottage shall content me in thy company. O my Loue, I will rather learne to spin hemp for thy shoo-threed, than liue without thee in the greatest pleasure.

I will not leaue thee my deare Loue (quoth he) by that faith I 15 vow, which I plighted to thee at our blessed mariage; and therefore be contented, and it shall not be long before I doe returne.

Leauing thus his sad Lady he came home, and secretly broke the matter vnto his Dame, desiring her counsell in this his extremity.

What, how now (quoth she) hast thou got a maide with child? 20 Ah thou whorson villaine, thou hast vndone thy selfe, how wilt thou doe now? thou hast made a faire hand; heere is now sixteene pence a weeke beside Sope and Candles, Beds, Shirts, Biggins, Wastcoats, Hedbands, Swadlebands, Crossecloths, Bibs, Taileclouts, Mantles, Hose, Shooes, Coats, Petticoats, Cradle and Crickets, and 25 beside that a standing-stoole, and a Posnet to make the Childe Pap; all this is come vpon thee, besides the charges of all her lying in. Oh *Crispine, Crispine,* I am heartily sorry for thee.

But in good faith, if I knew the queane that hath brought thee to this folly, I would haue her by the face I sweare to you: for 30 though I speake it before thee (*Crispine*) thou art a proper fellow, and thou mightest haue done full well if thou hadst had grace. God hath done his part on thee: and with that she began with kindnesse to weepe. Whereupon her husband comming in, asked what she ailed.   35

O man (said she) *Crispine!*

Why what of *Crispine?* tell me. Why speakest thou not?

---

[14] than liue] Q2-4; that liue Q1

131

Wee shall lose a good seruant, so we shall.

What seruant shall we lose foolish woman (quoth he?) Tell me quickly.

O husband! by Cock and Pye, I sweare, Ile haue her by the
5 nose.

Who wilt thou haue by the nose? What the Deuill art thou madde, that thou wilt not answer me?

Crispine, who at his Masters coming in shunned the room, lending an eare vnto these words, went vnto his Master, and said vnto
10 him, These four yeers haue I serued you, and the fifth draweth neere vnto an end; as I haue found you a good Master to me, so I trust you haue had no great cause to complain of me, tho' through ignorance I haue sometimes made offence: and knowing at this instant, no man so neere a friend vnto me as your selfe, I haue
15 thought good to impart my secret counsell to you: something I did presume vpon my Dames fauour: which made me open that vnto her, which now I wish I had not discouered. Notwithstanding, resting more vpon your discretion then her secrecy, I would desire your counsell in a matter that concernes me very neare.

20 Verily said his Master, if it bee a thing wherein I may doe thee good, thou shalt finde that I will not fall from thee in thy sorrowes, and therefore be not abashed to declare thy mind: for I sweare, if I may procure thee right, thou shalt put vp no wrong.

Why then sir, thus it is (quoth he) my will running before my
25 wit, I have gotten a Maiden with childe, and I wot not in this case what to doe, that I might preserue the Maide from shame, and my selfe from discredit: beside, I doubt if it be knowne, it will cost me my life: therefore in such case good Master be secret.

Tush man feare not (quoth he) it is a matter of nothing: but I
30 pray thee, now tell me, what a wanton Wagtaile is it that thou hast clapt thus vnder the apron?

O Master (quoth he) the Kings faire daughter *Vrsula* is my Loue, and she it is that liues in care for my sake.

Passion of my heart thou whorson Knave, quoth his Master, thou
35 art a dead man. I maruell how the deuill thou camest to bee so bold with her: Surely thou hast drawne on her shooes on Sunday, I may say, thou hast left so good a token behind: but intruth my boy I commend thee, that thou wouldest shoote at the fairest.

Yea sir, quoth *Crispine,* and I haue hit the marke I trow, and
40 doe verily beleeue, that none will shoot so neere againe.

132

Chapter Eight

Nay sweare not, said his Master, many may aime at faire markes, and more then one man hits them now and then: but what wouldest thou haue me to do in this case?

My good Master (quoth *Crispine*) the troth is, she is my wife; and the very same night my brother was prest to the wars, I was maried to her: and if you could tell me how shee might be deliuered of her burden without any suspition, I should not only remaine beholding to you while I liued, but would also gratifie your kindnesse in such sort as should content you.

His dame all this while listned to their talk, and when she vnderstood he spake of the Kings daughter, and that he had maried her, she said: Now Gods blessing on thy heart *Crispine,* that thou art so carefull for thy wife, but it maketh me wonder she would marry a Shoomaker, and a poore fellow too.

Master and Dame (quoth *Crispine*) seeing I haue begun, Ile shew you a further matter, as strange as the other. The necessity of these times makes many Noble personages to maske in simple habite, as *Iupiter* did in a shepheards weed, and the truth is, that Lady *Vrsula* is not ignorant, that by matching with me she hath wedded a Prince, and you may say that these fiue yeeres two Princes haue serued you obediently, vnder the simple borrowed names of *Crispine* and *Crispianus*.

Our Royall Father was slaine by the Emperor *Maximinus,* and the Queene our Mother lies yet imprisoned, and your poore house, and these leather garments, haue bin our life of defence against the blood-thirsty-tyrant. Now you see, that though there were hate towards vs in the Father, yet there is loue yeelded vs by the Daughter. This must be kept for a certaine time from the knowledge of him, lest our liues pay a deare ransome for our loues.

Well *Crispine* (quoth his Dame) be of good cheare, for I haue a deuice in my head, how to get thy Loue out of her Fathers Pallace, that shee may be brought to bed in mine owne house, without either hurt to thee, or dishonour to her, if thou wilt doe as I wish thee. When you do perceiue that shee growes neere vnto the time of her trauell, I would wish you to worke such means, as to set some tree on fire late in the night, that standeth somewhat neere one of the Beacons vpon the Seacoast, whereby it will follow, that such watchmen as watch at our Beacons, supposing the Beacons at the Seacoast to be of fire, will set theirs on fire also. Then will there be a great hurlie burlie, with the preparation of men at Armes on

133

all sides, to withstand a supposed foe, that which they shall neuer find: then (as you know) *Maximinus* with his houshold will be in most feare, because hee is most hated, so that whilest he is abroad, the rest of his houshold will euerie one of them seeke for their own
5 safegard, amongst the which, let faire *Vrsula* be one, who by that meanes singling her selfe alone, may take vp my house, and here she may closely bee kept till shee be deliuered, taking vpon her the name and habite of a simple woman.

But the troth of this matter (quoth *Crispine*) I doubt wil soone
10 be perceiued and found out, then how shall Lady *Vrsula* do, for she will straight be missed.

Tush thats no matter (quoth his Dame) and missed let her be, vntill such time as she is in better case to go abroad again, for in such a tumult as then will bee, they will suppose many things, that
15 one mischance or other is befalne her: or if she be in health, that she hath wandred into the woods, or some other vncouth place; where she might best prouide for safetie: and when she comes home againe, I warrant thee *Crispine* she will be welcome.

Then said his Master, I like my wiues deuice well; and therefore
20 by my consent put it in practice.

Whereunto *Crispine* consented, and so making the Lady priuy to the purpose; at length it was put in execution, at what time there was crying out on all sides, Arme, Arme, Arme: our enemies are comming vpon vs.
25 Where (quoth they?)

At *Rutupium* said one.

At *Aruvagus* Castle sayd another.

Quoth the third it is at *Doris.*

I tell you (quoth the fourth) it is at *Duur.*
30 And all this is but *Douer* (said the fifth man;) and at *Douer* it is vndoubtedly, therefore, hast, hast, and away; for neuer was there more neede. So that *Maximinus* was almost at his wits end, as one not knowing which way to turne, the cries of the people came so thicke, one after another: the waiting-gentlewomen left their Prin-
35 cesse and sought their owne saftie. Thus while some were busie in carying out the Kings treasure; others hiding the plate, and others the goods, *Vrsula* had an easie passage into the Shoomakers house.

The young Prince *Crispine* was gone with the rest of the town towards *Douer,* where when they came, there was nothing to doe,

134

which when *Maximinus* saw, he was not a little glad the wars were
so soone ended.

But when he came to the Court, and missed his daughter, there
was posting vp and downe in euery place to seeke her, but all in
vaine; for no man could meet with her, for which he made great   5
lamentation, making a Proclamation throughout the whole Country, That whosoeuer could bring her to him, hee should not onely
haue a Princely reward, but also if hee were a man of Noble blood,
hee should bee honoured with the mariage of his faire daughter.
This was good newes for *Crispine,* who was not to learn to make   10
profit thereof.

But by that time his Lady was light, *Crispianus* his eldest brother
arriued into *England* with great honor, as before you haue heard.
And before he went to the Court, he thought it good to visite his
old Master, who came also in good time to the christening of his   15
brothers childe, which when he with wonder beheld, noting what
a strange accident this was, that *Maximinus* daughter should be his
brothers wife.

But after that hee had in princely manner saluted the new de-
liuered Lady, taking the infant in his armes, he kissed it saying: 20
Now will I say and sweare (said he) that a Shoomakers sonne is a
Prince borne, ioyning in the opinion of *Iphicratis,* and henceforth
Shoomakers neuer shall let that terme die.

Then turning to his Master and Dame (he said) how much deere
Master and Dame are we bound to your fauors, that haue main-   25
tained our honors with our happinesse; for by this meanes, I hope
wee shall make a ioyfull conclusion of our sorrowfull beginning,
and I will so worke, that the Emperor shall confirme what is already begun, I meane the honour due to these Princely Louers, and
together with our happy fortunes procure our mothers liberty.   30

Hereupon, within a short time after, hee made preparation to
the Court; he attired himself in princely manner, and with a most
knightly grace he deliuered to *Maximinus,* the King of *Gaules* letter, where he certified the Emperor of the honorable deeds performed by *Crispianus,* whereupon he receiued him to great fauor,   35
and said vnto him: Right renowned Knight, for the great honor
thou hast done me in *France,* I will honour thee with any thing

*10 not to learn] Q1-4; not slow to learn   Lange

which thou shalt command, that standeth with the Maiestie and credit of an Emperour to giue.

Then I beseech your Highnesse (quoth he) to grant me the life and liberty of my deare mother, that late Queen of *Logria.*

5 Art thou her son said *Maximinus?* although thy father was my foe, yet I must needs say, hee was a most couragious and warlike Prince: thy sute is granted. And once I had a daughter worthy of thy loue, but vnconstant Fortune hath bereft mee of that blisse; but had it pleased the faire Heauens to haue left her me till this 10 day, I would haue made thee more honourable by her match: But seeing that my wishing doth nothing profit thee, take hence the richest iewell I haue, and be thou next my selfe in authority: with that he took from his owne necke a Coller of most precious Diamonds, and gaue it to *Crispianus,* saying, Be thou as fortunate as *Polic-* 15 *rates.*

CHAPTER IX.

How faire *Vrsula* came before her father with *Crispine* her
    husband, who was ioyfully receiued by him, and in the
    end had his good will to confirme the mariage be-
20   twixt them, whereupon there was great ioy on both
    sides. And the Shoomakers in honor of this happy
    day, made a ioyfull Song.

Within a certaine space after, word was brought to the Emperor, that his daughter was with a Shoomaker, come to the 25 Court; whereat *Maximinus* was stricken into a sudden ioy, saying: An Honourable Shoomaker may hee be that hath brought my faire daughter againe. Welcome my sweet *Vrsula,* and in good time welcome to thy father, and welcome also is this happy yong man, that hath so fortunately brought thee; and turning to *Crispianus* 30 he said: Noble sir Knight, take heere my daughter to wife.

Not so deare Father (quoth she) this man hath best deserued my loue, that hath preserued my life, and his wife will I be.

Why *Vrsula,* said her Father, wilt thou darken the sun-shine of

my ioy, with the clouds of foule obstinacie, and yoke thy selfe so
vnequally? This man is a Prince.

And this mans son is another (quoth she.)

That is strange said the Emperor; can that child be a Prince,
whose father is but a Shoomaker? 5

Then answered *Vrsula,* My Royall Father, a Shoomakers son is
a Prince borne.

Most gratious Lord (quoth *Crispianus*) the very like sentence did
I heare the renowned *Iphicrates* pronounce to the King of *Gaules,*
when he vpbraided him with his birth: with that *Crispines* Dame 10
presented the child to the Emperor; and faire *Vrsula* was very
diligent to vncouer the childs face, and held it to her Father.

Why daughter (quoth he) art thou not ashamed to honour a base
borne brat so much? hence with the Elfe, and therewithall pusht it
from him: whereat his daughters teares trickled down her cheeks, 15
and so kissing the child, gaue it againe to the woman.

What (said *Maximinus*) doest thou loue the childe so well, that
thou must kisse it, and weepe for it?

I haue cause deare Father (quoth she) for that this childes mother
lay in my mothers belly. 20

At these words the Emperor suspected somthing, and demanded
of *Crispine* of what parentage he was. And then knowing that hee
was *Crispianus* brother, all the controuersie was ended, and their
secret mariage confirmed openly, with great ioy and triumph: at
which time the Shoomakers in the same towne made holiday: To 25
whom *Crispine* and *Crispianus* sent most Princely gifts for to maintaine their merriment. And euer afterward, vpon that day at night
the Shoomakers make great cheare and feasting, in remembrance
of these two Princely brethren: and because it might not be forgotten, they caused their names to be placed in the Kalender for a 30
yeerly remembrance, which you shall find in the moneth of October, about three daies before the Feast of *Simon* and *Iude.*

The Shoomakers Song on Crispianus night.

Two Princely brethren once there was,
  right sonnes vnto a King; 35
Whose father tyrant *Maximus*
  to cruell death did bring:
Crispianus one was call'd,
  the eldest of the two;

137

Crispine was the others name,
  which well had learn'd to wooe.
These brethren then were after faine,
  from fathers house to flie:
Because their foes to spoile their liues
  in priuy waite did lie:
Into a kinde Shoomakers house,
  they suddenly stept in;
And there to learne the *Gentle Craft,*
  did presently begin.
And fiue yeeres they liued so,
  with great content of minde;
So that the Tyrant could not tell,
  whereas he should them finde:
Though euery day to Court they came,
  with shooes for Ladies feet:
They were not knowne by their attire,
  they vsed themselues so meet.
At length vnto the furious warres
  was *Crispianus* prest;
Whereas his knightly prowesse then
  he tryed with the best:
But *Crispine* found him better sport,
  would I had *Crispine* beene;
The Kings faire daughter lou'd him well,
  as it was after seene.
The length of this faire Ladies foot,
  so well did *Crispine* know,
That none but he could please her mind,
  the certaine truth is so:
Came he by night, or else by day,
  he was most welcome still;
With kisses sweet she did him pay,
  and thankes for his good will:
So oft these Louers twaine did meete,
  by day and eke by night:
That at the last the Lady said,
  she should be shamed quite;
What was the matter tell me true,
  that so her sorrow bred:

138

Her Shoomaker most daintily
  had got her Maidenhead.
But he at length so wisely wrought,
  as doth the Story tell:
Her fathers right good will he got,   5
  and euery thing was well.
And *Crispianus* came againe
  from warres victoriously:
Then Shoomakers made Holiday,
  and therefore so will I.   10
And now for *Crispianus* sake,
  this wine I drinke to thee,
And he that doth this marke mistake,
  and will not now pledge me:
He is not *Crispianus* friend;   15
  nor worthy well I wot,
To have a Lady to his Loue,
  as *Crispine* he hath got.

CHAPTER X.

How Sir *Simon Eyre* being at first a Shoomaker, became in 20
the end Mayor of *London,* through the counsell of his
wife: and how he broke his fast euery day on a Table
that he said he would not sell for a thousand pounds:
and how he builded *Leaden Hall.*

Our English Chronicles doe make mention, that somtime there 25
was in the honourable Citie of *London* a worthy Maior known
by the name of Sir *Simon Eyre,* whose fame liueth in the mouthes
of many men to this day, who albeit he descended of meane parentage; yet by Gods blessing in the end hee came to be a most
worthy man in the Common-wealth.   30
    This man being brought yong out of the North Countrey, was
bound prentice to a shoomaker bearing then the name of the

Gentle-Craft (as still it doth.) His Master beeing a man of reasonable wealth, set many Iourny-men and Prentices to work, who followed their busines with great delight, which quite excludeth all wearines, for when seruants doe sit at their work like dromedaries, then their
5 minds are neuer lightly vpon their busines: for it is an old prouerb;

> They proue seruants kind and good,
> That sing at their busines like birds in the wood.

Such fellowes had this yong Lad, who was not behind with many northerne Iigs, to answer their sothern Songs. This youth being
10 the yongest prentice in the house, as occasion serued, was often sent to the Conduit for water, where in short time he fell acquainted with many other prentices comming thither for the same intent.

Now their custome was so, that euery Sunday morning diuers of these prentices did vse to go to a place neer the conduit, to break
15 their fast with pudding Pies, and often they would take *Simon* along with them: but vpon a time it so fell out, that when he should draw mony to pay the shot with the rest, that he had none: whereupon hee merrily said vnto them: My faithfull friends, and Conduit companions, treasurers of the Water-tankerd, and maine
20 pillars of the pudding-house; I may now compare my purse to a barren Doe, that yeelds the Keeper no more good then her empty carcasse: or to a bad nut, which being opened hath neuer a kernell: therefore, if it wil please you to pardon me at this time, and excuse me for my part of the shot, I do here vow vnto you, that if
25 euer I come to be Lord Maior of this City, I will giue a breakfast vnto all the Prentices in *London*.

We will take your word (quoth they) and so they departed.

It came to passe, that *Simon* hauing at length worn out his yeers of Apprentiship, that he fell in loue with a Maiden that was a
30 neere neighbor vnto him, vnto whom at length he was maried, and got him a shop, and laboured hard daily, and his yong wife was neuer idle, but straight when she had nothing to doe, she sate in the shop and spun: and hauing liued thus alone a yeere or thereabout, and hauing gathered somthing together, at length he got
35 him some prentices, and a Iourni-man or two, and he could not

22 to a bad nut] Q2-4; to be a bad nut Q1
24 the shot] Q2-4; my shot Q1

make his ware so fast as he could haue sold it, so that he stood in
great need of a Iourny-man or two more.

At the last, one of his seruants spying one go along the street
with a fardell at his back, called to his Master, saying, Sir, yonder
goes S. *Hughes* bones, twenty pounds to a peny.   5

Run presently (quoth he) and bring him hither.

The boy running forth called to the man, saying; Good fellow,
come hither, here is one would speake with you.

The fellow being a Frenchman, that had not long bin in *England,* turning about, said: Hea, what you sea? Will you speake wed 10
me, Hea? what you haue? tell a me, what you haue, hea?

And with that comming to the stall, the good man askt him if
hee lackt work.

We par ma foy, quoth the Frenchman.

Hereupon *Simon* tooke him in, and to worke he went merrily, 15
where he behaued himselfe so well, that his Master made good account of him, thinking he had beene a Batcheller; but in the end
it was found otherwise.

This man was the first that wrought vpon the low cut shoo with
the square toe, and the latchet ouerthwart th'instep, before which 20
time in *England* they did weare a hie shoo that reached aboue the
ankles, right after the manner of our husbandmens shooes at this
day, saue onely that it was made very sharpe at the toe turning vp
like the taile of an Island dog: or as you see a cock cary his hinder
feathers.   25

Now it is to bee remembred, that while *Iohn Deneuale* dwelt with
Simon Eyre, it chanced that a Ship of the Ile of *Candy* was driuen
vpon our Coast, laden with all kind of Lawnes and Cambrickes,
and other linnen cloth: which commodities at that time were in
London very scant, and exceeding deare: and by reason of a great 30
leake the ship had got at Sea, being vnable to saile any further, he
would make what profit he could of his goods here.

And being come to *London,* it was *Iohn Deneuales* chance to
meet him in the streetes, to whom the Merchant (in the Greeke
tongue) demanded where he might haue lodging, for hee was one 35
that had neuer bin in *England* before; and being vnacquainted,
wist not whither to goe: but while he spake Greeke, *Iohn Deneuale*
answered him still in French, which tongue the Merchant vnderstood well: and therfore being glad that he had met with one
that could talke to him, he declared vnto him what tempests hee 40

had indured at Sea, and also how his ship lay vpon the Coast with such commodities as he would sell.

Truly sir, quoth *Iohn,* I am my selfe but a stranger in this Country, and vtterly vnacquainted with Merchants, but I dwell with
5 one in the City that is a very honest man, and it may be that hee
can helpe you to some that will deale with you for it, and if you
thinke it good, I will moue him in it, and in the meane space, Ile
bring you where you may haue very good lodging, and tomorrow
morning I will come to you againe.

10 Sir, said the Merchant, if you please to do me that fauour, ile
not only be thankfull vnto you for the same, but also in most
honest sort will content you for your paines: and with that they
departed.

Now so soone as *Iohn* the Frenchman came home, he moued
15 this matter vnto his Master, desiring him that hee would doe what
he could for the Merchant. When his Master had heard each cir-
cumstance, noting therwith the want of such commodities in the
Land, cast in his mind as he stood cutting vp his worke, what were
best to be done in this case, saying to his man *Iohn,* I will thinke
20 vpon it betwixt this and the morning, and then I will tell thee my
minde: and therewithall casting downe his cutting Knife, hee went
out of his shop into his chamber, and therein walking vp and
downe alone very sadly ruminating hereon: he was so farre in his
muse, that his wife sending for him to supper two or three times,
25 he nothing regarded the maides call, hammering still this matter in
his head.

At last his wife came to him saying: Husband, what meane you
that you doe not come in to supper? why speak you not man? Hear
you good husband, come away, your meat will be cold: but for all
30 her words, hee staid walking vp and downe still like a man that
had sent his wits a wool-gathering: which his wife seeing, pulled
him by the sleeue, saying: Why husband in the name of God, why
come you not? will you not come to supper to night? I called you a
good while agoe.

35 Body of me, wife (said he) I promise thee I did not heare thee.

No, faith, it seemeth so (quoth she) I maruell whereupon your
mind runneth.

Beleeue me wife, quoth he, I was studying how to make my selfe
Lord Maior, and thee a Lady.

25 he nothing] Q2-4; nothing Q1

Chapter Ten

Now God helpe you (quoth she) I pray God make vs able to pay euery man his owne, that we liue out of debt and danger, and driue the woolfe from the doore, and I desire no more.

But wife, said he, I pray thee now tell me, Doest thou not thinke that thou couldst make shift to beare the name of a Lady, if it shold be put vpon thee?

In truth husband (quoth she) ile not dissemble with you, if your wealth were able to beare it, my mind would beare it well enough.

Well wife (replied he) I tell thee now in sadnesse, that if I had money, there is a commodity now to be bought, the gaines whereof would be able to make me a gentleman for euer.

Alas husband, that dignity your trade allowes you already, being a squire of the *Gentle-Craft,* then, how can you be lesse than a gentleman, seeing your son is a Prince borne?

Tush wife (quoth he) those titles do only rest in name, but not in nature: but of that sort had I rather be, whose lands are answerable to their vertues, and whose rents can maintaine the greatnes of their minds.

Then sweet husband, tell me, said his wife, tell me, what commodity is that which you might get so much by? I am sure your selfe hath some mony, and it shal go very hard but ile procure friends to borrow one forty shillings, and beside that, rather then you shall lose so good a bargain, I haue a couple of crowns that saw no sun since we were first maried, and them also shall you haue.

Alas wife (said *Simon*) all this comes not neare that matter: I confesse it would do some good in buying a few backs of leather, but in this thing it is nothing: for this is Merchandise that is precious at this time and rare to be had, and I heare whosoeuer that will haue it, must lay downe 3000. pounds ready mony. Yea wife, and yet thereby he might get three and three thousand pounds profit.

His wife hearing him say so, was inflamed with desire therof, as women are (for the most part) very couetous: that matter running still in her mind, she could scant find in her heart to spare him time to goe to supper, for very eagernesse to animate him on to take that bargaine vpon him. Wherefore, so soone as they had supt, and giuen God thanks, she called her husband, saying: I pray you come hither I would speake a word with you: That man is not alwaies to bee blamed that sometimes takes counsell of his

143

wife: though womens wits are not able to comprehend the greatest things, yet in doubtfull matters they often helpe on a sudden.

Well wife, what meane you by this (said her husband?)

In truth quoth she, I would haue you plucke vp a mans heart,
5 and speedily chop vp a bargaine for these goods you speake of.

Who I? quoth he, which way should I doe it, that am not able
for three thousand pounds, to lay downe three thousand pence?

Tush man, quoth shee, what of that? euery man that beholds
a man in the face, knows not what he hath in his purse; and what-
10 soeuer he be that owes the goods, he will, no doubt, be content
to stay a month for his mony, or three weekes at the least: and I
promise you, to pay a thousand pounds a week, is a pretty round
payment, and I may say to you, not much to be misliked of.

Now husband, I would haue you in the morning goe with *Iohn*
15 the Frenchman to the Grecian Merchant, and with good discretion
driue a sound bargaine with him, for the whole fraught of the
ship, and thereupon giue him halfe a dozen Angells in earnest, and
eight and twenty dayes after the deliuery of the goods, condition to
deliuer him the rest of his money.

20 But woman (quoth hee) doest thou imagine that he would take
my word for so weighty a masse of money, and to deliuer his goods
vpon no better security?

Good Lord, quoth she, haue you no wit in such a case to make
shift? Ile tell you what you shall doe: Be not knowne that you
25 bargaine for your owne selfe, but tell him that you doe it in the
behalfe of one of the chiefe Aldermen in the City; but beware in
any case, that you leaue with him your owne name in writing,
hee being a Grecian cannot read English: and you haue no need
at all to shew *Iohn* the Frenchman, or if thou shouldst, it were no
30 great matter, for you can tell well enough that he can neither
write nor read.

I perceiue Wife (quoth he) thou wouldst faine be a Lady, and
worthy thou art to be one, that dost thus imploy thy wits to bring
thy husbands profit: but tell me, if he should be desirous to see
35 the Alderman to confer with him, how shall we do then?

Iesus haue mercy vpon us (quoth she) you say women are fooles,
but me seemeth men haue need to be taught sometimes. Before you
come away in the morning, let *Iohn* the Frenchman tell him, that

---

³⁶ quoth she] Q2-4; quoth he Q1

the Alderman himselfe shall come to his lodging in the afternoon; and receiuing a note of all the goods that be in the ship, he shall deliuer vnto him a Bil of his hand for the payment of his money, according to that time. Now sweetheart (quoth she) this Alderman shall be thine owne selfe, and ile goe borrow for thee all things 5 that are necessary against that time.

Tush (quoth her husband) canst thou imagine, that he seeing me in the morning, will not know me againe in the afternoon?

O husband, quoth she, he will not know thee, I warrant thee: for in the morning thou shalt goe to him in thy doublet of sheepe- 10 skins, with a smutched face, and thy apron before thee, thy thumb-leather and hand-leather, buckled close to thy wrist, with a foule band about thy necke, and a greasie cap on thy head.

Why woman (quoth he) to goe in this sort will be a discredit to me, and make the Merchant doubtfull of my dealing: for men of 15 simple attire are (God wot) slenderly esteemed.

Hold your peace good husband (quoth she) it shall not be so with you, for *Iohn* the Frenchman shall giue such good report to the Merchant for your honest dealing (as I praise God hee can doe no lesse) that the Grecian will rather conceiue the better of you, then 20 otherwise: iudging you a prudent discreet man, that will not make a shew of that you are not, but go in your attire agreeable to your trade. And because none of our folkes shall be priuy to our in-tent, to morrow weele dine at my coosin *Iohn Barbers,* in S. *Clem-ents* Lane, which is not far from the *George* in *Lumbard* street, 25 where the Merchants strangers lie. Now Ile be sure that all things shall be ready at my coosin *Iohns,* that you shall put on in the afternoone. And there he shall first of all with his sizzers, snap off all the superfluous haires, and fashion thy bushie beard after the Aldermans graue cut: then shall he wash thee with a sweet Camphire 30 Ball, and besprinkle thine head and face with the purest Rose-water; then shalt thou scoure thy pitchy fingers in a bason of hot water, with an ordinary washing ball: and all this being done, strip thee from these common weeds, and Ile put thee on a very faire doublet of tawny sattin, ouer which thou shalt haue a Cassock 35 of branched damask, furred round about the skirts with the finest foynes, thy breeches of blacke Veluet, and shooes and stockings fit for such array: a band about thy neck, as white as the driuen snow,

*11 smutched] Q2-4; smugged Q1

145

and for thy wrists a pretty paire of cuffes, and on thy head a cap of the finest blacke: then shalt thou put on a faire gown, welted round with veluet, and ouerthwart the backe thwart it shal be with rich foine, with a paire of sweet gloues on thy hands, and on
5 thy fore-finger a great seale ring of gold.

Thou being thus attired Ile intreat my coosin *Iohn Barber,* because he is a very hansome yong man, neat and fine in his apparell (as indeed all Barbers are) that he would take the paines to waite vpon you vnto the merchants, as if he were your man, which he
10 wil do at the first word. And when you come there, tis not for you to vse many words, because one of you cannot vnderstand the other, so that it will be sufficient with outward curtesie, one to greet another; and he to deliuer vnto you his notes, and you to giue to him your bill, and so come home.

15 It doth my heart good, to see how trimly this apparell doth become you, in good faith husband, me seemes in my mind, I see you in it already, and how like an Alderman you will looke, when you are in this costly array. At your returne from the Merchant, you shal put off all these clothes at my coosins againe, and come home
20 as you did goe forth. Then tell *Iohn* the Frenchman, that the Alderman was with the Merchant this afternoon; you may send him to him in the morning, and bid him to command that his ship may bee brought downe the Riuer: while she is comming about, you may giue notice to the linnen Drapers, of the Commodities you
25 haue comming.

Enough Wife (quoth he) thou hast said enough, and by the grace of God Ile follow thy counsell, and I doubt not but to haue good fortune.

CHAPTER XI.

How *Simon Eyre* was sent for to my Lord Mayors to sup-
    per, and shewing the great entertainment that he and
    his wife had there.

Anon after, supper time drew neare, she making her selfe ready 5
in the best manner she could deuise, passed along with her
husband vnto my Lord Maiors house: and being entred into the
great Hall, one of the Officers there certified to my Lord Maior,
that the great rich Shoomaker and his wife were already come.
Whereupon the Lord Maior in courteous manner came into the 10
Hall to *Simon,* saying: You are most heartily welcome good Master
Eyre, and so is your gentle bedfellow.

Then came forth my Lady Maioresse and saluted them both in
like manner, saying: Welcome good Master *Eyer* and Mistresse *Eyer*
both, and taking her by the hand, set her downe among the Gentle- 15
women there present.

Sir (quoth the Lord Maior) I vnderstand you are a Shoomaker,
and that it is you that hath bought vp all the goods of the great
Argozy.

I am indeed my Lord of the *Gentle-craft,* quoth hee, and I praise 20
God, all the goods of that great Argozy are my owne, when my debts
are paid.

God giue you much ioy of them, said the Lord Maior, and I
trust you and I shall deale for some part thereof. So the meat being then ready to be brought in, the guests were placed each one 25
according to his calling. My Lord Maior holding *Simon* by the
hand, and the Ladie Maioresse holding his wife, they would needs
haue them sit neare to themselues, which they then with blushing
cheekes refusing, my Lord said thus vnto them, holding his cap
in his hand: 30

Master *Eyer* and Mistresse *Eyer,* let me intreat you not to be
troublesome, for I tell you it shall be thus: and as for these Gentlemen here present, they are all of mine old acquaintance, and many

times wee haue bin together, therefore I dare be the bolder with them: and albeit you are our neighbour also, yet I promise you, you are strangers to my Table, and to strangers common courtesie doth teach vs to shew the greatest fauour, and therefore let mee rule you
5 in mine house, and you shall rule me in yours.

When *Simon* found there was no remedy, they sate them downe, but the poore woman was so abashed, that shee did eate but little meat at the Table, bearing herselfe at the table with a comely and modest countenance: but what she wanted in outward feeding, her
10 heart yeelded to with inward delight and content.

Now so it was, many men that knew not *Simon,* and seeing him in so simple attire sit next my Lord, whisperingly asked one another what he was. And it was enough for *Simons* wife with her eyes and eares, to see and hearken after euery thing that was said
15 or done.

A graue wealthy Citizen sitting at the table, spake to *Simon* and said; Sir in good will I drink to your good health, but I beseech you pardon mee, for I know not how to call your name.

With that my Lord Maior answered him, saying: his name is
20 Master *Eyer,* and this is the Gentleman that bought all the goods that came in the blacke Swan of Candy, and before God, though he sit heere in simple sort, for his wealth, I doe verily beleeue he is more sufficient to bear this place then my selfe. This was a man that was neuer thought vpon, liuing obscure amongst vs, of none
25 account in the eies of the world, carying the countenance but of a Shoomaker, and none of the best sort neither, and is able to deale for a bargaine of fiue thousand pounds at a clap.

We do want many such Shoomakers (said the Citizen), and so with other discourse droue out supper.
30 At what time rising from the Table, *Simon* and his wife receiuing sundry salutations of my lord Maior and his Lady, and of all the rest of the worshipfull guests, departed home to their owne house: at what time his wife made such a recitall of the matters; how brauely they were entertained, what great cheare was there,
35 also what a great company of Gentlemen and Gentlewomen were there, and how often they dranke to her husband and to her, with diuers other cricumstances, that I beleeue, if the night had beene six months long, as it is vnder the North pole, shee would haue found talke enough till morning.
40 Of a truth (quoth she) although I sate close by my Ladies side,

148

I could eat nothing for very ioy, to heare and see that we were so
much made of. And neuer giue me credit husband, if I did not
heare the Officers whisper as they stood behind me, and all demanded one of another, what you were, and what I was: O quoth
one, doe you see this man? marke him well, and marke his wife 5
well, that simple woman that sits next my Lady: What are they?
What are they quoth another? Marrie this is the rich Shoomaker
that bought all the goods in the great Argozie: I tell you there was
neuer such a Shoomaker seene in *London* since the City was builded.
Now by my faith (quoth the third) I haue heard much of him to- 10
day among the Merchants in the street, going betweene the two
Chaines: Credit me husband, of mine honesty this was their communication. Nay, and doe you not remember when the rich citizen dranke to you (which craued pardon, because hee knew not
your name) what my Lord Maior said? Sir (quoth he) his name is 15
Master *Eyer,* did you marke that? and presently thereupon he
added these words: This is the Gentleman that bought, and so
forth. The Gentleman vnderstood you, did you heare him speake
that word?

In troth wife (quoth he) my Lord vttered many good words of 20
me, I thanke his honor, but I heard not that.

No (quoth she) I heard it wel enough: for by and by he proceeded further, saying: I suppose, though he sit here in simple sort,
hee is more sufficient to beare this charge then my selfe. Yea thought
I, he may thanke his wife for that, if it come so to passe. 25

Nay, said *Simon,* I thanke God for it.

Yea, and next him, you may thanke me (quoth she.) And it did
her so much good to talke of it, that I suppose, if she had liued to
this day, she should yet be prating thereof, and if sleepe did not
driue her from it. 30

And now seeing that *Simon* the Shoomaker is become a Merchant, we will temper our tongues to giue him that title, which his
customers were wont to doe, and from henceforth call him Master
Eyer, who, while he had his affaires in hand, committed the gouernment of his shop to *Iohn* the Frenchman, leauing him to be a 35
guide to his other seruants, by meanes of which fauour, *Iohn*
thought himselfe at that time to be a man of no small reputation.

[29] she should] Q2; he should Q1; she would Q3,4

CHAPTER XII.

How *Iohn* the Frenchman fell in loue with one of his Masters Maides: and how hee was crossed through the craft of *Haunce* the Dutchman.

5 At the same time there was dwelling in the house, a iolly lusty wench, whose name was *Florence,* whom *Iohn* the Frenchman loued dearely well, and for her onely sake hee brought many a good bottle of wine into the house, and therwithall, so soone as their Master and Mistresse were gone to bed, they would often-
10 times make merry amongst themselues; which *Haunce,* a Iourney-man in the same house perceiuing, sought to crosse them as much as in him lay, thereby to bring his owne purpose the better to passe, which was to ioyne the Maidens fauour to his owne af-fection.

15 And because the Frenchman had greatest gaines vnder his mas-ter, and being thereof no niggard when he had got it, the maid did much delight in him, and little esteemed the Dutchman, though his good will were as great towards her as the other: for they could not be in any corner of the house together, nor could they meete
20 in any place abroad, but the Dutchman would still watch them.

Vpon a time, *Florence* being at Market, her loue *Iohn* went forth of the shop to meet her, and *Haunce* stayed not long behind, who at length espied them, and heard his fellow *Iohn* questioning with her in this sort.

25 What *Florence,* what you haue in your basket? hea, let mee see what you buy.

Marrie *Iohn* (quoth she) I haue bought Beefe and Mutton, and other things. Come, come, must you peep into my basket (quoth she) away for shame away.

30 Bee Got *Florence,* mee will see a little: ha, ha! *Florence,* you buy the budding, hea, you loue de buddings? *Florence* hea?

Yea sir (quoth shee) what if I doe loue puddings? what care you?

Chapter Twelve

Of my tra *Florence,* if I be your husband, mee will giue you budden shall warren.

My husband (quoth she) in faith sir no, I meane not to marry a Frenchman.

What *Florence,* de Frenchman be de good man: but come *Flor-* ence, mee will giue you a pinte of wine by my treat.

O, I cannot stay now, I thanke you *Iohn* (quoth she.)

What *Florence,* no stay with your friend? I shall make you stay a little time.

And so with that, taking her by the hand, into the Tauerne they goe, and *Haunce* the Dutchman following them, and sate close in the next roome, and by that meanes he heard all that they said, and that they appointed the next Sunday to goe to *Islington* together; and there to be merrie: and so the Maid hasting away, they departed.

Well (quoth *Haunce* secretly to himselfe) it shall goe hard but Ile disappoint you.

Sunday in the afternoone being come, *Iohn* the Frenchman, according to appointment, went before to *Islington,* leauing *Florence* to come after, with another Maid which dwelt in the same house, whilst he prepared good cheare for their comming; and the more to make her merrie, hee hired a Noise of Musicians to attend their pleasure.

And as it after hapned, his fellow *Haunce* preuented this sport, who watching in the fields for *Florence,* at length he spied her comming: to whom he said, Well met faire *Florence,* your friend *Iohn* hath changed his mind; for whereas he appointed you to meet him at *Islington,* you shall lose your labour so to doe, for hee is not there.

No, how so said *Florence?*

The reason is this (said *Haunce.*) So far as I can vnderstand by him, hee thinkes you are very fickle and inconstant; and because it was his chance this morning, to see you speake to a young man that passed by, he saith verily, that you are a maruellous great dissembler: and in this humor he is gone I know not whither.

And it is euen so, said *Florence?* Ile tell thee what *Haunce,* because he hath made thee so priuie to his mind, I will shew thee somewhat of mine. Doth he suspect me, because I did but speake to one? Nay, if he be so iealous now, what will he be hereafter? And therefore insomuch that it is so, let him goe to the deuill, hee

---

³² and inconstant] Q2-4; an inconstant Q1

shall very well find, that I will set as light by him, as he doth by me: Did the knaue get leaue of my Mistris for me to come abroad this day, and doth he now serue me thus? well, this shall teach mee wit, in faith; and so she turnes back againe.

5   Nay (quoth *Haunce*) seeing you are now abroad, let me intreat you to goe to *Hogsdon;* and I will bestow a messe of creame vpon you.

    In the end she was won, and as they walked together, *Haunce* spake thus vnto her: I doe not know what cause *Iohn* the French-
10 man hath giuen you, to beare him so much good will, as I perceiue you doe, but, in my minde, he is a farre vnmeete match for you. And thus much I know, he is of a very mistrustfull nature, a wauering minde, and deceitfull heart, he did professe great good will to you in outward shew, but I haue heard him speak most
15 shamefully of you behind your backe, making his vaunts, that hee had you at a becke of his finger, and how that for a pinte of wine, he could cause you to follow him vp and downe ouer all the Citie. *Florence,* I am a foole to tell you thus much, it may be you will scarce beleeue it, and for my part I will not vrge you thereunto:
20 but in troth, looke what I tell you, is for good will, because I haue beene sorry to see you so abused.

    I thanke you good *Haunce,* quoth she, I may beleeue it well enough: but from henceforth I know what I haue to doe: I confesse indeed, that I haue drunke with him abroad, but it was at his own
25 earnest entreaty, neither could I euer be in quiet for the knaue, he doth so follow me vp and downe in euery place; but seeing I know his dissimulation to be such, if I doe not requite him in his kind, trust me no more: and now I am heartily sorry that I was so foolish as to follow him this day at his appointment: but seeing
30 he hath serued me thus, hee shall not know of my comming out of doores, and therefore good *Haunce,* doe not tell him you met with me this day in the fields.

    Nay in faith *Florence* (quoth he) I will not only be secret to thee, but will also from henceforth acquaint thee with all my
35 proceedings.

    And hauing eaten their creame, *Haunce* brought her some part of the way homeward: and taking his leaue of her, he went back to see if he could meet with *Iohn* the Frenchman, who hauing stayed at *Islington* for *Florence* vntill almost night, and shee not
40 comming, hee and the Musicians together were faine to eate vp the

meate, without more company, which caused *Iohn* the Frenchman to sweare like a Turke.

As he was comming homeward ouer the field, chafing and fretting to himself, who should hee meet withall, but *Haunce* the Dutchman, who said to him: What, *Iohn*, who thought to meet 5 you here?

Here thou seest I am now, said *Iohn:* but when came you from home?

Marry but euen now (quoth *Haunce.*)

And who is at home, said *Iohn*? 10

The other answered, there was no bodie but their Mistresse, and the maide *Florence*, with the rest of the houshold.

Is *Florence* at home, said *Iohn*? The diuell take her for mee, shee hath made a right foole of me indeed.

How so, quoth *Haunce*? 15

Then the other in a great chafe, said: Bee Got shall be reuenged, *Florence* mocke an mee too mush, too mush shee make me beleeue she loue me, an me tinke so too, and be Got, she make me a iacke foole.

When *Haunce* heard him say so, hee said: Alas good *Iohn*, she 20 loue thee? if you thinke so, you are greatly deceiued: for shee is the scoffingest queane in *London:* And I haue heard her behinde your backe, to mocke and flout you, saying: Doth shitten *Iohn* thinke that I will marrie him? in faith sir no.

When the Frenchman heard this, hee stampt like a madman, 25 and bit his thumbe, saying; *Mordue* shall be reuenged be Got: shitten *Iohn*? call a shitten *Iohn,* hea? *A de pur in corroyna me shant,* shiten *Iohn,* no better name but shitten *Iohn*?

It is as I tell you quoth *Haunce:* and moreouer, she said, she scorned to come after you to *Islington,* saying, she would see you 30 hanged first.

Well, be no matra, she no loue me, me no loue she; but me shall go home; mee shall, and beat as a stockfish.

Nay, doe not so, said *Haunce,* but let her alone: for it is no credit to you to beat a woman: and besides that, if you should, 35 our Master would turne you out of doores; therefore be quiet a while, and be secret in that I haue told you, then shall you see how she vseth you.

[38] how] Q2-4; show Q1

In this humor they departed: at what time, *Iohn* full of melancholy, stood frowning by the fires side: and as the maid went vp and down the house about her busines, he cast looks on her, as fierce as a Panther; but shee, by reason of the Dutchmans tale to
5 her, shewed her selfe as scornfull as he was currish, and not once cast her eie towardes him, and thus they droue out the time for a senight or a fortnight.

CHAPTER XIII.

How Master *Eyer* was called vpon to be Sheriffe of *Lon-*
10 *don,* and how he held his place with worship.

In this space Master *Eyer* following his businesse, had sould so much of his merchandize as paid the Grecian his whole mony: and yet had rested to himselfe three times as much as hee had sold, whereof hee trusted some to one Alderman, and some to
15 another, and a great deale amongst substantiall Marchants; and for some had much readie mony, which he imployed in diuers merchandizes, and became Aduenturer at Sea, hauing (by Gods blessing) many a prosperous voyage, whereby his riches daily increased.
It chanced vpon a time, that being in a studie, casting vp his
20 accounts, he found himselfe to bee clearly worth 12. or 13. thousand pounds, which he finding to be so, he called his wife to him, and said: The last day I did cast vp my accounts, and I finde that Almighty God of his goodnesse hath lent me thirteen thousand pounds to maintaine vs in our old age; for which his gracious
25 goodnesse towards vs, let vs with our whole hearts giue his glorious Maiestie eternall praise; and therewithall pray vnto him, that we may so dispose thereof, as may be to his honour, and the comfort of his poore members on earth, and aboue our neighbours may not bee puffed vp in pride, that while wee thinke on our wealth, we
30 forget not God that sent it vs, for it hath bin an old saying of a

²⁵ let vs] Q2-4; let as Q1

154

wise man, That abundance groweth from riches, and disdaine out of abundance: of which God giue vs grace to take heed, and grant vs a contented mind.

So soone as he had spoken this, they heard one knocking hastily at doore: whereupon hee sent *Florence* to see who it was, the 5 Maiden comming againe, told her Master it was one of my Lord Maiors Officers that would speake with him. The Officer being permitted to come in, after due reuerence, he said: Sir, it hath pleased my Lord Maior, with the worshipfull Aldermen his brethren, with the counsell of the whole Communaltie of the honour- 10 able Citie, to chuse your worship Sheriffe of *London* this day, and haue sent me to desire you to come and certifie your mind therin, whether you be contented to hold the place or no.

Master *Eyer* hearing this, answered he would come to his Honor and to their Worships incontinent, and resolue them what hee was 15 minded to doe; and so the Officer departed.

His wife, which all this while listened vnto their talke, hearing how the case stood, with a ioyfull countenance meeting her husband, taking him about the necke with a louing kisse, said, Master Sheriffe, God giue thee ioy of thy name and place. 20

O wife (quoth he) my person is farre vnworthy of that place, and the name farre exceedes my degree.

What, content your selfe good husband (quoth shee) and disable not your selfe in such sort, but bee thankfull vnto God for that you haue, and doe not spurn at such promotion as God sendeth 25 vnto you; the Lord bee praysed for it, you haue enough to discharge the place whereto you are called with credit: and wherefore sendeth God goods but therewithall to doe him and your country seruice?

Woman (quoth he) it is an old Prouerb, Soft fire makes sweet 30 mault: for such as take things in hand rashly, repent as suddenlie: to bee Sheriffe of *London* it is no little cost. Consider first (said he) what house I ought to haue, and what costly ornaments belong thereto, as hanging of Tapistrie, cloth of Arras, and other such like, what store of Plate and Goblets of Gold, what costlie attire, 35 and what a chargeable traine, and that which is most of all, how greatlie I shall stand charge beside to our Soueraigne Lord the

*34 Arras] Q2-4; Orace Q1

155

King, for the answering of such prisoners as shall be committed to my custody, with an hundred matters of such importance, which are to such an Office belonging.

Good Lord Husband (quoth she) what neede all these repetitions?
5 you neede not tell me it is a matter of great charge: notwithstanding I verily thinke many heretofore haue with great credit discharged the place, whose wealth hath not in any sort been answerable to your riches, and whose wits haue bin as mean as your owne: Truly sir, shall I be plaine? I know not any thing that is to be spoken of,
10 that you want to performe it, but only your good will: and to lacke good will to doe your King and Countrie good were a signe of an vnworthy subiect, which I hope you will neuer be.

Well wife (said her husband) thou dost hold mee here with prittle prattle, while the time passeth on, tis high time I were gone
15 to Guild hall, I doubt I shal appear too vnmannerly, in causing my Lord Maior and the rest to stay my leisure.

And hee hauing made himselfe ready, meet to goe before such an Assembly as he went vnto, he went out of doore, at what time his wife called after him, saying: and holding vp her finger.
20 Husband, remember, you know what I haue said: take heed you dissemble not with God and the world, looke to it husband.

Goe to, goe to, get you in quoth he, about your businesse, and so away he went.

So soone as he was gone out of sight, his wife sent one of her
25 men after him to Guild hall to hearken and hear, whether her husband held his place or no; and if he do, bring me word with all possible speed.

I will Mistris, quoth her man.

Now when Master *Eyer* came to Guild-hall, the Lord Maior and
30 his brethren bade him heartily welcome, saying: Sir, the communaltie of the Citie hauing a good opinion of you, haue chosen you for one of our sheriffes for this yeare, not doubting but to find you a fit man for the place.

My good Lord, quoth he, I humbly thanke the City for their
35 courtesie and kindnesse, and I would to God my wealth were answerable to my good will, and my ability were able to beare it. But I finde my selfe insufficient; I most humbly desire a yeere respite more, and pardon for this present.

At these words, a graue Commoner of the City standing vp,
40 with due reuerence spake thus vnto the Maior: My good Lord, this

is but a slender excuse for Master *Eyre* to make: for I haue often heard him say, and so haue diuers others also, that he hath a Table in his house, whereon he breakes his fast euery day, that he will not giue for a thousand pounds: wherefore (vnder your Lordships correction) in my simple iudgement, I thinke he that is able to spare a thousand pounds in such a dead commoditie, is very sufficient to be Sheriffe of *London*.

See you now, quoth my Lord, I muse Master *Eyer,* that you will haue so lame an excuse before vs as to take exceptions at your owne wealth, which is apparently proued sufficient; you must know Master *Eyer,* that the Commons of *London* haue searching eies, and seldome are they deceiued in their owne opinion, and therefore looke what is done, you must stand to.

I beseech you my Lord, quoth Master *Eyer,* giue mee leaue to speake one word. Let it be granted, that I will not giue my Table whereon I breake my fast for a thousand pounds, that is no consequence to proue it is worth so much; my fancy to the thing is all: for doubtlesse no man here would giue me a thousand shillings for it when they see it.

All is one for that, quoth my Lord Maior, yet dare I giue you as much wine as you will spend this yeare in your Shriualtie to let mee haue it.

My good Lord quoth he, on that condition I will hold my place, and rest no longer troublesome to this company.

You must hold, said my Lord, without any condition or exceptions at all in this matter: and so they ended.

The Assembly being then broken vp, the voice went, Master *Eyer* is Sheriffe, Master *Eyer* is Sheriffe. Whereupon the fellow that Mistris *Eyer* sent to obserue how things framed, ranne home in all hast, and with leaping and reioycing said: Mistris, God giue you ioy, for you are now a Gentlewoman.

What, quoth she, tell me sir sawce, is thy Master Sheriffe, or no? and doth hee hold his place?

Yes Mistris, hee holds it now as fast as the stirrop doth the shooe while we sow it.

Why then (quoth she) I haue my hearts desire, and that I so long looked for, and so away she went.

Within a while after came her husband, and with him one of the Aldermen, and a couple of wealthy Commoners, one of them was he that gaue such great commendations of his Table, and comming to his dore, he said, You are welcome home good Master Sheriffe.

Nay, I pray you come in and drinke with me before you goe.

Then said he, Wife, bring me forth the Pastie of Venison, and set
5 me heere my little Table, that these Gentlemen may eate a bit with me before they goe.

His wife which had beene oft vsed to this terme, excused the matter, saying; The little Table! good Lord husband, I doe wonder what you will doe with the little Table now, knowing that it is
10 vsed already? I pray you good husband, content your selfe, and sit at this great Table this once. Then she whispered him in the eare, saying; What man, shall we shame our selues?

What shame (quoth he?) tell not me of shame, but do thou as thou art bidden, for we are but three or foure of vs, then what
15 should wee doe troubling the great Table?

Truly (answered shee) the little Table is not readie: now good husband let vs alone.

Trust me, we are troublesome guests (said the Alderman) but yet we would faine see your little Table, because it is said to bee
20 of such price.

Yea, and it is my mind you shall, quoth Master *Eyer:* therefore he called his wife againe, saying: Good wife, dispatch and prepare the little Table: for these Gentlemen would faine haue a view of it.

Whereupon his wife seeing him so earnest, according to her
25 wonted manner, came in; and setting herselfe downe on a lowe stoole, laid a faire Napkin ouer her knees, and set the Platter with the pastie of Venison therupon, and presently a chaire was brought for Master Alderman, and a couple of stooles for the two Commoners: which they beholding, with a sudden and hearty laughter,
30 said; Why Master Sherife, is this the table you held so deare?

Yes truly, quoth hee.

Now verily, quoth they, you herein haue vtterly deceiued our expectation.

Euen so did you mine, quoth hee, in making me Sheriffe: but
35 you are all right heartily welcome, and I will tell you true, had I not thought wondrous well of you, you had not seene my Table now. And I thinke, did my Lord Maior see it as you doe, he would repent his bargaine so hastily made. Notwithstanding I account of my Table neuer the worse.

Nor haue you any cause (quoth they) and so after much pleasant talke, they departed, spreading the fame of Master Sheriffes little table ouer the whole Citie.

But you must now imagine, that a thousand cares combred the Sheriffe, in prouiding all things necessarie for his Office: at what 5 time he put off his Shoomakers shop to one of his men, and set vp at the same time the signe of the Blacke Swan swimming vpon the Sea, in remembrance of that Ship, that first did bring him his wealth: and before that time the signe of the Blacke Swanne was neuer seene nor knowne in any place in or about the Citie of 10 *London.*

CHAPTER XIV.

How *Haunce* having circumuented *Iohn* the Frenchmans Loue was by him and others finely deceiued at the Garden.

15

Now by that time *Iohn* the Frenchman, and faire *Florence* were both at variance, as you heard before, by the Dutchmans dealing, by which subtiltie he sought meanes to win fauor for himselfe: which *Iohn* the Frenchman perceiued, and therefore went about not onely to preuent him, but to take reuenge on him for his 20 deceitfulnesse. And meeting *Florence* as shee went to the Garden for flowres, he began to talke thus vnto her.

What *Florence,* you goe to the Garden?

And how then, quoth she, what haue you to say to that?

Me sea nothing, but you be very short; you no speake a me; you 25 no looke a me; nor you no drinke with me, nor noting, ah *Florence,* how chance dat?

Goe get thee hence, prating foole, quoth she, I drinke with thee? thou shalt be pie peckt first.

Pie peckt? What be pie-peckt a hea? Be got *Florence,* you make 30 me a Iacke nape, you mock a me, and call me shitten *Ian,* and you

159

bee so proud, because *Haunce* loue you, dat shall be maruell: but and if you call mee shitten *Ian* any more, *par ma foy* shall not put vp, shall not take at your hands.

Who told you, that I called you shitten *Iohn,* quoth *Florence,*
5 I neuer called you so.

No *Florence!* you no call a mee shitten *Iohn?* a so me shant villain pulard *Haunce* tell a me so.

I neuer saide so, quoth *Florence.* But *Haunce* tolde mee that you made your boast that I was at a beck of your finger; and that you
10 could make mee follow you vp and downe the whole Citie for a pinte of Wine; no, I would you should well vnderstand, I wil not follow a better man then you.

Of me fet *Florence,* me neuer sea so.

No? yes, quoth she but you did, I can tell you by a good token,
15 for that verie time that I should haue met you at *Islington,* you said it, and made me a foole to come ouer the fields to you, and when all came to all, you sent *Haunce* to tell me you were gone there hence long a gone.

Ah cet tokin *Haunce,* quoth *Iohn,* be des ten bon, tis true, for
20 me tarrie deare more den one, two, tree houre, and had prouid shopon, de rabit, de creame, de buding pie, and twentie ding more.

Well, howsoeuer it was, I am sure I was made an asse betwixt you, and for that cause I will beware how I shew kindnesse againe to any: therefore *Iohn* I pray you bee gone, and seeke some other
25 company, for you shall not goe with me.

No said *Iohn?* Well den, adieu *Florence,* and so they parted.

Now it is to be vnderstood, that *Haunce* had promised *Florence* to meet her in the garden, and to bring with him a bottle of wine, and there in the presence of a maide or two more, to make them-
30 selues sure together: and she, for that purpose, had carried with her a good corner of a venison pastie. But there was an English Iourny-man in the house cald *Nicolas* that vnderstood thereof, who meeting with *Iohn* the French-man, he made him priuie there-unto, saying; Trust me *Iohn,* if thou wilt be ruled by mee, wee
35 will not onely disappoint this match, but also with their good cheere make our selues merrie.

Iohn, who was glad and readie to doe the Dutchman any iniurie, consented to follow *Nicolas* his counsell in any thing.

Then, quoth *Nicholas,* it shall be thus: I will goe to the Garden,
40 and stay for *Haunce* his comming with the wine, and in the meane

space doe thou hide thy selfe vnder one of the hedges of the Garden on the other side, and with thee take a couple of pots, and let
the one be empty, and the other filled with water, and when *Haunce*
is come into the Garden with his bottle of wine: now he will not
let mee see it by his good will, notwithstanding ile obserue well 5
where hee doth set it downe, and then will I find the meanes,
while they are busie in toying and talking, to conuey the bottle
of wine through the hedge to thee, and likewise the venison: then
emptying the bottle, thou shalt fill it with water, and thrusting it
through the hedge againe, it shall bee set where first it was found, 10
which being done, thou shalt hastily rap at the garden doore, at
what time they shal be told that it is my Master or Mistris, which
they hearing, will be in such a maze, that on a sudden they will
not know which way to turne themselues, especially for the con-
ueying away of *Haunce:* Now when you haue knockt twice or thrice, 15
and that you heare no bodie come to the doore, get you away, and
stay for mee at the Rose in *Barking,* and there we will drinke vp
their wine, eate vp the venison: and this being done, weele laugh
them to scorne.

Truly *Nicholas,* quoth *Iohn* the Frenchman, this will be braue, 20
and thereupon they prepared themselues to doe the feat.

Nicholas therefore got him into the garden, and by and by after
comes *Haunce* with the bottle of Wine, who knocking at the garden
doore, was straight let in: but seeing *Nicholas* there, hee secretly
set his bottle in a corner: but *Nicke,* who had as searching eies as 25
Argos in his businesse, quickly did as before hee had determined,
and instead of wine set the bottle downe againe, where hee first
found it, full of water.

Then comes *Iohn* and lustily knockt at the doore.

There is our Master or Mistris (quoth *Nicholas.*) 30

Alas quoth *Florence,* what shall we doe for *Haunce?* Then rapt
he at the doore againe; Alas, quoth she, get you ouer the hedge.

Shall I open the doore, quoth *Nicke?*

O no said *Florence,* not yet good *Nick.*

With that he knockt more hastily. Anon, anon, quoth she. Hence 35
Haunce: Go to the doore *Nicke.*

Who is there, quoth hee? And with that opening the doore found
iust no bodie. Truly *Florence,* said he, they are gone whosoeuer
they were. God be with you, I can stay no longer.

When he was departed, the Maides wished that *Haunce* had 40 beene there again. Alas poore fellow (quoth they) is he gone, and left his bottle behind him?

Marry I am glad that it is no worse, quoth *Florence:* And now, that the wine is here, wee will drinke it for his sake, and I haue
5 here a morsell of Venison, that will giue it a good relish: and therewithall looking for it, she found the cloake, but the meate gone. Now a vengeance on it (quoth she) one skuruy curre or other hath got into the garden, and tooke away the meat.

O God what ill luck is that (quoth the maid?) a murren on that
10 curre that got it: but seeing it is gone, farewell it.

Well, said *Florence,* here is the wine yet, I know it is excellent good: for hee told me he would bring a bottle of the best Renish wine that in *London* could be bought: and I am certaine he is as good as his word. But beleeue me *Ioane,* hee is as kind-hearted,
15 and as louing a fellow as euer professed loue to any: I assure you, that here is a cup of Wine that the King might drinke therof: but how shall vs do for a glasse?

Weele drinke it out of the bottle, said *Ioane.*

Not so (quoth *Florence*) I do loue to see what I drinke, and
20 therefore Ile borrow a glasse at the next house.

And while she goes for a glasse, said *Ioan* to her selfe, Ile haue a taste of it before she returnes againe: and then setting her hand vnto the bottle, and the bottle vnto her mouth, she dranke a good draught, and finding it to bee something thin in the going downe,
25 she said to *Besse* that sate by: Credit me now, but for the name of Wine, I haue drunke as good water.

It is Renish Wine (quoth *Besse*) and that is neuer strong.

It may be made of raine well enough, quoth *Ioane.*

At which words *Florence* entred with a glasse: and pouring it
30 out into the glasse, she extolled the colour, saying: See what a braue colour it hath, it is as cleare I doe assure you as rocke water: and therwithall drinking it off, she said, it drinks very dead: Of a troth (quoth she) this is but bad wine, it is euen as dead as a doore naile: and so filling the glasse againe, she gaue it vnto *Besse.*
35 She tasting thereof said: Passion of me, this is plaine water.

Water, sayd *Ioane?* is it water: let me taste of it once againe: by my Maidenhead it is water indeed (quoth she).

Water, said *Florence,* verily you haue plaid the drabs in drinking out the wine, and filling the bottle againe with water.
40 Of my faith (quoth *Ioane*) you say not true in so saying: I would

you did vnderstand, wee played not the drabs in any such sort, but *Haunce* rather played the knaue that brought vs water instead of wine.

Nay (quoth *Florence*) I dare sweare for him that he would not serue you so, for all the wealth my Master is worth. And I am per- 5 swaded it was no body but your selues that did it: but in faith you might haue dealt so with another, and not with me.

Nay then, quoth they, you needed not to serue vs so, to cause vs to drinke water in stead of wine: and wee would you should thinke, although you bee Master Sheriffes Maid, we loue our mouthes as 10 well as you doe yours for your life, and it was but an homely recompence for our good will, I tell you true; neither doe we care how little wee come to be thus deluded.

Go to, go to, said *Florence,* you are like to *Penelopes* puppie, that doth both bite and whine, I know you well enough. 15

Know vs (quoth *Ioane?*) What doe you know by vs? wee defie you for any thing you can say by vs. Know vs? Nay, it were well if thou didst know thy selfe, and hearest thou? though thou hast thy companions to meet thee at thy pleasure, and we haue not: no, know vs? we are knowne to be as honest as thou art, or else 20 wee should be sorrie: and so she departed in a chafe.

Now *Iohn* the Frenchman and *Nicholas* hauing eaten the venison, and drunke vp the wine, came backe againe time enough to heare all this strife, whereat they greatly reioyced. But so soone as *Florence* did meet with *Haunce* againe, she kept no small stir 25 for mocking her with a bottle of water: about the which they fell at variance, in such sort, that they were not friends for a long time after.

But during the time that *Haunce* was out of fauour, *Nicholas* sought the Maides friendship by all the meanes hee might, but in 30 vaine was his paines spent therein: for although *Florence* (outwardly) seemed much displeased, yet *Haunce* had her heart still, and in process of time obtained great fauour: the matter was growne so forward, that the performance of their mariage was forthwith appointed, which they intended should be celebrated at 35 the Abbey of *Grace* on Tower Hill. Notwithstanding, this matter was not kept so close, but that their secret dealings were knowne; and *Nicholas* purposing to deceiue the Dutchman, made *Iohn* the

37 dealings were] Q2-4; dealing was Q1

Frenchman priuy thereunto, saying; *Iohn,* it is so that this night at midnight Masse, *Florence* and *Haunce* doe intend secretly to be married, and they haue appointed the Frier to doe it so soone as the Tapers are all put out, because they will not be seene of any:

5 Therefore *Iohn,* if now you will be my friend, I doe not doubt but to marry her my selfe, and so to giue the Dutchman the slampam, and bore him through the nose with a cushin.

Ha (quoth *Iohn*) be Got me shall doe as you sea, and therefore *Nicholas* tell a mee what you doe.

10 Mary *Iohn* (quoth he) you know the Dutchman loueth to drinke well, and by that he loueth, weele cause him to lose his Loue, for we will get him out to the Tauerne, and there cause him to be disguised, that he shal neither be able to stand nor goe; and while he lies parbreaking his mind, Ile goe and marrie the Maide.

15 The Frenchman hearing this, scratcht his head, and rubbing his elbow, saide, *Ma foy, Nicholas,* dis be de fine tricke: how shall wee get him forth adoores?

Excellent well, quoth *Nicholas,* for there is a new Iourney-man come to Towne with S. *Hughes* bones at his backe, and you know,

20 that we being of the *Gentle Craft,* must go giue him his welcome, and I will tell *Haunce* thereof, who being now very iocund, by reason that his mariage is so neer, will not deny to come, I know. Therefore you and the strange Iourney-man shall go before to the Tauerne, and then I will goe fetch him.

25 *Abeene,* content, content, said *Iohn.*

And so to the Tauerne hee hasted with the strange man. Anone comes *Nicholas* and *Haunce,* and with them two or three Iourneymen more, and all to the new Iourney-man: sitting downe, they get *Haunce* in the midst, called for wine lustily, and such varietie,

30 as the Dutchman was soone set packing, for euery one sought to ouercharge him; and being himselfe of a good kinde to take his liquor, spared not to pledge euerie man. At what time in the midst of his cups, being wel whitled, his tongue ran at randome (as wine is the bewrayer of secrets) so it proued by him, for there he opened

35 to his companions all his whole mind, saying, My hearts, for all I sit here, I must be a married man ere morning.

God giue you ioy (quoth they).

But who shall you marry, sayd *Nicke, Florence?*

Yea, *Florence,* said the Dutchman, that is the lasse that I doe

164

loue, and all the world cannot deceiue me of her now, I am the man that must haue her maiden-head, and this night we must be maried at the Abbey of *Grace;* and if you be good fellowes, goe with me to Church, will you goe with me?

Will we goe with thee? (said *Iohn* Frenchman) that we will. 5

O *Iohn* (said *Haunce*) I haue wiped your nose, and *Nicks* too, you must weare the willow Garland.

Well, what remedie (quoth they) it is the better for you.

But in faith *Haunce,* seeing it is so (quoth *Nicke*) weele haue one bottle of wine more, that wee may drinke to the health of our 10 faire bride.

Ile pledge her if it be a gallon (quoth *Haunce.*)

Be my fet and trote, said *Iohn,* weele haue a gallon. Hea Drawer, where be you? I pray you bring me a gallon of de best Claret, and a gallon of de best Seck, shall make merry I fet: what *Florence* 15 bee merrie and I no know?

But by the time this Wine was drunke, *Haunce* was laid vp for walking any more that night. When *Nicke* perceiued that, he stole suddenly out of the Tauerne, and went to meet *Florence* at the appointed place: but *Iohn* quickly missing him, knew straight 20 whereabout he went, got him presently to the Constable of the Posterne Gate, and told him, that *Nicke* had laid a man for dead in Tower street, and that he was gone to saue himselfe vnder the priuiledge of the Abbey of *Grace,* but (quoth he) if you will goe along, I shall bring him out with faire words vnto you, and then 25 I desire you to clap him vp to answer this matter in the morning.

But where dwell you, said the Constable?

I do dwell with Master Alderman *Eyer* (quoth *Iohn*) and there you shall haue me at all times.

The Constable did as *Iohn* bade him, and committed *Nicholas* 30 to prison. In the meane space, *Florence,* and an old woman of Tower street, said that they did goe to a womans labour, and by that meanes they passed along by the Watch, and to the Abbey of *Grace* they came. They had not long been there, but that *Iohn* Frenchman meeting them, sayd; *Florence,* well met, here is a fit 35 place to finish that I haue long looked for.

Iohn (quoth she) thou art like an euill spirit that must be con-iured out before a body shall get any quietnesse, vrge not mee

---

[17] the time] Q2-4; that time Q1

vpon any such matters, for you be not the man I looke for, and therefore, as taking little pleasure in your presence, as of your proffers, I should be very glad to see your backe.

What, said *Iohn,* haue you no compassion vpon a poore man?
5 you be hard-hearted indeed.

But as hee was vttering these speeches, it was his wifes chance to heare his tongue, being newly come from the Barge at *Billingsgate,* and at that time going towards Saint *Katherines,* to see if she could meete with any of her Countrey folkes, that could tell her
10 any tidings of her husband, but as I said, hearing his tongue, and knowing him by his speech, she said, What, *Iohn Deneuale?* my husband *Iohn Deneuale?* What make you wed pretty wence hea?

At which words *Iohn* was stricken into such a dump, that he wist not what to say: notwithstanding, hearing *Florence* to aske if shee
15 were his wife, he answered and said, Yea.

O thou dissembling fellow, quoth she, is it euen so? did thou say thou wast a Batcheller, seeking to marrie me, and hast a wife aliue? now fie on thee: O good Lord, how was I blest to escape him? nay, now I see that *Haunce* may haue a wife in *Flanders* too,
20 though he be here: and therefore by the grace of God, I will not marrie a stranger.

O (quoth *Iohn*) I thought my wife had bin dead, but seeing shee is aliue, I will not lose her for twenty thousand crownes.

So *Florence* departed, and left *Iohn* with his wife.
25 Now, *Haunce* neuer waking vntill it was next day at noone: when hee saw he had ouerslept himselfe, being very sorry, hee went home, not knowing how to excuse his folly to *Florence,* whom shee now vtterly forsooke, as well in regard of his drunkennesse as for that being a stranger, he might (like *Iohn* Frenchman) haue an-
30 other wife liuing. But *Nicholas* (that all this while lay in prison) being brought before Alderman *Eyer,* rehearsed the truth, and crauing pardon for his offence, was without more adoe deliuered. And *Florence* being called before him, hee made vp the match betweene her and his man *Nicholas,* marying them out of his house
35 with great credit, giuing them a good stocke to begin the world withall: also for *Iohn* Frenchman hee did very much, and shewed himselfe a good Master to his man *Haunce,* and to all the rest of his seruants.

₃₈ seruants] Q2-4; seruant Q1

CHAPTER XV.

How Master Alderman *Eyer* was chosen Lord Maior of London, and how he feasted all the Prentices on Shroue-tuesday.

Within a few yeeres after, Alderman *Eyer,* being chosen Lord 5
Maior of *London,* changing his copie, hee became one of
the Worshipfull Company of Drapers, and for this yeare hee kept a
most bountifull house. At this time it came into his minde what
a promise once hee made to the Prentices, being at breakfast with
them at their going to the Conduit, speaking to his Lady in this 10
wise: Good Lord (quoth he) what a chance haue wee had within
these thirty yeares? and how greatly hath the Lord blessed vs since
that? blessed be his Name for it.

I doe remember, when I was a yong prentice, what a match I
made vpon a Shroue-tuesday morning, being at the Conduit, among 15
other of my Companions; trust me wife (quoth he) tis worth the
hearing. And Ile tell thee how it fell out.

After we had filled our Tankards with water, there was some
would needs haue me set downe my Tankard, and goe with them
to breakfast (as many times before I had done) to which I con- 20
sented: and it was a breakefast of Pudding-pies. I shall neuer forget
it: But to make short, when the shot came to be paid, each one
drew out his money, but I had not one penny in my purse, and
credit I had none in the place; which when I beheld, being abashed,
I said; Well my Masters, doe you giue me my breakfast this time; 25
and in requitall thereof, if euer I be Maior of *London,* Ile bestow
a breakfast on all the Prentices of the Citie: these were the words,
little thinking (God wot) that euer it would come to passe: but
such was the great goodnesse of our God, who setteth vp the
humble, and pulleth downe the proud, to bring whom he pleaseth 30
to the seat of honor. For as the scripture witnesseth, *Promotion
commeth neither from the East, nor from the West, but from him*

¹ XV] Q4; XVI Q1-3

that is the giuer of all good things, the mighty Lord of heauen and earth: Wherefore wife seeing God hath bestowed that vpon me that I neuer looked for; it is reason that I should performe my promise: and being able now, Ile pay that which then I was not able to do: for I would not haue men say that I am like the Ebon tree, that neither beares leaues nor fruit. Wherefore wife, seeing that Shrouetuesday is so neere at hand, I will vpon that day performe my promise; which vpon that day I made.

Truly, my Lord (quoth she) I shall bee right willing therunto. Then answered my Lord, As thou dost loue me let them lacke neither Pudding-Pies nor Pancakes, and looke what other good cheare is to be had, Ile referre all to your discretion.

Hereupon great prouision was made for the prentices breakfast: and Shrouetuesday being come, the Lord Maior sent word to the Aldermen, that in their seuerall Wards they should signifie his minde to the Citizens, to craue their fauours, that their Prentices might come to his house to breakfast; and that for his sake they might play all the day after.

Whereupon it was ordered, that at the ringing of a Bell in euery Parish, the Prentices should leaue worke, and shut in their shops for that day, which being euer since yearly obserued, it is called the Pancake bell. The prentices being all assembled my Lord Maiors house was not able to hold them, they were such a multitude; so that besides the great Hall, all the Garden was beset with Tables, and in the backeside Tables were set, and euery other spare place was also furnished: so that at length, the Prentices were all placed; and while meate was bringing in, to delight their eares, as well as to feede their bodies, and to drowne the noise of their pratlings, Drums and Trumpets were pleasantly sounded: that being ended, the Waits of the City, with diuers other sorts of Musicke played also to beguile the time, and to put off all discontent.

After the first seruice, were all the Tables plentifully furnished with Pudding-pies and Pancakes, in very plentifull manner, and the rest that remained was giuen to the poore. Wine and Ale in very great measure they had giuen; insomuch, that they had no lacke, nor excesse to cause them to be disordered. And in the middest of this their merriment, my Lord Maior in his skarlet gowne, and his Lady in like manner went in amongst them, bid-

---

[24] so that besides] Q2-4; so they beside Q1

ding them all most heartily welcome, saying vnto them, that his promise so long agoe made, he hath at length performed. At what time they (in token of thankfulnesse) flung vp their Caps, giuing a great showt, and incontinently they all quietly departed.

Then after this, Sir *Simon Eyer* builded *Leaden-Hall,* appointing 5
that in the middest thereof, there should be a Market kept euery
Monday for Leather, where the Shoomakers of *London,*
for their more ease, might buy of the Tanners, without
seeking any further. And in the end, this worthy
man ended his life in *London* with great Honour. **10**

FINIS.

THE GENTLE CRAFT, PART II

THE
GENTILE
CRAFT.

The second Part.

Being a moſt merrie and pleaſant
Hiſtorie, not altogether vnprofitable nor
any way hurtfull: verie fit to paſſe away the te-
diouſneſſe of the long winter evenings.

By *T. D.*

Newly corrected and augmented.

Haud curo invidam.

LONDON,
Printed by *Elizabeth Purſlow*, dwelling neere
Chriſt Church 1610.

To the Master and Wardens of the
worshipfull company of the Cordwaynors

in London, all continuance of health and perfect brotherly affection.

Once more hath good will emboldened me, to present vnto your 5
Worships, my worthles labour, to manifest the good affection
I beare to this fraternity: and finding, you lent a gentle looke on
the first part of this History, I have beene the more bolde to proffer
you the second: for having bound my selfe by promise to performe
it: and you perhaps clayming promise as a debt, expecting pay- 10
ment, I bent all my study to keepe touch: whereupon I tender this
small trifle vnto you, onely crauing at your worships hands, a good
opinion of my poore endevours. And albeit this pamphlet doth
not minister matter worthy your grave view: yet in regard of the
subject, I trust you will deigne to esteeme it, sith so well as I could, 15
though not so well as I would, I have sought herein to procure
your delight: and although you finde not all the men spoken of,
which is promised in the first part, yet thinke it no faintnes in me,
but fault of good instruction: and againe, for as much as these men
here mentioned were all of this Citie (whose story grew longer then 20
I supposed) and the other of the country: I thought good so to
breake off, and to defer their story to another time, when I may
more perfectly speake thereof. In the meane space I commend your
Worships to the protection of the most highest.

Your Worships in all he may.　25
T. D.

To the Courteous Readers
health.

Gentle Reader, you that vouchsafe to cast curteous lookes into this rude Pamphlet: expect not herein to find any matter of
5 light value, curiously pen'd with pickt words, or choise phrases, but a quaint and plaine discourse, best fitting matters of merriment, seeing wee have herein no cause to talke of Courtiers or Scholers. Notwithstanding, if you find your selfe over charged with melancholy, you may perhaps have here a fit medicine to purge
10 that humour, by conferring in this place with Doctor *Burket:* or if you meet with round *Robin,* he may chance ryme it away. I tell you among Shoomakers is some solace, as you shall see by *Tom Drums* entertainment, and other mad merry prankes playd by the Greene-King of S. Martins. If that will not suffice, you may in meet-
15 ing with *Anthony now now,* have such a fit of mirth, with his firking Fiddle, that it shall be a great cause to expell choler. And so I leave you to your owne liking, whether you will enter to see this sport or no: stand backe, I pray, roome for a Gentleman, for you cannot come in vnder a groat.

174

CHAPTER I.

Containing the History of
Richard Casteler:
and the first of his love.

The louely Maidens of the Citty of *Westminster,* noting what a 5
good husband *Richard Casteler* was and seeing how diligently
hee followed his businesse, judged in the end hee would prove a
rich man: for which cause many bore vnto him very good affection,
and few there was that wished not themselves to be his wife: insomuch that he hauing the custome of all the pretty Wenches in the 10
Citty, by that meanes knew the length of every Maidens foot so well,
that he aboue all other best pleased them: On the Sundayes when
he came into the Church, the Maides eyes were so firmely fixed on
him, that hee could neither looke forward, backeward, nor on any
side, but that he should be sure to haue a winke of one, a smile of 15
another, the third would give a nod: and to be briefe, they would
all cast on him such gracious lookes, that it was easie to guesse by
their outward countenance, their inward good will.

And when in his Holy-dayes attire he past along the streets, the
Maidens (after their businesse was done) standing at their Masters 20
doores and spying him, would say thus one to another: Now verily,
there goes a proper civill young man, wise and thrifty: yea such a
one as in time will prove wondrous wealthy, and without all doubt,
will come to great credit and preferment.

These and the like words would they vse of him continually, 25
whereby he had among them such a generall good opinion, that
as he stood a dayes at his cutting boord, he should be sure to haue
twenty cursies made him in an houre, by Maidens that past up and
downe: some would bestow on him dainty sweet nosegayes, of the
fairest flowers they could find, and other some would bring him 30
handkerchers of Cambrick, and divers such like favours, well bewraying their friendship towards him.

But among many that secretly affected him, I will onely tell of twaine, because aboue all the rest, their merriments doe onely remaine in memorie, the one of them was called *Margaret,* of the spread-Eagle, but more commonly knowne by the name of long
5 *Meg* of *Westminster:* The other was a proper neat wench named *Gillian* of the George, both of them as wily as they were witty, who among all the Maides in *Westminster* were reputed to be the best servants; having therefore good wages, they maintained themselues gallantly, and therwithall so honestly, that no man could quip them
10 with bad liuing, though afterward it fell out otherwise, as in this historie you shall heare.

Margaret was a maiden borne in *Lancashire,* in height and proportion of body, passing the ordinary stature of women, but therewithall very comely, and of amiable countenance, her strength was
15 agreeable to her stature and her courage as great as them both: she was of a quicke capacitie, and pleasant disposition, of a liberall heart, and such a one as would be sodainely angry, and soone pleased, being readier to revenge her wrongs by weapons, then by words: and therein did shee differ from the nature of other women, because
20 shee could not abide much brabling: and so heedfull was shee of her behaviour in her yonger yeeres, that her good properties far exceeding her portion, she was wooed by divers, but would be won by none, for the man whom shee most loved, least thought upon her. And albeit shee manifested her good will by diuers meanes, yet did
25 *Richard* little regard it, having his mind nothing bent vnto marriage, by meanes whereof *Margaret* grew into such sad conceits as changed her chery cheekes into a greene wan countenance: in-so-much that euery one wondred to see her pensiuenes.

At last it chanced that *Margaret* having occasion to go into *Lon-*
30 *don,* it was her good fortune to meet with *Gillian* of the George, whom her mistres had sent thither to buy Comfets, and Carawayes, with divers other sweet meates, for that they had a banket bespoken by divers gallant Courtiers, which that night appointed to come thither: but so soone as *Margaret* spied her, she smiled, saying:
35 *Gillian* now in good sadnes, wel met, (if thou beest met a maid.)

And ill met (quoth shee) not meeting so good a maid as my selfe.

Tush (said *Margaret*) it is good for vs to thinke well of our selves, for there is enough that think ill of vs.

Mary I defie them (quoth *Gillian*) that thinks ill of me, and I respect as little their speech, as they do my profit. For a woman with a good life, feares no man with an evill tung.

If you bee so hot (quoth *Margaret*) where the wind blows so cold, what will you be by that time supper is ready, where the fire will be as fierce as your choller is great? and mistake mee not good 5 *Gillian,* though I said men think ill of vs, I meane not thereby that any goe about to blemish our good names, but I suppose they thinke not so wel of vs as they might do that doe not love vs so well as to marry vs.

Nay (said *Gillian*) if that be all, I am at a good point; for 10 though my maiden-head be some what burdensom to beare, yet I had rather keepe it, then bestow it on a bad husband: but though I say it, though I be but a poore wench, I have choise of husbands enough, and such as I am assured in my conscience, would both love me well, and keepe me gallantly. 15

Wherefore then doe you not marry (quoth *Margaret*)? in my opinion it is the most pleasingst life that may be, when a woman shall have her husband come home and speake in this sort vnto her. How now Wife? how dost thou my sweet-heart? what wilt thou have? or what dost thou lacke? and therewithall kindly embracing 20 her, gives her a gentle kisse, saying: speake my prettie mouse, wilt thou have a cup of Claret-wine, White-wine, or Sacke to supper? and then perhaps he carues vnto her the leg of a Capon, or the wing of a Chicken, and if there be one bit better then other, shee hath the choise of it: And if she chance to long for any thing by 25 and by it is sent for with all possible speed, and nothing is thought too deare to doe her good. At last having well refresht themselues, she sets her siluer whistle to her mouth, and calles her maid to cleare the boord: then going to the fire, he sets her on his knee, and wantonly stroking her cheeke, amorously hee chockes her 30 under the chin, fetching many stealing toutches at her rubie lips, and so soone as he heares the Bell ring eight a clocke, he calles her to goe to bed with him. O how sweet doe these words sound in a womans eares? But when they are once close betweene a paire of sheetes, O *Gillian* then, then. 35

Why what of that (quoth she)?

Nay nothing (saith *Margaret*) but they sleep soundly all night.

Truly (quoth *Gillian*) there be many wiues, but few that meete with such kind husbands: but seeing you aske me why I marry not, in troth *Meg* I would tell thee, if I had time to stay: but I feare I have stood too long pratling here already, and therefore farewell good *Meg*, when I see thee againe, thou shalt know more of my mind.

5 Nay *Gillian* heare you (quoth she) go but a little way with me, and I will goe home with you as straight as a line, for I haue nothing to buy but a score of Quinces, and couple of Pomegranets, and that shall be done in a trice.

Gillian was contented for her good companies sake to stay a 10 while, and as soone as *Margaret* had made her market, they settled themselves to goe homeward, where by the way *Gillian* entred into this communication.

You did euen now demand a question of me, and very desirous you were to know why I did not marry when I was so well offered: 15 Trust me *Margaret*, I take you to be my friend, which makes me the more willing to vnfold my fancy, being as well perswaded of your secresie as I am of your amity, and there-upon I am the more willing to make you copartner of my counsailes. Fire in straw will not be hidden, and the flames of affection wil burst forth at length, 20 though it be long kept vnder. And truth it is that I haue forsaken good matches, for I might haue had Master *Cornelius* of the Guard if I would, who as you know is wealthy, and therwithall of very good conuersation, yet there was one thing made me refuse his kind offer.

25 What was that (quoth *Margaret*) I pray thee tell?

(Quoth she) he loued not me so well but I loued another tenne times better, and therefore it is not good for handes to joyne, where hearts agree not. No *Meg*, no, there is a youth in our street that nearer touches my heart and better pleases my mind, notwith- 30 standing he shall go namelesse, for it is an old prouerb, two may keep counsell if one be away.

Nay then (quoth *Meg*) if you dare not trust me tell no further, notwithstanding I have had credit in as great matters as yours, for many a man hath put his life in my hands, and found no hurt 35 thereby, and as many women have committed their secrets to me, as men have ventured their bodies with me.

Go to *Margaret*, you are disposed to iest (said *Gillian*) but sweare by thy Maidenhead that thou wilt never bewray my liking, nor prevent me in my love, and I will shew thee all.

40 Nay fie, do not so (quoth *Margaret*) shew not all for shame, least

178

more see it then my selfe, for so may they blush at thy boldnes, and nothing commend thy modesty: but it is happy that I have a maidenhead left to sweare by: else I perceiue I should know nothing of thee.

No trust me (quoth *Gillian*) for such a one as cannot keepe her 5 Maidenhead, wil neuer keep a secret, and that made *Katherine* of the Crane to be such a blab: but now *Meg* I will proceed to the matter. What doe you thinke by *Richard* of the Rose, the wakeful cock of *Westminster?*

Oh he (quoth *Meg*) is that the man? there is no reason I should 10 thinke amisse of him that euery man commends: neuerthelesse, he is no body in respect of riches, being but a yong housekeeper of one yeares standing, a man, God wot, vnacquainted with the worlds guise, and to speake truth, nothing comparable to Master *Cornelius.* 15

I will tell thee what (quoth *Gillian*) that man which needeth neither to flatter with his friends, nor borrow of his neighbours hath riches sufficient: and hee is most poore that hath least wit, by which arguments I am able to proove, that the Cock is as wealthy as he is wary, for he will sure be beholding to no body, or 20 to as few as he may, and it is al wayes to be noted that men of such mindes doe never prove beggers.

Margaret hearing *Gillian* so stoutly to take *Richards* part, perceiued by her vehement speeches the great affection she bore to him, and finding that she was sick of her owne disease, *Margaret* 25 sought means to remoue the cause of her griefe, and thereby thrust her selfe into the greater sorrow: And the policy she vsed most herein, was to speak altogether in *Richards* dispraise, seeking thereby to dislodge her love, and the more firmely to plant her owne, whereupon she vttered her mind in this sort. 30

Well *Gillian*, seeing you beare so good an opinion of *Richard* of the Rose, I would not for a bushel of Angels seek to disswade you: but because you request my opinion how I like the man, in troth I will tell thee my mind without fraud or flattery: I confesse that *Richard* is a gentle young man, curteous and kind, diligent 35 about his businesse, and wary in his dealings, which argues good husbandry. Notwithstanding, I like not these ouer couetous fellowes, of such greedy mindes, such penny fathers and pinchfistes,

---

[38] pinchfistes] Lange; pinchfoistes 1639

that will not part from the paring of their nailes, nor the dropping of their nose, if they thought it would yeeld them but the fourth part of a farthing. Tell me I pray thee what ioy should a woman haue with such a churle, that would grudge at every halfe-penny
5 that is laid out, that in a whole yeare would not leaue a farthing worth of mustard vnwritten in his booke: And such a one I feare will this Cocke prove, for me thinkes hee lookes with a hungry nose, and, howsoeuer you think of him, I know not, but I verily feare though hee be a Cocke by name, hee will never prove a Cock
10 of the game. Againe he is but a dwarfe in respect of a man, a shrimpe, a Wren, a hop of my thumbe, such a one as a body might hide in a wrinkle of their buttocks.

Well *Meg* (quoth shee) you are priuiledged to speake your pleasure, but should another thus mistearme him, I would teare her
15 face: I tell thee true I had rather haue a winner then a waster, a sparer, then a prodigall spender: for when a man in his youth, hath gotten something with paine, he may the better spend it in his age with pleasure, and farre better it is hee should be thought couetous, then carelesse; his stature and proportion of body pleases
20 me well enough, for it is no matter how great hee is, but how good hee is.

But *Margaret* seeing our talk hath indured so long, that it hath brought vs both home, let vs at our parting be mindfull of our promises, to keepe secret whatsoeuer hath been said, for little
25 knowes the young man the depth of my mind, and therefore would I keepe it close, till I saw some signe of good will proceeding from him, for it becommeth not maidens to be woers, though willingly they could wish to wed where they best fancie, and so farewell sweet *Margaret*.
30 Adue gentle *Gillian* (quoth *Margaret*) vntill our next meeting, when I hope I shall further vnderstand of your proceedings in your loue.

When *Meg* had thus vnderstood her mind, and saw how the matter went, she sought all meanes possible to preuent her, as
35 hereafter shall be shewen.

CHAPTER II.

How *Margaret* requested *Richard* to the eating of a Posset
at night: And how her Masters buttocks was scalded
therewith.

It chanced that against Whitsontide, *Margaret* stood in need of a 5
new paire of Shooes: Therefore in a morning betimes she came
to *Richard* of the Rose to bespeake them aforehand, and the
more to declare her kindnes, and to win his good will, she carried
with her a bottle of excellent good Muskadine, which one of the
Yeomen of the Kings wine seller had bestowed upon her: and to 10
make it relish the better, she carried with her a dainty peece of
powdred beefe, and the tender carkasse of a cold Capon, and thus
plesantly began to greet him.

All health to the kind cocke of *Westminster,* that with the Larke
greetes the Sun rising with a cheerefull note, and mounts aboue 15
many to the loue of pretty lasses. Tell me (quoth she) thou bonny
Lad, wilt thou take the length of my foote, and make me a good
payre of shooes against Sunday?

That I will *Margaret* (quoth he), therefore let me see thy foote:
There is both my foote and leg (said *Meg*), I am not ashamed 20
to shew either of them, for I am not legged like a Crane, nor footed
like a Flie, and therewith lift vp her cloathes to the knee.

Whereat *Richard* smiling said, a little higher *Meg* and shew all.

Whereupon she sodainly replied in this sort: soft, *Richard* not
so, for I will tell thee one thing. 25

> Euery Carter may reach to the garter,
> A Shoomaker he may reach to the knee,
> But he that creepes higher shall aske leaue of me.

Good reason (quoth *Richard*) leaue is light, which being obtained a man may be bold without offence, but this onely is my 30
griefe, I haue neuer a Last in my shop long enough for thy foot.

Then I would they were all fired (quoth *Meg*). He that will be counted a good workman must haue tooles to fit all persons, and I muse that you which strive to be counted excellent, will want necessaries: Fie *Richard* fie, thou shouldest neuer be vnprouided
5 especially for women.

Well *Meg* (quoth he) be contented, consider you are a woman of no ordinary making, but as in height thou ouerlookest all, so in the length of thy foot thou surpassest all: therefore I must haue a paire of Lasts made for the nonce, and that shall be done out of
10 hand.

I tell thee *Dicke* (quoth shee) as high as I am, I am not so high as *Paules* nor is my foot so long as *Graues-end* Barge.

Notwithstanding (quoth *Richard*) a paire of Lasts to fit thy foot will cost as much as a hundred of fagots which will not be bought
15 vnder ten groats.

If they cost a crown (quoth *Meg*) let me haue them; what man, rather then I will goe without shooes I will beare the charge thereof my selfe and in token that I mean troth, take there the money, thou shalt find me no Crinkler, but one that will reward
20 cunning to the vttermost: I loue not to pinch for a peny, or stand upon tearmes for two pence, if I find my shooes good I will not shrinke for a shilling.

In troth (quoth *Richard*) franke customers are worthy of good ware, and therefore *Meg* doubt not, for thou shalt haue as good a
25 shoe as euer was drawne upon womans foote.

God a mercy for that, sweet *Dicke* (quoth shee) and seeing thou saist so, I will bestow this bottle of wine on thee to breakfast, beside that, I haue brought here a modicome that will proue as good a shooing-horne to drawe downe a cup of Muskadine as may
30 be: and therewithall shee pluckt out her powdred beefe and her colde Capon.

Richard seeing this, with thankes to *Margaret* for her meat, reacht out a couple of ioyne stooles, and after that they had laid a cloth thereon, they downe did sit, at which time many merry speeches
35 did passe betweene them. And at that very time there was in the same shoppe, amongst a great many other men a pleasant iorney man called round *Robin,* being a wel trust fellow short and thicke, yet very actiue and pleasantly conceited: for singing hee was held

¹² *Graues-end*] Lange; *Graus-end* 1639

in high reputation among all the Shoomakers in *Westminster,* and
he would scant speake any thing but in rime. This iolly companion
seeing them bent so well to their breakfast, and nothing at all to
respect him, in the place where he sate cast out these merry speeches
vnto them.   5

> *Much good doe it you masters, and well may you fare,*
> *Beshroe both your hearts and if you do spare:*
> *The wine should be nought as I judge by the smell,*
> *And by the colour too I know it full well.*

Nay faith (quoth *Meg*) that's but a iest,   10

> *Ile sweare (quoth* Robin) *tis none of the best.*

Tast it (quoth *Meg*) then tell me thy mind:

> *Yea marry (quoth* Robin) *now you are kind.*

With that *Margaret* filling a cup brim full, gaue it into his hand
saying: Now tast it *Robin* and take there the cup.   15

> *Nay hang me (quoth* Robin) *if I drinke it not up.*

By my Maiden-head (quoth *Margaret*) I see that thou art a
good fellow: and to haue thee drinke it up, is the thing that I craue.

> *Then sweare (quoth* Robin) *by the thing you haue,*
> *For this to sweare I dare be bold:*   20
> *You were a maid at three yeares old.*
> *From three to foure, five, sixe, and seauen,*
> *But when you grew to be eleuen,*
> *Then you began to breed desire;*
> *By twelue your fancy was on fire:*   25
> *At thirteene yeares desire grew quicke,*
> *And then your maiden-head fell sicke:*
> *But when you came vnto fourteene,*
> *All secret kisses was not seene:*
> *By that time fifteene yeares was past,*   30
> *I guesse your maiden-head was lost.*

And I pray God forgiue me this,
If thinking so I thinke amisse.

Now by my honesty (quoth *Meg*) you doe me mighty wrong to thinke so ill of me: for though indeed I confesse, I cannot excuse
5 myselfe, for women are not Angels, though they haue Angels faces: for to speake the truth might I haue had my owne hearts desire when time was, I would rather haue chosen to lye with a man then a maid, but such merry motions were out of my mind many a deere day agoe, and now I vow that a maiden I will die.

10   *By this wine (quoth* Robin) *I dare sweare you lye,*
    For were I as my master by this good light,
    You would leese your maiden-head ere twelue a clock at night.
    With high derry derry,
    If it be not gone already.

15 Nay (quoth *Margaret*) your Master scornes me, he keeps all his gownes for *Gillian* of the George: a pretty wench I confesse, hauing a proper body but a bad leg, she hath a very good countenance but an ill coulour, and you talk of desire, but her desire I doubt will bring her the greene sicknesse, if your master like a good
20 Phisition giue her not a medicine against that malady.

Why *Margaret* (quoth *Richard*) hath she told you so much of her mind, that you know her griefe so well?

It may be she hath (quoth *Margaret*) but whether she did or no, it is sufficient that I know so much: But I thinke (quoth *Margaret*)
25 you are not so besotted to make any account of a Tallow cake.

    No, faith (quoth Robin) *a nut-browne girle,*
    Is in mine eye a Diamond and a Pearle:
    And shee that hath her cheekes cherry red,
    Is euer best welcome to a young mans bed.

30 Certainly (quoth *Richard*) which is the best or worst I know not yet, nor doe I meane hastily to prove; and as for *Gillian* of the George, as she hath no reason to hate me, so she hath no cause

5 faces] Lange; aces 1639
17-18 countenance] Lange; counteance 1639
31 for] Lange; *om.* 1639

184

to loue me: but if she doe, it is more favour then I did euer merit
at her hand, and surely were it but in regard of her good will, I am
not to scorne her nor for her favour to feed her with floutes, but
for her good thoughts of me to think well of her, though not so
well as to make her my wife.   5
Well said Master (quoth *Robin*).

> *In this sort grind you still,*
> *So shall we haue mo sackes to mill.*

Trust me (quoth *Margaret*) I speake not this so much to disgrace *Gillian,* as for the regard I haue to your credit: but to make 10
an end of *Gillian* and this iest altogether, let me entreat you soone
at night to come to our house; and thinke this, though your cheere
chance to be small, your welcome shall be great. I know that this
Summer (and especially against these holy-daies) you will worke
till ten, and I promise you by eleuen I will haue as good a posset 15
for you, as euer you did taste on in your life. My master is an old
man, and he commonly goes to bed at nine, and as for my mistris,
I know where she will be safe till midnight masse be ended, so
that for an houre we may be as merry as pope *Iohn:* what say you
Richard (quoth she), will you come?   20
In troth *Margaret* (quoth he) I heartily thank you for your
good will, I would willingly come but I loue not to be from home
so late.

> *I thinke so (quoth* Robin) *least you should misse* Kate,
> *But take my counsell, when you are with* Meg: 25
> *Suppose you haue got fine* Kate *by the leg.*

Robin (said he) thou art so full of thy rime, that often thou art
without reason; thou seest that *Margaret* hath been at cost with
vs to day, and it is more then good manners to charge her further,
before we haue made amends for this: and beside that, late walking 30
in the euening brings young men into much suspition.
Tush (quoth *Margaret*) once and vse it not, is not such a matter:
therefore sweet *Richard* you shall come, and you shall not say me
nay, therefore I charge you on paine of displeasure not to faile,
and forget not to bring round *Robin* with you, and so farewell.   35

No, faith (quoth Robin) *it shall not need,*
I am bidden already and so God speed.

Who bad thee (quoth *Margaret*)?

What are thy wits so vnsteady?
5   *You did bid me (quoth* Robin) *haue you forgot already?*

Why then I pray thee good *Robin* (said *Meg*) do not forget in
any case, and put thy Master in mind thereof if he should chance
to change his opinion, or ouerslip the time through greedines of
work, for, Ifaith *Robin* if thou bring him along with thee, I will
10 thinke the better of thee while I liue.
Why then (quoth he).

And as I am no knight,
We will come to eate the posset soone at night.

Now *Margaret* was no sooner gone, and *Richard* at his cutting
15 boord, and *Robin* set on his stoole, but in comes *Gillian* of the
George, bringing in her aporne the corner of a Venison Pastie, and
a good deale of a Lambe pye, who with a smyling countenance
entring the shop, bidding *Richard* good morrow, askt if he had
broke his fast?
20 Yes verily (quoth *Richard*) I thank long *Meg*, we haue beene at
it this morning, and had you come a little sooner you had found
her heere, for she went away but euen now, and I verily thinke
she is scant at home yet.

Tis a lusty wench (quoth Robin) *gentle and kind,*
25   *And in truth she beares a most bountifull mind.*

Gillian hearing *Robin* to enter into *Megs* commendations, began
to grow iealous of the matter: out upon her foule stammell (quoth
she) he that takes her to his wife shall be sure of flesh enough, let
him get bread where he can: tis such a bold betrice, she will ac-
30 quaint her selfe with euery bodie. Notwithstanding this I will tell
you *Richard* the lesse she comes in your company, the more it will
be for your credit. And howsoever shee deserues it, God knowes, I
cannot accuse her, but I promise you she hath but a hard report

186

among many. But letting her rest as she is, see here what I haue brought you, and with that she gaue him the Venison and the rest, and drawing her purse, she would needs send for a quart of wine.

Richard sought to perswade her to the contrary, but she would 5
not be intreated; what man, quoth she, I am able to giue you a quart of wine.

That's spoke like an Angell (quoth *Robin*).

> *And this I doe thinke,*
> *If you be able to giue it, we be able to drinke.*   10

Hereupon the wine was fetcht, and so they sate them downe to their meate, at what time they fed not so heartily on the Venison pasty, but *Gillians* eye fed as greedily on *Richards* favour: and as soone as the wine was come, she pluckt out of her pocket a good peece of sugar, and filling a glasse of wine tempered wel therwith, 15
she drank to him saying: here *Richard* to all that loue you and me, but especially to him whom I loue best.

Let it come (quoth *Richard*) I will pledge him, whosoeuer it be.

> *So will I (quoth* Robin) *without any faile,*
> *Were it the best* Hipocras, *I would turn it ouer my naile.*   20

Then *Gillian* looking round about spoke to this effect: verily *Richard,* heere is a pretty house, and every thing hansome by Saint *Anne,* I see nothing wanting but a good wife to keep all things in his due kind.

Whereunto *Robin* made this answer.   25

> *Now speake thy conscience, and tell me good* Gill,
> *Wouldst not thou be that good wife, with a good will?*

Who I? alas (quoth she) your Master scornes me, he looks for a golden girle, or a girle with gold, that might bring him the red ruddocks chinking in a bag, and yet possible he were better 30
to have one with lesse money, and more huswifery: for my owne part I thanke God, and in a good time may I speake it, I would not

---

[13] favour] Lange; faour 1639

187

come to learne of never a woman in *Westminster,* how to deale in such affaires.

I thinke no lesse (quoth *Richard*) and therefore I pray God send you a good husband, and one well deserving so good a wife.

5 With that *Gillian* fetcht a great sigh, saying; Amen I pray God, for it is a sinful thing to leade a sinfull life, except . . .

Nay, say your mind, speake your mind (quoth *Richard*).

Why (quoth she) it is written, that we shall giue an account for every idle word, and that ill thoughts are as bad as wanton 10 deeds:

It is true (quoth *Richard*).

Then God helpe vs all (quoth *Gillian*) but if I were married, I should remove a great many of them.

Why then marry me (quoth *Robin*) and thereby prevent the 15 perill of bad thoughts.

Harke in thy eare *Robin* (quoth she) I would thy Master would say as much and then he should soone know my mind.

> *Ha, ha (quoth* Robin) *I faith, you drab,*
> *And would you have him to stampe the crab?*

20 Why what is the matter (quoth *Richard*)?

Nay nothing (quoth *Gillian*) but that I was bold to jest with your man, and I hope you will not be offended if he and I talke a word or two.

There is no reason I should (quoth *Richard*) and therefore con- 25 ferre at your pleasure, and the whilest I will be busie with the Lambe pye.

Then *Gillian* rounding *Robin* in the eare, spoke in this sort vnto him. I perceiue you can spie day at a little hole: you may see *Robin,* love is like an vnruly streame that will over-flow the 30 banks if the course be once stopt, as by my speeches no doubt you have noted: neuerthelesse how forcible soeuer fancy is, it is thought small modesty in a maiden to lay open her heart in those cases, but I am of opinion that affection growing as strong in a woman as a man, they ought to haue equall priviledge, as well 35 as men to speake their minds. *Robin,* I take thee to be an honest fellow, and it is the part of a man in cases of honest love to as-

---

[8] quoth she ∧] Lange; quoth she? 1639

sist poore maidens: counsell, the key of certainty, which makes
me to require both thy counsaile and help. In truth *Robin* to be
plaine, I love thy Master with all my heart: and if thou wouldst
be so much my friend to break the matter vnto him and therewithall to procure his good liking to me, I would bestow on thee as 5
good a sute of apparell as euer thou wast master of in thy life.
Wherevnto *Robin* answered, saying,

> *Heer's my hand* Gillian, *at thy request*
> *Ile make a vow Ile doe my best,*
> *But for my apparell grant me this,* 10
> *In earnest first to give me a kisse.*

There it is (quoth *Gillian*) and I doe protest, that upon that
blessed day, when he gives his happy consent to be my husband,
at the deliuery of thy apparell I will make that one kisse twenty,
and hereupon shaking hands, they came to the table and set them 15
downe againe.

Richard marking all, said nothing, but at her approach to the
boord tooke the glasse and drunk to her, giuing her thankes for
her cost and kindnes: she gladly accepting the same, bending her
body instead of cursie, tooke it at his hands, and with a winke 20
drunk vnto *Robin,* and so taking her leave of them both as light
as a Doe she ran speedily home.

So soone as she was gone, *Robin* told his Master it was the
pleasantest life in the world to live a Batcheler, during which
time he could neither want good cheere nor good company. 25

I mary (quoth *Richard*) but what I get one way I spend another way, while I passe the time in trifling about nothing: you
see (quoth he) here is a forenoone spent to no purpose, and all by
the means of a couple of giglets, that haue greater desire to be
playing with a man, then to be mindfull to follow their busines: 30
but if I liue I will sodainly avoid both their delights and their
loues. I tell thee *Robin,* I account their favours full of frawd, and
their inticements daungerous, and therefore a man must not be
won with faire words as a fish with a baite.

Well Master (quoth *Robin*) all is one to me, whether you love 35
them or loath, but yet soone at night let not the posset be forgot.

Beleeve me (quoth *Richard*) if I rest in the mind I am in now,
I meane not to be there at all.

O then you will loose her love (quoth *Robin*) for euer and euer Amen.

That (said his Master) is the onely thing that I request, for the love of a shroe is like the shadow of a cloude that consumeth as
5 soone as it is seene, and such love had I rather loose then find.

> But yet (*quoth* Robin) *this once follow my mind*
> *Though by her love you set but light,*
> *Let vs eate the posset soone at night:*
> *And afterward I will so deale,*
> 10 *If you will not my trickes reveale:*
> *That they shall trouble you no more,*
> *Though by your love they set great store:*
> *For one another they shall beguile,*
> *Yet thinke themselves well pleas'd the while.*

15 Verily (quoth his Master) if thou wilt doe so, I wil be *Megs* guest for this once, and happy shall I thinke my self to be so well rid of them.

Hereupon being resolved, they plyde their worke hard till the euening, and when the Sunne was crept under the earth, and the
20 Stars up in the skies, *Richard* having his shop window shut in, and his doores made fast, he with his man *Robin* tooke their direct way to the spread Eagle, where they no sooner knockt at the doore, but *Margaret* came downe and let them in, with such a cheerefull countenance, as gave perfect testimony of their welcome.

25 Now *Richard* (quoth she) I will witnesse you are a man of your word, and a man that hath a respect of his promise: I pray you hartily come neere, for to have you come in my office, is my desire.

> But tell vs first (*quoth* Robin) *was your office never a fire?*

Y faith no (quoth she) you see the kitchin is large and the
30 chimney wide.

> But how many rookes (*quoth* Robin) *hath the goodnes of your kitchin tride?*

I know not (said *Meg*) how many or how few:

Chapter Two

Trust me (quoth Robin) *I thinke euen so.*

Goe to (quoth *Meg*) I smell out your knauery, and guesse at your meaning, but taking it to be spoken more for mirth, then for malice, I let them passe. Then taking *Richard* by the hand, she bad him sit downe, saying, good *Richard* think yourselfe welcome, 5 for in troth I have neuer a friend in the world that can be better welcome.

I thank you good *Margaret* (said he).

I thank her still (quoth Robin) *with thanks of every degree,*
For you that have all the welcome, shall give all thanks for mee.   10

Why *Robin* (quoth *Meg*) be not offended for thou art welcome to mee.

I faith (quoth he) you bid me welcome when you haue nothing else to do.

Herewithall *Margaret* very neately laying the cloth, with all 15 things necessary, set a dainty minst pie on the boord, piping hote, with a great deale of other good cheere, and having sent another maid of the house for a pottle of wine, they fell to their meat merrily, whereof when they had eaten and drunk, *Margaret* stepping from the boord went to reach the posset, but while she had 20 it in her hands she sodainly heard one comming down the stairs.

Gods precious (quoth she) my Master comes, what shift shall we make to hide the posset, if he chance to see it, we shall have more anger then ten possets are worth.

With that she quickly whipt into the yard and set the posset 25 downe upon the seat in the privy-house, thinking it there safest out of sight, for her Master being an old crabbed fellow, would often steale downe to see what his maids were a doing, but God wot that was not the cause, for the old man being raised by the loosenes of his body, came hastily downe to pay tribute to *Aiax,* where when 30 he was come, he clapt his buttocks into the posset, wherewith being grieuously scalded, he cried out saying, alacke, alacke, help maids, help, or I am spoild for euer; for some spirit or divell in the foule bottome of the priuie hath throwne up boyling leade upon my buttocks.   35

191

And in this case like one dauncing the trench more he stampt up and downe the yard, holding his hips in his hands.

Meg that better knew what the matter was then her master, ran into the house of office with a spit in her hand, as if she had 5 beene purposed to broch the divell, and there casting the well spiced posset into the midst of the puddle, taking the bason away, said, how now Master, what is the matter, who hath hurt you, or are you not hurt at all?

Hurt (quoth her master) I tell thee *Meg*, neuer was man thus 10 hurt, and yet I am ashamed to shew my hurt.

Bring me a Candle (quoth *Meg*) I tell you Master, it is better all should be shewen, then all should be spoyled: and therewith casting by his shirt, spied both his great cheekes full of small blisters, whereupon she was faine with all possible speed to make 15 him a medicine with sallet oyle and houseleeks, to asswage the fury of an vnseene fire. And by meanes of this vnhappy chance, *Richard* with his man was faine secretly to slip away, and to goe home without tasting the posset at all: which was to *Robin* no small griefe, and yet they could both of them scant stand for laughing, 20 to thinke how odly this ieast fell out.

> *I am (quoth* Robin) *forty yeares old and more,*
> *Yet did I never know posset, so tasted before:*
> *I thinke his eyes in his Elbowes he had,*
> *To thrust his arse in the posset, or else he was mad.*

25 His master answering said, beleeue me *Robin*, I neuer knew the like in my life, but by the grace of God I will neuer goe there no more to eate a posset: and so going to bed they slept away sorrow till morning.

At what time *Margaret* comming thither told them she was very 30 sorie they were so suddenly broke from their banket; but Y faith *Richard* (quoth she) another time shall make amends for all.

Chapter Three

CHAPTER III.

How the Cocke of *Westminster* was married to a Dutch
maiden, for which cause Long *Meg,* and *Gillian* of
the George wore willow Garlands.

*R*ichard Casteler liuing a long time a Batchelor in *Westminster,* 5
after many good proffers made vnto him, refusing all, hee at
last linked his loue to a young Dutch maiden dwelling in *London,*
who besides that, was of proper personage, and comely countenance, and could doe diuers pretty feates to get her owne living.
To this pretty soule went *Richard* secretly a wooing, who for halfe 10
a yeare set as light by him, as hee did by the Maidens of *Westminster.* And the more hee was denyed, the more desirous hee was
to seeke her good will, much like to an vnruly patient, that most
longes after the meate hee is most forbidden: and such is the fury of
fond Lovers, to esteeme them most precious, that are to them most 15
pernitious: he scornfully shunnes such as gently seekes him, and
wooes her earnestly that shakes him off frowardly: but while he was
thus busied to make himselfe blessed by matching with a Mayden
in *London,* round *Robin* cast in his mind how to set the Maydens
wittes a worke in *Westminster,* which he effected as occasion was 20
offred in this sort.

Margaret and *Gillian* comming often by the shop, cast many a
sheepes eye to spye out their beloued friend, and after they had
many times mist him from his busines, they thought either that
he was growne love-sick or lazie: but knowing him a man to be 25
mightily addicted to the getting of money, judged that it was not
idlenes, that withdrew him from his busines, but rather that he
was gone a wooing to one pretty wench or other, for loving hearts
have euer suspicious heades and iealousie is copartner with affection: whereupon *Margaret* entred into these speeches with round 30
Robin.

I muse much (quoth *Meg*) where your Master layes his knife a

193

boord now adayes, for seldome or never can I see him in his shop: trust me, I doubt, he is become thriftles, and will prove but a bad husband in the end: tell me *Robin* (said she) I pray thee say where doth the Cocke crow now?

5   *Not so (said* Robin) *my Master will not that allow,*
       I must not shew his secrets to one or other:
       Therefore you shall not know it though you were my mother,
       Yet thus much by thy speech I plainly do see,
       Thou thinkst not so well of him as he thinks on thee.

10   *Margaret,* hearing round *Robin* rime to so good purpose, asked if hee knew his Masters minde so much? truly (quoth shee) if I wist he bore any spark of love toward me, it should neither goe vnregarded nor vnrewarded, therefore sweet *Robin* let me know whereupon thou speakest; feare not my secrecie, for I will rather
15 loose my life then bewray his love.

Heereupon *Robin* said, that his Master was very well affected towards her, and that if it were not that *Gillian* of the George did cast searching eyes into his actions, he would long ere this have vttred his mind: but (quoth *Robin*) he is so haunted by that female
20 spirit, that he can take no rest in no place for her, and therefore the more to quiet his mind, he hath left his shop to my charg, and betaken himselfe to wander the Woods so wild.

These words vttered by *Robin* made *Margarets* heart leape in her belly: wherefore taking gently her leave of him, she thus began
25 to meditate on the matter: Now doe I well see that the tongue of a wise man is in his heart, but the heart of a foole is in his tongue: and *Richard* (quoth she) hast thou borne me such secret good will and would neuer let me know it? Iwis, Iwis, soone would thy sorrow be asswaged if thou soughtest remedie at my hand: well though
30 the fire be long supprest, at length it will burst into a flame, and *Richards* secret good will, at last will shew it selfe, till when I will rest my selfe contented, thinking it sufficient that I know he loves me: and seeing it is so, I will make him sue and serve, and daunce attendance after me: when he is most curteous, I will be most
35 coy, and as it were scorning his proffers, and shunning his presence, I will make him the more earnest to intreat my favour: when he sayes he loves me, I will laugh at him, and say he can faine and flatter well: if he affirme he be grieued through my disdaine, and

that the lacke of my good wil hath been his greatest sorrow, I will
say alas good soule, how long have you been love-sick? pluck out thy
heart man and be of good cheere, there is more maids then Malkin:
though I doe lightly esteeme thee, there are some that perhaps will
better regard both thy griefe, and thy good will: and therefore good 5
Dicke trouble me no more.

Thus must maides dissemble least they be counted too curteous
and shewing themselvs ouerfond, become the lesse favoured, for a
womans love being hardly obtained, is esteemed most sweet, therefore we must giue our lovers an hundred denials for fashion sake, 10
though at the first we could find in our hearts to accept their
proffered pleasures.

Thus in a jolly humor *Margaret* ietted home, flattering herselfe
in her happy fortune, in which delight we will leave her, and make
some rehearsall of *Gillians* ioy: who, comming in the like manner 15
to *Robin,* asking for his Master, was certified by him, that for her
sake onely he lived in such sorrow, that he could not stay in his
shop, and therfore was faine to driue away melancholy by marching
abroad.

O *Gillian* (quoth he) had it not bin for two causes, he would 20
long ere this haue vttered his mind vnto thee, for he loues thee
aboue measure.

Yfaith (quoth *Gillian*) is it true *(Robin)* that thou dost tell me?

Doubt not of that (quoth he) doe you think that I will tell you a
lye? I should gaine nothing by that I am sure: if then you will 25
beleeue me you may; if not, chuse, I meane not to intreat you
thereto.

Nay good *Robin* (quoth she) be not angry, though I credit thy
speeches, yet blame me not to aske a question.

Aske what you will (quoth *Robin*) I respect it not, and I may 30
chuse whether I will answere you or no: Swounds, now I haue
opened my masters secret, you were best blab it through all the
towne.

Nay good *Robin* that is not my mind (quoth *Gillian*) but I
beseech thee, let me know those two causes that keepes thy Master 35
from vttering his mind.

Nay soft, there lay a straw for feare of stumbling (quoth *Robin*).
Hold your peace *Gillian,* it is not good to eate too much hony,
nor to gorge you with too much gladnes: let it suffice that you
know what you know. 40

Nay good sweet *Robin* (quoth she) I pray thee make it not dainty now to tell me all, seeing you haue begun: the day may come that I may requite thy curtesie to the full.

Say you so, *Gillian* (quoth hee)? now by good *Crispianus* soule
5 I sweare, were it not that I am in hope you will prove kind to my Master, and be a good Mistresse to vs when you are married, I would not vtter one word more, no not halfe a word, nor one sillable.

Well *Robin* (quoth she) if euer I come to command in thy
10 masters house, and to carry the keys of his Cubberts gingling at my sides, thou shalt see I will not keepe a niggards Table, to haue bare platters brought from the boord, but you shall haue meate and drinke plenty, and be vsed as men ought to be vsed in all reasonable manner. And whereas you seeme to make doubt of my
15 kindnesse toward thy Master, ha *Robin,* I would thou knewest my heart.

Robin hearing this, told her this tale, that his master loved her intyrely, and would long since haue vttered his mind, but for two reasons: the first was, that he could never find fit oportunity to
20 doe it, because of Long *Meg,* whose loue to him was more then he could wish, and such as he would gladly remove if he might: for (saith *Robin*) though my Master do not care a straw for her, yet she casts such a vigilant eye upon him, that if he do but speake, or looke upon any, she by and by poutes and lowres, and many
25 times inveyes against the parties with disgracefull termes, which is to my Master such a griefe, that he is faine to keepe silent, what otherwise should be shown: and the second reason is this, that because he is not so wealthy as he could wish himselfe, you would disdaine his sute, and make no account of his good will.

30 Who I (quoth *Gillian*)? now by these ten bones it was never my mind to say him nay. I tell thee *Robin* I doe more respect his kindnes then his goods: he is a proper youth and well conditioned, and it is far better to have a man without money, then money without a man.

35 Why then good *Gillian* (quoth *Robin*) harken hither three dayes hence, and you shall heare more, but in the meane space looke you play mum-budget, and speake not a word of this matter to any creature.

I warrant thee *Robin* (quoth she) and so away she went being
40 as glad of this tydings as her Master was of a good Term.

196

Chapter Three

Now when his Master came home, his man *Robin* asked him how he sped in his suit?

Verily (quoth he) even as Cookes doe in baking of their pies, sometimes well, sometimes ill. *London* Maids are wily wenches: on Sunday my sweet-heart was halfe won, but now I doubt she is 5 wholy lost. Now she is in one mind, by and by in another, and to be briefe never stedfast in any thing.

Tush Master (quoth *Robin*) stoop not too much to a thistle, but take this comfort, that what one will not, another will. I tel you Master, Crabs yeeldes nothing but verjuice, a sower sauce good 10 for digestion but bad to the taste, and these nice minions are so full of curiosity, that they are cleane without curtesie: Yet well fare the gallant girles of *Westminster,* that will doe more for a man then he will doe for himselfe.

What is that (said his Master)? 15

Mary (quoth he) get him a wife ere he is aware, and give two kisses before he calles for one.

That indeed is extraordinary kindnes (quoth *Richard*) but their loves are like braided wares, which are often showne, but hardly sold. 20

Well Master (quoth *Robin*) you know your two old friends, *Meg* and *Gillian.*

I, what of them (quoth *Richard*)?

In troth (quoth he) I have made them both so proud, that they prance through the streets like the Kings great horses: for I have 25 made them both beleeue that you love them out of all cry.

And I beshroe thy heart for that (quoth *Richard*) for therein thou dost both deceive them, and discredit mee: I assure thee I like not such jesting.

> *Now gip (quoth* Robin) *are you griev'd at my talke?* 30
> *And if you be angry I pray you goe walke.*
> *Thus you doe never esteeme of a man,*
> *Let him doe for you the best that he can.*

Richard hearing his man so hot, pacified him with many cold and gentle speeches, wishing if he had begun any jest, that he 35 should finish it with such discretion, that no reproach might grow thereby unto him, and then he would be content: whereupon *Robin* proceeded in this sort.

Upon a time *Margaret* according to her wonted manner came thither, whom *Robin* perswaded that his Master was newly gone into *Tuttle field,* and that he left word if she came she should doe so much as to meet him there: but (quoth he) take heed in
5 any case least *Gillian* of the George spie you, and so follow to the place where my Master attends your comming, who I dare sweare would not for all the Shooes in his shop it should be so: and therefore good *Margaret* if you chance to see her, goe not forward in any case, but rather lead her a contrary way, or make some
10 queint excuse, that she may leave your company, and not suspect your pretence.

Tush (quoth *Margaret*) let me alone for that, if she follow me she were better no, for, Ifaith, I will lead her a dance shall make her weary before she have done, and yet shall she goe home as very
15 a foole as she came forth, for any goodnesse she gets at my hand: and therefore farewell, *Robin* (quoth she) for I will trudge into *Tuttle fields* as fast as I may.

But looke (quoth Robin) you loose not your Maiden-head by the way.

20 *Robin* presently thereupon runnes unto *Gillian,* saying what cheere *Gillian,* how goes the world with all the pretty wenches here? it is a long while since I have seene you.

Ifaith, *Robin* (quoth they) we rub out with the rest, but what is the news with thee?

25 *Small news (quoth Robin) yet somewhat I haue to say,*
All Maides that cannot get husbands must presently marry,
They that cannot stay,
But heare you Gillian *a word by the way.*

And with that (rounding her in the eare) he told her that incon-
30 tinent it was his Masters mind that she should meet him in *Tuttle fields,* charging her if she met *Margaret* of the Spread Eagle, that she should in no case goe forward, but turne her steps some other way, for (quoth he) my Master cannot abide that great rounsefull should come in his company.

*31 Spread Eagle] Mann; Crane 1639

198

Chapter Three

For that let me alone (quoth *Gillian*) but trust me *Robin,* it could not have come in a worse time this twelve moneth, for this day have we a mighty deale of worke to doe, beside a great bucke that is to be washt.

Why then let it rest till another time (quoth *Robin*).   5

Nay (quoth she) hap what hap will, I will goe to him, sith so kindly he sent for me; and thereupon making her selfe quickly ready, into *Tuttle fields* she got, where at last she espied *Margaret* with a hand-basket in her hand, who as sodainly had got a sight of her, and therefore made a shew as if she gathered hearbs in the   10 field.

I wis that craft shall not serue your turne (quoth *Gillian*) I will gather hearbs as fast as you, though I have as little need of them as your selfe.

But in the mean time *Robin* got him home, and hartily laught   15 to see what paines these wenches tooke for a husband. O (quoth he) what a merry world is this, when Maids runnes a madding for husbands, with hand-baskets in their hands? now may I well sweare what I have seene.

> Two Maides runne as fast as they can,   20
> A mile in the fields to meet with a man.

Then how can men for shame say that Maidens are proud, disdainfull or coy, when we find them so gentle, that they will run to a man like a Falcon to the Lure, but alas poore soules, as good were they to seek for a needle in a bottle of hay, as to search for   25 *Richard* of the Rose in *Tuttle fields:* but hereby doe I know their minds against another time, if my Master should chance to request their company.

Thus did round *Robin* deride them when he found their fondness to be such: but to leave him to his humor, we will returne to   30 the Maids that were so busie in picking up hearbs in the fields: when *Meg* saw that *Gillian* would not away at last she came unto her, asking what she made there?

Nay what doe you here (quoth she)? for my owne part I was sent for to seeke Harts-ease, but I can find nothing but sorrel.   35

Alack good soule (quoth *Meg*) and I come to gather thrift, but can light on nothing but thistles, and therefore I will get my waies home as fast as I can.

In doing so you shall doe well (quoth *Gillian*) but I mean to get some Harts ease ere I goe away:

Nay *Gillian* (quoth she) I am sure I shall find thrift as soone as you shall find Harts-ease, but I promise you I am out of hope to 5 find any to day.

I pray you get you gone then (quoth she).

What would you so faine be rid of my company (quoth *Meg*)? for that word I meane not to be gone yet: Ifaith *Gill* I smell a rat.

Then (quoth she) you haue as good a nose as our gray Cat: 10 but what rat do you smell, tell me? I doubt I doubt if there be any rat in the field, you would faine catch him in your trap, if you knew how; but Ifaith *Meg,* you shall be deceiued as cunning as you are.

Then belike (quoth *Meg*) you would not have the rat taste no 15 cheese but your owne.

All is one for that (said *Gillian*) but wheresoever he run I would have him creep into no corner of yours.

Your wordes are mysticall (quoth *Meg*) but if thou art a good wench, let us goe home together.

20 Not so (said *Gillian*) as I came not with you, so I meane not to goe with you.

No (quoth *Meg*)? before God I sweare I will stay as long as thou for thy life.

In troth (quoth she) I will make you stay till midnight then.

25 Yea (quoth *Meg*)? now, as sure as I live I will try that.

And in this humor sometimes they sat them downe, and sometimes they stalkt round about the field, till it was darke night, and so late, that at last the watch met with them, who contrary to *Gillians* mind, tooke paines to bring them home both together: at what 30 time they gave one another such privie flouts, that the watchmen tooke no little delight to heare it: But their Mistresses that had so long mist them from home though they were very angry with their long absence, yet were glad they were come againe. And asking where they had been so long, the watch-men answered, that the one 35 had beene to seeke Harts-ease, and the other to gather thrift and therefore that they should not blame them for staying so long to get such good commodities.

Verily (quoth their Mistresses) we will not, for no maruell if they stayed out till midnight about such matters, seeing we have sought it this seven yeares and could never find it: and in this sort this jest ended.

Within a while after this, *Richard* through his long woing, had gotten the good will of his sweet-heart, and therefore making all things ready for his marriage, the matter being known through *Westminster, Margaret* and *Gillian* had tydings thereof with the soonest, who comming unto *Richard,* said he was the most false and unconstant man in the world.

Have I (quoth *Meg*) set my whole mind upon thee to be thus serued?

Nay (quoth *Gillian*) have I loved thee so deerly, and indured such sorrow for thy sake, to be thus unkindly cast off?

And I (quoth *Meg*) that never thought any thing too much for thee, that loved thee better then my life, that was at all times ready at thy call, and ready to run or goe at thy commandement to be so vndeservedly forsaken, grieves not my heart a little.

Nay (quoth *Gillian*) could you make me leave my worke to waite upon thee in *Tuttle-fields?*

Nay did I waite there halfe a day together (quoth *Meg*) at thy request to be thus mockt at thy hand? Now I wish it from my heart, if thou marriest any but me, that thy wife may make thee as errant a Cuckold as *Iack Coomes.*

So you are very charitable (quoth *Richard*) to wish me no worse then you meane to make your husband: but when did I request thee to come into *Tuttle-fields?*

What have you so weake a memory (quoth she)? I pray you aske your man round *Robin* whether it were so or no.

Well (quoth *Robin*) how then? wherefore did you not speake with him at that present?

You know it comes in an houre, comes not in seven yeare,
Had you met him at that instant you had married him cleare.

A vengeance take her (quoth *Meg*) I could not meete him for *Gillian.*

And I could not meet him for *Margaret,* a morin take her (quoth *Gillian*).

Richard perceiving by their speech there was a pad lying in the straw, made this reply. It is a strange thing to see how you will blame me of discourtesie, when the whole fault lyes in your selves: had you come at the appointed time, it is likely I had marryed one of you, seeing my minde was as well addicted to the one as to the other.

5   Why may it not be yet (quoth they) if it please you?

Not so (said *Richard*) you speake too late, men gather no grapes in Ianuary, my wine is already provided, and my wife prepared: therefore I thanke you both of your good wills, though I be constrained of force to forsake you.

10   The maidens being herewith struck into their dumps, with water in their eyes, and griefe in their hearts went home, to whom *Robin* carryed two Willow garlands, saying

> *You pretty soules that forsaken be,*
> *Take here the branches of the Willow tree,*
> 15   *And sing loves farewell joyntly with me.*

Meg being merily inclined, shooke off sorrow in this sort, and gently taking the willow Garland, said: wherefore is griefe good? can it recall folly past? no: can it helpe a matter remedilesse? no: can it restore losses, or draw us out of danger? no: what then? 20 can griefe make unkind men curteous? no: can it bring long life? no: for it doth rather hasten our death, what then can it do: can it call our friends out of their graves? no: can it restore virginity if we chance to lose our maidenhead? no: Then wherefore should I grieve? except I went to kill my selfe: Nay seeing it is so, hang 25 sorrow, I will never care for them that care not for me, and therefore a Figge for the Cocke of *Westminster:* by this good day I am glad I have scapt him, for I doe now consider I should have never tooke rest after foure a clocke in the morning, and alas a young married wife would be loath to rise before eight or nine: beside 30 that I should never have gone to bed before ten or eleuen, or twelve a clocke at night by that meanes, what a deale of time should I have lost aboue other women: have him quoth you? now God blesse me, I sweare by *Venus,* the faire goddesse of sweet love, in the minde I am in, I would not have him, if he had so 35 much as would lie in *Westminster* Hall. And therefore *Robin* this Willow garland is to me right heartily welcome: and I will goe

32 aboue] Mann; about 1639

with thee to *Gillian* presently, and thou shalt see us weare them
rather in triumph, then in timerous feare.

Well said, in good sadnes (quoth *Robin*) thou art the gallantest
girle that ever I knew.

But when she came to *Gillian*, *Robin* staid for her at the staire
foot: they found her sicke in her bed, fetching many sore sighes,
to whom *Margaret* spake in this manner.

Why, how now, *Gillian*, what, sicke a bed? now fie for shame,
plucke up a good heart woman, let no man triumph so much ouer
thee, to say thou gavest the Crow a pudding, because love would let
thee live no longer: be content (quoth she) and take courage to
thee, death is a sowre crabbed fellow.

Ah no (quoth *Gillian*) death is sweet to them that live in sorrow,
and to none should he be better welcome then to me, who desires
nothing more then death to end my miseries.

What now (quoth *Margaret*) whose Mare is dead? art thou a
young wench, faire and comely, and dost thou despaire of life?
and all for love, and all for love. O fond foole worthy to weare
a coate with foure elbowes, this were enough if there were no
more men in the world but one, but if there were two, why shouldst
thou languish, much lesse knowing there is so many to be had.

O (quoth *Gillian*) what is all the men in the world to me now
I have lost *Richard*, whose love was my life.

I pray thee rise (quoth *Meg*) and let us go drinke a quart of
Sacke to wash sorrow from our hearts.

O (quoth shee) I cannot rise if you would give me a hundred
pound, nor will I rise for any mans pleasure.

What (quoth *Meg*) if your father sent for you, would you not
goe to him?

No (quoth she).

Would you not goe to your mother?

No.

But what if your brethren requested you to rise?

Yfaith I would not (quoth she).

Say that some of the Kings Gentlemen intreated your company?

Never prate, I would not goe to the best Lord in the Land (quoth
Gillian) nor to no man els in the world.

No (quoth *Meg*) I am sure you would.

(Quoth she) if I doe, say I am an errant queane, and count me
the veriest drab that ever trod on two shooes.

Nay (quoth *Meg*) seeing you say so, I have done, I was about to tell you of a matter, but I see it is to small purpose, and therefore Ile keep my breath to coole my pottage.

A matter (said *Gillian*)? what matter is it sweet *Meg* tell me?

5 No, no (quoth she) it is in vaine, I would wish you to couer your selfe close, and keepe your selfe warme, least you catch an ague, and so good night *Gillian*.

Nay, but *Meg* (quoth she) good *Meg* if ever thou didst love me, let me know what this matter is that you speake of, for I shall not
10 be in quiet till I know it.

Tush tis but a trifle, a trifle (quoth *Meg*) not worth the talke: your sweet heart *Richard*, hath sent his man *Robin* for you, and, as he tels me he hath a token to deliuer you.

What (quoth *Gill*) is that true? Where is *Robin*? why comes
15 he not up?

Truly (quoth *Meg*) he counts it more then manners to presse into a Maides chamber: beside he would be loath to give any cause of suspition to any of your fellowes, to thinke Ill of him or you, for now a dayes the world is growne to such a passe, that if
20 a Maide doe but looke merrily upon a young man, they will say straight, that either she shall be his wife, or that she is his harlot: but if they see a man come into a womans chamber, they will not sticke to sweare that they have been naught together; for which cause *Robin* intreated me to come unto you, and to certifie you
25 that hee stayed at the three-Tunnes for your comming: but seeing you are a bed I am sorry I have troubled you so much, and therefore farewell good *Gillian*.

O stay a little good *Meg* (quoth she) and I will goe along with you: and with that on she slipt her petticoate, and made such
30 hast in dressing her selfe, that she would not stay the plucking on of her stockings nor the drawing on of her shooes.

Why, how now *Gillian* (quoth *Meg*) have you forgot your selfe? remember you are Ill and sicke a bed.

Tush (quoth shee) I am well enough now.

35 But if you goe foorth to night you are an arrant drab, and a very queane (quoth *Meg*).

Tush tis no matter for that (said *Gillian*) griefe hath two

² matter] matt 1639
¹⁵⁻¹⁶ up? *new par.* Truly] Lange; up, truly 1639

tongues, to say, and to unsay, and therefore I respect not what you
prate, and therewithall shee ran downe the stayres after *Margaret*,
who got *Robin* to goe before to the three-Tunnes, where when
Gillian came, she asked him how his Master did, and what his
errand was to her.   5

> *Soft: First let us drinke (quoth* Robin) *and then let us talke,*
> *That we cannot pay for, shall be set up in chalke.*

You speak merrily (quoth *Margaret*) whatsoever you meane,
but I would I could see the wine come once, that I may drink
a hearty draught; for sorrow they say is dry, and I find it to be 10
true.

> *Then drinke hard (quoth* Robin) *and bid sorrow adue.*

Thus when they had whipt off two or three quarts of wine,
Gillian began to grow as pleasant as the best, and would needs
know of *Robin,* what it was he had to say to her.   15
Nothing, quoth he, but to doe my Masters commendation, and
to deliver you his token.
This token (quoth *Gillian*)? What, a Willow garland? is the
matter so plaine? is this the best reward hee can give me for all
my good will; had he no body to flout but mee?   20
Yes by my faith (quoth *Meg*) it was his minde that I should
beare you company, therefore, looke what he sent to you, he did
the like to mee, and that thou maiest the better believe me, see
where it is.
O intollerable iniury (quoth *Gillian*) did I take paines to rise 25
and come out of my warme bed for this? O how unfortunate have
I beene above all other in the world? Well, seeing I cannot recall
what is past, I will take this as a iust penance for my too much
folly; and if *Margaret* will agree, we will weare these disdainfull
branches on his marriage day to his great disgrace, though to our 30
continuall sorrow.
Content (quoth *Meg*) all is one to mee, looke what thou wilt
allow, I will not dislike, and so paying the shot, away they went.
At length, when the marriage day was come, and that the Bride,
in the middest of her friends was set downe to dinner, *Margaret* 35

and *Gillian,* attyred in red Stammell petticoats, with white linnen
sleeves, and fine Holland Aprons, having their Willow garlands on
their heads, entred into the Hall singing this song:

When fancie first fram'd our likings in love,
    sing all of greene Willow:
And faithfull affection such motion did move,
    for Willow, Willow, Willow.
Where pleasure was plenty we chanced to be,
    sing all of greene Willow:
There were we enthral'd of our liberty,
    and forced to carrie the Willow garland.

This young man we liked and loved full deere,
    sing all of greene Willow:
And in our hearts-closset we kept him full neere,
    sing Willow, Willow, Willow.
He was our hearts-pleasure and all our delight,
    sing all of greene Willow:
We judg'd him the sweetest of all men in sight,
    Who gives us unkindly the Willow garland.

No cost we accounted too much for his sake,
    sing all of greene Willow:
Fine bands and handkerchers for him we did make,
    sing Willow, Willow, Willow.
And yet for our good will, our travell and paine,
    sing all of greene Willow:
We have gotten nothing but scorne and disdaine;
    as plainly is prov'd by this Willow garland.

Then pardon our boldnesse, thou gentle faire Bride,
    sing all of greene Willow:
We speake by experience of that we have tride,
    sing Willow, Willow, Willow.
Our over much courtesie bred all our woe,
    sing all of greene Willow:
But never hereafter we meane so to doe,
    For this onely brought us the Willow garland.

Chapter Three

Their song being thus ended, the Bride said she was heartily sorry for their hard fortune in love, greatly blaming the Bridegroom for his unkindnes.

Nay, do not so (quoth *Meg*) for you shal find him kind enough soon at night: but seeing he hath disappointed me in this sort, it shall go hard, but I will make shift to lose my maiden-head as soone as you shall lose yours, and you shall make good haste, but I wil be before you. O God (quoth she) have I been so chary to keep my honesty, and so dainty of my maiden-head that I could spare it no man for the love I bore to hard-hearted *Richard,* and hath he serv'd me thus? Well *Gillian* (quoth she) let us go, never wil I be so tide in affection to one man again while I live; what a deale of time have I lost and spent to no purpose since I came to *London?* and how many kinde offers have I forsaken, and disdainfully refused of many brave Gentlemen, that would have bin glad of my good will? I thinke I was accurst to come into his company: Well, I say little, but hence forward hang me if I refuse reason when I am reasonably intreated; trust me, I would not for a good thing, that my friends in the country should know that one of my ripe age, bone and bignesse hath all this while liv'd in *London* idly, like an unprofitable member of the common-wealth; but if I live, they shall heare that I will be better imploy'd, and so adue good *Gillian.*

Thus *Margaret* in a melancholy humor went her waies, and in short time after she forsooke *Westminster,* and attended on the Kings army to *Bullen,* and while the siege lasted, became a landresse to the Camp, and never after did she set store by her selfe, but became common to the call of every man, till such time as all youthfull delights was banished by old age, and in the end she left her life in *Islington,* being very penitent for all her former offences.

Gillian in the end was well married, and became a very good house-keeper, living in honest name and fame till her dying day.

[26] *Bullen*] *Bullio* 1639 [*i.e., Boulogne*]

CHAPTER IV.

How round *Robin* and his fellowes sung before the King.

The Kings Maiesty having royally won the strong town of *Bullen,* victoriously he returned and came into *England,* and accord-
5 ing to his accustomed manner, lying at his Palace of *Whitehall,* divers of the Nobility, passing up and down *Westminster,* did many times heare the Shoomakers iournymen singing; whose sweet voyces and pleasant songs was so pleasing in the eares of the hearers, that it caused them to stay about the doore to hearken thereunto:
10 *Robin* above the rest, declared such cunning in his song, that he ever obtained the chiefest praise; and no marvell, for his skill in pricksong was more then ordinary, for which cause the Singing-men of the Abbey did often call him into the Quire.

Now you shall vnderstand, that by their often singing in the
15 Shop, the iourneymen of that house were noted above all the men in *Westminster,* and the report of their singing went far and neer, in so much that at the last, the Kings Maiesty had knowledge thereof, who hearing them so greatly commended, caused them to be sent for to the Court. Whereupon round *Robin* and his foure
20 fellows made themselves ready, and their Master being of a good mind, against the day that they should goe before our King, he suted them all at his owne proper cost, in doublets and hose of crimson Taffety, with black Velvet caps on their heads, and white feathers; on their legs they had fine yellow stockings, pumps and
25 pantofles on their feet: by their sides each of them wore a faire sword; and in this sort being brought before his Maiesty, upon their knees they craved pardon for presuming to come into his royall presence.

The King, seeing them to be such proper men, and attyred in
30 such Gentleman-like manner, bad them stand up: Why my Lords (quoth he) be these the merry minded Shoomakers you spake of?

They are most dread Soveraigne (said they).

208

Chapter Four

Certainly (said our King) you are welcome every one, but who among you is round Robin?

> *My Liege* (*quoth* Robin) *that man am I,*
> *Which in your Graces service will live and die:*
> *And these be my fellowes every one,*   5
> *Ready to waite your royall Grace upon.*

How now *Robin* (said our King). What, canst thou rime?

> *A little my Liege* (*quoth he*) *as I see place and time.*

His Grace laughing heartily at this pleasant companion, told him that he heard say he could sing well.   10

> *Trust me* (*quoth* Robin) *at your Graces request,*
> *You shall well perceive we will doe our best.*

Hereupon the King sate him downe, where many great Lords and Ladies of high estate attended on his Highnesse. And being in the Christmas time, after the master of merry disports had per- 15 formed all his appointed pastimes, *Robin,* with his fellowes had liberty to declare their cunning before our King, but the Maiesty of his Princely presence did so amate them, that they were quite dash'd out of countenance, which his Grace perceiving, gave them many gracious words of encouragement, whereupon they began in 20 this sort, singing a song of the winning of *Bullen.*

The Song of the winning of *Bullen* sung before the King by round *Robin* and his fellowes.

> In the moneth of October
> Our King he would to Dover: 25
>   By leave of Father and the Sonne:
> A great armie of men,
> Well appointed there was then,
>   Before our noble King to come;
>
> The valiant Lord Admirall,   30
> He was captaine Generall,

Of all the royall Navie sent by Sea:
The sight was worthie to behold,
To see the ships with shining gold,
    And Flags and Streamers sailing all the way.

5   At *Bullen* then arriving,
With wisdome well contriving:
    The armed men were set in battle ray;
And *Bullen* was besieged round,
Our men with Drum and Trumpets sound,
10   Before it march'd couragious that day.

Then marke how all things chanced,
Before them was advanced,
    The royall Standard in the bloodie field;
The Frenchmen standing on the walls,
15 To them our English Heralds calls,
    Wishing in time their Citie for to yeeld.

Our King hath sent to prove you,
Because that he doth love you,
    He profferd mercy if you will imbrace:
20 If you deny his kinde request,
And in your obstinacie rest,
    Behold you bring your selves in wofull case.

(Quoth they) wee doe deny you,
And flatly we defie you,
25   Faire *Bullen* is a famous Maiden towne;
For all the deeds that hath beene done,
By conquest never was she won,
    She is a Lady of most high renowne.

When they so unadvised,
30 His proffer had despised,
    Our Ordinance began to shoote amaine;
Continuing eight houres and more,
For why our King most deeply swore,
    Her Maiden-head that he would obtaine.

Chapter Four

When thus his Grace had spoken,
Hee sent her many a token,
    Firie balls, and burning brazen rings:
Faire broad arrowes sharpe and swift,
Which came among them with a drift,   5
    Well garnish'd with the gray goose wings.

This Maiden towne that lately
Did shew herselfe so stately,
    In seeking favour, many teares she shed:
Upon her knees then fell she downe,   10
Saying, O King of high renowne,
    Save now my life, and take my maidenhead.

Lo, thus her selfe she ventred,
And streight her streets wee entred,
    And to the market place we marched free: 15
Never a French-man durst withstand,
To hold a wepon in his hand,
    For all the gold that ever hee did see.

Their song being ended, our King cast them a purse with fifty
faire angells for a reward, commending both their skill and good 20
voyces, and after much pleasant communication, they had liberty
to depart; and when they came home, they told to their Master,
all their merriment before the King, and what reward his Grace
had bestowed on them; and powring the gold downe upon the
Table, the same being truly told by their Master, every mans 25
share came iust to five pound a piece. Which, when round *Robin*
saw, he swore he would bestow a supper upon his Master and
Mistresse that night, though it cost him two angels; which his
fellowes hearing, and seeing *Robins* liberall heart to be such, said,
they would ioyne with him, and laying their money together, 30
would have all the Shoomakers in *Westminster* to beare them
company.

    Content (quoth Robin) *with all my heart,*
    And twenty shillings I will spend for my part:
    And as I am true man, and sung before our King,   35
    As much shall each of you spend before our parting.

So shall we have musicke and gallant cheere,
Secke and Sugar, Claret wine, strong Ale and Beare.

This being concluded, they met all together at the signe of the
Bell, where they were so merry as might be, at what time *Robin*
5 began to blame his Master, that had not in three yeeres space
gotten his Mistresse with childe.

Hold thy peace (quoth he) all this while I haue but iested, but
when I fall once in earnest, thou shalt see her belly will rise like a
Tun of new Ale: thou know'st I am the Cocke of *Westminster*.

10 *I (quoth* Robin) *you had that name,*
More for your rising, than your goodnesse in Venus *game.*

The company at this laugh'd heartily, but seven yeeres after
this iest was remembred; for in all that space had not his wife
any child: Wherefore *Robin* would often say, that either his
15 Master was no perfect man, or else his Mistresse was in her in-
fancy nourished with the milk of a Mule, which bred such barren-
nesse in her; for till her dying day she never had child.

And after they had lived together, many yeeres, at last, *Richard*
Casteler dyed, and at his death he did divers good and godly
20 deeds: among many other things he gave to the City of *Westminster*
a worthy gift to the cherishing of the poore inhabitants for ever.
He also gave toward the reliefe of the poore fatherlesse children
of *Christs Hospitall* in *London,* to the value of forty pound land
by the yeere; and in the whole course of his life he was a very
25 bountifull man to all the decayed housekeepers of that place, leaving behind him a worthy example for other men to follow.

Chapter Five

CHAPTER V.

The pleasant Story of *Peachey* the famous Shoomaker of
Fleet-street in *London*.

M vch about this time, there lived in *London* a rich Shoomaker,
and a gallant housekeeper; who being a brave man of per- 5
son, bore a mind agreeable thereunto, and was therefore of most
men called lusty *Peachey:* hee kept all the yeere forty tall men on
worke, beside Prentises, and every one hee clothed in tawny coats,
which he gave as his livery to them, all with black caps and yellow
feathers; and every Sunday and holiday, when this gentleman-like 10
Citizen went to Church in his black gown garded with Velvet, it
was his order to have all his men in their liveries to wait upon
him, with every man his sword and buckler, ready at any time, if
need required.

It came to passe upon Saint *Georges* day, that this iolly Shoo- 15
maker (being servant to the Duke of *Suffolk*) went to the Court
with all his men after him, to give attendance upon his noble
Master, which some yong Gentlemen, more wanton than wise, beholding and envying his gallant mind, devised how they might
picke some quarrell, thereby to have occasion to try his manhood. 20

(Quoth they) Did you ever know a shoomaker, a sowter, a cobling
companion, brave it so with the best, as this fellow doth? see with
what a train of hardie squires he goes, what squaring lads they be:
they look as if they would fight with *Gargantua,* and make a fray
with the great Turk, and yet I durst lay my life they dare scantly 25
kill a Hedgehog: mark him I pray, I warrant you there is never a
Knight in this countrey that goes with so great a train.

Swounes (quoth one) it were a good sport to draw, and try what
they can do.

My Masters be advised (quoth another) and attempt nothing 30
rashly: I tell you this fellow is a hardy Coine, he is currant mettle
y-faith, and whensoever you try him, Ile warrant you shall finde
he will not flie a foot.

213

With that comes by lusty *Tom Stuteley* and *Strangwidge,* two
gallant Sea Captaines, who were attired all in Crimson Velvet, in
Marriners wide slops that reacht to the foot, in watched silk thrumb
hats and white feathers, having Pages attending with their weapons,
5 who seeing a cluster of Gentlemen in hard communication at the
Court gate, askt what was the matter?

Marry Captaine (quoth they) we are all beholding to yonder
lusty Gallant, that hath so many waiting on him with Tawny Coats.

Sblood, what is he (quoth *Stuteley*)?

10 He seemes to be a gallant man (said *Strangwidge*) whatsoever
he be: and were it not I see him in the Duke of *Suffolks* liverie,
I should have taken him by his train to be some Lord at the least.

Nay (quoth *Stuteley*) he is some Knight of good living.

Gentlemen (quoth they) how your iudgements deceive you: it is
15 certaine he is as good a Shooemaker as any is in *Fleetstreet.*

What? is he but a Shooemaker (quoth *Stuteley*)? O how that
word makes me scratch my elbo: Can a Shooemaker come to the
Court with more Servingmen at his heeles then Captaine *Stuteley*?
see how it makes my blood rise: O the passion of my heart, how
20 the villaine squares it out? see, see, what a company of handsome
fellowes follow him, it is twenty pound to a penny but they were
better borne then their Master.

Not so (quoth the Gentlemen) but I think their birth and bringing up was much alike, for they be all Shooemakers and his stoole
25 companions.

Now, by this iron and steell (quoth *Stuteley*) were it not that he
is attendant on the good Duke, I would have him by the eares
presently. I will lay an hundred pound, and stake it downe straight,
that Captaine *Strangwidge* and I will beat him and all his forty
30 men.

The Gentlemen being ready to set this match forward, greatly
commended the Captaines high courage: notwithstanding they
would not hazard their money on such a desperate match.

Well Gentlemen (quoth they) you say he dwels in *Fleetstreet,*
35 and that he is a Shoomaker, never trust us more if we become not
his customers, but the crossest customers shall he finde us that ever
came to his shop for shooes.

Nay (quoth *Stuteley*) we will bespeak Boots of him, and thus we
will raise our quarrell: when they are made, if they come not on
40 easie, and sit on our legs neatly, we will make them pluck them

off againe, and presently we will beat them in peeces about his pate, which if he seeme to take in dudgin, and with his men follow us into the street for revenge, if we make them not leap before us like Monkies, and force them run away like sheep-biters, let us lose our credits and Captainships for ever. 5

But what if you should chance to kill any of them (said the Gentlemen)?

Swounes (quoth they) what care we, we are bound to sea on a gallant voyage, wherein the King hath no small venture, and with-out us it cannot go forward, so that it is not the death of twenty 10 men can stay us at home, and therefore when they should be seek-ing of us in *Fleetstreet,* we would be seeking out the Coast of *Florida.*

You say well Captaines (quoth they) and no doubt if you do any such thing we shall heare of it: for the report thereof will be 15 famous through *London.*

Within a while after *Stuteley* and *Strangwidge,* having thus de-termined, came into *Fleetstreet,* and making inquiry for *Peachies* shop, they were by every man directed to the house: where, when they were come, they called for the good man of the house: the fore- 20 man of the shop demanded what their will was?

Why knave (quoth they) what carest thou, let us speak with thy Master.

Gentlemen (quoth he) if you lack any such commodity as we make, you shall finde me sufficient to serve you, for to that end 25 hath my Master set me in the shop.

Why, Iack-sauce (quoth *Stuteley*) you whorson peasant, know you to whom you speak?

The fellow being very cholerick, and somewhat displeased at these disdainfull speeches, made him this round answer: ask you 30 to whom I speak (quoth he)?

I, goodman flat cap (said *Strangwidge*) we ask to whom you speak?

Sir (quoth he) I speak to a Velvet foole, a silken slave that knowes not how to governe his tongue. 35

With that *Stuteley* swore like a madman and presently drew out a dudgin haft dagger that he had by his side, and began to lay at the fellow, which one of his fellowes seeing, flung a Last at his

---

[29] cholerick] Lange; chflecick 1639

head and feld him to the ground: *Strangwidge* thereupon drew his sword, but by that time the fellow had took downe his sword and buckler, which hung in the shop hard at hand, and therewith so well defended himselfe, that *Strangwidge* could do him no hurt:
5 and by that time *Stuteley* recovering crald up againe.

But *Peachie* hearing a great hurly burly in the shop, came forth and demanded the cause of the quarrell? his servants told him that those Gentlemen had given the Iourneymen very ill words.

How can they chuse but speak ill (quoth *Peachie*) for it may be
10 they never learn'd to speak well: whereupon he went unto them saying; how now, Captaines, how grew this quarrell twixt you and my men?

Thy men (quoth *Stuteley*)? thy Roags, and thy selfe is no better that brings them up.

15 Sir (quoth *Peachie*) you wrong me too much, and get you quickly from my doore, or, by this sunne that shines, ile set you packing, and therefore never think to outface me with great looks, for I tell thee *Stuteley* and *Strangwidge* both, did you look as big as the Devill I feare you not. And you forgot your maners too
20 much to give me such base tearms, for I would you well knew I keepe forty good fellowes in my house, that in respect of their manhood may seeme to be your equals.

O intollerable Comparison (quoth *Stuteley*) flesh and blood cannot beare such abuse. Ile tell thee what (quoth he) if we two
25 beat not thee and thy forty men, I durst be hangd up at thy doore.

Fie, fie, tis too much oddes (quoth *Peachy*) dare you two take ten? nay dare you fight with five?

Take that and try (quoth *Strangwidge*) and therewithall gave him a sound blow on the eare.

30 Nay this is too much (quoth *Peachy*) put up this and put up all. *Stuteley* and *Strangwidge* (quoth he) if you be men, meet me in *Lincolnes-Inne-fields* presently.

Content (quoth they) and thereupon went their wayes.

Peachie fetching straight his sword and buckler, call'd his man
35 *Iohn Abridges* to go with him, charging all the rest not to stir out of doores, and so into the fields they went, where immediately they met with these lusty Caveliers. The Captaines seeing him come only with one man, askt if that were all the helpe he had?

---

[15] you wrong] Lange; your wong 1639
[38] that were] there well 1639; there were   Lange

Chapter Five

I will request no more (quoth *Peachie*) to swinge you both out of the fields.

Brag is a good Dog (quoth *Stuteley*) but tell us, hast thou made thy Will, and set thy house in order?

What if I have not (quoth *Peachie*)?   5

Why then (quoth *Strangwidge*) for thy wife and childrens sake go home againe and do it, or else get more aide about thee to preserve thy life.

Why how now Master (quoth *Iohn Abridges*) come you into the field to fight with women? why these be two disguised butter 10 whores ile lay my life, that have more skill in scoulding then in fighting: but heare you (quoth he) if you be men, leave your foule words, and draw your faire weapons, and because I will spare your middle peece, if I strike a stroke below the girdle, call me Cut.

Sblood shall we be thus out-braved (quoth *Stuteley*)? and there- 15 with drawing their weapons, they fell to it lustily, where *Peachie* and his man laid so bravely about them, that they beat both the Captaines out of breath, in which fray, *Stuteley* was wounded in the head, and *Strangwidge* in the sword arme, but at last they were parted by many Gentlemen that came in good time to prevent 20 further mischiefe.

The Captaines got them straight to the Surgion, and *Peachie* with his man went directly home: and while they were a dressing, *Peachie* hearing how they were hurt, sent to *Stuteley* a kerchiefe by one of his men, and by another a scarffe to *Strangwidge*, by the 25 third he sent them a silver bottle of *Aqua vitae,* wishing them to be of good cheare, for hee intended to be better acquainted with them ere long. The Captaines finding these favours to be but flouts, were more grieved thereat, then at their hurt, and therefore with many disdainfull speeches, they refused his proffer'd curtesie.   30

And you shall understand that afterward *Peachies* men by two and two at a time, did often meet and fight with them, and so narrowly would they watch for them, that they could be in no place in peace, insomuch that the Captaines found fighting work enough, and a great deale more then willingly they would, whereby 35 they received many scarres and wounds in the body, so that lightly they were never out of Surgions hands. Upon a time it chanced that, being upon the point of their voyage, and shortly to go to

---

[26] sent them a silver] Folger; sent a 1639

217

sea: *Stuteley* and *Strangwidge* having beene at the Court, and newly come from my Lord-Admirals lodging, before they came to *Charing-crosse*, they were encountred by a couple of *Peachies* men, who presently drew upon them, and laid so freely about, that the two Cap-
5 taines were glad at length to house themselves for their refuge.

Now a plague on them (quoth *Stuteley*) shall we never be in quiet for these quoystrels? never were we so ferrited before, swownes we can no sooner look into the streets, but these shoomakers have vs by the eares: a pox on it that ever we medled with the rascals:
10 sblood they be as unluckie to be met, as a Hare on a iorney, or a sergeant on a Sunday morning, for ever one mischiefe or other followes it. Captaine *Strangwidge* (quoth he) there is no other shift but to seek their friendship, otherwise we are in danger every houre to be maimed, therefore to keep our lims sound against we
15 go to Sea, tis best to finde meanes to quiet this grudge.

Then (said *Strangwidge*) it were good to do so, if a man knew how: but you may be sure they will not easily be intreated, seeing we have so mightily abused them in speech.

Thus they cast in their mindes divers times by what meanes
20 they might be reconciled: and albeit they sent divers of their friends unto Master *Peachie* and his men, yet they would not yeeld, nor give consent to be appeased, nor to put up such wrong as they had received without further revenge: so that the Captaines were at length constrained to make sute to the Duke of *Suffolk* to take up
25 the matter: who most honorably performed their request: and so the grudge ended betwixt them, to the great credit of Master *Peachie*, and all his men.

12 it. Captaine] Folger; ⌣, ⌣ 1639
20 of] Folger; *om.* 1639
21 *Peachie* ∧ and his] Folger; *Peachie*, and by his 1639

Chapter Six

CHAPTER VI.

How *Harrie Nevell,* and *Tom Drum* came to serue *Peachey*
of *Fleet-street.*

The fame of *Peachey,* running through *England* by meanes of
the frayes which he and his men had with *Stuteley* and *Strang-* 5
widge, it made many of that occupation desirous to come and
dwell with him, for beside that he was a tall man of his hands,
he was also an excellent good workman, and therewithall a bountifull house keeper. Among many other that was desirous of his service, there was one called *Tom Drum,* that had a great minde to be 10
his man, a very odde fellow, and one that was sore infected with
the sin of cogging: this boasting companion, sitting on a time sadly
at work in his Masters shop at *Petworth,* and seeing the Sun shine
very faire, made no more to doe but suddenly shrowded up
S. *Hughes* bones, and taking downe his pike-staffe, clapt his pack at 15
his back, and called for his Master, who comming into the shop,
and seeing his man prepared to be prauncing abroad, demanded
what the matter was that he followed not his businesse.

O Master (quoth he) see you not how sweetly the Sun shines, and
how trimly the trees are deckt with green leaves? 20
Well and how then (quoth his Master)?
Marry sir (quoth he) having a great mind to heare the small
birds sing, and seeing the weather fitter to walk then to work, I
called you forth to take my leave and to bid you farewell, I hope
sir, I have no wages in your hand, have I? 25
Why no (quoth his Master) thou wilt be sure to take an order
for that, and therefore seeing thou wilt be gone, adue.
God be with you good master (quoth he) and farewell all good
fellowes of the gentle craft, and therewith he departed.
The iourneymen of the Towne hearing that *Tom Drum* went 30
away, according to their ancient custome they gathered themselves
together to drink with him, and to bring him out of town: and

25 wages] Folger; wager 1639   hand, have I?] Folger; hand. 1639

to this intent, up they go with him to the signe of the Crowne, where they parted not till they had drunk a Stand of Ale drie.

Which being done, they bring him a mile on his way, carrying a gallon of beere with them: and lastly there once againe they drink
5 to his good health, and to *Crispianus* soule: and to all the good fellowes of *Kerbfoord:* which being done, they all shook him by the hand, and with hollowing and whooping, so long as they can see him, they bid him a hundred times farewell.

So soone as he was gone out of their whooping, the sweat reek-
10 ing in his hand, and the Ale in his head, he trips so light in the highway, that he feeles not the ground he goes on: and therefore, being in a merry vaine, and desirous to drive out the weary way, as he walks he begins thus pleasantly to sing:

> The Primrose in the greene Forrest,
> 15   the Violets that be gay:
> The double Dazies and the rest,
>   that trimly decks the way,
> Doth move the spirits to brave delights,
>   where beauties Darlings be:
> 20   With hey tricksie, trim goe tricksie,
>   under the greenewood tree.

The singing of this song awaked a young Gentleman whom sorrow had laid asleepe on a greene bank by the high wayes side. Who having unadvisedly displeased his Parents, in a cholerick
25 humour departed from them, betaking himselfe to travell, thereby to try how fortune would favour him abroad: but having now spent all his money, he was in a wofull taking, not knowing what to do, for never had he beene brought up to any trade, whereby he might be able to get a penny at his need. Wherefore being in
30 this distresse, he was fully purposed to go to *London,* and there to learne some occupation, whereby he might keep himself a true man, and not to be driven to seek succour of his friends.

Now therefore when he heard *Tom Drum* so trimly tune it on the

5 *Crispianus*] Folger; *Chrispianus* 1639
7 hollowing] Folger; hallowing 1639
15 that] Folger; they 1639
18 to] Folger; with 1639
19 where] Folger; whose 1639

way, raising himselfe from the sad ground, he awaited his comming, at whose sudden sight *Tom Drum* started like one that had spied an Adder: and seeing him provided with a good sword and buckler, supposed he had beene one that waited for a fat purse: for which cause he began thus to enter parly with him.   5

Good fellow (quoth he) God give you good morrow, but ill speed.

Why saist thou so (quoth *Harrie*)?

Because (said *Tom*) by the good light of the day thou maist see to passe beside me, and that by thy speeding ill, I may speed the better.   10

What hast thou such store of money (quoth *Harrie*) that thou art loath to lose it?

No by my faith (quoth he) I have so little that I cannot spare it: for I assure thee all my store is but one poore pennie, and that thou maist see heere under my little finger.   15

Why then (quoth *Harrie*) if I were minded to assault thee, it should be more to rob thee of thy manhood then thy money: but tell me what pack is that thou bearest at thy back?

Marry they be Saint *Hughes* bones.

Saint *Hughes* bones (quoth *Harrie*) what is that?   20

A kind of commodity (said *Tom*) which I cannot misse, for they be my working tooles.

I pray thee (said *Harrie*) what occupation art thou?

Sir (quoth he) I am a Goldsmith that makes rings for womens heeles.   25

What meanest thou by that (said *Harrie*)?

I am (quoth *Tom*) of the Gentle Craft, vulgarly called a Shoo-maker.

The happier art thou (quoth *Harrie*) that thou hast a trade to live by, for by that means thou carriest credit with thee in every   30 place: but tell me good friend, what is thy name, and how far dost thou travell this way?

Sir (quoth he) I travell to the next towne, but my iorney is to *London*, and as for my name, I am not ashamed to shew it: For my name is a Nowne substantive that may be felt, heard, and   35 understood, and to speak the truth I am called: whoe there, I

---

15 heere] Folger; *om.* 1639
29 art thou] Folger; thou art 1639
35 and] Folger; or 1639

trust sir you ask for no hurt, you are no Bayliffe nor Bayliffs man, are ye?

No not I (said *Harrie*).

Gods blessing on you (quoth he) I love you the better: for I was
5 never so fraid lest my Hostesse of the *George* in *Petworth* had sent you to arrest me, for I think I owe her some ten Groats on the score, set up in very faire Chalk, as one of the principals of her house is able to testifie: but I pray God send her meat, for I verely think I shall never send her monie.

10 But yet (quoth *Harrie*) I know not how to call your name.

Verily (said he) I am called *Thomas Drum* or *Tom Drum*, chuse you whether.

Well *Thomas* (quoth *Harrie*) I perceive thou art a man and a good fellow, therefore I will not be strange to open my need unto
15 thee. I have beene unto my parents untoward, and more then that, not knowing when I was well, wilfully I came from them: and now that I have spent all my money and worne my selfe out of credit, I have vtterly undone my selfe, for I am not worth a groat, nor no man will trust me for two pence.

20 Why then (quoth *Tom*) thou art not worth so much as goodman *Luters* lame nagge, for my Lord of *Northumberlands* hunts-man would have given halfe a Crowne for him to have fedde his dogges: notwithstanding be of good cheere, if thou wilt goe to *London* with me, I will beare thy charges, and, Ifaith, at the next towne
25 we will be merry and have good cheere.

Alas (quoth *Harry*) how can that be, seeing you have but one penny?

Ile tell thee what (quoth *Tom*) wert thou a Shoomaker as I am, thou mightst goe with a single penny under thy finger, and trauell
30 all *England* over, and at every good towne, have both meate, drinke and lodging of the best, and yet have thy penny still in store, as when we come to *Gilford* you shall soone see.

Beleeve me (quoth *Harry*) that is more then any tradesmen in *England* els can doe.

35 Tush (quoth *Tom*). Shoomakers will not see one another lacke,

⁶ to] Folger; for to 1639   on] Folger; of 1639
²⁸ Ile] Folger; I 1639
³⁰ meate,] Folger; meate ∧ and 1639
³¹ still] Folger; *om.* 1639

for it is our vse if wee know of a good fellow that comes to towne, wanting either meate or money, and that he make himselfe knowne, he shall neede to take no further care, for he shall be sure that the jornymen of that place will not onely give him kinde wel-come, but also provide him all things necessary of free cost: And 5 if he be disposed to worke among them, he shall have a Master provided by their meanes, without any sute made by himselfe at all.

Verily (quoth *Harry*) thou dost rauish me with the good report of thy passing kind and curteous trade, and I would spend part of 10 my gentle bloud, to be of the gentle Craft: and for thy curtesie if thou wouldst teach it mee, I would annoint thee a gentleman for ever.

Wilt thou say and hold (quoth *Tom*)?

Or els hang me (said *Harry*). 15

Then (said he) annoint me a Gentleman, and I will shape thee for a Shoomaker straight.

Thereupon *Harry* tooke his knife, and cutting his finger, all besmeared *Tom-Drums* face with his bloud, that hee made him looke like the Image of *Bred-streete* corner, or rather like the 20 *Sarazines-head* without *New-gate.*

Tom Drum, seeing him doe so, said he might by that means as well annoint him a Ioyner, as a Gentleman.

Nay (said *Harry*) I do not deceiue thee I warrant thee, seeing this blood did spring from a Gentleman, if thou wilt not beleeve 25 me, aske all the men in Towne-malin, and they will say the like.

Well, Ile take thy word (quoth *Tom*). And therefore looke that presently thou strip thy selfe, for I will cast thee in a Shoomakers mould by and by.

Harry perceiving his meaning did what he willed, and so he 30 was suted in *Toms* attire, and *Tom* in his; so that *Harry* bore the pike staffe and Saint *Hughes* bones: and *Tom* swaggered with his sword and buckler; and comming in this sort to *Gilford,* they were both taken for shoomakers, and very hartely welcomed by the jorneymen of that place, especially *Harry,* because they never 35 saw him before: And at their meeting they askt him and if he could sing, or sound the Trumpet, or play on the Flute, or recon

*19 besmeared] to besmeared Folger; to smeared 1639
*26 Towne-malin] Folger; the towne-Malin 1639

up his tooles in rime, or manfully handle his pike staffe, or fight with sword and buckler?

Beleeve me (quoth *Harry*) I can neither sound the Trumpet, nor play on the Flute: and beshroe his nose that made me a shoo-
5 maker, for he never taught me to recon up my tooles in rime nor in prose.

Tom hearing him say so, told them that he made him of an old serving man a new shoomaker.

When was that (quoth they)?

10 Marry (saith he) when I was annointed a Gentleman, for I thinke this face can shew, that I have gentle blood about me.

Why then (quoth they) thou art but a painted Gentleman, but we must account this young man wise, that to auoid misery betakes himselfe to follow our mistery, for cunning continueth when for-
15 tune fleeteth, but it will be hard for such as never were brought up to bodily labour to frame their fine fingers to any course faculty.

Not a whit (quoth *Harry*) for labour by custome becommeth easie.

Thou saist true (said *Tom*) for I durst lay a good wager I have
20 made more shooes in one day then all the iorney-men here have done in a month.

With that one of the jorney-men began to chafe, saying, how many paire of shooes hast thou made in a day?

I made, quoth Tom, when the daies were at longest, eight score
25 paire of shooes in one day.

O monstrous detestable lye (quoth they) and thereupon one ran into the chimney and cried, come againe *Clement,* come againe.

Who calst thou (quoth *Tom*)?

I call *Clement carry lye,* that runnes Poste betwixt the Turke,
30 and the Devill; that he may take his full loading ere he goe, for the best jorneyman that ever I knew, never made aboue ten paire in a day in his life: and I will lay my whole yeeres wages with thee, that thou canst not make twenty paire in a day as they ought to be: I should be ashamed but to doe as much as another, and I

---

2 sword] Folger; a sword 1639
10 for] Folger; *om.* 1639
14 our] Folger; *om.* 1639
16 bodily] Folger; the bodily 1639
19 for] Folger; *om.* 1639
23 paire] Folger; a paire 1639
28 Who] Folger; Whom 1639

never saw him yet that could out worke me, yet dare not I take upon me to make a doozen paire of shooes in a day: but tis an old saying, they brag most that can doe least.

Why thou Puppie (quoth *Tom*) thou house Doue, thou Cricket, that never crept further then the chimney corner, tell me what Countries hast thou trauelled? 5

Far enough (quoth he) to prove as good a work-man as thou art.

I deny that (quoth *Tom*) for I have been where I have seene men headed like Dogs, and women of the same shape, where if thou hadst offered them a kisse, they would have beene ready to have snapt off thy nose: othersome I have seen, that one of their legs hath been as good as a penthouse to couer their whole bodies, and yet I have made them shooes to serve their feet, which I am sure thou couldest never do: nay if thou wilt go with me, if thou seest me not make an hundred paire of shooes from sunrising to sunsetting, count me worse then a stinking Mackrell. 10 15

Now verily thy talke stinkes too much (quoth they) and if thou canst do so, never make further jorney, but try the matter heere.

I tell you (quoth *Tom*) I cannot try it in *England,* nor yet in *France, Spaine,* or *Italy,* nor in any part of the low countries, nor in high *Germany, Sweathland,* or *Polonia.* 20

We think no lesse (quoth they) nor in any part of the world beside.

Yes (quoth *Tom*) I can do it as we trauell to *Russia,* for there every day is fiue and fiftie of our dayes in length: nay Ile tell you further, quoth *Tom,* in some parts of the world where I have been, it is day for halfe a yeare together, and the other halfe yeare is continually night: and goe no further, quoth he, but into the further part of *Scotland,* and you shall find one day there (in the month of Iune) to be foure and twenty houres long, and there-fore my Masters while you live, take heed how you contrary a traueller, for therein you shall but bewray your owne ignorance, and make your selves mocking stockes to men of knowledge. 25 30

And trauellers (quoth they) uncontrouled, have liberty to vtter what lies they list. 35

My masters tell me (quoth *Tom*) were you not borne in *Arcadia?*

² tis] Folger; it is 1639
⁴ Puppie] Puple Folger
³⁶ My] Folger; *om.* 1639

No (quoth they) but why aske you?

Because (said *Tom*) that countrey doth most abound in plenty of Asses, where they swarme as thicke as Bees in *Sicilly*.

We have cause to give you much thanks (quoth they) for calling us
5 Asses so kindly.

Not so (said *Tom*) I did but aske a question; but seeing you are so cunning, tell mee what Countrey breeds the best Hides, and Leather, and from whence have we the best Corke?

Our best Corke comes from *Portugall* (quoth they) but the best
10 Leather grows in our owne land.

I deny it (quoth *Tom*) there is I confesse good Corke in *Portugall*, but the best grows in *Sparta;* but for Hides and Lether there is none comparable to that in *Siciona:* where I have made a man a paire of shooes that hath lasted him a twelve month to toyle in
15 every day. O tis a gallant Countrey, for Ile tell you what, there is never a shoomaker in *England* that kept so many men as I did at that time.

Then said the rest, thou speakest thou knowest not what: Master *Peachy* of *Fleetstreete* keeps continually forty men a work, and the
20 green-King of *Saint-Martins* hath at this time little lesse then three-score journey men.

This is pretty well (quoth *Tom*) but what say you to him that for halfe a yeere together, kept waiting on him above a hundred men that never did him stitch of work? this was a shoomaker of
25 some account.

But who was that (quoth they)?

Marry (quoth *Tom*) simple though I stand heere, it was my selfe, and yet I never made brags of it.

O what a shamelesse lyer art thou (quoth they) we never knew
30 thee able to keep one man.

Now, by this bread (said *Tom*) you do me mighty wrong, and were it not that you be all of the gentle Craft, which science I doe so greatly love and reuerence, this Iron and steele should make it

---

² most] Folger; more 1639

³ Bees in *Sicilly*.] Bees ∧ in *Sicilly:* Folger; Bees, in *Cicily* ∧ 1639

⁴ much] Folger; *om.* 1639

¹⁵ Ile] Folger; I 1639

²² This] Folger; Then 1639

³² you] Folger; ye 1639   the gentle] Folger; this gentle 1639

good upon your flesh, for I tell you once againe, I have beene Master
of an hundred men, and put sixe-score to the hundred.

I pray you tell us (quoth they) what men were they?

What men were they (quoth *Tom*) they were vermin.

In troth (quoth they) we thought as much, and we commend 5
you for telling truth, and we suppose if you were well searcht we
should find twenty vermin waiting on you still. But tell vs *Tom,*
art thou minded to be Master *Peachies* man?

I am (quoth he) except he will make me his fellow.

By the Masse (quoth they) then wert thou best to have thy 10
wards ready, and thy hilts sure, for he receives no servant before
he tries his man-hood.

So much the better (quoth *Tom*) and for that purpose I poste up
to *London.*

Thus having had at *Gilford* very good cheere, the jorney-men 15
of the towne paid for all, and beside gave them money in their
purses to spend by the way, and so toward *London* they went with
all speed.

CHAPTER VII.

How the wilde Knight Sir *Iohn Rainsford* for burying a 20
Massing Priest alive, was faine to leave his Lady, and
forsake his house, till he had obtained his pardon of
the King: who meeting with *Harry Nevell,* and *Tom
Drum,* went with them to serve *Peachy* of *Fleetstreet,*
where for a while he became a Shoomaker. 25

You shall understand that at this time there lived a gallant
Knight called Sir *Iohn Rainsford,* who was for his courage
and valiant heart inferiour to few men liuing: he kept a bountifull

*2 sixe-score] Folger; sixteene score 1639
23 *Harry*] Folger; *Henry* 1639
24 them] Folger; him 1639
27 *Rainsford*] Folger; *Ransford* 1639
28 inferiour] Folger; inferour 1639

house, and a brave company of tall men to waite upon him. To all the poore round about where he dwelt, he was very charitable, releeving them daily both with money and meate; he was a famous Courtier, and in great favour with the King, and the onely thing
5 that disgraced his vertues, was this, that he was something wild in behaviour, and wilfull in his attempts, often repenting sadly what he committed rashly.

It came to passe upon a time, that as this couragious Knight was riding home to his own house, there was at a certaine village, a
10 corps carried to be buried, the deceased father of fiue small children and the late husband of a wofull Widow, whose pouerty was such, that she had no money to pay for his buriall: which thing Sir *Iohn* the parish Priest doubting, would not by any meanes doe his duty to the dead man, except he might first have his money.
15 The Widdow and her children, with many teares intreated him to do his office, but he would not be perswaded, saying: What you beggers, would you have me open my sacred lips to invocate and call upon the King of Heaven, to receiue thy husbands soule, and to perswade our great Grandmother the earth to wrap his cold
20 body in her warme bosome, for nothing? I tel thee no: first shall his soule frie in the flames of purgatory, till it be as thin as a pancake, and his body remaine aboue ground till the Crowes have pickt his carrion carkasse to the bare bones: and therefore leave your puling, and prate no more, least you make me as chollericke
25 as a quaile.

And therewithall, as he was going away, the poore Widdow falling on her knees, pluckt him by the gowne, saying: good Sir *Iohn,* for sweet Saint *Charity,* say one *Aue Maria,* or one *Pater noster,* and let my poore husbands corps be couered, though it be
30 but with one handfull of holy ground.

Nay dame (quoth he) do you remember at the last shrift how you served me? you would not, no forsooth you would not: and now good Mistris I will not: no penny, no *Pater noster,* that is flat: I pray you now see if your honesty be sufficient to keepe your
35 husband from the Crowes. I thought a time would come at length to cry quittance for your coynes: and with that word away he went.

The poore Widdow seeing his obstinacy, with a heavy heart

11 Widow] Folger; Widdw 1639
16 saying:] Folger; ∼? 1639

turned to the high wayes side, which was hard adioyning to the Church-yard, and there she and her children wofully begged of the passers by, some money to bury their fathers dead body.

At the last Sir *Iohn* came riding with all his men, of whom the poor Widdow in this manner began to aske his almes: good Sir 5 (quoth she) if ever womans misery mooved your heart to pitty, give me one penny for Gods sake, toward the burying of my poore husband: in like manner the children cried, saying, one penny for Christ his sake good Master, good Master one penny.

Sir *Iohn,* hearing their lamentable cry, and seeing the dead corps 10 lying there, askt why the Priest did not bury it?

O Sir Knight (quoth she) I have no money to pay for the buriall; and therefore the Priest will not doe it.

No (quoth Sir *Iohn*)? by Gods blessed mother I sweare, Ile make him bury the dead or Ile bury him alive: whereupon he willed 15 one of his men presently to goe to the Parsonage for the Priest, and to bring him thither immediately. His man did so, and foorth came Sir *Iohn,* in his gowne and corner cap, roughly demanding who would speake with him?

That would I (quoth Sir *Iohn Rainesford*): therefore tell me, 20 how comes it to passe, that according to order you put not this dead corps into the pit?

Sir (quoth he) because according to order they will not pay me for my paines.

Aboue all men (quoth Sir *Iohn*) Priestes should respect the poore, 25 and charitably regard the state of the needy, because they them-selves doe teach charity to the people, and perswade men unto works of mercy: and therefore Sir *Iohn,* seeing good deeds are meritorious, doe you win heaven by this good work, and let the dead possesse their due. 30

I, so they shall (said the Priest) so I may not loose my due: for I tell you further, I count it little better then folly, to fill my soule with pleasure by emptying my purse with coine.

Wilt thou not bury him (said the Knight)?

No, not without money (said the Priest). 35

---

¹ turned to] Folger; turned into 1639
⁴ At the last] Folger; At last 1639
⁹ good Master, good Master] Folger; good Master 1639
¹⁷ man] Folger; men 1639
²⁹ and let] Folger; let 1639

I pray thee (said the Knight) let me intreat thee for this time to doe it, because the woman is poor.

Then let me intreat you to pay me (quoth the Priest) because you are rich.

5　Sir *Iohn Rainsford* seeing him stand so peremptory on his points, swore a deep oath, that it were best for him to bury him, or (quoth he) Ile bury thee.

Bury me (said the Priest)? A fig for you, and bury blind bayard when he is dead, or the dogs that your Hauks will not eate.

10　The Knight at these words being maruelous angry commanded his men to take him up and cast him into the grave: his men made no more to do, but presently upon their Masters word tooke up the Priest, and wrapping him round in his gowne, put him quicke into the grave, and the rest cast earth upon him as fast as they

15　could, at what time the Priest cried out, hold, hold, for Gods sake, let me rise and I will bury him.

Nay soft (quoth the Knight) thou art not like to rise, no rising heere before the generall resurrection, that thou shalt rise to judgement.

20　And therefore quicke as he was they buried him, which being done, he commanded the Sexton to make another grave for the dead man, and sending for another Priest, he askt him if he wold bury the dead without money, who, making twenty legs, shivering and shaking with feare, answered: I forsooth with all my heart,

25　for they are knaves and no Christians that will not doe it.

Now when the dead man was buried, the Knight gave the poore Widdow an angell in gold to comfort her and her children, and so rode his way.

When he came home, he told to his Lady what he had done;

30　who greatly grieving thereat, wisht he had paid for twenty burials, rather then he had made that one buriall.

Tis done now (said the Knight) and undone it cannot be againe, though with griefe I should kill my selfe.

Now you shall understand that the Deane of the Dioces, having

35　word hereof, rode up presently to *London*, and made a great complaint thereof unto the King, which when his grace had considered, he was very wroth thereat, and therefore sent down pursevants to apprehend the Knight, but he before had forsaken

---

²⁹ told to] Folger; told 1639

his house, and wandred in disguise up and downe the Countrey.
His Lady in the meane space made great suite for his pardon, being therein assisted by divers grave Counsellors, and Noble Lords,
who much lamented the Knights case: notwithstanding they could
hardly forbeare laughing many times when they thought upon this 5
mad pranke.

But as Sir *Iohn* disguisedly wandred, he chanced twixt *Gilford*
and *London* to light in the company with *Harry Nevell* and *Tom
Drum:* But *Harry* vewing him well in the face, discried by his
countenance what he was, and maruelling much to see him in 10
such distresse, made himselfe not known, but sounded him in this
sort.

Sir (quoth he) whither do you wander this way, or to what place
trauell you?

Gentle youth (quoth he) fitly dost thou aske me whither I wander, 15
seeing indeed we doe all but wander in this vale of misery: dost
thou demand whither I trauell? nay rather aske wherefore I trauell,
or wherewith I trauell? and then could I soone answer thee.

Sbones (quoth *Tom*) I durst lay a haporth of Ale, that the
Peasant is in labour with love. 20

Nay (quoth Sir *Iohn*) hadst thou said I had trauelled with griefe,
and that I was in labour with sorrow, then hadst thou said right,
for I may say to thee, I have had a sore labour continuing this
month in paine, and yet is not the time of my deliuerance come,
wherein I should be freed from this untoward child of care: thou 25
didst thinke I was in love, O would to God it were so, for while I
was in love, my dayes ran foorth in plesant houres, but I am cast
off like a lumpe of earth from the gardiners spade: I love, but I am
not beloved, but rather hated and despised.

Tush (quoth *Tom*) bridle these foolish passions, for Ile tell thee 30
what, hunger asswageth love, and so doth time, but if thou be not
able to doe any of these, then to take an halter, which if thou
doest vse as it ought, if ever thou complaine more, of sorrow or
care, never trust my word for a cupple of blacke puddings.

Belike (said Sir *Iohn*) thou hast been some hangman that thou 35
art so cunning in the nature of an halter: but howsoever thou

³ grave] Folger; great 1639
²¹ had] Folger; *om.* 1639
²³ continuing] Folger; continually 1639

accountest it good, yet it is an Ill word foure times a yeer at *Newgate*, and as small comfort is it to me to heare it rehearst at this time.

Indeed (said *Harry*) these are unsauory tearmes to be spoken to
5 a sorrowfull man: neither have any of us great cause to be merry at this meeting, considering the hard cases wee are in, that are both masterlesse, and moneylesse, which if God doe not soone send us, will cause our sodaine misery.

With that the Knight turning his head, pluckt his hat to his eyes
10 to hide the teares that trickled down his face, saying, O my masters, want of money cannot make a man miserable, if he have health and liberty, to worke for his living, but indeed the frownes of a good Master, the displeasure of a good Master, the hate of a good Master, may easily make a servant miserable, as by mine own
15 experience I have seen, and to my grief but lately felt.

What man, be blith (said *Tom*) and never grieve so much for the Ill will of a Master. God keepe me from being of thy mind, for if I should have grieved at the Ill will of every Master that I have serued, I verely thinke I had kild a proper man long ere this; for
20 I am sure I have had as many Masters, as there are Market townes in *England*.

And yet perhaps (quoth *Harry*) none so good a Master as his was.

Never did man speake truer word, said the Knight, for he was
25 to me good, kind and liberall, but howsoever he hath banisht me his house, yet shall my heart serue him while I live: now doth it come in my mind, how happy they are that live in his favour: how blessed they be that enioy his presence; O were my head once againe shadowed under his faire roofe, it would expell all unquiet thoughts,
30 which like milstones presseth downe my hearts comfort.

What, would you goe dwell with him againe (quoth *Tom*)? fie, what a base mind doe you beare; were it to me, by this flesh and bloud, I would rather run as far as *Ierusalem* to seeke a Master.

Tom, Tom (said the Knight) I know this, wealth makes men
35 lofty, but want makes men lowly, and commonly gentle. Masters have proud servants, but had I beene as wise, as I was wilfull, I might have led a happy life, but if teares might satisfie for mine offence, I would quickly recouer his favour.

[19] had kild] Folger; should have kild 1639

Chapter Seven

Hereupon the wofull Knight would have parted their company, but *Harry* secretly conferring with him had knowledge how his griefe grew, and making themselves known the one to the other, agreed to goe to *London* together, and there to try what fortune would befall them. 5

The Knight tooke great comfort by this conference, and having good store of gold about him, made them great cheere at *King-stone,* and in the end was content to take their counsaile: and comming into *Fleet-streete, Tom Drum* brought them to *Peachies* house, where such meanes was made, that at last upon the tryall of 10 their manhood, they were all entertained; and so well did *Peachy* like of Sir *Iohn* that he vowed he should not be his man, but his fellow.

Within short time after the French-men had landed in the Ile of *Wight,* about two thousand men of warre, who burned and 15 spoyled the Country very sore, for which cause the King had made ready an army of men to goe thither. *Peachy* at his owne proper cost, set forth thirty of his owne servants, well armed at all essayes, and himselfe as Captaine over them mustred before the King: who liked so well of them, that he chose out seaven of that com- 20 pany for his owne Guard; at what time Sir *Iohn,* in disguised manner shewed there such good service, that thereby he won his Majesties high favour, and was by him most graciously pardoned. *Peachy* was hereupon made the King's Shoomaker, who lived long after in great favour and estimation, both with his Majesty and all 25 the honourable Lords of the Court.

⁷ good] Folger; *om.* 1639
¹¹⁻¹² did *Peachy* like] Folger; *Peachy* liked 1639

233

CHAPTER VIII.

Of *Tom Drums* vants, and his rare intertainment at Mistris *Farmers* house, the faire Widdow of *Fleet-street*.

Tere lived in *Fleet-streete* at this time a faire Widdow, who was
5 as famous for her beauty, as she was esteemed for her wealth, she
was beloved of many Gentlemen, and sued unto by divers Cittizens,
but so deepe was the memory of her late husband ingrauen in her
heart, that she vtterly refused marriage leading a sober and solemne
life.
10 *Harry Nevell* having his heart fired with the bright beams of
this blazing Comet, sought all meanes possible to quench the heate
thereof with the floudes of her favourable curtesie: and lacking
meanes to bring himselfe acquainted with so curious a peece, bewrayed by his outward sighs, his inward sorrows: which upon
15 a time, *Tom Drum* perceiving, demanded the cause of his late
conceiued griefe, saying, How now *Hal,* what wind blowes so bleake
on your cheekes now? tell me mad wag, hath *Cupid* and you had
a combate lately? why lookest thou so sad? hath the blind slave
giuen thee a bloody nose, or a broken head?
20 Oh, no *Tom* (quoth he) that little tyrant aimes at no other
part but the heart, therefore tis my heart, and not my head that
bleeds.
With whom *Hal,* with whom art thou in love, tell me man? it
may be I may pleasure thee more in that matter then my Lord
25 Maior: therefore, Ifaith *Harry* say who is it? never be afraid man
to unbuckle your Budget of close counsell to me, for if I bewray
your secrets call me dogs-nose, and spit in my face like a young
kitling. I tell the *Harry,* I am held in greater account among women

5 as famous] Folger; famous 1639
16 *Hal*] Folger; *Hall* 1639
23 *Hal*] Folger; *Hall* 1639
25 Maior] Folger; Major 1639
28 held in] heldin Folger; holden in 1639

then you are aware, and they will more willingly shew their secrets to me then to their ghostly father.

But art thou so in favour with fine wenches (quoth *Harry*)?

Ifaith Sir I (quoth *Tom*) for I tro I have not lived thus long, but I know how to make a woman love me, by a cunning tricke 5 that I have: I durst lay my life, I will make a dozen maids runne after me twenty mile for one nights lodging, striving among themselves who should first bestow her maiden-head upon me.

That tricke surpasses of all the trickes that ever I heard (quoth *Harry*). 10

Nay (quoth *Tom*) Ile tell thee once what a merry pranke I plaid, God forgive me for it: upon a time, on a Saterday in the evening, I went into *East-cheape* of purpose to spie what pretty wenches came to Market, where I saw a great many as fresh as flowers in May, tripping up and down the streets with handbaskets in their 15 hands, in red stammell petticoates, cleane neckerchers and fine holland aprons as white as a Lilly: I did no more but carry the right leg of a Turtle under my left arme, and immediately the wenches were so inamoured with my sight that they forsooke the butchers shops, and inticed me into a Tauerne, where they spent 20 all the money they should have laid out at Market, onely to make me merry: and never had I so much to doe, as to be rid of their company where they were ready to fall together by the eares, for the kisses they would have bestowed on me.

But it may be (quoth *Harry*) your art would faile you now, to 25 help your friend at a dead lift.

Not so (said *Tom*) and therefore if there be any in this street that thou hast a mind unto, thou shalt carry but the head of a dead crow about thee, and it shall be of force to bring her to thy bed, were it fine Mistres *Farmer* her self. 30

But art thou acquainted with her (quoth *Harry*) or dost thou thinke thou couldst prefer a friend to her speech?

---

⁴ for] Folger; and 1639
⁷ mile] Folger; miles 1639
⁷⁻⁸ among themselves] Folger; *om.* 1639
⁸ upon] Folger; on 1639
⁹ the trickes] Folger; *om.* 1639
¹² evening] Folger; morning 1639
²⁴ on] Folger; upon 1639
²⁵ you] Folger; me 1639

Me thinkes I should (quoth *Tom*), why I tell thee I am more familiar with her then with *Doll* our kitchen drudge: why man she will doe any thing at my request, nay, I can command her in some sort, for I tell thee she will not scant be seene in the street, though
5 some would give her twenty pound for every step, and I did but slightly request her to walke into the fields with me, and straight she went, and I never come into her house, but I have such entertainment as no man hath the like: for as soone as ever she sees me set footing on her checkquerd pavement, presently with a smiling
10 looke, she meetes me halfe way, saying, what my friend *Tom-Drum?* honest *Thomas*, by my Christian soule, hartily welcome: then straight a chair and a cushion is fetcht for me, and the best cheere in the house set on the table, and then sitting downe by my side in her silken gowne, she shakes me by the hand and bids me wel-
15 come, and so laying meate on my trencher with a silver forke, she wishes me frolicke, at what time all the secrets of her heart she imparts unto me, crauing my opinion in the premises.

I assure thee (said *Harry*) these are high favours, well bewraying the great friendship that she beares thee, and I much maruell
20 that thou, being a young man, wilt not seeke a wife that is so wealthy, and so make thy selfe famous, by marrying Mistris *Farmer*, for it is likely she could will a way to make him her husband, to whom she opens her hearts secrets.

Tis true (quoth *Tom*) and I know that if I spoke but halfe a
25 word she would never deny me: nay she would spend ten of her twelve silver Apostles, on condition I would vouchsafe to be her husband. But wot you what *Harry*, it is well known though Lillies be faire in shew, they be foule in smell, and women as they are beautifull so are they deceitfull: beside, Mistris *Farmer* is too old
30 for me.

Too old (quoth *Harry*)? why man she is not so old as Charing Crosse for her gate is not crooked, nor her face withered: but were she an hundred yeare old, having so strong a body and so faire

---

¹ Me thinkes I should] Folger; I 1639
² kitchen drudge] kitching drudge Folger; kithen-drudge 1639
⁷ her house] Folger; the house 1639
¹³ set] Folger; is set 1639
¹⁸ these] Folger; those 1639
²² will] well Folger, 1639
*³² withered] wethered Folger

a face, she were not in my opinion much to be mislikt; yet in my
conscience I thinke, since first her faire eyes beheld the bright
sunne, she never tasted the fruites of twenty flourishing Somers: nor
scant felt the nipping frostes of nineteene cold winters, and therefore her age need be no hurt to her marriage. 5

Ile tell thee my mind (quoth *Tom*) after a woman is past sixteene
yeeres old, I will not give fifteene blew buttons for her: but tell
me *Harry*, dost thou like her? if thou dost, say so, and I will warrant
her thy owne.

Gentle *Tom Drum* (quoth *Harry*) the true figure of unfained 10
friendship, and the assured Map of manhood, doe but prefer me
to her acquaintance, and I will request no greater curtesie.

Here is my hand (quoth *Tom*) it shall be done, and on Thursday
at night next we will goe thither, and then thou shalt see whether
Tom Drum can command any thing in Mistresse *Farmers* house 15
or no.

The day being thus set downe, *Harry* had prepared himselfe
a faire sute of apparell against the time, and beside had bought
certaine giftes to bestow on the faire Widdow: *Tom Drum* in like
sort had drest himselfe in the best manner he might, still bearing 20
Harry in hand that none in the world should be better welcome
then he to the Widdow: which God wot was nothing so, for she
never respected him but onely for the shooes he brought her: but
you shall see how it fell out.

The day being come, *Tom* taking *Harry* by the hand, and com- 25
ming to the Widdows doore, took hold of the Bell and rung thereat
so lustily, as if he had beene bound seaven yeeres Prentise to a
Sexton: whereupon one of the Prentises came straight to the doore,
saying, who is there?

Sirra (quoth *Tom Drum*) tis I, open the doore. 30

The fellow seeing it to be *Tom Drum,* with a frown askt him
what he would have? who answered, he would speake with his
Mistris.

My Mistris is busie (quoth the fellow) cannot I doe your errand?

No marry can you not (quoth *Tom*) I must speak with her my 35
selfe.

Then stay a little (said the boy) and I will tell her. And with that

---

²⁶ hold of] Folger; hold on 1639
³⁷ said] Folger; quoth 1639   her] Folger; *om.* 1639

in he went, leaving *Tom* still at the doore, where they sate till their feet waxt cold before the boy returned.

By the Masse (quoth *Harry*) whatsoever your credit with the Mistris is I know not, but the curtesie is small that is shewen you
5 by her man.

Tush (quoth *Tom*) what will you have of a rude unmannerly boy? if any of the Maids had come to the doore, we had beene long ere this brought to their Mistris presence: therefore once againe I will vse the help of the Bell-rope.

10 At his second ringing, out comes one of the Maids, saying with a shrill voyce: who the Divell is at the doore, that keepes such a ringing?

Why you queane (quoth he) tis I.

What *Tom Drum* (quoth shee) what would you have?

15 I would speak with your mistresse (quoth he).

Trust me (said the maid) you cannot speake with her now, for she is at supper with two or three that are sutors; Master Doctor *Burket* is one, and Master Alderman *Iaruice* the other.

Tut (quoth *Tom*) tell me not of sutors, but tell her that I am
20 here, and then good enough.

Well, I will (quoth shee) and with that, claps to the dore againe, and keepes them still without.

This geare workes but ill-favouredly yet (said *Harry*) and you are little beholding either to the men or the maids, for ought that
25 I see, that will not shew you so much favour to stay within dores.

'Tis no matter, *Harry* (quoth he) but if their Mistresse should know this, she would swinge their coats lustely for it.

And with that, one of the boyes opening the doore, told *Tom* that his mistresse wold have him send up his errand.

30 Sblood (quoth he) is she so stately that she will not come downe? I haue seene the day when she would have bin glad to have spoken with me.

I (quoth the fellow) it may be so, when you have brought her a new paire of shoes, that hath pincht her at the toes.

35 Come *Harry* (said *Tom*) I will take paines for this once to goe up to her.

16 for] Folger; *om.* 1639
20 and then] Folger; then 1639
24 or] Folger; or to 1639
35 paines] Folger; the paines 1639

Chapter Eight

By my faith but you shall not (said the fellow): and therefore keepe backe, for you come not in here.

Tom Drum, seeing himselfe thus disgrac'd before his fellow *Harry,* became very angry and askt if this was the best entertainment that they could affoord their Mistresses Friends? And therewithall 5 began to struggle with them: which their mistresse hearing, started from the table, and suddenly came to see what the matter was, who being certified of *Tom Drums* sawcinesse, began thus sharpely to check him: Why, fellow (quoth she) art thou mad, that thus un-civilly thou behavest thy self? what hast thou to say to me, that thou 10 art thus importunate?

No hurt (quoth he) but that this gentleman and I would have bestowed a galland of wine to have had three or foure houres talke with you.

I tell thee (said she) I am not now at leasure, and therefore good 15 honesty trouble me no more: neither is it my wont to be won with wine at any time.

Gods Lord (quoth he) are you grown so coy? if you and I were alone I know I should finde you more milde: what must no man but Doctor *Burket* cast your water? is his Phisicke in most request? 20 well I meane to be better entertained ere I goe, for there is never a Flemming of them all shall out face me, by the morrow Masse I sweare.

Mistris *Farmer* seeing him so furious, answered he should have present entertainment according to his desert; whereupon she made 25 no more to doe, but quietly went to her servants, and willed them to thrust him out by the head and shoulders: which presently they performed. But *Harry* was by her very modestly answered, that if he had occasion of any speech with her, the next day he should come and be patiently heard and gently answered: with which 30 words after she had drunke to him in a gobblet of Claret wine, he departed, and going home he told *Tom Drum* he was highly beholding to him for his curtesie in preferring his sute to Mistris *Farmer.*

² keepe] Folger; keepe you 1639

*³ *Drum,*] ∼ ∧ Folger, 1639   *Harry,*] ∼ ∧ Folger, 1639

*⁴ became] being Folger, 1639   and] *om.* Folger, 1639   was] Folger; were 1639

²² Flemming] flemming Folger; Felmming 1639

²⁴ *Farmer*] Folger; *Farmar* 1639

Surely (quoth hee) you are in very high favour with the faire
woman, and so it seemed by your great entertainment: I pray
thee *Tom* tell me how tasted the meat which she set on thy trencher
with her silver forke: and what secret was that which shee told
in thy eare? trust me, thou art precious in her eies, for she was as
glad to see thee, as if one had given her a rush, for when after
many hot wordes she heard thee draw thy breath so short, she for
very pitty tumbled thee out into the street to take more ayre.

Well, well (quoth *Tom*) floute on, but I am well enough served,
Ile lay my life had I not brought thee with me, never a man should
have had more welcome then I: and now I consider with my
selfe that it did anger her to the heart when she saw I was purposed to make another copartner of her presence: but it shall
teach me wit while I live, for I remember an old saying, love and
Lordship brookes no fellowship.

But when this matter was made known to the rest of the jorney-
men, *Tom-Drums* entertainment was spoke of in every place, insomuch that it is to this day a proverb amongst us, that where it
is supposed a man shall not be welcomed, they will say he is like
to have *Tom Drums* entertainment. And to auoid the flouts that
were daily given him, poore *Tom Drum* forsooke *Fleet-street,* and
at last went into *Scotland,* being prest for a Drummer at *Muskelborough* field, where the noble Duke of *Sommerset* and the Earle of
Warwick were sent with a noble army: where the Englishmen and
Scots meeting, there was fought a cruell battle, the victory whereof
fell to the Englishmen: at what time there was slaine of the Scots to
the number of foureteene thousand, and fifteene hundred taken
prisoners, where we will leave *Tom Drum* till his returne, making
mention how *Harry Nevell* behaved himselfe in the meane space in
London.

4 that which] Folger; that 1639
6 if] Folger; *om.* 1639
9 Well, well] Folger; Well 1639
22-23 *Muskelborough*] Folger; *Muskelbrough* 1639
24 army:] Folger; ~ ∧ 1639   the Englishmen] Folger; Englishmen 1639
27 foureteene thousand] Folger; 14. Thousand 1639

240

CHAPTER IX.

How *Harry Nevell* wooed Mistris *Farmer* and deceived
Doctor *Burket:* and how they were both beguiled by
a Prentice that dwelt in the house, who in the end
married her. 5

Mistris *Farmer* fiering the hearts of many with her faire beauty,
was wondrously wooed by Doctor *Burket,* who would give
unto her divers rich gifts, the which though they were faire and
costly, yet Mistris *Farmer* would hardly accept them, but even
what he in a manner by perforce constrained her to take, least by 10
his cunning he should insert therein some matter more then ordinary,
that might moove any motion of love, contrary to her naturall in-
clination.

Upon a time *Harry Nevell* comming thether, and finding the
Doctor very diligent to breed the Widdows content, whereby he 15
greatly hindred his proceedings, cast in his mind how he might
disburden the house of the Doctor and get opportunity to prefer
his owne sute. At last lighting on a device fit for the purpose, in
this sort he delt with the Doctor; there was an Egyptian woman that
at *Black-wall* was in trauell with child, and had such hard labour, 20
that she was much lamented among all the wives that dwelt thereabout. *Harry Nevell* comming that way, and hearing thereof,
thought it a fit matter to imploy Doctor *Burket* about, while in the
meane space he might the better bewray his affection to the Widdow.

Whereupon he sent one to him attyred like a serving man, booted 25
and spurd, who comming to the Widdows house all in a sweate,
laid load on the doore demanding for Master Doctor.

What would you with him (quoth one of the Maids)?

Marry (quoth he) my Lady *Swinborne* hath sent for him in all
post hast, and therefore I pray you let me speake with him. 30

⁶ faire] Folger; *om.* 1639
²⁹ *Swinborne*] *Sunborne* Folger, 1639

I will presently doe your errand (said the maid) whereupon running up she told him that my Lady *Swinborne* had sent a messenger in great hast to speake with him. Doctor *Burket* hearing that, and being well acquainted with the Lady *Swinborne*, took leave of the Widdow and went to the messenger, saying how now good fellow, what would my good Lady haue with me?

Sir (said the messenger) she would desire you if ever you did tender the life of a Lady, to make no delay, but presently to put your selfe a horse-back and come to her, for she is wondrous sick.

I am sory for that (said the Doctor), and surely I will make all the speed possible to come to her: whereupon the Doctor tooke horse and immediatly went with the seruingman.

Harry hearing of his departure, came to the Widdow with a smiling countenance and thus merily began to wooe her.

Now Mistris *Farmer*, happy it is that a yong man once in a moneth may find a moment of time to talk with you: truth it is that your good graces haue greatly bound me in affection to you, so that onely aboue all the women in the world I haue setled my delight in your love, and if it shall please you to requite my good will with the like kindnesse, I shall account my birth-day blessed, and remaine your faithfull friend for ever.

Gentle man (quoth she) for your good will, I thank you, but I would haue you understand, that the lesse you love me, the better I shall like you, for your delights and mine are not alike, I haue setled my fancy on a single life, being a Widdow unmeete to marry, and unapt to loue; once indeed I had learned that lesson, but my schole master being untimely dead that taught me, I grew forgetfull of all those principles, and then I swore neuer to follow that study more: wherefore if you will become a faithfull friend to me, let me be assured thereof by this, that from henceforth you will not any more trouble me with this matter, and thereby you shall bind me to think the better of you while I know you: and doe not think I speak this of any affection proceeding from myself to any other, or for the desire of any benefit proferred by any other to me.

Faire Mistris (quoth *Harry*) I know it is the custome of women to make their denials unto their louers, and strictly to stand on nice

2 *Swinborne* had] Folger; *Sunborne* hath 1639
3 great] Folger; very great 1639
10 all the] Folger; all 1639

242

points, because they will not be accounted easily won, or soone entreated: alack deere Dame, consider nature did not adorne your face with such incomparable beauty, and framed every other part so full of excellency, to wound men with woe, but to worke their content. Wherefore now in the *Aprill* of your yeares, and the sweet summer of your dayes, banish not the pleasures incident to bright beauty, but honour *London* streets with the faire fruite of your womb and make me blessed by being father to the issue of your delicate body; and though your beauty as the spring doth yet yearely grow, yet in the black winter of old age it will not be so, and we see by daily experience, that flowers not gathered in time rot and consume themselves: wherfore in my opinion you should doe the world intollerable wrong to live like a fruitlesse figtree.

Nay then Sir (quoth she) I perceive you will grow troublesome, and shew your selfe no such man as you professe your selfe: and seeing among many I request but one thing at your hands, and you refuse to doe it for my sake, I may say your frindship is more in words then in works; wherefore I perceive I must be constrained to call my Maid for a cup of voyding beere ere you will depart.

Nay Mistris (quoth he) I will saue you that labour, seeing your love commands me, and I pray God grant you a more favourable mind at our next meeting, and with these words he departed.

Now you shall understand, that this gallant Widdow had in her house a very proper youth which was one of her aprentices, who had a long time borne his Mistris great good will: whereupon he became so diligent and carefull about all things committed to his charge, that thereby he won much commendations among all the neighbors, and was for the same highly esteemed of his Mistris: who after he had long concealed his grief at last unburdened himselfe of some sorrow, by making a friend privy to his passions, who comforted him in this sort.

Tush man (quoth he) what though she be thy Mistris, and thou her prentise, be not ashamed to shew thy affection to her: she is a woman wise and modest, and one that however she answers thy demand, will not think worse of thee for thy good will: therefore try her, thou knowest not how fortune may favour thy sute, and the worst is she can but say thee nay.

O (quoth he) if I were out of my years, I could have some heart to wooe her, but having yet three quarters of a yeere to serve, it may be some hindrance to my freedome if she should prove froward.

Tush stand not on those tearms (said his friend *Francis*) she will never requite kindnes with such discurtesie, and therefore *William* prove not a foole by being too fearefull.

O my deare friend *Francis* (quoth he) how can I suppose I 5 should speed well, seeing she disdains Doctor *Burket,* and refuses Master Alderman, and will shew no countenance to gallant Master *Nevell.*

What a bad reason is this (quoth *Francis*) some cannot abide to eate of a Pig: some to taste of an Eele, othersome are sicke if 10 they see but a Crab, and divers cannot away with cheese: yet none of them all but doe live by their victuals, every man hath his fancy, and every woman will follow her own mind, and therefore though she find not an Alderman or a Doctor for her diet yet she may think *William* her man a fit morsell for her own tooth.

15 I wis (quoth *William*) thy reasons are good, and I have advantage aboue all other suters to follow my sute, being in the house daily with her, and every evening when they are away: beside she hath appointed me this after noone to come to her Closet, that I may shew her my reckoning and accounts and in what sort her state 20 standeth: wherefore seeing I have such occasion, I will no longer trifle out the time: but so soon as that businesse is ended, put my selfe to the hazard of my happy fortune: wherefore good *Francis* farewell till I see thee againe, and how I speed, at our next meeting thou shalt know.

25 The time at last being come that Mistris *Farmer* had appointed to have her books cast over, getting into her closet shee whistled for her Maid, and bad her call up *William;* (quoth she) let him bring his books of account with him.

The maid did as her Mistris commanded, and up comes *William* 30 with his books under his armes: and after he had very reuerently don his duty to his Mistris, she bad him sit downe saying, now *William* let me see these reckonings justly cast up, for it is long since I have cast an eye into mine estate.

Mistris (quoth he) doubt not but your estate is good, and your 35 accounts justly kept for I have had as great regard thereto as the goods had been my owne.

Therein (quoth she) I am the more beholding to thee, neither shal thy true service goe unrewarded if I live; or if I dye thou shalt not be altogether forgotten.

40 These kind speeches greatly comforted *Williams* heart, where-

upon he fell to his reckonings roundly, till his mind running too much on his Mistris beauty, sometimes he would misse and count three-score, and foure-score, nine-score.

Nay there you faile (quoth his Mistris) and over-tell forty, for three and foure is but seaven. 5

Tis true indeed Mistris (said he) and three times seaven is iust five and twenty.

I tell thee (quoth she) tis but one and twenty; what fellow, begin you to dote in your yong yeares?

O my deere Mistris (said he) blame me not if I doe so, seeing 10 your sweet presence hath made farre wiser then my self to dote: O my good Mistris pardon my presumption, for being thus bold to unburden my hearts griefe unto you, my hearty love to your sweet selfe is so great, that except you vouchsafe favourably to censure, and kindly to judge thereof, that the sorrowes of my mind will 15 wound my very soule, and make my life loathsome unto me.

Wherefore my good Mistris, despise not your poore servant, but yeeld unto him such succour, as may prolong his dayes with many blessed houres.

His Mistris obscuring her beauty with lowring browes, (like 20 foggy vapours that blot the sky) made him this answer: How now Sirra? hath my too much mildnesse made you thus sawcy? can you set your love at no lower a pitch, but you must mount to be Master of your Mistris?

No Mistris (quoth he) no master, but your servant for ever. 25

Goe to, leave your prating (quoth she) or I will breake thy head I sweare, have I refused as thou seest, a graue and wealthy Alderman that might make me a Mistris of worship and dignity, and denied master Doctor of his request, who as thou knowest is at this day esteemed the cunningest Physition in *London,* and diverse 30 other honest and well landed Gentlemen, and among the rest young Master *Nevell,* who as some say is descended of a noble house, and whose love I dare sweare is to me most firmely devoted, so that in my heart I am perswaded he loves the ground the better that I tread on: and should I (I say) forsake all these to make my foot my 35 head, and my seruant my superiour, to marry thee which art a Prentice boy?

Nay Sir (quoth she) seeing you are grown so lusty, tis time to tame you and looke to your steps: therefore I charge you leave the shop and get you into the kitchin to help the Maid to washe 40

the dishes and scowre the Kettles; and whereas since my husbands decease I have given foure nobles a yeare to a water bearer, I will make thee saue me that charges, for it is well seene, that too long the water Tankard hath beene kept from thy lazy shoulders, and if
5 thou scornest to doe this, get where thou wilt; but if thou wilt remaine with me, so long as thou hast a day to serve, thou shalt be thus imployed.

Hereupon she called up her man *Richard* to supplie his place, and to be fore-man of the shop, gracing him with the keyes of the
10 counting house: which *William* seeing, sadly went out of her sight, wofully to himselfe bewayling his hard fortune, but yet such was his love to his Mistris, that he rather chose to be drudge in her kitchin, then to change her service for any other. All the servants in the house much mused at this alteration: but to no creature did
15 his Mistris tell the cause thereof, but kept it secret to her selfe: toward the evening, foorth he must needs goe for water, at what time he wanted no flouts of all his fellows, nor of many of the neighbors servants: where meeting with his friend *Francis*, discoursed to him the whole cause of his disgrace: he greatly chafing thereat,
20 perswaded him never to endure such base drudgery, but rather to seeke preferment in some other place.

Notwithstanding *William* would not follow his counsell, but rather chose patiently to abide all brunts. Night being come, and supper ended, *William* was set to performe his penance for his pre-
25 sumption in love, that is to say, to scrape the trenchers, scowre the kettles and spits, and to wash up the dishes: which he went about with such good will, that it seemed to him rather a pleasure then a paine.

His Mistris closset joyning to the kitchin, had a secret place
30 therein to look into the kitchin, where closely sitting, she earnestly beheld her man how he bestirred himselfe in his busines: Whereupon she entered into this consideration with her selfe. Now fie for shame, how Ill doth it beseeme me to set so handsome a youth to such drudgery? if he bore a mans mind he would never indure
35 it, but being of a base and servile condition, he doth easily indure the yoake of servitude, and yet I am to blame so to thinke, for if he had stubbornly disobeyed my commandement, how could

23 brunts. Night] Lange; brunts ∧ night 1639
30 where] Lange; were 1639

246

I otherwise judge, but that in pride and disdaine he thought himselfe too good to be at any direction: some servants would in such
a case have given me many foule words, and rather malepartly
set me at nought, and forsake my service, then to have indured
the tearms of disgrace that he hath done by this means: but heereby 5
it is evident that love thinks nothing too much. Well *Will* (quoth
she) the vertue of thy mind shall breed better thoughts in thy
Mistris, which shall make her reward thy good will in a large
measure: see, see, how neately he goes through his work, how hand-
somely he handles every thing: and surely well may I suppose that 10
he which is so faithfull a servant, would certainly prove a kind husband, for this hath beene no slender triall of his constant heart.

With that, hearing the Maid and some other of the servants
talke with him, she lending a heedfull eare to their speech, heard
them speake to this purpose: good Lord *William* (quoth one) I 15
maruell much that you, being of so good parents and having so little
a while to serve, will be thus vsed at her hands? it were too much if
you were but this day bound prentice, to be set to such slavery.

I sweare (quoth another) I have three times longer to serve then
you and if she should bid me doe as thou dost, I would bid her 20
doe it herselfe with a morin.

Ile tell you what (quoth the third) Ile be plaine and vse but few
words, but I would see my faire Mistris with the black Devill before I would doe it.

Well well my masters (quoth *William*) you are mad merry wags 25
but I take it as great favour done me by my Mistris thus to imploy
me, that thereby I might have knowledge how to decke up a kitchen
that meeting with a bad huswife to my wife, I know how to instruct
her in houshold affaires.

I care for no such favour (said he). 30

Their Mistris hearing all, said nothing, but determined to try
them all what they would doe ere it were long: wherefore being
now greatly affectioned to her man, couered her love with such
discretion, that none could perceive it: For Master Doctor being
newly returned, came thither puffing and blowing, saying he was 35
never so served since he was borne; (quoth he) since I was here,
I have at least ridden an hundred miles with an arrant knave that
carried me I knew not whether: he rode with me out of *Bishopsgate* foorth right as far as *Ware,* and then compassing all *Suffolke*
and *Norfolke,* he brought me backe againe through *Essex,* and so 40

conducted me to *Black-wall* in *Middlesex* to seeke out my Lady
Swinborne, my good Lady and Mistris: at last I saw it was no such
matter, but the villaine being disposed to mocke me, brought me
to a woman Egiptian, as blacke as the great Divell, who lay in
5 child-bed and was but delivered of a child of her owne colour:
to the which in despite of my beard they made me be God-father,
where it cost me three crownes, and I was glad I so escaped, and
who was the author of all this deceipt but Master *Nevell?* but if
ever I come to give him Phisicke, if I make him not have the
10 squirt for five dayes, count me the veriest dunce that ever wore
veluet cap.

Master Doctor (quoth she) I am very sorie you were so vsed,
notwithstanding to make Master *Nevell* and you friends I will
bestow a breakefast upon you to morrow, if it please you to accept
15 my offer.

Faire Widdow (quoth he) never a one in the world would have
vrged me to be friends with him but your selfe, and I am contented for your sake to doe it: and thus till next morning he took
his leave.

20 Next day as soone as she was up she called up one of her men
saying, Sirra run quickly, take a basket and fetch me a bushel of
oysters from *Billinsgate.*

The fellow frowning said, I pray you send another, for I am
busie in the shop.

25 Why knave (quoth she) Ile have thee goe.

(Quoth he) make a drudge of some other and not of me, for to
be plaine I will not goe.

No (quoth she)? call me *Iohn* hither.

When he came, she desired him very gently to fetch her
30 a bushel of oysters.

Why Mistresse (quoth he) my friends set me not here to be a
Porter to fetch Oisters from *Billingsgate.* I tell you true, I scorne
you should require any such matter of me.

Is it true (quoth she)? very well, I will remember this when you
35 forget it.

Thus when she had tried them all, she called her man *William,*
saying: sirra goodman scullian take the great close basket, and

*28 *Iohn*] Lange; *Richard* 1639

fetch me a bushell of oysters from *Billinsgate,* and look you tarry not.

I will forsooth Mistris (quoth he) and presently away he went with such good will as none could go with better, being marvellous glad that she would request any thing at his hands.   5

When he was come againe, with a smiling countenance she said, what *Wilkin* art thou come already? it is well done, I pray thee bring some of them up into my Closset, that I may taste how good they be.

Yes forsooth (quoth *William*) and after her he went, the Maide 10 likewise carried up a couple of white manchets, and with a Diaper napkin covered the table.

Now Maid (quoth she) fetch me a pint of the best red wine.

I will forsooth (said the Maid).

Mistris (said *William*) if it please you, I will open your Oysters 15 for you.

I pray you do (quoth she).

Then taking a towell on his arme, and a knife in his hand, being glad he had gotten so good an office, shewed himselfe so feat and expert in his occupation, that he opened as fast as his Mistresse 20 could eat.

Beleeve me *William* (quoth she) you are nimble at an oyster, and quick in carving up shellfish, though dull in casting up accounts, I pray thee tell me how many shels are in three and thirtie oysters?   25

Threescore and six (said *William*).

You are a witty youth (quoth she) if thy speech be true it must then needs follow that I have eaten three and thirty oysters, have also devoured threescore and six shels, which is too much for one womans breakfast in a cold morning in conscience, and therefore 30 I had need quickly to give over, least I break my belly with oyster shels: whereupon she cald her maid, saying: come hither *Ioane,* and bring me a goblet of wine that I may wash *Williams* shels from my stomack.

Indeed Mistris (quoth he) if you take my words so, I spoke with- 35 out book.

It is true (quoth she) for they are alwaies without that are never within, and either thy knowledge is small, or thy blindnesse great, or oyster shels very soft, that I should eat so many and

249

never feele one: for surely, if there be threescore and six oystershels
in three and thirty oysters, there must needs be as many more in
three and thirty oysters: and to affirme my words true, behold
here the shels that were out of the oysters, now shew me those that
5 were within the oysters.

William seeing his Mistris thus pleasant, began to gather some
courage to himselfe, and therefore thus uttered his mind: Deare
Mistris, needs must I prove both blinde in sight, and dull in
conceipt, while your faire eyes that gives light to the Sunne obscure
10 themselves, and dark the glory of their shine, when I seek to receive comfort thereby: and the want of your good will makes my
wits so weak, that like a barren tree it yeelds no fruit at all.

True (quoth she): three times seven is iust five and twenty: but
tell me what is the cause that moves thee to desire my favour, and
15 to request my good will?

Good Mistris pardon me (quoth he) and I will tell you.

Whereupon she replied, saying, trust me *William,* my pardon is
easier to be gotten then the Popes, and therefore be not afraid to
proceed.

20 Why then my deare Mistris, seeing you have so graciously granted
liberty to my hearts advocate, to pleade at the bar of your beauty,
and to open the bill of my complaint: know this, that hope against
hope perswaded me to labour for your love, that gaining the same
I might be called a blessed man by winning such a wife.

25 What *Will* (quoth she) art thou not ashamed, that such a youth
as thy selfe, a lad, a stripling, a prentice boy, should in the ignorance of his age, cumber himselfe with the cares of the world, and
wantonly take a wife, that knowes not how to guide himselfe? I
tell thee fellow, first learne to thrive, and then wive.

30 O my deare Mistris (said *William*) let not pleasant youth which
is the glory of many be a disgrace to me: neither without triall
deere Mistris disable not my manhood, which now I take to be in
his chiefe prime.

Nay (quoth she) if thou wilt have thy manhood tried, prepare
35 thy selfe for the warres, and purchase honour by beating down
our countries foes, and so shalt thou weare the golden wreath of
honour for ever.

In troth Mistris (quoth he) I had rather have my manhood tried
in another place.

40 Yfaith where (quoth shee)?

Chapter Nine

By my troth (said he) in your soft bed, which is far better then the hard field.

Why thou bold knave (quoth she) it were a good deed to make you a bird of *Bridewell* for your saucinesse.

Beleeve me Mistris (quoth he) I am sorie you should be offended, 5 rather will I get me into a corner and die through disdaine, then stay in your sight and grieve you: and with that away he went.

She seeing him so hastily depart, called him againe saying: *William* come hither, turne againe you faint hearted coward, what, art thou afraid of *Bridewell?* use thy selfe well, and I will be thy 10 friend.

The young man that with these words was revived like a sick man out of a dead sound, turning merrily to his Mistris, gave her a kisse, saying: on that condition I give you this.

How now sir (quoth she) I called you not back to be so bold: 15 in good sadnesse do so againe, and I will give you on the eare.

Nay, Mistris (quoth he) if that be all the danger, take then another, and lay me on the eare (so I may lay you on the lips) and spare not.

Nay, then (said his Mistris) I see my too much softnesse makes 20 thee saucy, therefore for feare thou shouldest catch a surfet, I charge thee on paine of loves displeasure, to get you downe about your businesse, and see that all things be in readinesse against my friends come: why goe you not? what stand you in a maze? pack I say and be gone. 25

And thus my deare Mistris (quoth he) parts my soule out of Paradise, and my heart from heavens ioy: notwithstanding you command and I consent and alwayes let me finde favour, as I am forward to follow your precepts, and therewithall away he went.

He was no sooner gone, but she having determined what to 30 do, sent for her friends, at what time the Alderman comming thither, and Master Doctor, she had also invited Master *Peachie* and his Wife, and with them came gallant young *Nevill.*

When they were all set at the table, after they had well tasted of the delicates there prepared: Mistris *Farmer* told them for two 35 causes she had requested their companie that day to breakfast: the one was, that master Doctor and young *Nevill* might be made friends: and the other that in their sight she might make her selfe sure to her husband, that they might be witnes of their vowes.

The companie said, they should be very glad to see so good 40

a work performed: whereupon shee calling up all her men servants, spake to this purpose. My good friends and kinde neighbours, because I will have none ignorant, of that which is to be effected, I have presumed to bring my servants into your presence, that
5 they also may beare record of the reconciliation betwixt Master Doctor and Master *Nevill,* and therefore my Masters, if your hearts consent to an unitie, declare it by shaking hands, that it may not bee said, that my house was the breeder of brawles, and on that condition I drink to you both: the Gentlemen both
10 pledged her, and according to her request ended the quarrell.

When this was done, she merrily told them, that among her men she had chosen her Master: albeit quoth she, this matter may seeme strange in your sight, and my fancie too much ruled by follie, yet this my determination I purpose by Gods grace to follow,
15 hoping it shall breed no offence to any in the companie, in such a chance to make mine own choice.

Her man *Richard,* and the rest that supposed themselves most graced by her favours, began at this speech to look something peart, and all the companie held opinion that she bore the best
20 minde to the foreman of her Shop: for first of all turning her speech to him, she said: *Richard* come hither, thou hast greatly to praise God for making thee so proper a man, thou art a neat fellow, and hast excellent qualities, for thou art not proud, nor high minded, but hast a care to thy businesse, and to keepe the
25 Shop: and because I have committed great matters into thy hands, I pray thee go downe and look to thy charge, for I have nothing more to say to thee at this time.

The fellow at these words lookt as blew under the eyes, as a stale Codshead under the gill: and going downe the staires shook his
30 head like one that had a flea in his eare.

Now come hither *Iohn* (quoth she) I must needs say thou art come of good parents, and thou knowst they bound thee not Prentice to fetch oysters from *Billinsgate* like a Porter, nor to have thy daintie fingers set to drudgerie, therefore good *Iohn* get you
35 downe after your fellow, for here is nothing for you to doe at this time.

Her man *William,* that all this while was playing the scullion in the kitchin was then sent for, who comming before the companie with his face all begrim'd, and his cloathes all greasie, his Mistris
40 spake in this manner. What a slovenlie knave comes here? were not

this a fit man think ye to be Master of this house and Lord of my love?

Now by my troth (said Mistris *Peachie*) I never saw a more un-handsome fellow in my life: fie how hee stinkes of kitchin stuffe: what a face and neck hath he! a bodie might set Leekes in the very durt of his lips. I thinke in my conscience three pound of Sope, and a barrell of Water is little enough to scowre him cleane: the like flowts used all the rest at poore *William,* to which his Mistris made this answer.

Good Lord my masters, how much do your sights deceive you? in my sight he looks the loveliest of them all, having a pleasant countenance, and a good grace, and so pleasing is he in every part to my sight, that surely if hee will accept of mee for his wife, I will not refuse him for my husband: her friends looking one upon another, and marvelling at her speech, thought verily she had but iested, till such time she took him by the hand, and gave him a kisse.

Whereupon *William* spake thus unto her: faire Mistris, seeing it hath pleased you, beyond my desert, and contrarie to my expecta-tion, to make me so gracious an offer, worthie I were to live a beg-gar, if I should refuse such a treasure: and thereupon I give you my heart and my hand.

And I receive it (quoth she) for it is thy vertue and true humilitie that hath conquered my former conceipts, for few men would have wonne a wife as thou didst.

No, how did he win you (said *Harrie Nevill*)?

By fetching oysters from *Billingsgate* (quoth she) which I know you would not have done, seeing all the rest of my servants scorn'd to do it at my request.

Sblood (quoth *Harrie*) by feching of oysters: I would have fetcht oysters, and mustles, and cockles too, to have got so good a bargaine.

The Alderman and the Doctor lookt strangely at this matter: neverthelesse seeing it was not to be helpt, they commended her choice, saying it was better for a man in such a case, to be favour-able in a womans eyes, then to have much gold in his coffers.

Then did she set her black man by her white side, and calling the rest of her servants (in the sight of her friends) she made them

⁵ he!] Lange; ∼? 1639

do reverence unto him, whom they for his drudgerie scorned so
much before: so the breakfast ended, she wild them all next
morning, to beare him companie to Church, against which time,
William was so daintily trickt up, that all those which beheld him,
5 confest he was a most comely, trim, and proper man, and after
they were married, they lived long together in ioy and prosperous
estate.

   Harrie Nevill became so grieved hereat, that soone after he went
from Master *Peachie,* and dwelt with a Goldsmith, and when he
10 had beene a while there, committing a fault with his Masters
daughter, he departed thence and became a Barber-Surgion: but
there his Mistris and he were so familiar, that it nothing pleased
his Master, so that in halfe a yeare he sought a new service and
became a Cook: and then a Comfetmaker dwelling with master
15 *Baltazar,* where after he grew something cunning, having done
some shrewd turne in that place, he forsooke that service, and
became a Smith, where their maide *Iudeth* fell so highly in love
with him that he for pure good will which he bore her, shewed his
Master a faire paire of heeles: and then practised to be a Ioyner,
20 where he continued till hee heard his Father was sick, who for his
abominable swearing had cast him from his favour, but after he
had long mist him, and that he could heare no tidings of his
untoward and wilde wanton Sonne, hee sent into divers places to
enquire for him, and at last one of his servants lighted where he
25 was, by which meanes he came to his father againe: who in a few
yeares after, leaving his life, this sonne *Harrie* became Lord of all
his lands: and comming upon a day to *London* with his men waiting upon him, he caused a great dinner to be prepared, and sent
for all those that had been his masters and mistresses: who being
30 come, he thus began to commune with them. My good friends, I
understand that a certaine kinsman of mine was sometimes your
servant, and as I take it, his name was *Harrie Nevell:* who as I
heare, used himselfe but homely toward you, being a very wilde and
ungracious fellow, the report whereof hath beene some griefe to
35 me, being one that always wisht him well: wherefore look what
dammage he hath done you I pray you tell me, and I am content
with reason to see you satisfied, so that he may have your favours
to be made a freeman.

   ²⁴ his servants lighted] Lange; this servants lighed 1639

Surely sir (said *Peachie*) for mine own part I can say little, save only that he was so full of love, that he would seldome follow his businesse at his occupation: but that matter I freely forgive and will not be his hindrance in any thing.

Marry sir (said the Goldsmith) I cannot say so: for truly sir he 5 plaid the theefe in my house, robbing my daughter of her maiden-head, which he nor you is ever able to recompence, though you gave me a thousand pound, yet I thank God she is married and doth well.

I am the glader of that (said the Gentleman) and for that fault 10 I will give toward her maintenance forty pound.

The Barber hearing him say so, told him that hee had iniured him as much, and had beene more bold a great deale then became him, whereby (quoth he) I was made a scorne among my neighbours.

Tush you speake of ill will (said the Gentleman) if your wife will 15 say so I will beleeve it.

To which words the woman made this answer. Good sir, will you beleeve me there was neuer so much matter, the youth was an honest faire conditioned young man, but my husband bearing a naughty iealous minde, grew suspicious without cause, onely be- 20 cause he saw that his servant was kinde and gentle unto me, and would have done any thing that I requested: notwithstanding I have had many a fowle word for his sake, and carried some bitter blowes too, but all is one, I am not the first woman that hath suf-fered iniury without cause. 25

Alas good soule (said the Gentleman) I am right sorry for thy griefe, and to make thee amends, I will bestow on thee twentie Angels, so your husband will not take it in dudgin.

The woman with a low cursie gave him thanks, saying: truly sir I am highly beholding to you, and truly I shall love you the better 30 because you are so like him.

The smith likewise for his maide said all that he might, to whose marriage the Gentleman gave twentie pound.

Thus after hee had fully ended with them all, hee made himselfe knowne unto them, at what time they all reioyced greatly, and then 35 after he had bestowed on them a sumptuous dinner, they all departed. And ever after, this Gentleman kept men of all these occupations in his own house, himself being as good a workman as any of them all.

²⁷ amends,] Mann; ∼. 1639

CHAPTER X.

Of the greene king of S. *Martins* and his merry feats.

There dwelt in S. *Martins* a iollie Shooemaker, hee was commonly called the Greene king, for that upon a time he shewed
5 himselfe before King *Henry*, with all his men cloathed in greene,
he himselfe being suted all in greene Satten. He was a man very
humorous, of small stature, but most couragious, and continually
he used the Fencing-schoole. When he went abroad, he carried alwayes a two handed sword on his shoulder, or under his arme: he
10 kept continually thirtie or fortie servants, and kept in his house
most bountifull fare: you shall understand that in his young yeares,
his father dying, left him a good portion, so that he was in great
credit and estimation among his neighbours, and that which made
him more happie, was this, that God blest him with the gift of a
15 good wife, who was a very comely young woman, and therewithall
very carefull for his commoditie: but he whose minde was altogether
of merriment, little respected his profit in regard of his pleasure:
insomuch that through his wastefull expence he brought povertie
upon himselfe ere he was aware, so that he could not do as he was
20 accustomed: which when his daily companions perceived, they by
little and little shund his company, and if at any time he passed
by them, perhaps they would lend him a nod, or give him a good
morrow and make no more a doe.

And is it true (quoth the Greene king) doth want of money part
25 good company, or is my countenance chaunged, that they do not
know me? I have seene the day when neuer a knave of them all,
but would have made much of my dog for my sake, and have
given me twenty salutations on a Sunday morning, for one poore
pint of Muskadine: and what, hath a thred bare cloake scarde all
30 good fellowship? why though I have not my wonted habites, I
have still the same heart: and though my money be gone, my
mind is not altred: why then what Iacks are they, to reject mee?

---

8 Fencing-schoole.] Lange; ∼ ∧ 1639

Chapter Ten

I, I, now I finde my wives tale true, for then she was wont to say, Husband, husband, refraine these trencher flies, these smooth faced flatterers, that like drones live vpon the hony of your labour and sucke away the sweetnes of your substance. I wis, I wis, if once you should come in want, there is not the best of them all, that would trust you for ten groates: by which saying Ile lay my life she is a witch, for it is come as just to pas as *Marlins* prophesie. I would the other day but have borrowed 12 d. and I tride 13 frinds, and went without it: it being so, let them go hang themselves, for I wil into *Flanders*, that is flat, and leave these slaves to their servill conditions, where I will try if a firkin barrell of butter bee worth a pot of strong beere, and a loade of *Holland* cheese, better then a gallon of *Charnico:* and if it be, by the crosse of this sword I will neuer staine my credit with such a base commodity againe.

With that he went to his wife, saying: woman dost thou heare? I pray thee looke well to thy busines till I come againe: for why? to drive away melancholy, I am minded to walke a mile or twaine.

But husband (quoth she) were you there where you layd your plate to pawne? I pray you is it not misused? and is it safe?

Woman (quoth he) I was there, and it is safe I warrant thee, for euer comming into thy hands againe, thou knowest I borrowed but twentie marke on it, and they have sold it for twentie pound: tis gone wife, tis gone.

O husband (quoth she) what hard fortune have we to be so ill delt withall? and therewithall she wept.

Fie (quoth he) leave thy weeping, hang it up, let it goe, the best is, it neuer cost vs groate: were our friends living that gave us that, they would give us more: but in vaine it is to mourn for a matter that cannot be helpt, farewell wife, looke to thy house, and let the boyes plie their worke.

The greene king having thus taken his leave, went toward *Billings-gate,* of purpose to take Barge: where by the way hee met with *Anthony* now now, the firkin Fidler of *Finchlane.*

What master (quoth he) well met, I pray whither are you walking? and how doe all our friends in saint *Martins?* Will you not have a crash ere you goe?

Yfaith, *Anthony* (quoth he) thou knowest I am a good fellow, and one that hath not been a niggard to thee at any time, therefore if thou wilt bestow any musick on me, doe; and if it please

God that I return safely from *Flanders* againe, I will pay thee well for thy paines; but now I have no money for musick.

Gods-nigs (quoth *Anthony*) whether you have money or no, you shall have musick, I doe not allways request coyne of my friends
5 for my cunning: what, you are not euery body, and seeing you are going beyond sea, I will bestow a pinte of wine on you at the Salutation.

Saist thou so *Anthony* (quoth he) in good sooth I will not refuse thy curtesie, and with that they stept into the Tauern, where
10 *Anthony* cald for wine: and drawing forth his Fiddle began to play, and after he had scrapte halfe a score lessons he began to sing.

When should a man shew himselfe gentle and kinde,
When should a man comfort the sorrowfull minde?
O *Anthony* now, now, now.
15 O *Anthony* now, now, now.
When is the best time to drinke with a friend?
When is it meetest my money to spend?
O *Anthony* now, now, now.
O *Anthony* now, now, now.
20 When goes the King of good fellowes away?
That so much delighted in dauncing and play?
O *Anthony* now, now, now.
O *Anthony* now, now, now.
And when should I bid my Master farewell?
25 Whose bountie and curtesie so did excell?
O *Anthony* now, now, now.
O *Anthony* now, now, now.

Loe ye now Master (quoth he) this song have I made for your sake, and by the grace of God when you are gone I will sing it
30 every Sunday morning vnder your wives window, that she may know we dranke together ere you parted.

I pray thee do so (said the Greene king) and do my commendations vnto her, and tell her at my returne I hope to make merry.

Thus after they had made an end of their wine, and paid for the
35 shot, *Anthony* putting up his Fiddle departed, seeking to change musicke for money: while the Greene king of Saint *Martins* sailed

4 friends] Lange; feiends 1639

258

in *Gravesend* Barge. But *Anthony* in his absence sung this song so often in Saint *Martins,* that thereby he purchast a name which he neuer lost till his dying day, for euer after men called him nothing but *Anthony* now now.

But it is to be remembred that the Green kings wife became so 5 carefull in her businesse, and governed her selfe with such wisdome in all her affaires, that during her husbands absence she did not onely pay many of his debts, but also got into her house every-thing that was necessary to be had, the which her diligence won such commendations, that her credit in all places was verie good, 10 and her gaines (through Gods blessing) came so flowing in, that before her husband came home, she was had in good reputation with her neighbours: and having no need of any of their favours, every one was ready to proffer her curtesie, saying good neighbour if you want any thing tell us, and looke what friendship we may doe 15 you, be sure you shall find it.

I neighbour (quoth she) I know your kindnesse, and may speake thereof by experience: well may I compare you to him that would never bid any man to dinner, but at two of the clocke in the after noone, when he was assured they had fild their bellies before, 20 and that they would not touch his meate, except for manners sake: wherefore for my part I will give you thankes, when I take benefit of your proffer.

Why neighbour we speake for good will (quoth they).

Tis true (quoth shee) and so say they that call for a fresh quart 25 to bestow on a drunken man, when they know it would doe him as much good in his bootes as in his belly.

Well neighbour (quoth they) God be thanked that you have no cause to use friends.

Mary Amen (quoth shee) for if I had I think I should finde few 30 here.

These and the like greetings were often betwixt her and her neighbors til at last her husband came home, and to his great comfort found his estate so good, that he had great cause to praise God for the same, for a warme purse is the best medicine for a cold 35 heart that may be. The greene king therefore bearing himselfe as brave as ever he did, having sworne himselfe a faithfull companion to his two-hand sworde, would never goe without it.

Now when his auncient acquaintance saw him again so gallant,

---

[38] two-hand sworde] Lange; two hand-sworde 1639

every one was ready to curry favour with him, and many would proffer him the wine. And where before they were wont scornefully to thrust him next the kennell, and nothing to respect his poverty, they gave him now the upper hand in every place, saluting him
5 with cap and knee: but he remembring how sleightly they set by him in his neede, did now as sleightly esteeme their flattery, saying: I cry you mercy, me thinkes I have seene your face, but I never knew you for my friend.

No (quoth one) I dwell at *Aldersgate,* and am your neere
10 neighbor.

And so much the worse (said the Greene king).

Wherefore (quoth the other)?

Because (said he) I thinke the place meete for an honester man.

I trust sir (said his neighbour) you know no hurt by me.
15 Nor any goodnes (quoth the greene king) but I remember you are he, or one of them of whom once I would have borrowed fortie pence, yet could not get it, if thereby I might have saved fifty lives: therefore goodman hog, goodman cog, or goodman dog, chuse you which, scrape no acquaintance of me, nor come any
20 more in my company, I would advise you, least with my long sword I crop your cowards legs, and make you stand like Saint *Martins* begger upon two stilts.

The fellow hearing him say so, went his wayes, and never durst speake to him afterward.

25 ## CHAPTER XI.

How the Greene King went a walking with his wife, and got *Anthony* now now to play before them, in which sort hee went with her to *Bristow*.

The Green king being a man that was much given to goe abroad,
30 his wife upon a time, thus made her mone to him: good Lord, husband (quoth she) I thinke you are the unkindest man alive, for as often as you walke abroad, you were neuer the man that would

take me in your company: it is no small griefe to me, while I sit
doating at home, every Sunday and Holy-day, to see how kindely
other men walke with their wives, and lovingly beare them company into the fields, that thereby they may have some recreation
after their weekes weary toyle: this pleasure haue they for their 5
paines, but I poore soule could never get such curtesie at your
hands: either it must needs be that you love me but little, or else
you are ashamed of my company, and I tell you true you have no
reason either for the one or the other.

Certainly wife (said hee) I should be sorrie to drive any such con- 10
ceit into thy head, but seeing you find your selfe grieved in this
kinde, let me intreate thee to be content, and then thou shalt perceive that my love is not small toward thee, nor my liking so bad
to be ashamed to have thee goe by my side. Thursday next is Saint
Iames day, against which time prepare thy selfe to goe with me to the 15
faire, where by the grace of God Ile bestow a fat Pig upon thee,
and there I meane to be merry: and doubt not but I will walke
with thee till thou art weary of walking.

Nay (quoth shee) I should never be weary of your company,
though I went with you to the Worlds end. 20

God a mercy for that wife, quoth hee, but so doing I doubt I
should trie you a very good foote-woman, or a bad flatterer.

Thus it past till Thursday came, in the meane season meeting
with two or three other shoomakers, he asked them if they would
walke with him and his wife to Saint *Iames* faire. 25

That wee will with all our hearts.

But will you not like flinchers flie from your words (quoth he)?

To that (they said) if they did they would forfeit a gallon of
wine.

Tush (said the greene king) talke not to me of a gallon of wine, 30
but will you bee bound in twenty pound a peece to performe it?

Why what needs bands for such a matter (quoth they)? we trust
you will take our wordes for more then that.

My masters (said the greene king) the world is growne to that
passe, that words are counted but wind, and I will trust you as 35
little on your word as Long *Meg* on her honesty: therefore if you
will not be bound, chuse, I will make no account of your company.

The men hearing him say so, knowing him to be a man of a

12 then] Lange; when 1639
14 side.] Lange; ~, 1639

merry mind, after their wits were all washt with wine, to the Scriveners they went, and bound themselves in twenty pound according to his request.

They had no sooner made an end of this merry match, but as 5 they stumbled into another Taverne, who should they meet but *Anthony* now now: who as soon as he spide the green King smiling with a wrie mouth, he joyfully imbrac't him with both his hands, saying: what my good master well met, when came you from the other side the water? by my troth you are welcome with all my 10 heart.

God a mercy good *Anthony* (quoth he) but how chance you come no more into Saint *Martins?*

O Master (quoth he) you know what a dainty commoditie I made at your parting to *Gravesendbarge?*

15 Yes mary (said the greene king) what of that?

Why (quoth he) by singing it under your window, all the merry shoomakers in Saint *Martins* tooke it by the toe: and now they have made it even as common as a printed Ballad, and I have gotten such a name by it, that now I am called nothing but *Anthony* now 20 now.

Why Master ile tell you, it hath made me as well acquainted in Cheapeside, as the cat in the creame pan: for as soone as the Goldesmiths wives spie mee, and as I passe along by the Marchants daughters, the apes will laugh at me as passes: beside that 25 all the little boyes in the streets will run after mee like a sort of Emits. *Anthony* now now, says one: *Anthony* now now, another: good Lord, good Lord, you never knew the like: heare ye master? I am sure that song hath gotten mee since you went, more pence then your wife hath pins: and seeing you are come againe, I will 30 make the second part very shortly.

But hearest thou, *Anthony* (said he)? if thou wilt come to me on Saint *Iames* his day in the Morning, thou shalt walke with us to the faire, for I meane to make merry with my wife that day.

Master (quoth he) by cock and pie, I will not misse you. And 35 thus after they had made *Anthony* drinke, he departed.

Saint *Iames* his day at last being come, he cal'd up his wife betimes, and bad her make ready, if she would to the faire: who very willingly did so: and in the meane space her husband went to his cubbert, and tooke thereout forty faire soveraignes, and 40 going secretly to one of his servants, he willed him to take good

heed of his house, and to see that his fellowes plide their businesse: for (quoth he) I goe with my wife to Saint *Iames* faire, and
perhaps you shall not see us againe this sennight.

Well Master said the fellow, I will have regard to your busines
I warrant you.   5

Wherewith he cal'd his wife, saying: come wife will you walke?

With a good will husband (quoth she) I am ready.

With that *Anthony* now now, began to scrape on his treable
viall, and playing a huntsup, said good morrow master good morrow, foure a clocke and a faire morning.   10

Well said, *Anthony* (quoth he) we be ready for thy company,
therefore along before, and let us heare what musicke you can
make.

Fie husband (quoth she) take not the Fidler with you, for shame.

Tush be content (quoth he) Musicke makes a sad mind merrie. 15

So away they went, and at Saint *Giles* in the fields he met the
rest of his company.

Well found, my masters (quoth he) I perceive you have a care
of your bonds.

So away they went with the Fidler before them, and the Greene 20
king with his two-hand sworde marching like a master of Fence
going to play his prize: when they came to the high way turning
downe to *Westminster,* his wife said: yfaith husband we shall come
to the faire too soone, for Gods sake let us walke a little further.

Content wife (quoth he) whereupon they went to *Kensington,* 25
where they brake their fast, and had good sport by tumbling on
the greene grasse, where *Anthony* brake his Fiddle, for which cause
the Greene king gave him ten shillings, and willed him to goe back
and buy a new one.

And now my friends (quoth he) if you will walke with mee to 30
Brainford I will bestow your dinner upon you, because I have a
minde to walke with my wife.

They were content, but by that time they came there, the woman
began to wax somewhat wearie, and because the day was farre
spent before they had dined, they lay there all night: where he 35
told his friends that the next morning he would bring his wife
to see the George in *Colebrook,* and then would turne home: but
to be briefe, when he came there, he told them flatly he meant to

³² wife.] Lange; ∼? 1639

goe to Saint *Iames* his faire at *Bristow:* for (quoth he) my wife
hath longed to walke with me, and I meane to give her walking-
worke enough.

But sir (quoth they) we meane not to goe thither.

5 Before God but you shall (quoth hee) or forfeit your band.

The men seeing no remedy, went along to *Bristow* on foote,
whereby the poore woman became so weary, that an hundred times
she wisht she had not come foorth of doores: but from that time
till she died, she never intreated her husband to walke with her
10 againe.

An hundred merry feates more did he, which in this place is too
much to be set downe. For afterward *Tom Drum* comming from
the winning of *Mustleborow,* came to dwell with him, where he
discoursed all his adventures in the wars: and according to his
15 old cogging humor, attributed other mens deeds to himselfe, for
(quoth he) it was I that killed the first Scot in the battell, yet I was
content to give the honour thereof to Sir *Michaell Musgrave,* notwithstanding (quoth he) all men knowes that this hand of mine
kild *Tom Trotter* that terrible traytor, which in despite of us, kept
20 the Castell so long, and at last as he cowardly forsooke it, and
secretly sought to flye, with this blade of mine I broacht him like
a roasting pigge. Moreover, Parson *Ribble* had never made himselfe so famous but by my meanes. These were his daily vaunts,
till his lies were so manifest that hee could no longer stand in
25 them.

But after the Greene king had long lived a gallant housekeeper, at last being aged and blinde, he dyed, after
he had done many good deedes to
divers poore men.

FINIS.

THOMAS OF READING

THOMAS OF
Reading.

OR,

The sixe worthy yeomen
of the West.

Now the fourth time corrected and enlarged
By T. D.

Printed at London for T. P.
1612.

The pleasant Historie of the six
worthie Yeomen of the
West.

In the dayes of King *Henry* the first, who was the first king that
instituted the high court of Parliament, there liued nine men, 5
which for the trade of Clothing, were famous throughout all England. Which Art in those dais was held in high reputation, both
in respect of the great riches that therby was gotten, as also of the
benefite it brought to the whole Common wealth: the yonger sons
of knights and gentlemen, to whom their fathers would leaue no 10
lands, were most commonly preferred to learne this trade, to the
end that therby they might liue in good estate, and driue forth their
daies in prosperity.

Among all Crafts, this was the only chiefe, for that it was the
greatest marchandize, by the which our Countrey became famous 15
through all Nations. And it was verily thought, that the one halfe
of the people in the land liued in those daies therby, and in such
good sort, that in the Common-wealth there was few or no beggars
at all: poore people, whom God lightly blesseth with most children,
did by meanes of this occupation so order them, that by the time 20
that they were come to be sixe or seauen yeares of age, they were
able to get their owne bread: Idlenesse was then banished our
coast, so that it was a rare thing to heare of a thiefe in those dayes.
Therefore it was not without cause that Clothiers were then both
honoured and loued, among whom these nine persons in this Kings 25
dayes were of great credit, viz. *Thomas Cole* of Reading, *Gray* of
Gloucester, *Sutton* of Salisburie, *Fitzallen* of Worcester, (commonly
called *William* of Worcester) *Tom Doue* of Exceter, and *Simon* of
South-hampton, *alias Sup-broath:* who were by the King called, The
sixe worthy husbands of the West. Then were there three liuing in 30
the North, that is to say, *Cutbert* of Kendall, *Hodgekins* of Hallifax, and *Martin Byram* of Manchester. Euery one of these kept a
great number of seruants at worke, spinners, carders, weauers,
fullers, diars, sheeremen, and rowers, to the great admiration of all
those that came into their houses to behold them. 35

267

Now you shall vnderstand, these gallant Clothiers, by reason of their dwelling places, seperated themselues in three seuerall companies: *Gray* of Gloucester, *William* of Worcester, and *Thomas* of Reading, because their iorny to London was all one way, they
5 conuerced commonly together. And *Doue* of Exceter, *Sutton* of Salisburie and *Simon* of South-hampton, they in like sort kept company, the one with the other, meeting euer altogether at Bazingstoke: and the ijj northerne Clothiers did the like, who commonly did not meet, till they came to Bosoms Inne in London.
10 Moreouer, for the loue and delight that these westerne men had each in others company, they did so prouide, that their waines and themselues would euer meete vpon one day in London at Iarrats hall, surnamed the Gyant, for that he surpassed all other men of that age, both in stature and strength: whose meriments and
15 memorable deedes, I will set downe vnto you in this following discourse.

CHAPTER I.

How King Henry Sought the Fauour of all his subiects, especially of the Clothiers.

This King *Henry,* who for his great learning and wisedome was 5
called *Beauclarke,* being the third son to the renowned Conqueror: after the death of his brother *William Rufus,* tooke vpon
him the gouernment of this land, in the absence of his second
brother *Robert* Duke of Normandy, who at this time was at warres
against the Infidels, and was chosen King of Ierusalem, the which 10
he, for the loue he bare to his owne country, refused, and with
great honour returned from the holy Land; of whose comming
when King *Henry* vnderstood, knowing he would make clayme to
the crowne, sought by all meanes possible to winne the good-will
of his Nobility and to get the fauor of the Commons by curtesie: 15
for the obtaining whereof hee did them many fauours, thereby the
better to strengthen himselfe against his brother.

It chaunced on a time, as he, with one of his sonnes, and diuers
of his Nobilitie, rode from London towards Wales, to appease the
fury of the Welshmen, which then began to raise themselues in 20
armes against his authority, that he met with a great number of
Waines loaden with cloth, comming to London; and seeing them
still driue on one after another so many together, demaunded
whose they were.

The Waine-men answered in this sort: *Coles* of Reading (quoth 25
they.)

Then by and by the King asked an other, saying: Whose cloth
is all this?

Old *Coles* (quoth he.)

And againe anone after he asked the same question to other, and 30
still they answered, Old *Coles.*

And it is to be remembred, that the King met them in such a
place, so narrow and streight, that he with all the rest of his traine,

*[30] to other] to others Q2,3; of others Q4

were faine to stand vp close to the hedge, whilest the carts passed by, the which at that time being in number aboue two hundred, was neere hand an houre ere the King could get roome to be gone: so that by his long stay, he beganne to be displeased, although the admiration of that sight did much qualifie his furie; but breaking out in discontent, by reason of his stay, he said hee thought olde *Cole* had got a Commission for all the carts in the Countrey to carry his cloth.

And how if he haue (quoth one of the Wainemen) dooth that grieue you, good sir?

Yea, good sir, said our King, what say you to that?

The fellow seeing the king (in asking that question) to bend his browes, though he knew not what he was, yet being abasht, he answered thus: Why sir, if you be angry, no body can hinder you; for possible sir, you haue Anger at commandement.

The king seeing him in vttering of his words to quiuer and quake, laughed heartily at him, as well in respect of his simple answere, as at his feare: and so soone after the last waine went by, which gaue present passage vnto him and his Nobles: and thereupon entring into communication of the commoditie of clothing, the king gaue order at his home returne, to haue Old *Cole* brought before his Maiestie, to the intent he might haue conference with him, noting him to be a subiect of great ability. But by that time he came within a mile of Stanes, he met an other company of waines in like sort laden with cloth, whereby the King was driuen into a further admiration: and demanding whose they were, answer was made in this sort:

They be goodman *Suttons* of Salisbury, good sir.

And by that time a score of them were past, he asked againe, saying: whose are these?

Suttons of Salisbury (quoth they) and so still, as often as the King asked that question, they answerd, *Suttons* of Salisbury.

God send me many such *Suttons,* said the king.

And thus the farther hee trauelled westward, more waines and more he met continually: vpon which occasion he said to his Nobles, That it would neuer grieue a King to die for the defence of a fertile countrie and faithful subiects.

I alwayes thought (quoth he) that Englands valour was more

---

⁶ said hee] said, hee Q1,2; said, I Q3,4

than her wealth, yet now I see her wealth sufficient to maintaine her valour, which I will seek to cherish in all I may, and with my Sword keepe my selfe in possession of that I haue. Kings and Louers can brooke no partners, and therefore let my brother *Robert* thinke, that although hee was heyre to England by birth, yet I am 5 King by possession. All his fauourers I must account my foes, and will serue them as I did the vngratefull earle of Shrewsbury, whose lands I haue seized, and banisht his body.

But now we will leaue the King to his iourney into Wales, and waiting his home returne, in the meane time tell you of the meet- 10 ing of these iolly Clothiers at London.

CHAPTER II.

How *William* of Worcester, *Gray* of Gloucester, and old *Cole* of Reading, met all together at Reading, and of their communication by the way as they rode to Lon- 15 don.

Whe̵n *G̵r̵a̵y̵* o̵f̵ G̵l̵o̵u̵c̵e̵s̵t̵e̵r̵,̵ a̵n̵d̵ *W̵i̵l̵l̵i̵a̵m̵* o̵f̵ W̵o̵r̵c̵e̵s̵t̵e̵r̵ w̵e̵r̵e̵ c̵o̵m̵e̵ to Reading, according to their custome, they always called old *Cole* to haue his company to London, who also duly attended their comming, hauing prouided a good breakefast for them: and 20 when they had well refreshed themselues, they tooke their horses and rode on towards the Citie: and in their iourney *William* of Worcester asked them if they had not heard of the Erle of *Moraigne* his escape out of the land.

What is he fled, quoth *Gray*? I muse much of that matter, being 25 in such great regard with the king as he was.

But I pray you, do you not know the cause of his going, quoth *Cole*?

The common report, quoth *Gray*, is this, that the couetous erle, who through a greedy desire, neuer left begging of the King 30 for one thing or other, and his request being now denied him, of meere obstinacie and wilfull frowardnesse, hath banished himselfe

271

out of the land, and quite forsaken the Countrey of Cornewall, hauing made a vow neuer to set foote within England againe, and as report goeth, he with the late banisht Earle of Shrewsbury, haue ioyned themselues with *Robert* duke of Normandy, against the
5 king, the which action of theirs hath inflamed the kings wrath, that their Ladies with their children are quite turned out of doores succorlesse and friendlesse, so that as it is told me, they wander vp and downe the countrie like forlorne people, and although many do pittie them, yet few do releeue them.
10   A lamentable hearing, quoth *William* of Worcester and with that casting their eyes aside, they espied *Tom Doue* with the rest of his companions come riding to meete them, who as soone as they were come thither, fell into such pleasaunt discourses, as did shorten the way they had to Colebroke, where alwaies at their comming to-
15 wards London they dined: and being entred into their Inne, according to olde custome, good cheere was prouided for them: for these Clothiers were the cheefest ghests that trauelled along the way: and this was as sure as an acte of Parliament, that *Tom Doue* could not digest his meat without musicke, nor drinke wine with
20 out women, so that his hostesse being a merrie wench, would often times call in two or three of her neighbours wiues to keepe him companie, where, ere they parted, they were made as pleasant as Pies. And this being a continuall custome amongest them when they came thither, at length the womens husbands beganne to take
25 exceptions at their wiues going thither: whereupon great controuersie grew betweene them, in such sort, that when they were most restrayned, then they had most desire to worke their willes.
   Now gip (quoth they) must we be so tied to our taske, that we may not drinke with our friends? fie, fie, vpon these yellow hose,
30 will no other die serue your turne? haue wee thus long bin your wiues, and do you now mistrust vs? verily you eate too much salt, and that makes you grow cholericke, badde liuers iudge all other the like, but in faith you shall not bridle vs so like Asses, but wee will go to our friendes, when wee are sent for, and do you what
35 you can.
   Well quoth their husbands, if you be so head-strong, we will tame you, it is the duty of honest women to obey their husbands sayings.

²⁸ be so] Q2-4; so be Qɪ
³¹ too much] Q2-4; two much Qɪ

And of honest men (quoth they) to thinke well of their wiues; but who doo sooner impeach their credite, then their husbands, charging them, if they do but smile, that they are subtill, and if they doe but winke, they account them wily, if sad of countenance, then sullen, if they be froward, then are they counted shrewes, and sheepish, if they be gentle: if a woman keepe her house, then you will say she is melancholie, if shee walke abroade, then you call her a gadder, a Puritane, if shee be precise, and a wanton, if shee be pleasant; so there is no woman in the world that knowes how to please you, that wee thinke our selues accurst to be married wiues, liuing with so many woes. These men, of whose company you forwarne vs, are (for aught that euer we sawe) both honest and curteous, and in wealth farre beyond your selues; then what reason is there, why we should refraine to visite them? is their good will so much to be requited with scorne, that their cost may not be counteruayled with our company? if a woman be disposed to play light of loue, alas, alas, do you thinke that you can preuent her? Nay, wee will abide by it, that the restraint of liberty inforceth women to be lewd: for where a woman cannot be trusted, she cannot think her selfe beloued, and if not beloued, what cause hath she to care for such a one? therefore husbands, reforme your opinions, and do not worke your owne woes, with our discredit. These Clothiers, we tel you are iolly fellowes, and but in respect of our curtesie, they would scorne our company.

The men hearing their wiues so wel to plead for themselues, knew not how to answer, but sayd, they would put the burden on their consciences, if they dealt vniustly with them, and so left them to their owne willes. The women hauing thus conquered their husbands conceits, would not leaue the fauour of their friends for frownes, and as aboue the rest *Tom Doue* was the most pleasantest, so was he had in most reputation with the women, who for his sake made this Song.

> Welcome to towne, Tom Doue, Tom Doue,
> The merriest man aliue,
> Thy company still we loue, we loue,
> God grant thee well to thriue,
> And neuer will depart from thee,

¹⁴ visite] Q2-4; vsite Q1

273

For better or worse, my ioy,
For thou shalt still haue our good will;
Gods blessing on my sweete Boy.

This song went vp and downe through the whole countrey, and
5 at length became a dance among the common sort, so that *Tom*
Doue, for his mirth and good fellowship, was famous in euery
place. Now when they came to London, they were welcome to the
host *Iarrat* the Gyant, and assoone as they were alighted, they were
saluted by the Marchants, who wayted their comming thither, and
10 alwaies prepared for them a costly supper, where they commonly
made their bargaine, and vpon euery bargaine made, they stil vsed
to send some tokens to the Clothiers wiues. The next morning they
went to the hal, where they met the Northern clothiers, who greeted
one another in this sort.

15 What, my maisters of the West, wel met: what cheere? what
cheere?

Euen the best cheere our Marchantes could make vs, (quoth
Gray.)

Then you could not chuse but fare well, quoth *Hogekins.*

20 And you be weary of our company, adieu, quoth *Sutton.*

Not so, sayd *Martin* but shall wee not haue a game ere wee goe?

Yes faith for a hundred pounds.

Well sayd, olde *Cole,* sayd they: and with that *Cole* and *Gray*
went to the dice with *Martin* and *Hogekins;* and the dice running
25 on *Hogekins* side, *Coles* money began to waste.

Now by the Masse, quoth *Cole,* my mony shrinks as bad as
northerne cloth.

When they had played long, *Gray* stept to it and recouered
againe the money that *Cole* had lost. But while they were thus
30 playing, the rest being delighted in contrary matters, euery man
satisfied his owne humor.

Tom Doue called for musicke, *William* of Worcester for wine,
Sutton set his delight in hearing merry tales, *Simon* of South-
hampton got him into the kitchin, and to the pottage pot he goes,
35 for he esteemed more of a messe of pottage, than of a venison pastie.
Now sir, *Cutbert* of Kendall was of another minde, for no meate
pleased him so wel as mutton, such as was laced in a red petticoate. And you shall vnderstand, that alwayes when they went to

274

dice, they got into Bosomes Inne, which was so called of his name that kept it, who being a foule slouen, went alwayes with his nose in his bosome, and one hand in his pocket, the other on his staffe, figuring forth a description of cold winter, for he alwaies wore two coates, two caps, two or three paire of stockings, and a high 5 paire of shooes, ouer the which he drew on a great paire of lined slippers, and yet he would oft complaine of cold, wherfore of all men generally he was called *Old Bosome,* and his house Bosoms Inne.

This lump of cold ice had lately married a yong wife, who 10 was as wily as she was wanton, and in hir company did *Cutbert* onely delight, and the better to make passage to his loue, he would often thus commune with her:

I muse good wife, quoth he.

Good wife, quoth she? Verily sir, in mine opinion, there is none 15 good but God, and therefore call mee Mistresse.

Then said *Cutbert,* Faire Mistresse, I haue often mused, that you being so proper a woman, could find in your heart for to match with such a greasie Carle as this, an euill mannered mate, a foule lump of kitchin stuffe, and such a one as is indeed a scorne of men; 20 how can you like him that all women mislikes? or loue such a loathsome creature? me thinks verily it should grieue you to lend him a kisse, much more to lie with him.

Indeed sir, quoth she, I had but hard fortune in this respect, but my friends would haue it so, and truly my liking and my loue 25 toward him are alike, he neuer had the one, nor neuer shall get the other: yet I may say to you, before I married him, there were diuers proper young men that were sutors vnto me, who loued mee as their liues, and glad was he that could get my company, those were my golden dayes, wherein my pleasure abounded, but 30 these are my yeeres of care and griefe, wherein my sorrowes exceede. Now no man regards me, no man cares for me, and albeit in secret they might beare me good will, yet who dares shew it? and this is a double griefe, he carries ouer me so iealous a mind, that I cannot looke at a man, but presently he accuseth me of incon- 35 stancy, although (I protest) without cause.

And in troth quoth *Cutbert,* he should haue cause to complaine for somewhat, were I as you.

16 God] Q2-4; good Q1

As sure as I liue, and so he shal, quoth she, if he do not change his bias.

Cutbert, hearing her say so, beganne to grow further in request-ing her fauor, wishing he might be her seruant and secret friend,
5 and the better to obtain his desire, he gaue her diuers gifts, inso-much that she began something to listen vnto him: and albeit she liked well of his speeches, yet would shee blame him, and take him vp very short sometimes for the same, till in the end, *Cutbert* shewed himselfe to be desperate, saying he would drowne himselfe
10 rather then liue in her disdaine.

O my sweete heart not so, quoth she, God forbid I should be the death of any man: Comfort thy selfe, kind *Cutbert,* and take this kisse in token of further kindnesse, and if thou wilt haue my fauour, thou must bee wise and circumspect, and in my husbands
15 sight I would always haue thee to finde fault with my doings, blame my bad huswifery, disprayse my person, and take exceptions at euery thing, whereby he will be as well pleased, as *Simon* of South-hampton with a messe of Pottage.

Deare mistresse quoth he, I will fulfill your charge to the vtter-
20 most, so that you will not take my iest in earnest.

Shee answered, Thy foulest speeches I will esteeme the fayrest, and take euery dispraise to be a prayse from thee, turning ech word to the contrary: and so for this time adieu, good *Cutbert,* for sup-per time drawes neere, and it is meet for me to look to my meat.
25 With that down comes old *Bosome,* calling his wife, saying, Ho *Winifred,* is supper ready? they haue done playing aboue: There-fore let the Chamberlaine couer the table.

By and by husband, quoth shee, it shall be done straight way.

How now my masters who wins, quoth *Cutbert?*
30 Our mony walkes to the west, quoth *Martin: Cole* hath woon forty li. of me, and *Gray* hath gotten well.

The best is, quoth *Hogekins,* they will pay for our supper.

Then let vs haue good store of sacke, quoth *Sutton.*

Content, sayd *Cole,* for I promise you, I striue not to grow rich
35 by dice-playing, therefore call for what you will, I wil pay for all.

Yea sayd *Simon!* Chamberlaine, I pray thee bring a whole pottle of pottage for me.

Now *Tom Doue* had all the Fidlers at a beck of his finger, which

---

²⁴ look to] Q4; look for Q1-3
²⁹ *Cutbert?*] Q3,4; ∼. Q1,2

follow him vp and downe the citie, as diligent as little Chickens after a hen, and made a vowe, that there should want no musicke. And at that time, there liued in London a musician of great reputation, named *Reior,* who kept his seruants in such costly garments, that they might seeme to come before any Prince. Their Coates 5 were all of one colour; and it is sayd, that afterward the nobility of this Land, noting it for a seemely sight, vsed in like maner to keepe their men all in one liuery. This *Reior* was the most skilfullest musician that liued at that time, whose wealth was very great, so that all the instruments whereon his seruants playd, were 10 richly garnished with studdes of siluer, and some gold: the bowes belonging to their Violins were all likewise of pure siluer. He was also for his wisedome called to great office in the city, who also builded (at his owne cost) the priory and hospitall of *Saint Bartholomew* in Smithfield. His seruants being the best consort in the City, 15 were by *Tom Doue* appointed to play before the yong princes.

Then supper being brought to the boord they all sat down, and by and by after comes vp their host, who tooke his place among them: and anone after, the goodwife in a red piticoat and a wastcoat, comes among them as white as a Lilly, saying, My masters, 20 you are welcome, I pray you be merry.

Thus falling close to their meat, when they had well fed, they found leysure to talke one with another: at what time *Cutbert* began thus to finde fault: Ywis, my hoast, quoth he, you haue a wise huswife to your wife, heere is meate drest of a new fashion, 25 God sends meat, and the diuel sends cookes.

Why what ailes the meat, quoth she; serues it not your turne? better men then yourselfe are content withall, but a paultry companion is euer worst to please.

Away, you sluttish thing, quoth *Cutbert,* your husband hath 30 a sweete iewell of you: I maruell such a graue ancient man would match himselfe with such a young giglot, that hath as much handsomenes in her as good huswifry, which is iust nothing at all.

Well sir, sayd she, in regard of my husbands presence I am loth to aggrauate anger, otherwise I would tell thee thy owne. 35

Go to, what neede all this, quoth the company? in good faith, *Cutbert,* you are to blame, you find fault where none is.

15 Smithfield. His] Q2-4; Smithfield, his Q1
24 fault:] ~, Q1-4

277

Tush, I must speake my mind, quoth *Cutbert,* I cannot dissemble, I trust the goodman thinks neuer the worse of mee, so I haue his good will, what the foule euill care I for his wifes.

Enough, quoth *Tom Doue,* let vs with musicke remooue these
5 brabbles, we meane to be merry, and not melancholy.

Then sayd old *Cole,* Now trust me *Cutbert,* we will haue our hostesse and you friends ere we part: here, woman, I drinke to you, and regard not his words, for he is brabling wheresoeuer he comes.

Quoth the woman, nothing grieues me so much, as that he
10 should thus openly checke me: if he had found any thing amisse, he might haue spied a better time to tell me of it then nowe, ywis he neede not thrust my bad huswifery into my husbands head, I liue not so quietly with him, God wot: and with that she wept.

Come *Cutbert,* quoth they, drinke to her, and shake handes and
15 bee friendes.

Come on, you puling baggage, quoth he, I drinke to you; here will you pledge me and shake hands?

No (quoth shee) I will see thee choakt first, shake hands with thee! I will shake hands with the diuell assoone.

20 Go to, sayde her husband, you shall shake handes with him then, if you will not shake hands, Ile shake you: what, you young hus-wife!

Well husband, sayd she, it becomes a woman to obey her husband, in regard whereof, I drink to him.

25 Thats well sayd quoth the company: and so she took her leaue and went downe.

And within a while after, they payd the shot, and departed thence to Garrats hall, where they went to their lodging; and the next day they tooke their way homeward all together: and com-
30 ming to Colebroke, they took vp their lodging: and it was *Coles* custome to deliuer his money to the goodwife of the house to keepe it til morning, which in the ende turned to his vtter destruction, as hereafter shall be shewed.

[10] me:] Q3,4; ~, Q1,2
[23-24] husband, in] Q2-4; ~∧ ~ Q1

CHAPTER III.

How *Grayes* wife of Gloucester, with one or two more of
her neighbours, went to the fayre, where seruants
came to be hyred, and how shee tooke the Earle of
Shrewesburies Daughter into her seruice.   5

It was wont to be an old custome in Gloucestershire, that at a certaine time in the yeere, all such young men and maidens as
were out of seruice, resorted to a faire that was kept neare Gloucester: there to be ready for any that would come to hire them, the
yong men stood all on a row on the one side, and the maydens on 10
the other. It came to passe, that the Earle of Shrewsburyes daughter,
whose father was lately banished, beeing driuen into great distresse, and weary with trauayle, as one whose delicate life was
neuer vsed to such toyle, sate her downe vpon the high way side,
making this lamentation.   15

O false and deceitfull world, quoth she! who is in thee that
wishes not to be rid of thee, for thy extreamities are great? Thou
art deceitfull to all, and trusty to none. Fortune is thy treasurer,
who is like thy selfe, wauering and vnconstant, she setteth vp
tyrants, beateth downe kings, giueth shame to some and renowne to 20
others: Fortune giueth these euils, and we see it not: with her hands
she toucheth vs, and we feele it not, she treads vs vnderfoote, and
we know it not: she speaks in our eares, and we heare her not: she
cries aloud, and we vnderstand her not: And why? because we
know her not vntill misery doth make her manifest. 25

Ah my deare father, well maist thou do. Of all misfortunes it is
most vnhappy to be fortunate: and by this misfortune came my
fall. Was euer good Lady brought to this extremity? What is become of my rare Iewels, my rich array, my sumptuous fare, my
waiting seruants, my many friends, and all my vaine pleasures? 30
my pleasure is banisht by displeasure, my friends fled like foes,
my seruants gone, my feasting turned to fasting, my rich array
consumed to ragges, and my iewels decke out my chiefest enemies:

therefore of all things the meane estate is best, pouertie with surety, is better than honour mixed with feare: seeing God hath alotted me to this misery of life, I wil frame my heart to imbrace humility, and carry a mind answerable to my misfortunes, fie on this vaine
5 title of Ladyship, how little doth it auaile the distressed? No, no, I must therefore forget my birth and parentage, and think no more on my fathers house, where I was wont to be serued, now will I learne to serue, and plain *Meg* shall be my name: good Lord grant I may get a good seruice, nay any seruice shall serue, where I may
10 haue meat, drinke and apparell.

She had no sooner spoke these words, but she espied a couple of maidens more comming towards her; who were going to the faire; and bidding her good morrow, asked her if she went to the faire.

Yea mary quoth she, I am a poore mans child that is out of
15 seruice, and I heare that at the Statute folkes do come of purpose to hire seruants.

True it is said the maidens, and thither goe we for the same purpose, and would be glad of your company.

With a good will, and I am right glad of yours, said she, be-
20 seeching you good maidens you will doe me the fauour, to tell me what seruice were best for me; for the more too blame my parents, they would neuer put me forth to know any thing.

Why what can you do (quoth the maidens) can you brew and bake, make butter and cheese, and reape corne well?
25 No verily said *Margaret,* but I would be right glad to learne to do anything whatsoeuer it be.

If you could spin or card said another, you might do excellent well with a clothier, for they are the best seruices that I know, there you shall be sure to fare well, and to liue merily.
30 Then *Margaret* wept saying, alas, what shall I do? I was neuer brought vp to these things.

What can you doe nothing quoth they?

No truly (quoth she) that is good for any thing, but I can reade, and write and sowe, some skill I haue in my needle, and a little on
35 my Lute: but this, I see will profit me nothing.

Good Lord, quoth they, are you bookish? we did neuer heare of a mayde before that could read and write. And although you

---

³⁰ saying, alas,] Q4; saying (alas) Q1 ; saying ∧ alas ∧ Q2,3

can do no other thing, yet possibly you may get a seruice, if you can behaue your selfe mannerly.

I pray you quoth another, seing you are bookish, will you do so much as to read a loue letter that is sent me, for I was at a friends of mine with it, and he was not at home, and so I know not what is in it.

I pray you let me see it, quoth *Margaret,* and I will shew you. Whereupon she readeth as followeth.

> O *Ienny* my ioy, I die for thy loue,
> And now I heare say that thou dost remoue: 10
> And therefore, Ienney, I pray thee recite
> Where I shall meete thee soone at night.
>
> For why, with my master no more will I stay,
> But for thy loue I will runne away,
> O *Ienny, Ienny,* thou puttst mee to payne,   15
> That thou no longer wilt here remayne.
>
> I will weare out my shoes of Neats Leather,
> But thou and I will meete together,
> And in spite of Fortune, Rat, or Mouse,
> We will dwell in one house.   20
>
> For who doth not esteeme of thee,
> Shall haue no seruice done of me:
> Therefore good *Ienny,* haue a care
> To meete poore *Fragment* at the fayre.

Now alas, good soule (quoth *Ienny*) I thinke he be the kindest young man in the world.

The rest answered, that he seemed no lesse, and surely it appeareth that he is a pretty witty fellow, quoth one of them, how finely he hath written his letter in rime, trust me, I will giue you a good thing, and let me haue a copy of it to send to my sweet hart.

That you shall, with all my heart: and so comming to the faire, they took vp their standing.

Within a while after, goodwife *Gray* of Gloucester came thither to store her selfe of diuers commodities: and when shee had boght

what she would, she told her neighbor she had great need of a maid
seruant or twaine.

Therefore quoth she, good neighbor go with me, and let me haue
your opinion.

5 With a good wil, said her neighbor.

And together they went, and looking and viewing the maidens
ouer, she tooke speciall notice of *Margaret.*

Beleeue me, quoth she, there stands a very proper mayden,
and one of a modest and comely countenaunce.

10 Verily, said her neighbor, so she is, as euer I looked vpon.

The mayden seeing them to view her so well, was so abashed,
that a scarlet colour ouerspred her lilly cheeks; which the woman
perceiuing, came vnto her, and asked if she were willing to serue.

The mayd with a low curtesie, and a most gentle speach, aun-
15 swered it was the onely cause of her comming.

Can you spinne or card, said goodwife *Gray?*

Truely Dame, said she, though my cunning therein be but small,
my goodwil to learne is great, and I trust, my diligence shall content you.

20 What wages will you take, quoth good wife *Gray?*

I will referre that, said *Margaret,* to your conscience and curtesie,
desiring no more than what I shall deserue.

Then asking what country woman she was the maiden wept,
saying, Ah good Dame, I was vntimely borne in Shropshire, of
25 poore parents, and yet not so needy as vnfortunate, but death
hauing ended their sorrowes, hath left me to the cruelty of these
enuious times, to finish my parents tragedy with my troubles.

What maiden! quoth her Dame, haue you a care to do your
busines, and to liue in Gods feare, and you shall haue no care to
30 regard Fortunes frownes.

And so they went home together.

Now, so soone as the goodman sawe her, he asked his wife where
she had that maiden.

She said, at the faire.

35 Why then quoth he, thou hast brought all the faire away, and I
doubt it were better for vs, to send the faire to another towne, **than**
to keep the faire here.

Why man, quoth she, what meane you by that?

Woman I meane this, that she will proue a Loadstone, to draw

---

33 maiden.] Q2; ~ ∧ Q1; ~ Q3,4

the harts of al my men after her, and so we shal haue wise seruice
done of all sides.

Then said his wife, I hope husband, *Margaret* will haue a better
care both to her owne credit, and our commodity then so, and let
me alone to looke to such matters. 5

Is thy name *Margaret* (quoth her master?) proper is thy name
to thy person, for thou art a pearle indeed, orient, and rich in
beauty.

His wife hearing him say so, began to change her opinion.

What husband (quoth she) is the wind at that doore? Begin you 10
to like your maid so well? I doubt I had most need to look to your
selfe: before God, I had rather then an angell I had chosen some
other: but heare you mayd; you shall pack hence, I will not nourish
a snake in my bosome, and therefore get you gone, I will none of
you, prouide a seruice where you may. 15

The mayden hearing her say so, fell downe on her knees, and
besought her saying, O sweet dame, be not so cruell to mee, to
turne me out of doores now: alas, I know not where to go, or what
to do, if you forsake me. O let not the fading beauty of my face
dispoyle me of your fauor: for rather then that shall hinder my 20
seruice, this my knife shall soone disfigure my face, and I will
banish beauty as my greatest enemy.

And with that her abundant teares stopped her speech, that
she could not vtter one word more.

The woman seeing this, could not harbour anger longer, nor 25
could her master stay in the roome for weeping. Well *Margaret*,
sayd her dame (little knowing that a Lady kneeled before her)
vsing thy selfe well, I well keepe thee and thou shalt haue my good
will, if thou gouerne they selfe with wisdom.

And so she sent her about her businesse. 30

Her husband comming to supper, sayd, How now! wife, art thou
so doubtfull of me, that thou hast put away thy mayden?

I wis (quoth she) you are a wise man, to stand praysing of a
maydes beauty before her face.

And you a wise woman (quoth he) to grow iealous without a 35
cause.

So to supper they went, and because *Margaret* shewed her selfe
of finest behauiour aboue the rest, she was appointed to waite on
the table.

And it is to be vnderstood, that *Gray* did neuer eate his meate 40 alone but still had some of his neighbors with him, before whom he called his mayd, saying, *Margaret,* come hither.

Now because there was another of the same name in the house, she made answere.

5   I call not you maiden, quoth he, but *Margaret* with the lilly white hand. After which time she was euer called so.

CHAPTER IV.

How the Kings maiestie sent for the Clothiers, and of the sundry fauours which he did them.

10   K ing *Henry* prouiding for his voyage into France, against King *Lewis* and *Robert* Duke of Normandy his owne brother, commited the gouernement of the Realme in his absence, to the Bishop of Salisbury, a man of great wisdome and learning, whom the King esteemed highly, and afterward he thought good to send for the
15 chiefe Clothiers of England, who according to the kings appoyntment came to the court, and hauing licence to come before his Maiesty, hee spake to this effect.

The strength of a king is the loue and friendship of his people, and he gouerns ouer his Realme most surely, that ruleth iustice
20 with mercy, for hee ought to feare many, whom many do feare: therefore the gouernours of the common wealth ought to obserue two speciall precepts, the one is, that they so maintayne the profit of the commons, that whatsoeuer in their calling they do, they referre it thereunto: the other, that they bee alwayes as well care-
25 full ouer the whole common wealth, as ouer any part thereof, lest while they vpholde the one, the other be brought to vtter decay.

And forasmuch as I doe vnderstand, and haue partly seene, that you the Clothiers of England are no small benefit to the wealth publike, I thought it good to know from your owne mouths, if there
30 be any thing not yet graunted that may benefit you or any other thing to be remoued that doth hurt you.

The great desire I haue to maintayne you in your trades, hath moued me hereunto. Therefore boldly say what you would haue in the one thing or the other, and I will grant it you.

With that, they all fell downe vpon their knees, and desired God to saue his Maiesty, and withall, requested three dayes respit to put in their answere: which was graunted. And thereupon they de- 5 parted.

When the Clothiers had well considered of these matters, at length they thought meete to request of his Maiesty for their first benefit, that all the Cloth measures, through the land might be of one length, whereas to their great disaduantage before, euery good 10 towne had a seuerall measure, the difficulty thereof was such, that they could not keepe them in memory, nor know how to keepe their reckonings.

The second thing whereof they found themselues greeued, was this, that the people would not take crackt money, though it were 15 neuer so good siluer: whereupon it came to passe, that the Clothiers and diuers other receiuing great summes of money, do take among it much crackt money, it serued them to no vse, because it would not go currant, but lay vpon their hands without profite or benefit, whereof they prayed reformation. 20

The third was a griefe, whereof *Hodgekins* of Halyfax com-playned, and that was, that whereas the towne of Halyfax liued altogether vpon clothing, and by the reason of false borderers and other euill minded persons, they were oft robbed, and had their clothes carried out of their fieldes, where they were drying, 25 that it would please his Maiesty to grant the towne this priuiledge, that whosoeuer hee was that was taken stealing their cloth, might presently without any further triall be hanged vp.

When the day of their appearance approched, the Clothiers came before the King, and deliuered vp their petition in writing, 30 which his Maiesty most graciously perusing, sayd, he was ready to fullfill their request: and therefore for the first poynt of their peti-tion, he called for a staffe to be brought him, and measuring there-upon the iust length of his owne arme, deliuered it to the clothiers, saying, This measure shalbe called a yard, and no other measure 35 throughout all the Realme of England shall be vsed for the same, and by this shall men buy and sell, and we will so prouide, that whosoeuer he be that abuseth our subiects by any false measure,

---

[17] do take] Q2-4; to take Q1

that he shall not onely pay a fine for the same to the king, but also haue his body punnished by imprisonment.

And as concerning the second poynt of your petition, because of my sudden departure out of the land, I know not better how to
5 ease you of this griefe (of crackt money) this decree I make, because they account crackt money not currant: I say, none shalbe currant but crackt money. And therefore I will giue present charge, that all the money through the land shalbe slit, and so you shall suffer no losse.

10 But now for your last request for the towne of Halyfax, where by theeues your clothes are so often stolne from you, seeing the lawes already prouided in that case are not sufficient to keepe men in awe, it is indeed high time to haue sharper punishment for them.

With that *Hodgekins* vnmannerly interrupted the King, saying
15 in broad Northern speech, Yea gude faith, mai Liedge, the faule eule of mai saule, giff any thing will keep them whiat, till the karles be hangde vp by the cragge. What the dule care they for boaring their eyne, sea lang as they may gae groping vp and downe the countrey like fause lizar lownes, begging and craking?

20 The king, smiling to heare this rough hewne fellow, made this reply: Content thee *Hodgekins,* for we wil haue redresse for all: and albeit that hanging of men was neuer seene in England, yet seeing the corrupt world is growne more bold in all wickednes, I thinke it not amisse to ordaine this death for such malefactors:
25 and peculiarly to the towne of Hallifaxe I giue this priuiledge, that whosouer they find stealing their cloth, being taken with the goods, that without further iudgement they shalbe hanged vp.

Thus (sayd our king) haue I graunted what you request, and if hereafter you find any other thing that may be good for you, it
30 shall be granted; for no longer would I desire to liue among you, then I haue care for the good of the commonwealth: at which word ended, the King rose from his royall throne, while the clothiers on their knees prayed for both his health and happy successe, and shewed themselues most thankfull for his highnesse fauor. His
35 maiesty bending his body toward them, sayd that at his home re-turne, he would (by the grace of God) visit them.

²⁰ made] Mann; make Q1-4

286

CHAPTER V.

How the Clothiers had prouided a sumptuous feast for the
  Kings sonnes, prince *William* and prince *Richard* at
  Gerrards hall, shewing also what chaunce befell *Cut-*
  bert of Kendall at that same instant.   5

The Clothiers departing from the court in a merry minde, ioyfull of their good successe, each one to other praised and mag-
nified the Kings great wisedome and vertue, commending also his
affabilitie and gentle disposition, so that *Hodgekins* affirmed on
his faith, that hee had rather speake to the Kings maiestie, than to 10
many Iustices of peace.

Indeed (said *Cole*) he is a most mild and mercifull prince, and
I pray God he may long raigne ouer vs.

Amen said the rest.

Then said *Cole,* My masters, shall we forget the great curtesie 15
of the Kings sonnes, those sweet and gentle princes, that still shewed
vs fauour in our suite? in my opinion it were reason to gratifie
them in some sort, that we may not vtterly be condemned of in-
gratitude: wherefore (if you thinke good) we will prepare a banquet
for them at our hoast *Garrats,* who as you know, hath a faire 20
house, and goodly roomes: Besides, the man himselfe is of a most
couragious mind and good behauiour, sufficient to entertaine a
prince; his wife also is a dainty fine Cooke: all which considered,
I know not a fitter place in London.

Tis true, quoth *Sutton,* and if the rest be content, I am pleased 25
it shalbe so.

At this they all answered, Yea, for (quoth they) it will not be
passing forty shillings apeece, and that we shall recouer in our
crackt money.

Being thus agreed, the feast was prepared.   30

Tom Doue quoth they, we will commit the prouiding of musicke
to thee.

287

And I, said *Cole,* will inuite diuers of our marchants and their wiues to the same.

That is well remembred, said *Gray.*

Vpon this they called to their hoast and hostesse, shewing their
5 determination, who most willingly said, all things should be made ready.

But I would haue two days liberty, sayd the good wife, to prepare my house and other things.

Content, said the Clothiers, in the meane space we will bid our
10 gests, and dispatch our other affaires.

But *Simon* of Southhampton charged his hostise, that in any case shee should not forget to make good store of pottage.

It shall be done quoth shee.

It is to be remembred, that while this preparation was in hand,
15 that *Cutbert* of Kendal had not forgot his kindnes to his hostise of Bosomes Inne. Therefore finding time conuenient when her husband was ouerseeing his haymakers, he greeted her in this sort, Sweet hostesse, though I were the last time I was in towne, ouer bold with you, yet I hope it was not so offensiue to you, as you
20 made shew for.

Bold, my *Cutbert,* quoth she? thou hast vowd thy selfe my seruant, and so being, you are not to be blam'd for doing what I wild you. By my honesty, I could not chuse but smile to my selfe, so soone as I was out of their sight, to thinke how prettily
25 you began your brabble.

But now, quoth he, we will change our chidings to kissings, and it vexeth me that these cherry lippes should be subiect to such a Lobcocke as thy husband.

Subiect to him quoth she! In faith sir, no, I will haue my lips at
30 as much liberty as my tongue, the one to say what I list, and the other to touch whom I like: In troth, shall I tell thee, *Cutbert,* the churles breath smels so strong, that I care as much for kissing of him, as for looking on him tis such a misshapen mizer, and such a bundle of beastlynesse, that I can neuer thinke on him without
35 spitting. Fie vpon him, I would my friends had carried me to my graue, when they went with me to the Church, to make him my husband. And so shedding a few dissembling teares, she stopt.

What my sweete mistresse (quoth he) weepe you? Nay sit downe

---

¹⁴ to be] Q2-4; be to Q1

by my side, and I will sing thee one of my country Iigges to make
thee merry.

Wilt thou in faith (quoth she)?

Yes verily, sayd *Cutbert.*

And in troth, quoth she, if you fall a singing, I will sing with 5
you.

That is well, you can so suddenly change your notes, quoth
Cutbert, then haue at it.

Man.	Long haue I lou'd this bonny Lasse,	
	yet durst not shew the same.	10
Wom.	Therein you prou'd your selfe an Asse,	
Man.	I was the more to blame.	
	Yet still will I remaine to thee,	
	Trang dilly do, trang dilly,	
	Thy friend and louer secretly.	15
Wom.	Thou art my owne sweet bully.	
Man.	But when shall I enioy thee,	
	delight of thy faire loue?	
Wom.	Euen when thou seest that fortune doth	
	all maner lets remoue.	20
Man.	O, I will fold thee in my armes,	
	Trang dilly do, trang dilly,	
	And keepe thee so from sodaine harmes.	
Wom.	Thou art my owne sweet bully.	
Wom.	My husband he is gone from home,	25
	you know it very well.	
Man.	But when will he returne againe?	
Wom.	In troth I cannot tell:	
	If long he keepe him out of sight,	
	Trang dilly do, trang dilly,	30
	Be sure thou shalt haue thy delight.	
Man.	Thou art my bonny lassy.	

While they were singing this song, her husband being on a sudden
come home, stood secretly in a corner and heard all, and blessing
himselfe with both his hands, sayd O abominable dissimulation, 35
monstrous hypocrisie, and are you in this humor? can you brawle

together and sing together? Well quoth he, I will let them alone,
and see a little more of their knauery. Neuer did Catte watch
Mouse so narrowely, as I will watch them.

And so going into the Kitchin, he asked his wife if it were not
5 dinner time.

Euen by and by, husband (quoth she) the meat will be ready.

Presently after comes in *Hodgekins* and *Martin,* who strayght
asked for *Cutbert* of Kendall. Answere was made, that he was in
his Chamber. So when they had called him, they went to dinner:
10 then they requested that their host and hostesse would sit with
them.

Husband, said she, you may go if you please: but as for me, I
will desire pardon.

Nay, good wife, go vp said her husband. What woman, you must
15 beare with your ghests.

Why husband, quoth she, do you think that any can beare the
flerts and frumps which that Northern tike gaue me the last time
hee was in towne? now God forgiue me, I had as liefe see the diuell
as see him: Therefore good husband, go vp your selfe, and let me
20 alone, for in faith, I shall neuer abide that Iacke while I liue.

Vpon these words away went her husband, and though he sayd
little he thought the more. Now when he came vp, his ghests bade
him welcome.

I pray you sit downe, good mine hoast, quoth they, where is
25 your wife? what will not shee sit with vs?

No verily sayd he, the foolish woman hath taken such a displeasure against *Cutbert,* that she sweares she will neuer come in
his company.

Is it so, said the other? then trust me we are well agreed. And I
30 sweare by my fathers sale, quoth hee, that were it not more for
good will to you, than loue to her, I would neuer come to your
house more.

I beleeue it well, said old *Bosome.*

And so with other communication they droue out the time, till
35 Dinner was ended.

After they were risen, *Martin* and *Hodgekins* got them forth
about their affaires, but *Cutbert* took his host by the hand, saying,
My host, Ile go talk with your wife; for my part I thought we had

³¹ to you] Q2-4; o you Q1

beene friends: but seeing her stomacke is so big and her heart so great, I will see what she will say to me; and with that hee stept into the kitchin, saying, God speed you hostise.

It must be when you are away then, sayd she.

What is your reason sayd the other? 5

Because God neuer comes where knaues are present.

Gip gooddy draggletaile, quoth he, had I such a wife, I would present her tallow face to the diuell for a candle.

With that shee bent her browes, and like a fury of hel began to fly at him saying, Why, you gag-toothd Iack, you blinking com- 10 panion, get thee out of my Kitchin quickly, or with my powdered Beefe broth, I will make your pate as balde as a Friers.

Get me gone, quoth he? thou shalt not bid mee twise: out you durty heeles, you will make your husbands hayre growe through his hood I doubt. 15

And with that hee got him into the Hall, and sate him downe on the bench by his hoast, to whom he sayd: Tis pitty my host, that your aged yeeres that loues quietnesse, should be troubled with such a scolding queane.

I, God help me, God helpe me quoth the old man; and so went 20 toward the Stable; which his wife watching, sodainly stept out and gaue *Cutbert* a kisse.

Within an houre after, the old man craftily called for his Nag to ride to field: but as soone as he was gone, *Cutbert* and his Host-esse were such good friends, that they got into one of the Ware 25 houses, and lockt the doore to them: but her husband hauing set a spye for the purpose, sodainly turned backe, and called for a capcase which lay in the Warehouse. The seruant could not find the key by any meanes. Whereupon hee called to haue the lock broke open. Which they within hearing, opened the doore of their 30 owne accord.

So soone as her husband spied her in that place, with admiration he sayd O, the passion of my hart, what do you heer? what you two that cannot abide one another? what make you so close to-gether? is your chiding and rayling, brabling and brawling, come 35 to this? O what dissemblers are these!

Why, my hoast quoth *Cutbert* what need you take the matter so hotte? I gaue a Cheese to my country man *Hodgekins,* to lay vp, and deliuered it to your wife to bee kept; and then is it not reason, that she should come and seeke me my Cheese? 40

O, quoth the old man, belike the doore was lockt, because the cheese should not run away.

The doore said his wife vnknowne to vs clapt to it selfe, and hauing a spring lock, was presently fast.

5 Wel, hus-wife, quoth he; I will giue you as much credit as a Crocadile; but as for your companion I will teach him to come hither to looke for cheeses.

And with that he caused his men to take him presently, and to binde him hand and foote. Which being done, they drew him vp
10 in a basket into the smokie louer of the hall, and there they did let him hang all that night, euen till the next day dinner time, when he should haue beene at the banquet with the princes: for neither *Hodgekins* nor *Martin* could intreat their inflamed hoast to let him downe.

15 And in such a heate was he driuen with drawing him vp, that he was faine to cast off his gownes, his coats, and two paire of his stockings, to coole himselfe, making a vow he should hang there vij. yeares except the kings sonnes came in person to beg his pardon, which most of all grieued *Cutbert*. When *Cole* and the rest
20 of the westerne yeomen heard hereof, they could not chuse but laugh, to think that he was so taken tardy.

The yong princes hauing giuen promise to be with the clothiers kept their houre, but when al the rest went to giue them entertainment, *Simon* was so busie in supping his pottage, that he
25 could not spare so much time. Which when the princes sawe, with a smiling countenance they said, Sup *Simon,* theres good broath.

Or else beshrew our hostesse, quoth he, neuer looking behind him to see who spake, till the prince clapt him on the shoulder. But good Lord, how blanke he was when he spied them, knowing
30 not how to excuse the matter.

Well, the princes hauing ended their banket, *Garrat* coms, and with one of his hands took the table of 16 foot long quite from the ground ouer their heads, from before the princes, and set it on the other side of the hall, to the great admiration of all them
35 that beheld it.

The princes being then ready to depart, the Clothiers moued

⁷ looke for] looke Q1-4
²⁶-²⁷ broath. *new par.* Or] broath, or Q1,2; ~: ~ Q3,4
²⁷ hostesse,] Q3,4; ~: Q1,2

292

them in pleasant maner, to be good to one of their company, that
did neither sit, lie, nor stand.

Then he must needes hang, quoth the princes.

And so he doth, most excellent princes quoth they; and there-
withal told them the whole matter.   5

When they heard the story, downe to *Bosoms* inne they goe, where
looking vp into the roofe, spied poore *Cutbert* pinned vp in a
basket, and almost smoked to death, who although he were greatly
ashamed, yet most pittifully desired that they would get him
released.   10

What is his trespasse, said the prince?

Nothing if it shall like your Grace quoth he, but for looking for
a cheese.

But he could not find it without my wife, said the good man:
the villaine had lately dined with mutton, and could not digest   15
his meate without cheese, for which cause I haue made him to fast
these twenty houres, to the end he may haue a better stomacke to
eate his dinner, then to vse dalliance.

Let me intreate you quoth the prince, to release him: and if
euer hereafter you catch him in the corne, clappe him in the   20
pownd.

Your Grace shall request or commaund any thing at my hand,
said the old man.

And so *Cutbert* was let downe vnbound: but when he was loose,
he vowed neuer to come within that house more. And it is said,   25
the old man *Bosome* ordaind, that in remembrance of this deed
euery yeare once all such as came thither to aske for cheeses should
be so serued: which thing is to this day kept.

CHAPTER VI.

How *Simons* wife of South-hampton being wholy bent to
pride and pleasure, requested her husband to see
London, which being graunted, how she got good wife
5   *Sutton* of Salisbury to go with her, who tooke *Crab*
to go along with them, and how he prophecied of
many things.

The Clothiers being all come from London, *Simons* wife of South-
hampton who was with her husband very merry and pleasant,
10 brake her mind vnto him in this sort.

Good Lord husband, wil you neuer be so kind as let me go to
London with you? shall I be pend vp in South-hampton, like a
parrat in a cage, or a capon in a coope? I would request no more
of you in lieu of all my paines, carke and care, but to haue one
15 weeks time to see that faire citie: what is this life if it be not mixt
with some delight? and what delight is more pleasing than to see the
fashions and maners of vnknowne places? Therefore good husband,
if thou louest me, deny not this simple request. You know I am
no common gadder, nor haue oft troubled you with trauell. God
20 knowes, this may be the last thing that euer I shall request at your
hands.

Woman quoth he, I would willingly satisfie your desire, but
you know it is not conuenient for both of vs to be abroad, our
charge is great, and therefore our care ought not to be small. If
25 you will goe your selfe, one of my men shall goe with you, and
money enough you shall haue in your purse: but to go with you
my selfe, you see my busines will not permit me.

Husband said she, I accept your gentle offer, and it may be I
shal intreat my gossip *Sutton* to go along with me.

30   I shal be glad quoth her husband, prepare your selfe when
you will.

[8] *Simons*] Mann; *Suttons* Q1-4

Chapter Six

When she had obtained this licence, she sent hir man *Weasell* to Salisbury, to know of good wife *Sutton* if she would keep her company to London. *Suttons* wife being as willing to go, as she was to request, neuer rested till she had gotten leaue of her husband; the which when she had obtained, casting in her minde their pleasure would be small, being but they twayne; thereupon the wily woman sent letters by collerick *Crabbe* her man, both to *Grayes* wife, and *Fitzallens* wife, that they would meet them at Reading; who liking wel of the match, consented and did so prouide that they met according to promise at Reading, and from thence with *Coles* wife they went al together, with each of them a man to London, ech one taking vp their lodging with a seuerall friend.

When the Marchants of London vnderstood they were in towne, they inuited them euery day home to their owne houses, where they had delicate good cheere: and when they went abroade to see the commodityes of the City, the Marchants wiues euer bore them company, being attyred most dainty and fine: which when the Clothiers wiues did see, it grieued their hearts they had not the like.

Now when they were brought into Cheapeside, there with great wonder they beheld the shops of the Goldsmiths; and on the other side, the wealthy Mercers, whose shops shined of al sortes of coloured silkes; in Watlingstreete, they viewed the great number of Drapers; in Saint Martines, Shoomakers; at Saint Nicholas church, the flesh shambles; at the end of the old change, the fishmongers; in Candleweeke streete the Weauers; then came into the Iewes streete, where all the Iewes did inhabite; then went they to Blackwel hall, where the country clothiers did vse to meete.

Afterward they proceeded, and came to S. Pauls church, whose steeple was so hye, that it seemed to pierce the clouds, on the top whereof, was a great and mighty wethercocke, of cleane siluer, the which notwithstanding seemed as small as a sparrow to mens eyes, it stood so exceeding high, the which goodly weathercocke was afterwards stolen away, by a cunning cripple, who found meanes one night to climbe vp to the toppe of the steeple, and tooke it downe, with the which, and a great summe of mony which he had got together by begging in his life time, he builded a gate on the North-west side of the city, which to this day is called Criple gate.

1 *Weasell*] Q4; *Wessell* Q1; *Welsell* Q2,3
7 *Crabbe*] Mann; *Cracke* Q1-4

From thence they went to the Tower of London, which was builded by *Iulius Caesar,* who was Emperour of Rome. And there they beheld salt and wine, which had laine there euer since the Romans inuaded this land, which was many yeares before our
5 Sauiour *Christ* was borne, the wine was growne so thicke that it might haue bin cut like a ielley. And in that place also they sawe money that was made of leather, which in ancient time went currant amongst the people.

When they had to their great contentation beheld all this, they
10 repaired to their lodgings, hauing also a sumptuous supper ordained for them, with all delight that might be. And you shall vnderstand that when the country weauers, which came vp with their dames, saw the weauers of Candlewike-street, they had great desire presently to haue some conference with them, and thus one
15 began to challenge the other for workmanship.

Quoth *Weasell,* ile worke with any of you all for a crowne, take it if you dare, and he that makes his yeard of cloth soonest, shall haue it.

You shall be wrought withall, said the other, and if it were
20 for tenne crownes; but we wil make this bargaine, that each of vs shall wynde their owne quilles.

Content quoth *Weasell.*

And so to worke they went, but *Wesel* lost. Whereupon another of them tooke the matter in hand, who lost likewise: so that the
25 London weauers triumphed against the country, casting forth diuers frumps.

Alas poore fellowes, quoth they, your hearts are good, but your hands are ill.

Tush, the fault was in their legges, quoth another, pray you
30 friend were you not borne at home?

Whie doe you aske quoth *Weasell?*

Because, said hee, the biggest place of your legge is next to your shoe.

Crabbe hearing this, being cholericke of nature, chafed like a
35 man of law at the barre, and he wagers with them foure crowns to twain, the others agreed, to work they go: but *Crab* conquered them all. Whereupon, the London weauers were nipt in the head like birds, and had not a word to say.

*15 the other] Q2-4; thother Q1
34 *Crabbe*] Q4; *Cutbert* Q1-3

Chapter Six

Now faith *Crab* as we haue lost nothing, so you haue won nothing, and because I know ye cannot be right weauers, except you be good fellowes, therefore if you will go with vs, wee will bestow the ale vpon you.

That is spoken like a good fellow and like a weauer, quoth the 5 other. So along they went as it were to the signe of the red Crosse.

When they were set downe, and had drunk well, they began merrily to prattle, and to extoll *Crab* to the skies. Whereupon *Crab* protested, that he would come and dwell among them.

Nay, that must not be, sayd a London weauer. The king hath 10 giuen vs priuilege, that none shal liue among vs, but such as serue seuen yeeres in London.

With that *Crab,* according to his old manner of prophesying, sayd thus:

> The day is very neere at hand, 15
> When as a King of this faire land
> Shall priuiledge you more then so:
> Then weauers shall in scarlet go.

> And to one brotherhood be brought,
> The first that is in London wrought, 20
> When other trades-men by your fame,
> Shall couet all to doe the same.

> Then shall you all liue wondrous well,
> But this one thing I shall you tell:
> The day will come before the doome, 25
> In Candleweeke streete shall stand no loome.

> Nor any weauer dwelling there,
> But men that shall more credit beare:
> For clothing shall be sore decayed,
> And men vndone that vse that trade. 30

> And yet the day some men shall see,
> This trade againe shall raised be,

[10] weauer.] ~? Q1,2; ~: Q3,4
[13] prophesying] Q2-4; prophesing Q1

When as Bayliffe of Sarum towne,
Shal buy and purchase Bishops downe.

When there neuer man did sow,
Great store of goodly corne shall grow;
5   And woad, that makes all colours sound
Shall spring vpon that barren ground.

At that same day I tell you plaine,
Who so aliue doth then remaine,
A proper mayden there shall see,
10   Within the towne of Salisbury.

Of fauour sweete, of nature kind,
With goodly eies, and yet starke blind,
This poore blind mayden I do say,
In age shall go in rich array.

15   And he that takes her to his wife
Shall lead a ioyfull happy life,
The wealthiest Clothier shall he be,
That euer was in that country.

But clothing kept as it hath beene
20   In London neuer shal be seene:
For weauers then the most shal win,
That worke for clothing next the skin.

Til pride the commonwealth doth peele,
And causeth huswiues leaue their wheele.
25   Then pouerty vpon each side
Vnto those workemen shall betide.

At that time, from an Egles nest,
That proudly builded in the West,
A sort shal come with cunning hand,
30   To bring strange weauing in this land.

4 grow;] Q3,4; ~? Q1,2
13 say,] Q2-4; ~. Q1
26 betide.] Q3,4; be tide ∧ Q1,2

298

And by their gaines that great will fall,
They shall maynetaine the weauers hall:
But long they shall not flourish so,
But folly will them ouerthrow.

And men shall count it mickle shame,   5
To beare that kind of Weauers name,
And this as sure will come to passe,
As here is ale within this glasse.

When the silly soules that sate about him heard him speake in
this sort, they admired, and honoured *Crabbe* for the same.   10
Why my masters, said *Weasel,* do you wonder at these words?
he will tell you twenty of these tales, for which cause we call him
our canuas Prophet.
His attire fits his title, said they, and we neuer heard the like
in our liues; and if this should be true, it would be strange.   15
Doubt not but it will be true, quoth *Weasel,* for ile tell you
what, he did but once see our *Nick,* kis *Nel,* and presently he
powred out this rime.

That kisse O Nel, God giue thee ioy,
Will nine monthes hence breede thee a boy.   20

And Ile tell you what, you shall heare: we kept reckoning and
it fell out as iust as *Iones* buttockes on a close stoole, for which
cause, our maids durst neuer kisse a man in his sight.
Vpon this they broke company, and went euery one about his
busines, the London weauers to their frames, and the country   25
fellowes to their dames, who after their great banqueting and meriment went euery one home to their owne houses, though with lesse
money then they brought out, yet with more pride.
Especially *Simons* wife of South-hampton, who tolde the rest of
her gossips, that shee sawe no reason, but that their husbands   30
should mainetaine them, as well as the Marchants did their wiues:
for I tell you what, quoth she, we are as proper women (in my
conceit) as the proudest of them all, as handsome of body, as faire
of face, our legs as well made, and our feete as fine: then what

---

[19] thee] Q2-4; the Qɪ

reason is there (seeing our husbandes are of as good wealth) but we should be as well maintained?

You say true gossip, said *Suttons* wife: trust me, it made me blush, to see them braue it out so gallantly, and we to goe so
5 homely.

But before *God,* said the other, I will haue my husband to buy me a London gowne, or in faith he shall haue little quiet.

So shall mine, said another.

And mine too, quoth the third.

10 And all of them sung the same note: so that when they came home, their husbands had no little to do.

Especially *Simon,* whose wife daily lay at him for London apparell, to whome he sayd, Good woman, be content, let vs go according to our place and ability: what will the Bailiffes thinke,
15 if I should prancke thee vp like a Peacocke, and thou in thy attire surpasse their wiues? they would eyther thinke I were madde, or else that I had more money then I could well vse: consider I pray thee good wife, that such as are in their youth wasters, doe prooue in their age starke beggars.

20 Beside that, it is enough to raise me vp in the Kings books: for many times, mens coffers are iudged by their garments: why, we are country folkes, and must keepe our selues in good compasse: gray russet, and good home-spun cloth doth best become vs; I tell thee wife, it were as vndecent for vs to go like Londoners, as it is
25 for Londoners to go like courtiers.

What a coyle keepe you, quoth she? are not we Gods creatures as well as Londoners? and the Kings subiects, as well as they? then finding our wealth to be as good as theirs, why should we not goe as gay as Londoners? No husband, no, heere is the fault, we are
30 kept without it, onely because our husbands are not so kind as Londoners: why man, a Cobler there, keepes his wife better then the best Clothier in this country: nay, I will affirme it, that the London Oyster-wiues, and the very Kitchin-stuffe cryers, do exceed vs in their Sundayes attyre: nay, more then that, I did see the
35 Water-bearers wife which belongs to one of our Marchants, come in with a Tankerd of water on her shoulder, and yet halfe a dozen gold rings on her fingers.

You may then thinke, wife (quoth he) she got them not with idlenesse.

20 enough] Q2-4; inough Q1

Chapter Six

But wife, you must consider what London is, the chiefe and capitall City of all the land, a place on the which all strangers cast their eyes, it is (wife) the Kings chamber, and his Maiesties royall seate: to that City repaires all Nations vnder heauen. Therefore it is most meete and conuenient, that the cittizens of such a City should not goe in their apparell like Peasants, but for the credit of our countrey, weare such seemely habites, as doo carry grauity and comelinesse in the eyes of all beholders.

But if we of the countrey went so (quoth she) were it not as great credit for the land as the other?

Woman quoth her husband, it is altogether needlesse, and in diuers respects it may not be.

Why then I pray you, quoth she, let vs go dwell at London.

A word soone spoken, said her husband, but not so easie to be performed: therefore wife, I pray thee hold thy prating, for thy talke is foolish.

Yea, yea husband, your olde churlish conditions will neuer be left, you keepe me here like a drudge and a droyle, and so you may keepe your money in your purse, you care not for your credit, but before I will goe so like a shepheardesse, I will first goe naked: and I tel you plaine, I scorn it greatly, that you should clappe a gray gowne on my backe, as if I had not brought you two pence: before I was married you swore I should haue any thing that I requested, but now all is forgotten.

And in saying this, she went in, and soone after she was so sicke that needes she must goe to bed: and when she was laid, she draue out that night with many grieuous groanes, sighing and sobbing, and no rest she could take God wot. And in the morning when she should rise, the good soule fell downe in a swowne, which put her maidens in a great fright, who running downe to their master, cried out, Alas, alas, our Dame is dead, our Dame is dead.

The goodman hearing this, ran vp in all haste, and there fell to rubbing and chafing of her temples, sending for *aqua vitae,* and saying, Ah my sweete heart, speake to me, good wife, alacke, alacke, call in the neighbours, you queanes quoth he.

With that shee lift vp her head, fetching a great groane and presently swouned againe, and much adoe iwis, he had to keepe life in

---

⁴ repaires] Q2-4; repaires of Q1
³⁰ fright] Q4; flight Q1-3

her: but when she was come to her self, How dost thou wife quoth he? What wilt thou haue? for Gods sake tel me if thou hast a mind to any thing, thou shalt haue it.

Away dissembler (quoth she) how can I belieue thee? thou hast
5 said as much to mee an hundred times, and deceiued mee, it is thy churlishness that hath killd my heart, neuer was woman matcht to so vnkind a man.

Nay good wife, blame me not without cause; God knoweth how dearly I loue thee.

10 Loue me! no, no, thou didst neuer carry my loue but on the tip of thy tongue, quoth she, I dare sweare thou desirest nothing so much as my death, and for my part, I would to God thou hadst thy desire: but be content, I shal not trouble thee long: and with that fetching a sigh, she swouned and gaue a great groane.

15 The man seeing hir in this case was wondrous woe: but so soone as they had recouered her he said, O my deare wife, if any bad conceit hath ingendered this sickenes, let me know it; or if thou knowest any thing that may procure thy health, let me vnderstand thereof, and I protest thou shalt haue it, if it cost me all that euer
20 I haue.

O husband, quoth she, how may I credite your wordes, when for a paltry sute of apparell you denied me?

Well wife quoth he, thou shalt haue apparell or any thing else thou wilt request, if God send thee once health.

25 O husband, if I may find you so kind, I shall thinke my selfe the happiest woman in the world; thy words haue greatly comforted my heart, me thinketh if I had it, I could drink a good draught of renish wine.

Well, wine was sent for.

30 O Lord said she, that I had a peece of a chickin, I feele my stomacke desirous of some meat.

Glad am I of that said her husband, and so the woman within a few dayes after was very well.

But you shall vnderstand, that her husband was faine to dresse
35 her London-like ere he could get her quiet, neither wold it please her, except the stuffe were bought in Cheapeside, for out of Cheapside nothing would content her, were it neuer so good: insomuch, that if she thought a tailer of Cheapside made not her gowne, she would sweare it was quite spoiled.

40 And hauing thus won her husband to her will, when the rest of

the Clothiers wiues heard thereof, they would be suted in the like sort too: so that euer since, the wiues of South-hampton, Salisbury, of Glocester, Worcester, and Reading, went all as gallant and as braue as any Londoners wiues.

CHAPTER VII.   5

How the Clothiers sent the King aid into France, and how he ouercame his brother *Robert,* and brought him into England, and how the Clothiers feasted his Maiesty and his sonne at Reading.

The Kings maiesty being at the warres in Fraunce, against *Lewis*   10
the French king, and duke *Robert* of Normandy, sending for diuers supplies of souldiers out of England, the Clothiers at their owne proper cost set out a great number, and sent them ouer to the King.

Which *Roger* Bishop of Salisbury, who gouerned the realme in   15
the Kings absence, did always certifie the King thereof, with his letters written in their commendations.

And afterward it came to passe, that God sent his Highnes victory ouer his enemies, and hauing taken his brother prisoner, brought him most ioyfully with him into England, and appointed   20
him to be kept in Cardife castle prisoner, yet with this fauour, that he might hunt and hawke where he would vp and downe the countrey, and in this sort he liued a good while, of whom we will speake more at large hereafter.

The King being thus come home, after his winters rest, he made   25
his summers progresse into the west country, to take a view of al the chiefe townes: whereof the Clothiers being aduertised, they made great preparation against his comming, because he had promised to visite them all.

And when his Grace came to Reading, he was entertained and   30
receiued with great ioy and triumph: *Thomas Cole* being the chiefe man of regard in all the towne, the king honored his house with

his princely presence, where during the kings abode, he, and his
son, and nobles were highly feasted.

There the king beheld the great number of people, that was by
that one man maintained in worke, whose harty affection and loue
5 toward his maiestie did well appeere, as well by their outward
countenances, as their gifts presented vnto him. But of *Cole* himselfe the king was so well persuaded, that he committed much trust
to him, and put him in great authoritie in the towne. Furthermore
the king said, That for the loue which those people bore to him
10 liuing, that he would lay his bones among them when he was dead.

For I know not said he where they may be better bestowed, till
the blessed day of resurrection, than among these my friends which
are like to be happy partakers of the same.

Whereupon his Maiesty caused there to be builded a most goodly
15 and famous Abbey: in which he might shew his deuotion to God,
by increasing his seruice, and leaue example to other his successors
to doe the like. Likewise within the towne he after builded a faire
and goodly castle, in the which he often kept his court, which was a
place of his chiefe residence during his life, saying to the Clothiers,
20 that seeing he found them such faithfull subiects, he would be their
neighbor, and dwell among them.

After his Maiesties royal feasting at Reading, he proceeded in
progresse, til he had visited the whole West-countrie, being wondrously delighted, to see those people so diligent to applie their
25 busines: and comming to Salisbury, the Bishop receiued his
Maiesty with great ioy, and with triumph attended on his Grace
to his palace, where his Highnes lodged.

There *Sutton* the Clothier presented his Highnesse with a broad
cloth, of so fine a threed, and exceeding good workmanship, and
30 therewithall of so faire a colour, as his Grace gaue commendation
thereof, and as it is said, he held it in such high estimation, that
therof he made his parliament robes, and the first parliament that
euer was in England, was graced with the Kings person in those
robes, in requitall whereof his highnes afterward yielded *Sutton*
35 many princely fauours.

And it is to be remembred, that *Simon* of Southhampton (seeing
the King had ouerpast the place where he dwelt) came with his wife

³ There] Q2-4; Where Q1
²³ West-countrie] Q4; west countries Q1-3

and seruants to Salisbury, and against the King going forth of that city, he caused a most pleasant arbour to be made vpon the toppe of the hill leading to Salisbury, beset all with red and white roses, in such sort, that not anie part of the timber could be seene, within the which sate a maiden attired like a Queene, attended on by a faire train of maidens, who at the kings approach presented him with a Garland of sweet floures, yielding him such honour as the Ladies of Rome were wont to doe to their Princes after their victories: which the King tooke in gracious part, and for his farewell from that country, they bore him company ouer part of the Plaine, with the sound of diuers sweet instruments of musicke. All which when his Grace vnderstood was done at the cost of a Clothier, he sayd he was the most honoured by those men, aboue al the mean subiects in his land: and so his highnes past on to Exceter, hauing giuen great rewards to these maydens.

Thomas Doue and the residue of the Clothiers, against his Graces comming thither, had ordained diuers sumptuous shewes; first, there was one that represented the person of *Augustus Caesar* the Emperour who commanded after the Romane inuasion, that their City should be called Augustus, after his owne name, which beforetime was called Isca, and of latter yeeres, Exeter.

There his Maiesty was royally feasted seuen daies together, at the onely cost of Clothiers, but the diuers delightes and sundry pastimes which they made there before the King, and his Nobles, is too long here to be rehearsed. And therefore I will ouerpasse them, to auoide tediousnes.

His grace then coasting along the country, at last came to Gloucester, an ancient City, which was builded by *Gloue* a Brittish King, who named it after his own name, Gloucester. Here was his maiesty entertained by *Gray* the Clothier, who profest himselfe to be of that ancient family of *Grayes*, whose first Originall issued out of the ancient and honorable Castle and towne of Rithin.

Heere was the King most bountifully feasted, hauing in his company his brother *Robert* (although his prisoner the same time.) And his Grace being desirous to see the maidens carde and spinne, they were of purpose set to their worke, among whom was faire *Margaret* with the white hand, whose excellent beauty hauing pearst the eyes of that amorous Duke, it made such an impression in his heart,

[3] Salisbury] Q2-4; Shaftesburie Q1

that afterward he could neuer forget her: and so vehemently was his affection kindled, that he could take no rest, till by writing he had bewrayed his mind: but of this we will speake more in an other place: and the King at his departure sayd, that to gratifie them, hee
5 would make his son *Robert* their Earle, who was the first Earle that euer was in Gloucester.

Now when his Grace was come from thence, he went to Worcester, where *William Fitz-allen* made preparation in all honourable sort to receiue him, which man being borne of great parentage, was
10 not to learne how to entertaine his Maiesty, being descended of that famous family, whose patrimony lay about the towne of Oswestry, which towne his predecessors had inclosed with stately walles of stone.

Although aduerse fortune had so grieuously frowned on some of
15 them, that their children were faine to become tradesmen, whose hands were to them instead of landes, notwithstanding God raised againe the fame of this man, both by his great wealth and also in his posterity, whose eldest son *Henry*, the Kings god-son, became afterward the Mayor of London, who was the first Mayor that euer
20 was in that Citty, who gouerned the same 23. yeeres: and then his son *Roger Fitz-allen* was the second Mayor.

The Princely pleasures that in Worcester were shewen the king, were many and maruelous, and in no place had his Maiesty receiued more delight then here; for the which at his departure he did shew
25 himselfe very thankfull. Now when his Grace had thus taken view of all his good townes Westward and in that progresse had visited these clothiers, he returned to London with great ioy of all his commons.

[13] stone.] Q2-4; ~, Q1

CHAPTER VIII.

How *Hodgekins* of Halifax came to the Court, and complained to the King, that his priuiledge was nothing
worth, because when they found any offendor they
could not get a hangman to execute him: And how by 5
a Fryer a gin was deuised to chop off mens heads of
it selfe.

After that *Hogekins* had got the priuiledge for the town of *Halifax*, to hang vp such theeues as stole their cloth in the night,
presently without any further iudgement, al the clothiers of the 10
towne were exceeding glad, and perswaded themselues, that now
their goods would be safe all night, without watching them at al, so
that whereas before, the town maintayned certaine watchmen to
keepe their cloth by night, they were hereupon dismissed as a thing
needlesse to be done, supposing with themselues, that seeing they 15
should be straight hanged that were found faulty in this point,
that no man would be so desperate to enterprise any such act. And
indeede the matter being noysed through the whole countrey, that
they were straight to be hanged that did vse such theeuery, it made
many lewd liuers to refraine such theeuery. 20

Neuerthelesse, there was at that same time liuing a notable
Theefe named *Wallis*, whom in the North they called *Mighty
Wallis,* in regard of his valor and manhood: This man beeing most
subtill in such kind of knauery, hauing heard of this late priuiledge,
and therewithall of the townes security, sayd that once he would 25
venture his necke for a packe of Northerne cloth; and therefore
comming to one or two of his companions, he asked if they would
be partners in his aduenture, and if (quoth he) you will herein hazard your bodies, you shal be sharers in all our booties.

At length by many perswasions the men consented: whereupon 30
late in the night, they got them all to a Farriours shop, and called
vp the folks of the house.

What the foule ill wald you haue (quoth they) at this time of the night?

Wallis answered, saying, good fellowes, we would haue you to remooue the shooes of our Horses feete, and set them on againe, 5 and for your paines, you shalbe well pleased. The Smith at length was perswaded, and when he had pluckt off all the shooes from their horses feete, they would needes haue them all set on againe, quite contrary with the caukins forward, that should stand back-ward.

10 How fay, fay man, quoth the Smith. Are you sick fules? what the deell doo you meane to breake your crags? gud faith I tro the men be wood.

Not so, Smith, quoth they, do thou as wee bid thee, and thou shalt haue thy money: for it is an old Prouerbe,

15   Bee it better, or be it worse
        Please you the man that beares the purse.

Gud faith and see I sall, quoth the Smith, and so did as he was willed.

When *Wallis* had thus caused their Horses to be shod, to Hallifax 20 they went, where they without any let laded their Horses with cloth, and so departed a contrary way.

In the morning, so soone as the clothiers came to the field, they found that they were robd, whereupon one ranne to another to tell these tidings. Now when *Hogekins* heard thereof, rising vp 25 in haste, he wild his neighbours to marke and see, if they could not descrie eyther the footesteps of men or Horses. Which being done, they perceiued that horses had bin there, and seeking to pur-sue them by their footesteps, they went a cleane contrary way, by reason that the horses were shod backward: and when in vaine they 30 had long persude them, they returned, being neuer the neere. Now *Wallis* vsed his feate so long, that at length he was taken, and two more with him: whereupon according to the priuiledge of the Towne, they put Halters about the theeues neckes presently to hang them vp.

35 When they were come to the place appointed, *Wallis* and the rest being out of all hope to escape death, prepared themselues paciently to suffer the rigor of the law. And there with the rest laying open the lewdnesse of his life, greeuously lamenting for his sinnes, at

length commending their soules to God, they yeelded their bodyes
to the graue, with which sight the people were greatly mooued
with pitty, because they had neuer seene men come to hanging
before: but when they should haue beene tyed vp, *Hodgekins* willed
one of his neighbours to play the Hangmans part, who would not 5
by any meanes do it, although he was a very poore man, who for
his paines should haue beene possest of all their apparell. When
he would not yeeld to the office, one of those which had his cloth
stolen, was commaunded to do the deed, but he in like maner would
not, saying: When I haue the skil to make a man, I will hang a 10
man, if it chance my workmanship do not like me.

And thus from one to another, the office of the Hangman was
poasted off. At last a Rogue came by, whom they would haue com-
pelled to haue done that deed.

Nay, my Masters, qouth he, not so: but as you haue got a Priui- 15
ledge for the Towne, so you were best to procure a Commission to
make a hangman, or else you are like to be without for me.

Neighbor *Hogekins* quoth one, I pray you do this office your
selfe, you haue had most losse and therefore you should be the most
readie to hang them your selfe. 20

No not I (quoth *Hodgekins*) though my losse were ten times
greater than it is, notwithstanding look which of these theeues will
take vppon him to hang the other, shall haue his life saued, otherwise they shall all to prison till I can prouide a hangman.

When *Wallis* saw the matter brought to this passe, he began 25
stoutly to reply, saying, My masters of the towne of *Halifax,* though
your priuiledge stretch to hang vp men presently that are found
stealing your goods, yet it giues you no warrant to imprison them
till you prouide them a hangman, my selfe with these my fellowes
haue here yeelded our selues to satisfie the Law, and if it be not per- 30
formed, the fault is yours and not ours, and therefore we humbly
take our leaue: from the gallowes the xviij of August.

And with that he leapt from the ladder, and cast the halter at
Hodgekins face.

When the Clothiers saw this, they knew not what to say, but tak- 35
ing them by the sleeues, intreated to haue their owne againe.

Not so quoth *Wallis,* you get not the valew of a plack or a
bawby: we haue stolne your cloth, then why do you not hang vs?

[20] readie] Q2-4; readiest Qr

Here we haue made ourselues ready, and if you wil not hang vs, chuse. A plague on you quoth he, you haue hindred me God knowes what, I made account to dine this day in heauen, and you keep me here on earth where there is not a quarter of that good cheare. The
5 foule euill take you all, I was fully prouided to giue the gallows a box on the eare, and now God knowes when I shall be in so good a mind againe.

And so he with the rest of his companions departed.

When *Hodgekins* saw, that notwithstanding their theeuery, how
10 they flowted at their lenity, he was much moued in mind: and as he stood in his dumps, chewing his cud, making his dinner with a dish of melancholy, a grey Frier reuerently saluted him in this sort: All haile, goodman *Hodgekins,* happinesse and health be euer with you, and to all suppressors of lewd liuers, God send euerlasting
15 ioyes.

I am sory goodman *Hodgekins,* that the great priuiledge which our King gaue to this towne, comes to no greater purpose: better far had it bin, that it had neuer beene graunted, then so lightly regarded: the towne hath suffred throgh their owne peeuishnes,
20 an euerlasting reproch this day, onely because foolish pitty hath hindred iustice.

Consider, that compassion is not to be had vpon theeues and robbers: pitty onely appertayneth to the vertuous sort, who are ouerwhelmed with the waues of misery and mischaunce. What great
25 cause of boldnes haue you giuen to bad liuers, by letting these fel-lowes thus to escape, and how shall you now keepe your goods in safety, seeing you fullfill not the law which should be your defence? neuer thinke that theeues will make any conscience to carry away your goods, when they find themselues in no danger of death,
30 who haue more cause to prayse your pitty, then to commend your wisdome: wherefore in time seeke to preuent the insuing euill.

For my owne part, I haue that care of your good, that I would work al good means for your benefit, and yet not so much in re-spect of your profit, as for the desire I haue to vpholde iustice, and
35 seeing I find you and the rest so womanish, that you could not find in your hearts to hang a theefe, I haue deuised how to make a gin, that shal cut off their heads without mans helpe, and if the King will alow thereof.

When *Hogekins* heard this he was somewhat comforted in mind,
40 and sayd to the Frier, that if by his cunning he would performe

310

it he would once againe make suite to the King to haue his grant
for the same. The Frier willed him to haue no doubt in him: and
so when he had deuised it, he got a Carpenter to frame it out of
hand.

Hodgekins in the meane time posted vp to the Court, and told 5
his Maiesty that the priuiledge of Halifax was not worth a pudding.

Why so, sayd our King?

Because, quoth *Hodgekins,* we can get neuer a hangman to trusse
our theeues, but if it shall like your good Grace, (quoth he) there
is a feat Frier, that will make vs a deuice, which shall without the 10
hand of man cut off the cragges of all such Carles, if your Maiesty
will please to alow thereof.

The King vnderstanding the full effect of the matter, at length
granted his petition: whereupon till this day, it is obserued in Halifax, that such as are taken stealing of their cloth haue their heads 15
chopt off with the same gin.

CHAPTER IX.

How the Bailifes of London could get no man to be a
catchpole, and how certaine Flemings tooke that office
vpon them, whereof many of them were fled into this 20
Realm, by reason of certaine waters that had drowned
a great part of their country.

The City of London being at this time gouerned by Bayliffes,
it came to passe, that in a certaine fray two of their catchpoles were killed, for at that time they had not the name of Ser- 25
geants, and you shall vnderstand, that their office was then so much
hated and detested of Englishmen, that none of them would take
it vpon him so that the Bayliffes were glad to get any man whatsoeuer, and to giue him certayne wages to performe that office.

It came to passe, as I sayd before, that two of their officers, by 30
arresting of a man, were at one instant slaine, by meanes whereof
the Bayliffes were inforced to seeke others to put in their roomes,

but by no means could they get any, wherefore according to their wonted maner, they made proclamation, that if there were any man that would present himself before them, he should not onely be settled in that office during their liues, but also should haue such
5 maintenance and allowance, as for such men was by the City prouided: and notwithstanding that it was an office most necessary in the commonwealth, yet did the poorest wretch despise it, that liued in any estimation among his neighbours.

At last a couple of Flemings, which were fled into this land, by
10 reason that their country was drownd with the sea, hearing the proclamation, offered themselues vnto the Bailiffes, to serue in this place, who were presently receiued and accepted, and according to order had garments giuen them, which were of ij colors, blue and red, their coats, breeches and stockings, whereby they were known
15 and discerned from other men.

Within halfe a yeere after, it came to passe, that *Thomas Doue* of Exeter came vp to London, who hauing by his iollity and good felowship, brought himselfe greatly behind hand, was in daunger to diuerse men of the citie, among the rest, one of his creditors
20 feed an officer to arrest him. The dutch man that had not been long experienced in such matters, and hearing how many of his fellowes had bin killed for attempting to arrest men, stood quiuering and quaking in a corner of the street to watch for *Tom Doue*, and hauing long waited, at length he spied him; whereupon he
25 prepared his mace ready, and with a pale countenance proceeded to do his office, at what time comming behind the man, sodainly with his mace he knockt him on the pate, saying, I arrest you, giuing him such a blow, that he felld him to the ground.

The catchpole thinking he had killed the man, he left his Mace
30 behind him and ranne away: the creditor hee ran after him calling and crying that he should turne againe: But the Fleming would not by any means come backe, but got him quite out of the city, and took sanctuary at Westminster.

Doue being come to himselfe, arose, and went to his inne, no
35 man hindring his passage, being not a little glad he so escaped the danger. Yet neuerthelesse, at his next comming to London, another catchpole met with him, and arrested him in the Kings name.

Doue being dismayd at this mischieuous chance, knew not what
40 to do: at last he requested the catchpole that hee would not vio-

lently cast him in prison, but stay till such time as he could send
for a friend to be his surety; and although kindnes in a catchpole be
rare, yet was he won with faire words to do him this fauor: whereupon *Doue* desired one to goe to his host *Iarrat,* who immediatly
came vnto him and offred himselfe to be *Doues* surety.   5

The Officer, who neuer sawe this man before, was much amazed
at his sight: for *Iarrat* was a great and a mighty man of body, of
countenance grim, and exceeding high of stature, so that the catchpole was wonderfully afraid, asking if he could find neuer a surety
but the diuell, most fearefully intreating him to coniure him away, 10
and he would doe *Doue* any fauor.

What, wil you not take my word quoth *Iarrat?*

Sir quoth the Catch-pole, if twere for any matter in hel, I would
take your word as soone as any diuells in that place, but seeing it
is for a matter on earth, I would gladly haue a surety.   15

Why thou whorson criket (quoth *Iarrat*) thou magget a pie,
thou spinner, thou paultry spider, dost thou take me for a Diuell?
Sirra, take my word, I charge thee, for this man, or else goodman
butterfly, Ile make thee repent it.

The officer, while he was in the house, said he was content, but 20
so sone as he came into the street, he cried, saying: Help, help,
good neighbours, or else the Diuell will carry away my prisoner.

Notwithstanding, there was not one man would sturre to be the
Catchpoles aide. Which when he saw, he tooke fast hold on *Thomas
Doue,* and would not by any meanes let him go.   25

Iarret seeing this, made no more to doe; but comming to the
officer, gaue him such a fillippe on the fore-head with his finger,
that he felld the poore Fleming to the ground; and while he lay
in the streete stretching his heeles, *Iarret* tooke *Doue* vnder his
arme, and carried him home, where he thought himselfe as safe as 30
king *Charlemaine* in mount Albon.

The next morning *Iarret* conueied *Doue* out of towne, who
afterward kept him in the countrey, and came no more in the
Catchpoles clawes.

CHAPTER X.

How Duke *Robert* came a wooing to *Margaret* with the white hand, and how he appointed to come and steale her away from her masters.

5   The beautifull *Margaret,* who had now dwelt with her dame the space of foure yeeres, was highly regarded and secretly loued of many gallant Gentlemen of the countrey, but of two especially, Duke *Robert,* and Sir *William Ferris.* It chaunced on a time, that faire *Margaret* with many other of her Masters folkes,
10 went a hay-making, attired in a redde stamell petticoate, and a broad strawne hatte vpon her head, she had a hay forke, and in her lappe she bore her breakfast. As she went along, Duke *Robert,* with one or two of his keepers, met with her, whose amiable sight did now anewe kindle the secret fire of loue, which long lay smothering
15 in his heart. Wherefore meeting her so happily, he saluted her thus frendly.

Faire maid, good morrow, are you walking so diligently to your labour? Needs must the weather be faire, where the sun shines so cleare, and the hay holsome that is dried with such splendant raies.
20   Renowned and most notable Duke (quoth she) poore haruest folkes pray for faire weather, and it is the laborers comfort to see his work prosper, and the more happy may we count the day, that is blessed with your princely presence.

But more happy sayd the Duke, are they which are conuersant
25 in thy company. But let me intreat thee to turne back to thy masters with me, and commit thy forke to some that are fitter for such toile: trust me, me thinks thy dame is too much ill aduised, in setting thee to such homely busines. I muse thou canst indure this vile beseeming seruitude, whose delicate limmes were neuer framed to
30 proue such painefull experimentes.

Albeit, quoth she, it becommeth not mee to controule your iudiciall thoughts, yet, were you not the Duke, I would say, your

---

[32] iudiciall] Q2-4; iudicical Q1

opinion deceiued you: though your faire eyes seeme cleere yet I
deeme them vnperfect, if they cast before your mind any shadow
or sparke of beauty in me: But I rather thinke, because it hath
beene an old saying, that women are proude to heare themselues
praised, that you eyther speake this, to driue away the time, or to 5
wring from me my too apparant imperfections. But I humbly intreat pardon, too long haue I foreslowed my busines, and shewne
my selfe ouerbolde in your presence: and therewith, with a courtly
grace, bending her knees to the courteous Duke, she went forward
to the field, and the Duke to the towne of Gloucester. 10

When he came thither, he made his keepers great cheere, intreating them they would giue him respite to be a while with old *Gray*.

For we twaine must haue a game or two, quoth he: and for my
safe returne, I gage to you my princely word, that as I am a true
Knight and a Gentleman, I will returne safe to your charge againe. 15

The keepers being content, the Duke departed, and with old
Gray goes to the field, to peruse the workefolkes, where while *Gray*
found himselfe busie in many matters, he tooke opportunity to
talke with *Margaret*. She who by his letters before was priuy to his
purpose, gest before hand the cause of his comming: to whom he 20
spake to this effect.

Faire maide, I did long since manifest my loue to thee by my
letter; tel me therefore, were it not better to be a Dutches then a
drudge? a Lady of high reputation, then a seruant of simple degree? with me thou mightest liue in plasure, where here thou 25
drawest thy dayes foorth in paine; by my loue thou shouldst be
made Lady of great treasures: where now thou art poore and beg-
gerly; all manner of delights should then attend on thee, and whatsoeuer thy heart desired, thou shouldst haue: wherefore seeing it
lies in thy owne choise, make thy selfe happy, by consenting to my 30
suite.

Sir (quoth she) I confesse your loue deserues a Ladyes fauor,
your affection a faithfull friend, such a one as should make but one
heart and mind of two hearts and bodies; but farre vnfit is it that
the Turtle should match with the Eagle; though her loue be neuer 35

---

² deeme] Q4; deemed Q1-3
⁶ from me] Q4; me from Q1-3
¹¹ keepers] Q4; keeper Q1-3
²⁸ then] Q2-4; them Q1

so pure, her wings are vnfitte to mount so high. While *Thales* gaz'd
on the starres, he stumbled in a pit. And they that clime vnad-
uisedly, catch a fall suddenly; what auayleth high dignity in time
of aduersity? it neyther helpeth the sorrow of the heart, nor re-
5 moues the bodies misery: as for wealth and treasure, what are they,
but fortunes baits to bring men in danger? good for nothing but to
make people forget themselues: and whereas you alleage pouerty
to be a henderer of the hearts comfort, I find it in my selfe contrary, knowing more surety to rest vnder a simple habite, then a
10 royall robe: and verily there is none in the world poore, but they
that think themselues poore: for such as are indued with content,
are rich hauing nothing els: but he that is possessed with riches,
without content, is most wretched and miserable. Wherefore most
noble Duke, albeit I account my life vnworthy of your least fauour,
15 yet I would desire you to match your loue to your like, and let me
rest to my Rake, and vse my Forke for my liuing.

Consider, faire *Margaret* (quoth he) that it lies not in mans
power to place his loue where he list, being the worke of an high
deity. A bird was neuer seene in Pontus, nor true loue in a fleet-
20 ing mind; neuer shall I remoue the affection of my heart, which in
nature resembleth the stone Abiston, whose fire can neuer be
cooled: wherefore sweet mayden giue not obstinate deniall, where
gentle acceptance ought to be receiued.

Faire sir (quoth she) consider what high displeasure may rise
25 by a rash match, what danger a Kings frowns may breed, my
worthlesse matching with your royalty, may perhaps regaine your
liberty, and hazard my life; then call to mind how little you should
inioy your loue, or I my wedded Lord.

The Duke at these words made this reply, that if she consented,
30 she should not dread any danger. The thunder (quoth he) is driuen
away by ringing of belles, the Lions wrath qualified by a yeelding
body: how much more a brothers anger with a brothers intreaty?
By me he hath receiued many fauors, and neuer yet did he requite
any one of them: and who is ignorant that the princely crowne
35 which adorneth his head, is my right? all which I am content he
shall still enioy, so he requite my kindnesse. But if he should not,
then would I be like those men (that eating of the tree Lutes) forget the country where they were borne, and neuer more should
this clime couer my head, but with thee would I liue in a strange

land, being better content with an egge in thy company, then with al the delicates in England.

The mayden hearing this, who with many other words was long wooed, at last consented; where yeelding to him her heart with her hand, he departed, appointing to certifie her from Cardiffe Castle 5 what determination he would follow: so taking his leaue of *Gray,* he went to his keepers, and with them posted to Cardiffe.

Now it is to be remembred, that sir *William Ferres* within a day or two after came vnto *Graies* house, as it was his ordinary custome, but not so much I wis for *Graies* company, as for the mind 10 he had to *Margaret* his maide, who although he were a marryed man, and had a faire Lady to his wife, yet he layd hard siege to the fort of this maydens chastity, hauing with many faire words sought to allure her, and by the offer of sundry rich gifts to tempt her. But when she saw, that by a hundred denials she could not be rid of 15 him, she now chanced on a sudden to giue him such an answer, as droue him from a deceit into such a conceit, as neuer after that time he troubled her.

Sir *William Ferrers* being very importunate to haue her graunt his desire, and when after sundry assaults she gaue him stil the 20 repulse, he would needs know the reason why she would not loue him.

Quoth he, If thou diddest consider who he is that seeketh thy fauor, what pleasure he may doe thee by his purse, and what credit by his countenance, thou wouldst neuer stand on such nice points. 25 If I be thy friend, who dareth be thy foe? and what is he that will once call thy name in question for any thing? therefore sweet gerle, be better aduised, and refuse not my offer being so large.

Truly sir *William* (quoth she) though there be many reasons to make me deny your suite, yet is there one aboue the rest that 30 causes me I cannot loue you.

Now I pray thee, my wench, let me know that quoth he, and I wil amend it whatsoeuer it be.

Pardon me sir, said *Margaret,* if I should speak my mind, it would possibly offend you, and do me no pleasure, because it is a 35 defect in Nature, which no phisicke may cure.

Sir *William* hearing her say so, being abashed at her speech, said, Faire *Margaret,* let me (if I may obtaine no more at thy hands) yet

---

⁷ keepers] Mann; brothers Q1-4

intreat thee to know what this defect should be. I am not wry-neckt, crook-legd, stub-footed, lame-handed, nor bleare-eied: what can make this mislike: I neuer knew any body that tooke exceptions at my person before.

5 And the more sorie am I quoth she, that I was so malapert to speake it, but pardon my presumption, good sir *William,* I would I had beene like the Storke, tonguelesse, then should I neuer haue caused your disquiet.

Nay, sweet *Margaret,* quoth he, tell me deare loue, I commend
10 thy singlenesse of heart, good *Margaret* speake.

Good sir *William* let it rest quoth she, I know you will not be-lieue it when I haue reuealed it, neither is it a thing that you can help: and yet such is my foolishnesse, had it not beene for that, I thinke verily I had graunted your suite ere now. But seeing you
15 vrge me so much to know what it is, I will tell you: it is sir, your ill fauored great nose, that hangs sagging so loathsomly to your lippes that I cannot find in my hart so much as to kisse you.

What, my nose quoth he? is my nose so great and I neuer knew it? Certainly I thought my nose to be as comely as any mans: but
20 this it is, we are al apt to think wel of our selues, and a great deale better than we ought: but let me see, (my nose!) by the masse tis true, I do now feele it my selfe: Good Lord, how was I blinded before?

Hereupon it is certaine, that the knight was driuen into such
25 a conceit, as none could perswade him but his nose was so great indeed; his Lady, or any other that spake to the contrarie, he would say they were flatterers, and that they lied, insomuch that he would be ready to strike some of them that commended or spake well of his nose. If they were men of worship or any other that contraried
30 him in his opinion, he would sweare they flowted him, and be ready to challenge them the field. He became so ashamed of him-selfe, that after that day he wold neuer go abroad, whereby *Margaret* was well rid of his company.

On a time, a wise and graue gentleman seeing him grounded in
35 his conceit so strongly, gaue his Lady counsell, not to contrary him therein, but rather say that she would seeke out some cunning Phisition to cure him: for, said he, as sir *William* hath taken this conceit of himselfe, so is he like neuer to beare other opinion, till his owne conceit doth remoue it, the which must be wisely wrought
40 to bring it to passe.

Whereupon the Lady hauing conferred with a Phisition that bare
a great name in the country, hee vndertooke to remoue this fond
conceit by his skill. The day being appointed when the Phisition
should come, and the knight beeing tolde thereof, for very ioy he
would goe forth to meete him, when a woman of the towne saw 5
the knight, hauing heard what rumor went because of his nose,
she looked very stedfastly vpon him: the knight casting his eye
vpon her, seeing her to gaze so wistly in his face, with an angry
countenance, said thus to her, Why how now good huswife, can
you not get you about your busines?   10

The woman being a shrewish queane, answered him cuttedly.
No mary can I not quoth she.

No, you drab! What is the cause, said the knight?

Because, quoth she, your nose stands in my way.

Wherewith the knight being verie angry, and abashed, went 15
backe againe to his house.

The Phisition being come, he had filled a certaine bladder with
sheepes blood, and conueyed it into his sleeue, where at the issue
of the bladder he had put in a peece of a swans quil through the
which the blood should runne out of the bladder so close by his 20
hand, that he holding the knight by the nose, it might not be perceiued, but that it issued thence. All things being prepard he
told the knight, that by a foule corrupt blood wherewith the veines
of his nose were ouercharged, his impediment did grow, therefore
quoth he, to haue redresse for this disease, you must haue a veine 25
opend in your nose, whence this foule corruption must be taken;
whereupon it wil follow, that your nose will fall againe to his
naturall proportion, and neuer shal you be troubled with this griefe
any more, and thereupon will I gage my life.

I pray you master doctor said the knight, is my nose so big as 30
you make it?

With reuerence I may speake it, said the phisition, to tell the
trueth, and auoyd flattery, I neuer sawe a more mis-shapen nose so
foule to sight.

Loe you now Madam, quoth the knight, this is you that said 35
my nose was as well, as handsome, and as comely a nose as any
mans.

Alas sir quoth she I spake it (God wot) because you should not
grieue at it, nor take my words in ill part, neither did it indeed
become me to mislike of your nose.   40

All this we will quickly remedy, said the phisitian, haue no doubt.

And with that, he very orderly prickt him in the nose, but not in any veine whereby he might bleed: and presently hauing a tricke
5 finely to vnstop the quill, the blood ranne into a bason in great abundance: and when the bladder was empty, and the bason almost full, the Phisition seemed to close the veine, and asked him how he felt his nose, shewing the great quantitie of filthy blood which from thence he had taken.
10 The knight beholding it with great wonder, said he thought that no man in the world had beene troubled with such abundance of corrupt bloud in his whole body, as lay in his misshapen nose, and therewithall he began to touch and handle his nose, saying, that he felt it mightily assuaged. Immediatly a glasse was brought
15 wherein he might behold himselfe.

Yea mary quoth he now I praise God, I see my nose is come into some reasonable proportion, and I feele my selfe very wel eased of the burden thereof; but if it continue thus, thats all.

I will warrant your worship, said the phisition, for euer being
20 troubled with the like againe.

Whereupon the knight receiued great ioy, and the Doctor a high reward.

CHAPTER XI.

How *Thomas* of Reading was murdred at his hoasts house
25 of Colebrooke, who also had murdred many before him, and how their wickednes was at length reuealed.

*T*homas of Reading hauing many occasions to come to London, as wel about his owne affaires, as also the kings businesse, being in a great office vnder his Maiesty, it chanced on a time, that his
30 host and hostesse of Colebrook, who through couetousnes had murdred many of their ghests, and hauing euery time he came thither great store of his money to lay vp, appointed him to be the next

<hr>

26 and how] Q2-4; how Q1

fat pig that should be killed: For it is to be vnderstood, that when
they plotted the murther of any man, this was alwayes their terme,
the man to his wife and the woman to her husband.

Wife, there is now a fat pig to be had, if you want one.

Whereupon she would answere thus, I pray you put him in the 5
hogstie till to morrow.

This was, when any man came thither alone without others in his
company, and they saw he had great store of money.

This man should be then laid in the chamber right ouer the
kitchin, which was a faire chamber, and better set out then any 10
other in the house; the best bedsted therein, though it were little
and low, yet was it most cunningly carued, and faire to the eye: the
feet whereof were fast naild to the chamber floore, in such sort,
that it could not in any wise fall, the bed that lay therein was fast
sowed to the sides of the bedsted: Moreouer, that part of the cham- 15
ber whereupon this bed and bedsted stoode, was made in such sort
that by the pulling out of two yron pinnes below in the kitchin,
it was to be let downe and taken vp by a draw bridge, or in maner
of a trappe doore: moreouer in the kitchin, directly vnder the place
where this should fall, was a mighty great caldron, wherein they 20
vsed to seethe their liquor when they went to brewing. Now, the
men appointed for the slaughter, were laid into this bed, and in the
dead time of the night when they were sound a sleepe by plucking
out the fore said iron pinns, downe would the man fall out of his
bed into the boyling caldron, and all the cloathes that were vpon 25
him: where being suddenly scalded and drowned, he was neuer able
to cry or speake one word.

Then had they a little ladder euer standing ready in the kitchin,
by the which they presently mounted into the sayd chamber, and
there closely tooke away the mans apparell, as also his money, in 30
his male or capcase: and then lifting vp the sayd falling floore which
hung by hinges, they made it fast as before.

The dead body would they take presently out of the Caldron and
throw it down the riuer, which ran neere vnto their house, whereby
they escaped all danger. 35

Now if in the morning any of the rest of the ghests that had talkt
with the murthered man ouer eue, chanst to aske for him, as hauing
occasion to ride the same way that hee should haue done, the goodman would answere, that he took horse a good while before day,

and that he himselfe did set him forward: the horse the goodman would also take out of the stable, and conuay him to a hay-barne of his, that stood from his house a mile or two, whereof himselfe did alwaies keepe the keies full charily, and when any hay was to
5 be brought from thence, with his owne hands he would deliuer it: then, before the horse should go from thence, he would dismarke him: as if he ware a long taile, he would make him curtall, or else crop his eares, or cut his maine, or put out one of his eyes; and by this meanes he kept himselfe a long time vnknowne.

10 Now *Thomas* of Reading, as I sayd before, being markt, and kept for a fat pig, he was laied in the same chamber of death but by reason *Gray* of Gloucester chaunst also to come that night, he escaped scalding.

The next time he came, he was laid there againe, but before he
15 fell asleepe, or was warme in his bed, one came riding through the towne, and cried piteously, that London was al on a fire, and that it had burned downe *Thomas Beckets* house in West cheape, and a great number more in the same streete, and yet (quoth he) the fire is not quencht.

20 Which tidings when *Thomas* of Reading heard, he was very sorrowfull, for of the same *Becket* that day had he receiued a great peece of money, and had left in his house many of his writtings and some that appertained to the king also: therfore there was no nay but he would ride back againe to London presently, to see how
25 the matter stood; thereupon making himselfe ready, departed. This crosse fortune caused his hoast to frowne.

Neuerthelesse the next time (quoth he) will pay for all.

Notwithstanding, God so wrought, that they were preuented then likewise, by reason of a great fray that hapned in the house betwixt
30 a couple that fel out at Dice, insomuch as the murderers themselues were inforced to cal him vp, being a man in great authority, that he might set the house in quietnes, out of the which by meanes of this quarell, they doubted to lose many things.

Another time when he should haue beene layd in the same place
35 he fell so sicke, that he requested to haue some body to watch with him, whereby also they could not bring their vile purpose to passe. But hard it is to escape the ill fortunes wherunto a man is allotted: for albeit that the next time that he came to London his horse

12 that] Q2-4; ~: Q1

Chapter Eleven

stumbled and broke one of his legges, as he should ride homeward, yet hired he another to hasten his owne death: for there was no remedy but he should go to Colbrook that night: but by the way he was so heauy a sleepe, that he could scant keepe himselfe in the saddle; and when he came neere vnto the Towne his nose burst 5 out suddenly ableeding.

Wel, to his Inne he came, and so heauy was his heart, that he could eate no meate: his hoost and hoastise hearing he was so Melancholy, came vp to cheere him, saying, Iesus, Master *Cole,* what ayles you to night? neuer did wee see you thus sad before: will it 10 please you to haue a quart of burnd sack?

With a good wil (quoth he) and would to God *Thomas Doue* were here, hee would surely make me merry, and we should lacke no musick: but I am sory for the man withall my heart, that hee is come so farre behind hand: but alasse, so much can euery man say, 15 but what good doth it him? No no, it is not wordes can helpe a man in this case, the man had neede of other reliefe then so. Let me see: I haue but one child in the world and that is my daughter, and halfe that I haue is hers, the other halfe my wifes. What then? shall I be good to no body but them? In conscience, my wealth is 20 too much for a couple to possesse, and what is our Religion without charity? And to whom is charity more to be shewne then to decaied housholders?

Good my hoast lend me a pen and inke, and some paper, for I will write a letter vnto the poore man straight, and something I 25 will giue him: that almes which a man bestowes with his own hands he shalbe sure to haue deliuered, and God knows how long I shall liue.

With that, his hoastise dissemblingly answered, saying: Doubt not, Master *Cole,* you are like enough by the course of nature to 30 liue many yeeres.

God knowes (quoth he) I neuer found my heart so heauy before.

By this time, pen, inke and paper was brought, setting himselfe to writing, as followeth.

In the name of God, Amen, I bequeath my soule to God, and my 35 *body to the ground, my goods equally betweene my wife Elenor, and Isabel my daughter. Item I giue to Thomas Doue of Exeter one hundred pounds, nay that is too little, I giue to Thomas Doue two*

---

³⁵ *Amen,*] Q2; ~_∧ Q1; ~: Q3,4

323

hundred pounds, in money, to be payd vnto him presently vpon his demaund thereof by my sayd wife and daughter.

Ha, how say you my hoast (quoth he) is not this well? I pray you reade it.

5 His hoast looking thereon, sayd, why Maister *Cole,* what haue you written here? you sayd you would write a letter, but me thinkes you haue made a will, what need haue you to doe thus? thanks be to God, you may liue many fayre yeeres.

Tis true (quoth *Cole*) if it please God, and I trust this writing 10 cannot shorten my dayes: but let me see, haue I made a will? Now I promise you, I did verily purpose to write a letter: notwithstanding, I haue written that that God put into my mind: but look once againe my hoast, is it not written there, that *Doue* shall haue two hundred pounds, to be payd when he comes to demand it?

15 Yes indeed, sayd his hoast.

Well then, all is well, sayd *Cole,* and it shall go as it is for me. I will not bestow the new writting thereof any more.

Then folding it vp, he sealed it, desiring that his hoast would send it to Exeter. He promised that he would, notwithstanding *Cole* 20 was not so satisfied: but after some pause, he would needs hire one to carry it. And so sitting downe sadly in his chaire againe, vpon a sudden he burst foorth a weeping: they demanding the cause thereof he spake as followeth:

No cause of these teares I know: but it comes now into my minde 25 (sayd *Cole*) when I set toward this my last iourney to London, how my daughter tooke on, what a coyle she kept to haue me stay: and I could not be rid of the little baggage a long time, she did so hang about me: when her mother by violence tooke her away, she cried out most mainely, O my father, my father, I shall neuer see him 30 againe.

Alas, pretty soule, said his hostesse, this was but meer kindnesse in the girle, and it seemeth she is very fond of you. But alasse, why should you grieue at this? you must consider that it was but childishnesse.

35 I, it is indeed, sayd *Cole,* and with that he began to nod.

Then they asked him if he would go to bed.

No sayd he, although I am heauy, I haue no mind to go to bed at all.

With that certaine musicions of the towne came to the chamber, and knowing Master *Cole* was there, drue out their instruments, and very solemnely beganne to play.

This musicke comes very well (said *Cole*) and when he had listned a while thereunto, he said, Me thinks these instruments sound like the ring of S. Mary Oueries bells, but the base drownes 5 all the rest: and in my eare it goes like a bell that rings a forenoones knell, for Gods sake let them leaue off, and beare them this simple reward.

The musicions being gone, his hoast asked if now it would please him to go to bed. 10

For (quoth he) it is welneare eleuen of the clocke.

With that, *Cole* beholding his hoste and hostesse earnestly, began to start backe, saying, what aile you to looke so like pale death? good Lord, what haue you done, that your hands are thus bloudy?

What my hands, said his host? Why you may see they are neither 15 bloudy nor foule: either your eies do greatly dazell, or else fancies of a troubled mind do delude you.

Alas my hoast, you may see, saide he, how weake my wits are, I neuer had my head so idle before. Come, let me drinke once more, and then I will to bed, and trouble you no longer. 20

With that he made himselfe vnready, and his hostesse was very diligent to warme a kerchefe, and put it about his head.

Good Lord said he I am not sicke, I prayse God, but such an alteration I find in my selfe as I neuer did before.

With that the scritch owle cried pitteously, and anone after the 25 night rauen sate croking hard by his window.

Iesu haue mercy vpon me, quoth he, what an ill fauored crie do yonder carrion birds make!

And therewithall he laid him downe in his bed, from whence he neuer rose againe. 30

His host and hostesse, that all this while noted his troubled mind, began to commune betwixt themselues thereof. And the man said, he knew not what were best to be done. By my consent (quoth he) the matter should passe, for I thinke it is not best to meddle on him.

What man (quoth she) faint you now? haue you done so many, 35 and do you shrinke at this?

Then shewing him a great deale of gold which *Cole* had left with her, she said, Would it not grieue a bodies heart to loose this? hang the old churle, what should he do liuing any longer? he hath too much, and we haue too little: tut husband, let the thing be done and then this is our owne.

Her wicked counsell was followed, and when they had listned at his chamber doore, they heard the man sound asleepe.

5   All is safe, quoth they.

And downe into the kitchin they goe, their seruants being all in bedde, and pulling out the yron pins, downe fel the bed, and the man dropt out into the boyling caldron. He being dead, they betwixt them cast his body into the riuer, his clothes they hid away, 10 and made all things as it should be: but when he came to the stable to conuey thence *Coles* horse, the stable doore being open, the horse had got loose, and with a part of the halter about his necke, and straw trussed vnder his belly, as the ostlers had dressed him ore eeue, he was gone out at the backe side, which led into a great field 15 adioyning to the house, and so leaping diuers hedges, being a lustie stout horse, had got into a ground where a mare was grasing, with whom he kept such a coile, that they got into the high way, where one of the towne meeting them, knew the mare, and brought her and the horse to the man that owd her.

20   In the meane space the Musitians had beene at the Inne, and in requitall of their euenings gift, they intended to giue *Cole* some musicke in the morning. The goodman told them he tooke horse before day: likewise there was a guest in the house that would haue borne him company to Reading; vnto whom the hoste also an- 25 swered, that he himselfe set him vpon horse-backe, and that he went long agoe.

Anone comes the man that owed the mare, inquiring vp and downe to know and if none of them missed a horse, who said no. At last hee came to the signe of the Crane where *Cole* lay: and call- 30 ing the hostlers he demanded of them if they lackt none: they said no.

Why then said the man, I perceiue my mare is good for something; for if I send her to field single, she wil come home double.

Thus it passed on all that day and the night folowing. But the 35 next day after, *Coles* wife musing that her husband came not home, sent one of her men on horse-backe, to see if he could meet him.

And if (quoth she) you meet him not betwixt this and Colebrooke, aske for him at the Crane, but if you find him not there,

---

[16] stout] Q2-4; stond Q1

then ride to London; for I doubt he is either sicke, or else some mischance hath fallen vnto him.

The fellow did so, and asking for him at Colebrooke, they answered, he went homeward from thence such a day. The seruant musing what should be become of his master, and making much inquiry in the towne for him; at length one tolde him of a horse that was found on the high way, and no man knew whence he came. He going to see the horse, knew him presently, and to the Crane he goes with him. The hoast of the house perceiuing this, was blanke, and that night fled secretly away. The fellow going vnto the Iustice desired his help, presently after word was brought that *Iarman* of the Crane was gone; then all the men said he had surely made *Cole* away: and the musitions told what *Iarman* said to them when they would haue giuen *Cole* musicke. Then the woman being apprehended and examined confessed the truth. *Iarman* soone after was taken in Winsor forest. He and his wife were both hangd after they had laid open al these things before expressed. Also he confessed, that he being a carpenter made that false falling floore, and how his wife deuised it. And how they had murdred by that means lx. persons. And yet notwithstanding all the money which they had gotten thereby, they prospered not, but at their death were found very farre in debt.

When the king heard of this murder, he was for the space of vij. dayes so sorrowfull and heauy as he would not heare any suite, giuing also commaundement, that the house should quite be consumed with fire wherein *Cole* was murdred, and that no man should euer build vpon that cursed ground.

Coles substance at his death was exceeding great, he had daily in his house an hundred men seruants, and xl. maids; he maintaind beside aboue two or three hundred people, spinners and carders, and a great many other housholders. His wife neuer after married; and at her death she bestowed a mightie summe of money toward the maintaining of the new builded monastery. Her daughter was most richly married to a gentleman of great worship, by whom shee had many children. And some say, that the riuer whereinto *Cole* was cast, did euer since carry the name of *Cole*, being called, The riuer of *Cole*, and the towne of Colebrooke.

12 all the men] Q2-4; all man Qi
31 neuer after] Q3,4; after neuer Q1,2

CHAPTER XII.

How diuers of the Clothiers wiues went to the churching of Suttons wife of Salisbury, and of their meriments.

Suttons wife of Salisbury which had lately bin deliuered of a
5 sonne, against her going to Church, prepared great cheare: at
what time *Simons* wife of South-hampton came thither, and so did
diuers other of the Clothiers wiues, onely to make merry at this
Churching feast: and whilest these Dames sate at the Table, *Crab,*
Weasell, and *Wren* waited on the boord, and as the old Prouerbe
10 speaketh, Many women many words, so fell it out at that time: for
there was such pratling, that it passed: some talkt of their husbands
frowardnes, some shewed their maids sluttishnes, othersome desci-
phered the costlines of their garments, some told many tales of
their neighbors: and to be briefe, there was none of them but would
15 haue talke for a whole day.

But when *Crab, Weasell,* and *Wren* saw this, they concluded betwixt themselues, that as oft as any of the women had a good bit
of meat on their trenchers, they offring a cleane one, should catch
that commodity, and so they did: but the women being busie in
20 talke, marked it not, till at the last one found lesure to misse her
meat: whereupon she said, that their boldnes exceeded their diligence.

Not so forsooth, said *Weasell,* there is an hundred bolder than
we.

25 Name mee one, said the woman, if you can.

A flea is bolder, quoth *Crabbe.*

How will you proue that said the woman?

Because quoth he, they will creepe vnder your coates, where we
dare not come, and now and then bite you by the buttocks as if they
30 were brawne.

But what becomes of them quoth the woman? their sweet meat

⁶ *Simons*] Q2-4; *Suttons* Q1

hath sowre sauce, and their lustines doth often cost them their liues, therefore take heed.

A good warning of a faire woman, said *Wren,* but I had not thought so fine a wit in a fat belly.

The women seeing their men so merry said it was a signe there 5 was good ale in the house.

Thats as fit for a churching quoth *Weasell,* as a cudgell for a curst queane.

Thus with pleasant communication and merry quips they droue out the time, till the fruit and spice cakes were set on the boord: 10 At what time one of them began to aske of the other, if they heard not of the cruell murder of *Thomas* of Reading.

What, saide the rest, is old *Cole* murdred? when I pray you was the deede done?

The other answered, on friday last. 15

O good Lord, said the women, how was it done, can you tell?

As report goeth said the other, he was rosted aliue.

O pittifull! was he roasted? Indeede I heard one say, a man was murdred at London, and that he was sodden at an Inholders house, and serued in to the ghests in stead of porke. 20

No neighbour, it was not at London, said another: I hear say twas comming from London, at a place called Colebrooke, and it is reported for truth, that the Inholder made pies of him, and penny pasties, yea, and made his owne seruant eate a piece of him. 25

But I pray you, good neighbour, can you tell how it was knowne? some say, that a horse reuealed it.

Now by the masse (quoth *Grayes* wife) it was told one of my neighbors, that a certaine horse did speake, and told great things.

That sounds like a lye, sayd one of them. 30

Why, sayd another, may not a horse speake, as well as *Balaams* asse?

It may be, but it is vnlikely, said the third.

But where was the horse when he spake?

As some say (quoth she) he was in the field, and had broke out of 35 the Stable, where he stood fast lockt in mighty strong iron fetters, which he burst in peeces, as if they had beene strawes, and broke downe the Stable doore, and so gotte away.

The good man comming in at these speeches, asked what that was they talkt of. 40

Mary, sayd his wife, we heare that *Cole* of Reading is murdred: I pray you, is it true?

I, sayd *Sutton*, it is true, that vile villaine his hoast murdered him, in whose house the man had spent many a pound.

5 But did they make pies of him, sayd his wife?

No no, quoth her husband: he was scalded to death in a boyling caldron, and afterward throwne into a running riuer that is hard by.

But, good husband, how was it knowne?

By his horse, quoth hee.

10 What, did he tell his master was murthered? could the horse speake English?

Iesus, what a foolish woman are you (quoth he) to aske such a question? But to end this, you are all heartily welcome, good neighbors, and I am sorry you had no better cheere.

15 So with thanks the women departed. Thus haue ye heard the diuers tales that wil be spred abroad of an euill deed.

CHAPTER XIII.

How Duke *Robert* deceiued his keepers, and got from
them: how he met faire *Margaret,* and in carrying her
20 away, was taken, for the which he had his eyes put out.

Duke *Robert,* hauing as you heard, obtained the loue of faire *Margaret,* did now cast in his mind, how he might delude his keepers, and carry her away. In the end he being fully resolued what to doe, sent his letter vnto her, wherein he requested, that she 25 would be ready to meete him in the forest, betwixt Cardiffe and Gloucester.

The young Lady hauing secretly receiued his message, vnknowne to her master or dame, in a morning betime made her readye and got foorth, walking to the appointed place, where her loue should 30 meete her.

During her aboad there, and thinking long ere her loue came, she

330

entered into diuers passions, which indeed presaged some disaster fortune to follow.

O my deere Loue, sayd shee, how slacke art thou in perfourming thy promise! why doe not thy deeds agree with thy inditing? see, these are thy words, Come my deere *Margaret,* and with *Cupids* swift wings flie to thy friend, be now as nimble in thy footing, as the Camels of Bactria, that runne an hundred miles a day, I will waite and stay for thee, so I stay not too long. There is no countrey like Austria for ambling horses, and to carry thee I haue got one.

O my Loue (quoth she) heere am I, but where art thou? O why doest thou play the trewant with Time, who like the winde slides away vnseene? An ambling gennet of Spaine is too slow to serue our turnes. A flying horse, for flying Louers were most meete.

And thus casting many lookes through the Siluane shades, vp and downe to espie him, she thought euery minute, an houre, till she might see him, sometimes she would wish herselfe a bird, that she might flye through the aire to meet him, or a pretty squirell to clime the highest tree to discry his comming: but finding her wishes vaine, she began thus to excuse him and perswaded her selfe, saying.

How much to blame am I, to finde fault with my friend? Alasse, men that lacke their liberty, must come when they can, not when they would, poore prisoners cannot doe what they desire, and then why should I be so hasty? Therefore if safely I may lay me downe, I will beguile vnquiet thoughts with quiet sleepe: it is sayd that *Galino* breedes no Serpents, nor doth Englands forrests nourish Beares or Lions, therefore without hurt I hope I may rest a while.

Thus leauing fayre *Margaret* in a sweete slumber, we will returne to Duke *Robert,* who had thus plotted his escape from his keepers.

Hauing liberty of the King to hawke and hunt, he determined on a day, as he should folow the chase, to leaue the hounds to the Hart, and the hunters to their hornes and being busie in their sport, himselfe would fly, which he perfourmed at that time, when hee appointed *Margaret* to meete him, and so comming to the place, his Horse all on a water, and himselfe in a sweate, finding his Loue a sleepe, he awaked her with a kisse, saying: Arise, fayre *Margaret,*

*7 Bactria] Q2-4; Bractria Q1
17-18 to clime] Q2-4; no clime Q1
32 at that] Q1BM, Q2-4; atthat is Q1HN
34 all on] Q1BM, Q2,3; all in Q1HN, Q4

331

now comes the time wherein thou shalt bee made a Queene: and presently setting her on horsebacke he posted away.

Now when the Keepers saw they had lost his company, and that at the killing of the game, he was not present, they were among
5 themselues in such a mutiny, that they were ready one to stabbe another.

It was thy fault, sayd one, that he thus escapt from vs, that hadst more minde of thy pleasure, then of thy prisoner, and by this meanes we are all vndone.

10 The other sayd as much to him, that he had thought he had followed him in the chase: but leauing at last this contention, the one posted vp to the King, while the others coasted vp and downe the countrey to search for the Duke, who hauing kild his horse in traueling, was most vnhappily met on foote with fayre *Margaret,*
15 ere he could come to any Towne, where he might for money haue another. But when he spyed his Keepers come to take him, he desired *Margaret* to make shift for her selfe, and to seeke to escape them. But she being of a contrary mind, sayd, she would liue and dye with him.

20 The Duke seeing himselfe ready to bee surprised, drew out his sword, and sayd, he would buy his liberty with his life, before he would yeeld to be any more a prisoner; and thereupon began a great fight betwixt them, insomuch that the Duke had killed two of them: but himselfe being sore wounded, and faint with ouer-
25 much bleeding, at length fell downe, being not able any longer to stand: and by this meanes the good Duke was taken with his fayre loue, and both of them committed to prison.

But in the meane space, when *Graies* wife had mist her mayde, and saw she was quite gone, she made great lamentation for her
30 among her neighbours: for she loued her as dearely as any child that euer she bore of her owne body.

O *Margaret* (quoth she) what cause hadst thou thus to leaue mee? if thou didst mislike of any thing, why didst thou not tell me? If thy wages were too little, I would haue mended it: If thy apparell
35 had beene too simple, thou shouldest haue had better: If thy worke had beene too great, I would haue had help for thee.

Farewell, my sweete *Meg,* the best seruant that euer came in any mans house, many may I haue of thy name, but neuer any of thy

⁷ hadst] Q1 BM, Q2-4; had Q1 HN

nature, thy deligence is much, in thy hands I laid the whole gouernment of my house, and thereby eased my selfe of that care which
now will cumber me.

Heere she hath left mee my keies vnto my chests, but my comfort
is gone with her presence, euery gentle word that shee was wont to 5
speake, comes now into my mind, her courteous behauiour shall I
neuer forget: with how sweete and modest a countenance would
shee qualifie my ouer-hasty nature? It repents my hart that euer I
spoke foule word vnto her. O *Meg*, wert thou here againe, I would
neuer chide thee more: but I was an vnworthy dame for such a 10
seruant: what will become of me now, if I should chance to be
sicke, seeing shee is gone, that was woont to be both my Apoticarie
and Phisition?

Well, quoth her neighbours, there is no remedy now, but to rest
content, you shall one day heare of her, doubt you not, and thinke 15
this, that shee was not so good, but you may get another as good,
and therfore do not take it so heauily.

O neighbour, blame me not to grieue, seeing I haue lost so great
a iewell, and sure I am perswaded, that scant in a bodies life time,
they shall meete with the like. 20

I protest, I would circuit England round about on my bare feete
to meete with her againe. O, my *Meg* was surely stole away from
me, else would she not haue gone in such sort.

Her husband on the other side grieued as much, and rested not
night nor day riding vp and downe to seeke her: but shee, poore 25
soule, is fast lockt vp in prison, and therefore cannot be met withall.

But when the King vnderstood of his brothers escape, he was
maruellous wroth, giuing great charge and commandement when
he was taken, that both his eies should be put out, and he kept in
prison till his dying day; appoynting also, that the maid should lose 30
her life for presumption in louing him.

This matter being rumored ouer all England, it came to the
eares of *Gray* and his wife, who hearing that *Margaret* also was
there in prison appointed to die, the good aged woman neuer rested
til she came to the court, where kneeling before the King, with 35
many teares she besought his Maiesty to spare the maidens life,
saying, Most royall king consider I humbly beseech you, that the
duke your brother was able to intice any woman to his loue, much

²⁸ wroth] Q2-4; wrath Q1

more a seely maiden, especially promising her marriage, to make
her a Lady, a Dutchesse, or a Queene, who would refuse such an
offer, when at the instant they might get both a princely husband
and a high dignitie? if death be a Louers guerdon, then what is due
5 to hatred? I am in my heart persuaded, that had my poore *Margaret*
thought it would haue bred your highnes displeasure, she would
neuer haue bought his loue so deare. Had your Grace made it
knowen to your commons, that it was vnlawful for any to marry
the duke your brother, who would haue attempted such an action?
10 if she had wilfully disobeyed your Graces commandement, she
might haue bin thought worthy of death; but seeing ignorantly
she offended, I beseech your Grace recall the sentence, and let me
still inioy my seruant, for neuer will I rise till your Maiestie haue
graunted my petition.
15 His Highnes, who was of nature mercifull, beholding the womans
aboundant teares, tooke pitty on her, and graunted her suite; which
being obtained, she went home with all haste possible. And from
thence, she with her husband taking their iorny to Cardiffe castle,
they came at that very instant when the maiden was led toward hir
20 death, who went in most ioyfull sort to the same, saying, that they
were not worthy to be accounted true Louers, that were not willing
to die for loue.
And so with a smiling countenance she passed on, as if she had
eaten *Apium Risus,* which causeth a man to die laughing: but her
25 dame *Gray* seeing her, fell about her necke, and with many kisses
imbraced her, saying, Thou shalt not die my wench, but goe home
with me, and for thy deliuerie, behold heere the Kings letters; and
with that she deliuered them vp to the gouernor of the Castle, who
reading them found these words written: We pardon the maids
30 life, and graunt her libertie, but let her not passe, till she see her
louers eies put out, which we wil haue you do in such sort, that
only the sight may perish, but the eie continue faire, for which
cause I haue sent downe doctor *Piero* that he may execute the same.
The gouernour of the Castle hauing read the Kings letter, said
35 thus to the maiden: The Kings maiesty hath pardoned thy life, and
allowed thy liberty, but you must not passe before you see your
louers eies put out.
O sir, said the maiden, mistake not your selfe, they are my eies

---

[31] you do] Q1BM, Q3,4; you to do Q1HN
[31-32] that only] Q4; that not only Q1-3

that must be put out, and not the Dukes: as his offence grew by my meanes, so I being guiltie, ought to receiue the punishment.

The kings commaundement must be fulfilled, said the gouernor.

And therewithall Duke *Robert* was brought forth, who hearing that he must lose his eies, said thus: the noble mind is neuer con- 5 quered by griefe, nor ouercome by mischance: but as the Hart reneweth his age by eating the serpent, so doth a man lengthen his life with deuouring sorrow: my eyes haue offended the King, and they must be punished, my heart is in as great fault, why is not that killed? 10

The Kings maiesty said the gouernor, spares your life of meere loue, and onely is content to satisfie the Law with the losse of your eies, wherefore take in good part this punishment and thinke you haue deserued greater than is granted.

With this *Margaret* cried out, saying, O my deare loue, most 15 gentle Prince, well may you wish that I had neuer bin borne, who by seeing of me must lose your sight; but happie should I count my selfe, if it so please the King, that I might redeeme thy eies with my life, or else, that being an equal offendor, I might receiue equall punishment: hadst thou sustained this smart for some Queen 20 or Princesse of high bloud, it might with the more ease be borne, but to indure it for such a one as I, it must needs cause a treble griefe to be increased.

Content thee faire *Margaret* said the duke, for honor ought to be giuen to vertue, and not riches: for glory, honor, nobility and 25 riches, without virtue, are but clokes of maliciousnes. And now let me take my leaue of thy beauty, for neuer must I behold thy face: notwithstanding I account my eies wel lost, in that I do forgo them for so peerlesse a paragon. Now faire heauens, farewell, the Sunne, Moone and Starres shall I in this world neuer behold againe; and 30 farewel also the fruitfull earth: wel may I feele thee, but those poore windowes of my body are now denied to view thee any more: and though the world hath euer bin my foe, yet wil I bid it fare-well too, and farewell all my friends; whiles I liue here in this world, I must suppose to sleep, and wake when I come in heauen, 35 where I hope to see you all againe. Yet had it pleased the King, I had rather haue lost my life than my eies. Life, why what is it but

19 with my life] Q2-4; to my selfe Q1
33 euer] Q2-4; neuer Q1

a floure, a bubble in the water, a spanne long, and full of miserie? of such small account is life, that euery souldier will sell it for six pence. And trust me I doe now detest life, worse than a goate doth hate basill.

5 With that the Doctor prepared his instrument, and being ready to set to the Dukes eies, he said, O stay master doctor, till I haue conueyed my loues countenance downe into my heart: Come hither my sweete, and let me giue thee my last kisse, while my eies may direct me to thy cherry lippes.

10 Then imbracing her in his armes, he said, O that I might giue thee a kisse of xx yeares long, and to satisfie my greedie eies with thy faire sight: yet it doth somwhat content me, because thou art present at my punishment, that I may hold thee by the hand, to comfort my heart at the sodaine pricke of my eie.

15 This being said, the Doctor performed his duetie, and so put out the cristall sight; at what time Duke *Robert* started vp, and with a most manly courage said, I must thanke his Maiesty, that though he depriueth me of my sight, yet he leaueth me eies to weep for my sinnes.

20 But so soone as *Margaret* beheld the deede, she fell downe in a swowne, and much adoe her dame had to recouer hir life: which when the duke vnderstood, he was wondrous woe, groaping for her with his bleeding eies, saying, O where is my loue? for Gods sake haue regard to her. And I pray you most heartily good goodwife

25 *Gray*, let her haue this fauour for my sake, that she may be vsed kindly.

And with that the Keepers led him into the castle, and *Margaret* was caried away wondrous sicke and ill: but her dame was most tender ouer her, and would suffer her to lacke nothing. When she

30 was somewhat well recouered, her dame *Gray* set her on horse backe: and at her comming to Gloucester there was no small ioy.

13-14 to comfort] Q1BM, Q2-4; the comfort Q1HN

CHAPTER XIV.

How *Tom Doue* being fallen to decay, was forsaken of his
friends, and despised of his seruants: and how in the
end he was raised againe through the liberality of the
Clothiers.   5

Such as seeke the pleasure of this world, follow a shaddow
wherein is no substance: and as the adder Aspis tickleth a man
to death so doth vaine pleasure flatter vs, till it makes vs forget
God, and consume our substance, as by *Tom Doue* it is apparant,
who had through a free heart, and a liberall mind wasted his   10
wealth, and looke how his goods consumed, so his friends fled
from him: And albeit he had beene of great ability, and thereby
done good vnto many, yet no man regarded him in his pouerty, but
casting a scornefull countenance vpon him, they passed by him
with slender salutation: neither would any of his old acquaintance 15
do him good, or pleasure him the value of a farthing; his former
friendship done to them was quite forgot, and he made of as much
account, as *Iob* when he sate on the dunghill.

Now when his wicked seruants sawe him in this disgrace with
the world, they on the other side beganne to disdaine him. Not- 20
withstanding that hee (to his great cost) had long time brought them
vp, yet did they nothing regard it, but behinde his backe in most
scornfull sort derided him, and both in their words and actions
greatly abuse him, reuerence they would do none vnto him, but
when they spake, it was in such malapert sort, as would grieue an 25
honest mind to heare it.

At last it came to passe, that breaking out into meere contempt,
they said they would stay no longer with him, and that it was a
great discredit to them, to serue a person so beggarly: whereupon
they thought it conuenient to seeke for their benefits elsewhere. 30

*20 the other] Q1BM, Q2-4; thother Q1HN

When the distressed man found the matter so plaine, being in great griefe, he spake thus vnto them.

Now doe I find, to my sorrow, the small trust that is in this false world. Why my masters (quoth he) haue you so much forgotten
5 my former prosperitie, that you nothing regarde my present necessity? in your wants I forsooke you not, in your sicknes I left you not, nor despised you in your great pouerty: it is not vnknowne, though you doe not consider it, that I tooke some of you vp in the high way, other some from your needy parents, and brought the rest
10 from meere beggery to a house of bounty, where from paltry boyes, I brought you vp to mans estate, and haue, to my great cost, taught you a trade, whereby you may liue like men. And in requitall of all my curtesie, cost and good will, will you now on a sodaine forsake me? is this the best recompence that you can find in your
15 hearts to yeeld me?

This is farre from the minds of honest seruants. The fierce Lion is kind to those that do him good: plucke but one thorne out of his foote, and for the same he will shew manifold fauors. The wilde Bull will not ouerthrow his Dam: and the very Dragons are duti-
20 full to their nourishers. Bee better aduised, and call to mind, I beseech you, that I haue not pluckt a thorne out of your feete, but drawne your whole bodies out of perils, and when you had no meanes to help your selues, I only was your support, and he, that when all other forsooke you, did comfort you in all your extremities.
25 And what of all this, quoth one of them? because you tooke vs vp poore, doth it therefore follow, that wee must bee your slaues? We are young men, and for our partes, we are no further to regard your profit, then it may stand with our preferment: Why should we lose our benefit, to pleasure you? If you taught vs our trade,
30 and brought vs vp from boyes to men, you had our seruice for it, whereby you made no small benefit, if you had as well vsed it, as we got it. But if you be poore, you may thanke your selfe, being a iust scourge for your prodigalitie, and it is my opinion plaine, that to stay with you, is the next way to make vs like you, neither
35 able to help our selues, nor our friends, therefore in briefe, come pay me my wages, for I will not stay, let the rest doe as they will for I am resolued.

Well sayd his Master if needs thou wilt be gone, here is part of

³⁴ vs ∧] Q2-4; ∼, Qᵢ

thy wages in hand, and the rest, so soone as God sends it, thou
shalt haue it.

And with that, turning to the rest, he sayd: Let me yet intreat
you to stay and leaue me not altogether destitute of helpe: by
your labours must I liue, and without you I know not what to doe. 5
Consider therefore my neede, and regard my great charge. And if
for my sake you will doe nothing, take compassion on my poore
children, stay my sliding foote, and let me not vtterly fall, through
your flying from me.

Tush (quoth they) what do you talke to vs? we can haue better 10
wages, and serue a man of credit, where our fare shal be far better,
and our gaines greater: therefore the world might count vs right
coxcomes, if we should forsake our profit, to pleasure you: therefore adieu, God send you more mony, for you are like to haue
no more men: and thus they departed. 15

When they were gon, within a while after they met one with
another, saying, What cheere? are you all come a way?

In faith I, what should we doe else (quoth they); but hear'st
thou, sirra, hast thou got thy wages?

Not yet saith the other, but I shall haue it, and that is as good, 20
tis but x. shillings.

Saist thou so (said he) now I see thou art one of God almighties
idiots.

Why so, said the other?

Because (quoth he) thou wilt be fed with shales: but Ile tell thee 25
one thing, twere best for thee quickly to arrest him, lest some other
doing it before, and there be nothing left to pay thy debt: hold
thy peace, faire words make fooles faine and it is an old saying,
One bird in hand is worth two in bush: if thou dost not arrest him
presently, I will not giue thee two pence for thy ten shillings. 30

How shall I come by him (quoth the other)?

Giue mee but two pots of ale, and Ile betray him saieth he.

So they being agreed, this smooth-fac'd Iudas comes to his late
Master, and told him that a friend of his at the doore would speak
with him. The vnmistrusting man thinking no euill, went to the 35
doore, where presently an Officer arrested him at his mans suite.

20 as good] Q1BM, Q2-4; a good Q1HN
22 said] Q1BM, Q2-4; quoth Q1HN
24 said] Q1BM, Q2-4; saith Q1HN
27 and there] Q1BM, Q2-4; there Q1HN

The poore man seeing this, being strucken into a sudden sorrow, in the griefe of his heart spake to this effect: Ah thou lewd fellow, art thou the first man that seekes to augment my misery? Haue I thus long giuen thee bread, to breede my ouerthrow? and
5 nourisht thee in thy neede, to worke my destruction? Full little did I thinke, when thou so often didst dippe thy false fingers in my dish, that I gaue foode to my chiefest foe: but what booteth complaints in these extremes? go wife, quoth he, vnto my neighbours, and see if thou canst get any of them to be my baile.
10 But in vaine was her paines spent. Then he sent her to his kinsfolks, and they denied him: to his brother, and he would not come at him, so that there was no shift, but to prison he must: but as hee was going, a messenger met him, with a letter from Master *Cole,* wherein, as you heard, he had promised him two hundred pounds:
15 which when the poore man read, he greatly reioyced, and shewing the same to the officer, he was content to take his owne word.
Whereupon *Tom Doue* went presently to Reading, where, at his comming, he found all the rest of the Clothiers lamenting *Coles* vntimely death, where the wofull widdow paid him the money,
20 by which deede all the rest of the Clothiers were induced to do something for *Doue.* And thereupon one gaue him ten pounds, another twenty, another thirtie pounds, to begin the world anew: and by this meanes (together with the blessing of God) he grew into greater credit than euer he was before. And riches being thus
25 come vpon him, his former friends came fawning vnto him, and when he had no neede of them, then euery one was ready to proffer him kindnesse. His wicked seruants also that disdained him in his distresse, were after glad to come creeping vnto him, intreating with cappe and knee for his fauour and friendship. And albeit he
30 seemed to forgiue their trespasses done against him, yet he would often say, he would neuer trust them for a straw. And thus he euer after liued in great wealth and prosperitie, doing much good to the poore, and at his death, left to his children great landes.

CHAPTER XV.

How faire *Margaret* made her estate and high birth knowne
   to her master and dame: and for the intire loue she
   bore to Duke *Robert,* made a vow neuer to marry, but
   became a Nun in the Abbey at Glocester. 5

After faire *Margaret* was come againe to Glocester, neuer did she
behold the cleare day, but with a weeping eye: and so great
was the sorrow which she conceaued for the losse of Duke *Robert*
her faithfull Louer, that she vtterly despised all the pleasures of
this life, and at last bewraid her selfe in this sort vnto her Dame. 10

O my good Master and Dame, too long haue I dissembled my
parentage from you, whom the froward destinies do pursue to
deserued punishment. The wofull daughter am I of the vnhappie
Earle of Shrewsbury, who euer since his banishment haue done
nothing but drawne mischance after me: wherfore let me intreate 15
you (deere Master and Dame) to haue your good wills, to spend the
remnant of my life in some blessed Monasterie.

When *Gray* and his wife heard this, they wondred greatly, as
well at her birth, as at her strange demaund. Whereupon her dame
knew not how to call her, whether Maiden or Madam, but said O 20
good Lord, are you a Lady and I knew it not? I am sory that I
knew it not before.

But when the folkes of the house heard that *Margaret* was a
Lady, there was no small alteration: and moreouer her Dame said,
that she had thought to haue had a match betweene her and her 25
sonne: And by many perswasions did seeke to withdraw her from
being a Nun saying in this manner, What *Margaret,* thou art young
and faire, the world (no doubt) hath better fortune for thee,
whereby thou mayst leaue an honourable issue behind thee, in
whom thou mayst liue after death. 30

These and many other reasons did they alleadge vnto her, but
all in vaine, she making this replie, Who knoweth not that this
world giueth the pleasure of an howre, but the sorrow of many

daies? for it payeth euer that which it promiseth, which is nothing
els but continuall trouble and vexation of the mind. Do you thinke,
if I had the offer and choice of the mightiest princes of Christendome, that I could match my selfe better then to my Lord Iesus?
5 No no, he is my husband, to whom I yeeld my selfe both body and
soule, giuing to him my heart, my loue, and most firme affection:
I haue ouerlong loued this vile world: therefore I beseech you
farther dissuade me not.

When her friends by no meanes could alter her opinion, the
10 matter was made knowne to his Maiestie, who against the time that
she should be receiued into the monasterie, came to Gloucester with
most part of his Nobility, to honour her action with his princely
presence.

All things being therefore prepared the yong Lady was in most
15 princely wise attired in a gowne of pure white sattin, her kertle
of the same, imbrodered with gold about the skirts, in most curious
sort, her head was garnished with gold, pearles, and precious
stones, hauing her haire like threeds of burnisht gold, hanging
downe behind her, in maner of a princely bride: about her iuory
20 necke iewels of inestimable price were hung, and her handwreasts
were compassed about with bracelets of bright shining diamonds.

The streets through the which she should passe, were pleasantly
deckt with greene oaken boughs. Then came the yong Lady most
like an heauenly Angell out of her masters house; at what time all
25 the bells in Gloucester were solemnly rung, she being led betwixt
the Kings maiesty, hauing on his royall robes and imperiall crowne,
and the chiefe Bishop wearing his Miter, in a Cope of cloth of gold,
ouer her head a Canopy of white silke, fringed about in princely
manner: before her went an hundred priests singing, and after her
30 all the chiefe Ladies of the land: then all the wiues and maidens
of Gloucester followed, with an innumerable sort of people on
euerie side standing to behold her. In this sort she passed on to the
cathedrall church, where she was brought to the Nunry gate.

The Lady Abbesse receiued her: where the beautiful maiden
35 kneeling downe, made her praier in sight of all the people: then
with her own hands she vndid her virgins faire gowne, and tooke
it off, and gaue it away to the poore: after that, her kertle, then
her iewels, bracelets and rings, saying, Farewell the pride and

7 world:] Q3,4; ~? Q1,2
21 bracelets of] Mann; bracelets or Q1-4

342

vanity of this world. The ornaments of her head were the next she gaue away: and then was she led on one side, where she was stripped, and instead of her smocke of soft silke, had a smocke of rough haire put vpon her.

Then came one with a paire of sheares, and cut off her golden 5 coloured lockes, and with dust and ashes all bestrewd hir head and face. Which being done, she was broght again into the peoples sight barefoot and barelegd, to whom she said: Now farewell the world, farewell the pleasures of this life, farewell my Lord the King, and to the Dukes sweet loue farewell; now shall my eies weep for my 10 former transgressions, and no more shal my tongue talke of vanity: farewell my good master and dame, and farewell all good people.

With which words she was taken away, and neuer after seene abroad. When duke *Robert* heard thereof, hee desired that at his death, his body might be buried in Gloucester: in that towne, 15 quoth he, where first my cleare eies beheld the heauenly beuty of my loue, and where for my sake she forsooke the world: which was performed accordingly.

The King also at his death requested to be buried at Reading, for the great loue he bare to that place, amongst those Clothiers, 20 who liuing, were his hearts comfort. *Gray* dying wonderous wealthy, gaue land to the monastery, whereinto *Margaret* was taken. *William Fitzallen* also died a most rich man, hauing builded many houses for the poore, whose sonne *Henry* after was the first Maior that euer was in London. 25

Sutton of Salisbury did also at his death much good, and gaue an hundred li. to be yearely lent to poore weauers of the towne to the worlds end. *Simon* of South-hampton gaue a most bounteous gift towards the building of a monasterie at Winchester. *Hodgekins* of Halifax did also great good, and so did *Cutbert* of Kendall, who 30 had married xxiij couples out of his owne house, giuing ech of them x.li. to beginne the world withall. *Martin Byram* of Manchester gaue toward the building of a free schoole in Manchester, a great masse of money. And thus (gentle Reader) haue I finished my Storie of these worthy men, desiring thee to take 35 my paines in good part, which will incourage me to greater matters, perceiuing this curteously accepted.

FINIS.

343

EXPLANATORY NOTES [1]

JACK OF NEWBURY

The first edition of *Jack of Newbury* was read out of existence so cleanly that one must depend on the Stationers' Register for the approximate date. Thomas Millington made the entry on 7 March 1597 (Arber, III, 81), and then signed over his rights to Humfrey Lownes on 25 May of the same year (Arber, III, 84). *Jack* may have appeared in print between March and July, for on 8 July 1597 Millington entered "a ballad intituled *the ffirst parte of Iacke of Newberye*" (Arber, III, 87); the ballad seems to be an attempt to exploit the popularity of an already published and fast selling novel.

But the earliest extant edition is that of 1619, and there seems to be no reference within the last century and a half to an earlier edition. W. Carew Hazlitt, in his *Hand-Book to the Popular, Poetical, and Dramatic Literature of Great Britain* (1867) referred to the 1619 edition as the earliest extant, but for some reason he did not give its location. In 1912 Mann noted (p. 506) that he had seen Hazlitt's reference to a 1619 edition but that he had been unable to find it and therefore was using the 1626 edition, the unique copy of which was in the possession of the Earl of Ellesmere (though it has since been bought by the Huntington Library).

In 1920 the location of the 1619 edition became generally known, for on 14 June of that year the library of Britwell Court, Buckinghamshire, sold the only extant copy to the Huntington Library.

Q1 in the footnotes, collation notes, and explanatory notes is the 1619

[1] In the following notes several works are referred to a number of times. Edward Arber, *A Transcript of the Registers of the Company of Stationers of London, 1554-1640* (London, 1875-77) is referred to as "Arber"; *Dictionary of National Biography*, ed. Leslie Stephen and Sidney Lee (London, 1885-1901), as "DNB"; Richard Grafton, *Chronicle* [ed. Sir Henry Ellis] (London, 1809), as "Grafton"; Raphael Holinshed, *Chronicles* (London, the 1587 edition), as "Holinshed"; *The Gentle Craft, Parts I and II*, ed. Alexis F. Lange, *Palaestra*, XVIII (Berlin, 1903), as "Lange"; *The Works of Thomas Deloney*, ed. Francis Oscar Mann (Oxford, 1912), as "Mann"; *The Works of Thomas Nashe*, ed. Ronald B. McKerrow (London, 1904-[10]), as "Nashe"; Sir James A. H. Murray, *Oxford English Dictionary* (Oxford, 1888-1933), as "OED"; John Stow, *Survey of London*, ed. Charles Lethbridge Kingsford (Oxford, 1908), as "Stow"; and Edward H. Sugden, *A Topographical Dictionary to the Works of Shakespeare and His Fellow Dramatists* (Manchester, 1925), as "Sugden."

edition; Q2 is the 1626 edition; Q3, 1630; Q4, 1633; and Q5, 1637. These five comprise all the early extant editions through the first half of the seventeenth century. Latter seventeenth and eighteenth century editions were emended so freely that they have no textual validity.

The collation and contents of Q2 are identical with Q1. Yet within an individual page the wording of Q2 often is quite different from Q1. The reason is not entirely clear. On the title pages Q1 claims to be the eighth edition and Q2 the tenth. It seems likely, therefore, that the compositor of Q2 is not setting from Q1 but from an intermediary edition that is now lost and that appeared between 1619 (Q1) and 1626 (Q2). If a lost edition separates Q2 from Q1, then the differences between the two extant editions are partly explained. But collation reveals another factor: the compositor of Q2 (or is it the compositor of the lost edition, or of both?) emends somewhat freely. In fact, at times he takes the phrase on the title page, "corrected and enlarged," somewhat literally. He inserts an adjective whenever he pleases; he turns round expressions like "so is it" to "so it is"; he loves to expand on the original when he comes to a passage of dialect; and in general he prefers his own grammar and punctuation to that of Q1. Occasionally, as the footnotes show, he contributes an emendation that a critical edition cannot refuse; but usually his changes are merely whimsical, and often they result from misinterpretations. He has a good eye for consistency, but sometimes it gets him into trouble—as, for example, in the scene on page 36, where Jack relates to the king the allegory concerning the ants and the butterflies. In Q1 (and in the present text) Jack says that the ants summoned their chief peers to a parliament on the "one and thirtith" day of September in the city of Dry Dusty. The Q2 compositor apparently reflects that there are only thirty days in September; therefore, he changes "thirtith" to "twentith," and in one stroke the date becomes an unnecessary detail and the humor loses some of its edge.

The next edition in point of time, that of 1630 (Q3), is derived from Q2, as a glance at the collation notes show. Consider the following (page and line references are to the present edition):

Page and line numbers	Q1	Q2,3
5, 17	found acquaintance	found many acquaintance
6, 3	I doubt some	I thinke some
6, 15	streight dyes	presently dyes
24, 33	to his bed	to his bed side
34, 19	woon [i.e., won]	worne
40, 27	Broome	Broomes
40, 29	amitie	unity

Explanatory Notes

Each of the Q1 readings above is retained in the present text and appears also in Q4 and Q5.

Q4 claims to be the ninth edition; in other words, the typesetter for some reason apparently does not recognize the existence of Q2 and Q3 (the tenth and eleventh editions, according to their title pages), to say nothing of the lost edition, Qx. The copy text for Q4 is Q1, the eighth edition, as the following readings show:

Page and line numbers	Q1	Q2,3	Q4
6, 6	truth	true	truth
7, 10-11	labour and trauaile	labour and painful trauel	labour and trauaile
7, 14-15	and the great	as also the great	and the great
7, 30-31	faint souldiers	some soldiers	faint soulders
36, 38	thirtith	twentith	thirtith
41, 32	watch	march	watch
56, 16	Spinners	Spinsters	Spinners
65, 1	vertuous people	vertuous minded people	vertuous people
82, 30	ought to defend	ought much rather to defend	ought to defend

On the title page of Q5 is "the tenth time Imprinted," which means what it seems to mean—that Q5 follows Q4. Collation establishes the relationship with a vengeance, for Q5 occasionally follows Q4 in simple misprints like "out credites," when "our credites" appears in Q1-3. The name Primislas appears twice on one page of Q1-3. When he sets the name the first time, the Q4 compositor spells it Brimislas, substituting by mistake a "B" for a "P." But when he comes to the second use of the name, he sets it, correctly, with a "P." The Q5 compositor, seeing the inconsistency in Q4, compounds the error by making both readings "Brimislas." He guesses wrong with an even chance and thus reveals that he has not seen Q1-3, where the only spelling is "Primislas."

A diagram makes clear the genetic order of the early editions of *Jack of Newbury:*

```
        Q1
      ╱    ╲
    Qx      Q4
    ┆       │
    Q2      Q5
    │
    Q3
```

Q1 (1619) is thus the only substantive edition among those extant. The lost edition between Q1 and Q2 is represented by "Qx" and by dotted

347

lines of derivation. Note that Q2 has no more authority than Q5; after Q1, the extant edition of most authority is Q4.

1619 (Q1). STC(PRJ) 6559. *Title page:* THE | PLEASANT HI- | STORY OF IOHN | Winchcomb, in his younger yeares | *called* Iack *of* Newberie, *the famous* | and worthy Clothier of England: declaring | *his life and loue, together with his charitable* | deeds and great hospitality: | And how hee set continually fiue | *hundred poore people at worke, to the* | great benefit of the Common-wealth: | *worthy to be read and regarded.* | Now the eight time Imprinted, corrected, and inlarged, | by *T. D.* | *Haud curo inuidiam.* | [*printer's orn.,* McKerrow 278] | AT LONDON, | Printed by *Humfrey Lownes,* and are to bee sould at the | signe of the Star on Bredstreet hill. | 1619.

Collation: Quarto, A-L⁴, M². No page numbers.

Contents: [A1ʳ], title; [A1ᵛ], blank; A2ʳ-A2ᵛ, dedication to the cloth workers; A3ʳ-M2ʳ, text; [M2ᵛ], blank.

Copy used: Huntington Library (only extant copy).

1626 (Q2). STC(PRJ) 6560. *Title page:* The pleasant Historie | OF | IOHN WINCHCOMB, | In his yonguer yeares called | IACK of NEWBERY, | The famous and worthy Clothier of | England; declaring his life and loue, | together with his charitable deeds | and great Hospitalitie. | And how hee set continually fiue hundred poore | people at worke, to the great benefite of | the Common-wealth. | Now the tenth time Imprinted, corrected and enlarged | by *T. D.* | *Haud curo invidiam.* | [*rule*] | [*orn.*] | [*rule*] | LONDON, | Printed by H. LOWNES, and are to be sold by *Cuthbert* | *Wright* in S. *Bartholomews,* neer the entrance | into the Hospitall. 1626.

Collation and contents: Identical with the 1619 edition.

Copy used: Huntington Library (only extant copy).

1630 (Q3). STC(PRJ) 6561. *Title page:* THE PLEASANT | HISTORY | OF | Iohn Winchcomb, | IN | His younger yeares called IACK | of *Newbery,* | The famous and worthy Clothier of | England; declaring his life and loue, | together with his charitable deedes | and great Hospitality. | And how he set

---

[2] In the following descriptions—of *Jack of Newbury* here and of the other three novels as they are taken up in the explanatory notes—"STC(PRJ)" means *Short-Title Catalogue . . . 1475-1640,* first compiled by A. W. Pollard and G. R. Redgrave (London, 1926), and now in the process of revision by William A. Jackson. "STC(W)" means *Short-Title Catalogue . . . 1641-1700,* compiled by Donald G. Wing (New York, 1945-51). The descriptions are made largely from photostat and microfilm.

continually fiue hundred poore | people at worke, to the great benefite of | the Common-wealth. | The eleuenth Edition, corrected and enlarged | by *T. D.* | *Haud curo inuidiam.* | [*rule*] | LONDON, | Printed by H L. and R Y. and are to be sold by | IOHN HARRIGAT at the Holy Lamb in Pater- | noster Row. *An.* 1630.

Collation and contents: Identical with the 1619 edition.

Copy used: Bodleian Library (only extant copy).

1633 (Q4) . STC (PRJ) 6562. *Title page:* THE | PLEASANT | HISTORY OF JOHN | WINCHCOMB, in his younger | *yeares called* Jacke *of* Newberie, *the fa-* | mous and worthy Clothier of England: | *declaring his life and love, together with his* | charitable deeds and great | hospitality; | And how hee set continually five | *hundred poore people at worke, to the* | great benefit of the Common-wealth; | *worthy to be read and regarded.* | Now the ninth time Imprinted, corrected, | and inlarged, by *T. D.* | *Haud curo invidiam.* | [*printer's orn.*] | LONDON, | Printed by *Robert Young,* and are to be sold by | *Cuthbert Wright.* 1633.

Collation and contents: Identical with the 1619 edition.

Copy used: British Museum (only extant copy).

1637 (Q5). STC(PRJ) 6563. *Title page:* THE | PLEASANT | HISTORIE OF JOHN | WINCHCOMB, in his younger | yeeres called *Jacke* of *Newberie,* the | famous and worthy Clothier of England: | declaring his life and love, together | with his charitable deeds and | great hospitality; | And how hee set conti- | nually five hundred poore people | at worke, to the great benefit | of the COMMON-WEALTH; | worthy to be read and | regarded. | Now the tenth time imprinted, corrected, and inlarged, by *T. D.* | *Haud curo in-vidiam.* | [*rule*] | [*orn.*] | [*rule*] | LONDON, | Printed by *Robert Young,* and are to be sold | by *Cuthbert Wright,* 1637.

Collation: Quarto, A-L4. No page numbers.

Contents: [A1r], title; [A1v], blank; A2r-A2v, dedication to the cloth workers; A3r-L4r, text; [L4v], blank.

Copy used: Huntington Library (only extant copy).

1672. STC(W) 963. Now the 13th time imprinted. By E. Crowch, for Thomas Passinger, 1672. Quarto. (Bodleian; Newberry)

1680? STC(W) 964. Printed by W. Wilde for Thos. Passenger, [1680?]. Quarto. (British Museum)

1684. STC(W) 958. By H. B. for W. Thackeray, 1684. Octavo. (Magdalene College)

1700? STC (W) 965. Printed for Eben. Tracy at the Three Bibles, [1700?]. Quarto. (British Museum, Cambridge)

MODERN EDITIONS

Following is a list of the nineteenth- and twentieth-century editions of the complete novel. No attempt has been made to list anthologies in which only parts of *Jack of Newbury* have been printed.

1859. *The History of John Winchcomb, Usually Called Jack of Newbury, the Famous Clothier. Written A. D. 1597*. Edited by James O. Halliwell [-Phillips]. London: T. Richards, 1859. In a note at the beginning, dated November, 1859, Thomas Richards, the printer, certifies that only twenty-six copies were printed. The 1633 edition was used as copy text.

1903. *Thomas Deloney. Eine studie über balladenlitteratur der Shakspere-zeit. Nebst neudruck von Deloney's roman "Jack of Newbury."* Edited by Richard Sievers. Weimar: R. Wagner, 1903. Reissued in 1904 by Mayer and Müller, Berlin [*Palaestra*, XXXVI]. Copy text: the 1630 edition.

1912. *The Works of Thomas Deloney*. Edited by Francis Oscar Mann. Oxford: Clarendon Press, 1912. Copy text: the 1626 edition.

1920. *Thomas of Reading and John Winchcombe*. Edited by W. H. D. Rouse. London: Blackie, 1920. Copy text: Mann's edition of 1912.

1929. *Shorter Novels*. Vol. I. Edited by Ernest Rhys. London: Dent (Everyman), 1929. Copy text: the 1626 edition.

1953. *Elizabethan Fiction*. Edited by Robert Ashley and Edwin M. Moseley. New York: Rinehart (paperback), 1953. "The text is taken from a 1626 printing of *Jack of Newbury* in Mann's edition of Deloney's *Works*."

NOTES

Page 3, *15*. **John Winchcombe:** Not mentioned by Richard Grafton or Raphael Holinshed. Thomas Fuller, in his *Worthies of England* (1662), writes glowingly that John Winchcomb was "the most considerable clothier England ever beheld." See the edition by John Freeman (London, 1952), p. 28. But Fuller leans too heavily on local Newbury tradition, if not on Deloney's novel. The best account is in the *DNB*. There were two John Winchcombs (alias Smallwood), father and son; and Deloney seems to combine the two—or perhaps oral tradition already had combined them—with emphasis on the son. The father died in 1520 and the son in 1558. Their wills are filed in Somerset House, London, under 27 Ayloffe and F.26 Noodes, respectively. It is highly doubtful that either of the Winchcombs aided importantly at Flodden Field, or that either entertained Henry VIII and Catherine in his house. But following are some of the ascertainable facts: both were pioneers in the manufacture of clothing in Newbury, Berkshire, where the father was buried in the parish church; on 20 January 1544-45 the son became a member of parliament for West Bedwin, Wiltshire; in 1549 he was granted a coat of arms; and on 8 February 1552-53 he was returned to parliament for Reading, Berkshire.

Page 8, *36*. **Spinhome-land:** i.e., Speenhamland, a suburb of Newbury, Berkshire, and now within the deanery of Newbury. See Peter H. Ditchfield and William Page, eds., *The Victorian History of Berkshire* (London, 1906-24), II, 48. Wallingford and Hungerford are also within a few miles of Newbury.

Page 10, *23-24*. **Gratis the Shepheard:** the story of Gratis is from Fortescue's translation of *The Forest*, sig. E1r. Fortescue spells the name with a "C," "Cratis." See the explanatory note for page 53, line 1.

Page 11, *2*. **For feare to haue Acteons head:** Acteon, a hunter in mythology, accidentally came upon Artemis (or Diana) bathing; she was so offended at being seen naked that she turned Acteon into a stag. Once a stag, he had horns—which to an Elizabethan suggested cuckoldry. For a similar reference to Acteon, see *Titus Andronicus*, II, iii, 63. All the Shakespeare references are to the one-volume G. B. Harrison edition (New York, 1952).

Page 12, *14*. **quills:** pieces of reed or hollow stem forming a bobbin or spool for the winding of yarn.

*19. **pecking vp:** the Q4 compositor saw that "pecking vp" in line 19 should be consistent with "to pecke vp" in line 21. The compositors of Q1-3 were content with "picking vp" and "to pecke vp."

Page 13, *22*. **sure to thee:** betrothed to thee.

32. **as ciuill as the nine Sibbels:** literally, as sober or grave as the nine, often ten, sibyls, who were women of antiquity capable of divining the future. Deloney is a good euphuist and likes the play on words.

34. **Bartholmew day:** 24 August, a festive day in honor of Bartholomew, one of the twelve Apostles.

36. **Fayring:** a present given at a fair or brought from a fair, as in the prologue "to the Kings Maiesty" of Jonson's *Bartholomew Fair* (1631). "Your Maiesty is welcome to a Fayre. . . . The Maker doth present: and hopes, to night | To giue you for a Fayring, true delight." See *Ben Jonson*, ed. Herford and Simpson (Oxford, 1925-52), VI, 11.

Page 14, *5*. **fine and briske in his apparell:** when applied to clothing, "brisk" meant "spruce" or "smartly dressed." "Fine," as now, had a vaguely disparaging or complimentary meaning, according to the context; here it simply means "well dressed" and reinforces "brisk."

26. **noyse of Musitions:** band of musicians.

30. **The beginning of the World:** a popular song in the 16th and 17th centuries. William Chappell, in *Popular Music of the Olden Time* (London, n.d.), I, 69, gives the music for it.

37. **Speen:** Speenhamland.

38. **corner cap:** a cap, with either three or four corners, that was worn in the 16th and 17th centuries by divines and members of the universities.

*Page 15, 27. **them:** The Q4 typesetter, intent on correcting what seemed to be a grammatical error, changed "them" to "him." But perhaps the colloquial "them" in this case is part of the widow's verbal game. In effect, she says, "If you meant 'him,' why didn't you say so; you said 'them.' " Thereafter the suitors do say "him," and probably with a great deal of emphasis.

Page 19, *5-6*. **Parsons are but newly suffered to haue wiues:** Deloney seems to be telescoping reigns the way he telescopes the two John Winchcombs; or perhaps he thinks the joke so good that historical fact should stand aside for it. But since the fact is not mentioned by Grafton or Holinshed, Deloney may have come by his information through oral tradition, which would explain the confusion. What actually happened is that Henry VIII insisted on the clergy's celibacy throughout his reign. It was not until the late 1540's, during the reign of Edward VI, that the Six Articles were repealed and full liberty of marriage granted the clergy. Then, with Mary, the right was virtually denied; and Elizabeth, while allowing marriage, imposed very rigorous restrictions. See Henry C. Lea, *History of Sacerdotal Celibacy in the Christian Church* (London, 1932), pp. 378-426.

13. **drie bobs:** here the meaning of dry bob is taunt or bitter jibe of a verbal nature. Another meaning was trick or practical joke. See *Dobsons Drie Bobbes* (1607), ed. E. A. Horsman (Oxford, 1955), p. vii.

Page 20, *28*. **Link:** torch. Falstaff says to Bardolph: "I never see thy face but I think upon hell fire. . . . O thou art a perpetual triumph, an everlasting bonfire-light! Thou hast saved me a thousand marks in links and torches, walking with thee in the night betwixt tavern and tavern." (*1 Henry IV*, III, iii, 31 ff.)

Page 21, *6*. **as good as George a Green:** apparently a fairly common saying that remained current as late as 1663, when Ralpho uses it in addressing his master in Butler's *Hudibras*, Part II, Canto II, line 505 (ed. A. R. Waller, Cambridge, 1904, p. 142). George a Green was indeed the best of men if we may believe an anonymous play of the same name. He outfought Little John and Robin Hood one after the other, but unlike them he remained on the side of the law. He was the pinner (*i.e.,* pinder, or impounder of stray beasts) of Wakefield in Yorkshire. In the course of his duties as pinner, he captured three high-ranking traitors, thereby breaking up a rebellion and gaining the favor of the king. J. C. Collins, editor in 1905 of Robert Greene's plays and poems, includes *George a Green* in Robert Greene's canon. According to Greg (ed. *Henslowe's Diary*, II, 158), the play went through five performances by the Earl of Sussex' men in December, 1593, and January, 1593-94. It was entered in the Stationers' Register on 1 April 1595 but apparently not published until 1599.

Page 22, *36* to page 24, *27*. Mann notices (p. 507) a similarity between this incident, in which Mistress Winchcomb turns the tables on Jack, and the Fourth Tale of the Seventh Day in *The Decameron*. In Boccaccio's story the wife is the younger, and she is cuckolding her husband. Suspecting her game, the husband locks her out. But when she feigns suicide, he lets her in, only to be locked out himself.

Page 24, *2-3*. **Spirit of the Butterie hunt after Crickets:** "buttery" was used in the 16th century in two senses—storeroom for provisions, and storeroom for liquor. "Spirit of the buttery" was a common phrase, according to the *OED*, for "spirit of wine"; but Mistress Winchcomb does not seem to be using the phrase in that sense, and the part about the crickets is even less clear. Apparently the 1626 compositor was puzzled, too, for he changed "Spirit" to "Spright."

26-27. **you . . . your:** the Q2-5 compositors understandably substitute "thou" and "thy"; but Deloney may have wanted to emphasize a loss of intimacy by having the widow change from "thou" to the more formal "you."

33. **Cawdell:** usually spelled "caudle"; a warm drink made of thin gruel mixed with wine or ale, and a little spice and sugar added. In his only two references to it in *Dyetary of Helth* (1542), Andrew Boorde recommends the mixture as a soothing drink for a man who is sick in bed. See the E. E. T. S. edition, Extra Series, No. X (1870), pp. 264, 302.

36. **Ilyris:** Illyria, or Illiria, was a district on the east coast of the Adriatic, apparently in the northern part of present-day Yugoslavia.

Page 25, *9.* the fish Scolopendra: Deloney found this wondrous fish in Stephen Batman's *The Doom* (1581), sig. B7. Batman reports that the Scolopendra is a hundred feet long and "whosoeuer toucheth it, shall be presently infected with an itch, as if he were stoong with Nettles." See the explanatory note for page 53, line *1.*

*Page 26, 4. **one hundred and fifty men:** the correct figure probably is 150, rather than the 250 in Q1-5. Whoever wrote this summary at the beginning of Chapter II probably was confused by the information on page 30, lines 23 ff. But page 40, line 5, gives the total number intended.

Page 27, *6.* peticoates of stammel red: stammel was a coarse woolen cloth that usually was dyed red.

34. **Fulling mill:** a mill where cloth is tread or beaten in order to cleanse and thicken it.

Page 28, *9.* turne the broaches: turn the spits, pointed rods of wood or iron, on which meat is roasted.

16. **woad and madder:** woad, according to the *OED,* is often called Dyer's or Garden Woad, the leaves of which produce a blue dye. From the root of madder, or Dyer's Madder, comes the so-called "turkey red."

17. **broad cloathes and kersies:** broadcloth and kersey differed both in size and in quality. According to the *OED,* a statute of 1465 fixed a broadcloth as 24 yards long and 2 yards wide while limiting a kersey to 18 yards by 1 yard and a nail. Broadcloth was a finer cloth than kersey. See page 35, line 10: Jack wears a pair of breeches made of heavy, durable kersey cloth.

38. **sheepes russet:** russet worn by shepherds. Russet was a coarse woolen cloth of grey or reddish brown that country folk wore. "Country russet" and "sheep's russet" were synonymous in the 16th and 17th centuries.

39. **kertle:** usually a gown; but here it apparently is a skirt or an outer petticoat worn over the gown. **—billiment of gold:** in this case a head band with jewels in it. But it could be almost any kind of ornament worn around the neck or on the head. Even a bonnet or a French hood, according to the *OED,* was regarded as a billiment.

Page 29, *4.* Bride laces and Rosemary: a bride-lace was a piece of lace made of gold or silver, and it was customarily used to bind up sprigs of rosemary at weddings. Hamlet tells Ophelia (IV, v, 174-175) what rosemary means: "There's rosemary, that's for remembrance."

5-6. **Sir *Thomas Parrie* . . . Sir *Francis Hungerford:*** both the Parries and the Hungerfords were well known Berkshire families throughout the 16th century. Sir Thomas Parrie died in 1560 shortly after receiving great favor from Elizabeth—a knighthood (in 1558), a seat on the privy council, and the manor of Hampstead Marshall in Berkshire. See the *DNB.*

21. **Stilyard:** also spelled "Stilliard" and "Steelyard." It was a hall on the north bank of the Thames, about 400 to 500 yards west of London Bridge, where foreign merchants did their trading. Kingsford notes that "Steelyard" probably is an erroneous translation of "Stahlhof," which was a Dutch word meaning an office where cloth was stamped (Stow, II, 318-20). According to Sharpe, Queen Elizabeth closed the Steelyard in 1598 because British merchants were not getting fair treatment abroad (*London and the Kingdom*, I, 565). See also Sugden, p. 487.

Page 30, *17-18.* **armed with Pikes and two Calieuers:** the pike was a long wooden shaft with a pointed head of iron or steel. The caliver, invented in the 16th century, was a light musket or hand gun that was somewhat larger than a pistol.

26. **fiftie shot:** fifty soldiers armed with firearms, probably muskets.

29. **Barbed Horse:** a war horse furnished with a barb; that is, the breast and flanks are covered with a protective and ornamental material.

34.* **he had discouered: "discouered" here means "reuealed" or "disclosed," a meaning that did not occur to the Q3 compositor, who changed "he" to "they." Jack reveals that he himself is a worthy clothier who had taken the initiative to equip 150 men for combat—an action that the justices commend.

Page 31, *20.* **Sir** *Henery Englefield:* there seems to be no record of this particular Englefield, but the family is well known in Berkshire history. See *The Victoria History of Berkshire.* According to the *DNB*, a Sir Thomas Englefield was sheriff of Berkshire during the reign of Henry VIII.

Page 32, *8-9.* **Cynomolgy:** in *The Doom,* sig. B1, Batman maintains that the "Cinomolgi are a people that are headed like dogges, whose voyces are as the barking of Houndes, by the whyche they doe bewray themselues, and in theyr natures and conditions appeare the same that they resemble." See the explanatory note for page 53, line 1.

28. *Flodden:* the battle of Flodden Field was fought several miles south of the River Tweed in September, 1513. Note Deloney's use of historical detail. He omits all reference to dates; yet his sweeping generalizations about the battle are straight from contemporary historians. See Grafton, II, 274 ff. But the private scenes, the scenes in which the queen speaks to Jack and others, are of course Deloney's invention.

Page 33, *19.* *The Song:* Deloney preserved two traditional ballads, this one and "The Fair Flower of Northumberland," which Deloney calls "The Maidens Song." (See pp. 43 ff. and the corresponding explanatory note.) F. J. Child reprints "The Song" as ballad No. 168 in his collection. He uses the 1633 edition; for variant readings, see the collation notes of the present edition. The last stanza, beginning with "Iacke with a feather," seems tacked on; but Child does not question its belonging with the rest of the ballad.

Page 35, *8.* **faced with Sarcenet:** trimmed with sarsenet, a material made of fine silk, in various colors and either plain or twilled.

10. **without welt or gard:** without ornamentation. "Welt" and "guard," according to the *OED*, mean approximately the same thing—the trimming, often some kind of frill or fringe, sewn on the edge of a garment. The word "guard," however, suggests that originally the trimming may have served to keep the edge of the garment from fraying.

11. **slops:** wide and baggy breeches or hose that usually came down no further than the knees. Notice, however, that in Chapter V of *The Gentle Craft, Part II,* Deloney tells us that the slops of Captains Stuteley and Strangwidge reach their feet. **—codpeece, wheron hee stucke his pinnes:** Harrison, in the introduction to his edition of *Shakespeare's Works* (New York, 1952), p. 93, writes the following description: "The codpiece covered the opening in front of the breeches (hose). This accessory to male attire was often indelicately prominent. It was made in various forms, such as a bow of silk, a flap tied to the hose with laces, a small padded sausage-shaped cushion ornamented with pins, or a small bag used as a pocket."

19.* **Garter King at armes: see the *DNB;* Stow, I, 302-303; and Holinshed, III, 823: sig. 4K2. Sir John Writhe (or Wriothesley), who died in 1504, and his son Sir Thomas, who died in 1534, were both Garter king-of-arms. Sir Thomas' brother William was the great-grandfather of Henry Wriothesley (1573-1624), Shakespeare's patron.

Page 36, *16.* **a Lyon in the field:** a bit of lore from Fortescue's *The Forest,* sig. 2A3: "The mightie Lyon dreadeth and feareth the Cock." See the explanatory note for page 53, line 1.

38.* **one and thirtith day of September: Q2, followed by Q3, missed the point here; half the humor of the allegory depends on there not being thirty-one days in September.

*Page 39, *15.* **pages and foot men:** Q1 and Q4 placed a comma after "pages"; but the comma should be left out to make it clear that the pages and the footmen are in one group together.

27.* **stucke: the sense appears to be "fastened upon." "Stocke" in Q1 may be a typographical error, or it may be the substantive, meaning goods or possessions in general. Q2 and Q4 independently preferred the emendation "stucke."

28. **Herostratus:** the story is from Fortescue's translation of *The Forest,* sig. 2k2v. Deloney adds one detail, that Herostratus is a shoemaker. See the explanatory note for page 53, line 1.

Page 40, *4.* **seassed:** assessed. In the 16th century the infinitive was often "seas" or "sess," although the modern "assess" was in fairly common use, too.

9. **Will Sommers:** see the *DNB* for the best account. Sommers became Henry VIII's fool in 1525 and soon was on intimate terms with him. Apparently Sommers and Wolsey had such flytings as Deloney invents.

9-10. **Empson** and **Dudley:** Sir Richard Empson and Edmund Dudley were beheaded at the Tower for treason in 1510. See Holinshed, III, 809: sig. 4I. Holinshed calls Empson and Dudley "caterpillers to the commonwealth." In the allegory of the ants and the butterflies (the latter are golden caterpillars) Jack sees Cardinal Wolsey in much the same way.

27. **While Conscience went not selling Broome:** as Mann points out, the Elizabethans regarded selling brooms the lowest of occupations. See Nashe, I, 280 (*Strange News,* 1592): "Broome boyes, and cornecutters (or whatsoeuer is more contemptible). . . ." Deloney may have seen a phrase in Greene's *A Quip for an Upstart Courtier* (1592), ed. Grosart, *Life and Works of Greene* (London, 1881-83), XI, 238: "when veluet was worne but in kinges caps, then conscience was not a brome man in Kent streat but a Courtier, then the farmer was content his sonne should hold the plough, and liue as he had done before: Beggars then feared to aspire, and the higher sortes scorned to enuie."

Page 42, *33*. **as buls doe eate their meate:** Fortescue, *The Forest*, sig. Q3, reports that the bull "feedeth contrary to all others, for in taking his repast he goeth alwaies backwardes all others of what soeuer kinde, marching still onwards." See the explanatory note for page 53, line 1.

Page 43, *2*. **the stockes at Sir *Amias Paulets:*** Holinshed reports that Paulet put Wolsey in the stocks when Wolsey attempted to take possession of a benefice given him by the Marquess of Dorset (III, 918: sig. 4S1ᵛ). But Albert F. Pollard in *Wolsey* (London, 1929), p. 13, notes that, according to tradition, Wolsey was put in the stocks for "exuberant behavior after a fair."

9. ***The Maidens Song:*** one of the traditional ballads Deloney preserves in *Jack of Newbury*. It appears in Child's collection as ballad No. 9, "The Fair Flower of Northumberland." Child uses the 1633 edition of *Jack of Newbury*. The present text is from an earlier edition, that of 1619; for variant readings, see the collation notes, below.

Page 50, *1-2*. **a mans minde is a Kingdome to himselfe:** an echo of the first line of Sir Edward Dyer's famous poem, "My Mind to Me a Kingdom Is," which was first published in William Byrd's *Psalms, Sonnets and Songs* (1588).

Page 51, *29-30*. **the huge Elephant was neuer more fearefull of the silly sheepe:** according to Fortescue, *The Forest*, sig. 2A3ᵛ, "the monstrous and huge Elephant . . . trembleth at the presence and sight of a Sheepe."

Page 53, *1*. **King named *Viriat:*** Viriat, and the other famous men in Chapter V, Deloney found in Thomas Fortescue's translation of Pedro Mexia's *Silva* (1540). This translation, based on Claudio Gruget's French version of 1552, appeared first in 1571, with a second edition in 1576. All references to *The Forest* in the explanatory notes are to the 1576 edition. Hyder E. Rollins pointed out Deloney's borrowings in "Thomas Deloney's Euphuistic Learning and *The Forest*," *PMLA*, L (1935), 679-686; and "Deloney's Sources for Euphuistic Learning," *PMLA*, LI (1936), 399-406. *The Forest* is a compendium of useful information gathered by Mexia from Pliny, Plutarch, and others; and Fortescue's translation was virtually a poor man's college education for tradesmen like Deloney. Rollins shows that Deloney made use of two other compendiums—Stephen Batman's *The Doom* (1581) and Thomas Johnson's *Cornucopiae* (1595). Almost any fairly learned-sounding reference in Deloney (especially to ancient Greece or Rome) is traceable to one of these three contemporary books.

Deloney's heaviest borrowing is in Chapter V, during the writing of which he had Fortescue's compendium open before him; see *The Forest*, sigs. V4ᵛ-X3. Yet even in Chapter V there are important changes. The picture idea is Deloney's. Fortescue merely lists the 15 famous men as historical examples of poor men who rose to great office. Deloney at once unifies and subordinates the information from Fortescue by introducing the pictures on the wall of Jack's parlor.

Deloney and Fortescue (or, rather, Mexia) seem to have had a meeting of minds that goes deeper than a mutual love of miscellaneous information. Both wanted to "animate men to aspire to great matters," to quote Fortescue; and both felt, with Deloney, that labor is in itself a good: "there is nothing base, but that which is basely vsed."

*Page 54, 7. **Galerus:** in Fortescue, Deloney's source, the name is Galerus. There was no Roman emperor by the name of Gabienus (the spelling in Q1, 4, and 5) or Gabianus (the spelling in Q2 and 3); but Galerius Valerius Maximianus, son of a shepherd, was emperor from A.D. 305 to 311. See Jacob Burckhardt, *The Age of Constantine the Great,* trans. Moses Hadas (New York, 1949), pp. 45, 380-381.

36-37. **most artificially drawne:** drawn in such a way as to display special art or skill.

*Page 55, 8. *Primislas:** a glance at the collation notes shows that in this second use of the name "Primislas" in Chapter V, the compositor of Q5 is the only one who emends to "Brimislas." What seems to have happened is that Q5, seeing that Q4 spells the name the first time with a "B" (see page 54, line 36) and then the second time with a "P," decides to be consistent and use "B" twice. If he had seen Q1, or even Q2 or Q3, he would have known that "Brimislas" in Q4 was a typographical error, and that "Primislas" in Q4 was an accurate following of Q1.

*Page 58, 7. **clothier:** The emendation of Q4 and Q5 is accepted here, and the Q1 reading rejected, to avoid ambiguity. The Q1 typesetter often uses a plural subject and a singular predicate, and there has been no attempt to modernize his grammar—except, as in this case, where the grammar is misleading. "Clothiers" could be possessive, and the reader must go over the passage several times before determining that the possessive is not intended.

38. **Patch:** the real-life servant and fool of Wolsey, though little is known about him. Hilaire Belloc, in *Wolsey* (Philadelphia, 1930), p. 289, stresses Master Patch's loyalty to Wolsey after the latter's fall.

*Page 60, *17.* **thereof:** Q2 and Q4, each following Q1, make an understandable mistake in emending to "hereof." In Q1 a space appears between the "t" and the "h" in "thereof" (and the phrase reads "ioyfull t hereof"). Q3 and Q5, blindly following Q2 and Q4, respectively, also print "hereof."

*Page 62, *3.* **box:** Q2 and Q4 both change "box" to "pox." The pun is consistent with the jestbook kind of wit that appears in the rest of the passage, but the question is whether "pox" has any authority. One possibility is that it appeared in a lost edition, antedating Q1, that the compositors of Q2 and Q4 could have seen. But Q1 could hardly have seen the same edition, for the emendation would not go the other way, from "pox" to "box." Another possibility is that Q4 prints from Q2, at least in this passage. But the best explanation seems to be that "pox" is an obvious pun, and that the setter of Q4 needed no help in discovering it.

10-24. **spring in *Arcadia* . . . sweate of a mule . . . water in *Boetia* . . . the riuer *Cea* . . . stones in *Pontus:** all this miscellaneous information Deloney took from Fortescue's *The Forest,* sigs. 2D2, S4, and T1v. See the explanatory note for page 53, line 1.

Page 64, *15-16.* **maintaine her selfe in brauerie:** dress herself in fine clothes and costly jewelry. **—occupiers:** traders or merchants who deal in money or goods, with the implication that the dealing is somewhat "shady."

Page 67, *5.* **partlet:** a neckerchief, collar, or ruff worn, chiefly by women, round the neck and upper part of the chest.

*Page 68, *3.* **fine Lordly attendants:** Q2 emends ingeniously by changing "fine" in Q1 to "fiue." But surely Deloney did not have the five senses in mind, for some of them hardly would be used in greeting friends.

15. **cacke:** Q4 changes "cacke" in Q1 to "cake." As Q4 surmises, Benedick really means cake, which presumably would improve "Joan's" breath. But the emendation eliminates a pun that Deloney almost certainly intended. The literal meaning of "cacke" was bowel movement, as every Elizabethan knew well enough.

22. **bee Gossen:** by God. In the *OED* Henry Bradley notes that "goss," like "gosh," is a mincing pronunciation of "God."

24. **mutton:** the pun involves a slang usage of mutton for prostitute or loose woman; a whoremonger was often termed a muttonmonger.

28. **shacke:** jack, or common fellow.

Page 70, *14.* **french hood:** where the English hood sat forward to cover the entire head, the French hood was small and worn far back. It curved forward to cover the ears, but otherwise exposed the hair. Deloney has his dates right: the French hood was popular during the reign of Henry VIII, but was unfashionable after 1580. For descriptions and illustrations of the French hood and of other 16th century attire, see Willett and Phillis Cunnington, *Handbook of English Costume in the Sixteenth Century* (London, 1954).

Page 71, *17.* **Whitsontide:** the season of Whit Sunday, beginning on the seventh Sunday after Easter and lasting for several days.

Page 72, *5.* **browne bread:** Deloney gives a fuller description of brown bread than Harrison or Boorde, or perhaps anyone else in the 16th century. Note that the best brown bread, and the most expensive, was made of wheat and rye, and that a less expensive and less highly regarded kind was made of barley or of rye mixed with pease.

16. **gathers:** the heart, liver, and lungs of an animal; often called "pluck."

Page 74, *20.* **Misery is troden downe by many:** All five quartos agree on this reading, except that Q3 substitutes "of many" for "by many." At first it appears that a transposition has taken place; "Many are troden downe by misery" would seem to make better sense. But the meaning is made clear by a passage from Chapter V of *The Gentle Craft, Part I:* "Alas sir (sayd *Crispianus*) necessitie is despised of euery one, and misery is troden downe of many; but seldome or neuer relieued. . . ." (p. 118) In this sentence "troden downe of many" is practically synonymous with "despised of euery one." Thus everyone shows contempt for necessity and misery, but unfortunately few are able to do anything about them.

27. **wash buckes:** buckwashing was a method of washing coarse and unusually dirty clothes. First the clothes were boiled in buck (or alkaline lye), and then they were rinsed in clear water. Deloney apparently thinks of bucks as the dirty clothes themselves rather than the lye.

31. **lee:** lye.

Page 75, *8.* **slip shooes:** slippers; shoes that fit loosely, and therefore slip off and on easily.

13-14. **the spread Eagle at Iuiebridge:** the Spread Eagle is the inn where Long Meg of Westminster is a servant in *The Gentle Craft, Part II.* See Stow for several references to Ivybridge in Westminster.

29. **poynt:** a lace or cord made of twisted yarn, silk, or leather; by means of points, which often were used instead of buttons, the hose could be attached, or trussed, to the doublet.

Page 77, *25-26*. **chosen Sheriffe:** one of Deloney's many departures from historical fact; there is no record of a Randoll Pert's being sheriff of London.

Page 78, *28*. **poudred biefe:** beef sprinkled with salt for preserving. Andrew Boorde writes: "Olde beefe and koweflesshe doth ingender melancolye and leporouse humoures. yf it be moderately powderyd, that the groose blode by salte may be exhaustyd, it doth make an Englysshe man stronge. . . ." (*Dyetary of Helth,* E.E.T.S. edition, p. 271.) Nashe (II, 311) mentions special tubs in which the salting was performed.

*Page 79, *10*. **Now assure you:** Q2-5 emend this phrase. But Mistress Frank is drunk and may find "Now I assure" a bit too unwieldy for a thick tongue.

37. **mistresse *Winchomb:*** here again Mistress Frank may be having trouble with her pronunciation; on the other hand, "*Winchomb*" may be a typographical error, for she seems to have no difficulty saying "*Winchcomb*" later in the same speech.

Page 80, *1*. **codlings:** The Elizabethans used the word in at least two senses—a variety of hard apple, or any unripe apple. In *Twelfth Night,* I, i, 167 ff., Malvolio has the latter sense in mind when he describes the disguised Viola: "Not yet old enough for a man, nor young enough for a boy, as a squash is before 'tis a peacod, or a codling when 'tis almost an apple." Mistress Frank, however, seems to be referring to a variety of hard apple.

4. **se-reuerence:** also commonly "sa-reuerence," "saue your reuerence," and "sir-reuerence"; an expression that precedes an unpleasant comment that needs preparing for.

25. **one of the Towne:** a prostitute; the usual punishment was a public ride in a cart. Ursula in *Bartholomew Fair,* IV, v, 80-81, apparently had an exciting ride: the bottom of the cart fell out.

Page 81, *35*. **cucking stools:** a favorite instrument of punishment for small offenses. It was a chair, which often took the form of a close-stool or privy. While the bystanders laughed and jeered, a scold or disorderly woman was placed in a cucking stool, carried to a pond, and ducked.

Page 82, *3*. ***Morlesse:*** Morlaix, on the north coast of Brittany, was taken by Surrey in July, 1522. See Grafton, II, 324-326; Holinshed, III, 874: sig. 4O3v; and Sugden, p. 354. Deloney's spelling of the names is very similar to Grafton's. As one might expect, Sir Edward Rigley is mentioned as receiving a knighthood; but Sir George, his brother, is not (and therefore probably is Deloney's creation).

10. **without coyne:** without forcing themselves on private persons for food and drink. In *A View of the State of Ireland* Spenser differentiates between "liverye" (food for horses) and "coygnye" (food for men). See the edition by Rudolf Gottfried in *Spenser's Prose Works* (Johns Hopkins Press, 1949), pp. 78-80.

*Page 83, *2*. **abie:** Both Q2 and Q4 emend to "abide." But the Q1 reading, "abie" (also spelled "aby" and "abye"), meaning to pay for, makes better sense.

Page 84, *27*. **Terme time:** there were four terms, or periods, during which the law courts were in session—Hilary, Easter, Trinity, and Michaelmas. The specific dates varied slightly from year to year; but, in general, during Henry VIII's reign the Hilary term came in the last two weeks of January; Easter in the latter part of April and the first of May; Trinity, the latter part of May and early

June; and Michaelmas, the middle weeks of November. See Sir William Holdsworth, *A History of English Law* (5th ed.; London, 1942), III, 674-675.

*32. **London,** because he: This is the Q2 and Q3 emendation of Q1's "*London
who. . . .*" The antecedents in Q1 often are not very clear, but this passage is
unusually tangled. The sense is that Master Winchcomb could not spare any of
his own servants to wait on Widow Loveless, and therefore he had to borrow a
few servants from another master.

The first printed record of *The Gentle Craft, Part I,* appears in the Stationers' Register for 19 October 1597: "Raphe Blore. Entred for his Copie vnder th[e h]andes of master Dix and master Man a booke called the gentle craft intreating of Shoomakers. vjᵈ" (Arber, III, 93). Lange (p. xxi) suggests that the first edition, for good business reasons, might have appeared by 25 October (St. Crispin's Day) of the same year. In 1840, in his Camden Society edition of Kemp's *Nine Daies Wonder,* Alexander Dyce describes what he claims to be a copy of the 1598 edition of both parts of *The Gentle Craft.* But Dyce does not say where the book can be found; and to this day its location, if any, is unknown. W. Carew Hazlitt, in his *Hand-Book* (1867), refers to a two-part 1598 edition, but one suspects that he got his information from Dyce. If Dyce's information is correct, the edition he saw could hardly have been the first edition, for the dedication to *Part II* clearly indicates that *Part I* already had appeared and that its sales prompted the author to be bold in offering *Part II.* It is possible that 1597, as Lange suggests, could be the date of the first edition of *Part I* and 1598 the date of the second edition of *Part I* and the first edition of *Part II.* Certainly by 1600 each part had been published at least once, as an entry in the Stationers' Register for 14 August 1600 (Arber, III, 169) makes clear. There would be no reason to refer to the "fyrste part" of *The Gentle Craft* unless the second already had been published.

But the earliest extant edition is that of 1627, the only extant copy of which was given to the University of Sheffield Library in 1931 by Sir Charles Harding Firth. The 1627 edition is the copy text of the present edition and therefore will be referred to as Q1. Q2 is the 1637 edition, Q3 the 1640 edition, and Q4 the 1648 edition. Later editions were emended so freely that they have no textual validity.

A word about the genetic order of the four early editions. Q1 is the only substantive extant edition. The setters of Q2, Q3, and Q4 did not see an edition earlier than Q1, for if they had they would not have omitted three lines that appear in Q1. (See the collation notes for page 111, lines 33-34; for page 121, lines 26-27; and for page 146, lines 10-11.) What happened is that Q2 (or an edition, no longer extant, between Q1 and Q2) mistakenly omitted the lines; then Q3, seeing nothing earlier than Q2, had no choice but to omit the lines; and, finally, Q4, seeing nothing earlier than Q3, could not know that the lines ever existed.

The collation notes give ample proof that Q3 derives from Q2 and Q4 from Q3. On page 94, line 12, Q2 changes "remoue" in Q1 to "turne"; similarly, on page 99, line 7, Q2 changes "a melancholy man" to "melancholy men." In both cases (and in many others) the Q2 reading continues in Q3 and Q4. In these examples it would appear possible that Q4 followed Q2. But one need only look a bit further: on page 103, lines 14-15, the reading in Q1 and Q2 is "vnkind Winifred, whose disdaine hath wrought my destruction." Q3 changes "wrought" to "brought" and Q4 follows suit.

An interesting clause on page 148, lines 38-39, reveals why Q1 gets us closer than the other extant editions to Deloney's text; it also shows one aspect of the relationship of the four early editions to each other. In Q1 the reading is "shee would haue found talke enough till morning." In Q2 the "s" in "shee" is changed to "t," resulting in a meaningless "the would haue found . . ." (an error Q2 makes again on page 162, line 35). Q3 follows Q2, despite the fact that "the" makes no sense. Then the setter of Q4, with Q3 before him, probably reasoned that the word should be either "they" or "she"; he guessed wrong and chose "they."

EARLY EDITIONS

1627 (Q1). STC(PRJ) 6554.5. *Title page:* THE | GENTLE CRAFT. | A | DIS-COVRSE CON- | TAINING MANY MAT- | TERS OF DELIGHT, VERY | pleasant to be read: shewing what | famous men haue beene Shoomakers | in time past in this Land, with their wor- | *thy deeds and great Hospitality.* | DECLARING THE CAVSE WHY | it is called the GENTLE CRAFT: and | also how the Prouerbe first grew; | *A Shoomakers sonne is a Prince borne.* T. D. | With gentlenesse iudge you, | At nothing here grudge you; | The merry Shoomakers delight in good sport: | What here is presented, | Be therewith contented; | And as you doe like it, so giue you report. | *Haud curo inuidiam.* | [*rule*] | [*type orn.*] | [*rule*] | Printed at London for *E. Brewster.* 1627.

Collation: Quarto, A-I4 (with C1 and C4 missing, and the bottom 9 lines of E3 torn off). No page numbers.

Contents: [A1r], title; [A1v], blank; A2r, dedication to the yeomen of the gentle craft; A2v, dedication to the readers; A3r-I4r, text; [I4v], blank.

Copy used: University of Sheffield Library (only extant copy).

1637 (Q2). STC(PRJ) 6555. *Title page:* The Gentle Craft. | A DISCOVRSE | Containing many matters of Delight, | *very pleasant to be read:* | Shewing what famous men have beene | SHOOMAKERS in time past in this Land, | *with their worthy deeds and great Hospitality.* | Declaring the cause why it is called the GENTLE | CRAFT: and also how the Prouerbe first grew; | [*rule*] | *A Shoomakers sonne is a Prince borne.* T. D. | [*rule*] | With gentlenesse judge you, | At nothing here grudge you; | The merry Shoomakers delight in good sport; | What here is presented, | Be therewith contented; | And as you doe

like it, so give your report. | [*rule*] | *Haud curo invidiam.* | [*rule*] | [*orn.*] |
LONDON: | Printed for ROBERT BIRD, 1637.

Collation and contents: Identical with the 1627 edition, except that no leaves
are missing or damaged.

Copy used: British Museum (only extant copy).

1640 (Q3). STC(PRJ) 6555.3. *Title page:* The Gentle Craft. | A DISCOURSE |
Containing many matters of De- | *light, very pleasant to be read:* | Shewing
what famous men have | been SHOOMAKERS in time past in | *this Land,
with their worthy deeds and* | great Hospitality. | Declaring the cause why it is
called the GENTLE | CRAFT: and also how the Proverbe first grew: | [*rule*] |
A Shoomakers Son is a Prince born. T. D. | [*rule*] | With gentlenesse judge
you, | At nothing here grudge you; | The merry Shoomakers delight in good
sport. | What here is presented, | Be therewith contented; | And as you doe
like it, so give your report. | [*rule*] | *Haud curo invidiam.* | [*rule*] | [*orn.*] |
LONDON. | [Printed] for Robert Bird, 1640. [*A small tear in the last line of
the title page probably has taken away the word "Printed" before "for Robert
Bird, 1640."*]

Collation: Quarto, A-I4 (with C3 missing and C4 defective). No page numbers.

Contents: Identical with the 1627 edition.

Copy used: British Museum (only extant copy).

1648 (Q4). STC (W) 953. *Title page:* The Gentle Craft. | A | DISCOURSE | Con-
taining many matters of Delight, very | pleasant to be read: | Shewing what
famous men have been SHOO- | MAKERS in time past in this Land, with |
their worthy deeds and great Hospitality. | *Set forth with Pictures, and variety
of Wit and Mirth.* | Declaring the cause why it is called the GENTLE |
CRAFT: and also how the Proverb first grew. | [*rule*] | *A Shoomakers Son is a
Prince born.* T. D. | [*rule*] | With gentlenesse judge you, | At nothing here
grudge you; | The merry Shoomakers delight in good sport. | What here is
presented, | Be therewith contented; | And as you do like it, so give your
report. | [*rule*] | *Haud curo invidiam.* | [*rule*] | LONDON, Printed for *John
Stafford,* and are to be sold at his | house in Saint *Brides* Church-yard. 1648.

Collation: Quarto, A-H4, I2 (I2r incorrectly signed H2). Leaves numbered
beginning with A4r; 62 pp. (pp. 60 and 61 incorrectly numbered 52 and 53).

Contents: [A1], missing but presumably blank; [A2r], title; [A2v], blank; A3r,
dedication to the yeomen of the gentle craft; A3v, dedication to the readers;
A4r-I2v, text of the novel (pp. 1-62); [I3, I4], two poems: "A new love Sonnet"
and "How a Shoomakers widdow fell in love with her man." I3r is numbered
63; I3v is numbered 56; I4r and I4v are not numbered, though they may have
been originally; the corner of the leaf where the pagination would occur has
been torn away and repaired with new paper. Woodcuts one-third the size of
the leaf appear at the beginning of each chapter.

Copy used: British Museum (only extant copy).

1652. STC(W) 954. Printed for John Stafford and are to be sold at his house at the sign of the George at Fleet Bridge. 1652. Quarto. (Bodleian)

1672. STC(W) 955. 1672. Quarto. (Bodleian)

1675? STC(W) 960. Printed for H. Rhodes at the Star, the corner of Bride-Lane, Fleet Street, [1675?]. Quarto. (British Museum, Cambridge)

1678. STC(W) 944. Printed by T. M. for William Thackery in Duck Lane, near West-Smith-field, 1678. Quarto. (British Museum)

1680? Not listed in STC; see Mann, p. 521. [Title page lost. 1680?] Quarto. (British Museum)

1685. STC(W) 945. By J. Millet, for W. T. to be sold by J. Gilbertson, [1685]. Quarto. (Magdalene College)

1690. STC(W) 961. For H. Rhodes, [1690]. Quarto. (British Museum; Huntington, Newberry, Columbia, Yale)

1696. STC(W) 962. Tenth edition. W. Wilde and sold by P. Brooksby, J. Deacon, J. Back, J. Blare, and E. Tracy, 1696. Quarto. (Bodleian; Newberry)

MODERN EDITIONS

Following is a list of the twentieth-century editions of the complete novel; there were none in the nineteenth century. No attempt has been made to list anthologies in which only parts of *The Gentle Craft, Part I,* have been printed.

1903. *The Gentle Craft* [both parts], *by Thomas Deloney.* Edited by Alexis F. Lange. Berlin: Mayer and Müller, 1903 [*Palaestra,* XVIII]. Copy text: the 1648 edition.
1912. *The Works of Thomas Deloney.* Edited by Francis Oscar Mann. Oxford: Clarendon Press, 1912. Copy text: the 1648 edition.
1928. *Deloney's Gentle Craft, the First Part.* Edited by Wilfrid J. Halliday. Oxford: Clarendon Press, 1928. "A modernized version of the edition of 1648, corrected by comparison with the edition of 1637" (preface).

NOTES

Page 92, 2. **Saint *Hugh:*** The main source for Saint Hugh probably was the life of St. Winifred. See the note on Winifred, below. But also, as Lange suggests (pp. xxxiv-xxxvi), Deloney may have seen *Guy of Warwick,* an edition of which appeared about 1560, and the life of St. George in Caxton's *Golden Legend* (of which there were at least 13 editions between 1535 and 1586).

2-10. Powis . . . Donwallo . . . Tegina . . . Pont Varry . . . Sichnaunt: For much of the information contained in this foreword to his readers, Deloney went not to Grafton and Holinshed, his usual bibles for background material, but (as Mann notes, p. 524) to Humphrey Llwyd, *The Breuiary of Britayne* (1573), sigs. K4ᵛ ff.

4. **the faire Virgin *Winifred:*** Deloney's portrait of Winifred, as Mann notes (p. 522), derives from Jacobus de Voragine's *Legenda Aurea* (c. 1470). Deloney was perfectly capable of reading it in Latin, but William Caxton's translation (the first edition appeared in 1483, and there were at least seven other editions by 1527) must have been quite accessible. From the life of St. Winifred come the main details of Winifred's character, the idea for Winifred's Well, and the tragic issue. From the story of St. Ursula and the virgins comes the basic situation of the Winifred-Hugh relationship. Both hero and heroine are of high birth. When he asks for her hand in marriage, she consents but only on condition that he be baptized and over a period of three years become well informed concerning the Christian religion. The hero accepts the condition very willingly—too willingly, Deloney apparently thought, for he changes this part and has Hugh complain about it.

Page 95, 35. **tonguelesse like a Storke:** An expression from Thomas Johnson's *Cornucopiae* (1595), sig. D1ᵛ. See the explanatory note for page 53, line 1.

Page 98, *25.* **from thence hee went into *Italy:*** Elizabethans thought of Italy as a den of iniquity, and Deloney capitalizes on their prejudice (which he shared to some extent). Deloney's readers must have enjoyed the poetic justice of *Jack of Newbury*, Chapter VII, in which Master Benedick, an Italian merchant, gets run out of Newbury for attempting to seduce an English wife.

Page 104, *15.* **a place called *Harwich:*** A seaport in Essex, 70 miles northeast of London.

Page 108, *9.* **staine:** excel. In *Histrio-Mastix* (1610), the jeweler says: "This those excells as farre, | As glorious Tytan staines a silly Starre" (III, i). See *The Plays of John Marston,* ed. H. Harvey Wood (Edinburgh, 1934-39), III, 272.

Page 110, *23-24.* **shadowed with a sheet of pure Lawne:** a "lawn" in this sense is a kind of fine linen, like cambric. "Shadowed" means veiled. Thus Winifred turns pale; she looks the way a rose would look through a thin sheet of white linen.

Page 111, *6-7.* **thy gore blood fully gorged:** Doubtless the alliteration appeals to Deloney, though "gore blood" was a common phrase meaning thick blood, flowing in great profusion.

Page 113, *14.* **Runnet:** Sometimes spelled "rennet," a mass of curdled milk that is found in the stomach of an unweaned calf and that may be used to curdle milk in the making of cheese.

27. **Mother *Bumby:*** Perhaps a reference to the fortune teller in Lyly's comedy, *Mother Bombie* (1594), for which Lyly's editor, R. Warwick Bond, was unable to find any direct sources.

39. **a sort of shoomakers:** A group or company of shoemakers.

Page 114, 12. **to pull out shoo-threed we must despise:** "Devise," the emendation in Q3, makes sense. But Deloney's meaning surely is that the thread should be sewn tightly enough not to pull out; the shoemaker would be loath to see his thread come loose.

33. **Posie:** A motto inscribed on a knife or within a ring; ordinarily it is just one line of verse, but here the shoemakers refer to a whole poem as a posy. Perhaps they do not mean "motto" at all, but simply "poesy."

Page 115, *11.* **Crispianus and his brother** *Crispine:* The lives of Sts. Crispin and Crispinian follow, in Caxton's *Golden Legend,* the story of St. Ursula. From the former come the names of the heroes and the name of the tyrant, Maximinus; from the latter comes the name Ursula, who in Deloney's narrative becomes the daughter of Maximinus. From the former comes also the main outline of the plot: Crispin and Crispinian in Jacobus de Voragine's story are persecuted by Maximian; they escape to Soissons, where they "exercised the craft of making shoes." Mann suggests (p. 523) that Crispine and Ursula are patterned after Romeo and Juliet.

12. **Logria:** As Sugden notes (p. 310), Deloney thinks of Logria as Kent; but Spenser (*F.Q.,* II, 10, 14) thinks of Logris as England. The derivation apparently was from Locrine, the son of Brute. For the place names, at least, Deloney's source probably was Llwyd's *Breuiary;* see signatures C1v-C7 for various references to Logria and Durovernum.

Page 118, *13.* **misery is troden downe of many:** See the note, above, for page 74, line 20.

Page 119, *9.* **Rochester Castle:** In Q2-4 "Rochester" becomes "Colchester." As towns, both are mentioned by Llwyd, but there were no castles in either place as early as the Roman occupation. Rochester, Kent, would seem to fit better into the background of Deloney's story than Colchester, Essex.

Page 125, *4.* **Saint** *Gregories* **Chappell:** The chapel of St. Gregory's priory in Canterbury.

Page 127, *6.* **fine is the silken twist:** Literally a silken twist is a thread or cord made of two or more fibers of silk; figuratively, it is the intimate union that marriage affords.

27. **she giues him brawne and sowse:** Brawn is the pickled flesh of a boar or pig, usually pig's head, feet, legs, or tongue. Sowse is any pickled food, but usually fish, or pig's feet.

Page 131, *23.* **Biggins:** Caps worn by children. The word derives from the Beguine religious order founded by Lambert Bègue, a Liège priest of the 12th century. See the *OED.*

24. **Crossecloths:** Linen cloths worn across the forehead by babies. Apparently women wore them on their heads, too. See Fynes Moryson's *Itinerary* (1617), ed. James MacLehose (Glasgow, 1907-08), IV, 211. —**Taileclouts:** Swaddling bands or clothes wrapped round a newborn infant.

26. **standing-stoole:** A stool for the support of a child who is learning to walk. In *The Weakest Goeth to the Wall* (1600), Hernando says of Epernon: "Get him a standing stool, | And then, perhaps, the child will learn to go" (IV, i). See *The Dramatic Works of John Webster,* ed. William Hazlitt (London, 1857), IV, 272. —**Posnet:** A small metal pot or cup, with a handle and three feet, for boiling. —**Pap:** A soft food for infants, made of bread or meal and moistened with water or milk.

Page 132, *4.* **by Cock and Pye:** A curious oath, with neither word meaning what the present day reader thinks it does. "Cock" is a corruption of "God"; according to the *OED* there was an intermediate form, "gock." "Pie" here means the collection of rules that were used before the Reformation to determine how to commemorate special religious occasions. Shakespeare uses the oath at least twice; see *Merry Wives,* I, i, 316, and *2 Henry IV,* V, i, 1.

30. **Wagtaile:** A familiar or contemptuous epithet; in this case it is contemptuous, meaning harlot or courtesan.

Page 133, *34-35.* **the time of her trauell:** "Travail" was the word the Elizabethans usually employed to denote labor of childbirth, but "travel" (meaning journey, too, of course) was not uncommon.

Page 134, *28.* **Doris:** Dubris was really the Roman town on the site of which Dover was built. As Mann notes (p. 527) Deloney spells it "Doris" because Llwyd spells it that way in *The Breuiary,* sig. C6v.

*Page 135, *10-11.* **was not to learn to make profit thereof:** Lange emends by inserting "slow" before "learn," but the sense is that Crispine did not need to learn. See page 306, lines 9-10, where William Fitzallen "was not to learne how to entertaine his maiesty."

Page 136, *14-15.* **as fortunate as *Policrates:*** apparently the Polycrates of Samos who was "fortunate" enough to have things his own way on the island of Samos from about 535 to 515 B.C. His fleet of a hundred ships was the scourge of the Aegean basin, and to the Greeks he was notorious for piracy. Deloney seems to think favorably of him; perhaps he has in mind Polycrates' numerous public works and patronage of the arts (Anacreon lived at his court). But in 515 B.C. he died by crucifixion at the hands of his enemies.

Page 139, *20.* **Simon Eyre:** Deloney also spells it "Eyer." Simon Eyre is the most famous of Deloney's historical characters. He was sheriff of London in 1434 and mayor in 1445. He died in 1458. See Stow, I, 153-154. For further information see Merritt E. Lawlis, "Another Look at Simon Eyre's Will," *N&Q,* CXCIX (1954), 13-16.

Page 140, *11.* **to the Conduit for water:** Stow uses "conduit" and "cesterne" synonymously (II, 41). There were several fountains in London, each one at a convenient place. The water for the one at Lothbery, Stow reports, was "conueyed in great abundance from diuers springes lying between Hoxton and Iseldon" (I, 283).

Page 144, *10.* **owes:** One sense of the word was "ownes," as in line 10 of Shakespeare's sonnet 18: "Nor lose possession of that fair thou ow'st."

*Page 145, *11.* **smutched:** blackened or made dirty. In Q1 the word is "smugged," which meant to smarten up or to make trim—the opposite of what Mistress Eyre has in mind.

33. **washing ball:** or wash ball; a ball of soap, often perfumed or medicated. The Elizabethan used it for washing his hands and face and for shaving.

36-37. **furred round about the skirts with the finest foynes:** Foines (the plural form) are trimmings or garments made of fur. In the singular it is the animal itself, a stone (or beech) marten.

Page 149, *11-12.* **betweene the two Chaines:** Mann surmises that these are the chains surrounding St. Paul's Churchyard. Stow refers (II, 12-13) to "Paul's chain."

Page 151, *13.* **Islington:** Sugden (p. 274) notes that Islington, a suburb north of London, was one of the popular places to go for an outing.

Page 152, *6.* **Hogsdon:** Also spelled Hogsden, and now Hoxton. Like Islington, it was a district north of London to which London citizens went for an outing. The Pimlico was a famous tavern there. See Sugden, p. 251.

Page 153, *33*. **beat as a stockfish:** i.e., beat her as I would a stockfish. Cod, haddock and certain other fish were called stockfish, and they commonly were split open and, without salting, dried hard in the open air. Then just before cooking they were beaten to make them tender.

*Page 155, *34*. **Arras:** The Q2-4 reading is "Arras" and the Q1 "Orace," very likely different spellings of the same town in the province of Artois, France, noted for the manufacture of an excellent tapestry fabric.

Page 157, *21*. **Shriualtie:** Or shrieualtie; pertaining to the office or jurisdiction of the sheriff. What the mayor is referring to is the wine Eyre will "spend" while performing his duties as Sheriff of London.

34. **stirrop:** A device for the cobbler to hold a shoe firmly on his knee while working. Often it was a strap that passed under the foot and over the knee; in the 19th century, at least, it was attached to the last, over which the shoe fitted.

Page 159, *29*. **pie peckt:** A common expression used to indicate great contempt; literally, pecked by a magpie, a bird of ill omen.

Page 163, *36*. **the Abbey of *Grace:*** Deloney's is the only Elizabethan reference to the Abbey of Grace that Sugden (p. 229) was able to find. In having Florence and Haunce plan their wedding there, presumably toward the middle of the 15th century, Deloney is not at all anachronistic: the Abbey was built in 1359, and in 1539—some sixty years before the publication of *The Gentle Craft, Part I*—it was dissolved, pulled down, and replaced by a storehouse for the Navy.

Page 164, *6-7*. **to giue the Dutchman the slampam:** To play a trick on him; often spelled "slampant."

7. **bore him through the nose with a cushin:** To bore someone through the nose is to cheat or swindle him. "Cushion" here means drinking cup. In other words, Nicholas will get Haunce drunk: he will cheat Haunce out of marrying Florence by means of a drinking cup.

14. **while he lies parbreaking his mind:** To parbreak means to vomit; to parbreak his mind, as line 35 indicates, is to speak loosely, to say all that is on his mind.

Page 165, *22*. **Posterne Gate:** The gate just north of the Tower.

Page 168, *22*. **Pancake bell:** The bell rung on Shrove Tuesday at 11 a.m. announcing the cessation of work, the beginning of the holiday, and the frying of pancakes.

Page 169, *11*. **FINIS:** Q1-3 end here, but in Q4 appear two ballads—"A new love Sonnet" and "How a Shoomakers widdow fell in love with her man." Neither is relevant to *The Gentle Craft, Part I;* almost certainly, neither is by Deloney.

THE GENTLE CRAFT, PART II

On 14 August 1600 *The Gentle Craft, Part I,* was entered in the Stationers' Register (Arber, III, 169) as the property of Thomas Pavier. Such a reference to *Part I* indicates that *Part II* already had been published—perhaps in 1598. But there was no entry in the Stationers' Register for *Part II* in 1597 or 1598.

The earliest extant edition is still that of 1639, and therefore the copy text of the present edition is the same one Mann used in 1912. There are two copies of the 1639 edition, one in the British Museum and one in the Bodleian Library. I have used the former as a copy text, but of course I have collated the latter. There are no substantive differences between the two copies; the Bodleian copy was helpful only in restoring the full title of the dedication on page 265. The title is "To the Master and Ward[ens of the] | worshipfull company of the Cord-[waynors] | in London, all continuance of health and [per] | fect brotherly affection." The parts in brackets, all appearing in the upper right hand corner of the printed page, were torn off the British Museum copy.

The 1639 edition is the only extant edition of any textual validity, for the 1660 edition was emended very freely. The Folger Shakespeare Library possesses, however, two fragments of a very early edition, perhaps even the first. For this portion of the text I have retained the accidentals of the 1639 edition while accepting the substantive readings of the fragments (which are referred to as "Folger" in the footnotes and collation notes).

EARLY EDITIONS

1598? STC(PRJ) 6555.7. Two fragments.

Collation: Quarto. H-I4 and K4L1. No page numbers.

Contents: H1r-L1v, the two fragments fitting together to form one continuous sequence, beginning with "by another a scarffe to *Strangwidge,*" toward the end of Chapter V (page 217, line 25, in the present edition) and ending early in Chapter IX with "whereupon the Doctor tooke horse and immediatly" (page 242, line 12).

Copy used: Folger Shakespeare Library (only extant copy).

1639. STC(PRJ) 6556. THE | GENTILE | CRAFT. | [*rule*] | *The second Part.* | [*rule*] | Being a most merrie and pleasant | Historie, not altogether vn-

profitable nor | any way hurtfull: verie fit to passe away the te- | diousnesse
of the long winter evenings. | By *T. D.* | Newly corrected and augmented.
| *Haud curo invidam.* | [*orn.*] | [*rule*] | LONDON, | Printed by *Elizabeth
Purslow,* dwelling neere | Christ Church[,] 1639[.] [*The bookbinder, in cutting
or cropping the edges of the book for binding, left only the upper half of the
last line visible. The punctuation is conjectural, but the date is almost certainly 1639.*]

Collation: Quarto, A-L⁴. No page numbers.

Contents: [A1ʳ], title; [A1ᵛ], blank; A2ʳ, dedication to the master and wardens
of the company of cordwainers; [A2ᵛ], dedication to the "Courteous Readers
health"; A3ʳ-L4ᵛ, text.

Copy used: British Museum.

1660. STC(W) 954a. Printed by G. P. for I. Andrews at the White Lyon in Pye-
Corner. 1660. Quarto. Harvard University Library.

MODERN EDITIONS

Following are the two twentieth-century editions of the complete novel;
there were none in the nineteenth century. No attempt has been made to
list anthologies in which only parts of *The Gentle Craft, Part II,* have
been printed.

1903. *The Gentle Craft* [both parts], *by Thomas Deloney.* Edited by Alexis F.
Lange. Berlin: Mayer and Müller, 1903 [*Palaestra,* XVIII]. Copy text: the 1639
edition.
1912. *The Works of Thomas Deloney.* Edited by Francis Oscar Mann. Oxford:
Clarendon Press, 1912. Copy text: the 1639 edition.

NOTES

Page 174, *10.* **Doctor *Burket:*** As Mann notes (p. 535), the reference in Henry
Chettle's *Kind harts dreame* (1593), ed. G. B. Harrison (London, 1923), p. 13,
seems to indicate that Dr. Burket was a well known physician of the time.
11. **round *Robin:*** See the note for page 198, line 29.
12-13. **Tom *Drums* entertainment:** Apparently a kind of proverbial phrase
that everyone knew; in some references the first name was Jack or John. "Entertainment" is ironic, for it consists of being thrown out as an unwelcome guest.
In the story that follows (in Chapter VIII) Deloney illustrates the well known
phrase. Shakespeare refers to Drum twice in *All's Well;* both references (III,
vi, 41 and V, iii, 322) indicate that the audience was familiar not only with the
name but with the "entertainment."

15. Anthony now now: Mentioned by Chettle in *Kind harts dreame*, p. 12, as a contemporary ballad singer.

Page 175, *2-3. Richard Casteler:* Next to Simon Eyre, perhaps the best known of Deloney's historical characters. He was a prominent shoemaker of West-minster in the 1550's and died in 1559. In his will he requested that Richard Grafton, the chronicler, look after Mrs. Casteler. Grafton apparently was a good friend and hence the paragraph on Casteler in the *Chronicle*, II, 531. From Grafton comes three bits of information that Deloney uses: (1) the "Cock of Westminster" phrase; (2) the knowledge that Casteler married but had no children, and (3) the knowledge that Casteler made a gift to Christ's Hospital. Holinshed has the same information, but he gets it word for word from Grafton. See Holinshed, III, 1083: sig. 5L6ᵛ, and Merritt E. Lawlis, "Thomas Deloney and Richard Casteler," *N&Q*, CXCVIII (January, 1953), 4-7. Stow omits Casteler.

31. **handkerchers of Cambrick:** "Handkercher," according to the *OED*, was common in literary use as late as the 17th century; then after "handkerchief" became the written form, "handkercher" remained in speech as late as the 1860's. Cambric was a fine white linen made in Cambray, Flanders, though it could be an English imitation made of hard-spun cotton yarn.

Page 176, *3-5. Margaret,* **of the spread-Eagle . . . long** *Meg* **of** *Westminster:* As Mann suggests (p. 531), Deloney probably saw the anonymous jestbook, *The Life and Pranks of Long Meg of Westminster* (1582). But she was such a well known figure by the end of the century that all the information about her life and pranks were common knowledge. On 27 August 1590 "A Ballad of longe Meg of Westminster" was entered in the Stationers' Register (Arber, II, 561). Still another ballad was "The madd merye pranckes of Long Megg of Westminster," entered on 14 March 1595 (Arber, II, 293). "The Life of long Megg of Westminster," entered on 18 August 1590 (Arber, II, 559) apparently was another edition of the jestbook of 1582.

6. **Gillian** **of the George:** Apparently a fictitious name and perhaps one of the few unhistorical characters in *The Gentle Craft, Part II*.

Page 178, *21.* **Master** *Cornelius* **of the Guard:** Mann suggests (p. 536) that he may have been Cornelius van Dun, a yeoman of the guard for Henry VIII, Mary, and Elizabeth (according to Stow, II, 123).

Page 179, *32.* **a bushel of Angels:** The angel was a gold coin that in the 1550's, when Casteler was a prominent shoemaker in Westminster, was worth about 10s.

Page 181, *2.* **Posset:** A drink made of hot milk and ale or wine, often with sugar and spices added. Boorde recommended it for tertian fever (*Dyetary of Helth*, E.E.T.S. edition, p. 97). Apparently it was taken as a nightcap, too (*Macbeth*, II, ii, 6). A posset was very similar to a caudle, which contained gruel instead of milk.

9. **excellent good Muskadine:** "Muscadine" is "muscatel," a strong sweet wine made from the muscat grape (the feminine form of which is *muscade* in Provençal).

12. **powdred beefe:** See the note for page 78, line 28.

Page 182, *12.* **Graues-end** **Barge:** An example of Deloney's tendency to get into his novel all topical allusions he can; this one is to the daily barge service from

London to Gravesend, a port in Kent on the south bank of the Thames, some 30 miles south of London. See Sugden, p. 230.

19. **thou shalt find me no Crinkler:** A crinkler is one who fails to carry out his intention; from the obsolete verb, to crinkle. Deloney seems to have invented the noun; at least it is not listed in the *OED,* and neither Nashe nor Harvey seems to have used it.

33. **ioyne stooles:** Originally "joined stool"; a stool consisting of parts joined or fitted together, sometimes with the implication that a professional joiner did the fitting and not someone less qualified.

Page 184, *15-16.* **he keeps all his gownes for *Gillian:*** i.e., he gives green gowns to Gillian, meaning euphemistically that he dallies with her on the grass until her dress is stained green. See Greene's *George a Greene* (1599), ed. Grosart, 1881-83, XIV, 140, where Ienkin says of Madge: "And first I saluted her with a greene gowne, and after fell as hard a-wooing as if the Priest had bin at our backs, to have married vs."

25. **Tallow cake:** A lump of congealed fat, with pointed reference to Gillian.

Page 185, *24.* **Kate:** Perhaps Katherine of the Crane (page 179, lines 6-7).

Page 186, *27.* **out upon her foule stammell:** In the 18th century, and perhaps earlier, "stammel" in slang meant "lusty, strapping Wench," "overgrown bouncing Wench," or "overgrown robust Wench"—all of which certainly apply to Long Meg. More literally, Meg probably was the wearer of a stammel petticoat (a petticoat of coarse woolen cloth, usually dyed red).

29. **a bold betrice:** So far as I know, the author of *Much Ado About Nothing* never uses the word "betrice" in Deloney's sense. But Mann shows (pp. 537-538) that Beatrice was used upon occasion as a nickname for a brazen woman. See *Maroccus Extaticus* (1595), Percy Society (London, 1843), XI, 16, and Dekker's *The Batchelars Banquet* (1603), in *The Non-Dramatic Works of Dekker,* ed. Grosart (London, 5 vols., 1884-86), I, 176.

Page 187, *20.* **Hipocras:** A cordial made of strained wine mixed with spices. The name comes from Hippocrates, who was the famous Greek physician of the 5th century B.C. "Hippocrates' sleeve" was the sleeve or bag through which wine was strained to make it clear. —***turn it ouer my naile:*** As Mann observes, "ouer my nail" is explained by a printed note in the outer margin of a page in Nashe's *Pierce Penilesse:* "Drinking *super nagulum,* a deuise of drinking new come out of Fraunce; which is, after a man hath turned vp the bottom of the cup, to drop it on his naile, & make a pearle with that is left; which, if it shed, & he cannot make stand on, by reason thers too much, he must drinke againe for his pennance" (I, 205).

Page 188, *18.* ***I faith:*** In faith. The expression appears at least four different ways in *The Gentle Craft, Part II:* "I faith," "y faith," yfaith," and "y-faith."

19. ***stampe the crab:*** The phrase literally means to press or crush crabapples in order to extract juice. It would seem to have a figurative meaning, too.

27. **rounding *Robin* in the eare:** Whispering in Robin's ear. See the note, below, for page 198, line 29.

Page 190, *27.* **come in my office:** That part of the house—in Meg's case, the Spread Eagle Inn—where the servants work. Kitchen, pantry, scullery, and laundry are included in the word "office."

31-32. ***how many rookes . . . hath the goodnes of your kitchin tride:*** Literally, how many rooks have been cooked in this kitchen? Pies were made with young rooks (or crows). But Robin intends a pun, too, and Meg says she understands it. But the 20th century reader has some difficulty. According to the *OED*, "rook" meant "knave," "cheat," or "gull" when applied to persons. None seems to apply here if in Robin's first question he is asking Meg whether her quarters were ever afire with sexual passion.

Page 191, *18*. **pottle:** Two quarts or half a gallon. It could also mean the pot or vessel that contained the half gallon of liquid. When Nashe meant the latter, however, he wrote "pottle pot" (Nashe, III, 32).

22. **Gods precious:** A common asseveration, now obsolete, with "blood" or "body" understood.

30. **to pay tribute to** *Aiax:* To go to the privy; in this sense often spelled "a iakes." Probably a pun (as in *Love's Labor's Lost*, V, ii, 581), Deloney intending to suggest not only a privy but also Ajax, the Greek hero who fights Hector in a duel and later wrestles Odysseus.

Page 195, *13*. *Margaret* **ietted home:** To jet was to walk along in a prancing swaggering manner. Nashe writes in *Pierce Penilesse:* "Mistris Minx, a Marchants wife, . . . iets it as gingerly as if she were dancing the Canaries" (I, 173).

37. **lay a straw:** Desist. Robin tells Gillian to stop inquiring or she may go too far (and "stumble").

Page 196, *37*. **play mum-budget:** A "budget" is a pouch or wallet, usually of leather, but "to open one's budget" means to speak one's mind. "Mumbudget" is silence. According to the *OED*, originally there may have been a children's game called "mumbudget." Nashe uses the word most colorfully in *Have with You to Saffron-Walden* (1596) when he says of Harvey: "no villaine, no Atheist, no murdrer, no traitor, no Sodomite hee euer read of but he hath likend mee too . . . for no other reason in the earth but because I would not let him go beyond me, or be won to put my finger in my mouth & crie mumbudget, when he had baffuld mee in print throughout *England*" (III, 128-124).

40. **a good Term:** The meaning could be "a good law term," as Mann suggests—a term financially profitable to Meg's master, implying that he engages, sometimes successfully, in law suits. There were three or four periods or terms each year for the sitting of certain law courts. But "term" also meant term day, or the day on which rents were paid; a good day of collecting rents would make the master glad enough.

Page 197, *19*. **braided wares:** Goods that have faded or become tarnished.

30. *gip:* An exclamation of anger, perhaps originally "By Mary Gipsy" ("by St. Mary of Egypt"). It is equivalent to "get out" or "get along with you."

Page 198, *3*. *Tuttle field:* An open field in Westminster on the left bank of the Thames. See Sugden, p. 535.

29. **rounding her in the eare:** Whispering to her. In naming Round Robin, a flat character, Deloney seems to have seized upon his characteristic trait of sly whispering; all that remained was the alliteration: hence "Robin."

31. *Margaret* **of the Spread Eagle:** As Mann notes (p. 539), Deloney for the moment confuses Margaret with Katherine of the Crane whom he had mentioned on page 179, lines 6-7.

33. **rounsefull:** Rounceval; a large, boisterous woman.

The Gentle Craft, Part II [Pages 199-214]

Page 199, *3-4*. **a great bucke that is to be washt:** See the note, above, for page 74, line 27.

25. **a needle in a bottle of hay:** "Bottle" here is from the OF *botel,* a diminutive of *bot,* meaning bundle. To find a needle in a bundle of hay, then, is like finding one in a haystack—an impossible task.

35. **to seeke Harts-ease, but I can find nothing but sorrel:** Both plants offer Gillian suitable puns. Heartsease in the 16th century, when applied to a flower or plant, meant pansy or wallflower. But sorrel was an unattractive and sour tasting plant the leaves of which were used in medicine and salads.

Page 201, *21-22.* **as errant a Cuckold as** *Iack Coomes:* Apparently a notorious person, but there seems to be nothing in print about him.

36-37. **pad lying in the straw:** Literally, a toad lying in the straw; a lurking or hidden danger.

Page 202, *17-24.* **wherefore is griefe good . . . should I grieve:** Meg's soliloquy, as Lange suggests (p. 36), may be a parody of Falstaff's "catechism" on honor in *1 Henry IV,* V, i, 131-143.

Page 203, *19.* **a coate with foure elbowes:** A fool's coat. Nashe explains the phrase in his preface to *Have with You to Saffron-Walden:* "like a fooles coat with foure elbowes" (III, 23).

Page 208, *3.* **The Kings Maiesty . . . town of Bullen:** Henry VIII captured Boulogne in 1544. Whitehall, mentioned in line 5, was the palace of English kings from Henry VIII to William III (Sugden, pp. 70, 564).

24-25. **pumps and pantofles:** Both were indoor slippers. Pumps were low-heeled, single-soled, and tight-fitting (without a fastening of any kind), while pantofles were high-heeled and loose-fitting. Apparently some of Robin's group wore pumps while others wore pantofles.

Page 213, *2. Peachey:* As Mann observes (p. 540), the name appears several times in Holinshed; but no one whom Holinshed describes seems to be the model for Deloney's hero.

21. **sowter:** From the Latin *sutor,* shoemaker. F. P. Wilson suggests that "sowter" means "ignorant shoemaker," judging from a passage in *The Wonderful Year* (1603): "thou shewst thy selfe to be a right Cobler & no Sowter" (*Dekker's Plague Pamphlet,* Oxford, 1925, p. 50).

23. **squaring:** Swaggering. To square or to square it out meant to strut or swagger.

Page 214, *1. Tom Stuteley* **and** *Strangwidge:* Holinshed describes "Thomas Stukeleie" as a "defamed person" and a "faithlesse beast" for being the ringleader of a rebellion against Queen Elizabeth in 1584 (*Chronicles,* III, 1359: sig. 6O6ᵛ). Mann cites (p. 533) a ballad by William Birch on Strangwidge: "A new balade of the worthy service done by Maister Strangwige in Fraunce" (1563), reprinted by the Percy Society. Then of course Deloney himself wrote a ballad on the subject in 1591; it was called "The Lamentation of Mr. Pages Wife." See the introduction, p. xxvi.

3-4. **watched silk thrumb hats:** Silk hats that are watchet colored or light blue and thrummed (having a nap or shaggy surface). But thrummed could also indicate (1) a fringe round the brim or (2) ornamented with thrums, which were tufts of some material like yarn.

374

Page 215, *2*. **to take in dudgin:** To take with a feeling of anger or resentment.

32. **goodman flat cap:** As Stow notes (II, 194-195), flat caps came into fashion when Henry VIII started wearing one toward the end of his reign. Made of black woolen yarn, flat caps were small and inexpensive. But at the end of the 16th century the Spanish felt hat was more fashionable. Apprentices who persisted in wearing the old-fashioned flat cap were laughed at by dapper men like Captain Strangewidge.

37. **dudgin haft dagger:** A dagger with a handle made of boxwood.

Page 216, *35*. *Iohn Abridges:* Again, there are various references to the family name, but none to a John Abridges, servant of a shoemaker.

Page 217, *10-11*. **butter whores:** Apparently butter-women, women who made or sold butter, often had very abusive tongues; and it is this characteristic that "butter-whore" or "butter-quean" denoted. She was, in other words, a scold (and no more).

14. **call me Cut:** John Abridges probably is distinguishing between a thrusting movement and a cutting or slashing stroke. "Cut" also means to castrate or circumcise, a meaning Abridges clearly has in mind.

25. **by another a scarffe:** With these words the two fragments in the Folger Library begin. The two fragments fit together and form a continuous text to page 242, line 12, in Chapter IX. The final words are "the Doctor tooke horse and immediatly."

Page 218, *7*. **quoystrels:** Spelled also coistrel and custrel, a knave or base fellow.

Page 219, *13*. **Petworth:** As Mann notes (p. 541), it is in Sussex, about 15 miles south of Guildford.

15. **pike-staffe:** A walking stick with a metal point at the lower end.

Page 220, *6*. **Kerbfoord:** Mann (p. 541) thinks this a misspelling of "Kirdford," a village five miles north of Petworth.

Page 221, *35-36*. **my name is a Nowne substantive that may be felt, heard, and understood:** A drum, the punning answer to Tom Drum's riddle, can be "felt, heard, and understood" and thus is a noun substantive as defined by William Lily in *A Short Introduction of Grammar* (1567), sig. A5r.

Page 222, *7*. **set up in very faire Chalk:** The amount of Tom Drum's debt at the George is, according to custom, written down plainly in chalk, probably on the door.

20-21. **goodman** *Luters* **lame nagge:** Apparently well known at the time, but there seems to be nothing in print that would offer an explanation.

*Page 223, *18-19*. **all besmeared** *Tom-Drums* **face:** In the Folger copy (1598?) the reading is "all to besmeared"; the 1639 typesetter, trying to correct the phrase, left out the wrong syllable and set "all to smeared." He should have dropped "to" rather than "be-".

20. **the Image of** *Bred-streete* **corner:** Mann suggests (p. 542) that Deloney has a monument in mind—the one of Thomas Tomlinson at "Breadstreet corner the north East end" (Stow, I, 34).

20-21. **the** *Sarazines-head* **without** *New-gate:* A saracen's head was the sign of a popular tavern on the north side of Snow Hill without Newgate. According to Sugden, p. 451, in 1522 it had 30 beds and stables for 40 horses.

*26. **Towne-malin:** Town Malling, as Lange notes (p. 61), near Maidstone in Kent.

Page 224, 29. ***Clement carry lye:*** Perhaps a well known person, though the name does not seem to appear in other writings of the time. If Deloney created the name, he is not nearly so successful as he is with other names, for the meaning of the word "clement" does not seem to reinforce what we know about the person.

*Page 227, 2. **sixe-score to the hundred:** In the 16th century six score often meant a "great hundred" or a "long hundred."

10-11. **to have thy wards ready:** Be ready to assume the correct defensive postures or movements in fencing. George Silver writes in *Paradoxes of Defence* (1599): "All single weapons haue foure wardes, and all double weapons haue eight wardes. The single sword hath two with the point vp, and two with the point downe." (Shakespeare Association Facsimiles No. 6, London, 1933, sig. E1ᵛ. The introduction is by J. Dover Wilson.)

20. **Sir *Iohn Rainsford:*** Grafton, II, 326, and Holinshed, III, 874: sig. 403ᵛ, report that a Sir John Rainsford was knighted in 1522 after helping Surrey at Morlaix. The will of (another?) Sir John Raynesford was probated in 1521; see Somerset House, 21 Maynwaryng. The historians say nothing, of course, about this episode concerning the widow and the priest.

Page 228, *13.* **Sir *Iohn:*** A familiar and often contemptuous name for a priest.

Page 230, *8.* **bury blind bayard:** A facetious taunt, combining the ingenious use of alliteration with the humorous connotation of "bayard," which in Charlemagne's time had been the proper name of a magic horse but which had come to mean (1) any horse and (2) a horse that symbolized blind recklessness.

Page 231, *19.* **haporth of Ale:** Halfpennyworth of ale.

Page 232, *1-2.* **an Ill word foure times a yeer at *Newgate:*** A reference to the four law terms. See the note, above, for page 84, line 27.

Page 233, *7-8.* ***Kingstone:*** Tom seems to have taken the main road, from Petworth through Guildford and Kingston to London (Mann, p. 543).

Page 235, *26.* **at a dead lift:** In a crisis or emergency. The earliest usage recorded in the *OED* is 1624.

Page 236, *9.* **checkquerd pavement:** Squares of stone, brick, tile, or wood arranged in different colors, like a chess board. Here Tom seems to be referring to the floor inside Mistress Farmer's house.

26. **twelve silver Apostles:** Silver spoons, the handles of which ended in figures of the Apostles; often they were given as presents by sponsors at baptisms. The apostle spoons came in sets of twelve.

*32. **her face withered:** The meaning may be "weathered" rather than "withered"; either would make sense.

Page 238, *18.* **Alderman *Iarvice:*** Deloney's reference to him seems to be the only one of the period; perhaps it is, therefore, one of the few fictitious names in *The Gentle Craft, Part II*.

*Page 239, *3-4.* ***Tom Drum** . . . **entertainment:*** Since Tom is the one who is angry, the passage calls for emendation.

20. **cast your water:** "To cast," a very popular Elizabethan verb with more than a dozen meanings, here means to diagnose disease; apparently a kind of urinalysis was part of the routine diagnosis.

Page 240, *6.* **as if one had given her a rush:** A very common plant with straight, bare stalks, often used to spread on the floors of apartments. Hence something of little value. The word often appeared in such negative expressions as "not to care a rush" or "not worth a rush."

26-27. **there was slaine of the Scots to the number of foureteene thousand:** As Mann notes (p. 544), Deloney takes his information from Holinshed (III, 988: sig. 5C6v).

Page 242, *11-12.* **the Doctor tooke horse and immediatly:** These are the final words of the fragments in the Folger Library. See the note, above, for page 217, line 25.

*Page 248, *28.* **call me *Iohn* hither:** Lange is right in emending "Richard," in the 1639 edition, to "Iohn." See page 252, lines 31-33; what Mistress Farmer says there makes it clear that she is referring to John here.

Page 251, *4.* ***Bridewell:*** Stow notes that in 1553 Bridewell became "a Workhouse for the poore and idle persons of the Citie" (II, 44-45). For a brief history, see Sugden, pp. 76-77.

Page 252, *28-29.* **a stale Codshead under the gill:** The mere physical analogy is striking, but "Codshead" also had the connotation of "stupid fellow" or "blockhead."

Page 254, *14-15.* **master *Baltazar:*** In using this name Deloney may be trying once again to account for a first occurrence; he seems to have a genuine historical mind, attempting always to find information about the beginnings of an industry in England or the first use of a phrase. Mann points out (p. 545) that Deloney's master Baltazar may be the Spaniard, Balthaser Sanches, perhaps the first confectioner in England. Mann refers to *The Beauties of England and Wales* (1816), X, 792.

Page 257, *7.* ***Marlins* prophesie:** Presumably Deloney is referring to Merlin, the magician, and to his prophesying in general as accurate (not to any particular prophecy); by analogy, the wife of the Green King was accurate in predicting the defection of the Green King's friends.

34. **firkin:** In this usage, it means "moving about briskly." Anthony probably dances while he fiddles.

Page 258, *6-7.* **the Salutation:** According to Sugden (p. 448) a tavern on the south side of Newgate Street. The sign may have represented the "salutation" between Gabriel and the Virgin Mary.

Page 261, *20.* **Worlds end:** The capital "W" suggests a pun on the World's End, a tavern in Spring Gardens, Knightsbridge, London (Sugden, p. 571).

Page 263, *9.* **a huntsup:** A song that is sung or a tune that is played to awaken someone early in the morning. Originally it was a particular song and tune to awaken huntsmen.

31. ***Brainford:*** Brentford, eight miles west of London. Perhaps the Green King has in mind the famous hostelry in Brentford called the Three Pigeons. See Sugden, p. 73.

Page 264, *17.* **Sir *Michaell Musgrave:*** Again Deloney uses a surname that was well known (and mentioned in Grafton and Holinshed); but there seems to be no record of a Sir Michael.

19. **Tom Trotter:** Mentioned briefly in Holinshed (III, 981: sig. 5C3), but not in Grafton. Holinshed reports that his information comes from "maister Patten."

22. **Parson** *Ribble:* Mann suggests (pp. 546-547) that Deloney has in mind Parson Keble, who is mentioned by Holinshed (III, 988: sig. 5C6^v). But Holinshed's account is so brief that, without further evidence, it is impossible to tell whether the two references are to the same man

THOMAS OF READING

The first record of *Thomas of Reading* in the Stationers' Register is for 19 April 1602, when Thomas Pavier "entred for his copies by assignement from Thomas Millington" not only *Thomas of Reading* but the first two parts of *Henry VI* and *Titus Andronicus* (Arber, III, 204). Millington had owned the rights to *Jack of Newbury* (see above, p. 345), and we may presume that he had published both novels by 1600. Certainly *Thomas* was published after *Jack,* for in the dedication of the latter Deloney promises that he will write *Thomas* if *Jack* is well received. Enough time elapsed between the writing of the dedication and the writing of *Thomas* for Deloney to change some of the names of the characters whom he mentions in the dedication. The second edition of *Thomas* probably came out in 1602 and the third between 1602 and 1612.

But the earliest extant edition is that of 1612. If we may believe what we read on the title page, the 1612 edition was the fourth. There are two copies extant. The one owned by the Huntington Library has been used as the copy text. The British Museum copy has been collated; but as the collation notes show, there are very few variant readings. Q1 in the collation notes indicates the 1612 edition and the agreement of both copies; when their readings are different, Q1HN is the Huntington copy and Q1BM is the British Museum copy. Q2 is the 1623 edition; Q3, 1632; and Q4, 1636.

Q1 is the only substantive edition among the four early editions that are extant. Q2, the fifth edition according to the title page, probably was set from Q1; see, for example, page 298, line 26, where Q2 follows Q1 in an obvious misprint, "shall be tide" (i.e., shall betide). Q2 makes important emendations that are accepted in the present edition (as the collation notes show), but many Q2 emendations are either arbitrary or careless. Q3, the sixth edition, follows Q2; and Q4, presumably the seventh edition, follows Q3—with the result that a number of the readings to the right of the brackets are "Q2-4." See, for example, page 300, lines 18-19, where the Q1 reading is "such as are in their youth wasters, doe prooue in their age starke beggars." Q2 mistakenly sets "masters" for "wasters," and the error is repeated in Q3 and Q4. But Q4 is more critical than Q3; on page 283, line 25, the Q1 reading is "could not harbour anger longer." Q2 carelessly sets "any" for "anger." Q3 blindly follows Q2, but in this case Q4 sees that "harbour any longer" does not make sense and changes "harbour" to "forbeare." The change shows not only that Q4 recognizes the error in Q3 but also that Q4 does not have access to Q1.

EARLY EDITIONS

1612 (Q1). STC(PRJ) 6569. *Title page:* THOMAS OF | Reading. | *OR,* | The six worthy yeomen | of the West. | Now the fourth time corrected and enlarged | By T. D. | [*printer's orn.,* McKerrow 345] | Printed at London for T. P. | 1612. [*According to the Huntington Library, the notation, in ink, in the upper right hand corner, is probably a shelf mark of a former owner. The notation reads:* AO M / 5].

Collation: Quarto, A-I⁴, K². No page numbers.

Contents: [A1^r], title; [A1^v], blank; A2^r-K2^v, text.

Copy used: Huntington Library, though it has been collated with the other extant copy owned by the British Museum.

1623 (Q2). STC(PRJ) 6570. *Title page:* THOMAS | OF | READING | OR, | The sixe worthie Yeomen | of the West. | Now the fift time corrected and enlarged | By T. D. | [*printer's orn.,* McKerrow 345] | LONDON, | Printed by W. I. for T. P. | 1623.

Collation and contents: Identical with the 1612 edition.

Copy used: Huntington Library (only extant copy).

1632 (Q3). STC(PRJ) 6571. *Title page:* THOMAS | OF | READING: | OR, | The sixe worthie Yeomen | of the West. | Now the sixth time corrected and enlarged | By *T. D.* | [*printer's orn.,* McKerrow 345] | LONDON, | Printed by ELIZ. ALLDE for | ROBERT BIRD. | 1632.

Collation and contents: Identical with the 1612 edition.

Copy used: Huntington Library. There are also copies in the British Museum, National Library of Scotland, Bodleian, Bristol University; Folger, Boston Athenaeum, Harvard, Yale.

1636 (Q4). STC (PRJ) 6572. *Title page:* THE | PLEASANT HISTORY OF | Thomas of Reading, | OR, | The six worthy Yeomen of the West. | Corrected and inlarged by *T. D.* | [*printer's orn.,* McKerrow 202c] | AT LONDON, | Printed for Robert Bird. 1636.

Collation and contents: Identical with the 1612 edition.

Copy used: Huntington Library. There are also copies in the London Library, Exeter Cathedral, and Peterborough Cathedral.

1672. STC (W) 966. Printed for William Thackeray and are to be sold at his shop in Duck-lane. 1672. Quarto. Bodleian.

Explanatory Notes

MODERN EDITIONS

Following are the nineteenth- and twentieth-century editions of the complete novel. No attempt has been made to list anthologies in which selections from *Thomas of Reading* have appeared.

1812. *Thomas of Reading*. [Editor's name not given]. Edinburgh: J. Ballantyne, 1812. Copy text: the 1632 edition.
1828. *A Collection of Early Prose Romances*. Vol. I. Edited by W. J. Thoms. London: William Pickering, 1828. Copy text: the 1632 edition.
1903. *Thomas Deloney: His Thomas of Reading, and Three Ballads on the Spanish Armada*. Edited by Charles Aldrich and Lucian Swift Kirtland. New York: J. F. Taylor, 1903. Copy text: the 1632 edition.
1912. *The Works of Thomas Deloney*. Edited by Francis Oscar Mann. Oxford: Clarendon Press, 1912. Copy text: the 1623 edition.
1912. *Some Old English Worthies*. Edited by Dorothy Senior. [London]: Stephen Swift, 1912. Copy text: the 1632 edition (modernized).
1920. *Thomas of Reading and John Winchcombe*. Edited by W. H. D. Rouse. London: Blackie, 1920. Copy text: Mann's edition of 1912.
1929. *Shorter Novels*. Vol. I. Edited by Ernest Rhys. London: Dent (Everyman), 1929. Copy text: the 1623 edition.

NOTES

Page 267, *4-5*. **Henry the first . . . instituted the high court of Parliament:** this bit of information is in Holinshed (III, 38: sig. D5ᵛ), but not in Grafton. The historical Henry I (1068-1135) had at least two connections with Reading: he founded an abbey there, and was buried in the abbey.

5-7. **there liued nine men, which for the trade of Clothing, were famous throughout all *England*:** Perhaps none of the names, given in lines 26 ff., is completely fictitious; certainly Fitzallen and Byram are names that crop up in Grafton and Holinshed. But there is no evidence that anyone by either name was in the clothing industry. The first names appear to be fictitious and alliterative; perhaps Deloney first chose the town—Worcester, for example—and then chose a name, William, to go with it. In the dedication to *Jack of Newbury*, where Deloney promises another novel, the name had been Richard of Worcester.

But the name Thomas of Reading may be historical, in spite of Thomas Fuller's doubts (*Worthies of England*, 1662, ed. Nuttall, I, 137). Cole was at least legendary, and the name probably was familiar to Deloney's readers. William Chappell (*Popular Music*, II, 633) suggests that Cole may be the Old King Cole of the nursery rhyme. Iona and Peter Opie (*Oxford Dictionary of Nursery Rhymes*, pp. 134-5) agree that the nursery rhyme may concern a real Thomas Cole, but they offer no evidence.

Page 268, *9*. **Bosoms Inne:** Sugden (p. 69) contends that Bosom's Inn was a corruption of Blossom's Inn, for the sign was St. Laurence surrounded by a border of flowers or blossoms. Whatever the correct name, the site was Laurence Lane, off Cheapside. Sugden adds that Deloney is incorrect in deriving the name of the inn from the host, Old Bosom. In other words, Deloney creates a character to fit the name of the inn. Surely Dickens could not have done better.

13. **Iarrats hall:** In *Thomas of Reading* the spelling is "Iarrats," "Gerrards," and "Garrats." Sugden (p. 218) refers to it as Gerard's Hall, a merchant's house on the south side of Basing Lane off Bread Street, Cheapside. Naturally, Deloney was quick to seize upon a legend connected with the hall; according to legend, Gerard's Hall was named after a giant who was so big that he used a 40-foot fir-pole for a walking staff. The account in Stow (I, 348) is not so hyperbolic: the 40-foot pole was a jousting staff.

Page 269, *8.* ***Robert*** **Duke of Normandy:** Robert Curthose, Duke of Normandy (*c.* 1054-1134), eldest son of William the Conqueror. William gave him the nickname "Curthose" because of his short, fat build. Note that Deloney never refers to the nickname; he implies that Robert was handsome as well as heroic. About his heroism there was no question. In 1099, with Godfrey of Bouillon and Robert of Flanders, he captured Jerusalem from the Turks. But apparently he was not actually offered the rulership of Jerusalem, as Deloney has it (from Grafton, Holinshed, and a number of English chroniclers beginning with William of Malmesbury). See Charles Wendell David, *Robert Curthose* (Cambridge, Mass., 1920), pp. 110-114.

*30. **to other:** The use of the singular is ungrammatical to us (as perhaps it was to the compositors of Q2 and Q4), but it is used throughout *Thomas of Reading* and may very well be what Deloney actually wrote.

Page 271, *23.* **Erle of *Moraigne:*** Robert, Count of Mortain (*d.* 1091?). With Bishop Odo, he helped Robert Curthose in the latter's rebellion against William Rufus in 1088. Deloney telescopes Robert Curthose's two attempts to gain the English crown; the one against William Rufus was in 1088 and the one against Henry I was in 1101, probably after the Count of Mortain's death. See David, *Robert Curthose*, pp. 47-52. See also the *DNB;* Holinshed, III, 32: sig. D2v; and Grafton, I, 181. Holinshed does not specifically report, as Grafton does that the earl joined forces with Duke Robert in Normandy against the king. But Holinshed is the one who supplies the information that the earl had a "willfull and stubborne mind" and, "exiling himselfe," went back to Normandy. Deloney apparently invents the part about the ladies and children being "turned out of doores."

Page 272, *14.* **Colebroke:** Deloney spells it "Colebroke" or "Colebrook," and he suggests that the town (really Colnbrook on the Coln about 5 miles east of Windsor) as well as the river got their name from Thomas Cole. As Sugden is quick to point out (p. 125), Deloney's derivation is not historically accurate.

29. **yellow hose:** To say that a person wears yellow hose is to say that he is jealous.

Page 274, *26-27.* **my mony shrinks as bad as northerne cloth:** Apparently a common belief. In *The Terrors of the Night* (1594) Nashe, on the subject of witches, remarks that "if a man have the least heart or spirite to with-stand one fierce blast of their brauadoes, he shall see them shrinke faster than Northern cloath, and outstrip time in dastardly flight" (I, 383-4).

Page 276, *27*. **Chamberlaine:** An attendant at an inn, now an obsolete meaning of chamberlain. Here he seems to be a waiter, but the task often involved care of bedchambers.

Page 277, *4*. *Reior:* Rahere (*d.* 1144). In March, 1123, he started building the priory and hospital of St. Bartholomew in Smithfield. See the *DNB* account; Holinshed, III, 31: sig. D2; Grafton, I, 180; and Stow, II, 25.

Page 278, *3*. **foule euill:** According to the *OED* "foul evil" often meant epilepsy or syphilis; Cutbert apparently intends a fairly strong oath.

Page 279, *11*. **the Earle of Shrewsburyes daughter:** The Earl of Shrewsbury was Robert of Bellême (fl. 1098); he was one of Duke Robert's allies against Henry I, but there is no record in Grafton or Holinshed of his having a daughter Margaret. Deloney's departure from history creates an interesting relationship: lover and father are fellow rebels, as Mortimer and Glendower are in *I Henry IV*. One wonders why Deloney happened to name his heroine Margaret and why he often refers to her as "Margaret of the white hand." Neither Grafton nor Holinshed mentions the fact that Duke Robert in his youth was engaged to Margaret, the beautiful sister of Count Herbert II of Maine (a province to the south of Normandy, to the east of Brittany, and to the southwest of the White Main River). Could "Margaret of Maine" ("Marguerite du Maine" in French) and the White Main have suggested "Margaret of the white hand" to Deloney? Ordericus Vitalis' *Historia Ecclesiastica* was not the source, for it did not appear in print until 1619. (For other sources of information about Robert and Margaret see David, *Robert Curthose*, pp. 205-210). Drayton does not mention Margaret in *The Tragical Legend of Robert, Duke of Normandy* (1596); Lodge's *The Famous, True, and Historical Life of Robert, Second Duke of Normandy* (1591) concerns a different Duke Robert—the 8th-century Robert (or Robin) the Devil, son of Duke Aubert.

Page 285, *23*. **borderers:** Those who live near the border of England and Scotland. Here and in other 16th-century allusions there seems to be the intimation that borderers are neither fish nor fowl, neither English nor Scottish, and therefore especially deserving of scorn.

35. **This measure shalbe called a yard:** Deloney got this fanciful bit of information from Holinshed, III, 28:C6ᵛ or Grafton, I, 179. The *OED* gives a more reliable account: through the first half of the 14th century, and earlier, the ell (45 inches) was a standard unit of measurement. But in 1353 (in the reign of Edward III) the ell was replaced by the *verge*, and yard is merely the English equivalent of *verge*.

Page 290, *30*. **sale:** Soul. Hodgkins, with his "broad Northerne speech," apparently is the speaker.

Page 292, *10*. **the smokie louer:** Louver, or opening in the roof to permit smoke to escape from the hall. The laths of some louvers in the 16th century were arranged in an overlapping way so that smoke could go out and fresh air come in while excluding rain.

Page 294, *14*. **carke and care:** "Cark and care" had become a cliché by the 1590's. Cark is a vague word implying a troubled state of mind. Boorde writes in *Dyetary of Helth*, E.E.T.S. edition, p. 240: "Thus a man . . . shall not be in rest nor peace, but euer in carke and care, for his purse will euer be bare."

Page 295, *25.* **flesh shambles:** To the Elizabethan, either a stall for the sale of meat or else a brothel. Here it is the former.

26. **Iewes streete:** Stow (I, 281) refers to the Old Jewry as a street. For more details as to the streets and buildings in this paragraph, see the *Survey* and the map at the end of volume II. See also Sugden.

38. **Criple gate:** Stow (I, 33) reports that he read "in the historie of *Edmond* King of the East Angles, written by *Abbo Floriacensis,*" that Cripplegate got its name from "Criples begging there." Sugden (p. 138) takes this explanation with a grain of salt.

*Page 296, *15.* See the explanatory note for page 337, line 20.

Page 298, *2.* **Bishops downe:** Mann (p. 554) identifies this place as Bishopstone, a small village about 4 miles northwest of Salisbury.

Page 305, *21.* **Isca:** As Mann points out (p. 555), Deloney took this information about Isca, and the information in lines 28-29 and 32 about Gloucester and Rithin, from Llwyd's *Breuiary.* See sigs. D1v-D3r and K3.

Page 307, *22.* ***Wallis:*** William Wallace (1272?-1305) of Scottish history. In calling him a "notable Theefe" Deloney expresses the English point of view; but Wallace nevertheless emerges from Deloney's story as a hero of the Robin Hood variety.

Page 308, *8.* **caukins:** Calkins, the turned down ends of a horseshoe which raise the horse's heels from the ground. As Mann notes (p. 555) Deloney probably found this incident in Holinshed, II, 213: sig. S5r (the history of Scotland). But Holinshed gives the credit to Robert Bruce. Since Wallace and Bruce are mentioned on the same page, it is possible that Deloney really thought that Wallace was the one who had the horses "shodde backwarde." It would seem more likely, however, that Deloney intentionally combined the two men, the way he combined the two Winchcombs, father and son, in creating Jack of Newbury.

Page 309, *13.* **poasted off:** To "post over" or "post off" was to transfer a duty or responsibility to another, as in Nashe's colorful sentence in *Christ's Tears:* "Post ouer the Plague to what naturall cause you will, I positiuelie affirme it is for sinne" (II, 158).

37-38. **the valew of a plack or a bawby:** A plack in the 15th and 16th centuries was a small Scottish copper coin that was worth 4 pennies Scots. The bawbee was a Scottish coin of the 16th century; it was made of base silver and was worth 3 pennies Scots. Each was nearly equivalent to a half-penny or "copper" in English money.

Page 312, *9.* **a couple of Flemings . . . fled into this land:** Grafton (I, 182) reports the catastrophe, but Holinshed (III, 34: sig. D3v) is the real source: he notes that the "Flemings" came to England "by reason their countrie was ouerflowne with the sea." The part about the bailiffs and the coats appears to be Deloney's invention.

Page 313, *16.* **magget a pie:** Magpie, the common European bird that is known for its raucous chatter and its signification of ill omens. "Magget" or "maggot" is from "Margot," the pet name for "Margaret." "Maggot-pie," "maggot-a-pie," and "margot la pie" are common forms.

Page 314, *8.* **Sir *William Ferris:*** The name, as Mann notes (p. 556), crops up in Holinshed (III, 33: sig. D3r). But no definite source has been found for the story itself—Sir William's nose and the power of suggestion. Mann refers us to the

Decameron (Third Tale of the Ninth Day) but the similarity is not very close. Perhaps there was no definite literary source. Deloney's particular version may be as "original" as Boccaccio's or any other.

Page 322, *17*. **Thomas Beckets house in West cheape:** See Sugden's comments (pp. 512-513 and 559) on this passage in Deloney. Clearly Deloney is guilty of anachronism: Becket was archbishop in Henry II's reign (not Henry I's) and his place of birth had no significance until the latter part of the 12th century.

Page 323, *5-6*. **his nose burst out suddenly ableeding:** A nosebleed was one of the omens that Renaissance writers of tragedy used again and again. For a short analysis of the various omens used in Elizabethan tragedy, see Theodore Spencer, *Death and Elizabethan Tragedy* (Cambridge, Mass., 1936), pp. 191-4.

Page 325, *5*. **the ring of S. Mary Oueries bells:** There were twelve bells, and they were famous for the beautiful sound they gave in the Southwark area. But the bell tower dates from the 16th century, not the early 12th. See Sugden, p. 335.

Page 328, *8*. **Churching feast:** Churching is part of the Anglican ritual. Beginning in 1552, the title of the service became "The Thanksgiving of Women after Childbirth, commonly called The Churching of Women." As the title suggests, "churching is a mother's return to church privileges after her enforced absence due to childbirth." See George Harford and Morley Stevenson, eds., *The Prayer Book Dictionary* (London, 1925), p. 203.

Page 331, 7. **Bactria:** The Q1 spelling, Bractria, seems to be a typographical mistake. The usual spelling was "Bactria" or "Bactriana," which formed the northeastern part of modern Afghanistan. See Sugden, p. 42.

29. **Hauing liberty of the King to hawke and hunt:** As George Paterson shows, in a paper as yet unpublished, Deloney gets this information from Grafton (I, 181), who writes that the duke "was permitted by the kinges licence to hawke, hunt, and vse al other pastimes what he would for his disport & recreation. . . ." Holinshed (III, 33: sig. D3) merely states that Robert had "libertie to walke abroad in the kings forrests, parks, and chases neere the place where he was appointed to remaine. . . ."

Page 337, 20. **the other side:** In the Huntington Library copy of Q1, the copy followed in the present edition as a copy text, the reading is "thother." In general, there has been no effort to emend the "accidentals" (spelling and punctuation) of the copy text. But there is a second copy of Q1 in the British Museum, and in this second copy "thother" has been changed to "the other."

COLLATION NOTES[1]

JACK OF NEWBURY

CHAPTER I

Page 3, *9.* considered] consider Q3
  17. sake] sakes Q4,5
  18. take] took Q2,3

5, *13.* not at any time] not any time Q2,4,5
  17. found acquaintance] found many acquaintance Q2,3

6, *2.* of the Towne] in the town Q3
  3. I doubt some] I thinke some Q2,3
  6. truth] true Q2,3
  14-15. of the Herring] of a Herring Q2,3
  15. streight dyes] presently dyes Q2,3
  31. its] tis Q4; 'tis Q5

7, *2.* heere?] ~, Q2-5
  3. cheer.] ~? Q2-5
  6. commendations] commendation Q4,5
  8. profit;] Q4,5; ~? Q1; ~: Q2,3
  10-11. labour and trauaile] labour and painfull trauel Q2,3
  12. cast very] cast a very Q2,3
  14-15. and the great] as also the great Q2,3
  30-31. faint souldiers] some Souldiers Q2,3
  32. makes] maketh Q2,3   to want fauour] want fauour Q5
  35. Womankind] Q2-5; Womenkind Q1

8, *4.* amongst] among Q2,3
  4-5. house and well furnished] house well furnished Q2,3
  14. pray ye who] pray who Q2,3
  16. loue] Q5; loues Q1,4; louers Q2,3
  18. Taylor, dwelling] Taylor, and dwelling Q2,3
  27. for so much as] forasmuch as Q5
  29-30. better a choice] better choice Q4,5
  31. there be] there is Q4,5
  32. like of him] like him Q5   long] large Q2,3

9, *17.* ye] you Q4,5

[1] An asterisk (*) in the collation notes, as explained in the introduction, p. xxxi, means that the entry is a footnote to the text and that a discussion of the entry appears in the explanatory notes.

18. fauour?] ∼. Q4,5

37. beside] besides Q4,5

10,   *10.* there be] there is Q4,5

18. turne] turnes Q2,3   solemnesse] sullennesse Q4,5

28. wreathen] wreathed Q4,5

33. should] would Q5

11,   *1.* faire I dare] Q2-5; fare I daire Q1

7. foule, little] foule, yea little Q4,5

19. For why?] ∼, Q4,5

23. sure] true Q4,5

25. loth ∧] loth, Q2-5

33. towarde] towards Q2-5

34. beside ∧] ∼, Q2,3; besides ∧ Q5

12,   *5.* seruant, that] seruant, and that Q2,3

6. inconueniences] inconueniencies Q2,3

*19. pecking] Q4,5; picking Q1-3

26. perceiued] perceiuing Q4,5

27. lighted] lights Q2,3

37. die, except in time] die in time, except Q2,3

13,   *4.* my Loomes] the Loomes Q2,3

5. ill] Q2-5; til Q1

21. of our] other Q5

33. humour she continued] Q4,5; humour continued Q1-3

35. towne)] Q2-5; ∼ ∧ Q1

37. it] him Q3

14,   *7.* hers, to] Q2-5; hers ∧ to Q1

29. you] ye Q4,5

35. thy] the Q4,5

37. spoke] spoken Q2,3

15,   *19.* but those] but such as Q4,5

22. there be] there is Q4,5   loues] loue Q4,5

*27. them] him Q4,5

28. in] of Q4,5

16,   *6.* at first] at the first Q5

20. hee] shee Q4

22. dozen Chickens] dozen of chickens Q5   beside]
besides Q5

24. receiuing] receiued Q4,5

39. so is it] so it is Q2,3

17,   *9.* fauours] fauour Q2-5

12. woman] women Q4

15. chiefe] chiefest Q2-5

22. company] drinking Q2,3

40. of Goose] of a Goose Q2,3

388

18,   *5.* of tender] of a tender Q2,3
       18. sutors] Q2-5; sutor Q1
19,   *4.* yet lost] yet haue lost Q2,3
       7. our] your Q2-5
       8. bad purpose] bad a purpose Q4,5   before:] Q2-5; ~? Q1
       10. her and me] her and I Q2,3
       11. the iolly] this iolly Q2,3
    12-13. neuer haue put vp] neuer put vp Q3
       35. husbands] Q2-5; husbads Q1
       37. you] Q2-5; yun Q1
20,   *27.* rose] arose Q2,3
       32. his Clark] the Clark Q4,5
       38. was?] ~. Q5
21,   *5.* widow?] Q2-5; ~, Q1
       8. trowe.] ~? Q5
    17-18. somthing] somewhat Q2,3
    24-25. and openly to laugh] and then openly laughed Q4 5
22,   *6.* young man] young a man Q5
       13. returne] Q2-5; returns Q1
       19. which] that Q2,3
       35. fustian] fustion Q2,3
23,   *1.* out of the] out the Q5
       3. keepes] keepe Q4,5
       4. night‸] Q2-5; ~, Q1
       11. prepare] repaire Q2,3
       19. like.] Q2-5; like‿ Q1
       22. as hee was] Q2-5; as hee as was Q1
24,   *2.* Spirit] Spright Q2,3
       3. Crickets?] Q4,5; ~, Q1-3
       5. any] no Q2,3
       9. my] mine Q2,3
    24-25. vnto yee] for you Q2,3; vnto you Q5
   *26-27. you . . . your] thou . . . thy Q2-5
       33. bed] bed side Q2,3
       34. did.] ~? Q2,4
       36. Ilyris] Illyris Q2-5
25,   *1.* mee‿ wife,] ~, ~‿ Q1
       14. nature of a woman] nature of women Q4,5

CHAPTER II

26,   **4.* one] two Q1-5
       11. carefull] carefulnesse Q2,3; to be careful Q4,5

11-12. dealing, and an] dealing, an Q2,3
   13. besides] beside Q2-5
   17. this motion] his motion Q3
   19. *Alesburie*] Q2,3; *Alisburie* Q4,5; *Alseburie* Q1
27, *16.* roome] loome Q4
28, *15.* hee was] was he Q2,3
   20. bominable] hominable Q4
   29. condemnation] condemnations Q3
   35. were] was Q2-4
   39. wosted] woosted Q2-4
29, *2-3.* pleated; . . . dayes,] ~, . . . ~: Q2-5
   6. faire] Q2-5; farie Q1   gilt] gelt Q5
   36. Christs] Christ Q4
30, *2.* should] would Q3   before] chefore Q3
   17. Iustices] Iustice Q4,5
 34. he had discouered] they had discouered Q3; he discouered Q5
31, *7.* eare] ere Q2-5
   12. in *Barkshire*] of *Barkshire* Q2-5
   26. there is] there are Q5
   33. I am] am I Q4,5
32, *6.* so bescratcht] to be scratcht Q4,5
   10. poysoned teeth] Q2-5; poysoned tooth Q1
   11. his breath] and his breath Q5
   14. come] came Q3-5
   16. field?] Q2-5; ~. Q1
   26. would to doe] would do Q4,5
33, *11.* shepheards] heards Q4,5
   14. wonne] won it Q5
   24. *Iames* his day] Q2-5; *Iames* day Q1
   28. bespoke] bespake Q2-5
   29. eye] eyes Q2,3
   30. Leaue off] Leaue of Q3
34, *19.* woon] won Q4,5; worne Q2,3
   25. many a fatherlesse] many fatherlesse Q4,5
   33. FINIS.] *omitted* Q4,5

CHAPTER III

35, *3.* a progresse] in progresse Q2,3
   10. stockings] stockens Q2,3
 19. *Garter*] Q5; *Garret* Q1-4
   20. Good fellowes,] Goodfellow ∧ so Q4; Goodfellow, Q5

21. with your swords] with swords Q4,5
30. Sommer] Summers Q3   winters] winter Q5
36,   *4.* stand] stands Q2,3
        27. see∧] ~, Q2,5
        30. our] my Q4,5
      38. thirtith] twentith Q2,3
37,   *11.* haue] Q2,4,5; haus Q1,3
        14. these] this Q2,3
        24. being King] being a King Q2,3
        31. humbly I yeeld] humbly yeeld Q2,3
        35. visite thy] Q2-5; visity the Q1
38,   *6.* also of gold curiously made] also made of gold curiously
            Q2,3; also gold curiously made Q4,5
        21. are they] they are Q4,5   mount by] mount with Q2,3
        24. womans] womens Q2
        31. especially] especiall Q3
        37. into] unto Q5
39,   *7.* set∧] ~, Q3,5   his Councell] the Councell Q2,3,5
      15. pages∧] Q2,3,5; ~, Q1,4
        19. Then] Thus Q2,3
        21. redounded] redowned Q3
        22. gall'd] galde Q2,3
        23. would] should Q2-5
      27. stucke] Q2-5; stocke Q1   himselfe∧] ~, Q2-5
40,   *10.* or] nor Q2-5
        13. subtiltie] subtilties Q4,5
        14. broke] brake Q4,5
        20. an] a Q2,3
        21. working in] working on Q2,3
        27. Broome] Broomes Q2,3
        29. amitie] unity Q2,3
41,   *6.* *Golias*] *Goliahs* Q2-5
         7. braines] braine Q2,3
        22. not] Q2-5; nor Q1
        25. trees indure] tree indures Q2,3
        26. on hie] not hie Q2,3
        27. Weauers liue] Weauer liues Q2,3
        29. doth] did Q5
        32. watch] march Q2,3
42,   *7.* and] nor Q2,3
     12-13. make good chear] make cheere Q2,3
     26-27. in remembrance] in a remembrance Q2,3
        28. spinners] spinsters Q2,3
43,   *2.* *Amias*] *Amie* Q2,3

11. leape] come Q4,5
15. leape] come Q4,5
19. come] leap Q3
27. my loue, come] my come Q3
29. flower of *Northumberland*] flower *Northumberland* Q5

44,   *11.* thy] the Q4
20. faire] merry Q2,3
21. be a Lady] be Lady Q2,3
22. ouer] our Q3

45,   *9.* the prisoner] this prisoner Q2,3
20. *Northumberland?*] ∼. Q2-5

46,   *8.* chiefest] chieft Q3
11. Where] Whether Q2,3
19. on foote] a foote Q2,3
20. to] at Q5
24. *Northumberland?*] Q2-5; ∼. Q1

47,   *13.* And] All Q2,3
15. them] him Q2,3
22. to Lady] nor Lady Q3-5
27. also were] were also Q2-5
31. The life] Q2-5; the life Q1

48,   *8.* vpon] on Q2-5
16. into] in Q5
17-18. the body] her body Q5
24. pittilesse,] Q2,3,5; ∼∧ Q1,4

49,   *13.* opinion, thinking] opinion, in thinking Q2,3
15-16. to Uniuersities] to the Uniuersities Q2,3
37. whence] Q2-4; when Q1,5

50,   *5.* kisse,] ∼: Q1
14. Maidens] Maides Q2-5

Chapter IV

21. serued] deserued Q2,3
22. hand and foote] Q5; hand and feete Q1,4; hands and feete Q2,3
29. hoste] house Q2,3

51,   *14.* Washing] Gods ounds Q2-5
38. It is] Is it Q2-5   they:] Q1,2; ∼, Q3; ∼? Q4,5
40. *Will*] *William* Q2,3

52,   *12.* but I] Q2-5; I Q1
13. giue to] giue Q2-5

CHAPTER V

25. about] round about Q2-5
26. 15.] fifteene Q2-5
53,   *15.* third] Q2-5; 3. Q1
       17. man] Q2-5; then Q1
       27. This was] *not a new paragraph* Q2,3,5; *begins a new paragraph*
           Q1,4
       28. most famous] famous Q2,3
       30. Valentinian] *begins a new paragraph* Q5; *not a new paragraph*
           Q1-4
   30-31. also was] was also Q2,3
54,   *1.* eighth] Q2-5; eight Q1
       2. so wise and prudent an Emperour:] both a wise and prudent
          Emperour, Q5   yet was he] and yet Q4,5
       7. *Galerus*] *Gabienus* Q1,4,5; *Gabianus* Q2,3
   11-12. twenty two] 22. Q2,3
       14. Sextus] *Sixtus* Q2,3
       19. hung] held Q2,3
       20. is] was Q2,3
       23. somewhat] softly Q2,3
       24. the better] better Q5
       25. though newly] though then newly Q2,3
       27. king] Q2,3; prince Q1,4,5
       29. it] him Q2,3
       30. after] afterward Q2,3
       31. honoured] fauoured Q2,3
       33. his succession] succession Q5   vnto] vntill Q2,3
       36. Primislas] *Brimislas* Q4,5
55,   *3.* among] amongst Q2,3
       5. with a most] with most Q2,3
      *8. Primislas] *Brimislas* Q5   was then] then was Q4,5
       9. plough:] ~, Q2,3
      15. and companion] a companion Q3
      16. a Taylor] and Taylor Q3
       20. of] Q2-5; if Q1
       26. their] Q2,3,5; his Q1,4

CHAPTER VI

56,   7. warres our] warres which our Q2,3
       9. and also] as also Q2,3
      10. dealing] dealings Q2,3

393

12. that the money] Q2-5; that money Q1

13. scarcely] scantly Q2,3   and] an Q2

14. thought] sought Q2,3

15. away their] away many of their Q2,3

16. Spinners] Spinsters Q2,3

17. 50.] fifty Q2,3

20. an hungry] a hungry Q2,3

28. means] Q2-5; meane Q1

29. thereon] hereon Q2,3

57,   *4.* hate] hates Q4

11. excellency] excellence Q2,3

19. Court] Courts Q4,5

23. daily bee] bee daily Q2,3

28. and Weauers] and the Weauers Q2-5

35. vnto] to Q2,3

41. griefe] griefs Q2

58,   *1.* the best] my best Q2,3

*7. clothier] Q4,5; clothiers Q1-3

28. side of the sea] side the sea Q2,3

31. best not] not best Q2,3

33. purpose. Sometimes] ~: sometime Q2,3; ~. Sometime
        Q4,5

59,   *5.* It is . . . *Patch:*] Is it . . . *Patch?* Q2-5

11. leisure] leasury Q2

12. cary] beare Q2,3

23. and a lofty] and loftie Q4,5

31. should] would Q2,3

32. least it bred] lest it did breed Q2,3; lest it breed Q4,5

60,   *5.* before] afore Q2,3

*17. thereof] hereof Q2-5

18. in] within Q2,3

19. againe was] was againe Q2,3

CHAPTER VII

25. were] was Q2-5

29. Spinners] Spinsters Q2,3

61,   *18.* sigh, sob] sigh, or sob Q2-5

20. women] woman Q2-5

22. spoke] spake Q2-5

25. Mettressa] Mistresse Q2; Metressa Q3   loue a mee] loue
        mee Q4,5   by my fa] by me fa Q3

26. shall] sal Q3   nothing] noting Q2-5

27. de fin] de fin fin Q2-5   de turd] the turd Q2

394

28. shall] sal Q3
30. Mettressa] Metresse Q2,3
31. you are] you be Q2,3   not chafe] no chafe Q2-5   with|
    wid Q3   your] you Q2,3
33. care] cares Q2,5
35. not minded] minded not Q4,5
36. to] in Q2-5
40. Ahah] Ah ha Q2-5   is] bee Q5   hould] hole Q3

62,   1. holde] hole Q3   there is] dere is Q3   crowne] crowne s
           Q5
         4. them] dem Q3
       *5. box] pox Q2-5
        17. some of the water] some water Q5
        22. *Cea*] *Ces* Q5
        24. *Pontus*] *Fontus* Q3
        26. fond] found Q5
        28. hands] hand Q2,3
        33. that will] till hee Q5
        35. his language] his own language Q5

63,   1. reuenged of] reuenged on Q3
        8. hundreth] hundred Q2-5
        15. him] Q2,3; them Q1,4,5
        24. of precious] of most precious Q2,3
        35. which] that Q2,3
   35-36. harts affection] hearts ardent affection Q2,3

64,   6. may] can Q2,3
        8. are to bee] may be Q3
        15. minding] purposing Q2,3
        16. occupiers] traders Q4,5
        19. hee perceiuing that,] which hee perceiuing ∧ Q2,3
        26. began] she began Q5
        28. my] this Q2,3
        31. *Bucephalus*,] Q2,3; ~∧ Q1,4,5
        33. *Artemisia*] *Artemisa* Q2,3

65,   1. vertuous people] vertuous minded people Q2,3
        2. forgiue me my] forgiue my Q2-5
        4. was thus] thus was Q5
        5. like a Riuer] like vnto a Riuer Q2,3
        9. said] Q2-5; sad Q1
        15. the tong] thy tongue Q2,3
        21. Wife,] Q2,3; ~? Q1,4,5
        30. selfe ∧] Q2-5; ~, Q1
        33. you queane] thou queane Q2,3

66,   4. is?] ~. Q2,3,5

9. my] our Q2-5

10. like] like vnto Q2,3

19. that euening] the euening Q2-5

24. them] him Q2,3

28. therefore] wherefore Q2,3

30. much] very much Q2,3

32. my great] my very great Q2,3

32-33. I did at length win] I have at length won Q2,3

34-35. is fallen] so fallen Q4,5

35. cannot alter] cannot now alter Q2,3

67,   *1.* to her bed] Q2,3; to bed Q1,4,5

7. not] no Q3-5

8. clothes for a towsand pound] clodes for a towsan poun Q3

9. then my wife] den me veife Q3

19. fit] fits Q2,3

20. tis no such] its no sush Q2,3

21. will] well Q4,5   the darke] de darke Q3,5

22. entring in] entring in at Q3

24. shall] sall Q3   pound] poun Q3

25. beds side] bed side Q2,3

32. mee deare] my deare Q2-5

36. (why . . . hart?)] Q4,5; (~ ∧) Q1; Why . . . hart, Q2,3
    parentheses omitted

68,   *1.* Alabaster] Alablaster Q2,3

*3. fine] fiue Q2,3

4. was] wast Q2-5

14. sicke? Mistris] sick, be Got mistris Q2; shick, be Got metressa Q3

15. breath] breat Q2-5   *cacke] cake Q4,5

20. matter.] ~? Q4,5

21. Poh mee] God ound Q2; Got ound Q3; Poh met Q5
    the great] de great Q3-5

22. dee play] you play Q2,3   the knaue] de knafes Q3

23. reuenged on you] reuenge be Got Q2,3

24. loue] loued Q2,3

28. owleface,] ~ ∧ Q2,3

29. wife] veife Q2-5   not bee] no bee Q2,3   mee loue] my loue Q2,3

30. till] tell Q2,3   I shall make] be Goz bode, I make Q2,3

32. laught] laughing Q4,5

Chapter VIII

69,   *6.* morrow Gossip] morrow good Gossip Q2,3
          8. fa] fay Q5
          12. you sit] you to sit Q2,3
          13. indeede] in troth Q2,3
          17. fine] good Q2,3
          20. you Gossip] you good Gossip Q2,3
          22. heartily Gossip] heartily good Gossip Q2,3   hear you|
              good Q2,3
          26. truth] troth Q2,3
          28. yet] *omitted* Q3
70,   *1.* Gods blessing] Mary Gods blessing Q2,3
          6. you of] Q2-5; of you Q1
          17. an] one Q4
          20. you?] ~, Q3-5   Gossip.] ~? Q3-5
          36. not to feare] not fear Q4,5
          38. possible] possibly Q4,5
71,   *3.* that] this Q3
          7. our] out Q4,5
          33. 20.] twenty Q5
          36. housewife] huswife Q2-5   hath but] hath had but Q2-5
          37. should] would Q3
72,   *14.* driues] driue Q4,5
          15. beside∧ that,] ~, ~∧ Q3
          21. in manner] in a manner Q2,3,5
          27. another saith this] another this Q5
          34. crumme] crummes Q2,3
73,   *4.* of] for Q4,5   make] makes Q2,3
          8. is a sinne] is sinne Q2-5
          16. checkt thee,] ~? Q4,5   mee?] ~, Q4,5
          24. you] thee Q4,5
          25. so long as she] so as she Q5
          27. hath alwayes] alwayes hath Q4,5

Chapter IX

74,   *20.* neerer] neere Q4,5   by many] of many Q3
75,   *6.* hauing an] having on an Q4,5
          10. started] stared Q3
          28. breech] breeches Q5

76,   7. mine] my Q2-5
       9. was:] ~, Q5
       12. but I] but that I Q2,3
       15. did as much] did much Q4,5
       17. thinke being] thinke by being Q4,5
       30. thee] you Q4,5
       37. am] are Q2-5
77,   5-6. forgiue it him] forgive him Q4,5
       11. should] would Q4,5
       26. at what] what Q4,5

CHAPTER X

78,   6. tittle-tattle] ~, ~ Q3; ~_∧ ~ Q2,4,5
       21. he_∧)_∧] ~)? Q4; ~?) Q5
       33. gambon] gammon Q2-5
79,   1. dranke] drunke Q2,3
       8. in *Newberie*] in all *Newberie* Q2,3
      *10. Now assure you] Now I assure you Q4,5; Now by my troth
           Q2,3
       12. my] mine Q2,3
       15. Lamb] Lambs Q2-5
       18. an Asse] both an Asse Q2,3
       30. tis] its Q2,3
       32. hath forgot] hath quite forgot Q2,3
       34. shee.] ~? Q2-5
       36. tis] its Q2,3
80,   1. go to, go to] go too, go too Q2,3
       2. I am sure] I thanke God Q2,3
       4. se-reuerence] sir-reuerence Q2,3; ser-reverence Q5
       5. now she goes] she goes now Q5
       6. her?] ~: Q4; ~, Q5
       10. the glasse] her glasse Q5
     12-13. they consented] they all consented Q2,3
       19. the starting] his starting Q2,3
       21. now,] ~? Q4,5
       23. *Tweedle:*] ~, Q2-4; ~? Q5
       24. its] 'tis Q2,3; tis Q4,5
       25. surelie] in troth Q2,3
       27. Why?] ~_∧ Q2-5
       39. go] get Q2,3
       40. possible] possibly Q4,5

81,   *7.* Well,] Ifaith∧ Q2,3
      14. shee∧] ∼? Q3-5   spake] spoke Q2,3
      15. spake] spoke Q2,3
      16. laughing] laughter Q2,3
      28. mee,] ∼? Q2-5
      29. braines were] braine was Q2,3
  33-34. and to stick] and stick Q2,3

CHAPTER XI

82,   *2.* maydens] maides Q2,3
    6-7. surpassed] surpasse Q4,5
      24. saying] in this manner Q2,3
      30. ought to defend] ought much rather to defend Q2,3
83,   *1.* but] for Q2,3   trust mee∧] by heauen I sweare, Q2,3
     *2. abie] abide Q2-5
      5. The] This Q4,5
      7. And] But Q2,3
    9-10. many checkes] many bitter checks Q2,3
  10-11. shee opened] opened Q5
      14. quoth hee∧] quoth he! Q5
      19. and hope] and I hope Q2,3
      23. death hath bereft] death bereft Q4,5
      27. this is the] Q2-5; this the Q1
      28. xii.] twelue Q2,3,5
      36. dwels] dwelleth Q2,3
84,   *2.* said] answered Q2,3
      6. delay . . . is] delayes . . . are Q2,3
      18. wilt thou] will you Q2,3
    *32. *London,* because he] Q2,3; *London*∧ who Q1,4,5
      33. seruants∧ at that time:] Q2,3; ∼: ∼∧ Q1,4,5
85,   *7.* draue] droue Q2-5
      10. thus] then Q5
      31. *Rigley*] Q2,3,5; *Regly* Q1,4
86,   *10.* *Winchcombes*] *Winchcomb* Q2
      29. too good] to good Q2
      30. in making] to make Q2,3
      31. it no] it in no Q3
      34. comst] camest Q2,3
  35-36. what friend] what a friend Q4,5

Page 91,   *10.* leaue] learne Q2-4
            11. this Land] the Land Q2-4
            36. should] would Q2-4
       92, *19.* where] Q2-4; wherein Q1
            26. nor] and Q2-4

Chapter I

       93,   *1.* Chapter I.] *heading om.* Q1-4
            18. fainest] feignest Q2-4
            27. into] in Q2-4
            28. my] *om.* Q2-4
       94,   *2.* accept] accept it Q2-4
             3. No] Now Q2-4
            10. wearied] wearie Q2-4
            12. remoue] turne Q2-4
            23. farther] further Q3,4
            24. desire] desire it Q2-4
            26. but] *om.* Q2-4
            28. nothing] not Q2-4
            34. I] Q3,4; *om.* Q1,2
       95,   *1.* on] one Q2,3
            34. friends] freind Q4
           *35. Storke?] Mann; Stocke; Q1; Stocke: Q2; Stocke? Q3,4
           37f. him. What] Q2-4; ∼, ∼ Q1
       96,   *9.* off] of Q4

Chapter II

       97, *10.* reading in] Q2-4; reading on Q1
            19. rests] rest Q4
            37. in vaine] on vaine Q3,4
       98, *32.* bring] bringing Q3,4
       99,   *6.* wide] wilde Q2-4
             7. a melancholy man] melancholy men Q2-4
            14. vnto their] to their Q2-4
            26. sung] sang Q3,4
            33. fond] *om.* Q4

100,   *2.* lay] lye Q2
         15. And] Add Q2
         26. all speed] speed Q2-4
         30. well] Q2-4; will Q1
         31. fauours] fauor Q4

101,   *1.* ran] run Q2-4   as suspitious] so suspitious Q2-4
         8. scornfulnesse,] Lange; ~; Q1-4
         11. and to them] to them Q2-4
         14. breeds] Q2-4; breede Q1
         15. neither] never Q4
         31. danger] dangers Q4
         33. what] which Q3,4
         37. so long] long Q2-4

102,   *5.* and anon] anon Q2-4
         11. ouer] our Q3
         22. taken] token Q2-4
         27. driuen vpon] driuen by Q4
         29. ship] Q3,4; ships Q1,2
         32. that placed] Q2-4; were placed Q1
         37. in darke] Q2-3; the darke Q1
         37f. and so passing vp the country in darke night, in the end he
               lost his way,] *om.* Q4

103,   *1-2.* a great darke] the dark Q2-4
         6. all] *om.* Q4
         7. vp to] vp into Q4
         11. suffer me] sufferest thou me Q3,4
         15. wrought] brought Q3,4
         25. wrinkling] wringing Q2-4
         27. at what time] what time Q2-4
         30. blood,] Q2-4; ~: Q1

104,   *1.* the shedding] shedding Q2-4
         2. hearts blood] Q2-4; heart bloods Q1
         6. wandring] wandred Q2-4
         7. passages] Q2-4; passage Q1
         19. where] Q2-4; were Q1

Chapter III

105,   *1.* III] Q4; II Q1-3
         10. by the] Q3,4; by diuers the Q1,2
         11. of diuers woluish] Q3,4; of woluish Q1,2
         16. wrought] wrote Q4
         23. his affection] his affections Q4

26-27. *Carchaedonis*] *Charchaedonis* Q2-4
29. will they] they will Q4
106,   6. sung] sang Q3,4
107, *10.* Sig. C1 is missing in Q1; beginning with "of which kind-
        nesse" and ending with "miseries, and in-" (page 109,
        line 20) the copy text is Q2.
      33. throats,] Q3; ∼. Q2 [*This stanza omitted in Q4*]
108, 25. on] Q3,4; one Q2
109,   *1.* like two] like to Q4
      13. to heauen] for heauen Q3
      16. affection] affections Q4
      17. thee life] thee thy life Q4
      23. haue I] I haue Q4
      24. our loues] our selues Q4
      32. gall-dying] gall, a dying Q2-4
      38. and I] I Q3,4
110,   *1.* deemed] doomed Q2-4
       7. to his teeth] at his teeth Q2-4   as small] a small Q4
      12. sprung] sprang Q3,4
      17. sprung] sprang Q3,4
      18. bearest] barest Q2,3
      27. caused it] caused Q2
111,   *1.* ill-sauoring] Q2-4; insauoring Q1
       8. coales] Q2-4; cooles Q1
      12. Caudle] Q2-4; Candle Q1   any true] my true Q2-4
      13. Louer] Louers Q4
      22. potion] portion Q3,4
      26. him] Q2,4 (*sig. C3 missing in Q3*); me Q1
33-34. the dearest draught of drinke that euer man tasted of] *om.*
        Q2,4
112,   2. life] selfe Q2,4

CHAPTER IV

      18. backe,] Q4; ∼: Q1,2
27-28. in remembrance] to remembrance Q2,4
      28. the Legacie] his Legacy Q2,4
113,   5. of them receiued] receiued of them Q2,4
      13. bee] being Q2
      15. euer] *om.* Q4
      17. them] them to Q4
      27. carrieth] carried Q2,4

114,   *3.* Sig. C4 is missing in Q1; beginning with "My freinds" and ending with "swift time ouerslip" (page 116, line 15) the copy text is Q2.

        8. squared] Q3,4; sqared Q2

    12. despise] devise Q3,4

      27. shrowd] shrowded Q3,4

115,   *1.* the Sword] his Sword Q4

      2. play] a play Q3,4

      8. departed.] Q4; ∼∧ Q2 [*This section of leaf torn off in Q3*]

Chapter V

    21. possible] possibly Q3

    24. danger] dangers Q4

116,   *7.* seeing] seeing that Q4

    15. Tyrant is] Tyrants Q3

    16. sct] sets Q4

    18. whither] whether Q2,3

117,   *4.* make] makes Q3,4

    5. can] doth Q2-4

    17. gentle] louing and Q4

    22. come] comes Q4

    25. and then I] and then we Q4

    27. thy company, thy company,] thy company, &c. Q4

    28. adowne] dery Q4

    36. knocked] knocking Q4

118,   *6.* seruice] Q2-4; seruices Q1

    10. shoemaker] shoemakers Q2-4

    18. often] *om.* Q4

  31-32. the good man] good-man Q4

    32. at his] by his Q2-4   See] *om.* Q4

119,   *4.* the reason] reason Q4

    9. laid prisoner in *Rochester*] layd in prison in *Colchester* Q2-4

    19. would] should Q4

    33. the trade] their trade Q2-4

Chapter VI

120,   *24.* vnpossible] impossible Q3,4

    26. did by] did to Q2-4

121,   *1.* clothed in] clothed with Q4

    5. often be] be often Q2-4

    7. like vnto a flame] like a flame Q2-4

11-12. enter in communication] enter into communication Q2-4

    14. which] what Q3,4

    15. gently] greatly Q2-4

    16. found] had found Q2-4

26-27. how shee might breake out her mind at *Crispines* next com-
      ming,] *om.* Q2-4

    28. her tongue] the tongue Q2-4

    36. therewithall] therefore Q3,4

    40. as Sun-shine is] as Sun-shine Q2-4

122,   *6.* giuing] given Q4

    15. counted] accounted Q2-4

23-24. owne part] one part Q4

    28. that for] for Q2-4   delight haue] delight hath Q2,3;
      light hath Q4

    39. worthy] *om.* Q3,4

123,   *8.* goe not] Q2,3; goes not Q1; goe out Q4

    9. therewith] with it Q2-4

    10. will] would Q2-4

    12. aside, priuately] ~∧ ~, Q2-4

    19. not danger] no danger Q2-4

    20. if so] so Q2-4

    23. that if] but if Q2-4

124,   *10.* ashes] the ashes Q2-4

    17. wee may] wee Q2-4

    31. God] Good Q4

    39. in secret] secret Q2-4

125,   *13.* Masters] Master Q2-4

    17. should] would Q3; will Q4

    23. forlocke] Q2-4; foreclock Q1

    27. quoth he] quoth she Q3

126,   *2.* on] vpon Q3,4

    5. True] Truly Q2-4   as little] a little Q3

    6-7. can see] cannot see Q4

CHAPTER VII

    20. busie] busied Q2-4

    23. full] full of Q2-4

    24. the house] his house Q2-4

    25. hapned, and] hapned. And Q1-4

    26. bin. They] been, they Q1-4

127,   *3.* commendation] communication Q4

            7. most] much Q4

128,   *1.* be but] but be Q2

            4. were] are Q2-4   lewdly] Q2-4; lewly Q1

            6. thereof] therefore Q2-4

            17. insolent] insulting Q3,4

            20. vnsatiate] unsatiable Q4

            35. fortunes] fortune Q4

            37. alarum] a alarum Q4

129,   *5.* into] in Q2-4

            7. this answer] his answer Q4

            8. my secrets] by secrets Q4

            24. most] *om.* Q3,4

            28. him] *om.* Q4

            29. his Colours] Q4; that Colours Q1-3

            31. followers] fellowes Q3,4

            38. such] such a Q3,4   rescued] reserued Q3,4

130,   *12.* willing] willingly Q2-4

Chapter VIII

131,   *4.* grief] griefes Q2-4

            13. shoo-threed] shop threed Q3,4

            14. than liue] Q2-4; that liue Q1

            17. doe returne] returne Q2-4

            27. all her] her Q4

            31. speake] spake Q4

            37. Why what] Why, Why what Q3,4

132,   *8.* coming in] comming Q2-4

            9. these words] those words Q2-4

            10. These four] Sir, these foure Q2-4

            11. as I] and as I Q2-4

            16. did presume] presume Q2-4

            30. what a wanton] what wanton Q2-4   is it that] is that Q4

133,   *9.* should] would Q4

            13. would] should Q4

            24. lies yet] yet lies Q2-4

            32. mine owne] my owne Q2-4

            39. of fire] on fire Q2-4

134,   *1.* a supposed] the supposed Q4

            3. so that whilest] that whilest Q2-4

            7. closely bee] be closely Q2-4

            9. doubt] doubt it Q2-4

            13. better] a better Q2-4   for] so Q4

18. will] shall Q2-4

19. deuice] counsell Q2-4   and therefore] therefore Q2-4

27. Aruuagus] *Arugagus* Q4

30. said] saith Q4

31. hast, hast, and] hast, hast Q2-4

34-35. their Princesse] the Princesse Q2-4

135,   *5.* great] a great Q2-4

10. for *Crispine*] to *Crispine* Q2-4   *not to learn] Q1-4; not slow to learn   Lange

17. this was] there was Q2-4

23. neuer shall] shall neuer Q2-4   that terme] their terme Q2-4

26. this meanes] that meanes Q4

136,   *6.* most] *om.* Q3,4

7. daughter] daughter was Q3,4

CHAPTER IX

137,   *27.* euer afterward] euer after Q2-4

34. there was] there were Q2-4

138,   *10.* presently] present Q4

22. tryed with] tried aboue Q2-4   best] rest Q2-4

139,   *16.* nor] not Q3,4

CHAPTER X

27. the name] name Q2

28. descended of] descended from Q2-4

140,   *19.* treasurers] treasures Q4

21. her empty] an empty Q4

22. to a bad nut] Q2-4; to be a bad nut Q1

24. the shot] Q2-4; my shot Q1

27. will take] doe take Q2-4

29-30. a neere] neere Q3,4

141,   *11.* tell a me] tell mee Q4

142,   *1.* had indured] endured Q2-4

5. the City] this City Q4

8. haue very] haue a very Q2,3; gaue a very Q4   and to-morrow] tomorrow Q2-4

14. so soone] as soone Q4

15. this matter] that matter Q2-4

20. tell thee] tell you Q2-4

22. walking] walked Q2-4

406

25. he nothing] Q2-4; nothing Q1   still] *om.* Q2-4
28. come in] come Q2-4

143,   *18.* minds] mind Q2-4
23. shall] should Q4
27. a few backs] some backs Q2-4
29-30. whosoeuer that] that whosoeuer Q2-4
33. desire] the desire Q2-4

144,   *1.* womens] womans Q3
4. plucke] to plucke Q2-4
14. goe] *om.* Q4
29. thou shouldst] you should Q2-4
34. husbands] husband Q2-4
36. quoth she] Q2-4; quoth he Q1

145,   6. are necessary] shall be necessary Q2-4
**11.* smutched] Q2-4; smugged Q1
26. Merchants] Merchant Q2-4
35. which] the which Q2-4

146,   *3.* round] about Q2-4
10-11. word. And when you come there, tis not for you to vse many
words,] *om.* Q2-4
13. to him] him Q3,4

CHAPTER XI

147,   *3.* that he] he Q2-4
8. certified to] certified Q2-4
13. my Lady] the Lady Q2-4
21. that great] the great Q2-4
26. his calling] their calling Q2-4
29. thus] *om.* Q2-4

148,   *2.* neighbour] neighbours Q2-4
38. shee would] the would Q2,3; they would Q4
40. close by] closely by Q2-4

149,   *24.* thought] though Q4
27. she] he Q4
28-29. to this] till this Q2-4
29. she should] Q2; he should Q1; she would Q3,4
35-36. a guide] guide Q3,4

CHAPTER XII

150,   *3.* Masters] Mistres Q3,4

   13. fauour] fauours Q4

16-17. maid did much] Maids did most Q2-4

   25. you haue] haue you Q2-4

   28. into my] in my Q2-4

   31. budding . . . buddings] pudding . . . puddings Q2-4

151,   *2.* budden] pudden Q2-4

   5. come] *om.* Q2-4

   7. (quoth she.)] *om.* Q2-4

   8. What] (Quoth he) What Q2; What (quoth he) Q3,4

18-19. according to] according to his Q4

   32. and inconstant] Q2-4; an inconstant Q1

   37. thee so] thee Q2-4

152,   *9.* doe not know] know not Q2-4

   10. much] *om.* Q3,4

   20. is for] it is for Q2-4

   21. so abused] abused Q2-4

   25. in quiet] at quiet Q2,3; quiet Q4

   31. tell him] tell him that Q2-4

31-32. with me] me Q2-4

   32. in the fields] on the fields Q2-4

153,   *3.* As hee] And as he Q2-4   field] fields Q2-4

   10. home] whome Q4

   13. home] whom Q4

   27. *pur*] *put* Q2-4

   32. matra] matre Q3; matter Q4

   35. credit to] credit for Q2-4

   38. how] Q2-4; show Q1

154,   *2.* fires side] fire side Q2-4

   5. shewed] shewes Q2-4

   6. time for] time of Q2-4

CHAPTER XIII

   8. XIII] XIV Q2,3

   13. had rested] had resting Q2-4

   19. a studie] his studie Q2-4

   25. let vs] Q2-4; let as Q1

   29. in pride] with pride Q2-4

30. forget not] forget Q2-4
155, *15.* and to] and Q2-4
17. vnto] to Q4
27. whereto] whereunto Q4
30. it is an old Prouerb,] *om.* Q4
32. it is] is Q3,4   said] quoth Q2-4
34. thereto] thereunto Q2-4   *Arras] Q2-4; Orace Q1
37. shall stand charge] stand charged Q2-4
156, *17.* himselfe] herselfe Q2
18. doore] doores Q2-4
22. Goe to, goe to] Goe too, goe to Q1; Goe too, goe too Q2-4
24-25. her men] his men Q2-4
35. I would] would Q2-4
37. yeere] yeeres Q3,4
157, *12.* owne] *om.* Q3,4
13. stand to] stand to it Q2-4
21. Shriualtie] Shriualry Q2-4
34. shooe] shooes Q4
158, *14.* but three] three Q2-4
15. should wee doe] we doe Q3; do we Q4
17. vs alone] it alone Q2-4
20. price] prize Q3,4
23. faine] faigne Q2-4
35. heartily] *om.* Q2-4

Chapter XIV

159, *12.* XIV] XIII Q2,3
16. by that] at that Q2-4
25. very short] discontent Q2-4
160, *2. par ma] parmy* Q4
13. me fet] my fet Q4
19. Ah cet tokin] Ahcet toking Q2-4
26. parted] departed Q4
161, *6.* will I] I will Q2-4
26. Argos] Argoes Q2; *Argus* Q3,4
29. knockt] knocks Q4
30. Master or] Master and Q2-4
35. quoth she] quoth he Q4
162, *7.* on it] one it Q4
9. on that] one that Q4
13. in *London* could be bought] could be bought in *London* Q3,4
          [*In Q3 sig. I1 is at the end of the book, just before the last leaf, I4*]

409

17. shall vs] shall we Q2-4
35. She] the Q2
38. verily] *om.* Q4

163,   4. dare] dare not Q2
         8. needed] neede Q2-4
         9. to drinke] drinke Q2-4
        37. dealings were] Q2-4; dealing was Q1

164,   9. tell a mee] tell me Q4
    14-15. mind, Ile goe and marrie the Maide. *new par.* The French-
             man] *om.* Q4
        23. strange] stranger Q3,4
        29. get] got Q3,4   varietie] varieties Q2-4

165,   5. we goe] we ged Q2-4
        10. bottle] pottle Q2-4
    10-11. our faire] your faire Q2-4
        15. Seck] Sack Q4
        17. the time] Q2-4; that time Q1   this] that this Q4
        20. missing] missed Q4

166,   3. I should] I would Q2-4
         6. wifes] wives Q4
         9. with any] with some Q2-4
    14-15. shee were] she was Q2-4
        16. is it] it is Q2
        20. though] although Q2-4
        35. great] *om.* Q3,4
        38. seruants] Q2-4; seruant Q1

CHAPTER XV

167,   1. XV] Q4; XVI Q1-3
        11. chance] change Q4
        27. on all] one all Q4
        28. would] should Q2-4

168,   7. day performe] day fulfill Q2-4
         9. I shall] I will Q2-4
        10. lacke] want Q4
        12. Ile referre] I will referre Q2-4
        19. Whereupon] Hereupon Q2-4
        20. shut in] shut up Q2-4
        24. so that besides] Q2-4; so they beside Q1   Garden was
             beset] gardens were set Q2-4
        26. the Prentices] they Q4
        37. my Lord] the Lord Q2-4

169,   6. Market] Market place Q2-4

410

THE GENTLE CRAFT, PART II

Chapter I

Page 175,   *5-6.* a good] Lange; a good a 1639
             12. aboue] Mann; about 1639
     179,   *38.* pinchfistes] Lange; pinchfoistes 1639

Chapter II

     182,   *12. Graues-end*] Lange; *Graus-end* 1639
     184,   *5.* faces] Lange; aces 1639
          17-18. countenance] Lange; counteance 1639
             31. for] Lange; *om.* 1639
     187,   *13.* favour] Lange; faour 1639
     188,   *8.* quoth she∧] Lange; quoth she? 1639

Chapter III

     198,   **31.* Spread Eagle] Mann; Crane 1639
     202,   *32.* aboue] Mann; about 1639
     204,   *2.* matter] matt 1639
          15-16. up? *new par.* Truly] Lange; up, truly 1639
     207,   *26. Bullen] Bullio* 1639 [*i.e., Boulogne*]

Chapter V

     215,   *29.* cholerick] Lange; chflecick 1639
     216,   *15.* you wrong] Lange; your wong 1639
             38. that were] there well 1639; there were   Lange
     217,   *26.* sent them a silver] Folger; sent a 1639
     218,   *10.* on a iorney] in a iorney   Folger
             12. it. Captaine] Folger; ∼, ∼ 1639
             20. of] Folger; *om.* 1639
             21. Peachie∧ and his] Folger; Peachie, and by his 1639

411

CHAPTER VI

219,   *25.* wages] Folger; wager 1639   hand, have I?] Folger; hand.
              1639
220,   *4.* drink] drunke Folger
        5. *Crispianus*] Folger; *Chrispianus* 1639
        7. hollowing] Folger; hallowing 1639   whooping]
              whopping Folger
        9. whooping] whopping Folger
        15. that] Folger; they 1639
        18. to] Folger; with 1639
        19. where] Folger; whose 1639
221,   *15.* heere] Folger; *om.* 1639
        29. art thou] Folger; thou art 1639
        35. and] Folger; or 1639
222,   *5.* sent] set Folger
        6. to] Folger; for to 1639   on] Folger; of 1639
        28. Ile] Folger; I 1639
        30. meate,] Folger; meate ∧ and 1639
        31. still] Folger; *om.* 1639
223,   **19.* besmeared] to besmeared Folger; to smeared 1639
        *26. Towne-malin] Folger; the towne-Malin 1639
224,   *2.* sword] Folger; a sword 1639
        10. for] Folger; *om.* 1639
        14. our] Folger; *om.* 1639
        16. bodily] Folger; the bodily 1639
        19. for] Folger; *om.* 1639
        23. paire] Folger; a paire 1639
        24. longest, eight] longe, steight Folger
        28. Who] Folger; Whom 1639
225,   *2.* tis] Folger; it is 1639
        4. Puppie] Puple Folger
        36. My] Folger; *om.* 1639
226,   *2.* most] Folger; more 1639
        3. Bees∧ in *Sicilly*.] Bees∧ in *Sicilly*: Folger; Bees, in *Cicily* ∧ 1639
        4. much] Folger; *om.* 1639
        15. Ile] Folger; I 1639
        16. that kept] that that kept Folger
        22. This] Folger; Then 1639
        32. you] Folger; ye 1639   the gentle] Folger; this gentle
              1639
227,   **2.* sixe-score] Folger; sixteene score 1639

412

CHAPTER VII

23. Harry] Folger; *Henry* 1639
24. them] Folger; him 1639
27. Rainsford] Folger; *Ransford* 1639
28. inferiour] Folger; inferour 1639
228,   *11.* Widow] Folger; Widdw 1639
16. saying:] Folger; ∼? 1639
229,   *1.* turned to] Folger; turned into 1639
3. passers∧ by,] ∼, ∼∧ Folger
4. At the last] Folger; At last 1639
9. good Master, good Master] Folger; good Master 1639
17. man] Folger; men 1639
29. and let] Folger; let 1639
230,   *13.* wrapping] wrapped Folger
17. not] *om.* Folger
26. buried, the∧] buried∧ the, Folger
29. told to] Folger; told 1639
231,   *3.* grave] Folger; great 1639
11. sounded him] sounded in him Folger
13. whither] whether Folger
15. whither] whether Folger
17. whither] whether Folger
21. had] Folger; *om.* 1639
23. continuing] Folger; continually 1639
232,   *19.* had kild] Folger; should have kild 1639
35. gentle. Masters] ∼∧ masters Folger
233,   *7.* good] Folger; *om.* 1639
11-12. did *Peachy* like] Folger; *Peachy* liked 1639

CHAPTER VIII

234,   *5.* as famous] Folger; famous 1639
16. Hal] Folger; *Hall* 1639
23. Hal] Folger; *Hall* 1639
25. Maior] Folger; Major 1639
28. held in] heldin Folger; holden in 1639
235,   *4.* for] Folger; and 1639
7. mile] Folger; miles 1639
7-8. among themselves] Folger; *om.* 1639
8. should] *om.* Folger   upon] Folger; on 1639
9. the trickes] Folger; *om.* 1639   heard] should heard Folger

413

   12. evening] Folger; morning 1639

   24. on] Folger; upon 1639

   25. you] Folger; me 1639

236,   *1.* Me thinkes I should] Folger; I 1639

   2. kitchen drudge] kitching drudge Folger; kithen-drudge 1639

   7. her house] Folger; the house 1639

   13. set] Folger; is set 1639

   18. these] Folger; those 1639

   22. will] well Folger, 1639

  *32. withered] wethered Folger

237,   *26.* hold of] Folger; hold on 1639

   37. said] Folger; quoth 1639 her] Folger; *om.* 1639

238,   *15.* your] you Folger he] her Folger

   16. for] Folger; *om.* 1639

   19. me not] not me Folger

   20. and then] Folger; then 1639

   24. or] Folger; or to 1639

   34. her] he Folger

   35. paines] Folger; the paines 1639

239,   *2.* keepe] Folger; keepe you 1639

  *3. *Drum,*] ~ ∧ Folger, 1639 *Harry,*] ~ ∧ Folger, 1639

  *4. became] being Folger, 1639 and] *om.* Folger, 1639

    was] Folger; were 1639

   22. Flemming] flemming Folger; Felmming 1639

   24. *Farmer*] Folger; *Farmar* 1639

240,   *4.* that which] Folger; that 1639

   6. if] Folger; *om.* 1639

   9. Well, well] Folger; Well 1639

  22-23. *Muskelborough*] Folger; *Muskelbrough* 1639

   24. army:] Folger; ~ ∧ 1639 the Englishmen] Folger; Eng-
    lishmen 1639

   27. foureteene thousand] Folger; 14. Thousand 1639

CHAPTER IX

241,   *6.* faire] Folger; *om.* 1639

   11. insert] insort Folger

   29. *Swinborne*] *Sunborne* Folger, 1639

242,   *2.* *Swinborne* had] Folger; *Sunborne* hath 1639

   3. great] Folger; very great 1639

   10. all the] Folger; all 1639

246,   *23.* brunts. Night] Lange; brunts ∧ night 1639

   30. where] Lange; were 1639

248,   *28. Iohn]* Lange; *Richard* 1639
253,   *5.* he!] Lange; ∼? 1639
254,   *24.* his servants lighted] Lange; this servants lighed 1639
255,   *27.* amends,] Mann; ∼. 1639

CHAPTER X

256,   *8.* Fencing-schoole.] Lange; ∼∧ 1639
258,   *4.* friends] Lange; feiends 1639
259,   *38.* two-hand sworde] Lange; two hand-sworde 1639
261,   *12.* then] Lange; when 1639
         14. side] Lange; ∼, 1639
263,   *32.* wife.] Lange; ∼? 1639

Page 267,   *16.* through all] thorowout all Q3,4

                  18. was] were Q2-4

                  19. blesseth] blessed Q3,4

                  22. then] *om.* Q4

                  28. Exceter] Excester Q2-4

268,   *7-8.* Bazingstoke] Basingstoke Q4

                  9. Bosoms] Bosome Q2

                  12. one day] a day Q3,4

Chapter I

269,   *8.* second] elder Q4

                  10. against] amongst Q2-4

                  21. armes] armies Q2

                  23. on] *om.* Q2-4

               30. to other] to others Q2,3; of others Q4

                  33. all] *om.* Q2-4

270,   *1.* vp] as Q2,3; *om.* Q4

                  6. said hee] said, hee Q1,2; said, I Q3,4

                  11. Yea] Yes Q2-4

271,   *10.* you of] you Q2-4

Chapter II

                  14. all together] altogether Q2

                  25. that] this Q2-4

272,   *7.* that as] that Q3,4

                  14. way] long way Q2-4

                  15. being] being once Q2-4

                  17. trauelled] trauailed Q2,3

                  28. be so] Q2-4; so be Q1

                  31. too much] Q2-4; two much Q1

                  32. other] others Q2-4

                  38. sayings] saying Q4

273,   *4.* wily] willy Q2

                  5. are they] they are Q2-4

                  14. refraine] restraine Q2-4   visite] Q2-4; vsite Q1

                  18. will] shall Q2   inforceth] inforces Q4

23. These] The Q2-4
27. dealt] deale Q2,3

274, 22. a hundred] an hundred Q2-4
35. more of a] more a Q2-4

275, 7. he would ∧ oft] ∼: ∼ Q3; would he ∧ ∼ Q4
16. God] Q2-4; good Q1
18. so proper a] a proper Q2-4
20. such a] such an Q4
21. mislikes] mislike Q4
26. alike] like Q4
31. are my] om. Q3,4

276, 16. huswifery] huswifries Q2,3; huswifrie Q4
24. look to] Q4; look for Q1-3
29. Cutbert?] Q3,4; ∼. Q1,2

277, 15. Smithfield. His] Q2-4; Smithfield, his Q1   consort] con-
sorts Q2-4
24. fault:] ∼, Q1-4
25. fashion,] ∼: Q2; ∼? Q3,4
27. turne] turnes Q3,4
36. neede] needs Q3,4

278, 2. mee,] ∼: Q2-4
6. our] your Q2-4
8. brabling] babling Q2-4
10. me:] Q3,4; ∼, Q1,2
19. thee!] ∼? Q2-4
23-24. husband, in] Q2-4; ∼ ∧ ∼ Q1

CHAPTER III

279, 6. Gloucestershire] Gloustershire Q2
33. decke] deckes Q2

280, 1. meane estate] meanest state Q2-4
7. my fathers] fathers Q4
11. spoke] spoken Q3,4
23. maidens ∧] ∼? Q3,4
29. to liue] so liue Q2-4
30. saying, alas,] Q4; saying (alas) Q1; saying ∧ alas ∧ Q2,3

281, 1. possibly] possible Q2,3
12. I shall] shall I Q2-4
20. dwell] dwell together Q2-4

282, 28. What ∧ maiden!] ∼? ∼ ∧ Q3,4
33. maiden.] Q2; ∼ ∧ Q1; ∼? Q3,4
35. faire] Faire Q2-4

417

283,   *5.* me] her Q2-4
           25. harbour anger] harbour any Q2-3; forbeare any Q4
           34. maydes] maidens Q2-4

CHAPTER IV

284,   *22.* speciall] especial Q4
           28. wealth] weal Q4
285,   *17.* other] others Q2-4   do take] Q2-4; to take Q1
      26-27. priuiledge, that] ∼, That Q2,3; ∼. That Q4
           27. whosoeuer] whatsoeuer Q2-4
           37. shall men] shall all men Q4
286,   *5.* this griefe] your griefe Q4
           17. hangde vp by] hanged by Q2-4
           20. made] Mann; make Q1-4
           28. haue I] I haue Q3,4
           31. word] words Q3,4
           34. highnesse] Highnesses Q3,4
           35. toward] towards Q3,4   sayd] *om.* Q3

CHAPTER V

287,   *3.* *Richard*] *Robert* Q3,4
           6. minde] mood Q4
288,   *14.* to be] Q2-4; be to Q1
           25. your] to Q2-4
           29. she!] ∼? Q4
           33. him ∧ tis] him: t'is Q2; him: it is Q3,4
289,   *7.* notes] note Q4
           11. prou'd] proue Q2-4
           17. hee,] the ∧ Q4
           28. troth] truth Q2-4
           36. brawle] braule Q2
290,   *1-2.* alone, and] alone, to Q2-4
           19. as see] as to see Q3,4
           22. the more] more Q2
           25. will not] will Q3,4
           26. such] sure Q4
           29. are] are all Q4
           30. more] meere Q2-4
           31. to you] Q2-4; o you Q1
           32. more] meere Q2-4

291,   7. gooddy] goodly Q2-4
        10. gag-toothd] gag-tooth Q2-4
        17. sayd] *om.* Q4
        33. the passion] passion Q3,4
292,   7. looke for] looke Q1-4
        21. so taken] taken Q4
    26-27. broath. *new par.* Or] broath, or Q1,2; ~: ~ Q3,4
        27. hostesse,] Q3,4; ~: Q1,2
293,   7. into] in Q4
     9-10. him released] his released Q2; him release Q3,4
        16. to fast] fast Q4

Chapter VI

294,   8. *Simons*] Mann; *Suttons* Q1-4
        14. lieu] lien Q2,3
        24. great] so great Q2-4
295,   1. *Weasell*] Q4; *Wessell* Q1; *Welsell* Q2,3
         4. rested] resting Q2
         7. *Crabbe*] Mann; *Cracke* Q1-4
        22. shined of] shined with Q2-4
        27. went] came Q2-4
    33-34. was afterwards] afterwards was Q4
    37-38. North-west side] North-side Q2-4
296,   3. laine] lien Q2; lyen Q3,4
         7. money] the money Q2-4
       *15. the other] Q2-4; thother Q1
        17. take it] take Q2,3; take me Q4
        34. *Crabbe*] Q4; *Cutbert* Q1-3
        35. wagers] wages Q4
297,   2. ye] you Q3,4
         6. along] long Q2
        10. weauer.] ~? Q1,2; ~: Q3,4
        11. shal] should Q2-4
        13. prophesying] Q2-4; prophesing Q1
        16. a King] the King Q2-4
        20. that is] is Q2,3
298,   2. Shal] Sall Q3,4
         3. When] Where Q4
         4. grow;] Q3,4; ~? Q1,2
         9. there] they Q2-4
        11. of nature] and nature Q2-4
        13. say,] Q2-4; ~. Q1

419

26. betide.] Q3,4; be tide ∧ Q1,2
27. from an] from Q3,4

299,   7. will] shall Q2-4
   11. Why] What Q4
   19. thee] Q2-4; the Q1

300,   *10.* sung] sing Q3,4
   18. wasters] masters Q2-4
   20. enough] Q2-4; inough Q1   books] booke Q2-4
   23. home-spun] hemp-spun Q2-4
   30. husbands are] husbands be Q2-4
   33. Oyster-wiues] Oyster-wines Q2

301,   *4.* repaires] Q2-4; repaires of Q1
   30. fright] Q4; flight Q1-3
   36. lift] left Q3

302,   *5.* as much to mee] to me as much Q2-4
   9. dearly] heartily Q3,4
   10. me!] ∼? Q3,4
   36. were bought] was bought Q2-4
   39. it was] it were Q2-4

303,   *1.* thereof] hereof Q4

CHAPTER VII

   16. alwayes] *om.* Q2-4   thereof] of Q4

304,   *1.* abode,] ∼; Q2,3
   3. There] Q2-4; Where Q1
   7. much] such Q2,3
   9. bore to] bore Q3,4
   23. West-countrie] Q4; west countries Q1-3
   33. euer was] was euer Q2-4

305,   *3.* Salisbury] Q2-4; Shaftesburie Q1
   18. represented] presented Q2-4
   20. Augustus] Augusta Q4
   21. latter] later Q2-4
  31-32. the ancient] that ancient Q3,4
   32. Rithin] Kithin Q2
   37. the white] her white Q2-4
   38. that amorous] the amorous Q2-4

306,   *13.* stone.] Q2-4; ∼, Q1
   27. all his] his Q2-4

CHAPTER VIII

307,   *19.* did] *om.* Q3,4
        20. refraine] restraine Q3
        31. all to] all into Q2,3
308,   *10.* How_∧] How? Q2-4   you] ye Q2,3
        21. so departed a] so departed Q2,3; departed a Q4
        24. tidings] things Q3,4
        31. his] this Q4
        36. all] *om.* Q3,4
        37. there with] therewith Q2-4
309,   *2.* with which] at which Q4
        3. come] *om.* Q4
        8. those] them Q4
        20. readie] Q2-4; readiest Q1
        27. vp men] men vp Q2-4
        28. stealing] stealing of Q3,4
        33. cast] hurl'd Q2-4
        37. plack] packe Q2-4
310,   *2.* on you_∧] vpon you, Q3,4
        30. to commend] commend Q2-4
        40. would performe] could performe Q4
311,   *7.* our King] the King Q2-4

CHAPTER IX

        23. this time] that time Q2-4
        25. name of] name Q2
        30. officers] offices Q2
312,   *3.* he should] they should Q4
        23. *Tom*] *Thomas* Q2-4
        26. do] *om.* Q3,4
        28. felld] fell Q2,3
        29. he left] left Q4
        32. come] turne Q2-4
        37. arrested] arrests Q4
        39. chance] mischance Q2-4
313,   *5.* vnto] with Q3,4
        7. a mighty] mighty Q3,4
        8. high] big Q4
        13. twere] it were Q2-4

421

16. magget a pie] maggat-a-pie Q2; maggat-apie Q3,4
21. so sone] soone Q2; as soon Q3,4
26. to doe] adoe Q3; a doe Q4
27. fillippe] fillop Q2,3; fillip Q4
28. felld] fell Q2,3

CHAPTER X

314,   *7.* loued] beloued Q2-4   gallant] gallant and worthy Q2-4
            two] two most Q2-4
      11. she had] she had also Q2-4
      12. bore] did carry Q2-4
      14. kindle] re-inkindle Q2-4
      18. where] when Q2-4
      20. notable] noble Q4
      32. iudiciall Q2-4; iudicical Q1

315,   *1.* seeme] seemed Q4
       2. deeme] Q4; deemed Q1-3
       6. from me] Q4; me from Q1-3
      11. keepers] Q4; keeper Q1-3
      20. gest] guest Q2-4
      23. then a] then Q2,3
      27. Lady] a Lady Q2-4
      28. then] Q2-4; them Q1
      29. desired] desireth Q2-4
      33. should make] could make Q2-4
      34. is it] it is Q2-4

316,   *8.* it in] it Q3,4
      14. life] selfe Q4
      20. shall I] shall Q3,4

317,   *7.* keepers] Mann; brothers Q1-4
      23. diddest] didst but Q2-4
      26. dareth] dare Q4
      36. may] can Q2-4
      37. her say so] on her so Q2,3

318,   *6.* pardon my] pardon me my Q3,4
      11. she] hee Q4
      21. (my nose!)] *no paren.* Q2-4
      28. commended or] commended and Q2-4
      38. beare] heare Q2,3

319,   *9-10.* can you not] cannot you Q2-4
      19. swans] swane Q2
      24. his impediment] this impediment Q4

320,   *3-4.* in any] in a Q3,4
         7. asked him] asked Q4

CHAPTER XI

         26. and how] Q2-4; how Q1
         30. hostesse] his hostesse Q4
         31. their ghests] the guests Q2-4
321,   *7.* man] *om.* Q4
         10. better] the better Q3
         11. best] *om.* Q4
         13. whereof] thereof Q4
         22. the slaughter] slaughter Q4
         24. would] will Q3,4
         30. tooke] take Q2-4
         39. took∧] Q2-4; ~: Q1
322,   *2.* him to] him by Q2-4
          9. a long time] *om.* Q3,4
         12. that∧] Q2-4; ~: Q1
         21. had he] he had Q3,4
323,   *2.* there was] there is Q2-4
          4. so heauy] heauy Q2-4
          5. neere vnto] neere to Q4
         12. *Thomas*] *Tom* Q2-4
         17. had neede] hath neede Q4
         22. shewne] she wine Q4
         34. to writing] in writing Q2-4
         35. *Amen,*] Q2; ~∧ Q1; ~: Q3,4
324,   *3.* my hoast] hoast Q2-4
         20. so satisfied] satisfied Q3,4
         24. teares] feares Q2-4
326,   *2.* then] *om.* Q4
          9. hid] made Q3,4
         10. things as] things at Q2
         13. trussed] trusted Q2
         16. stout] Q2-4; stond Q1
         24. borne] bore Q2-4
         29. last] the last Q3,4
327,   *5.* be become] become Q4
         12. all the men] Q2-4; all man Q1   surely] sure Q2-4
      26-27. should euer] should Q4
         31. neuer after] Q3,4; after neuer Q1,2

CHAPTER XII

328,   *3.* meriments] meriment Q2-4
    6. Simons] Q2-4; *Suttons* Q1
    7. other] others Q2-4
329,   *11.* aske of] aske Q3,4
    17. goeth] goes Q2-4
    20. serued in] serued it Q2-4
    28. it was] it is Q4
    37. as if] as Q2-4

CHAPTER XIII

330,   *23.* away] quite away Q2-4   fully] absolutely Q2-4
    24. his letter] this letter Q3,4
331,   **7.* Bactria] Q2-4; Bractria Q1
    10. art] are Q3
    17-18. to clime] Q2-4; no clime Q1
    32. at that] Q1BM, Q2-4; atthat is Q1HN
    34. all on] Q1BM, Q2,3; all in Q1HN, Q4
332,   *7.* hadst] Q1BM, Q2-4; had Q1HN
    22. to be any more] any more to be Q4
    33. thou not] not thou Q4
333,   *28.* wroth] Q2-4; wrath Q1
    29. he kept] be kept Q2-4
    31. in louing] of louing Q3,4
334,   *12.* recall] to recall Q2-4
    17. home with] home in Q3,4
    31. you do] Q1BM, Q3,4; you to do Q1HN
    31-32. that only] Q4; that not only Q1-3
    36. thy liberty] thee liberty Q4
335,   *19.* with my life] Q2-4; to my selfe Q1
    25. riches] to riches Q4
    33. euer] Q2-4; neuer Q1   bid it] bid thee Q3,4
    36. pleased] please Q3
336,   *7.* loues] Louers Q4
    8. my eies] mine eies Q2-4
    12. faire] *om.* Q3,4
    13-14. to comfort] Q1BM, Q2-4; the comfort Q1HN

CHAPTER XIV

337,
6. this world] the world Q3,4
13. no man] not a man Q4
15. old] former Q3,4
*20. the other] Q1BM, Q2-4; thother Q1HN
24. abuse] abused Q4
29. to them] for them Q3,4
30. benefits] benefit Q4

338,
11. estate] state Q2,3
14. find in] find Q3
27. partes] part Q3,4
33. and it is] and is Q2,3
34. vs∧] Q2-4; ∼, Q1

339,
1. so soone] as soone Q2-4
7. on my] of my Q3,4
20. as good] Q1BM, Q2-4; a good Q1HN
22. said] Q1BM, Q2-4; quoth Q1HN   almighties] Amighties Q2
24. said] Q1BM, Q2-4; saith Q1HN
26. best] better Q2-4
27. and there] Q1BM, Q2-4; there Q1HN
32. saieth] said Q2-4

340,
1. strucken] strucke Q4
7. booteth] boote Q3,4
10. sent her] sent Q3,4

CHAPTER XV

341,
21. knew] know Q2-4
32. knoweth] knowes Q2-4

342,
6. most] my most Q2-4
7. world:] Q3,4; ∼? Q1,2
19. behind her] behind Q2-4   in maner] in the manner Q4
21. bracelets of] Mann; bracelets or Q1-4
30. maidens] Maides Q4

343,
25. euer was] was euer Q3,4
32. Byram] *Briam* Q2,3; *Brian* Q4
36. incourage] ingage Q3,4

INDEX [1]

char. = character(s)
GCI = The Gentle Craft, Part I
GCII = The Gentle Craft, Part II
JN = Jack of Newbury (and *1619 JN* = the 1619 edition of *Jack of Newbury*)
note on 376 = There is a note, on the item being indexed, on page 376 in the Explanatory Notes.
xxv *n.* = There is a footnote, on the item being indexed, at the bottom of page xxv in the Introduction.
SR = Stationers' Register
TD = Thomas Deloney
TR = Thomas of Reading

Abbey, Westminster, choir of, 208
Abbey of Grace: on Tower Hill, 163, *note on* 368; had privilege of sanctuary, 165
abie, *pay for*, 83, *note on* 359
Abiston, a stone 'whose fire can neuer be cooled,' 316
Abridges, John, char. in *GCII*, 216, 217, *note on* 375
accent, foreign: Benedick's Italian accent, 61-68; John Denevale's French accent, 141, 150-154, 159-166. *See* dialect
Acteon, a hunter in Greek mythology, 11, *note on* 351
Adam, 'our old father,' 96
Aesop, his dog in the manger, 32
affected, *aspired to*, 176; *disposed (in love)*, 194

Agathocles (361-289 B.C.), tyrant of Syracuse, self-styled king of Sicily, son of a potter, 53
Agilmand, King, saves Lamusius' life, 54
Agnes, Countess of Mansfield, wife of the Archbishop of Cologne, xxiv
Ajax, Long Meg's master pays tribute to him in *GCII*, 191, *note on* 373
Albouina, King of Lombardy, 'when all came to ruine,' 54
Alchemist, The. See Jonson
aldermen, of London. *See* London
Aldersgate. *See* London
Aldrich, Charles, and Lucian Swift Kirtland, eds. in 1903 of *TR*, 381
ale: 6, 18, 28, 29, 39, 69, 168, 220, 231, 299, 329; 'rise like a Tun of new Ale,' 212. *See also* beer, wine

---

[1] Information about Deloney's London printers and booksellers is from the following: R. B. McKerrow *et al.*, *A Dictionary of Printers and Booksellers . . . 1557-1640* (London, 1910); Henry R. Plomer, *A Dictionary of the Booksellers and Printers . . . 1641-1667* (London, 1907) and *A Dictionary of the Printers and Booksellers . . . 1668-1725* (Oxford, 1922). If a Deloney proverb or saying is listed in Morris Palmer Tilley's *A Dictionary of the Proverbs in England in the Sixteenth and Seventeenth Centuries* (Ann Arbor, 1950), Tilley's designation (such as A172) is given in parentheses after the proverb; if listed in Warren E. Roberts' "Folklore in the Novels of Thomas Deloney" (*Studies in Folklore*, Bloomington, Ind., 1957), Roberts' name is given in parentheses. Miscellaneous information about Elizabethan London place names is mainly from Edward H. Sugden, *A Topographical Dictionary to the Works of Shakespeare and His Fellow Dramatists* (Manchester, 1925).

Alesbury, Buckinghamshire, xiv, 26

Alexander the Great, Iphicrates is accused of being like, 128

Allde, Elizabeth: bookseller in London, 1628-40; printer of *1632 TR*, 380

All's Well that Ends Well, two references to Drum, 370

amate, *daunt, dishearten*, 209

anachronism, regarding Thomas à Becket, 385

Andrews, J[ohn], bookseller at the White Lion near Pie Corner, 1654-63. *See 1660 GCII*, 370

angel, *gold coin*, 179, *note on* 371

animals: 'tonguelesse like a Storke,' 'as blind as a Flie in October,' etc., 95-96; lions, bears, bulls, elephant, dragon in Sicily, 103, 104; virtue found in the brains of a weasel, the tongue of a frog, 113; love among the, 122; lion, bull, dragon, more grateful than men, 338

answerable to, *in proportion to*, 156; answering of, *answering for, responsibility for*, 156

Anthony-now-now, a fiddler in *GCII*, 174, 257-264, *note on* 371

Apium Risus, to eat of it 'causeth a man to die laughing,' 334

Apostles, twelve silver, *silver spoons*, 236, *note on* 376

apprentices, breakfast given by Mayor of London to, on Shrove Tuesday, 167-169. *See also* shoemaking

Arabia, 63

Arcadia, 62, 225, 226, *note on* 357

Arcadia. See Sidney

Argus, the mythological herdsman with eyes all over his body, 161

Armin, Robert, ballad writer, xxvii

armor. *See* weapons

Arras, France, 155, *note on* 368

arrows. *See* weapons

Artaxerxes, King of Persia, son of a cobbler, 53

Artemis (Diana), the story of Acteon, 351

Artemisia, a heathen lady who drank her husband's ashes, 64

artificially, *with art or skill*, 54, *note on* 357

Artois, France, where tapestry fabric made, 368

Aruvagus Castle. *See* Dover

Ashley, Robert, and Edwin M. Moseley, eds. in 1953 of *JN*, 350

Aspis (*asp*), an adder that 'tickleth a man to death,' 337

As You Like It, sources of, xii

Augustus. *See* Exeter

Austria, for ambling horses, 331

B., H.: ? the same 'H. B.' who printed *Rome's Thunder Bolt* in 1682 for J. Conyers; printer of *1684 JN*, 349

Babington, Anthony, of Babington conspiracy, xxvi

Back, J[ohn]: bookseller, 1682-1703, at the Black Boy on London Bridge; seller of *1696 GCI*, 364

Bactria, *an ancient country, now part of Afghanistan*, 331, *note on* 385

baies (bayes), *bay leaves*, 48, 64

bailiffs, of London. *See* London

Baker, E. A., *The History of the English Novel* (1924-39): TD's use of dialect and malapropism, xiv; TD's characterization, xxiii

Balaam's ass, a talking animal, 329

ballads: *Strange Histories*, collection of TD ballads, xxi, xxvii; printing of TD ballads, xxv; as newspaper of time, xxv-xxvi; have historical subjects, xxvi; *The Garland of Good Will*, collection of TD ballads, xxvi; ballad on scarcity of grain troubles authorities, xxviii; 'even as common as a printed Ballad,' 262

—Deloney ballads by title or subject: on money, 6-8; on jealousy, 11; describing cloth-making, 26-28; 'The Weauers Song,' 40-42; 'To all the good Yeomen of the Gentle Craft,' 91; 'The Curtizans Song of Venice,' 99-100; on Winifred, 106; on the Gentle Craft, 107-108; of St. Hugh's bones, 114; shoemakers' song on love, 116-117; on marriage, 127; 'The Shoomakers Song on Crispianus night,' 137-139; of green willow, 206; 'The Song of the winning of *Bullen* sung before the King by round *Robin* and his fellowes,' 209-211; song on flowers, 220; Anthony-now-now's song for the Green King, 258;

song by women for Tom Dove, 273-
274; of Jenny, 281; country jig, 289;
weaver's prophecy, 297-299
—Deloney ballads mentioned: 'Salomons good housewife in the 31 of
his Proverbes,' xx; 'Lamentation of
Beckles,' xxv; 'The Winning of
Cales,' xxvi *n.;* 'The faire Lady
Rosamond,' xxvi; 'Shores Wife,'
xxvi; 'A proper new Ballad breefely
declaring the Death and Execution
of fourteen most wicked Traitors,'
xxvi; 'The Lamentation of Mr. Pages
Wife,' xxvi, 374
—Deloney ballads and traditional ballads by first lines: 'A maiden faire
I dare not wed,' 11; 'Among the
ioyes on earth, though little ioy
there bee,' 127; 'In the moneth of
October,' 209-211; 'It was a Knight
in *Scotland* borne,' 43-47; 'King
Iamie had made a vowe,' 33-34;
'Long haue I lou'd this bonny
Lasse,' 289; 'My freinds, I pray you
list to me,' 114; 'My Masters I thank
you, its time to pack home,' 6-7;
'Of Craft and Crafts-men more and
lesse,' 107-108; 'O *Ienny* my ioy, I
die for thy loue,' 281; 'The day is
very neere at hand,' 297-299; 'The
pride of Britaine is my hearts delight,' 106; 'The Primrose in the
greene Forrest,' 220; 'Two Princely
brethren once there was,' 137-139;
'Welcome to towne, Tom Doue,
Tom Doue,' 273-274; 'Welcome to
Venice, gentle courteous Knight,' 99-
100; 'When fancie first fram'd our
likings in love,' 206; 'When *Hercules* did vse to spin,' 40-42; 'When
should a man shew himselfe gentle
and kinde,' 258; 'Within one roome
being large and long,' 26-28; 'Would
God that it were holiday,' 116-117;
'You that the Gentle Craft professe,
list to my words both more and
lesse,' 91
—Other ballads mentioned: 'The beginning of the World,' 14, *note on*
351; 'A new love Sonnet,' 368; 'How
a Shoomakers widdow fell in love
with her man,' 368; 'The madd

merye pranckes of Long Megg of
Westminster,' 371; 'A Ballad of
longe Meg of Westminster,' 371;
by William Birch on Strangwidge,
374
—Traditional ballads: 'The Song,' 33-
34, *note on* 354; 'The Maidens Song,'
43-47, *note on* 356
Ballantyne, J., publisher in 1812 of
TR, xviii *n.,* 381
Ballard, John, of Babington conspiracy, xxvi
balls, 'firie-balls.' *See* weapons
Baltazar, Master, a comfetmaker, *GCII,*
254, *note on* 377
band, *bond,* 261, 264
banket, *banquet,* 192
Barber, John, cousin to Mistress Eyre
in *GCI,* 145, 146
barbers: work described, 145; all are
neat and fine, 146; barber-surgeon,
254; mentioned, 51, 255
Barkeshire (Berkshire): mentioned, 31;
visit of Henry VIII to, 35. *See also*
Englefield, Sir Henry; Greenham;
Hungerford; Newbury; Reading;
Spinhome-land; Wallingford
Barnstable, Devonshire, xxvi
Bartholomew Fair. See Jonson
Bartholomew's Day, fair on, 13, *note
on* 351
basilisks, whose poisoned breath kills
from afar, 32
Batman, Stephen, *The Doom* (1581):
TD's source for the Scolopendra,
353; for Cynomolgy, 354; a compendium TD uses, 356
bawby, *bawbee, a Scottish silver coin,*
309, *note on* 384
bayard, 'bury blind bayard,' 230, *note
on* 376
bayes. *See* baies
Bazingstoke (Basingstoke), Hampshire,
268
beacons, on the seacoast of England,
133
bears, in Sicily, 103
Becket, Thomas à, his house in West
Cheap, 322, *note on* 385
Beckles (Beccles), Suffolk, xxv
beef, salting, 78, *note on* 359
beer: 28, 29, 212, 220, 257; 'voyding

beere,' 243; brewing, 321. *See also* ale, wine

Bègue, Lambert, founder of Beguine religious order, 366

beguiled, *cheated*, 241

Belloc, Hilaire, his *Wolsey* (1930), on Patch's loyalty to Wolsey, 357

Benedick, Master, an Italian merchant in *JN*, 61-68, 365

Berkshire. *See* Barkeshire

beshroe, *beshrew, a light oath*, 69, 183, 197, 224

Besse, a servant in *GCI*, 162

best, 'you were best blab it,' 195

betimes, *early*, 262

betrice, *Beatrice, brazen woman*, 186, *note on* 372

bewray, *reveal*, 164, 175, 178

Bible, Scripture quoted, xxi, 167

biefe, poudred, *powdered beef*, 78, 181, 291, *note on*, 359

biggins, *caps worn by children*, 131, *note on* 366

bil (bill) of hand, *I O U*, 76, 145

billiment, *head band*, 28, *note on* 353

Billingsgate. *See* London

Birch, William, ballad on Strangwidge, 374

Birchin Lane. *See* London

Bird, Robert, bookseller, 1621-38, at the Bible in St. Lawrence Lane, Cheapside. *See 1637* and *1640 GCI*, 363; *1632* and *1636 TR*, 380

Bishops downe (Bishopstone), a village near Salisbury, 298, *note on* 384

Bishopsgate. *See* London

Blackie, publisher in 1920 of *JN* and *TR*, 350, 381

Black Swan, name of a Greek ship, 148, 149; also name of Simon Eyre's shop in London, 159

Blackwall. *See* London

Blackwell (Bakewell) Hall. *See* London

blanke, *pale*, 327

Blare, J[osiah], or J[oseph]: bookseller, 1683-1706, at the Looking Glass on London Bridge; seller of *1696 GCI*, 364

Blore (or Blower), Ralph: printer and bookseller, 1595-1618, near the Middle Temple Gate, Fleet St.; enters *GCI* in SR (19 October 1597), 361

Boccaccio, Giovanni, *Decameron*, possible source for *JN* incident, 352

bodkin, 61

Bodleian Library: owner of copies of *1630* and *1672 JN*, 348-349; of *1652*, *1672*, and *1696 GCI*, 364; and of *1632* and *1672 TR*, 380

Boetia (Boeotia), in ancient Greece, where the water extinguishes affection, 62, *note on* 357

Bond, R. Warwick, ed. Lyly, on 'Mother Bumby,' 365

Boorde, Andrew, *Dyetary of Helth* (1542): recommends a caudle, 353; on powdered beef, 359; a posset for tertian fever, 371

borderers, 285, *note on* 383

Bosom, Old, char. in *TR*, xix, 275-278

Bosom's Inn, Cheapside, London, 268, 275, 288-293, *note on* 381-382

Bosom's wife (Winifred), char. in *TR*, 275-278

Boston Athenaeum, owner of copy of *1632 TR*, 380

bottle, *bundle*, 199, *note on* 374

Bouillon, Godfrey of, captured Jerusalem in 1099, 382

Boulogne, France. *See* Bullen

Bowers, Fredson, his edition of Dekker's dramatic works, xxx-xxxi

box, 62, *note on* 357

brabbles, *quarrels*, 278, 288; brabling, *quarreling*, 176, 278, 291

braided wares, *goods that have faded or become tarnished*, 197

Brainford (Brentford), Middlesex, a town 8 miles W. of London, 263, *note on* 377

brake their fast, *breakfasted*, 263

Bramstone-green, place where James of Scotland was slain at Flodden Field, 34

bravery, *fine dress*, 64, 98, *note on* 357

brawn, *pickled flesh of a pig*, 127, 328, *note on* 366

bread, brown, 72, *note on* 358. *See also* manchet

Bread Street Corner, image of, 223, *note on* 375

Bread Street Hill, where *1619 JN* was sold, 348

Brentford. *See* Brainford

Breuiary of Britayne, The. See Llwyd

Brewster, E[dward], bookseller, 1621-47. *See 1627 GCI*, 362

bride cakes, 29

bride cup, 29

bride laces, 29, *note on* 353

Bridewell, London, 'to make you a bird of Bridewell for your sauciness,' 251, *note on* 377

brisk (in apparel), 14, *note on* 351

Bristol University Library, owner of copy of *1632 TR*, 380

Bristow (Bristol), England, 264

British Museum, owner of copies of *1633, 1680?,* and *1700? JN*, 349-350; of *1637, 1640, 1648, 1675?, 1678, 1680?* and *1690 GCI*, 363-364; of *1639 GCII*, 370; of *1612* and *1632 TR*, 380

Britwell Court, library of, Buckinghamshire, former owner of only extant copy of *1619 JN*, 345

broach, *stick, pierce,* 192, 264; broaches, *spits,* 28, *note on* 353

broad cloathes, *broadcloth,* 28, 29, 39, 304, *note on* 353

broch. *See* broach

broke with, *revealed (his plan) to,* 124

Brooksby, P[hilip], bookseller, 1672-96, next to the Ball, West Smithfield, etc.; seller of *1696 GCI,* 364

broom, *selling it is the lowest of occupations,* 40, *note on* 355

brothel. *See* flesh shambles

Bruce, Robert, Holinshed on his having horses 'shodde backwarde,' 384

Bucephalus, steed of Alexander the Great, 64

buckes, wash, *buckwash,* 74, *note on* 358; bucke, 'a great bucke that is to be washt,' 199

Buckinghamshire, mentioned, 30. *See also* Alesbury, Stony Stratford

buckler, *a shield worn on the arm. See* weapons

budget, *purse, bag,* 234

Bullen (Boulogne), France, 207, 208, *note on* 374; ballad on, 209-211

bulls, 'buls do eate their meate,' 42, *note on* 356; in Sicily, 103; more grateful than men, 338

Bumby, Mother, mentioned as a witch, 113, *note on* 365

Burket, Doctor, char. in *GCII*, xxi, 174, 238-254, *note on* 370

Butler, Samuel, his *Hudibras,* on George a Green, 352

butter whore, *scold,* 217, *note on* 375

buttery, spirit of the, 24, *note on* 352

Byram, Martin, of Manchester, a clothier in *TR,* 267, 274, 290-293, 343, *note on* 381

Byrd, William, his *Psalms, Sonnets and Songs* (1588), 356

C. mery Talys, A (1525?): its looseness of form, xvi; as source for *JN,* xvii; as compared to *The Mirrour of Mirth,* xxv

cacke, 68, *note on* 358

Caesar, Augustus, gave his name to Exeter, 305

Caesar, Julius, built Tower of London, 296

Cain, the cursed seed of, 128

caliver. *See* weapons

Calvary, mount of, Hugh is far from it, 97

cambrick, *cambric, fine linen cloth,* 141, 175, *note on* 371

Cambridge, Cambridgeshire, in *Dobsons Drie Bobbes,* xvi

Cambridge University Library: owner of copy of *1700? JN,* 350; of *1675? GCI,* 364

camphire ball, *a ball of soap treated with camphor,* 145

camree (French accent), *cambric,* 61

Candlewick (now Cannon) Street. *See* London

Candy (Candia, now Crete), Isle of, home of Greek merchant in *GCI,* 141, 148

cannon. *See* weapons

Canterbury (or Durovernum), Kent, England, 115; mentioned in ballad, 116; Christ Church, 124; St. Gregory's Chapel, 125

canvas, 'canuas Prophet,' *prophet in working clothes,* 299

cap, 'saluting him with cap and knee,' 260; 'intreating with cappe and knee for his fauour,' 340; corner cap, *a cap with either three or four corners,* 14, 229, *note on* 351; flat cap, a small cap made of black woolen yarn, 215, note on 375

capcase, *a kind of valise*, 291, 321

Cardiff Castle, Wales, where Duke Robert is held prisoner, 303, 317, 330, 334

cards, *toothed instruments for carding, in making cloth*, 51

careful, *anxious, care-burdened*, 107, 133

carke, *a troubled state of mind;* 'carke and care,' 294, *note on* 383

carl, *base fellow*, 311

cast, 'cast your water,' *diagnose disease by urinalysis*, 239, *note on* 376-377

Casteler, Richard, hero of *GCII*, 175-212, *note on* 371

Castor and Pollux, two bright stars (Winifred and Hugh in *GCI* are like them), 109

catchpole, *a policeman*, 311; a despised office, 312; uniform described, 312

Cateratus, led captive to Rome, 119

Catherine of Aragon, Queen, 1st wife (1509-33) of Henry VIII: mentioned, 26; conducts war against Scots, 30-32; her gifts after victory at Flodden Field, 32-33; entertained by Jack, 38-50; presents gift to Jack's wife, 50

caukins, *calkins*, 308, *note on* 384

cawdell (caudle), *a warm drink*, 24, 111, *note on* 353

Caxton, William, his *Golden Legend*, from which TD takes story of Crispin and Crispianus, 366

Cea, a river whose water makes men witless, 62, *note on* 357

Cecil, William, receives letter about TD from Mayor Slany, xxviii

Centaur, in his labyrinth, 104

certify, *make known*, 155; *inform*, 195, 204, 239, 317

chafe, *angry humor*, 163

chaines, the two, ? surrounding St. Paul's Churchyard, 149, *note on* 367

chalk, 'set up in very faire Chalk,' *as evidence of a debt*, 222, *note on* 375

challenge the field, *challenge to a duel*, 318

chamberlain, *attendant at an inn*, 276, *note on* 383

changing copy, *in Simon Eyre's case, changing legally or officially from shoemaker to draper*, 167

Chappell, William, *Popular Music of the Olden Time:* gives music for 'The Beginning of the World,' 351; suggests Thomas Cole may be Old King Cole, 381

characterization: widow in *JN*, xvii; idealization of historical characters, xviii, xix; tradesmen heroes idealized, xix; of women, xix-xxi; vitality of minor characters, xix, xxi-xxiii; flat characters, xxi-xxiii; naming characters, xxii; E. A. Baker on, xxiii; combining, or telescoping, of characters, as the two Winchcombs, father and son, 350-351, and Robert Bruce and William Wallace, 384. *See also* women

chargeable, *costly, expensive*, 155

charged, *loaded, burdened*, 174

Charing Cross. *See* London

Charlemagne: 8th c. Frankish king, emperor, 313; in his time 'bayard' was proper name for 'magic horse,' 376

charms: brains of a weasel, tongue of a water-frog, mugwort, houseleek, pimpernel, 113; love charms, right leg of a turtle, head of a dead crow, 235

Charnico, *charneco, a wine from Charneco, Portugal*, 257

Cheapside. *See* London

check, *rebuke*, 120

checkered pavement, *pavement in squares, like a chessboard*, 236, *note on* 376

Chettle, Henry, *Kind harts dreame* (1593), ed. G. B. Harrison (1923), on Doctor Burket and Anthony-now-now, 370-371

Child, F. J.: TD's 'The Song' is No. 168 in his ballad collection, 354; TD's 'The Maidens Song' is No. 9 in his ballad collection, 356

child labor: turning spits, 28; picking wool, 27, 49; in clothing industry, 267

chop up, *accomplish quickly*, 9, 124

Christianity: Winifred accepts it, 96;

comes to England in time of Diocletian, 105

Christ's Hospital. *See* London

Christ's Tears. See Nashe

churching, *return of women to Anglican service after absence due to
childbirth,* 328-330, *note on* 385

Cicilie. *See* Sicily

Circes (Circe): she is bewitching, 62;
enchantress who turned men into
swine (Italian women are like her),
98

Clement-carry-lie, carries lies 'betwixt
the Turke, and the Devill,' 224,
note on 376

clime, *a quarter of the sky,* 316

close basket, ? *a closed basket, one
with a lid on it,* 248

close stool, *chamber pot,* 299

cloth: broadcloth, 28, 29, 39, 304, *note
on* 353; cambrìc (cambrick, camree),
61, 141, 175, *note on* 371; canvas,
299; damask, 145; holland, 206, 235;
kersey, 28, 35, *note on* 353; lawn,
110, 141, *note on* 365; linen, 206;
russet, 18, 28, 35, 49, 64, 300, *note
on* 353; sarsenet, 35, 48, *note on*
354; satin, 145, 256, 342; silk thrumb,
214, *note on* 374; stammel, 27, 186,
206, 314, *note on* 353, 372; taffeta,
84, 208; tawny (the color, or tawny-
colored cloth) 14, 213, 214; velvet,
115, 116, 208, 213, 214; wool, 28;
worsted, 28; 'fine is the silken twist,'
127, *note on* 366; lawns and cam-
brics scant in London, 141; 'handkerchers of Cambrick,' 175, *note on*
371; 'foule stammell,' 186, *note on*
372; 'a Velvet foole, a silken slave,'
215; 'shrinks as bad as northerne
cloth,' 274, *note on* 382; colored silks
in drapers' shops, 295; gift of broadcloth to King, 304; stealing of cloth,
307-310. *See also* dress, welt

clothiers: Henry I's attitude toward,
xix; dedication of *JN* to, 3; household of a clothier, 26-28, 327; supplication to King, 56-57; nine famous
clothiers listed, 267; requests to
Henry I for standard measure of
cloth, etc., 285; banquet for King's
sons given by, 287; 'Blackwel hall,
where country clothiers did vse to

meet,' 295; send soldiers to King,
303; fête King on his visit, 303-306.
See also cloth, clothing industry,
cloth workers, Byram, Cole, Cutbert, Dove, Fitzallen, Gray, Hodgkins, Simon, Sutton, Winchcomb

clothing. *See* dress

clothing industry: rise of middle class
came with development of, xvi;
trouble over foreign labor, xxvii-
xxviii, 56-57; gives living to poor,
3, 47, 267; child labor in, 27, 28,
49, 267; wooden shuttles, 31; looms,
40; size of, 57, 267, 270; bargaining
for cloth, 61; 'Merchants strangers,'
145; made England famous, 267;
younger sons of knights and gentlemen in, 267; hanging first allowed
as punishment for stealing cloth,
285-286; origin of yard measure,
285, *note on* 383; prophecy concerning in ballad, 297-299. *See also*
cloth, clothiers, cloth workers, drapers, mercers, weavers

cloth workers: kinds of workers listed
(spinners, carders, etc.), 267; carders,
27, 41, 42, 56, 60, 64, 305, 327; dyers,
27, 47; fulling mill, 27, 47, *note on*
353; 'foure score Rowers,' 27; shear-
ers, 27, 56; spinners, 27, 42, 56, 60,
305, 327; wool pickers, 27, 49, 267;
dress of cloth workers described, 27.
See also cloth, clothing industry,
weavers

clown, *a rustic, boor, common fellow,*
80

coat, with four elbows, *a fool's coat,*
203, *note on* 374; to swing [some-
one's] coat, *to reprimand severely,*
238

Cock and Pye, by, *an oath,* 132, *note
on* 366-367

cock of the game, *a fighting cock; a
man who is very masculine,* 180

Cock of Westminster. *See* Casteler,
Richard

codling, *a variety of hard apple,* 80,
note on 359

codpiece, *a covering for the opening
in front of the breeches,* 35, *note
on* 355

codshead, *stupid fellow, blockhead,*
252, *note on* 377

433

Cofetua, a king who loved a beggar, 120

cogging, *boasting, bragging, lying, cheating, deceiving,* 219, 260, 264

coil, *fuss, to-do,* 300, 324, 326

coin, 'a hardy Coine,' *a sterling character, pure gold,* 213; 'cry quittance for your coynes,' *get even (with you) for your treatment,* 228; 'without coyne,' 82, *note on* 359

coistrel. *See* quoystrel

Colchester Castle. *See* Rochester Castle

Cole, Thomas: his murder in Chap. XI of *TR* discussed, xv; clothier mentioned in dedication to *JN,* 3; as hero of *TR,* 267, 268, 269-278, 287-293, 303-304, 320-327, 329, 340, *note on* 381; Fuller doubts that he is historical, Chappell suggests he may be Old King Cole, 381

Colebrook (Colnbrook): town five miles east of Windsor, *note on* 382; the George, an inn there, 263; where the clothiers of the West stopped on way to London, 272; Cole is murdered at the Crane there, 320-327

Cole's wife (Elinor): accompanies Gray's and Fitzallen's wives to London, 295-296, 299-303; mentioned in Cole's will, 323; sends a servant to find her missing husband, 326-327

collation notes: *JN,* 387-399; *GCI,* 400-410; *GCII,* 411-415; *TR,* 416-425

Collier, John Payne, on the death of TD's son, xxv

Collins, J. C., ed. Robert Greene's plays and poems, 352

Colman, Nicholas, printer of 'The Lamentation of Beckles,' xxv

Colnbrook. *See* Colebrook

Coln River, gets its name from Thomas Cole, 327

Columbia University Library, owner of copy of *1690 GCI,* 364

combred, *encumbered,* 159

comfetmaker, *maker of comfits, sweetmeats,* 254

commons, shorter, *smaller portions (of food),* 73

Commons of London. *See* London

compass, 'keepe our selues in good compasse,' *keep ourselves within bounds,* 300

conceipt, dull in, *dull witted,* 250

conceit, *idea, notion,* 22, 93, 108; conceited, *witty,* 182

conditioned, *behaved,* 196, 255

conduit, *fountain. See* London

Consitt, Frances, *The London Weavers' Company* (1933), on a complaint against immigrant weavers, xxvii-xxviii

consort, *band of musicians,* 277

content, *happiness,* 97; contented, *calmed,* 131; be content, *be calm,* 263; 'Content wife,' *Agreed, wife,* 263

Coomes, Jack, 'as errant a Cuckold as *Iack Coomes,*' 201, *note on* 374

copy. *See* changing copy

cordwaynor, *cordwainer, a shoemaker, esp. one who works with cordovan leather; GCII* dedicated to the Company of Cordwainers, 173

Cornelius, Master, of the Guard, mentioned as suitor of Gillian in *GCII,* 178, *note on* 371

corn fed, *well fed, corn meaning wheat, as opposed to rye or the coarser grains,* 72

Coromandae, whose men were tongueless, 61

costume. *See* dress

courtship: of Jack by widow, 7-21; jealousy, ballad on, 11; gifts sent, 16; by Sir George Rigley, 85-86; of Hugh and Winifred, 93-98; of Ursula and Crispine, 122-124; jealousy, 151; of Richard Casteler by Gillian and Meg, 176-207; 'it becommeth not maidens to be woers,' 180; of Dutch maiden by Richard Casteler, 193; of widow Farmer, 234-254; of Margaret by Duke Robert, 314-317. *See also* marriage, weddings, women

coy, *scornful,* 73

coyle. *See* coil

coyne. *See* coin

Crab, char. in *TR,* 294-299, 328

crab, stamp the, 188, *note on* 372

Craftes, the tanner, widow's suitor in *JN,* 8, 14-19

Crane, Sign of the, tavern in Coln-brook, 327

crash, *a bout of music,* 257

Crete. *See* Candy

cricket, *small wooden stool,* 131

crinkler, *one who fails to carry out his intention,* 182, *note on* 372

Cripplegate, why so named, 295, *note on* 384. *See also* London

Crispianus: his mother discussed, xx; a hero in *GCI,* 115-139, *note on* 366; 'by good *Crispianus* soule,' a shoe-makers' oath, 196; Tom Drum and Harry Nevell drink to his soul, 220

Crispianus' Night, ballad on, 137-139

Crispine: his mother discussed, xx; a hero in *GCI,* 115-139, *note on* 366

crosscloths, *linen cloths worn across the forehead by babies,* 131, *note on* 366

crow, the head of a dead crow, car-ried for a love charm, 235

Crowch (or Crouch), E[dward]: printer, 1641-67, at Hosier Lane, Snow Hill; printer of *1672 JN,* 349

cry, 'out of all cry,' *excessively,* 197

cry quittance, 'cry quittance for your coynes,' *get even (with you) for your treatment,* 228

cucking stool, 81, *note on* 359

cuckold, 'as errant a Cuckold as *Iack Coomes,*' 201, *note on* 374; cuck-oldry implied, 42, 127

Cunnington, Willett and Phillis, on English costume in 16th c., 358

Cupid: 'hath Cupid and you had a combate lately?' 234; has swift wings, 331

curiosity, *fastidiousness,* 197

curious, *careful, particular, scrupu-lous,* 13

currant mettle, *current metal, good money; hence a stalwart fellow, a sterling fellow,* 213

cursie, *curtsy,* 175, 189, 255

curtall, *curtal, a horse with a docked tail,* 322

cushin, *cushion, drinking cup,* 164, *note on* 368

custom, 'hauing the custome,' *having as customers,* 175

cut, 'call me Cut,' 217, *note on* 375

Cutbert of Kendal, one of the three

clothiers of the North in *TR,* 267, 274-278, 287-293, 343, *note on* 381

Cyclopes, 'monstrous men that had but one eie a piece,' 102

Cynomolgy, people with bodies of men but dogs' heads, 32, *note on* 354

Cynthia (Artemis or Diana), 'shaped her course to seeke out *Sol,*' 125

dance. *See* morrice, trench more

David, Charles Wendell, *Robert Curt-hose* (1920), for biographical details about Robert, Duke of Normandy, 382

David, King, kills Goliath, in 'The Weauers Song,' 41

Deacon, J[ohn]: bookseller, 1682-1701, at the Rainbow, Holborn, etc.; seller of *1696 GCI,* 364

Decameron. See Boccaccio

Defoe, Daniel, *Dobsons Drie Bobbes* a precursor of his biographical novels, xvi

Dekker, Thomas: his plays ed. Fred-son Bowers, xxx; *Dekker's Plague Pamphlet,* ed. F. P. Wilson (1925), on the word 'sowter,' 374; *The Bachelors Banquet* (1603), in *Non-Dramatic Works,* ed. Alexander Grosart (1884-86), on use of 'be-trice,' 372

Deloney, Thomas:
1. Life: date of birth unknown, xxiii; death, xxiii; occupation, xxiii, xxv; education, xxiv; religion, xxiv; liv-ing in London, 1586, xxv; death of son, xxv; as journalist, xxv-xxvi; in-volvement in weavers' controversy over foreign labor, xxvii-xxviii; im-prisoned, xxviii; helps draft weav-ers' complaint, xxviii; trouble with authorities, 1596, xxviii-xxix; disap-pears, 1596-1600, xxix
2. Writings: as novelist, xi-xviii; pop-ularity of his novels, xi; primarily concerned with life of artisans, xi; *The Forest* as source, xii; indebted-ness to drama, xii-xvi; use of solil-oquy, xiii; stage-like humor, xiv; use of dialogue, xiv-xv; first to use dialect in novel, xiv; first to use malapropism, xiv; tragic scene in

435

TR, xv; realism, xv; his novel structure like jest-biographies, xvi; as translator of Des Périers' *Les contes (Mirrour of Mirth)*, xvi, xxv; influence of jestbook, xvi-xviii; his sympathy for women, xix-xxi, xxvi; proof of authorship of novels, xxiii; called the 'balletting silke-weauer,' xxiii; novels printed, xxix-xxx

—*Jack of Newbury,* first dramatic novel in English, xii; four-fifths dialogue, xiv; like jest-biography, xvii; Chap. VI reflects TD's 1595 experiences, xxviii; Henry as ideal ruler in Chap. VI, xxviii-xxix; entered in SR, estimated publication date, xxix; text, 1-87; explanatory notes, 345-360; collation notes, 387-399

—*The Gentle Craft, Part I,* entered in SR, estimated publication date, xxix; text, 88-169; explanatory notes, 361-368; collation notes, 400-410

—*The Gentle Craft, Part II,* Meg's soliloquy in, xiii; estimated publication date, xxix-xxx; text, 170-264; explanatory notes, 369-378; collation notes, 411-415

—*Thomas of Reading,* idealized characters in, xi; possible borrowing of Shakespeare and Webster from, xv; rise of middle class in, xvi; like a play, xvii; as an historical novel, xviii; Scott a possible editor of, xviii *n.;* Henry I as ideal ruler in, xxix; estimated publication date, xxix-xxx; text, 265-343; explanatory notes, 379-385; collation notes, 416-425

See also ballads, characterization

demilances. *See* weapons

Denevale, John, a French shoemaker in *GCI,* 141-154, 159-166

Dent (Everyman), publisher in 1929 of *TR,* 381

Des Périers, Bonaventure, *The Mirrour of Mirth and Pleasant Conceits,* ? trans. TD (1583), showing that TD knew French and was acquainted with jestbook literature, xvi, xxiv

Devonshire. *See* Exeter

dialect: TD first to use it in novel, xiv; rural Buckinghamshire dialect,

28-30; Hodgkins' 'broad Northern speech,' 267, 274, 285-293, 307-311, 343. *See also* accent, foreign

dialogue: TD's crisp dialogue, xi; dialogue the making of Cole's death scene, xv

Diana, temple of: burned by Herostratus, 39; goddess of chastity, 48

diaper napkin, 'the Maide . . . with a Diaper napkin covered the table,' 249

dice: Cole and others gamble at Bosom's Inn, 274-275; 'a couple that fel out at Dice,' 322

Dickens, Charles: TD has gift for particularity like Dickens', xvi; TD comparable in individualizing char., xxi; TD comparable in naming char., xxii; Dickens is TD's only superior in drawing flat char., xxiii

Dioclesian (Diocletian), Roman emperor 284-305 A.D., his picture in Jack's parlor, 53; causes death of Winifred and Hugh in *GCI,* 105-112

disable, *belittle, disparage,* 155

Ditchfield, Peter H., and William Page, eds., *The Victoria History of Berkshire,* 351

doating, *acting foolishly,* 261

Dobsons Drie Bobbes (1607): its structural unity, xvi; ed. Horsman (1955), 352

Doll, a 'kitchen drudge' in *GCII,* 236

Donwallo, King of Tegina, mentioned as father of Winifred in *GCI,* 92, *note on* 365

Doom, The. See Batman

door nail, 'as dead as a doore naile,' 162

Doris (Dubris). *See* Dover

Dorset, Marquess of, gives Wolsey a benefice, 356

doubt, *fear,* 132, 194, 197; doubt not, *fear not,* 182; 'you will make your husbands hayre growe through his hood I doubt,' *don't doubt,* 291

Dove, Tom, of Exeter: his 'tag,' calling for music, xxii; char. in *TR,* 267-268, 272-278, 287-293, 305, 312-313, 323, 337-340, *note on* 381

Dover, Kent, also called Rutupium,

Doris, Duur (Aruvagus Castle is there), 134, *note on* 367

drab, *loose woman*, 23, 188, 203, 204; *a woman to be scorned for any reason*, 52, 162, 163, 319

draggle tail, *untidy*, 'I knew her a draggle tayle girle,' 79

dragon: in Sicily, 103; more grateful than men, 338

drapers: linen drapers, 146; Worshipful Company of, 167; shops of, 295. *See also* clothing industry

dress: men of simple attire are 'slenderly esteemed,' 145; 'mens coffers are iudged by their garments,' 300
—of children: in pageant for the King, 48; infants' necessities listed, 131. *See also* biggins, crosscloths, taileclouts
—of country people: women of country demand London apparel, 299-303; 'we are country folkes . . . gray russet, and good home-spun cloth doth best become vs,' 300; for hay-making, 314
—of fools: 'a motley Ierkin,' 52; 'coate with foure elbowes,' 203, *note on* 374
—headwear: 'and though she goe in her hood . . . she is but a girle to mee,' 79; Spanish felt hat, fashionable at end of 16th c., 375. *See also* billiment; cap, corner; cap, flat; French hood; thrumb
—of men: 'holy daie apparell,' 6, 175; wandering musicians, 14; a tailor, 18; 'slipt on his shooes and came downe in his shirt,' 23; 'he made himselfe vnready [for bed], and his hostesse was very diligent to warme a kerchefe and put it about his head,' 325; soldiers, 30; clothier's servants for military service, 35; clothier to greet the King, 35; singers before the King, 208; merchant, 77; leather garments of shoemaker, 133; shoemaker (doublet of sheepskins, apron, etc.), 145; poor shoemaker, 145; poor man, 75; 'What neuer a shoo to thy foot, hose to thy legge, band to thy necke, nor cap to thy head,' 76; London alderman, 145-146; Mayor of London, 168;

'Fine bands and handkerchers for him we did make,' 206; 'kerchiefe' and 'scarffe' as gifts, 217; 'Duke of Suffolks liverie,' 213-214; origin of livery, 277; sea captains, 214; velvet cap of physician, 248; Old Bosom 'alwaies wore two coates, two caps, two or three paire of stockings, and a high paire of shooes, ouer the which he drew on a great paire of lined slippers,' 275; Cutbert 'was faine to cast off his gownes, his coats, and two paire of his stockings, to coole himselfe,' 292; catchpoles, 312. *See also* codpiece, handkercher, point, slops
—of religious: parish priest (gown and corner cap), 229; a bishop, 342; for taking nun's vows, 342-343
—shoes: description of high and low cut shoes, 141; 'booted and spurd,' 241; shoes of neat's leather, 281. *See also* pantofles; pumps; shoes, slip
—of women: well-to-do woman, 16, 70, 84, 236; 'maidens' while spinning, 27; 'pretty wenches' at market, 235; Meg and Gillian at Richard's wedding, 206; wedding apparel, 28, 29; 'nor turne her head aside, for feare of hurting the set of her neckenger,' 74; 'the goodwife in a red piticoat and a wastcoat,' 277. *See also* bride laces, frog, gowns, kertle, partlet
See also barbers, brisk, cloth, foynes, gard, jewelry, shoemaking. For descriptions and illustrations of 16th c. dress, see Willett and Phillis Cunnington, *Handbook of English Costume in the Sixteenth Century* (1954)

dress him in his kind, ? *treat him as he deserves*, 66

drie bob (dry bob), *taunt, bitter jibe*, 19, *note on* 352

droyle, 'like a drudge and a droyle,' 301

Drum, Tom: his remark about Arcadia, xi; introduces himself, in dialogue, xv; his 'sin of cogging,' xxii; his 'entertainment,' 174, 240, *note on* 370; char. in *GCII*, 174, 219-240, 264

Duchess of Malfi, The. See Webster

Duck Lane, where *1672 TR* was sold, 380

dudgin, *boxwood,* 'dudgin haft dagger,' *a dagger with a handle made of boxwood,* 215; 'in dudgin,' *with a feeling of anger or resentment,* 215, 255

Dudley, Edmund, beheaded, 40, 355

duelling, a duel, 216-217. *See also* challenge the field, fencing

Dun, Cornelius van. *See* Cornelius

Dunham, in *Dobsons Drie Bobbes,* xvi

Dunnington Park, the King's domain, 42

Durovernum. *See* Canterbury

Duur. *See* Dover

Dyce, Alexander, ed. in 1840 of Kemp's *Nine Daies Wonder,* 361

Dyer, Sir Edward, an echo from his 'My Mind to Me a Kingdom Is,' 50, 356

Dyetary of Helth. See Boorde

ear: 'have vs by the eares,' 218; 'to fall together by the eares,' 235; 'lay me on the eare,' *strike me on the ear,* 251

earnest, *a sum paid in advance to bind the bargain,* 189

East Cheap, a London street, 235

Easter, one of the four terms when courts are in session, 359

Ebsworth, J. W., author of *DNB* account of TD, xxiii

Egyptian woman, 'as blacke as the great Divell,' 241, 248

eke, *also,* 138

elbow, 'scratch my elbo,' *a gesture of increasing anger or irritation,* 214

Elderton, William, his death, xxvii

elephant, in Sicily, 103

Elizabeth I, Queen of England, in a TD ballad, xxviii-xxix

ell, replaced by *verge* (yard) in 1353, 383

Ellesmere, Earl of, former owner of *1626 JN,* 345

emits, *emmets, ants,* 'the little boyes . . . will run after mee like a sort of Emits,' 262

Empson, Sir Richard, sent to Tower for treason, 40, *note on* 355

Englefield, Sir Henry, of Berkshire, 31, *note on* 354

englischen Schwankbücher, Die. See Schulz

Essex, Dr. Burket rides through Essex, 247. *See also* Harwich

Eumenes, a captain under Alexander the Great, 53

Euphues. See Lyly

euphuism, TD's acquaintance with, xi

evil, foul. *See* foul

Exeter, Devonshire: first called Isca, then Augustus, then Exeter, 305, *note on* 384; king's visit to, 305. *See* Dove, Tom, of Exeter

Exeter Cathedral, owner of copy of *1636 TR,* 380

explanatory notes: *JN,* 345-360; *GCI,* 361-368; *GCII,* 369-378; *TR,* 379-385

Eyre, Mistress, a char. in *GCI,* xix-xx, 140-149, 154-159, 167-169

Eyre, Simon, a tradesman-hero in *GCI,* xix-xx, 139-149, 154-159, 167-169, *note on* 367

fain, *gladly,* 144, 158, 200; *forced, obliged, oblige,* 138, 192, 194, 195, 196

fair: in Newbury on Bartholomew's Day, 13; in Westminster and Bristol on St. James' Day, 261-264; 'St. Iames faire,' *fair on St. James' Day,* 261; Cardinal Wolsey's alleged behavior after a fair, 356. *See also* fairing, statute

'Fair Flower of Northumberland, The.' *See* ballads, 'The Maidens Song'

fairing, *present given at a fair,* 13, *note on* 351

Falstaff: his 'catechism' on honor compared with Meg's soliloquy, xiii, *note on* 374; quoted on links and torches, 352

fardel, *bundle, burden,* 141

Farmer, Mistress, Dr. Burket fails to win her, xxi; 'faire widdow of *Fleetstreet,*' char. in *GCII,* 234-254

feat, *skillful, dexterous,* 249; featly, *skillfully,* 27; feats, *tricks,* 256, 264

fell, *fierce, cruel, savage,* 11

fencing, school, the Green King uses it, 256. *See also* duelling, prize, wards

Ferris, Sir William, char. in *TR,* 314, 317-320, *note on* 384-385 ferrited (ferreted), *harassed,* 218

Feversham, Kent, where Crispine and Crispianus become shoemakers, 115-116

fie, *exclamation of disgust or dislike,* 257, 263

fig, 'a Figge for the Cocke of *Westminster,'* 202; 'A fig for you,' 230

fillippe (fillip), *a blow by a finger that is held by the thumb and then released quickly,* 313

Finch Lane. *See* London

fired, *consumed or destroyed by fire,* 182

firking, *moving about briskly,* 'with his firking Fiddle,' 174; 'firkin Fidler of *Finchlane,'* 257; 'firkin barrell,' *one-quarter barrel,* 257

Firth, Charles Harding, Regius Professor of History at Oxford, donator of copy of *1627 GCI* to University of Sheffield Library, 361

Fitzallen, William, of Worcester: from Oswestry, son Henry was first Mayor of London, son Roger second Mayor of London, 306; char. in *TR,* 267-268, 271-276, 306; dies a rich man, 343; *note on* 381

Fitzallen's wife, visits London, 295-296, 299-303

Flanders: Haunce's home, 166; where the Green King goes, 257-258

Fleet Bridge, where *1632 GCI* was sold, 364

Fleet Street. *See* London

Flemings, fled to England because their country was flooded, 311-312, *note on* 384

flesh shambles, *stalls for the sale of meat,* 295, *note on* 384

Flintshire: formerly called Tegina, 92; where Hugh goes to see Winifred, 107

flocks, *woolen or cotton waste,* 28

Flodden (a village in Northumberland) Field: Jack prepares to fight against the Scots, 26, 30, 350; Queen's army marches toward Flodden, 32-33, *note on* 354; ballad about, 33-34. *See also* ballads, 'The Song'

Florence, char. in *GCI,* 150-155, 159-166

Florida, coast of, to which Stutely and Strangwidge would escape, 215

fly, 'as blind as a flie in October,' 96

foins. *See* foynes

Folger Library: owns copy of two fragments of *1598? GCII,* 369; of *1632 TR,* 380

food: for workers, 27-28, 71-73; served to King in glass, 39; gambon of bacon, 78; roast beef, 78; powdered beef, 78, 181, *note on* 359; powdered beef broth, 291; brawn and sowse, 127, *note on* 366; brown breads, 'wheate and rie mingled,' 'barlybread,' 'or rie mingled with pease,' less fine than wheat bread, 72, *note on* 358; 'a couple of white manchets' (fine wheat bread shaped like muffins or small rolls), 249; a 'firkin barrell of butter,' 257; fruit and spice cake, 329; capon, 16, 17, 69, 177, 181; 'looked so sowrely vpon another, as if they had beene newly champing of Crabs,' 18; caudle, 24, 111, *note on* 353; cheese, 291, 293; a load of Holland cheese, 257; chicken, 16, 17, 18, 177, 302; cockles, 253; comfits and caraways, 176; mess of cream, 152, 160; goose, 16, 17, 18; honey, 195; meat for servants, 'neckes and poynts of beefe,' 'peece of bacon or pork [in] pottage,' 'midriffes of the Oxen, and the cheekes, the sheepes heads, and the gathers,' 72, *note on* 358; mussels, 253; mustard, 180; shoulder of mutton, 16; oysters, 248, 253; pancakes, 168; pap, 131, *note on* 366; pennypasties, 329; pies, 329; pudding pies, 140, 160, 168; lamb pie, 186, 188; 'minst' pie, 191; pomegranates, 178; pork, 16, 329; pottage, 72, 274, 276, 288 ff.; beef and mutton puddings, 150; quinces, 178; rabbit, 16, 160; runnet, with which women make their cheese, 113; preparation of stockfish, cod, etc., *note on* 368; one-half pound of sugar, 16; venison pasty, 158, 160, 186, 187, 274; 'Bachelors in Pigs flesh take such delight,' 17; 'shorter commons, and courser meate,' 73; 'as Cookes doe in baking of their pies,' 197; 'never trust my

word for a cupple of blacke puddings,' 231; 'laying meate on my
trencher,' 236; 'some cannot abide
to eate of a Pig: some to taste of
an Eele,' 244; 'God sends meat, and
the diuel sends cookes,' 277. *See also*
corn fed
fool, motley dress of, 52; coat with
four elbows, 203, *note on* 374. *See
also* Patch and Sommers, Will
footman, *walker*, 125
Forest, The. See Fortescue
forsooth, *certainly, indeed, for truth,*
230, 249
Forster, E. M., on flat characters, xxi-
xxii
Fortescue, Thomas, *The Forest* (1571):
TD's direct source for euphuism,
xii; source for Gratis, 351; for story
of Herostratus, 355; for Chap. V in
JN, 356; source for Galerus, 357; miscellaneous information from, 357
foul, 'what the foule euill care I,' 278,
note on 383; 'What the foule ill,'
308
Four Letters. See Harvey
foynes (foins), *trimmings made of fur,*
145, 146, *note on* 367
Fragment, Jenny's lover in *TR*, 281
France: fights with England against
invading Persians in *GCI*, 128-130;
King of, 130, 135, 137
Francis, friend of William's in *GCII*,
244, 245
Frank, Mistress, friend of 2nd Mistress
Winchcomb's in *JN*, xiv, 69-73, 78-
81, *notes on* 359
frank, *free, liberal-handed,* 182
fraught, *cargo, load,* 144
French hood, 70, *note on* 358. *See also*
billiment
frog (French accent), *frock,* 'for make
you a Frog,' 61; *leaping animal,*
'tongue of a water-frog hath such
great force,' 113
froward, *refractory, perverse, rebel-
lious,* 93, 105, 243; frowardly, 193
frumps, *gibes,* 296
Fuller, Thomas, *Worthies of England*
(1662): on John Winchcomb, 350;
doubts Thomas Cole is historical,
381

fulling mill, 27, *note on* 353
fustian, *gibbering,* 22

gage, *to pledge,* 315, 319
gag-toothed, *with projecting teeth,*
'Why, you gag-toothd Iack,' 291
Galerus (Galerius), Roman emperor
305-311 A.D., 54, *note on* 357
Galino, a place that 'breedes no Serpents,' 331
gambling. *See* dice
gambon, *gammon, leg (of bacon),* 78
gard, *guard, trimming,* 35, 213, *note
on* 354
Gargantua, Peachy's men would fight
with, in *GCII*, 213
Garland of Good Will, The. See ballads
Garter king-of-arms, messenger in *JN*,
35, *note on* 355
gathers, 'cheekes, the sheepes heads,
and the gathers,' 72, *note on* 358
gear, *matter, affair, stuff,* 238
gennet (*jennet*), 'an ambling gennet of
Spaine,' 331
Gentle Craft, The, originally planned
as trilogy, xxx. *See also* Deloney
George, a tavern in Colnbrook, 263
George, the Sign of the, where *1652
GCI* was sold, 364
George a Green, the pinner of Wakefield, 21, *note on* 352
George of Gloucester, clothier mentioned in dedication to *JN*, 3
Gerard (spelled by TD 'Gerrard,'
'Garrat,' 'Jarrat,' and 'Jarret'), the
giant in *TR*, 268, 274, 278, 287, 292,
313, *note on* 382
Gerard's Hall. *See* London
ghostly father, *priest,* 235
giglet, *frivolous girl,* 189, 277
Gilbertson, J.: bookseller, 1684 ff., at
the Sun and Bible on London
Bridge; seller of *1685 GCI*, 364
Gilford (Guildford), Surrey, town between Petworth and London, 222,
223, 227, 231
Gillian, servant at the George in *GCII*,
xiii, xix, 176-207, *note on* 371
Gillian, wife of weaver in *JN*, 63-68
gilliflower (gillyflower), children give
them to the King, 48; 'Roses flourish

in Iune, and Gilliflowers in August,' 101

gin, *mechanical device,* 'to chop off mens heads,' 307, 310

gip, *get out,* 197, *note on* 373

Gloucester, Gloucestershire: named after King Gloue, 305; Henry I visits, 305-306; Henry I makes his son first Earl of, 306; Duke Robert visits, 315; Margaret agrees to meet Robert between Cardiff and, 330; TD gets information about Gloucester from Llwyd, 384. *See also* Gray of Gloucester

Gloucester Abbey: Margaret becomes a nun there, xx, 341-343; Robert asks to be buried there, 343

Gloucestershire, has old custom of hiring servants at fair, 279

Gloue, King of England, who gave name to Gloucester, 305

go to, *go away (an exclamation of protest),* 163

God's nigs ('nigs' not defined in *OED*), *an oath,* 258

God's precious, 'Gods precious [blood] (quoth she),' 191, *note on* 373

Golden Legend. See Caxton

Goliath, his strength, 41

gore blood, *thick blood,* 111, *note on* 365

Gossen, 'bee Gossen,' *by God,* 68, *note on* 358

gowns, 'he keeps all his gownes for *Gillian*,' 184, *note on* 372

Grafton, Richard, *Chronicle:* xviii, xxvi, 345 *n.;* source for TD's treatment of Flodden, 350; on the taking of Morlaix, 359; apparently a good friend of Casteler's, 371; on the origin of 'yard,' 383; reports the Flemings coming to England, 384

Gratis, the shepherd, mentioned by widow in *JN,* 10, *note on* 351

Gravesend barge. *See* London

Gray of Gloucester, clothier in *TR,* 267-268, 271-276, 282-284, 288-293, 305, 315-317, 322, 333-336, 341-343

Gray's wife, char. in *TR,* 279-284, 295-296, 299-303, 329, 332-336, 341-343

Greece, ancient, TD's references to, 356

Greek merchant, owner of the Black Swan ship, in *GCI,* 141-148

Greene, Robert: TD not indebted to his realism, xi; his *Pandosto* (1588) a source for *The Winter's Tale,* xii; his death and Harvey's *Four Letters,* xxvii; his *A Quip for an Upstart Courtier* (1592) quoted from, 355; his *George a Greene* quoted from, 372

Green King, of St. Martin's, char. in *GCII,* xii, 174, 226, 256-264

Greenham, Berkshire, a town near Newbury, 80

green sickness, *a reference to any strong emotion which makes one look ill, as 'green with envy'; chlorosis, an anemic disease of young women characterized by a greenish hue of the skin,* 184

Greg, W. W., ed. *Henslowe's Diary,* reference to the play *George a Green,* 352

Gregory XIII, Pope, TD translates his Latin letters, xxiv

Griffith, Hugh's brother in *GCI,* 95, 96

Grosart, Alexander, his ed. of Greene, 355. *See* Dekker

guerdon, *reward,* 334

Guildford. *See* Gilford

Guildhall. *See* London

Halifax, Yorkshire: hanging as criminal punishment first allowed in, 285, 286; a thief escapes hanging, 307-311. *See also* Hodgkins of Halifax

Halliday, Wilfrid J., ed. in 1928 of *GCI,* 364

Halliwell-Phillips, James O., ed. in 1859 of *JN,* 350

halter, take an, *marry,* 231

Hampshire, soldiers of, 31. *See also* Bazingstoke, Simon of Southampton

Hampstead Marshall, manor of, given Sir Thomas Parrie by Elizabeth, 353

hand, bill of, *I O U,* 76, 145; out of hand, *at once,* 182; of his hands, *in action, in fight,* 219; bearing in hand, *reminding,* 237

handkercher, *handkerchief,* 175, *note on* 371

hand-leather, ? *a protective covering for the hand, made of leather*, 145

handwrist, *wrist*, 342

hanging: four times a year at Newgate, 231-232; 'of men was neuer seene in England,' 286, 309; of murderers, 327; of thieves, 307-311; finding a hangman, 309

hang it up, *stop it*, 257

hap, *chance, luck*, 23, 117, 118; 'hap what hap will,' 199

haporth, *halfpennyworth*, 231

Harford, George, and Morley Stevenson, eds. *The Prayer Book Dictionary* (1925), on 'churching feast,' 385

hark in thy ear, *an expression preparing one for a whisper*, 188

Harrigat, John, bookseller, 1624-35, at the Holy Lamb in Paternoster Row. *See 1630 JN*, 349

Harrison, G. B.: his one-volume ed. used for all references to Shakespeare, 351; his description of codpiece, 355. *See also* Chettle

harts-ease, *heartsease, an herb*, 199, *note on* 374

Harvard University Library: owner of copy of *1660 GCII*, 370; of *1632 TR*, 380

Harvey, Gabriel, *Four Letters* (1592), his attack on Elderton and Greene, xxvii

Harwich, Essex, 104, *note on* 365

Hassell, J. Woodrow, Jr., xxiv *n*.

Haunce, the Dutchman, char. in *GCI*, 150-154, 159-166

Have with You to Saffron-Walden. See Nashe

Hazlitt, W. Carew, ed.: *Shakespeare Jest-Books* (1846), xvii *n.; Hand-Book* (1867), 345, 361

Heart of Midlothian. See Scott

Hector of Troy, Crispianus fights like, 128

heels, 'out you durty heeles,' 291

Helen of Troy, 41

Henry I (1068-1135): rise of clothing industry during reign, xvi; conflict with older brother, Duke Robert, xviii-xix; as ideal governor, xxviii-xxix; institutes Parliament, 267, *note on* 381; why called Beauclerk, 269; (youngest) son of William the Con-

querer, sought good will of nobility and commons, 269; delayed by clothiers' wains, 270; 'I am King by possession,' 271; speaks to clothiers, 284, 285; originates yard measure, 285; first to punish by hanging, 286; clothiers give feast for his sons, 287; at war in France, 303; builds castle and abbey in Reading, 304; 'summers progresse into the west country,' 303-306; makes son Robert first Earl of Gloucester, 306; grieves at Cole's death, 327; captures Duke Robert and has his eyes put out, 332-336; sees Margaret enter monastery in Gloucester, 342; dies and is buried in Reading, 343; mentioned, 311

Henry IV, Part I: Falstaff's soliloquy on honor, xiii; quoted from, on links and torches, 352; Long Meg's soliloquy may be a parody of Falstaff's, 374

Henry VIII (1491-1547): as historical char., xviii; as ideal governor, xxviii-xxix; 'In the daies of King Henery the eight,' 5; visits Newbury and John Winchcomb, xix, 35-50; goes to war in France, 30-32; in a ballad, 'The Song,' 33; as 'Defender of the Faith,' 60; gives Sir George Rigley a living, 87; captures Boulogne, 208, *note on* 374; mentioned in Chaps. IV, VII, and X of *GCII*, 208-211, 227, 228, 230, 232, 233, 256

Henslowe's Diary, ed. Greg, reference to *George a Green*, 352

herbs: heartsease, sorrel, thrift, thistle, 199-200, *note on* 374; basil, 'worse than a goate doth hate basill,' 336. *See also* rosemary

Hercules, Greek hero 'did vse to spin,' 40

Herford and Simpson, eds. Ben Jonson, on 'Fayring,' 351

Herostratus, burned down the temple of Artemis (Diana) in 356 B.C., 39, *note on* 355

Hilary, one of the 4 terms when courts were in session, 359

hilts, 'to have thy wards ready, and thy hilts sure,' 227

hippocras, *a cordial*, 187, *note on* 372

Hippocrates' sleeve, 372
History of the English Novel, The.
   See Baker
Histrio-Mastex. See Marston
Hodgkins, of Halifax, char. in *TR*,
   267, 274, 285-293, *note on* 381, 383
Hogsdon (Hoxton), a district north of
   London, 152, *note on* 367
hold, 'you must hold,' *you must wager,*
   157
Holdsworth, Sir William, *A History of
   English Law* (5th ed., 1942), on terms
   when courts were in session, 360
Holinshed, Raphael, *Chronicles:* xviii,
   xxvi, 345 *n.;* on Garter king-of-arms,
   355; on the beheading of Empson
   and Dudley, 355; on Paulet's putting
   Wolsey in stocks, 356; on the taking
   of Morlaix, 359; copies Grafton on
   Casteler, 371; uses the name
   'Peachey' several times, 374; TD's
   source for number of Scots slain
   at Musselburgh Field, 377; mentions Tom Trotter, 378; as TD's
   source on Count of Mortain, 382;
   on the origin of 'yard,' 383; source
   for incident in *TR* about horses
   'shodde backwarde,' 384; name 'Ferres' appears in, 384; source for information in *TR* regarding the
   Flemings coming to England, 384
holland (cloth), 206, 235
Holy Lamb, where *1630 JN* was sold,
   349
honest, *chaste,* 65; honesty, *chastity,* 64,
   65
hood, French. *See* French hood
hop of my thumb, *a very diminutive
   person,* 180
horn, *the mark of a cuckold,* 10, 42,
   64, 127
Horsman, E. A., ed. in 1955 of *Dobsons Drie Bobbes,* 352
host cloth, 50
house furnishings: of widow in *JN*, 20;
   rushes, tapestries, tables, etc., 38-39;
   pictures, 53-55; necessary for sheriff
   of London, 155, *note on* 368; bed
   and bedstead, 321. *See also* cricket,
   'joyne' stools, standing-stool
house of office, *privy,* 192
Howard, Lord Thomas, in ballad, 34

Hudibras, a reference to George a
   Green, 352
Hugh, Sir or Saint. *See* Saint Hugh
*Hundred Merry Tales, A. See C. mery
   Talys, A*
Hungerford, Berkshire, where tailor
   lives, in *JN,* 8
Hungerford, Sir Francis, his son at
   Jack's wedding, 29, *note on* 353
Huntington Library: owns copies of
   1619, 1626, and *1637 JN,* 348-349; of
   1690 GCI, 364; of *1612, 1623, 1632,*
   and *1636 TR,* 380
huntsup, *a song sung to awaken some-
   one,* 263, *note on* 377
husband, *careful manager,* 175

I, *aye;* I mary, *aye, Mary,* 189; I thank
   her still, *aye, thank her still,* 191;
   197, 230, 259
Iacke nape (Italian accent), *jacka-
   napes, a monkey,* 159
'Iacke of Newberye,' a ballad, 345
I faith (or I-faith, y-faith), *in faith,*
   188, *note on* 372
Ilyris (Illyria or Illiria), where people
   kill with their looks, 24, *note on* 353
image of *'Bred-streete* corner,' 223,
   note on 375
imbracements, *embraces,* 129
incontinent, *at once,* 16, 23, 110, 155
India, 63
indue, *provide, furnish, endow,* 124
Ione. *See* Joan
Iphicrates, an Athenian, general of the
   Persians, 53, 126, 128-130, 135, 137
Isca. *See* Exeter
Islington, a suburb north of London,
   151, 153, 207, *note on* 367
Italy, 98-100, *note on* 365
Itinerary. See Moryson
I wis, *certainly,* 9; iwis, 301; ywis, 277,
   278

jack, *a term of deprecation,* 153, 256,
   290; 'iacke foole,' 153; 'Iack-sauce,'
   215
Jack of Newbury. *See* Winchcomb,
   John
Jackson, William A., reviser of *Short-
   Title Catalogue,* 348 *n.*

J[aggard], W[illiam], printer and bookseller, 1594-1623; printer of *1623 TR*, 380

jakes. *See* Ajax

James IV, King of Scotland, invades England, 30; at Flodden Field, 32-34

Jarman, of the Crane, Colnbrook, char. in *TR*, 320-327

Jarrat. *See* Gerard

Jarrats hall. *See* London, Gerard's Hall

Jarvice, Alderman, suitor of Mistress Farmer in *GCII*, 238-254, *note on* 376

Jenny, friend of Margaret's in *TR*, 281

Jerusalem, captured by Robert, Duke of Normandy, 232, 382

jestbook: TD as translator, xxiv-xxv; *The Life and Pranks of Long Meg of Westminster* (1582), 371

Jesus, mentioned by Margaret in *TR*, 342

jetted, *walked in a prancing, swaggering manner*, 195, *note on* 373

jewelry: silver pins, 16; chain of gold, Queen's gift, 33; Queen's gift of diamond, emeralds, rubies, 50; pearls, 63; bracelets of diamonds, 63, 342; collar of diamonds, 136; rings, 300

Jew's (Old Jewry) Street. *See* London

Joan, char. in *JN*, loved by Benedick. *See* Jone

Joan (Mistress Loveless), employee of Jack's in *JN*, whom Sir George Rigley weds, 82-87

Joan, friend of Florence's in *GCI*, 162-163

Joan, Mistress Farmer's maid in *GCII*, 249

Job, Tom Dove ignored by people the way Job was, 337

John, a servant of Mistress Farmer's in *GCII*, 248, 252

John, Pope, 'as merry as pope *Iohn*,' 185

John XXII, Pope, his father a shoemaker, 54

John, Sir, *a familiar or contemptuous name for a priest*, 20, 228

John, Sir, parish priest in *GCII*, 228-230

John, Sir, priest in *JN* who marries Jack and widow, 20

Johnson, Thomas, *Cornucopiae* (1595): a compendium TD uses, 356; source for 'tonguelesse like a storke,' 365

Jone, char. in *JN*, loved by Benedick, 61-68

Jonson, Ben, *The Alchemist*: dialogue in *JN* as racy and colloquial as, xiv; *Bartholomew Fair* quoted from, 351

joyne stools, 182, *note on* 372

Judas, thirty silver plates for betrayal, 65-66; a servant, Judas-like, betrays Tom Dove, 339

Judith, a maid who falls in love with Harry Nevell in *GCII*, 254

Jupiter, the god, disguises himself in a shepherd's clothes, 133

Katherine, of the Crane: mentioned in *GCII*, 179; ? the same girl, called 'Kate,' 185; TD confuses Margaret with her, 373

Katherine, Queen. *See* Catherine

Keble. *See* Ribble

Kemp, Will, *Nine Daies Wonder* (1600), mentions TD's death, xxiii-xxiv

Kendal, Westmoreland. *See* Cutbert of Kendal

kennel, *gutter*, 'thrust him next the kennell,' 260

Kensington, a village to the W. of Hyde Park, now a London suburb, 263

Kent (or Logria), King of, father of Crispine and Crispianus, 115. *See also* Canterbury, Dover, Feversham, Logria, Towne-malin

Kerbfoord (? Kirdford, Sussex), 220, *note on* 375

kercher, *kerchief*, 'milke-white kerchers on their head,' 27

kersey, *a cloth similar to broadcloth, but more durable*, 28, 35, *note on* 353

kertle, *an outer petticoat*, 28, 342, *note on* 353

ketha, *quotha, indeed, forsooth*, 'Leaue her company ketha?' 73

Kind harts dreame. See Chettle

King's books, ? *used for purposes of taxation*, 300

Kingsmile, Master, into whose cellar Will Sommers falls, 42

Kingstone (Kingston), Surrey, town between Guildford and London, 233, *note on* 376

Kirtland, Lucian Swift. *See* Aldrich

Lais, takes her lovers' purses, 100

Lamusius, King of Lombardy, 'son of a common strumpet,' 54

Lancashire, where Long Meg was born, 176. *See also* Byram, Martin, of Manchester

lance. *See* weapons

Lange, Alexis F.: ed. in 1903 *GCI* and *GCII*, 345, 364, 370; emends 'Richard' to 'John,' 248, *note on* 377; mentioned, xiii, 361, 374, 376

latchet, *leather strap* (*of a shoe*), 141

lawn, *fine linen, like cambric*, 110, 141, *note on* 365

lay a straw, *desist*, 195, *note on* 373

Lea, Henry C., *History of Sacerdotal Celibacy*, 352

Leadenhall. *See* London

lee, *lye*, 74

Legenda Aurea. See Voragine

legs, making, *bowing*, 230

Lethe, lake of, 49

lift, at a dead, *in a crisis or emergency*, 235, *note on* 376

lightly, *easily*, 217

Lily, William, *A Short Introduction of Grammar* (1567), defines 'Nowne substantive,' 375

lin, *cease*, 27

Lincoln's Inn Fields. *See* London

link, *torch*, 20, 21, *note on* 352

lion: in the field, 36, *note on* 355; in Sicily, 103; more grateful than men, 338

Llwyd, *The Breuiary of Britayne* (1573): from which TD borrows for background material in *GCI*, 365; source of Logria and Durovernum in *GCI*, 366; on Doris, Roman town, 367; source for information about Isca, Gloucester, and Rithin, 384

lobcocke, *a country bumpkin*, 288

Lodge, Thomas, *Rosalynde* (1590), source for *As You Like It*, xii

Logria (Kent), 115, *note on* 366

Logria, Queen of, char. in *GCI*, 115, 116, 119, 120, 136

London:

—Abbey of Grace on Tower Hill, 163, 165, *note on* 368

—Aldermen of: 'in their seuerall wards,' 168; Randoll Pert dies an Alderman, 77

—Aldersgate: one of the four oldest gates and a street running S. from the gate to St. Martin's-le-Grand. Mentioned, 260

—Bailiffs, 'The City of London being at this time gouerned by Bayliffes,' 311

—Billingsgate: the chief of the old water-gates, on N. side of the Thames; at its wharf fishing and other boats docked. Oysters from B., 248; barge at B., plied between B. and Gravesend, 166, 257

—Birchin Lane, a street occupied chiefly by drapers and second-hand clothes dealers, 77

—Bishopsgate, one of the old gates in N.E. London, 247

—Black Swan, Simon Eyre's shop, 159

—Blackwall, a suburb of London, on N. side of river, 4 miles E. of St. Paul's, 241, 248

—Blackwell (Bakewell) Hall, Basinghall St., 57, 295

—Bread Street Hill: where *1619 JN* was sold, 348; 'hee made him looke like the Image of *Bred-streete* corner,' 223, *note on* 375

—Bridewell, on W. side of Fleet Ditch, 251, *note on* 377

—Candlewick (Canwick, later Canning, now Cannon) Street, 'Canweeke street,' 77, 'Candlweeke streete,' 295, 296, 297

—Charing Cross, so-called because Edward I had a cross erected wherever the body of his queen, Elinor, rested on its journey to burial at Westminster. The village of Charing lay between London and Westminster. Mentioned, 218, 236

—Cheapside (West Cheap): the old market place, between St. Paul's and the Poultry; shops of goldsmiths and mercers there, 262, 295;

best tailors' shops, 302; Thomas à Becket's house, 322, *note on* 385

—Christ's Hospital: a school for poor children on the N. side of Newgate St.; R. Casteler's bequest to the 'poore fatherlesse children of *Christs Hospitall*,' 212

—'Commons of *London*,' 157; 'Communaltie of the Citie . . . haue chosen you for one of our sheriffes,' 156

—Company of Cordwainers, *GCII* dedicated to, 173

—conduits (or fountains), built in principal streets as early as 14th c. to supply water for citizens. Mentioned, 140, 167, *note on* 367

—Cripplegate, one of the N. gates (pulled down in 1760), 295, *note on* 384

—East Cheap, a street with many butchers' shops, 235

—Finch Lane, running from Cornhill to Threadneedle St., 257

—Fleet Street, 213, 214, 215, 219, 233, 240

—Gerard's Hall, Cheapside, 268, 274, 278, 287, *note on* 382

—Gravesend barge, 182, 259, 262, *note on* 371-372. Gravesend: a port on the Thames 30 miles below L. A barge plied between G. and Billingsgate; from G. ships went to foreign ports

—Guildhall, where the 'Commons of *London*' meet to choose Eyre as sheriff, 156-157

—Jew's (Old Jewry) Street, 'where all the Iewes did inhabite,' 295, *note on* 384

—Leadenhall: built by Simon Eyre, a market for leather, 169; it stood at the intersection of Gracechurch St. and Cornhill at the S.E. corner (and was taken down in 1812)

—Lincoln's Inn Fields, the square immediately W. of Lincoln's Inn. Men executed there, xxvi; the site of a duel, 216

—Marshalsea Prison: stood on the E. side of Borough High St., Southwark; where clothiers imprisoned, 59

—Mayor of L.: Stephen Slany, xxviii-xxix; Simon Eyre made mayor, 139, 167-169; Simon Eyre visits Lord Mayor's house, 147-148; first mayor of L. is Henry Fitzallen, second is Roger Fitzallen, 306

—Newgate: one of the old gates; used as a prison, xxviii, 232, *note on* 376

—Old Change Street, 'at the end of old change, the fishmongers,' 295

—Pancake Bell, its origin, 168, *note on* 368

—Postern Gate (Tower Postern), at the S. end of L. Wall, N. of the Tower of L., built when the Tower was erected and taken down in 1720; a constable of, 165

—St. Bartholomew, priory and hospital, Smithfield, built by Rahere, 277

—St. Bride's Churchyard, where *1648 GCI* was sold, 363

—St. Clement's Lane (now Clement's Lane), 145

—St. Giles Church, Cripplegate, xxv

—St. Giles-in-the-fields, a village near London (S. of what is now New Oxford St.), 263

—St. James's Park, opposite St. James's Palace, 57

—St. Katherine's, a hospital which stood on the Thames immediately E. of the Tower of L., 166

—St. Martin's: an area around church of St. Martin's-le-Grand, which stood on E. side of St. Martin's Lane; the church was destroyed during reign of Henry VIII. Mentioned, 256, 257, 259, 262

—St. Martin's Lane (now St. Martin's-le-Grand), location of shoemakers' shops, 295

—St. Mary Overies, (now St. Saviour's), a church in Southwark, 325, *note on* 385

—St. Nicholas' Shambles: a church on N. side of Newgate St., pulled down at the Reformation; 'at Saint Nicholas church, the flesh shambles,' 295

—St. Paul's Cathedral, 149, *note on* 367; 182, 295

—Sheriff of L.: Randoll Pert made sheriff, 77, *note on* 359; Eyre made sheriff, 154-159; things necessary to have for office of S., 155-156. *See also* shriualtie

—Stilyard, hall where merchants of the Hanseatic League had their headquarters, on N. bank of Thames near L. Bridge, 29, 60, *note on* 354

—Temple: the two Inns of Court, the Inner and Middle T., 85; the name derives from the Knights Templars who once held the land occupied by the T.

—term time, 84, *note on* 359

—Tower of L.: Empson and Dudley sent there, 40; a marriage there, 86; built by Julius Caesar, 296

—Tower Street (now Great Tower St.), 165

—the watch, 165, 200

—Watling Street: the famous Roman Road which ran from Dover through London to Chester. A draper of W.S., 74; in W.S. 'they viewed the great number of Drapers,' 295
See also taverns, Westminster

London Library, owns copy of *1636 TR*, 380

London Weavers' Company, The. See Consitt

long sword. *See* weapons

lotus tree. *See* Lutes

louer, *louver*, 292, *note on* 383

Louis VI, King of France, 284, 303

Loveless, Mistress. Jack borrows servants to wait on her, 84, *note on* 360. *See* Joan

Lownes, Humfrey: printer and bookseller, 1587-1629, at the W. Door of St. Paul's and later at the Star on Bread St. Hill; receives rights to *JN*, 345; printer of *1619* and *1630 JN*, 348, 349

lucre, *covetousness*, 40

Luter, goodman, his lame nag, 222, *note on* 375

Lutes (lotus), a tree the fruit of which makes men forget the country where they were born, 316

Luther, Martin, mentioned, 59

Lyly, John, *Euphues* (1578): pervasive influence, xi-xii; characterization, xxiii

M., T., ? Thomas Moore, printer of *1678 GCI*, 364

Macbeth: its similarity to murder scene in *TR*, xv; referred to for meaning of 'posset,' 371

mace, of catchpole. *See* weapons

McKerrow, Ronald B.: *Printers' and Publishers' Devices in England and Scotland, 1485-1640* (London, 1913), for ornaments on title pages, 348, 380; ed. *The Works of Thomas Nashe* (1904-[10]), xxvi *n.*, xxvii *n.*, 345

MacLehose, James. *See* Moryson

madder, *a red dye*, 28, *note on* 353

madding, *raving, wild*, 'Maids runnes a madding for husbands,' 199

Magdalene College, owner of copy of *1684 JN*, 349; of *1685 GCI*, 364

magget a pie, *magpie*, 313, *note on* 384

maidenhead, of an unconquered town, 210, 211

maiden town, an unconquered town (Boulogne), 210, 211

Maine (France), Count Herbert II of, *note on* 382

malapert, *saucy*, 37, 318, 337

malapropism, TD first to use it in novel, xiv; example of, 28

male, ? *a kind of valise*, 'male or capcase,' 321

malkin, *a kind of mop; a slatternly woman*, 195

man, 'he should not be his man, but his fellow,' 233

Manchester, Lancashire. *See* Byram

manchet, *small loaf or roll of finest kind of wheat bread*, 249

manhood, 'upon the tryall of their manhood,' 233

Mann, Francis Oscar, ed. in 1912 of TD's *Works*, xxv, 345, 350, 352, 355, 364, 365, 367, 369, 370, 371, 372, 373, 374, 375, 376, 377, 378, 381, 384

Marcus Aurelius, Roman emperor 169-180 A.D., 54

Margaret, daughter of Earl of Shrewsbury: char. in *TR*, compared with Sidney's Pamela, xi; an angelic woman, xx; her name means 'pearl,' 283; 'with the lilly-white hand,'

284; 279-284, 305, 314-318, 330-336, 341-343, *note on* 383

Margaret, Queen of Scotland, sister of Henry VIII, 33

Margaret of the Spread Eagle (or Long Meg of Westminster), char. in *GCII*, xiii, xiv, xix, xx, 176-207, *note on* 371

Marlin (Merlin), 'it is come as just to pas as *Marlins* prophesie,' 257, *note on* 377

marriage: TD's conception of a good wife, xxi; jealousy in, 10, 255, 275, 283, 289-293; between old and young, 12; of social unequals, 12, 120-121, 245, 315-316; priests recently allowed to marry, 19, *note on* 352; 'shee would take him downe in his wedding shooes,' 22; wifely virtues, 26, 123; dowry, 28, 29, 86; disagreement between husband and wife, 73; after seduction, 82-87; ballad on ('fine is the silken twist'), 127, *note on* 366; baby's necessities listed, 131; 'many wiues, but few that meete with such kind husbands,' 177; discussion of, between two maids, 177-180; 'it is far better to have a man without money, then money without a man,' 196; 'first learne to thrive, and then wive,' 250; 'as errant a Cuckold as *Iack Coomes*,' 201; 'if every horne-maker should be so plagued by a horned beast, there should bee less hornes made in *Newberie* by many in a yeare,' 10; 'that they may giue their wiues the hornes,' 42; 'shall I giue my husband hornes,' 64; 'And when he comes, she giues him brawne and sowse, . . . and oftentimes the horne,' 127; 'to carry the keys of his Cubberts,' 196; wives' right to freedom, 272-273; 'you will make your husbands hayre growe through his hood,' 291. *See also* courtship, halter, weddings, women

marry (or mary), *by the Virgin Mary, but used as a light interjection (indeed, to be sure, why)*, 153, 162, 183

Mars, danced naked with Venus, 65

Marshalsea Prison. *See* London

Marston, John, *Histrio-Mastix* (1610),

in *Plays*, ed. Wood, on use of word 'stain,' 365

Maximinus: Roman emperor 235-238 A.D., 54; char. in *GCI*, a tyrant who rules England, 115, 119-137

Mayer and Müller: publishers in 1904 of *JN*, 350; in 1903 of *GCI* and *GCII*, 364, 370

Mayor, of London. *See* London

mean season, *meantime*, 261

medicine, of 'sallet oyle and house-leeks,' for a burn, 192

meet, *fit*, 156

Meg, Long. *See* Margaret of the Spread Eagle

Memoirs of the Principal Actors in the Plays of Shakespeare. See Collier

mercers, shops of, in Cheapside, 295, 302. *See also* clothing industry

mercy, 'I cry you mercy,' *I beg your pardon*, 260

Merie Tales of Skelton, The (1567), a jest-biography, xvi

Merlin. *See* Marlin

Merry Wives of Windsor, The, use of 'Cock and Pye,' 367

Mexia, Pedro, Spanish author of *Silva* (1540), trans. Thomas Fortescue in 1571, 356

Michaelmas, 29 September (feast of archangel Michael), 79; one of the four terms when courts were in session, 359

mickle, *much*, 26, 41, 127

middle class: rise of, due to growth of industries, xvi; gentlemen jealous of Jack's wealth, in *JN*, 31; Queen Catherine's attitude toward Jack's wealth, 31, 32; opposition of Cardinal Wolsey to, 36-39, 58-60; clothiers give feast for King's sons, 287; Henry I approves of rise of middle class, 269-271

Middlesex, England: 'and so conducted me to *Black-wall* in *Middlesex*,' 248; 'if you will walke with mee to *Brainford* [Brentford],' 263, *note on* 377. *See also* Stanes

Millet, J[ohn], printer, 1683-92; printer of *1685 GCI*, 364

Millington, Thomas: bookseller in London, 1593-1603, under St. Peter's

Church in Cornhill; enters *JN* in SR, 345; sells his rights to *TR*, 379

mind, *intention*, 164

Mirrour for Magistrates, The (1559), as a probable source, xxvi

Mirrour of Mirth, The. See Des Périers

modicome, *modicum*, 182

Mogunce, invisible being who flung stones at men, 32

mome, *blockhead*, 6, 34

money: ballad on, 6-7; Simon Eyre worth more than £12,000, 154; corpse not buried for lack of, 228-229; cracked money made current, 285-286; made of leather, 296; Cole murdered for, 320-327; King's gift of, 42, 211

—attitudes toward: 'O glorious gold . . . how sweete is thy smell? how pleasing is thy sight? Thou subduest Princes, and ouerthrowest kingdomes,' 64; 'I am not worth a groat, nor no man will trust me for two pence,' 222; 'no penny, no *Pater noster*,' 228; 'wealth makes men lofty, but want makes men lowly,' 232; 'doth want of money part good company?' 256; 'a warme purse is the best medicine for a cold heart that may be,' 259; 'more pence than your wife hath pins,' 262; 'mens coffers are iudged by their garments,' 300; 'of such small account is life, that euery souldier will sell it for six pence,' 336

—credit: bill of hand (*I O U*), 76, 145; buying on credit, 144; notes and bills, 146; 'That we cannot pay for, shall be set up in chalke,' 205, 222, *note on* 375; books of account, 244. *See also* occupiers

—kinds mentioned: angel, 57, 63, 144, 179, 211, 255; bawbee, 309, *note on* 384; crown, 5, 42, 63, 143, 182; half-crown, 222; farthing, 180, 337; groat, 64, 182, 222, 257; mark, 50, 257; noble, 28; penny (d.), 6, 27, 77, 182, 257; half-penny, 180, *see also* haporth; plack, 309, *note on* 384; portigue (portague), 64, 65; pound (li.), 13, 63, 74, 114, 143, 211, 236, 255,

276, 323, 343; shilling, 6, 63, 143, 182, 211; sovereign, 262

—value of: 12 pence = 1 shilling, 'And twelue pence a Sunday . . . , to fifty two shillings amounts in the yeare,' 6; 2 angels = £1, 20 shillings = 2 angels or £1, 208-211; penny, day's pay for child wool-pickers, 27; finest wool 'valued at an hundred pound a cloath,' 39; jewelry worth 900 marks, 50; 'I would saue 20. pound a yeare' (on food for household), 71; two pence for bearing a trunk, 75; four angels, payment to friar for a secret wedding, 124; 'hast thou got a maide with child? . . . heere is now sixteene pence a weeke besides Sope, and Candles . . . ,' 131; 'a hundred of fagots which will not be bought vnder ten groats,' 182; poor widow given an angel in gold, 230; four nobles a year to a water bearer, 246; cost three crowns to be godfather, 248; plate (silver) pawned for 20 marks, sold for £20, 257; 10 shillings for new fiddle, 263; banquet for king's sons cost nine clothiers 40 shillings apiece, 287

—wagers: by Queen, 40; between weavers, 296; £20 to a penny, 141, 214. *See also* shot, 'to pay the shot'

Moraigne, Earl of. *See* Mortain, Robert, Count of

morin. *See* murren

Morlesse (Morlaix), France, captured by Earl of Surrey in 1522, 82, *note on* 359

morrice (morris) dance, mentioned in ballad, 34

Mortain, Robert, Count of (d. 1091?), joins Robert Curthose against Henry I, 271-272, *note on* 382

Moryson, Fynes, *Itinerary* (1617), ed. James McLehose (1907-08), on 'cross-cloths,' 366

Moseley, Edwin M. *See* Ashley

Mount Albon, 'as safe as king *Charlemaine* in mount Albon,' 313

Muggins, William, helps TD draft a complaint, xxviii

mumbudget, *silence*, 'looke you play mum-budget,' *see that you keep silent*, 196, *note on* 373 murren, *murrain, plague,* 162, 201, 247

muse, *to wonder, be surprised,* 182

Musgrave, Sir Michael, mentioned by Tom Drum in *GCII,* 264, *note on* 377-378

music: at tavern, 14, 325; at wedding, 29; military drums and trumpet, 32, 128, 210; ditty and burden (of a song), 'two of them singing the Dittie, and all the rest bearing the burden,' 43; 'himselfe sung the Ditty, and his fellowes bore the burthen,' 127; shoemakers should be able to play flute, sound trumpet, and sing 3-part song, 115, 223-224; northern jigs, southern songs, 140; drums and trumpets at breakfast, 168; choir of Westminster Abbey, 208; for king, 208-211, 305; at supper for shoemakers, 212; fiddle, cost of, 263; treble viol, 263; 'makes a sad mind merrie,' 263; *'Anthony* now now, the firkin Fidler of *Finchlane,'* 257; *'Anthony . . .* seeking to change musicke for money,' 258; fiddlers follow Tom Dove 'up and down the citie,' 276-277; Rahere, eminent musician, 277, *note on* 383; instruments garnished gold and silver, 277. *See also* Anthony-now-now, ballads, consort, crash, huntsup, noise, pricksong, waits

muskadine, *muscatel,* 181, *note on* 371

Muskelborough (Musselburgh, Scotland) Field, battle of, 240, 264, *note on* 377

mutton, *prostitute or loose woman,* 68, *note on* 358

'My Mind to Me a Kingdom Is.' *See* Dyer

nail, 'turn it ouer my naile,' *a method of drinking,* 187, *note on* 372

Narcissus, in love with his reflection, 101

Nashe, Thomas: *Christ's Tears* (1593), quoted from, for 'post ouer,' 384; *Have with You to Saffron-Walden* (1596), refers to TD as 'Balletting Silke-weauer,' xxiii, refers to TD's *The Garland of Good Will,* xxvi *n.,* on use of 'mumbudget,' 373, quoted from on 'coat with foure elbowes,'

374; *Pierce Penilesse* (1592), quoted from, 372, 373; *Strange News* (1592), TD mentioned in the Harvey-Nashe quarrel, xxvii, quoted from, regarding broom boys, 355; *The Terrors of the Night* (1594), quoted from, on the shrinking of Northern cloth, 382; *The Unfortunate Traveler* (1594), realism alien to TD, xi, reference to salting beef, 359

National Library of Scotland, owns copy of *1632 TR,* 380

neat's leather, *cowhide,* 281

Nevell, Harry, semi-historical character in *GCII,* xv, xxiv, 219-255

Newberry Library: owns copy of *1672 JN,* 349; of *1690* and *1696 GCI,* 364

Newbury, Berkshire: where *JN* takes place; St. Bartholomew's Chapel in, 20

Newbury, Jack of. *See* Winchcomb, John

Newgate prison. *See* London

Nicholas, char. in *GCI,* 160-166

nick, 'in the nick' (of time), 81

Nine Daies Wonder. See Kemp

noise of musicians, *band of musicians,* 14, 29, 151

nonce, for the, *for the special occasion,* 182

Norfolk, mentioned, 247. *See also* Norwich

Normandy, Robert Curthose, Duke of. *See* Robert, Duke of Normandy

Northumberland: Earl of, in ballad 'The Maidens Song,' 43-47; 'Lord of *Northumberlands* hunts-man,' 222. *See also* Flodden Field

Norwich, Norfolk: once thought to be TD's birthplace, xxiii; TD ballad printed there, xxv

nose, 'bore [one] through the nose,' *to cheat or swindle,* 164, *note on* 368; wipe your nose, *to cheat,* 165; 'he lookes with a hungry nose,' 180; jest of a nose too large, 317-320; 'nose burst out suddenly ableeding,' *an ill omen,* 323, *note on* 385

nowne substantive, 221, *note on* 375

noyse. *See* noise

occupiers, *traders, merchants,* 64, *note on* 357

Odo, Bishop, aids Robert Curthose against Henry I, 382

office, *rooms where servants work*, 190, *note on* 372

Old Change Street. *See* London

omens, TD's use of in *TR*, 323 ff., 385

once, 'once and vse it not, is not such a matter,' 185

one of the town, *a prostitute*, 80, *note on* 359

Opie, Iona and Peter, *Oxford Dictionary of Nursery Rhymes*, suggest Old King Cole may be Thomas Cole, 381

order, to take an, *to arrange*, 219

ordinance. *See* weapons

Oswestry, Shropshire, a walled town, 306

overcharge, *overburden, overload*, 'euery one sought to ouercharge him [with wine],' 164

owe, *own*, 144, *note on* 367

Oxford University Press: publisher in 1912 of TD's *Works*, ed. Mann, 350, 364, 370, 381; in 1928 of *GCI*, ed. Halliday, 364

packing, set, ? *drunk*, 'Haunce . . . called for wine lustily . . . as the Dutchman was soone set packing,' 164

pad, *toad*, 201, *note on* 374

Page, a miser, in a ballad, xxvi

Pallas, Greek goddess, '*Pallas* wrought vpon the Loome,' 40

Pancake Bell. *See* London

Pandosto. See Greene

pantofles, *indoor slippers*, 208, *note on* 374

pap, *a soft food for infants*, 131, *note on* 366

Paradoxes of Defence. See Silver

parbreaking, *vomiting*, 164, *note on* 368

Paris, France, Hugh goes there, 98

Paris of Troy, Helen was his 'trull,' 41

Parliament: Jack chosen burgess in, 70; instituted by Henry I, 267, 304, *note on* 381

Parrie, Sir Thomas, his son at Jack's wedding, 29, *note on* 353

Parson of Speen (Speenhamland), suitor of widow, in *JN*, 8, 14-19

partlet, *neckerchief*, 67, *note on* 357

passed, *happened*, 328

Passinger, Thomas, the First: bookseller, 1664-88, at the Three Bibles on London Bridge; *see 1672* and *1680? JN*, 349

Patch, Cardinal Wolsey's servant and jester, in *JN*, 58-59, *note on* 357

Paternoster Row, where *1630 JN* was *sold*, 349

Paterson, George, shows that TD uses Grafton on Duke Robert, 385

Paulet, Sir Amias, ? put Wolsey in the stocks, 43, *note on* 356

pavement. *See* checkered pavement

P[avier], T[homas]: draper and bookseller, 1600-25; enters *GCI* in SR, 369; enters *TR* in SR, 379; seller of *1612* and *1623 TR*, 380

Peachy, of Fleet Street, char. in *GCII*, 213-218, 219, 226-233, 251-255, *note on* 374

Peachy's wife, 251, 253

Penelope, wife of Odysseus: '*Penelope* apace did spin,' 41; has been wooed but has given no answer, 65

Penelope's puppy, 'that doth both bite and whine,' 163

penny fathers, *misers, skinflints*, 179

Pert, Randoll, char. in *JN*, xxii, xxiii, 74-77, 359

Pertinax, Aelius, (? Publius Helvius Pertinax, Roman emperor 193 A.D.), 53

Peterborough Cathedral, owner of copy of *1636 TR*, 380

Petworth, Sussex: Tom Drum a shoemaker there, 219; Tom drinks at the 'signe of the Crowne,' 220; Tom owes money to the 'Hostesse of the George,' 222; *note on* 375

Pickering, William, publisher in 1828 of *TR*, 381

pie, ? *magpie*, 'as merrie as a Pie,' 6; pie peckt, *pecked by a magpie*, 159, *note on* 368

Pie Corner, Giltspur St. and Cock Lane, in W. Smithfield, where *1660 GCII* was sold, 370

Piero, Doctor, who put out Duke Robert's eyes, 334

pike, 'armed with Pikes,' 30, *note on* 354

pike-staffe, *a walking stick with a metal point at the lower end*, 219, 224

Pimlico, The, famous tavern at Hoxton, 368

Piper, Dick, mentioned as a cuckold, 113

pippin, *a seedling apple*, 79

plack, *a small Scottish copper coin worth 4 pennies*, 309, *note on* 384

Pliny, a source of Mexia's *The Forest*, 356

pluck, or gather, *the heart, liver and lungs of an animal*, 358

Plutarch, a source of Mexia's *The Forest*, 356

Plymouth, England, home of Page in ballad, xxvi

poast (post) off, *transfer a duty to another*, 309, *note on* 384

Policrates (Polycrates), tyrant of Samos in 6th c. B.C., 136, *note on* 367

Pollard, Albert F., his *Wolsey* (1929), on Wolsey in the stocks, 356

Pollard, A. W., and G. R. Redgrave, *Short-Title Catalogue, 1475-1640* (1926), 348 *n.*

Polonia (Poland), 225

Pont Varry, a place name from Llwyd, 92, *note on* 365

Pontus (ancient name for the Black Sea): where stones burn in water, 62, *note on* 357; a bird was never seen in, 316

Popham, Sir John, Lord Chief Justice, xxviii

Popular Music of the Olden Time, by William Chappell, 351

portigue, *portague, a Portuguese gold coin of the 16th c., variously estimated as worth from £3½ to £4½ sterling*, 64, 65

Portugal, good cork in, 226

posie, *motto*, 114, *note on* 366

posnet, *metal pot or cup for boiling*, 131, *note on* 366

posset, *a drink made of hot milk and ale or wine*, 181, *note on* 371

Postern Gate. *See* London

post hast, *posthaste, immediately*, 241

pottle, *two quarts or half a gallon*, 191, *note on* 373

poverty: 'Misery is troden downe by many,' 74, *note on* 358; scares people away, 256; brings loss of friends, 337-340

Powis (Powes or Powys): one of 3 principalities of Wales before it was united in 10th c.; place name from Llwyd, 92, *note on* 365; King of Powis, father of Sir Hugh in *GCI*, 92

pox, used as a pun, 357

point, *used to attach hose to doublet*, 75, *note on* 358

prattling, *talking, chattering*, 168

Prayer Book Dictionary, The. See Harford

prefer, *present, advance, promote*, 235, 239

prentice, *apprentice*, 167

Priam, King of Troy, mentioned in ballad, 41

pricksong, *song with written notes*, 208

Primislas, King of Bohemia, mentioned in *JN*, 54-55, *note on* 357

prison: debtors', Randoll Pert sent there, 74; Tom Dove almost has to go, 339-340. *See also* London, Marshalsea, Newgate

privy, *secret*, 138, 200; privy to, *aware of, familiar with*, 125, 134, 145

prize, 'to play his prize,' *to take part in a contest or exhibition (of fencing)*, 263

Probus, Roman emperor 276-282 A.D., 53

protest, *proclaim, declare*, 189

Proverbs, proverbial comparisons, and sayings:

'Abundance groweth from riches, and disdaine out of abundance' (Roberts), 155;

'All things are not as they seeme' (Tilley, T199), 7;

'As errant a Cuckold as *Iack Coomes*' (Roberts), 201;

'As good as George a Green' (Tilley, G83), 21;

'A warme purse is the best medicine for a cold heart that may be,' 259;

'A womans love being hardly obtained, is esteemed most sweet,' 195;

Proverbs, proverbial comparisons, and sayings (Cont.):

'Bee it better, or be it worse/Please you the man that beares the purse' (Tilley, P646), 308;

'Being so long a ranger, he would at home be a stranger,' 8;

'Brag is a good Dog' (Tilley, B587), 217;

'Call me Cut' (Tilley, C940), 217;

'Doth want of money part good company?' 256;

'Faint souldiers neuer find fauour' (Roberts), 7;

'First learne to thrive, and then wive' (Tilley, T264), 250;

'God sends meat, and the diuel sends cookes' (Tilley, G222), 277;

'Hap what hap will' (Tilley, C529), 199;

'Hee is most poore that hath least wit' (Roberts), 179;

'He was a tall man of his hands' (Tilley, M163), 219;

'Hee will bee so bent to his books, that he will haue little minde of his bed,' 9;

'Howsoever things doe frame,/Please well thy Master, But chiefly thy Dame' (Roberts), 119;

'It is euen as dead as a doore naile' (Tilley, D567), 162;

'Tis an old saying, they brag most that can doe least' (Tilley, B591), 225;

Like Aesops dogge lying in the maunger, will doe no good himselfe, nor suffer such as would to doe any' (Tilley, D513), 32;

'Love and Lordship brookes no fellowship' (Tilley, L495), 240;

'Many haue runne neere the goale and yet lost the game' (Roberts), 19;

'Many women many words' (Tilley, W686), 328;

'Men gather no grapes in Ianuary' (Roberts), 202;

'Mens coffers are iudged by their garments,' 300;

'More maids then Malkin' (Tilley, M39), 195;

'More pence than your wife hath pins,' 262;

Proverbs, proverbial comparisons, and sayings (Cont.):

'No penny, no *Pater Noster,*' (Tilley, P199), 228;

'One bird in hand is worth two in bush' (Tilley, B363), 339;

'One Swallow makes not a Sommer' (Tilley, S1025), 15;

'Poore people, whom God lightly blesseth with most children' (Roberts), 267;

'Profered ware is worse by ten in the hundred than that which is sought' (Roberts), 8;

'Put up this and put up all' (Tilley, A172), 216;

'Rich preyes do make true men theeues,' 125;

'Soft fire makes sweet mault' (Tilley, F280), 155;

'Store is no sore' (Tilley, S903), 8;

'Such as are in their youth wasters, doe prooue in their age starke beggars' (Roberts), 300;

'The longer she liues the worse shee is' (Roberts), 24;

'The maried sort, that for a dram of delight haue a pound of paine' (Tilley, D582), 122;

'There goes Saint *Hughes* bones' (Tilley, S44), 112;

'There lay a straw for feare of stumbling' (Tilley, S919), 195;

'They are worthy to knowe nothing, that cannot keepe something' (Roberts), 9;

'They proue seruants kind and good,/That sing at their busines like birds in the wood' (Tilley, S240), 140;

'Thou art not worth so much as goodman *Luters* lame nagge' (Roberts), 222;

'Three things are to small purpose, if the fourth be awaie' (Roberts), 17;

'Two may keep counsell if one be away,' 178;

'You are like to *Penelopes* puppie' (Roberts), 163;

'You can spie day at a little hole' (Tilley, D99), 188;

'You stand like Saint *Martins* begger upon two stilts' (Roberts), 260;

Proverbs, proverbial comparisons, and sayings (Cont.):

'Wealth makes men lofty, but want makes men lowly,' 232;

'Where much talke is, must needes bee some offence,' 65;

'Where true loue remaines, there is no discontent,' 122;

'Women are not Angels, though they haue Angels faces' (Roberts), 184;

'Womens tongues are like Lambes tayles, which sildome stand still,' 65

Proverbs XXXI, Biblical source for one of TD's ballads and his attitude toward women, xxi

pulard, *poulard, chicken,* 160

pumps, *indoor slippers,* 208, *note on* 374

pursevant, *pursuivant, a king's messenger,* 230

Purslowe, Elizabeth: printer, 1633-46, at the East End of Christ Church; printer of *1639 GCII,* 370

P[urslowe?], G., printer of *1660 GCII,* 370

quarter staff. *See* weapons

quean, *harlot,* 65; 'an errant queane,' 203; 'an errant drab and a very queane,' 204; *term of contempt applied to a woman,* 153, 319

quill, *bobbin, spool,* 12, 13, 41, 296, *note on* 315

Quip for an Upstart Courtier, A (1592), Greene's, quoted from regarding 'brome man,' 355

quittance, cry, *get even,* 228

quoystrel, *coistrel, custrel, a knave or base fellow,* 218

Rahere (d. 1184), eminent musician, built priory and hospital of St. Bartholomew, 277, *note on* 383

Rainsford, Sir John, a wild knight in *GCII,* 227-233, *note on* 376

Ralpho, on George a Green, in *Hudibras,* 352

razed, *erased,* 108

Reading, Berkshire: clothiers meet there before going to London, 271; clothiers' wives meet there before going to London, 295; King's visit to, 303-304; King buried there, 343

Reading, Thomas of. *See* Cole

Reading Abbey, founded by Henry I, 304; Henry I buried there, 343

Reading Castle, Henry I built it and lived there, 304

realism: of Nashe and Greene, xi; TD's details of everyday life, xv

Red Cross, Sign of the, in London, Crab goes there for a drink, 297

Redgrave, G. R. *See* Pollard

Reior. *See* Rahere

resolve, *clear up [one's] doubts,* 155

respect, *heed,* 183

Rhodes (or Rodes), H[enry]: bookseller, 1681-1709, at the Star on Fleet St., etc. *See 1675? GCI* (which perhaps should bear a later date), 364; *see also 1690 GCI,* 364

Rhys, Ernest, ed. in 1929 of *TR,* 381

Ribble (? Keble), Parson, mentioned by Tom Drum, 264, *note on* 378

Richard, Prince, son of Henry I, 287, 292-293

Richard, servant of Mistress Farmer's, char. in *GCII,* 246

Richard of Worcester, clothier mentioned in dedication to *JN,* 3

Richards, T., publisher in 1859 of *JN,* 350

Rigley, Sir Edward, mentioned in *JN,* 82, 359

Rigley, Sir George, char. in *JN,* 82-87, 359

Rinehart, publishers in 1953 of *JN,* 350

Rithin: a castle and town, 305; information about, from Llwyd, 384

Robert Curthose, Duke of Normandy (1054-1134), eldest son of William the Conqueror: compared to Sidney's Musidorus, xi; as an historical char., xviii-xx; refuses to be King of Jerusalem, 269; heir to English throne, 271; plots to take English throne, 272, 284; captured, and imprisoned at Cardiff Castle, 303; meets Margaret, 305; in Gloucester with Henry I, 305; proposes to Margaret, 314-317; escapes, is recaptured, has eyes put out, 330-336; desires to be buried at Gloucester, 343; *notes on* 382, 385

Robert, 1st Earl of Gloucester, son of Henry I, 306

Robert of Bellême. *See* Shrewsbury, Earl of

Robert of Flanders, captured Jerusalem in 1099, 382

Robin, Round, char. in *GCII*, xxii, 174, 182-212, *note on* 373

Robin Hood, TD conceives of Wallace as a kind of Robin Hood, 384

Rochester Castle, where Queen of Kent is imprisoned, 119, *note on* 366

Roger, Bishop of Salisbury, 303, 304

Rollins, Hyder E., author of two articles on TD's sources, 356

Rome: Winifred's father sent there, 92; Cateratus led captive to, 119; TD's references to, 356

rook, *literally crow, but also 'knave,' 'cheat,' or 'gull,'* 190, *note on* 372-373

Rosalynde. See Lodge

rosemary, used at wedding, 29, *note on* 353

rounding, *whispering,* 188, 198, *note on* 373

rounsefull, *rounceval, a large, boisterous woman,* 198

Rouse, W. H. D., ed. in 1920 of *JN* and *TR*, 350, 381

rowers, *those who put a nap on cloth,* 27

rub out, *? go on in spite of difficulties,* 198

ruddocks, *gold,* 187

runnagate, *renegade, traitor,* 128

runnet, *rennet, curdled milk,* 113, *note on* 365

rush, *something of little value,* 240, *note on* 377

russet, *a coarse woolen cloth. See also* cloth

Russia, length of days there, 225

Rutupium. *See* Dover

St. Anne, Gillian swears by her in *GCII*, 187

St. Bartholomew, priory and hospital, Smithfield, 277

St. Bride's Churchyard, London, where *1648 GCI* was sold, 363

St. Clement's Lane (now Clement's Lane), London, 145

St. George, likes his horse and fights the dragon, 114

St. Giles, Cripplegate, a church in London, with references to TD in its parish register, xxv

St. Giles-in-the-fields. *See* London

St. Gregory's Chapel, Canterbury, 125, *note on* 366

St. Hugh: char. in *GCI*, 92-115, *note on* 364; bequeathes his bones to shoemakers, 112. *See also* shoemaking (St. Hugh's bones)

St. James's Park, London, 57

St. Katherine's. *See* London

St. Martin's: an area of London where the 'Greene King' lived (*see* London); 'and make you stand like *Saint Martins* begger upon two stilts,' 260

St. Martin's Lane. *See* London

St. Mary Overies. *See* London

St. Nicholas' Church. *See* London

St. Paul's: the cathedral church of London, 182; ? the chains surrounding the churchyard, 149, *note on* 367; its weathercock stolen, 295

St. Ursula, her life in *Golden Legend* is basis for Winifred-Hugh relationship in *GCI*, 365

St. Winifred, her life in *Golden Legend* is basis for TD's Winifred in *GCI*, 365

sale (dialect), *soul,* 290, *note on* 383

Salisbury, Bishop of, Henry I leaves government in his hands, 284

Salisbury, Wiltshire, Henry I visits, 304-305. *See also* Sarum, Sutton of Salisbury

Salutation, a tavern in Newgate St., London, 258, *note on* 377

Sarazines-head (Saracen's Head), a tavern without Newgate, 223, *note on* 375

sarcenet, *sarsenet, a cloth of fine silk, plain or twilled,* 35, 48, *note on* 354

Sarum Town (Salisbury), the capital city of Wiltshire, 298

sayings. *See* proverbs

'sblood, *God's blood (an oath),* 214, 217, 238

Schulz, Ernst, *Die englischen Schwankbücher bis herab zu Dobson's Drie Bobs* (1912), analysis of jestbook form, xvi, xxv

Scolopendra, a fish dangerous to touch, 25, *note on* 353
Scotland: a day in June is light for 24 hours, 225; Muskelborough (Musselburgh) Field, where 14,000 Scots slain, 240, *note on* 377. *See also* Flodden Field, James IV, Wallis
Scott, Sir Walter, *Heart of Midlothian*, his use of historical char. compared to TD's, xviii
seassed, *assessed*, 40, *note on* 355
seethe, *boil*, 321
Senior, Dorothy, ed. in 1912 of *TR*, 381
sennight, *seven night, week,* 263
se-reverence, 80, *note on* 359
sergeants, *police, formerly called catchpoles*, 311
set, 'set me at nought,' 247; 'set packing.' *See* packing
Sextus (Sixtus) IV, Pope 1471-84, 54
shacke (Italian accent), *jack, common fellow,* 68
shadowed, *veiled,* 110, *note on* 365
Shakespeare, William, his use of sources, xii
shale, *shell (of a nut),* 339
shambles. *See* flesh shambles
Sharpe, Reginald R., *London and the Kingdom* (London, 1894-95), on 'Stilyard,' 354
Sheffield, University of, Library, owner of copy of *1627 GCI*, 361
sheriff of London. *See* London
shoemaking: ballad to shoemakers, 91; why called the 'Gentle Craft,' 105, 107; a shoemaker's son is a prince born, 126, 128, 135, 137, 143; leather garments of shoemaker, 133, 145; 'The Shoomakers Song on Crispianus night,' 137-139; shoemakers' holidays, on Crispianus' Night, 137, 139, and on Shrove Tuesday, 168-169; 'first wrought upon the low cut shoo with the square toe, and the latchet overthwart the instep,' 141; 'there should be a Market kept euery Monday for Leather,' 169; Company of Cordwainers, 173; shoemakers' oath, 'by good Crispianus soule,' 196; shoemakers sing for the King, 208-211; how many shoes made in a day, 224, 225; shoes

that last a twelve month, 226; King's shoemaker, 233; shops in St. Martin's Lane, 295
—apprentices and journeymen: the ideal journeyman, 114-115, 223-224; bound for seven years, 118; work done by an apprentice, 119; camaraderie of journeymen, 219-220, 222-223; number of shoemakers employed by one man, 226, 256
—tools and materials: St. Hugh's bones, why tools of shoemaker so called, 112-115; mentioned, 105, 141, 219, 221; tools listed in ballad, 114; sole-leather, 123; spun hemp for shoe thread, 131; cutting knife, 142; stirrop, 157, *note on,* 368; last, 181; where best hides, leather, and cork found, 226; shoes of neat's leather, 281
See also dress
shoes, slip, *slippers,* 75, *note on* 358
shoe thread, 114, 131, *note on* 365
shot, *tavern reckoning,* 'to pay the shot,' *to pay the bill,* 15, 16, 140, 167, 205, 258; 'fiftie shot,' 30, *note on* 354. *See also* weapons
Shrewsbury, Robert of Bellême, Earl of (fl. 1098): *note on* 383; banished by Henry I, 271-272; his Lady and children homeless, 272; Margaret, char. in *TR,* is his daughter
shrift, *confessional,* 228
shriualtie, 157, *note on* 368
shroe, *shrew,* 190
Shropshire, 282. *See* Oswestry
Shrove Tuesday, annual breakfast on, given by Mayor for apprentices, 168
shrowded up, *covered up,* 219
Sibyls, nine, prophetesses of antiquity, 13, *note on* 351
Sichnaunt, Valley of, 92, 102, *note on* 365
Sicily: 'monstrous men that had but one eie a piece, and that placed in the midst of their foreheads,' 102; 'as thicke as Bees in,' 226
Siciona (Sicyon, in ancient Greece), best hides and leather from, 226
Sidney, Sir Philip, *Arcadia* (1590, 1593), his idealized characters, xi, xxiii

Sievers, Richard, ed. in 1903 of *JN*, 350

silken twist, 127, *note on* 366

Silver, George, *Paradoxes of Defence* (1599), quoted on 'wards,' 376

Simon and Jude, feast of, 137

Simon of Southampton, alias 'Supbroth,' char. in *TR*, xxii, 267, 268, 274, 288-293, 300-302, 304-305, 343, *note on* 381

Simon's wife, char. in *TR*, 294-296, 299-303, 328-330

Sirens, seek Ulysses' destruction, 99, 100

sirra, *derogatory form of sir*, 24, 75, 313

Six Articles, repealed, 352

six-score to the hundred, 227, *note on* 376

slampam, give the, *to play a trick on*, 164, *note on* 368

Slany, Stephen, mayor of London, xxviii, xxix

sleepy drench, *sleeping potion*, 66

sleight, *trick*, 13

slops, *wide and baggy breeches or hose*, 35, 214, *note on* 355

smutched, *blackened*, 145, *note on* 367

sodden, *boiled*, 329

Somerset, Duke of: char. in *JN*, 58, 59; mentioned in *GCII*, 240

Somerset House, London, where the Winchcomb wills are filed, 350

Sommers, Will, Henry VIII's fool, in *JN*, xvii, 40, 42, 50-52, *note on* 355

sorrel, *an herb*, 199, *note on* 374

sort, *group or company*, 113

sound, *swoon*, 251

Southampton, Hampshire. *See* Simon of Southampton

sowsc, *any pickled food*, 127, *note on* 366

sowter, *shoemaker*, 213, *note on* 374

Spain, an ambling jennet of, 331

Sparta, where best cork grows, 226

speak, 'I spoke without book,' 249

Spencer, Theodore, *Death and Elizabethan Tragedy* (1936), on the omens used in Elizabethan tragedy, 385

Spenser, Edmund, *A View of the State of Ireland*, ed. Rudolf Gottfried

(1949), on 'liverye' and 'coygnye,' 359

Spinhome-land (Speenhamland), a suburb of Newbury, Berkshire, called Speen, 8

spirit of the buttery. *See* buttery

Spread Eagle at Ivybridge, Westminster, 75, *note on* 358

squaring, *swaggering*, 213

Stafford, John, bookseller, 1637-64. *See* *1648* and *1652 GCI*, 363-364

staine, *excel*, 108, *note on* 365

stammel, *a coarse woolen cloth*, 'out upon her foule stammell,' 186, *note on* 372. *See also* cloth

Stanes (Staines), Middlesex, a town on the Thames, 17 miles W. of London, 270

stand (of ale), *a cask, tub, or large barrel*, 220

standing-stool, 131, *note on* 366

Star, Sign of the, on Bread Street Hill, where *1619 JN* was sold, 348

starved, 'starued in my bed,' *perishing with cold*, 20

statute, 'at the Statute,' *at the fair* (which is held at a time ordained by statute or charter), 280

Steven, who was stoned, 60

still, *ever, always, constantly*; 'stiltossed bed,' *always turning in bed, sleepless*, 100

Stilyard. *See* London

stirrop, *a cobbler's tool*, 157, *note on* 368

stockfish, beat as a, 153, *note on* 368

Stony Stratford, Buckinghamshire, 52 miles N.W. of London, 31

stools, join, *joined stools*, 182, *note on* 372

stork, 'tonguelesse like a Storke,' 95

Stow, John, *Survey of London* (1598): referred to in notes as 'Stow,' 345; on the Stilyard, 354; references to Ivybridge, 358; on 'Paul's chain,' 367; on Cornelius van Dun, 371; notes that Bridewell became a 'Workhouse for the poore,' 377; on Gerard the giant, 382; refers to Old Jewry as a street, 384; on the origin of 'Cripplegate,' 384

Strange Histories, TD ballad collection, xxvii

Strange News. See Nashe
Strangwidge, a sea captain in *GCII*, 214-218, *note on* 374
straw, lay a, *desist*, 195, *note on* 373; 'care a straw,' 196; 'a pad lying in the straw,' *a lurking or hidden danger*, 201, *note on* 374
Stubs, Phillip, ballad writer, xxvii
stuck, 39, *note on* 355
Stuteley, Tom, a sea captain in *GCII*, 214-218, *note on* 374
Suffolk, Duke of, Peachy is his servant in *GCII*, 213, 214, 218
Suffolk, mentioned, 247. *See also* Beckles
Sugden, Edward H.: *Topographical Dictionary*, referred to in notes as 'Sugden,' 345; suggests 'Bosoms Inne' a corruption of 'Blossoms Inn,' 381
superstitious, *religious*, 96
sure, *betrothed, engaged*, 13, 160, 251
surety, *bail*, 313; *confidence in [one's] safety*, 316
Surrey, Earl of, 82, 359
Surrey. *See* Gilford, Kingstone
Sussex. *See* Kerbsfoord, Petworth
Sutton of Salisbury, char. in *TR*, 267, 268, 270, 274, 287-293, 304, 330, 343, *note on* 381
Sutton's wife, char. in *TR*, 294-296, 299-303, 328-330
Sweathland (Sweden), 225
Swift, Stephen, publisher in 1912 of *TR*, 381
Swinborne, Lady, mentioned in *GCII*, 241, 242, 248
sword. *See* weapons
swownes (or swownds), *God's wounds (an oath)*, 195, 213, 218
Sympson, Gabriell, printer of weavers' complaint in 1595, xxviii

taileclouts, *swaddling bands*, 131, *note on* 366
tailor, unnamed suitor of widow in *JN*, 8-19
tall, *valiant, fine*, 'tall man of his hands,' 219
tallow-cake, *a lump of congealed fat*, 184, *note on* 372
Taprobana (Taprobane), the old Greek name for island of Ceylon, 61

Tartaria (or Tartary), home of the Tatars, a vast, indefinite area in Asia west of Mongolia and north of the Himalayas, 62
taverns: the Bell in the Strand, London, 84; Sign of the Bell, Westminster, 212; Bosom's Inn, Cheapside, London, 268, 275, 288-293, *note on* 381; the Crane, Westminster, 179; Sign of the Crane in Colnbrook, 327; Sign of the Crown, Petworth, 220; the George in Colnbrook, 263; the George in Lombard Street, London, 145; the George at Petworth, 222; the George in Westminster, 176; Gerard's Hall, Cheapside, London, 268, 274, 278, 287, *note on* 382; the Pimlico at Hoxton, *note on* 368; Sign of the Red Cross, London, 297; the Rose in Barking, London, 161; the Salutation, Newgate St., London, 258, *note on* 377; Saracen's Head, without Newgate, London, 223, *note on* 375; the Spread Eagle at Ivybridge, Westminster, 75, 176, 190, *note on* 358; the Three Pigeons at Brentford, 377; the Three Tuns, Westminster, 204, 205; the World's End, in Spring Gardens, Knightsbridge, London, 261, *note on* 377
tawny, *tanned by the sun*, 'till he looked like a tawnie Moore,' 51; tawny coats, *tan-colored coats*, 14, 213, 214
taxation. *See* King's books
Taylor, J. F., publisher in 1903 of *TR*, 381
Tegina, 'which is now called Flintshire,' 92, *note on* 365
Temple. *See* London
tenters, *stretchers for cloth*, 28
term time, *period when law courts were in session*, 84, *note on* 359; 'a good Term,' 196, *note on* 373; 'an Ill word foure times a yeer,' 232, 376
Terrors of the Night, The. See Nashe
text, explanation of: editions used, xxx; collation, xxx; textual footnotes, xxxi-xxxii; emendations, xxxii; explanation of print used, xxxii. *See also* collation notes and explanatory notes

458

T[hackeray], W[illiam]: bookseller at the Angel in Duck Lane, etc., 1664-92. *See 1684 JN,* 349; *1678* and *1685 GCI,* 364; and *1672 TR,* 380

Thales, Greek Astronomer of 7th c. B.C., while he 'gaz'd on the starres, he stumbled in a pit,' 316

Theophrastus, a philosopher, son of a tailor, 55

Thoms, W. J., ed. in 1828 of *TR,* 381

Three Bibles, where *1700? JN* was sold, 350

Three Pigeons, at Brentford, England, 377

thrumb, silk, *silk having a nap or shaggy surface,* 214, *note on* 374

thumb-leather, ? *a protective covering for the thumb, made of leather,* 145

thunder, 'driuen away by ringing of belles,' 316

tike, ? *dog,* 290

time, 'tooke hold of Time's forlocke,' *rose early,* 125

Titus Andronicus, reference to Acteon, 351

to doe, *ado,* 219, 239, 256

tomble, *tumble,* 67

Tom Jones (1749), by Henry Fielding, combines best elements of *JN, TR,* and *Dobsons Drie Bobbes,* xvii

Tomlinson, Thomas, whose monument TD may be referring to in *GCII,* 375

Tower of London. *See* London

Tower Street. *See* London

Towne-malin (Town Malling), Kent, 'aske all the men in Towne-malin,' 223, *note on* 376

Tracy, Eben[ezer]: bookseller, 1695-1719, at the Three Bibles on London Bridge; seller of *1700? JN,* 350; seller of *1696 GCI,* 364

train, *group of attendants,* 155, 214

travail, *labor,* 'diligent labour and trauaile,' 7; labor of childbearing, 133, 241, *note on* 367

trencher, *wooden plate,* 236, 246

trencher flies, 'these trencher flies, these smooth faced flatterers,' 257

trench more, *a lively, boisterous country dance,* 192

Trinity, one of the terms when courts were in session, 359

tro, *trow, believe, think,* 235

troth, *truth,* 134, 152, 162

Trotter, Tom, mentioned by Tom Drum in *GCII,* 264, *note on* 378

Troy, besieged by the Greeks, 41

Turk, 'to sweare like a Turke,' 153; 'betwixt the Turke, and the Devill,' 224

Turney (Tournay), France, where Henry VIII fought, 33

Turwin (Thérouanne), France, where Henry VIII fought, 33

Tuttle Fields, in Westminster, 198, *note on* 373

Tweedle, one of Jack's servants in *JN,* xiv, 78-81

two-hand sword. *See* weapons

Ulysses, his destruction sought by the Sirens, 100

Unfortunate Traveler, The. See Nashe

unmeet, *unfit,* 152, 242

unready, *undressed,* 68

unseparately, *inseparably,* 124

Ursula, char. in *GCI,* xx, 120-139

Valentinian, 'who also was crowned [Roman] Emperor,' 53

vaunts (or vants), *boasts,* 152, 234, 264

Venice, Italy: where courtesans sing Hugh a song, 99; 'finest silke that is made in Venice,' 63

ventred, *ventured, risked,* 211

Venus: danced naked with Mars, 65; wrongly matched with Vulcan, 120; Long Meg swears by her in *GCII,* 202; her game (love), 212

Victoria History of Berkshire, The, for references to the Englefield family, 354

View of the State of Ireland, A, by Spenser, on 'liverye' and 'coygnye,' 359

Viriat, King of Portugal, 53, *note on* 356

voiding beer, *beer drunk immediately before departing,* 243

Voragine, Jacobus de, *Legenda Aurea* (c. 1470): from which TD takes story of Winifred in *GCI,* 365; source of Crispine and Crispianus story, 366

vouchsafe, *condescend,* 174

Vulcan, foul, wrongly matched with Venus, 120

wag, *a term of endearment,* 'tell me mad wag,' 234
Wagner, R., publisher in 1903 of *JN,* 350
wagtail, *harlot,* 'what a wanton Wagtaile,' 132, *note on* 367
waits, *musicians,* 168
Waldburg, Gebhard Truchsess von, Archbishop of Cologne, xxiv, xxvii
Wales, revolt against Henry I, 269. *See also* Powis
Waller, A. R., ed. *Hudibras,* 352
Wallingford, Berkshire, where tanner in *JN* lives, 8, 351
Wallis (Wallace), William (1272?-1305), Scottish hero who escapes hanging in *TR,* 307-310, *note on* 384
wards, 'have thy wards ready,' 227, *note on* 376
Ware, Hertfordshire, 'out of *Bishopsgate,* foorth right as far as *Ware,*' 247
warrant, *guarantee,* 40, 80, 126
Warwick, Earl of, mentioned by Tom Drum in *TR,* 240
washing ball, *a ball of soap,* 145, *note on* 367
watch, 'they passed along by the Watch,' 165; 'the watch' brings Gillian and Meg home, 200
watched, *watchet, light blue,* 214, *note on* 374
Watling Street. *See* London
Weakest Goeth to the Wall, The. See Webster
weapons: pikes, demilances, shot, armor, lance, calivers, 30; sword and buckler, 35, 213, 216, 221, 223, 224; cannon with iron balls, 65; sword and buckler, long sword, quarter staff, 115; quarter staff, 118; lances, 128; 'Ordinance began to shoote,' 210; 'firie-balls, and burning brazen rings . . . arrowes sharpe and swift,' 211; pike staff, 219, 224; two-handed sword, 256, 259, 263; mace (of a catchpole), 312; a dudgin haft dagger, 215
wear the willow garland (as an emblem of disappointment in love), 165, 202, 206
weasel, virtue found in the brains of, 113
Weasel, servant of Simon's wife in *TR,* 295-299, 328-329
weaver, a, unnamed husband of Gillian and kinsman of Jone in *JN,* 63-68
weavers: controversy over foreign labor, xxvii-xxviii; Weavers' Company, xxvii; weaving room, 26; weavers' song (ballad), 40-42; out of work, 56; 'in Candleweeke streete the Weauers,' 295; contest between weavers, 296; 'wynde their owne quilles,' 296; 'The king hath giuen vs [weavers] priuilege, that none shal liue among vs, but such as serue seuen yeeres in London,' 297; 'Then weauers shall in scarlet go,' 297; 'In Candleweeke street shall stand no loome,' 297; weavers' prophecy (ballad), 297-299; 'They shall maynetaine the weauers hall,' 299; bequest of £100 yearly to, 343. *See also* clothing industry, clothiers, cloth workers
Webster, John, *The Duchess of Malfi:* its similarity to murder scene in *TR,* xv; *The Dramatic Works of,* ed. William Hazlitt (1857), on 'standing-stoole,' 366
weddings: of Jack and widow, 21; detailed description, mentioning bride cakes, bride cup, bride laces, garlands of wheat, rosemary, 28-30, *note on* 353; of Joan and Sir George Rigley, 86; secret wedding of Crispine and Ursula, 126. *See also* courtship, dress, marriage
welt, *trimming,* 35, 146, *note on* 354
West Cheap. *See* London, Cheapside
Western Islands, Hugh goes there in *GCI,* 101
Westminster: setting of story about Richard Casteler, 175-212; Long Meg a servant at the Spread Eagle, 176; Gillian a servant at the George, 176; Tuttle Fields, 198, 199, 201, *note on* 373; Westminster Hall, 202; Robin, Meg, and Gillian drink at the Three Tuns, 204, 205; Palace of Whitehall,

208; the choir of Westminster Abbey, 208; Casteler's bequest to poor of, 212; Robin drinks at the Sign of the Bell, 212; 'the high way turning downe to *Westminster*,' 263; where catchpole takes sanctuary, 312

Westmoreland. *See* Cutbert of Kendal

wheels, *spinning wheels*, 'you haue made our wheeles cast their bands,' 51

whit, 'not a whit,' 224

Whitehall, the palace of Henry VIII, 60, 374

White Lion, in St. Paul's Churchyard, where *1660 GCII* was sold, 370

whitled, *plied with liquor*, 164

Whitsuntide, *season of Whit Sunday*, 71, 181, *note on* 358

whore, butter, *a scold*, 217, *note on* 375

whoreson, *base, worthless*, 'thou whorson villaine,' 131, 132, 215, 313

widow, Jack's 1st wife in *JN*, 5-25

Wight, Isle of, invaded by French, 233

Wilde, W.: a jobbing printer, 1687-96; printer of *1680? JN* (which perhaps should bear a later date), 349; and of *1696 GCI*, 364

William, char. in *GCII*, apprentice, suitor of Mistress Farmer, 243-254

William, Prince, son of Henry I, 287, 292-293

William of Salisbury, clothier mentioned in dedication to *JN*, 3

William Rufus, 2nd son of William the Conqueror, after whose death Henry I becomes king, 269, 382

William the Conqueror, father of Robert Curthose, William Rufus, and Henry I, 382

Willington, helps draft weavers' complaint (1595), xxviii

willow garland. *See* wear the willow garland

Wilson, F. P., his article on jestbooks mentioned, xvi. *See* Dekker

Wiltshire, soldiers from, appear before the Queen, 31. *See also* Bishops downe, Salisbury

Winchcomb, John (Jack of Newbury): meets father-in-law, xiv; a figurehead, xix; his 1st wife, xxi; Jack

and Randoll Pert, xxii-xxiii; hero of *JN*, 3-87, *note on* 350

Winchcomb, the first Mistress, char. in *JN*, xix, 5-25

Winchcomb, the second Mistress (Nan), char. in *JN*, 26-87

Winchcomb's unnamed father-in-law: his use of dialect and malapropism, xiv; his speech is his 'tag,' xxii, 26-30

Winchester, where Simon of Southampton builds a monastery, 343

Windsor Castle, King sends emblem of beehive to Windsor Castle, 38

Windsor Forest, where Jarman is captured, 327

wine: *aqua vitae*, 217, 301; caudle, 24, 111, *note on* 353; charnico (charneco), 257; claret, 15, 17, 39, 110, 165, 177, 212, 239; hipocras (hippocras), 187, *note on* 372; muskadine (muscatel), 181, 256, *note on* 371; posset, 185-191, *note on* 371; red wine, 249; Rhenish, 29, 39, 162, 302; sack, 16, 20, 39, 78, 165, 177, 203, 212, 276; burned sack, 323; white wine, 177; wine and sugar, 15, 187, 212; toasts, 18, 139, 252, 278, ? women drink only when pledged first by a man, 17; drunkenness, 79-81, 259; 'pottle of wine,' 115, 191, *note on* 373; 'as wine is the bewrayer of secrets,' 164; 'turn it ouer my naile' or drinking *super nagulum*, 187, *note on* 372; wine left in Tower of London by the Romans, 296; mentioned, 14, 50, 63, 64, 69, 115, 150, 151, 160, 164, 168, 205, 239, 258, 261, 262, 272. *See also* ale, beer

Wing, Donald G., *Short-Title Catalogue, 1641-1700* (1945-51), 348 n.

Winifred, char. in *GCI*, xx, 92-112, *note on* 365

Winifred's Well, a spring in the neighborhood of Holywell in the county of Flint, N. Wales; 'there sprung vp suddenly a christal stream . . . whereof this Virgin did daily drinke,' 92; mentioned, 96, 109

Winter's Tale, The, sources of, xii

wipe [someone's] nose, *to cheat*, 'I haue wiped your nose, and *Nicks* too,' 165

461

wishly, or wistly, *fixedly, intently,* 118, 319

wist, *knew,* 141, 166, 194

withered, 'her face withered,' 236, *note on* 376

woad, *blue dye,* 28, *note on* 353; 'that makes all colours sound,' 298

Wolfe, John, London printer, xxiv

Wolsey, Cardinal: char. in *JN,* 37-42, 58-59; blamed for clothiers' financial difficulties, 38; mentioned, 355, 356, 357

women: TD's view of, xix-xxi; as wives, 25; 'The sweet Rose doth florish but one moneth, nor Womens beauties but in yong yeers,' 64; soliloquy on marriage, chastity, etc., 64-65; a green housewife, 71; one reluctant to be loved, 93; inconstant, 98; French vs. English, 98; of Italy, 98, 99-100; earthly love vs. heavenly love, 109; very covetous, 143; 'are not Angels, though they haue Angels faces,' 184; 'ought to haue equall priviledge, as well as men to speake their minds' [in love], 188; 'a womans love being hardly obtained, is esteemed most sweet,' 195; 'after a woman is past sixteene . . . , I will not give fifteene blew buttons for her,' 237; an Egyptian woman 'in trauell with child,' 241; 'mutton, such as was laced in a red petticoate,' 274, *note on* 358; a wanton wife, 275-278, 288-293; a lady in distress, 279-280; duties of servant girls, 280; 'I will banish beauty as my greatest enemy,' 283; country wives demand London apparel, 299-303; 'womens tongues are like Lambes tayles, which sildome stand still,' 65; 'many women, many words,' 328; marriageable women, 7, 9-10. *See also* courtship, dress, marriage, weddings

Wonderful Year, The. See Dekker

wont, *custom,* 239, 257; wonted, *accustomed,* 158, 198, 256

Wood, A. Harvey, ed. *The Plays of John Marston* (1934-39), use of word 'staine,' 365

woodcuts, in *1648 GCI,* 363

Worcester, Worcestershire, visited by Henry I, 306. *See also* Fitzallen of Worcester

World's End, a tavern in Spring Gardens, Knightsbridge, London, 261, *note on* 377

worship, *honor,* 'men of worship,' 318; 'gentleman of great worship,' 327

wot, *know, knows,* 'I wot,' 139; 'God wot,' 191, 237

Wren, a servant in *TR,* 328

Wright, Cuthbert: bookseller, 1613-39; seller of *1633* and *1637 JN,* 349

Wriothesley, Henry (1573-1624), Shakespeare's patron, 355

Wriothesley, Sir John (d. 1504), Garter king-of-arms, 355

Wriothesley, Sir Thomas (d. 1534), Garter king-of-arms, 355

Wriothesley, William, great-grandfather of Henry Wriothesley, 355

Xenocrates, 'sufficient to allure chaste hearted *Xenocrates* vnto folly,' 99

Yale University Library: owns copy of *1690 GCI,* 364; of *1632 TR,* 380

yard, origin of, as unit of measurement, 285, *note on* 383

yellow hose, *jealousy,* 'fie, fie, vpon these yellow hose,' 272

Yorkshire. *See* Halifax

Y[oung], R[obert]: printer, 1625-43, and important member of Company of Stationers; printer of *1630, 1633,* and *1637 JN,* 349